Africa *PROBLEMS IN*
ECONOMIC DEVELOPMENT

Africa

PROBLEMS IN ECONOMIC DEVELOPMENT

Edited by

J. S. Uppal and Louis R. Salkever

The Free Press, New York
Collier-Macmillan Limited, London

The Free Press
A Division of The Macmillan Company
866 Third Avenue, New York, New York 10022

Collier-Macmillan Canada Ltd., Toronto, Ontario

Library of Congress Catalog Card Number: 78–169240

printing number
1 2 3 4 5 6 7 8 9 10

Contents

v

Preface

During the last two decades there has been a burgeoning literature on the socio-economic problems of the newly emerging African countries. Many important contributions are scattered throughout professional journals, books, and other publications all over the world, especially in Africa and Europe.

International organizations, notably the Food and Agricultural Organization, the International Labour Office and the United Nations Economic Commission for Africa, have also made important contributions to our knowledge of Africa, particularly in the area of problems and processes of Africa's economic development. It is difficult and time-consuming for students and teachers to select pertinent material from these numerous and scattered sources. Therefore, we felt that bringing selections together in one volume would greatly assist students, teachers and others interested in Africa. This anthology includes several articles and excerpts chosen specifically to meet the needs of undergraduate and graduate students interested in the economic development of Africa.

We gave preference to articles using an interdisciplinary approach, in order to make the information comprehensive and useful to the reader, be his background in economics, political science, sociology or history. The articles in this collection deal with the problems of Africa as a whole, rather than those of individual countries; it is hoped that this will enable readers to understand how, within diverse socio-economic and cultural settings, different societies in the continent are pursuing the common and difficult task of economic development. The twenty-one selections in the anthology have been grouped in six parts. Each part starts with an introduction interrelating the selections and highlighting their main points.

The editors wish to thank the authors and publishers for their permission to use the selections that constitute this anthology.

State University of New York at Albany

J. S. Uppal
Louis R. Salkever

Africa

PROBLEMS IN ECONOMIC DEVELOPMENT

The Setting

BETWEEN THE COMPLETION of colonial partition and the rise of political emancipation, Africa, the largest of the world's continents, has been the victim of a conspiracy of silence; except for the work of a handful of scholars, little was written about her. Since the artificial curtain of "darkness" has lifted, more is known about this vast land of diversity—in natural endowment, historical heritage, political organization, as well as in social and economic development. Moreover, with political independence Africa has obtained power and importance in world affairs.

The key to the shape of the world's political future may well be in African hands. This huge continent, possessing an abundance of vital metals and minerals and a potentially colossal supply of hydroelectric power, can no longer be ignored by the rest of the world. Because of the mines of Katanga, in 1960 we stood on the brink of another world war when the Congo (Kinshasha) was plunged into the chaos of civil strife. Since then, as more independent African states are admitted to the United Nations, Africa's political presence is enhanced.

However, African leaders are well aware that their political power can easily be sapped through economic dependence. In fact, many believe as does Kwame Nkrumah, that this has already occurred. Hence, everywhere in Africa, despite differences in the conceived path, economic development is regarded as the *sine quo non* of overall advancement.

The leaders of the new states know well that they cannot create modern nations without rapid social and economic development; mass poverty, disease, and ignorance must be eradicated. They are coming to know too that the process of economic development in an underdeveloped country is beset with problems. The obstacles to economic advancement in Africa are tougher and more intricate than elsewhere. Apart from the problems of maintaining internal security and political stability, there are impediments to economic development from colonial arrest, cultural incompatibilities, and institutional rigidities.

Africa is still a land of many ethnic groups and a multiplicity of languages with accompanying social and cultural differences. The ethnic group in Africa is still an effective social, spiritual, and economic institution and commands loyalties as

1

a source of individual security as well as the embodiment and the fortress of the past. Modernization and development must start with a reconciliation of tradition and change, a shifting of loyalties from ethnic groups to the nation states. These groups will have to be transformed into building blocks rather than road blocks to advancement.

Among the many other obstacles to African economic development are illiteracy among masses (literacy rates in most countries in tropical Africa are below 6 per cent); shortage of technical, managerial, and administrative personnel; lack of capital; inadequate available power; poor transportation; poor health and sanitation; overdependence on one or two key export commodities; low agricultural productivity. These obstacles to economic development stem mainly from the paucity of social and economic infrastructure that undergirds the economic development of any country. African countries badly need sound institutional structure in government, education, agriculture, trade, industry, and practically every other aspect of their economies.

The articles in this section deal with the present state of African economies, prospects of their development, and the social and cultural environments within which the process of economic development is taking place. The articles by Berg, the U.N. Economic Commission for Africa, and Kamarck focus on the principal characteristics of African economies and the major economic and social problems facing them. They provide a comprehensive view of the present state and the probable future development of the economies of Africa.

The article by Dalton explains the ways in which the traditional African societies differ from the advanced countries. The difference is not only in technology, but in structural aspects, including the organization of production. The article highlights the absence of a market-dependence, economic organization as in Western economies. African forms of market entail social control of production by kinship, religion, and tribal organizations. Allocation and organization of factors of production in such settings are not motivated by economic considerations, but are expressions of social obligation, social affiliation, and social right. Social relationships and cultural values are important determinants of work arrangements; sexual division of labor is maintained, and magic and religion impinge on work schedules.

In the article "Economic Development and Economic Incentives," Neumark examines often-made statements concerning the lack of response of producers and wage earners in underdeveloped countries to ordinary economic incentives. He divides the problems of incentives into specific categories, and finds that in most cases African workers respond to economic incentives in a normal fashion. Where the expected response to economic incentives seems lacking, the answer is one or more of the following: "praedial larceny"; labor immobilities and shortages; scarcity of tools; lack of transport facilities; and distance from market. Neumark makes the point that, where the lack of incentives or response arise from constraints and/or unfavorable circumstances, these must be removed and/or altered as a prerequisite for development.

Overall Economic Development: Recent Trends

After the winning of political independence, two problems move to the center of the African stage: political integration and economic development. The two are obviously related. Leaders of the new states know they cannot create modern nations without the resources that economic development makes available. They must build more roads, schools, and hospitals, not only because their people want these things, but because without them there can be no national construction, no replacement of local feelings by wider allegiances.

The immediate post-colonial years in other parts of the world, particularly in Asia, were not notable for economic achievement. Many observers see a desperate decade or two ahead for Africa, or at best a period of stagnation. Obstacles to rapid growth in Africa are enormous, and there are many question marks about African ability to overcome them. But the picture is not without its brighter features, and the pervasive pessimism which characterizes much contemporary discussion of Africa's economic future is not altogether justified by the facts.

The Pattern of Economic Development

THE BREVITY OF MODERN ECONOMIC CONTACTS

The modern economic history of Africa is extremely short. Except for North Africa, which had long been in economic contact with Europe and the Middle East, Africans lived in near economic isolation from the outside world until very recently. South of the Sahara, there were only four points of contact with the outside as late as 1880: the ancient trans-Sahara trade between the western Sudan and North Africa; European trading posts on the western coast of Africa; Arab settlements on the east coast; and the European settlements on the southern tip of Africa.

Goods and ideas had trickled into Africa for hundreds of years through these points of entry, but they had little impact on the lives of most Africans. South Africa had moved further in the direction of intensified

1

The Character and Prospects of African Economies

Elliot J. Berg

From Walter Goldschmidt, The United States and Africa *(New York : The American Assembly, Columbia University, 1963), pp. 115–155. Reprinted with permission.*

contact than other areas, although before diamonds were discovered, in 1869, it was not much different from the rest of Africa. Subsistence agriculture occupied many of its white residents; in the 1870's, sheep raising was their predominant income-earning activity. Penetration inland had taken place only to the depth of some 150 miles.

West Africa, with its ancient trans-Sahara trade, had in some ways a more intensive experience with money economy than had South Africa. Important commercial centers such as Kano, scattered throughout this part of Africa, impressed European explorers in the early eighteenth century. The West African slave trade also led to the development of active monetized sectors, towns like Whydah (in Dahomey), and Lagos (in Nigeria). African trading groups were to be found all along the coast in the late 1800's; by 1860, peanuts were exported from Senegal, and rubber and palm products from Ghana and Nigeria.

Trade in East Africa was probably less substantial than in West Africa. Though Livingstone saw evidence of trading activity in addition to the slave trade, markets were generally less prevalent in East and Central Africa than in the West, and experience with the money economy appears to have been much less intensive.

By 1880, then, Africa was a continent of subsistence production—that is, production for self-consumption rather than for sale in markets. European dealings with Africa for over three centuries were based mainly on the trade in slaves and did not require European movement beyond the coastal areas; they failed to work any fundamental transformation in African societies. When the European powers carved up Africa, they found economic systems that had undergone few changes in basic structure for as long as men could remember. Until 1900 or so, occupation of the area, political consolidation, and the establishment of settled administrations absorbed most of the colonizers' energies. But from the turn of the century, economic matters began to claim major attention.

THE GROWTH OF THE MONEY ECONOMY

It is widely believed that not much happened in African economic life until after World War II. The report of the International Bank Mission to Nigeria, for example, speaks of the "leisurely pace of the pre-war economy." But development before World War II was hardly leisurely either in Nigeria or in other African areas. Indeed, the rate of economic change and growth from 1900 to 1930 was relatively rapid by most criteria. World War I slowed it down somewhat, and the depression of the 1930's even more. But the performance of most African economies over a period of some 60 years has been remarkable.

It is hard to measure long-term rates of growth because long series of national income data exist for only a few countries. Between 1911 and the mid-1950's, the national income of the Union of South Africa grew at a rate of about 4.5 per cent a year. In the Congo, from 1920 to the mid-1950's, the rate was over 4 per cent a year. For a shorter span of time, the years 1923 to 1939, it has been estimated that Kenya's economy expanded at a rate of about 2.7 per cent a year in real terms. For at least these countries, then, the rate of economic growth over the past few decades has been among the highest in the world.

Export statistics indicate a similar rapid expansion in much of Africa. In the decade

before World War I, the value of exports doubled in French West Africa and in Nigeria, more than quadrupled in Ghana, Kenya, and Tanganyika, rose over sixfold in Nyasaland, and increased more than tenfold in Uganda. Even more impressive is the expansion of the 1920's. The value of exports rose by at least 200 per cent in most of the continent during the 1920's. It doubled in Ghana and Nyasaland, tripled in Northern Rhodesia, Uganda, and Tanganyika, quadrupled in Kenya, rose five times in French Equatorial Africa and the Belgian Congo, about eight times in French West Africa, and over fifteen times in Nigeria.

The buoyant expansion of the 1920's came to an abrupt halt at the end of the decade. The Great Depression dealt Africa a staggering blow; export prices plummeted and the pace of economic change slowed markedly. The 1930's were a decade of retrenchment in most parts of the continent, at least during the first half of the decade; government services were cut, employment fell, land brought into production for the market was turned back to the subsistence sector.

The rhythm of growth of the 1920's was recaptured and, in many cases, exceeded after World War II. The years between 1947 and 1960 represented for most of Africa a period of tremendous economic expansion. The export sector paced the advance. In value terms, exports in many African countries were between ten and fifteen times greater in the late 1950's than they had been in the late 1930's, whereas general price levels rose only about three times over the same period. Investment also increased markedly after 1946. In French Africa, for example, more public capital assistance was received from France between 1947 and 1958, than in the previous fifty years of the French presence. While the rate of increase was perhaps more spectacular here than in some other areas, it was impressive in most, and Africa as a whole did better than underdeveloped areas generally. Rates of gross capital formation—the proportion of national income invested in fixed capital—exceeded 40 per cent in the Rhodesias during some years, were in the neighborhood of 30 per cent in the Belgian Congo throughout the early 1950's, and were less than 15 per cent in only a few countries. These capital formation rates, moreover, understate the true rate of investment in most cases, since they generally exclude peasant investment in cash crop agriculture.

Three main factors account for the rapid rate of growth of the postwar decade. First, world prices and market conditions were generally favorable for Africa's exports, despite some weakening of prices in 1954 and in the late 1950's. High world prices created greater private incomes for both export crop growers and wage earners, and larger flows of income which could be taxed away (through export duties and marketing board surpluses) and used for development purposes. Secondly, high earnings and optimistic expectations (as well as the inflow of European immigrants into white-settler Africa) led private individuals and business firms to undertake new investments, and encouraged the reinvestment of earnings by established firms. Finally, a new urgency to development arose due in part to the "New Deal" which typified postwar colonialism. The most notable examples were in the Belgian Congo, where more than a billion dollars were invested under a ten-year plan (1950–59), and in French West Africa, where public investment during the years 1947–57 (mostly provided by metropolitan France in the form of grants) reached nearly a billion dollars (1956 value). In the Congo, as in English-speaking Africa, most investment came from internal sources, though the British colonies in Africa were helped by grants from the half-billion dollar Colonial Development and Welfare Fund established in 1946, and by U.K. government loans.

Beginning about 1958, a new and less hopeful phase began for many African countries. Prices of some of Africa's chief exports (notably coffee and cocoa) fell sharply, and rates of growth of export earnings declined; in some cases export earnings stagnated or even fell. Political independence or turbulence had inevitable effects on capital flows. In the Congo during 1959 and in 1960, there was a massive hemorrhage of private capital, and South Africa in 1959 was also shaken by large-scale capital flight. In East Africa and Southern Rhodesia there were the same tendencies, though on a smaller scale. Everywhere the enthusiasm of private capital for African investment has diminished. The result of all this has been a general slowing down of economic growth in the past several years, though continuing increases in the volume of exports have in most countries offset price declines and maintained the level of export earnings. Considering these price movements, and the fact that the years since 1957 have witnessed political transformations of unparalleled magnitude, it is remarkable that the economic transition has been as smooth as it has.

FORMS OF DEVELOPMENT

Economic development took different forms in different parts of Africa. Everywhere, however, it involved either the activation of unused resources or the transfer of resources out of subsistence agriculture into money-earning activity. The two general models of economic development into which most African countries fit are:

1. Economies whose base is either mining or European agricultural production. In these countries, development occurred by the relatively large-scale inflow of capital from abroad into mining and agriculture. Generally non-African settlers are found in these countries (although not invariably; in the Congo, for example, there was a substantial European agricultural sector but few real settlers). In these countries, the African has entered the money economy primarily as a wage earner. Typical of this group are the countries in North Africa, South Africa, Northern and Southern Rhodesia, Kenya, the Congo, and the Portuguese areas.

2. Peasant-producer economies, where development has been by African peasant production of cash crops for export. In these economies there are relatively few large-scale expatriate enterprises, few or no European settlers, and relatively few African wage earners. The role of the European in these countries has been essentially that of a trader

or administrator. Most of West Africa and Uganda fall into this category.

These categories are simplified models. Not all countries fit easily into them. Guinea, for example, has a mineral export sector of growing importance since 1960; of its chief export crops, coffee is produced by African peasants, bananas by European and Levantine planters. Tanganyika, similarly, has a relatively large plantation sector (sisal), but its coffee is peasant-grown. Liberia's rubber is mainly produced on expatriate plantations, but there is a growing African planter group.

Despite such cases, the broad distinction is useful, and reflects a number of important factors. The portion of Europeans tends to be substantially greater in the mining expatriate-agriculture economies. South Africa, of course, has the greatest number of Europeans—about 3 million; Southern Rhodesia had 270,000 Europeans (in 1960) to 3 million Africans; Northern Rhodesia, 73,000 to 2.4 million Africans; the Belgian Congo (in 1959), 110,000 to 13 million Africans. Elsewhere (with the exception of Angola, which had 110,000 Europeans and 4.5 million Africans in the late 1950's), the proportion of Europeans is much smaller: in Ghana, 7,000 to 7 million Africans; in Nigeria, 15,000 to 50 million Africans; in Nyasaland, 9,000 to 2.9 million Africans. Senegal, with almost 50,000 Europeans to 2.3 million Africans, and the Ivory Coast, with almost 15,000 to 3 million, are the peasant-producer countries with the highest proportion of Europeans.

Capital investment throughout most of the colonial period was concentrated in the mining, expatriate-agricultural economies. According to Professor Frankel's calculations (*Capital Investment in Africa*), South Africa was the site of some 42 per cent of the total foreign investment in Africa south of the Sahara between 1880 and 1936. The two Rhodesias received another 18 per cent, the Belgian Congo, 11 per cent, Kenya and Uganda together, about 4 per cent. Ghana and the French West African territories received less than 3 per cent each.

The incidence of wage earning is substantially greater in the mining expatriate-

agricultural economies. In South Africa and Southern Rhodesia, over one-quarter of the resident African population is in "modern" paid employment; in Kenya, Northern Rhodesia, and the Congo, the proportion is about 10 per cent; in most of the rest of the continent it is below 5 per cent; and in Nigeria and the former territories of French West Africa it is about 2 per cent (or 4 per cent, if we include Africans working for African farmers).

The figures of national income distribution are probably the clearest indications of the differences between the two groups of countries. In South Africa, Northern Rhodesia, Kenya, and the Congo, less than one-third of the total money income generated in the late 1950's was African income; this indicates the large portion of total market activity in the hands of non-African factors of production. In Nyasaland, Uganda, and most of the West African countries, African incomes are about two-thirds of total money income.

Finally, the countries differ in the proportion of African income derived from wage earning. In South Africa, the Federation of Rhodesia, and the Congo, between 65 and 90 per cent of the aggregate money income accruing to Africans comes from wages. Even in Kenya, which is mainly agricultural, over 80 per cent of African money incomes in the late 1950's was earned through wage employment; in Nyasaland, in 1958, about 65 per cent. In Uganda, on the other hand, only about 25 per cent of African money income is derived from wages, and in Ghana, probably less than 20 per cent.

These differing forms of development have some obvious consequences for Africa's future. The economies that rest on a mining and European agricultural base are generally richer, more industrialized, and have had higher rates of capital formation in the recent past; their national output has in general grown faster than that of the peasant-producer economies. They also have generally denser networks of social overhead capital. At the same time, the "enclave" character of these economies is more marked and they are politically less developed. The peasant-producer countries have a more even racial distribution of income, a wider participation of Africans in economic decision-making, and more political experience. Peasant-producer economies are thus in one sense more resilient: They are less exposed to withdrawal of expatriate skill and capital; they are more "African." At the same time, their economic institutions are less complex, and hence more manageable.

Despite great diversity, most African economies share certain common characteristics. They are mainly agricultural economies. They all have large subsistence sectors. They are all "open" and most are specialized in the production of a few export commodities. In the modern sector of the economy, non-African capital and skills predominate; the continent is particularly poor in trained human resources. Economic development has been unevenly distributed geographically within countries. Most of Africa, finally, remains relatively underpopulated.

THE PRIMACY OF AGRICULTURE AND THE DOMINANCE OF THE SUBSISTENCE SECTOR

In most African countries, between 80 and 90 per cent of the population is found in rural areas engaged in agriculture. As column (2) of Table 1 shows, agriculture accounts for between one- and two-thirds of national output, except in the Central African Federation, where it is only 20 per cent, and in South Africa, where it is 12 per cent. Mineral production rivals agriculture only in the Rhodesias, the Congo, and South Africa, while manufacturing generates 10 per cent or more of the national income only in South Africa, Morocco, Tunisia, Southern Rhodesia, the Congo, and Kenya.

Within the agricultural sector, subsistence farming remains the predominant activity. According to United Nations' estimates, in the late 1940's over 70 per cent of the land under African cultivation was in subsistence crops, and less than 10 per cent in crops wholly for export. Estimates for the late 1950's still indicate that more than half of the African agricultural area is devoted mainly to subsistence farming, though there are very wide differences between countries: In the peasant-producer economies of West Africa, well over half of the cultivated land is probably now given over to production for the market.

Table 1—Gross Domestic Product by Industrial Origin (in per cent)

	Year	Agriculture	Of which Subsistence Agriculture	Mining	Manufacturing	Construction	Transport and Communication	Commerce	Services (including Public Utilities)
	(1)	(2)	(3)	(4)	(5)	(6)	(7)	(8)	(9)
Senegal	1959	27		2	9	4	4	27	28
Ivory Coast	1960	54			4	4	5	32	1
Ghana	1958	60–65	30–33	4	3	4		29	
Nigeria	1958	63	30–33	1	2	11	15		8
Sudan	1958–59	58			2	8	14		19
Ethiopia	1959	62	50		2	3	5	13	15
Congo (Leopoldville)	1958	31	12	16	10	4	9	7	23
Federation of Rhodesia and Nyasaland	1958	20	9	14	12	8	6	16	24
Kenya	1958	42	25	1	10	4	8	13	22
Uganda	1956–59	67	27	1	4	3	3	10	12
Tanganyika	1958	65	41	4	4	3	7	7	11
Tunisia	1955–58	32		4	11	4	8	20	20
Republic of South Africa	1959	12		13	25		8	12	31

Source: *Economic Bulletin for Africa*, Vol. II, No. 2 (June, 1962), and national accounts, various countries. Totals of more than 100 per cent are due to rounding.

What is true of land resources is equally true of labor. Most Africans spend most of their time bound up in the village economics. In the continent as a whole, there are probably no more than 10 million Africans who work for wages during any part of the year. Only in southern Africa is there more than 10 per cent of the population engaged in modern wage-earning employment. In most of the continent, the greater part of these wage earners are migrant workers, only temporarily in paid employment, who return to the villages after a spell as wage workers.

The continuing predominance of the subsistence sector is indicated in column (3) of Table 1, which shows that in most African countries subsistence production accounts for between a quarter and a half of total output.

EXPORT ORIENTATION AND SPECIALIZATION

African economies are "open" or export economies in which a substantial proportion of what is produced for sale is exported and many non-food consumer goods are imported. Only the northern and southern tips of the continent, with their relatively dense European populations, have well developed internal markets. Elsewhere, between 25 and 60 per cent of marketed production is exported.

These countries tend to send abroad only a narrow range of goods, almost exclusively raw materials in unprocessed or semi-processed form. Thus Senegal, Mali, and Niger are almost totally dependent on peanuts, which make up over 80 per cent of the value of their exports. Cocoa and coffee provide 75 per cent of the Ivory Coast's export earnings, cocoa over half of Ghana's. Copper exports are 90 per cent of Northern Rhodesia's sales abroad. Some countries have a somewhat more diversified list of export commodities: Nigeria (peanut products, palm products, cocoa, tin); the Congo (copper, coffee, cotton, cobalt, tin); Southern Rhodesia (tobacco, asbestos, gold). And some other areas have brought new exports into production in recent years: Liberia (iron ore, in addition to rubber); Guinea (processed bauxite, in addition to coffee, bananas,

and iron ore); Gabon (manganese and iron ore, in addition to wood products). But most African economies remain very narrowly based.

THE PREDOMINANCE OF EUROPEAN
CAPITAL AND SKILL

Except in the agricultural sectors of the peasant-producer economies, the African role in modern economic life has been restricted to the provision of unskilled and semiskilled labor, petty trading, and some handicraft production. In the private sector, the entrepreneurial role, management, and high-level technical skills—all of these have been the near monopoly of non-Africans. This was true everywhere until very recent years, and remains true in much of East, southern, and Central Africa.

The private non-agricultural sector of most African economies consists of a cluster of expatriate enterprises, usually large in size, small in number, and international in character, surrounded by a constellation of smaller enterprises—small manufacturers, transporters, and trading firms—sometimes African in management, but most commonly managed by members of immigrant communities—Syrians, Lebanese, Greeks, Levantines, and Asians (particularly in East and Central Africa). Thus in the Congo, several dozen large, diversified firms (and through financial control, one firm in particular—the *Societé Générale de Belgique*) centralize control over a large segment of the modern economy. In Northern Rhodesia, two mining groups are in control of the copper-belt copper mines. In Liberia, Firestone and a dozen other firms (mainly American) are dominant. In the rest of West Africa, a handful of great trading firms (some of which have become more diversified organizations with interests in mining and manufacturing) control the channels of external and, to a lesser extent, internal trade (The United Africa Company, the *Societé Commerciale Ouest Africaine*, etc.).

The "commanding heights" in the money economy, then, are occupied by expatriate organizations even in peasant-producer countries, while in the mining and European agricultural economies, the capital and management of the basic producing units are also non-African in origin.

Thus, positions of skill and decision-making responsibility in the private sector have until very recently been occupied exclusively by non-Africans. The situation was not much different in the public sector, until a decade ago. In Nigeria, for example, of the more than 3,000 senior posts in the civil service in 1951, less than 700 were held by Africans. Changes in this respect have come quickly in the past few years. As of the beginning of 1961, some 90 per cent of the senior civil service posts (those usually requiring some college training) in Western Nigeria were held by Africans. In Ghana, the proportion was comparable, though slightly lower. In French-speaking areas and in East, Central and southern Africa, the rate of Africanization has been much slower. In Senegal, in 1961, there were still some 1,500 French technical assistance personnel in the country, and in Kenya and Tanganyika, less than 20 per cent of the senior posts of the civil service were held by Africans in 1961. In West Africa and the ex-Belgian Congo, Africans do most skilled work below the foreman level, but in East Africa many of these jobs are held by Asians, and everywhere expatriates fill many, if not most, of the lower level supervisory jobs—even in Ghana, in 1960, 300 out of that country's 900 foremen were expatriates.

UNEVEN GEOGRAPHICAL DEVELOPMENT

Within most African countries, the geographical pattern of economic development has been exceedingly uneven. It is a continent dotted with islands of modern economic development. In West Africa, for example, the region extending some 200 miles inland has moved rapidly into the money economy, whereas the vast interior regions (where most of the people live) have been relatively little touched by modern economic advance. The interior territories of French-speaking West Africa and the northern regions of Ghana and Nigeria have lagged behind the coastal areas both economically and socially. This pattern appears throughout the continent. The Buganda area in Uganda is well ahead of the rest of the country. The Gabon Republic, in

ex-French Equatorial Africa, is much richer than the other parts of that area; two provinces, Leopoldville and Katanga, generated most of the income arising in the ex-Belgian Congo. In Northern Rhodesia, there is the copper-belt, and not much else; European farming areas straddle the railway, but most of the rest of the country remains untouched by modern communications and by modern economic activity. In white-settler Africa generally, economic development has largely bypassed the "native Reserves."

RELATIVE UNDERPOPULATION

The African continent below the Sahara in general does not have any serious population problem. There are some areas where population presses on the land (parts of Kenya and Tanganyika, Ruanda, Burundi, Nigeria), and population growth is almost everywhere high, probably about 2 per cent a year. But land remains relatively abundant in most of the area.

It is not generally very good land. About one third of Africa's land mass is desert or semidesert, and much of the area is infested with tsetse fly, which makes it uninhabitable for men and beasts. Great areas are not well watered. But even when account is taken of the low carrying capacity of African land under present technological conditions, it remains true that the continent is not over-peopled.

Thus, despite occasional famine in certain areas and chronic malnutrition in many, there is little rural misery of the kind found in much of the Middle East and parts of Asia. Recent publications of the Food and Agricultural Organization have claimed that in the decade of the 1950's, food consumption per capita declined in Africa. This is a dubious proposition; it rests on scattered and altogether unreliable estimates of food-production trends in the subsistence sector. Bad crop years in North Africa and flood and drought in Tanganyika in 1961 did lead to some difficulties in those areas, but there is no convincing evidence that the ordinary

African today eats less food than he did a decade or two ago, and there is a great deal of evidence that some portions of the population are eating a more varied and abundant diet than ever before.

The Economic Prospects: Viability and Growth

The question is often raised about the new African states: Are they economically "viable"? Strictly speaking, the question has little meaning. Almost any political unit can be viable if viability means mere capacity to survive economically. In African conditions, with only scattered population pressure and an economy still largely subsistence-oriented, this is no real concern. If, however, by "viability" we mean something more—the capacity of an economy to maintain a customary or expected level of income, or to increase it—then clearly a number of African countries are not presently viable, and some may never be able to become so.

It is easy to be gloomy about the economic prospects for the new Africa. All the old obstacles and restraints to development remain: an ungracious nature and a delicate agriculture; an imperfect commitment to money earning in the villages; inadequate transport facilities in a large land mass; uncertain resource endowments; low levels of money income, and hence limited domestic sources of saving; uncertainties about price prospects for African exports on world commodity markets. To these have been added new and different problems: administrative inadequacies arising from rapid Africanization in the face of terrible scarcities of technical and administrative abilities; political turbulence, with consequent capital flight or hesitancy of potential private investors; the new costs of sovereignty; some tendencies towards economic adventurism by new governments.

On top of all this, independence, or its approach has unloosed powerful new ambitions. This can be seen in the new development plans which have sprouted in the post-independence period: Senegal hopes to find $370 million in investment resources over the years 1961–64, $200 million of which is public investment. Mali's Four-Year Plan anticipates investment of $250 million. Guinea's Three-Year Plan, founded in 1960, involves planned investment of $155 million; Nigeria's 1962–67 plan counts on $1.8 billion, and Tanganyika's Three-Year Plan on $67 million. Ghana's new Seven-Year Plan aims at government expenditure of $1.4 billion.

All of these plans have two features in common: They involve capital expenditures at rates substantially greater than that occurring in the recent past, and they rely on outside aid for at least half of their total investment resources. The Tanganyika plan is particularly illuminating. A World Bank Mission to Tanganyika in 1960 recommended a plan of $47 million. The Tanganyika government regarded this as too conservative, and increased its size by over 40 per cent. At the same time, Tanganyika counts on external loans and grants for more than 80 per cent of total planned expenditure.

Most of the new plans mention increases in real income of 3 to 5 per cent per capita per year. This is a substantial growth rate. Since population is increasing at a rate close to 2 per cent a year in most of the continent, and more in a number of countries, it means increasing aggregate income by between 5 and 7 per cent a year. Such a rate of economic growth is not impossible; output in Germany, Austria, Japan, Israel, Greece, and the Eastern European Communist countries grew at a rate of more than 6 per cent a year during the decade of the 1950's. In Africa, the Rhodesias and Nyasaland, during the latter half of the 1950's, had income growth of 6.8 per cent a year in the aggregate and 4.1 per cent per capita. But these are uncommonly high rates of growth. The Congo, during the extraordinary boom of the 1950's, expanded its output at an aggregate rate of over 5 per cent a year, or 2.5 per cent per capita. And total real output in Nigeria during the 1950's increased at about 4 per cent a year, which is a rate much closer to average African performance during these years.

To maintain, much less increase, these rates of growth during the decade ahead will be a strenuous task. In weighing the prospects, it is essential to emphasize that intercountry differences are very great: The economic prospects for the Upper Volta, Chad, or Nyasaland are hardly comparable to those of the Ivory Coast or Northern Rhodesia.

Obstacles to Growth

THE SCARCITY OF TRAINED MANPOWER

The experience of the Congo, left at independence without a single African doctor, lawyer, engineer, or army officer, dramatically brought the African manpower problem to world attention. Many African countries are better endowed with high-level manpower than was the Congo in 1960, but in all of them there exists a critical need to develop the skills and raise the level of education of their people. In all of Africa below the Sahara, there were in 1958 not more than 10,000 Africans studying in universities at home and abroad, and 6,500 of these came from Ghana and Nigeria. In the same year, only a few other countries had more than 200 students in universities. Since 1958, the rate of intake into universities has markedly increased, but a recent report on Nigeria stated that even if an educational program (which is far beyond Nigeria's present financial possibilities) were introduced, it would be more than a decade before that country could meet its normal needs for trained manpower from domestic sources. During the decade of the 1960's, Nigeria would have to import almost 7,000 man-years of secondary-school teachers—and Nigeria is educationally one of Africa's most advanced countries.

The problem of university-trained people is most striking, but the principal bottleneck is on the secondary-school level. In all of sub-Saharan Africa there were in the late 1950's only about 8,000 Africans graduating from general academic secondary schools, of which about 40 per cent were in Nigeria and Ghana alone. Vocational and teacher training school graduates swell the number, but it is still true that in the late 1950's, more people graduated from Chicago's high school than from all the high schools of Africa.

This scarcity of trained human resources is a major constraint on rates of economic development in Africa. It means that African governments lack the administrative ability to execute large and complex development schemes, and that governments and private firms must continue for years to import expensive foreign manpower. It means also that African countries must devote substantial resources to education and the development of skills. Although investments in education are productive, they involve reductions in investment in fixed capital. Investment in people, moreover, yields little increase in the output of society in the short run, at the same time that it adds a great and growing budgetary burden in the form of teacher salaries and school maintenance costs.

Until recently, primary education has received most attention, and this has created delicate problems of imbalance in educational systems. For the thousands of youths now graduating from primary and junior high schools, there are few places in high schools. Nor are these boys able to find the clerical jobs once open to primary school graduates. They thus remain idle, living with relatives and friends in town. To an important extent this is a transitional problem, due to the rapidity of change; but until agricultural employment or unskilled manual work is accepted as suitable for literate men, a serious potential social problem will exist.

There is something more. Relatively large portions of public revenues are already being devoted to education. In the southern regions of Nigeria, to take the most striking example, almost half of total government current expenditures now go to education. Few African governments spend less than 15 per cent, and in all of them the proportion is rising rapidly. Now a great step forward must be taken in the area of secondary and higher education, at potentially staggering cost. It has been estimated that in one West African country (Senegal) the total cost of turning out a primary-school graduate is about $350, whereas the cost of a secondary-school graduate (boarding school) is over $6,000. This illustrates the problem: At a time when most African budgets are already groaning under educational expenditures, tremendous new demands will arise due to the increase in secondary education.

CAPITAL SCARCITY

In order to increase money income in any country, it is usually necessary that the individuals or enterprises in that country set aside some portion of their current incomes for investment. This is not the only way that capital formation takes place. Every time an African farmer plants a cocoa tree or clears a new piece of ground for planting, capital formation occurs, even though it involves no "saving" in the conventional sense. But the setting aside of a part of current money income is basic to development.

In the postwar period, we saw earlier, many African countries experienced high rates of capital formation because of favorable world prices for African exports, loans and grants from colonial powers, and high rates of reinvestment of earnings by private companies in some of the countries. But for these rates of capital formation to continue and to increase, it is necessary that savings of Africans provide a larger portion of investment funds. The capacity to draw off significant amounts of savings from the domestic economy, however, is limited by the low level of African money incomes. Per capita average annual money incomes are less than $100 in most African countries, between $100 and $200 in some, and over $300 only in the Republic of South Africa.

Though these figures should be used cautiously, they are useful in indicating the difficulty of raising local resources for the financing of economic development. These difficulties are often exaggerated. In British Africa and the Belgian Congo, the respectable rates of capital formation over the postwar period were in large measure financed from domestic sources—in British Africa, mainly through levies on the export earnings of peasant producers. It is also true that, compared with peasant producers of export crops, much of the African population tends to be undertaxed, particularly the higher level African civil servant group, and comparable employees in the private sector. Nonetheless, even with higher rates of taxation and with continuing levies on export crop growers, the possibilities for financing development from domestic sources are restricted by low levels of taxable money incomes.

Furthermore, it is worth emphasizing something that is often forgotten: A major economic problem in Africa is to induce men to shift their energies from "leisure" (non-income-earning activities) and subsistence production, to income-earning activity. The possibility of higher levels of consumption is one of the major instruments for accomplishing this, so that potential incentive-destroying effects of taxation in the agricultural sector must be guarded against. The failure of Ghanaian cocoa output to expand more during the 1950's, for example, is not unrelated to the high rates of taxation imposed through marketing boards and export duties on the cocoa industry. Even the taxation of higher-level African employees is subject to the restraint created by the existence of an international market in high-level manpower; high taxes on incomes of African technicians can add another element to the bundle of inducements that already encourages them to take jobs in other countries.

THE DIFFICULTIES OF AGRICULTURAL DEVELOPMENT

Agricultural development is the key to general economic growth. Since most Africans are agriculturalists, and since land is relatively plentiful, expansion of agricultural incomes is the main way open to expand the local market. Furthermore, expansion and diversification of agricultural output is essential to any basic improvement of African health and welfare since, though adequately fed in terms of caloric intake, most Africans are badly fed. In particular, they lack protein, which reduces their general resistance to disease. The production and consumption of more protein-rich foods is thus indispensable for an improvement in the general health and well-being of the majority of people.

Obstacles to increasing the quantity and

diversity of agricultural production are for-midable. First, African soils generally tend to be exceedingly delicate; it has been estimated that only about 10 per cent of the total land area of the continent can be cultivated with-out special attention. The lush forest areas, once regarded as endlessly fertile, are sus-ceptible to leaching of chemical nutrients and to massive erosion when cleared and exposed to burning sun and hammering rain. This is equally true of the wooded prairie in the savannah regions, of which much of the interior consists.

Second, cultural or social factors obstruct agricultural change and growth. Under tra-ditional forms of land tenure arrangements, land is held "communally"; it is also held in unconsolidated pieces; and where matrilineal inheritance patterns exist, fathers pass their improved land (cocoa farms, for example) to nephews, not sons. These patterns of landholding and inheritance tend to reduce incentives to improve land and, more important, lack of clear-cut ownership claims exposes land titles to uncertainty and makes it difficult to establish systems of agricultural credit.

Third, economic and technological ob-stacles exist. Foremost is the scarcity of transport and marketing facilities. The essential motor for the expansion of agri-culture must be an increase in effort by villagers now devoting themselves to sub-sistence production, or to non-productive activity. This cannot come about until there are ways for villagers to get their crops to market at relatively low cost, and marketing facilities which will allow villagers to pur-chase consumer goods conveniently and cheaply. While in some parts of Africa both transport and markets have been provided, particularly in the last decade, in many countries vast areas remain isolated. The presence of adequate transport is particu-larly significant with respect to the marketing of local foods; these tend to be heavy in weight and without low-cost transport, the return from their sale is not sufficient to stimulate production. Improved transporta-tion, therefore, is a prerequisite to agricultural development.

Wider use of mechanization in agriculture is another frequent prescription. Experience with mechanized agriculture, however, has revealed serious pitfalls. Many African soils contain widespread rock formations, are particularly hard in texture, or have dense underlying root systems—all of which make the use of tractors and plows extremely hazardous. Visitors to the site of the famous Tanganyika Groundnut Scheme, where many of these difficulties were encountered, said it resembled a battlefield, strewn with wrecked and abandoned equipment. Some kinds of functions, moreover, are not readily per-formed by agricultural machinery perfected in industrialized countries; one of the major problems in large-scale African agricultural projects, for example, is the digging out of tree stumps, but no machine has yet been designed which can adequately perform this job. There is furthermore a great deal that is as yet unknown about the effects of mechani-zation on African soils. It is not even known whether continued plowing in tropical heat and moisture leads to declining fertility through oxidization of organic matter.

The economics of mechanized agriculture raises other questions. Operating costs of machinery are very high. Wear and tear in physical terms is great. There are few skilled drivers available, particularly drivers aware of the subtleties of machine maintenance. Maintenance costs for machinery are thus exceedingly high, partly because skilled labor costs so much, and partly because repairmen must often be brought long distances to repair damaged machines.

Finally, despite some growth of agri-cultural research and extension services, there is still a vast ignorance about much that is relevant to agricultural development: the nature of African soils, the long-term effects of plowing, the suitability and economics of fertilizer use. This lack of knowledge is one of the major factors blocking the expansion of African agriculture.

THE COLONIAL HERITAGE

A number of obstacles to expansion arise from the peculiar set of ideas and practices passed on to Africans by the colonizers. This is a many-sided issue which can only be touched on here. But it is at least as important as most of the questions so far considered.

One feature of this heritage is an all-pervasive paternalism in economic matters. Everyone recognizes that in political terms a colonial system is profoundly authoritarian. What is not always equally recognized is that colonial economic systems, with a few exceptions and some differences in degree, are equally authoritarian. To an astonishing extent, economic policy in most of Africa has been paternalistic, "*dirigiste*," anti-individualistic. As often as not, African peasants have been told what to produce, when and how to produce it, to whom and at what price it must be sold. Colonial internal economic policy in most African countries was typified by a passion for "order" and "organization" on the part of the officials responsible for economic policy. The freely competitive market was in general regarded with a sour eye. To colonial administrators it was a symptom of economic disorder to have two sellers where there might be one, or to have spirited competition between railways and roads; it was a symptom of conspiracy when retail prices rose. Markets had to be "organized," and the flow of commodities and labor "regularized." The paraphernalia of state controls flowered almost everywhere, ranging from price supports and marketing boards to sales quotas, price controls, monopolistic allocations of sales and purchases, regulation of entry into trade and industry, provision of "rations" as part of wage payments, and compulsory "deferred saving" schemes of various sorts in the wage sector.

Economic controls were often ineffective for their explicit aims. But whatever their effect in determining the pattern of development, the world view from which the attempts at controls arose had important effects in shaping African economic attitudes. For one thing, it slowed the growth of a sense of responsibility among Africans. The competitive market, whatever its shortcomings, is a great educator; the countless decisions demanded of individuals in a market economy provide a training ground for the growth of a sense of individual responsibility. In Africa, traditional economic policy under colonial rule made the emergence of this sense of responsibility much more difficult than it would otherwise have been. It is probably no accident that English-speaking West Africa, where economic paternalism rested with a lighter hand, is characterized by a general vitality of economic behavior distinctive in the continent.

Perhaps a more significant consequence is that African elites bring to their new political responsibilities little warmth for or understanding of the operation of the market mechanism, and an implicit faith in the efficacy of economic controls. There are of course many other reasons why this is so, but the colonial economic tutelage is one of the more important ones. It is in part for this reason that so much African thinking on economic policy runs in terms of state enterprise, state control over production and marketing, "suppression of intermediaries," and so forth. The motives underlying these policies may be different, yet in one fundamental sense at least they represent a continuation of the past: They reflect skepticism and distrust of individual initiative in the free market. Having seen so little of it in the past, few African leaders are disposed to try it now.

Another aspect of the inheritance in attitudes relates to employee behavior in the wage-earning sector. In the colonial period, African wage earners, whether of low place or high, regarded their employers as separate and distant—as "they." This was of course hardly irrational. Non-Africans were in fact in control of almost all private and public economic power and decision-making. The colonial situation with its vast gap between the managers and the managed thus stunted the growth of a sense of common enterprise. This was reflected in careless work performance, cheerful neglect of the ordinary rules of machine maintenance, and a general lack of personal commitment to craftsman-like ideas. In the postindependence period this has led to serious problems on state-run enterprises, the railway system in Guinea having had particularly severe difficulties of this kind. For this reason, pleas for a "decolonization" of work habits have arisen.

Another facet of the colonial heritage is the wage structures left to independent African states. Where the supply of trained and educated manpower is scarce, the wages of trained people tend to be very high in comparison to that of unskilled workers. This is simply a matter of supply and demand, the demand for skilled and educated manpower is great while the supply is sparse. This would be enough in itself to create a very "wide wage structure." This natural situation is exacerbated in Africa because the educated people were lacking and it was necessary to pay the rates obtainable in European countries for skilled labor, plus some premium to compensate for the so-called discomforts and hazards of service in Africa. These already handsome base salaries were matched with a whole range of attractive fringe benefits—housing allowances, car allowances, long vacations in Europe, etc. This caused no particular problem so long as there were few or no Africans in comparable positions. As the colonial era came to an end and more and more Africans began to assume responsible positions, African replacements began to demand the same privileges which it was politically necessary to grant (with somewhat fewer fringe benefits). Table 2

Table 2—Civil Service Salary Structures (Monthly Rates in United States dollars, 1958)

	Lagos (Nigeria)	Accra (Ghana)	Abidjan (Ivory Coast)
Primary or Middle School Graduate, Entering Rate	26.60	25.70	67.00
Secondary School Graduate	35.00	37.30	162.00
University Graduate	140.00	158.00	240.00

suggests what this meant in terms of the wage structure. In these West African countries, a university graduate entering the civil service receives something in the order of five times the wages of the lower-paid civil servant; in the United States, the ratio is about 1.2 to 1.

The consequence of this has been that as African governments assume power, one of the first tasks they find themselves faced with is that of "taming" civil servants. Civil service salaries are often taking enormous portions of the budget and it therefore becomes necessary to bring civil service wages, indeed the wages of all highly skilled people, into line with the general level of wages in the country. In most cases, it is the abundant fringe benefits that are aimed at; in 1962, the Ivory Coast, for example, eliminated housing allowances for senior civil servants. But the market forces of supply and demand tend to keep the highly skilled wage up, and habits of the past as well as political factors tend to restrict the possibilities for reductions.

Another aspect of the colonial heritage, peculiar to ex-French Africa, is a heavy dependence on direct subsidies from the metropole, especially since the end of World War II. The substantial development programs of the postwar years were financed almost wholly by France. The total of French grants and loans (most of it was in the form of grants) for investment purposes between 1947 and 1958 amounted to about 700 billion French francs. (Changes in the value of the franc and difficulties in finding an appropriate rate of exchange make it hard to put a meaningful dollar figure on this total; converted at the exchange rate of the mid-1950's—350 francs to a dollar—it comes to about $2 billion). It made possible a rate of capital formation in French Tropical Africa estimated at close to 20 per cent of national income. It also bred in some French–African political leaders an unwillingness to come to grips with some of the hard problems of financing development from internal sources.

Moreover, French Africa has traditionally been more intimately bound up in trade relations with the metropolitan country than other African areas. In the postwar period, some 70 per cent of total African trade has usually been within the franc zone. Because of high tariffs and exchange controls, Africans in these areas have been forced to buy consumer and capital goods from high-priced French suppliers, but as a counter-balance, African producers have enjoyed over most of the postwar period a protected market in France where they sell their crops at higher prices than could be obtained in the open world market. Over most of the past decade, peanuts have enjoyed a price advantage between 10 and 30 per cent, and coffee about 20 per cent. This dependence has grown greater, not less, since political independence. With the collapse of the world coffee market after 1958, the French granted to the Ivory Coast, the main franc-zone producer of coffee, a high degree of protection: Coffee from the Ivory Coast sold in France in 1961 at about twice the price that could be obtained on other world markets. All of this means that French African producers have grown up in a kind of hot-house atmosphere, isolated from the rigors of world competition.

ECONOMIC IDEOLOGIES

It was noted above that African thinking on economic policy has been in part shaped by the economic experience of paternalism under colonial rule. Even more important in determining economic policy is the "socialism" that so many African leaders proclaim. "Socialism" of one variety or another is indeed the dominant postindependence ideology. There are many reasons for its prevalence: the identification of capitalism with "exploitation" and with colonialism; the ideological tendencies absorbed by African students in metropolitan capitals, particularly in Paris; the belief (expressed by President Nkrumah, for one) that capitalism is "too complicated" for Africa; the view that socialism is more compatible with the communal traditions of African society.

African varieties of socialism are generally extremely vague. Only one thing is clear about them; they are heretical. For Mr. Senghor of Senegal, socialism is a mixture of Marxism, Christian humanitarianism, and Negritude. President Sekou Touré of Guinea, who has been most articulate in these matters, rejects a basic tenet of orthodox Marxism—the class struggle; in Africa, he says, there is only one major conflict—between the colonizers and the colonized. All Africans are united in this struggle.

"African socialism" expresses itself mainly in two concrete ways in the area of economic policy. First, with respect to agricultural development, interest tends to be placed on large-scale state-run efforts, such as the state farms Ghana is experimenting with at the present time, and the rural enterprises envisaged in Guinea's planning. Secondly, and more important, there is an inclination to give the state a much greater role in internal and external commerce through the creation of state trading corporations. Ghana and Senegal have begun to make some halting steps in this direction, and in Mali state trading firms now control some 30 per cent of the total external trade.

This development has gone furthest in Guinea. Shortly after independence, Guinea set up state trading firms which were to monopolize the export and import trade. Though local retail trade was to remain much as before, it was not long before it, too, was under the control of the state monopolies. State retail outlets and widespread price regulations were introduced. The result was disastrous. Meat and fish disappeared from markets in Conakry, the capital city; fishermen sold their catches in neighboring Sierra Leone, where prices were better, and cattlemen from Northern Guinea shipped their animals across to Liberia. Mismanagement of state stores led to waste on a large scale. Soon corruption began to appear. By March, 1961, organized trading had practically ground to a halt. Conakry was badly provided with products of the interior; the interior lacked imported goods, which were piling up on the docks in Conakry. It was finally necessary to mobilize all available trucks in the country to bring goods to the countryside. Shortly thereafter the state trading agency was decentralized and private traders given a freer hand. But the damage was enormous, in morale as well as in money.

Certain conclusions emerge. The expanded role of the state demands trained personnel in large numbers. They are not present in most African countries, and are not likely to be present for at least a decade. Under colonial rule, the role of the state had been great; about half of the wage-earning labor force was employed by the state in most African countries. The operation of the state sector, even in its pre-independence size, is a task to strain all the meager resources in trained manpower which the African countries possess; to expand the role of the state into new areas is to place an intolerably heavy load on the cadre of trained men available and to invite trouble. Management of the economy under African conditions is exceedingly difficult, for reasons including the long frontiers over which smugglers can roam at will, and the universal difficulties of regulating the economic behavior of intractable peasants and crafty traders. The common tendency to give the state more than it can do with its present resources in manpower is one of the most ominous features of the African landscape.

POLITICAL DECOMPOSITION

One of the accompaniments of independence has been the breakup of political and economic units created under colonial rule. In 1960, the Belgian Congo was a centralized state with six administrative provinces. In 1963, some twenty states appear to be emerging in a Congolese federation with a central government of uncertain powers. In 1958, the eight territories in French-speaking West Africa, and four in Central Africa formed part of the federations of French West Africa and French Equatorial Africa. In 1963, there are twelve independent states.

Economic disengagement has paralleled these political changes. The vast free trade area of French-speaking Africa broke up after 1958. The common currency, airlines, and research organizations of British West Africa have disappeared. The economic unit that was formed by the Central African Federation is undergoing changes as a result of the withdrawal of Nyasaland and Northern Rhodesia. Only in East Africa do the pre-independence economic institutions (a common market and the Common Services Organization) persist.

Although the real economic consequences of these changes are usually exaggerated,

they have had several negative effects. First, with larger political units many public services could be provided more cheaply per person, and all could be manned more efficiently when government was able to draw on a wider labor market for its personnel. Secondly, the replacement of larger political units with smaller ones has entailed some competitive expenditure in the military and diplomatic fields, increasing the charges of sovereignty. Thirdly, in the larger political unit and the larger market associated with it, there may have occurred a larger volume of private investment than would otherwise have taken place. Manufacturing enterprises in Senegal, for example, were established with a capacity designed for a wider, all-French West African market. The same is true in Kenya, Southern Rhodesia, and Leopoldville Province of the Congo. Similarly, certain public investment decisions could be coordinated so as to reduce duplication of investment—notably in statistical and research facilities and in general administrative overheads.

These have been the general costs of the new political arrangements. There have been more specific costs for some of the individual states involved. As was to be expected, the relatively poorer states have suffered most. Formerly they relied on subsidies from their richer partners; many now subsist only with greater subsidies from abroad. This is particularly the case in the ex-French territories; presently the French government is financing not only the development expenditures of most of these states, but part of their ordinary expenditures as well. Dahomey is a good example. Its 1961 budget was in the neighborhood of $25 million, but only $18 million could be raised from local resources—just enough to cover the salaries of civil servants. The situation in Nyasaland is not much different. Once outside of the Central African Federation, it will have to depend on Britain for the $8 million to $11 million annual subsidization it formerly received within the Federation.

The real or imagined advantages of larger

economic units and the fact that so many Africans give at least verbal support to Pan-Africanism account for the variety of organizations that have sprung up in the past few years aimed at bringing about closer economic cooperation: The Organization of African States, the Union of African and Malagasy States, the Ghana–Guinea–Mali Union, and others. The "Casablanca" powers have taken steps towards the formation of a common market and a common military command. But it is the eighteen ex-French states in the African Malagasy Union (UAM) that have gone furthest. They have created an economic organization (*Organisation Africaine et Malgache pour le Coopération Economique*, or OAMCE), a defense organization, a tourist organization, and a common airline. They are making efforts to extend their cooperative ventures in such areas as joint development banks, shipping lines, common diplomatic organization at the United Nations and elsewhere, and common recruitment of technicians.

These inter-African organizations notwithstanding, the main trend has so far been toward less, rather than more, actual economic integration. The old French African free trade area has been disrupted by unilateral commercial policies; the barriers between franc and sterling zone countries have not notably diminished—the lowering of barriers between Ghana and the Upper Volta in 1961 is the only exception.

There are a number of economic reasons why closer economic integration has not yet become more of a reality. First, cooperation between ex-French and ex-British African countries has been hindered by the continuing connection of the ex-French territories with the franc zone and the European Economic Community. The rules of the game within the franc area and the EEC preclude departures in monetary and fiscal policy and restrict action in the area of commercial policy; associated countries cannot, for example, form customs unions with nonassociated African neighbors. Secondly, French-speaking Africans desire to retain the privileges they enjoy through association with the EEC (economic aid and tariff

preferences on tropical products), and this limits the extent to which they are disposed to cooperate with nonassociated African countries in economic matters. Finally, economic integration is not unambiguously advantageous for all combining states or regions. The record of the common markets or free trade areas with which Africa has had experience suggests the following observations. (1) A relatively rich agricultural country is not likely to benefit from economic union with its poorer neighbors, since it will have to help pay for the public services of the poorer partners, and not have much compensatory benefit in the form of larger markets for manufactures. This was the experience of the Ivory Coast in the old Federation of French West Africa, and to a lesser extent of Gabon in ex-French Equatorial Africa. (2) The advanced member state which has an industrial head start will benefit; its industrial sector will grow faster than that of its partners, and its income will rise faster. This is what has happened in Kenya (within the East African customs union) and in Southern Rhodesia (within the Central African Federation).

In both types of situation there is likely to be reluctance on the part of some states to continue the economic association; for example, the Ivory Coast has been the least willing of any West African state to join in closer economic arrangements with other states. There has been considerable grumbling in Uganda and Tanganyika that Kenya has gotten most of the benefits of economic union, while Uganda's and Tanganyika's industrialization has been slowed. Although there is probably not much substance to the latter charges, the fact that they exist is important.

All of this means that economic unification is not likely to be easy, at least in the near future. This in turn means that a number of the African states will remain "client" states forced to rely on outside help to maintain themselves. The French-speaking states of the interior (Mali, Niger, Upper Volta, Chad, Central African Republic, etc.), the small coastal states (Togo and Dahomey), the Central African states of Ruanda, Burundi, Nyasaland, the High Commission territories—these territories cannot be maintained at their present levels of living, much less develop in new directions, without support from somewhere. They will either continue as wards of the world community, or they will find their place within a wider African grouping of states.

Favorable Elements

The list of pitfalls and obstacles to be overcome by African countries on their way to economic modernization is long. It is no surprise that there are many observers who see a dim economic future for most of the continent. But the scales are not without their counterweights.

POPULATION

There is first of all the population factor. The fact that land exists in relative abundance in much of the continent is an advantage of great significance. Aside from reducing the harshness or misery of village life, the life that most Africans still lead, it means that the "population explosion" is less of an economic menace than elsewhere in the underdeveloped world. In parts of Africa, increased population may in fact stimulate the growth of income per head; it can increase the intensity of cultivation in certain areas and render certain investments (notably in roads) more economical.

Furthermore, the existence of adequate land tends to exercise a levelling influence on African societies, giving to most of these societies a relatively equalitarian cast. This is not true in some areas; in the hierarchical societies of the Sudanese belt of West Africa, and in parts of East and Central Africa, class structure tends to be fairly rigid. But sharp and durable division in traditional societies tends to be a function of land scarcity; where each man has access to land, such divisions form with difficulty. Related to this is the fact that most of Africa, unlike most of Asia and Latin America, lacks a landlord problem; there is no need to confront the economic and political dilemmas created by a system of landholding which leaves most of the land to the few.

ECONOMIC STRUCTURE

The economic structure of most African countries is such as to create an apparently high degree of resiliency, an ability to weather extraordinary economic and political upheaval. For example, partly because much of the wage-earning labor force in the continent consists of "migrant" or temporary workers, slowdowns in economic activities and urban unemployment, such as occurred after 1958 in many African countries, can be absorbed without inordinate shock. Men return earlier to the villages and fewer come out for employment. The rest are cared for by extended family members or by friends in town. In short, the absence of a large, permanently committed work force has prevented the emergence of a true proletariat of any size, and in a period of turbulence and change, this introduces an element of flexibility which does not exist in many other parts of the world.

Similarly, the "enclave" character of some African economies has itself provided an element of stability in times of disturbance. In those countries where economic or political conditions deteriorated after independence, expatriate enterprises were able to maintain output. In Guinea, FRIA, the large bauxite processing firm, began production and expanded its output in the years following independence, at a time when the surrounding economy was faltering badly. And more striking still, many enterprises in the Congo, although sitting on a powder keg of potential inflation and civil disorder approaching anarchy, have managed to do surprisingly well; exports from the Congo in 1962 were only about 25 per cent below those of several years earlier—an extraordinary performance, given the political circumstances.

QUALITY OF LEADERSHIP

The quality of African political leadership is another positive factor. This may seem a surprising statement. African leadership has been subject to considerable criticism, and even derision. There seem to be too many parades, too much conference-going, too great a diversion of energies to political exercises in general. African cabinet ministers are accused of living too stylishly, of moving too eagerly into the villas of their former overlords, or building new and better ones, and of driving too often in shiny new Mercedes autos. Corruption and graft have been pointed to and, as the recent Coke Commission Investigation in Nigeria made plain, they have occurred on a large scale. Everywhere there seems to be a marked penchant for setting up unprofitable national air lines. Africa is filled with talk of rapid industrialization and forced draft growth, much of which seems unrealistic.

Yet the fact is that on the whole, African political leadership is dedicated, honest, moderate, responsible, and intelligent. It is indeed a remarkably able leadership, far more responsible than might have emerged, given the pace of political change, the degree of training and preparation available to Africans in many parts of the continent, the nature of the colonial situation and the psychological scars it has left, and the political premium on radicalism. It is a leadership practically everywhere dedicated to rapid modernization; nowhere in the continent is there to be found a ruling group which aims at slowing the modernization process, as in other parts of the undeveloped world. Similarly, if corruption has appeared in a number of African countries, it is worth emphasizing that it rarely exists in Africa on a scale comparable to that found in many parts of the world, particularly in Asia. Vigorous efforts, moreover, are made to deal with it. In how many countries of the world could a Coke Commission fail to find dirty linen in abundance?

It is in the area of economic attitudes that, as we saw earlier, the most serious questions have arisen regarding the new political elites. Nontheless, except in the Congo, moderation and restraint have so far prevailed even here. In fiscal and monetary policies, most African leaders (the Congo provides a notable exception) have roared like lions but acted more like lambs—partly, it is true, because they have had no alternative. Their develop-

ment plans have in practice contained relatively little fat or waste. Showplace schemes are few. Industrial white elephants on the Asian scale are relatively unknown. The counsels of the cautious have most often been followed; transportation, education, agriculture, and public health have been at the center of public investment programs. Economists can look with justifiable concern at the growing current obligations required to maintain expanding educational systems, but these are responses to political pressures not easily contained. It is well to recall, moreover, that in the past four or five years more Africans have won access to secondary and university education than in all the previous years of the colonial presence, and that the rate of output of university graduates is already two or three times greater in some countries (Kenya for example) than was predicted only two or three years ago.

Finally, most African leaders have attacked with courage and vigor problems which all European observers have decried for decades. They are trying to reform work habits, and have urged more effort, responsibility, and dedication on all their people. They are preaching the virtues of manual labor in general, and agricultural work in particular. They are pushing technical and vocational training. They spend little —usually less than 3 per cent of their budgets—on military expenses (except in Ethiopia). They have introduced, at least in a number of cases, tax reforms from which the colonial regimes shrank. They have for the most part adopted policies of wage restraint and have tried to breach the citadel of privilege in the civil service. They are trying to spread literacy and the gospel of modernization throughout their countries. Lethargic leadership is rarely a problem. Indeed, the real danger is that they will try to do too much, too quickly.

RESOURCES

The fragility of African agriculture and the difficulties inherent in its improvement were described earlier. But the agriculture sector is not without its promise. First, it is essential to remember that the African villager has been an economic orphan, neglected for decades by economic policy makers. Outside of the peasant-producer countries, and even there to a certain extent, he was given little encouragement and few of the instruments required for his entry into the modern economy. Transport facilities remain very rudimentary in most African farming areas. Marketing facilities are far from abundant. Price policies for export crops and consumer goods have often been such as to discourage the growth of incentives for the expansion of agriculture. In Central and southern Africa, hesitations to improve land arose from fears of European expropriation.

Second, the knowledge of African soils and general agricultural potentials remains rudimentary. Increased research will certainly open up new possibilities. At the same time, the widening of primary education may well increase the receptivity of ordinary villagers to new ideas for the development of money-earning agricultural activities within the framework of village society.

Third, and most important, African agriculture is at such a low stage of technology that relatively slight changes can have enormous impact. It is not in large-scale change of a revolutionary sort that the greatest future expansion can be anticipated, but in the small things—new seeds, new rotations, the application of known fertilizers, the use of hybrids and better strains, the control of plant disease through spraying, etc. Examples of such changes abound. In Ghana, the recent introduction and spread of capsid spraying on a wide scale has probably led to a 15 per cent increase in cocoa yields at low cost. In parts of southern Africa, animal fertilizer has vastly increased corn yields on nearly exhausted lands—in some cases by as much as 300 per cent. Experiments with chemical fertilizers in parts of West Africa have shown comparable results. There is enough evidence, moreover, to show that African farmers will adopt these changes when they are convinced of their efficacy. There is in fact general evidence that the African peasant is prepared to work small revolutions if he is given the means and the incentive. For example, in the Ivory Coast, where roads were slashed through the forest region so that African cocoa and coffee farmers could go to work readily and market

their crop, coffee output tripled in ten years, making the country the world's third largest coffee producer. Kenya promises to give a similar testimony to peasant energy; in the last few years there has occurred remarkable expansion of African-grown export crop production, as a result of new attention shown some African farmers by the Kenya government.

With respect to nonagricultural resources, the variation in the continent is so great as to rule out brief or easy treatment. Bauxite is scattered throughout Africa, and potential water power is abundant—an estimated 40 per cent of the world's total. The potentials for aluminum production are therefore widespread. Rich iron ore deposits have been found in various parts of West Africa; manganese in Gabon and Ghana; iron in Liberia, Guinea and Southern Rhodesia; copper in Mauritania; oil in Nigeria, Libya and the Gabon. It would be risky to base future predictions on great mineral strikes now unforeseen: It is not certain that the African subsoil contains a great store of mineral wealth. But it is a fact that geological exploration is in its infancy in much of the area, and even places formerly believed to be geologically uninteresting have offered surprises. It was not, for example, until after World War II that rich new gold fields were discovered in South Africa—one of the best prospected areas in the world. As late as 1950, it was the sober opinion of the most technically competent people that the Sahara was devoid of profitable minerals. And in the mid-1950's, Libya was cited in a United Nations report and in textbooks on economic development as an example of a country without resources, and hence a country which could not go anywhere; Libyan oil today flows abundantly.

One good mineral find is no guarantee of rapid growth. But it can provide a big push. In a land of 2 or 3 million people it does not take much of a mineral find to light up the future. And minerals hold out special hope because mineral exploration and exploitation is perhaps the only activity in Africa that receives sustained interest from private enterprise in the non-Communist world. African governments, moreover, whatever their ideological complexion, are increasingly disposed to encouraging private capital in this area.

THE SIZE OF STATES AND ECONOMIC
DEVELOPMENT

Africa now has more nation-states per square mile than any other continent. This is a dubious distinction. We noted earlier some of the inconveniences it causes, but the existence of numerous small states instead of larger units is probably a much less substantial barrier to economic growth than is commonly supposed.

It is not at all clear that over-all growth is adversely affected by the kind of political and economic breakup that we have witnessed in Africa since 1958. The poorer countries suffer, but the richer ones gain—they are able to devote to their own development resources formerly allocated to their poorer partners in larger units. In these circumstances, over-all growth for the two areas together is retarded only to the extent that: (1) public and private capital flows to the separate states are smaller than they would be if the two states were joined together, and (2) the productivity of public investment in the poorer states is greater than the productivity of investment in the richer ones. The first possibility is likely, but there is little evidence that it has in fact occurred, and the experience of the Ivory Coast and Gabon (two of the best-endowed states in ex-French Africa) certainly does not bear it out; they have probably had more, not less, private and public investment since their separation from the former federations. The second possibility is most unlikely. In fact, the presumption would be to the contrary—that public investment in the richer area will almost surely, at present stages of development, yield greater returns than investment in the poorer area. A road in the Ivory Coast, for example, will tend to increase output more than a road in the Upper Volta. What this means is that it is not inconceivable that

over-all incomes will grow faster in the absence of larger units than with them; but this income will be distributed differently.

Coordinated planning and investment policy—one of the major possibilities pointed to as an advantage in larger political units, is not demonstrably easier within such units than outside of them. This is particularly the case when the larger unit is a federation. It is thus not obvious that in federated Nigeria, investment coordination occurs to any greater extent than in fragmented ex-French Africa. Within the common market area of East Africa, each of the three territories tries to lure its own new industrial investment.

The smaller size of markets, one possible consequence of economic separatism, is not necessarily a heavy burden. The effect of small market size on investment and growth depends on the way average unit costs of production vary with output. Put another way, it depends on the extent to which "economies of scale" can be realized by larger output. If a relatively large volume of output is needed before a plant can produce near its top efficiency, market size clearly sets sharp limits on industrial development. If, however, costs per unit of product do not fall much with larger outputs (once a relatively small volume of output is reached), then larger markets are not so vital. Now it is obvious that in some lines of production economies of scale are substantial—in steel or autos, for example. Economists are in disagreement as to the significance of scale economies in many lines of production, but studies in industrial countries suggest that in much manufacturing industry, and particularly in the kind of light manufacturing which presents the greatest possibilities for African countries in the near future, relatively small plants are not notably less efficient than large ones. It is, therefore, only under certain conditions that small market size, due to political and economic fragmentation, will retard industrial development: (1) if economies of scale exist in the production of specific goods which might be manufactured locally, and potential national markets are too small to absorb that volume of output which allows firms to produce near their lowest cost points, and (2) if at the same time these firms are prevented by tariffs or other means from marketing part of their output in neighboring countries because competing firms have been created there. While these are not unlikely circumstances, neither are they universal.

Finally, many of the more obvious costs of small state size can be dealt with without important political reshuffling—through common diplomatic representation, joint ventures in the banking and transport area, etc. Nor is it clear that the higher administrative costs normally attributed to small state size are avoided when political integration occurs; federation, which is the only realistic alternative in most of Africa, is not famous for low-cost administration.

None of this is to say that small state size is beneficial. It is simply that it is not obvious that such political arrangements need be serious obstacles, at least at present, to overall growth. What political separatism does is to make clear the precarious position of the poorer regions of the continent. It also has the negative effects noted earlier. But none of these is of overwhelming significance.

FOREIGN AID

The flow of foreign economic aid has not been reduced with independence; indeed, it has increased. The European Economic Community countries made available to African states associated with them a total of $580 million in the period 1958 to 1962, and have since promised an additional $730 million for the period 1963 to 1967. This is in addition to substantial bilateral aid: $675 million from France in 1962, $109 million from West Germany, $152 million from the United Kingdom, $45 million from other Western European countries, and $123 million from other sources (the International Bank, the United Nations, etc.). To this should be added the indirect aid from France in the form of price supports for exports; under EEC arrangements these are to be extended until 1967, though at lower levels, at which time they will be abandoned. The pace of United States aid has markedly increased in the past several years. Between 1946 and 1962, the United States provided a total of $1.7 billion of aid in all forms to African countries, but in 1962 alone, U.S. aid in all forms amounted to more than half a billion dollars. The Soviet Union similarly has contributed to African assistance programs. Total Soviet and other bloc aid commitments between 1959 and 1962 amounted to $678 million, having grown from very little ($3 million) in 1959, to $236 million in 1962. The total foreign aid inflow to Africa in 1962 was close to $2 billion, which is more than the average annual aid during the booming 1950's. Thus the world community has continued to provide support on a large scale. Despite a certain restiveness among all aid-giving countries, it is not likely that Africa will be abandoned in the decade ahead.

African Economic Development in Summary

To set out these more hopeful facets of the African economic picture is not to underestimate the magnitude of the obstacles to African development, nor to ignore the darker trends and tendencies which cloud the future. The specter of political turbulence, absent nowhere in the continent, is particularly ominous in the states of East, Central and Southern Africa. Political experience in these areas is slight, the ranks of African elites are thin, there are acute tribal differences in some areas, and little political consensus among existing parties. The price prospects for some African commodities on world markets remain uncertain, even after discounting the endemic pessimism of economists and African political spokesmen. The dangers of economic adventurism, particularly by overloading the state with tasks that it is not now capable of performing, are real. The threat of reductions in foreign economic aid, arising in part because of dissatisfaction with the political dividends yielded by aid to Africa, cannot be dismissed; the Clay Report, which urged sharp curtailment of U.S. aid efforts in Africa, and some recent trends within the Communist bloc which indicate similar Soviet views, are not to be taken lightly. Finally, there is the danger that African political leadership will not recognize the potentials of peasant agriculture and will strike out in other directions; this would put the development prospect in another light.

But the economic obstacles, the policy shortcomings, the errors, the economic illusions circulating in the continent—these have received wide attention. Other considerations of a more hopeful nature are also present, and emphasis on these is needed in order to put into better perspective the economic outlook for Africa. For the prospects are by no means uniformly bleak. In many important respects, they are better for Africa as a whole than for either Asia or Latin America. Latin America must contain and channel a rising storm of social revolution. Much of Asia has population pressures and/or military and social problems crippling to its development efforts. These are not African concerns—at least not yet.

All of this means that it would be a tragic mistake if we in the U.S., and in the West generally, began an economic withdrawal from Africa on the grounds either that the economic or political returns are too small. In the long run, the economic and political pay-off for our aid efforts may well be greater in Africa than anywhere else.

2

The Economic Setting in Africa

United Nations Economic Commission for Africa

From Industrial Growth in Africa *(New York, United Nations Economic Commission for Africa, 1963), pp. 1–6.*

Africa embraces nearly one-fourth of the land surface of the world. Its 240 million people account for about 8 per cent of the world's population. Compared with the industrial countries in Western Europe, the area of land under cultivation per head of the entire population in the continent is three times as high, livestock units *per caput*[1] nearly twice as high, and the grazing area per unit of the livestock nearly seven times as high. Even the very inadequate surveys of its other natural resources suggest a vast potential. The continent already produces nearly one-seventh of the world's mineral output—much more if coal is excluded. Its energy resources—principally coal in the south, hydropower in the centre and oil and gas in the north—are considerable.

Owing to the delayed adoption of high labour productivity techniques, however, the continent's share in world output is only 2 per cent. The net value of its annual output may be estimated to be 26,000 million dollars—or about one-half of that of the United Kingdom and almost equal to that of Italy. *Per caput* income at £110 per year is less than one-tenth of that in the industrial countries.

Owing to special characteristics of its economic development, Africa's share in world exports—at about 5 per cent—is much higher than in world income. Annually, Africa exports commodities worth 6,600 million dollars. Its imports almost approximate 8,000 million dollars. *Per caput* level of foreign trade comes to £29 for exports and £35 for imports. Exports are thus about one-fourth and imports one-third of its output. Its foreign trade dependence is considerably greater even than that of the United Kingdom, where exports and imports form 18 and 22 per cent, respectively, of national output. Since nearly one-third of the continent's output originates in subsistence agriculture, its relative dependence on foreign trade is even greater than indicated by these shares.[2]

The data in Table 1 give only an inadequate and, in many respects, a misleading picture of the African economy. One country, the Republic of South Africa, accounts for nearly one-fifth of its total output, although its share in the continent's population is only 6 per cent. If it were excluded, the income of the rest of Africa would be about 21,000 million dollars. The *per caput* income would be approximately £90 per year, or not much different from that of most of Southeast Asia. As can be seen from Table 1, there are significant differences in income levels in Africa. The group of countries in North Africa have twice as high a *per caput* income as in South and East Africa (excluding the Republic of South Africa), whereas the West African countries are in between these extremes.

Long-Term Changes

The main currents of industrial growth over the last century have so far had relatively little impact on this continent south of the Mediterranean. The output per head of subsistence farmers may be assumed not to have changed much during these years. There has been considerable expansion of commercial crops and of mineral output for export and also of manufacturing output, particularly in recent years. But much of it has been concentrated in a few countries. Moreover, the share of these sectors in total output in Africa (excluding South Africa) is still small.

During this period the economic landscape

27

in the countries north of the Mediterranean has radically altered. Halfway through the nineteenth century, the average *per caput* income in Western Europe was $150–170, or one-and-a-half times that in Africa now. Part of this difference may be attributed to higher economic values for the larger requirements of food, shelter and clothing in the colder climate. Economic setbacks caused by wars and depressions notwithstanding, *per caput* real income in the industrial countries increased by about 1.8 per cent per year. The real output per person expanded seven-fold over the last century— or by more than in the entire preceding history of mankind. In the process, the age-old afflictions of poverty and want were swept away, except in some sections of the population and some depressed areas. Poverty, as an urgent problem, moved from the centre to the fringe.

The economic distance between the continents separated by the Mediterranean has widened faster during the last century than ever before. Its origin lay in a steady growth of *per caput* income by 1.8 per cent per year in most of western Europe compared with a very much slower rate in Africa. This century-old process appears, as can be seen from Table 2, to have continued over the last two decades.

Per caput output in Africa (excluding the Republic of South Africa) increased by perhaps 10 to 20 per cent over the last two decades (see Table 2). In the industrial countries, on the other hand, it is now over 60 per cent above the prewar level.[3] Even the limited expansion in Africa seems to have been concentrated largely in the sectors catering to foreign trade, a substantial portion of the income from which goes to peoples of non-African origin. The real average income level in Africa has changed but little. The economic trends in Africa are thus not altogether different from those in other underdeveloped countries. The economic distance that divides the rich and the poor countries has continued to lengthen in this continent, as elsewhere.

This is the setting for the world-wide concern for future economic growth in Africa as well as elsewhere. If political independence

Table 1—Selected Economic Indicators in Africa

Region or Country[b]	Population in Millions	Exports	Imports	National Income (in U.S. $)	Total	Agriculture	Mining	Manufacturing	Rest
							(in '000million U.S. $)		
North Africa	63	24	45	130	8.15	2.65	0.25	0.95	4.31
West Africa	65	22	27	110	7.25	4.35	0.15	0.60	2.15
South and East Africa[b]	89	21	20	65	5.56	2.23	0.48	0.48	2.12
Total above[a]	217	22	29	95	20.96	9.23	0.88	2.03	8.58
Rest of South Africa	14	130	112	360	5.05	0.60	0.60	1.20	2.60
Total Africa	231	29	35	110	26.01	9.85	1.50	3.25	11.20
Former French West Africa	19	14	18	144	2.73	1.64	0.03	0.34	0.73
UAR (Egypt)	28	18	23	95	2.62	0.87	0.03	0.32	1.42
Algeria	10	38	127	250	2.50	0.55	0.08	0.28	1.59
Nigeria	32	14	19	70	2.26	1.42	0.03	0.06	0.76
Morocco	10	30	36	154	1.54	0.52	0.09	0.28	0.65
Rhodesia and Nyasaland	8	67	55	155	1.23	0.23	0.26	0.12	0.62
Ghana	5	64	72	245	1.22	0.73	0.02	0.10	0.37
Congo (Leo)	14	35	25	85	1.17	0.30	0.19	0.14	0.54
Total above[b]	126	26	36	121	15.27	6.26	0.73	1.64	6.68
Total Rest of Africa[b]	91	16	21	62	5.69	2.97	0.15	0.39	1.90

Note : Gross domestic product figures for the latest year available are rounded to the nearest 5 or 10.
[a] Arranged in descending order of total national income.
[b] Excluding the Republic of South Africa.

has been the watchword in Africa for the last ten years, rapid economic growth will no doubt be the overriding preoccupation for the years to come. The disparity in the rates of economic growth of different areas persisted at a time when stagnation or slow growth was unquestioningly accepted. But the newly independent states of Africa are now shaping an image of the continent from which poverty and economic backwardness would be eliminated as rapidly as possible. The aspirations, vague in the early stages, are rapidly being transformed into concrete plans.

More than ever before, governments are formulating plans, programmes and projects aimed at bringing about the economic transition from poverty to relative well-being. There is thus a continuing need to assess the progress already made and the problems and perspectives for the future. This study attempts to review the state of industrial growth in Africa and to indicate the broad contours along which it might proceed in the future.

Structure of the African Economy

The statistical information so far available for Africa is inadequate to define precisely its economic structure. Some of the general characteristics of the African economy may, however, be suggested. Although

the picture is only approximate, it may serve as a useful analytical tool. The over-all picture for the continent can hardly be expected to correspond to economic reality in the individual countries.

A comparison of the structural characteristics of Africa with those of the industrial countries may help to give some idea of the economic distance which separates them. It could also suggest the main lines along which the African economies might advance in the years to come. The pattern of economic development of one country at one time can hardly be repeated in the same fashion in another place at another time. Africa need not follow exactly the economic trail traversed by the industrial countries. Nor is it necessary for the economic image of the Africa of the future to be merely a carbon copy of the industrial countries today. The tempo of growth may differ. Africa's particular cultural, political and social traditions and natural endowments will no doubt leave their special imprint on its future economic development. And yet, it is reasonable to suggest that economic growth in Africa would involve an increase in the output of goods and services which advances in science and technology have made possible in the industrial countries.

Table 2—Major Economic Changes in Africa,[a] Prewar to 1960

Item	Index numbers: 1938[b] = 100		Annual compound percentage change	
	1950	1960	Prewar to 1960	1950 to 1960
Population[b]	115	140	1.7	1.9
Agricultural output[b]	130	150	1.8	1.4
Industrial output	220	345[c]	6.7[c]	6.4[c]
Total commodity output[d]	130	160	2.1	2.1
Per caput commodity output	112	115	0.6	0.2
Quantum of exports	125	195	3.0	4.7
Quantum of imports	145	234	3.9	5.0

Sources: United Nations, *Economic Survey of Africa since 1950.*
United Nations Statistical Yearbook 1961.
United Nations Demographic Yearbook 1960–1961.
United Nations, *FAO Production Yearbook, 1958, 1960.*

[a] Including the Republic of South Africa.
[b] Base years for index of population is 1940, and of agricultural output average for 1934–1938.
[c] Terminal year is 1957.
[d] Derived by combining, as a weighted basis, the index numbers of agricultural and industrial output of small-scale industry assumed to have changed in line with population.

The data assembled in Table 3 attempt such a comparison. It may be emphasized again that the magnitudes are illustrative— adequate only for assessing the broad order of differences and indicating the main direction of change. Despite their approximate character, they suggest at once a number of observations.

The average *per caput* income in Africa (excluding the Republic of South Africa) is under one-twelfth of that in the industrial countries combined as a group. But it is being increasingly recognized that the estimates of *per caput* incomes for areas with significantly different output structures and price relatives cannot be readily used for comparative purposes. Many authors have suggested that the *per caput* incomes in poor countries have to be raised significantly to assure a measure of realistic comparison.[4] The adjustments in Table 3 are rough and ready and intended only to serve as broad indicators rather than precise measurements.

Over forty per cent of the income in Africa (excluding South Africa) originates in agriculture. The comparative proportion for the industrial countries is only about ten per cent. Agricultural output on a *per caput* basis for the whole population would amount to about $40 in Africa and $120 in the industrial countries. The prices at which the contribution of agricultural output (particularly of subsistence agriculture) is computed are usually lower than in the industrial countries.

If African agricultural output were to be expressed in the relative prices of industrial countries, it would require a marked upward revision. With an upward adjustment by about one-half (column (b) in Table 3), the *per caput* net agricultural output in the industrial countries would be only twice as high as in Africa for the population as a whole. The comparison of *per caput* industrial production in Africa and in the industrial countries, however, reveals a very wide gap indeed. Its level in the industrial countries is nearly twenty-five times as high as in Africa. Without any price adjustments, these ratios would be 3:1 for agricultural and over 30:1 for industrial output for the population as a whole.

The service sector is the most difficult to adjust for comparative purposes. The usual difficulties are magnified in Africa where the non-African population has an unusually high weight in this sector. Its scale of remuneration is often higher than in its country of origin. Only fragmentary indicators are available for income distribution between the African and the non-African

Table 3—Illustrative Measurement of the Economic Distance Between Africa[a] and the Industrial Countries, 1960

Output by industrial origin	Africa In African prices ($) (a)	Africa In US relative prices ($) (b)	Industrial countries (c)	Ratio of per caput[c] output in industrial countries and in Africa (c):((b) (d)	Rates of growth and period needed by Africa to reach the 1960 level of industrial countries Annual per caput rate of growth in per cent (e)	Rates of growth and period needed by Africa to reach the 1960 level of industrial countries Years (f)
Agriculture	40	60	120	2	1.5–2	40–50
Industry	15	20	480	25	7–8	40–45
Commodity output	55	80	600	8	5	40–50
Other sectors	35	...[b]	600	...	?	?
Total output	90	(150)[b]	1,200	(8)	(5)	(40–50)

Source: Computed from Surendra J. Patel, *Economic Distance between Nations: Its Origin, Management and Outlook,* The Journal of Modern African Studies, Vol. 2, No. 1 (1964), pp. 329–349.

Note: The figures, based on domestic product at factor cost, are very rough and have therefore been rounded to the nearest 5 or 10. Adjustments in column (b) are purely notional in character.

[a] Excluding South Africa.
[b] Relative prices in the service sector are difficult to compare nearly everywhere but more so in Africa where, owing to the predominance of the non-African population in this sector, the remuneration is relatively high. The figure for total output in column (b) is therefore purely arbitrary.
[c] Of the whole population, not according to sectors.

population. They suggest that the latter account for a little over one per cent of the population in Africa (excluding the Republic of South Africa), but nearly 20 to 25 of its output.[5] The adjusted figure for the total *per caput* output in Table 3 is therefore purely arbitrary in character.

The statistical foundation of the adjustments in Table 3 is undoubtedly weak. But it is not likely that any improvements in statistics would alter significantly the broad relationships outlined above—that is, the agricultural distance between countries in Africa and the industrial countries is of the order of 2 to 1, whereas the industrial distance is about 25 to 1. The distance is not as incredible as it may appear at first sight. The demand for food is largely limited by the size of the body, climatic conditions, levels of activity, and a variety of diet, while the demand for industrial raw materials is likely to be less than that for food. But when these factors are taken into consideration, it would seem that a doubling of *per caput* agricultural supplies in Africa for the whole population would bring the figure near to the level in the industrial countries.

At this point, it should be made clear that *per caput* output is used here as a broad guide to both total agricultural output and total industrial output. *Per caput* output refers to the output per head of the whole population and must be distinguished clearly from labour productivity in agriculture or labour productivity in industry, which are measured by dividing total output in the sector concerned by the labour force employed in that sector. Comparative figures of labour productivity are not readily available, but it is evident that the gap between labour productivity in the two continents is very much greater than 2:1. It is outside the scope of this report to argue the need for an increase in labour productivity in agriculture in Africa of the order of twenty-fold. An increase in agricultural production is clearly necessary as a means of releasing labour from agriculture for employment in industry, as a source of capital for investment in the economy, and to increase purchasing power for the products of industry.

The dimension of agricultural growth in the industrial countries over the last century

was not in fact altogether dissimilar. During this period, the population of these countries increased a little under three-fold, and total agricultural output four- to five-fold. *Per caput* agricultural output thus rose by only a little over one-half. Industrial output, on the other hand, expanded during these years over forty-fold, or nearly fifteen-fold on a *per caput* basis.[6]

Economic Image Over the Decades To Come

The main object of economic growth in any country has always been to increase the supply of goods and services available for present consumption and of investible resources to assure future development. In this respect, the experience of the industrial countries has considerable relevance for Africa. The indicators put together in Table 3 could be used as general guideposts—but no more than that—to outline the broad contours of Africa's future growth. The indicators for Africa as a whole would, of course, have to be adjusted to fit the economic structure and potential of each individual country.

To raise the low *per caput* output in Africa and other industrially less developed areas to the output of the industrial countries is now generally accepted as a long-term objective of economic development. The implications of such a transition are therefore of considerable operational significance. The approximate indicators in Table 3 could be used to suggest the dimensions of time and pace that this economic transition would entail.

Many of the countries in Africa are now in the process of formulating economic plans. In any such formulation, the characteristics and resources of each individual country must play a decisive role. Some of the comparative data presented here may serve as a useful economic background for setting concrete targets for the expression of each sector. Stated in a summary fashion, the economic transition in Africa would involve increasing the output of two major sectors roughly by these orders: doubling of agricultural output and a twenty-five-fold increase in industrial output *per caput* for the whole population. These dimensions suggest at once the sector where the leeway between Africa and the industrial countries is the greatest. A very rapid industrial expansion would have to form the core of any programme for raising the income level in Africa to that in industrial Europe,[7] assuming that industrial production and incomes per worker in Africa would be much higher than production and incomes in agriculture. More than doubling *per caput* agricultural output without a simultaneous expansion of industries, as suggested above, would create problems of marketing for which solutions are not easily predictable at present.

How rapidly could this economic distance be covered? The answer obviously depends on the pace of economic growth. As shown above, the process took, in general, about a century in the industrial countries—as an annual growth rate of *per caput* output of 1.8 per cent. Whether it would be faster in Africa is a question that can be decided only at national level.

The pace of economic growth has generally quickened for each of the new entrants into the field of industrialization. There are many reasons for this. The most important is the possibility that latecomers benefit from the vast accumulation of technical knowledge. Their pace need not be cramped by the tempo of technical development, or hampered by economic fluctuations. They can readily draw upon the amassed technical knowledge of the world. The rate of their economic growth would thus depend mainly on the ability and speed with which they assimilate, adapt, and spread modern knowledge and a scientific outlook among their peoples.

The right-hand columns in Table 3 give an illustrative idea of the dimensions of time and pace that such a translation could entail. The economic distance that separates Africa from the industrial countries could be covered in forty to fifty years if *per caput*

output could be increased at 1.5 to 2 per cent for agriculture and 7 to 8 per cent for industries.[8] These dimensions are not meant to be taken literally, but they do indicate that, given such growth rates, the economic transitions need not cover centuries. These growth rates are indeed higher than those that prevailed during the century of industrialization in Western Europe.[9] But even at West European growth rates, economic transition in Africa would need no more than a century to reach the present level of Western Europe.

In recent decades many countries have experienced much higher growth rates for fairly long periods of time. If these could be attained in Africa and maintained for three to four decades (preferably higher in the earlier period and lower afterwards), then the transformation of Africa from an industrially backward economy to an advanced one could take place within half a century.

Notes

1. *Per caput* is used in this paper to refer to the whole population, not just to those engaged in the sector or activity in question.
2. "Industrialization and Foreign Trade," United Nations Economic Commission for Africa, 1963, Chap. II, para. 54 *et seq.*
3. Estimate derived by regression (growth backward) of *per caput* income and known growth rates of these countries, and by using a weighted average and straight-line extrapolation in time. See Simon S. Kuznets, *Six Lectures on Economic Growth* (Beverly Hills, Calif.: Glencoe Press, 1959), p. 27.
4. For details see S. S. Kuznets, "National Income and Industrial Structure" in *Economic Distance*, Vol. XVII, Supplement (July, 1949), p. 209; Gilbert and Kravis, *Comparative National Products and Price Levels* (OEEC Paris) National Bureau of Economic Research, *Problems in the International Comparison of National Accounts* (Princeton, N.J.: Princeton University Press, 1957), p. 384; Harry Starks, *Infirmities of per capita Income Estimates* (Coral Gables, Fla.: University of Miami Press).
5. Estimate based on information in United Nations ECA, *Economic Survey of Africa Since 1950* (New York, 1959), p. 87.
6. Based on Surendra J. Patel's study, *Economic Distance between Nations: Its Origin, Management and Outlook.*
The following annual compound growth rates (in percentages) for the industrial countries as a

group could be derived from it for the period 1850 to 1960:

	Per caput	Over-all
National income	1.8	2.7
Agricultural output	0.5	1.4
Industrial output	2.6	3.5

These growth rates appear modest, but when cumulated over a long period, they bring about the massive expansion indicated in the paragraph above. This is because of the relentless force of growth at compound rates over a period of time—particularly towards the end of the period.

The table below gives an illustrative idea of the possible expansion in initial output (taken as 1), if it grows at rates varying from 1 to 10 for years indicated.

Annual Compound Percentage Rate of Growth	Period in Years			
	10	20	50	100
1	1.10	1.22	1.6	2.7
2	1.22	1.49	2.7	7.2
3	1.34	1.8	4.4	19
4	1.48	2.2	7.1	50
5	1.63	2.7	11.5	130
6	1.79	3.2	16	340
7	1.97	3.9	30	870
8	2.16	4.7	47	2200
9	2.37	5.6	74	5530
10	2.59	6.7	120	14000

Drawing attention to the astonishing increase involved in compound rates of growth, Keynes once illustrated this by the probable growth of the treasure of £40,000—the prodigious spoils of the *Golden Hind*—with which Captain Drake returned to England in 1580. "Now it happens," he wrote, "that £40,000 accumulating at $3\frac{1}{4}$ compound interest approximately corresponds to the actual volume of England's foreign investments at various dates and would actually amount today to the total of £4,000,000,000 which I have already quoted as being what our foreign investments now are. Such is the power of compound interest." See his "Economic Possibilities for our Grandchildren (1930)" in *Essays in Persuasion* (London, 1931), p. 362.

7. In the early stages of industrialization, agriculture contributed twice as much as industry to total output in the industrial countries. But its share in the increase of commodity output in these countries over the following hundred years was only about one-sixth.

8. Agricultural growth potential is not the subject of this study. For a discussion of the feasibility of a high rate of agricultural growth see ECE, *Economic Survey of Europe in 1959*, Chap. VII, pp. 7–23 and 46–50.

9. Economic growth during this century was not continuous. It was often interrupted and even reversed by wars and depressions. During these hundred years, the industrial countries faced six to seven business cycles, one major agricultural depression, the Great Depression, and two world wars.

3

African Economic Development: Problems and Prospects

Andrew M. Kamarck

From Africa Report Magazine, *Vol. 14, No. 1 (1969), pp. 16–20 and 37. Reprinted with permission.*

> *"And he gave it for his opinion, that whoever could make two ears of corn or two blades of grass grow upon a spot of ground where only one grew before, would deserve better of mankind, and do more essential service to his country than the whole race of politicians put together."*
> —The King of Brobdingnag, in Jonathan Swift's *Gulliver's Travels*

> *"What's past is prologue; what to come, In yours and my discharge."*
> —William Shakespeare, *The Tempest*

ANY FACTUAL APPRAISAL of economic progress and potential in Africa is bound to present only a partial picture, since much of what is most important in developing countries is not measurable in figures—or at least, is not usually measured in figures.

There is no regular series of statistics, for example, that measures changes in attitudes toward life and work; no measurement of the degree to which the average African has become oriented toward problem solving; no easy way even to measure the gains in knowledge of the African natural environment and of how to master it. How do we assess precisely the progress made in creating national unity, or the degree of political stability, or the people's sense of security about the future? In spite of what Jonathan Swift said, politicians can make a substantial contribution to Africa—for the restructuring of societies is closely intertwined with economic development.

We do have figures on growth in gross domestic product. The GDP is a generally useful, summarizing figure in looking at economies and I do not want to discard it. But for countries in the economic stage of most of those in Africa, the GDP and other statistics derived from it must be used with caution. The GDP of countries with a large subsistence sector is likely to be underrated because the value of the subsistence output is underpriced; this means that at least a part of the economic growth that appears in the GDP statistics when production is monetized is illusory. Even the relative position of countries as shown by their per capita GDP's must be interpreted with care. It is extremely doubtful that a country that has a GDP of $80 equivalent per capita is really twice as well off as a country with a GDP per capita of $40; but it can be taken that it is better off.

We also know that the relative distance between the per capita incomes of the African countries and the industrialized countries exaggerates the real differences. As countries develop, for example, the prices of services go up without a real increase in the productivity or the satisfaction provided (e.g., a haircut which costs $2.50 in the United States is not likely to provide 10 times the satisfaction of a haircut that costs 25 cents in an African country). In terms of the real purchasing power over the goods and services that can be purchased, the U.S. per capita GDP of $4,000 is not 100 times the per capita GDP of $40 in Rwanda, but perhaps more like 20 to 40 times. The relative ranking remains, and the differences are still enormous, however, and this is why the figures still remain useful.

While there are no absolute standards that one can apply to a country's growth performance, it is of some value to compare the growth rates in Africa to other regions. The data in Table 1 indicate that for the period 1960 to 1966 (and 1967 and 1968 are likely to be about the same), the gross domestic product in Africa as a whole grew at about the same rate as that of South Asia. It is not surprising that neither Africa nor South

Table 1—Real Gross Domestic Product, Population, and Gross Domestic Product Per Capita—Regional Summary (Average Annual Rates of Growth— per cent)

	1950–1960	1960–1966
Africa		
GDP	4.4	3.3
Population	2.2	2.3
GDP per capita	2.2	1.0
South Asia		
GDP	3.6	3.4
Population	1.9	2.5
GDP per capita	1.7	0.8
East Asia		
GDP	5.1	4.9
Population	2.5	2.7
GDP per capita	2.5	2.1
Southern Europe		
GDP	5.6	7.7
Population	1.4	1.4
GDP per capita	4.1	6.2
Latin America		
GDP	4.9	4.7
Population	2.9	2.9
GDP per capita	1.9	1.7
Middle East		
GDP	5.6	7.2
Population	3.1	2.9
GDP per capita	2.4	4.2
Industrialized Countries		
GDP	4.0	5.1
Population	1.2	1.2
GDP per capita	2.8	3.9

Source: *World Bank Annual Report* 1967/68.

Note: Estimates in this table are for:

Fifty-six developing countries covering approximately 90 per cent of GDP of all developing countries. In *Africa :* Algeria, Congo–Kinshasa, Ethiopia, Ghana, Kenya, Malawi, Morocco, Nigeria, Rhodesia, Sudan, Tanzania, Tunisia, Uganda, UAR, Zambia account for 76 per cent of the aggregate GDP of the region. In *South Asia :* Burma, Ceylon, India, Pakistan cover 100 per cent. In *East Asia :* Republic of China, Malaysia, Philippines, Thailand, Indonesia cover 68 per cent. In *Southern Europe :* Cyprus, Greece, Portugal, Spain, Turkey, Yugoslavia cover 100 per cent. In *Latin America :* Argentina, Bolivia, Brazil, Chile, Colombia, Costa Rica, Dominican Republic, El Salvador, Ecuador, Guatemala, Haiti, Honduras, Jamaica, Mexico, Nicaragua, Panama, Paraguay, Peru, Trinidad and Tobago, Uruguay, Venezuela cover 73 per cent. And in the *Middle East :* Iran, Iraq, Israel, Jordan, Syria cover 73 per cent.

Twenty-one industrialized countries. In *North America :* United States, Canada. In *Western Europe :* Austria, Belgium, Denmark, Finland, France, Federal Republic of Germany, Italy, Netherlands, Norway, Sweden, Switzerland, United Kingdom, Ireland, Iceland, Luxembourg. *Other industrialized countries :* Australia, Japan, New Zealand, South Africa.

Asia did as well as the other developing regions. Africa and South Asia are the regions where per capita income is the lowest in the world.

In general, the growth rate of a developing country tends to accelerate as per capita income moves up into the $300–600 bracket per capita. Table 2 shows some of the reasons for this. The percentage of their GDP that the African countries save to finance investment is the lowest of any of the regions of the world, around 10 per cent; Southern Europe has the maximum, around 21 per cent. While there is much more to growth than rate of investment, it is not surprising that Southern Europe is also the region in the developing world that is growing the fastest and is in fact beginning to catch up to the developed countries.

While the growth rate of GDP in Africa and South Asia is about the same, in terms of per capita GDP, Africa has been growing faster than the South Asia rate: one per cent compared to somewhat under one per cent. This is primarily because the rate of population growth in South Asia is higher than it is in Africa. (These figures, of course, are for the region as a whole and they are not necessarily true of any one individual country.)

In 1960 certain African countries, for various historical and natural reasons, had per capita GDP's of $200 or over; that is, considerably above those of the other African countries. These select countries were Senegal, Ghana, Gabon, Southern Rhodesia, and Mauritius. Of these, only Gabon has had uninterrupted and rapid growth since then, based on continued development of its various mineral resources. The growth of the other countries of this group slowed down or halted, mainly due to political events—in the case of Senegal, the major factor being the breakup of the French West African Federation, of which Dakar was the political and economic center.

Since 1960, this group of $200+ GDP per capita countries has been joined by Ivory Coast, Liberia, Swaziland and Zambia, and approached by Angola. Except for the Ivory Coast, the main reason for this growth in the countries concerned was the development of mineral resources. (See Table 3.) Of the other African countries south of the Sahara, good

Table 2—Economic Indicators for 63 Selected Developing and Industrialized Countries—Regional Summary

			Average Annual Rates of Growth (Per Cent), 1960–1966					Per Cent of GNP Average, 1960–1966			
Region	Population (1)	Total GDP (2)	GDP Per Capita (3)	Agricultural Production (4)	Manufacturing Production (5)	Exports[d] (6)	Imports[d] (7)	Total Gross Investment (8)	Gross Investment (9)	Savings (10)	Current Account Deficit (11)
Developing Countries	2.5	4.8	2.3	2.1	7.3	7.4	7.8	8.6	17.4	15.2	2.2
Africa[a]	2.3	3.3	1.0	2.5	5.9	5.3	4.8	5.7	13.7	10.1	3.6
South Asia	2.5	3.4	0.5	1.0	7.0	2.2	2.8	7.5	13.8	11.0	2.8
East Asia	2.7	4.9	2.1	2.1	5.9	7.2	6.6	9.3	13.4	12.0	1.4
Southern Europe	1.4	7.7	6.2	2.8	10.8	14.7	18.4	17.2	23.8	21.0	2.8
Latin America[b]	2.9	4.7	1.7	2.7	5.6	5.3	4.3	3.7	18.0	16.9	1.1
Middle East[c]	2.9	7.2	4.2	4.1	9.3	10.1	9.5	5.7	19.3	14.4	4.9
Industrialized Countries	1.2	5.1	3.9	1.5	6.3	7.8	8.0	6.3	20.9	21.4	−0.5

Source: *World Bank Annual Report* 1967/68.

Note: The data pertain to the same countries as those included in Table 1, except as shown in footnotes [a] to [d].

[a] Columns 4 through 11 exclude Algeria, Republic of Congo, Malawi, Rhodesia, UAR, and Zambia.
[b] Columns 4 through 11 exclude Bolivia, Costa Rica, Haiti, and Trinidad and Tobago.
[c] Columns 4 through 11 exclude Syria.
[d] Goods and services at current prices.

Table 3—Population, Total GNP, and GNP Per Capita in U.S. Dollars for African Countries and Territories, 1966[a]

Country	Mid-Year Population (Thousands)	Total GNP (U.S. $ Million)	GNP Per Capita (U.S. $)
Nigeria	59,700	4,895	80
Ethiopia	23,000	1,357	60
Congo (Kinshasa)	15,986	1,007	60
Sudan	13,940	1,366	100
Morocco	13,725	2,306	170
Algeria	12,147	2,709	220
Tanzania	11,833	887	70
Kenya	9,643	887	90
Ghana	7,945	1,851	230
Uganda	7,740	782	100
Mozambique	7,040	704	100
Malagasy Republic	6,200	577	90
Cameroon	5,350	478	110
Angola	5,225	909	170
Upper Volta	4,955	268	50
Mali	4,654	293	60
Tunisia	4,460	905	200
Rhodesia, Southern	4,400	915	210
Malawi	4,035	206	50
Ivory Coast	3,920	878	220
Zambia	3,827	704	180
Guinea	3,608	289	80
Senegal	3,580	763	210
Niger	3,433	268	80
Chad	3,361	222	70
Burundi	3,274	154	50
Rwanda	3,204	128	40
Somalia	2,580	129	50
Dahomey	2,410	183	80
Sierra Leone	2,403	351	150
Togo	1,680	166	100
Libya	1,677	1,078	640
Central African Republic	1,437	161	110
Liberia	1,090	228	210
Mauritania	1,070	139	130
Lesotho	865	49	60
Congo (Brazzaville)	850	151	180
Mauritius	759	162	210
Botswana	575	34	60
Portuguese Guinea	528	—	—
Gabon	468	187	400
Reunion	408	—	—
Swaziland	375	107	290
Gambia	336	30	90
Cape Verde Islands	228	—	—
Comoro Islands	225	24	100
Rio Muni	198	—	—
Ceuta and Melilla	160	—	—
French Somaliland	84	48	570
Fernando Póo	74	—	—
São Tomé and Principe	60	—	—
Ifni	53	—	—
Seychelles Islands	48	—	—
Spanish Sahara	48	—	—

[a] Ranked by size of population.

37

rates of growth have been shown by Cameroon, Ethiopia, Kenya, the Malagasy Republic, Mauritania, Mozambique, Nigeria (prior to the civil war), Sudan, and Uganda. Again, the particularly favorable rates of Mauritania, Mozambique, and Nigeria were due mostly to mineral development.

All the indications are that Africa is entering a period not only of a high growth rate of population, but an accelerating growth rate. Population is still one of the fields on which little information is available in Africa, but there is sufficient evidence from a number of countries to show that the birth rate is almost 50 per thousand, and that the average total fertility for tropical Africa is about 6.5 children per female. The high mortality rate that has heretofore run parallel with these extremely high fertility rates is dropping.

The most thorough study of population yet carried out in Africa was made recently in Kenya. The government demographer estimates that birth rates in Kenya are around 50 per thousand and death rates 20 per thousand, with a natural increase of at least three per cent per year. The death rate, still twice that in the industrialized countries, will certainly come down. But even assuming that the natural rate of increase continues at only three per cent a year, this means that Kenya's present population of 9 million would have risen to 30 million in A.D. 2000 and to 144 million in less than a century. The problem of educating, housing, and providing jobs for this population increase would be almost insuperable, even without contemplating any increase in per capita income. Based on this analysis, the Kenya Government is now planning to take action to try to reduce the birth rate.

All other things being equal, a country with a lower rate of population growth can increase its per capita GDP more rapidly than a country with a higher rate of population growth. The figures in Table 1 can be used as an example: In 1960 to 1966, GDP in the industrialized countries grew at 5.1 per cent a year, and population at 1.2 per cent; per capita GDP grew at 3.9 per cent per year. At this rate, per capita GDP would

double in 19 years. During the same period, GDP in Latin America grew at 4.7 per cent a year, almost equal to the developed countries, population at 2.9 per cent, and per capita GDP at 1.7 per cent. These figures suggest it would take *42 years* for Latin American per capita GDP to double. The process is cumulative: about 65 per cent of total investment in developing countries must now be devoted to maintaining per capita income at its present low level, as compared with less than 25 per cent in the developed countries. Thus the developed countries can use over $75 out of every $100 invested to raise per capita incomes, while only $35 can be used for this purpose in the developing countries. This is one of the reasons why the gap between the rich and poor countries is widening.

But the position of African countries will be even worse than Latin America's. The bulk of the increase in population consists primarily of children, and the proportion of dependents to the whole population shoots up year by year. The proportion of savings available for increasing the standard of living sinks even below the 35 per cent mentioned above.

Most governments and peoples in Africa have not yet become conscious of the seriousness of the population problem facing them. It may well be that the most important decision which will influence the pace of economic development in individual African countries for the rest of this century will be the decision governments and individuals take in regard to controlling the explosive rate of population increase.

Practically all economic analysis of development problems in Africa comes out with the conclusion that a necessary condition for faster industrial growth in most countries is a larger size market, and that the small economic size of most African countries is a severe handicap to establishing industry. The initial impact of independence was to destroy most of the existing larger economic units, such as the federations in West Africa, and the monetary unions under the West African and East African Currency Boards. The East African Common Market of Uganda, Kenya, and Tanzania has in large part been preserved through the Treaty for

East African Cooperation which came into effect on December 1, 1967, and it may be expanded to include Zambia and possibly Ethiopia. However, there are still problems of implementation.

Of the other initiatives at economic integration, the Union Douanière et Economique de l'Afrique Centrale (UDEAC) was severely strained in 1968 by the withdrawal of Chad. The Central African Republic withdrew and then returned to the group of Cameroon, Gabon, and Congo (Brazzaville). In West Africa, Dahomey, Ivory Coast, Mauritania, Togo, Senegal, and Upper Volta remain in a multinational currency union, and the four Equatorial states and Cameroon form another. Various other initiatives—for example the Union Douanière et Economique de l'Afrique de l'Ouest, consisting of Mauritania, Senegal, Mali, Niger, Upper Volta, Ivory Coast and Dahomey—are still mostly at the beginning stage, or even the declaration of intention or planning stage.

Aside from the political will to set them up and make them work, economic unions, common markets, or customs unions need to have as a base a better inter-African infrastructure. It would do little good to combine Ethiopia and Kenya into a common market, for example, if there is no easy transport link between them. A step in this direction has

been taken in recent years with the creation of a working group consisting of the African Development Bank, the Economic Commission for Africa, the United Nations Development Program, and the World Bank to plan improvements in the inter-African network of transport, telecommunications, and power. One concrete result of this joint planning has been the decision to construct power lines from Ghana to Togo and Dahomey by which the Volta Project in Ghana will provide electricity to the other two countries. There is also some progress being made in beginning the improvement of roads between countries. Work is going ahead, for example, on the building of roads to join Ethiopia and Kenya and on improving the road between Tanzania and Zambia.

Over the next 10 years, world technological progress is likely to make possible a big step forward in bringing African countries into closer communication with each other. The jet airplane in its "jumbo" phase should reduce air transport costs considerably and may well make air transport much more economic in large parts of Africa than the road or rail alternatives. For a continent

Table 4—Value of Exports from Developing Countries by Main Commodity Groups

	Average Annual Values 1963–1965 ($ billions)	Average Annual Rates of Growth of Values of Exports 1958–1960 to 1963–1965 (per cent)
Food, beverages and tobacco	11.3	4.2
Raw materials :	8.3	3.4
Textile fibers	2.1	4.1
Other agricultural materials	2.1	−1.4
Total agricultural materials	4.7	0.9
Non-metallic minerals	0.4	5.9
Metals, ores and scrap	1.5	7.1
Non-ferrous metals	1.7	8.2
Total non-agricultural materials	3.6	7.5
Total food and raw materials	19.6	3.9
Fuels	10.5	7.0
Total primary commodities	30.0	4.9
Manufactures	3.9	12.4
Total exports	34.1	5.6

Source: UNCTAD, "Recent Developments and Long-Term Trends in Commodity Trade," TD/9, November, 1967.

with large empty spaces separating centers of development, air transport is peculiarly well suited since it eliminates the need for large expenditures of funds to build roads or rails traversing long distances over empty land where little traffic is generated. Communications by satellite should also be peculiarly suited to Africa because of the savings on laying wire or building microwave towers over vast distances with little intermediate traffic. Indeed, it may be more economic to use these most modern means of transport and communications in Africa than in many of the presently developed countries, which have existing large investments in transport and communication networks.

While an improved inter-African infrastructure and economic unions are important steps toward African economic development, even after they are created progress is bound to be slow since the selfreinforcing character of poverty will still continue. The creation of some additional industry may become possible when two African countries combine their markets, but the fact that there is a market of 10 million people instead of two single markets of, say, 5 million people each, is still not going to result in explosive industrialization if the 10 million have average per capita incomes of $100 or under, and still have to spend the bulk of their incomes on simple food and shelter. The market for manufactures is highly income-elastic; it is only as people's incomes go up into higher levels that their demand for manufactures increases rapidly. This reinforces the gains that can come from a slower rate of population increase: one man having an income of $200 a year represents a total larger market for manufactures than that of four men, each of whom has an income of $50 a year.

The African Development Bank created in 1966 is an important advance, but it has been severely hampered by lack of funds and lack of staff. This is in striking contrast to the Asian Bank, which was started later, profited from the African institution's experience, and avoided some of its mistakes. The Asian Bank, for example, did not restrict its membership to nations in the region; indeed it recruited nonregional members while maintaining a majority control for the countries in the region. It has a capital of $1.1 billion, and its 13 non-regional members, all capital-exporting countries, are putting up $175 million of paid-in capital, plus $175 million of callable capital which can be used as guarantees for borrowing in the capital markets of the world. The African Bank, on the other hand, will have a maximum of $250 million of nominal capital, of which $125 million is paid in, and all of this subscribed by the poor, capital-importing countries in Africa. The Asian Bank's non-regional membership has also been a source of personnel to supplement staff drawn from the region in building up a permanent Bank staff. (And within the region, of course, are Japan, Australia, and New Zealand—all substantial contributors of capital as well as of experienced staff.)

Finally, it should be mentioned that the United Nations regional agency for Africa, the Economic Commission for Africa, has during the last 10 years built up an effective organization and one which is making an increasingly valuable contribution to the area.

The most important economic tie African countries have outside the region is that of the 18 African associate members with the European Common Market. This association began in 1957, was extended in 1964 for a period of five years expiring May 31, 1969, and is now being negotiated for renewal. The associated African countries have benefited from the aid, largely in grant form, that derived from these arrangements—totalling in the 1960's around $1 billion—as well as from the protected market that provided most of their products in the European Economic Community countries.

A limited association with the EEC has also been negotiated by Nigeria and by the three East African countries, and these arrangements too are due for renegotiation in 1969. These "limited association agreements" provide for duty-free entrance of goods into the EEC under certain limits. For East Africa, the duty-free privilege applies to all exports except coffee, cloves, and canned pineapple. For Nigeria, it applies to all products except groundnut oil, palm oil, cocoa, veneer, and plywood, which are subject to quantitative restrictions for volumes above the average of imports 1962–64. The duty free import of these latter products is to be increased by three per cent a year. In return, the East African countries are to grant tariff preferences to nearly 15 per cent of EEC exports, and Nigeria to an even more limited list.

Economic growth in the African countries, as in most less-developed countries, is closely related to the growth of exports. The economies of developing countries experiencing a rapid increase in exports not only are stimulated directly by this growth, but are also given an indirect stimulus, since the additional revenues provided to the government help growth in the non-export sector. While some countries have wide latitude in developing export possibilities, most developing countries, and certainly most African countries, have a limited range of choice. Africa's export markets, like those of most less-developed countries, are primarily in the developed countries and primarily in Western Europe. In Table 4, which summarizes the rates of growth experienced by the different kinds of exports from the less-developed countries since 1958, the recent high rate of growth in the export of manufactures from the developing countries is of particular interest. While the African countries are not yet in a position to take advantage of this opportunity, economic integration that would make possible the establishment of competitive industry could have a second payoff in building up exports.

The rapid rate of growth of exports in fuels—oil and natural gas—is expected to continue. So far in Africa, only Libya, Algeria, Nigeria, and, to a more limited extent, Gabon and Angola, have experienced this new wealth. Libya, in fact, has had an explosive growth as a result of the exploitation of its petroleum resources, as indicated in a jump in per capita GDP from under $100 a decade ago, to the vicinity of $1,000 in 1968. In Nigeria, the development of oil and natural gas is still in the early stages of exploitation, and has been hampered by the civil war. With the restoration of peace, Nigeria should almost certainly become a major oil exporter within a very few years, with all the opportunities for development

that large foreign exchange earnings from this source make possible.

With fuels, the most rapid rates of growth have been in the non-ferrous metals and ores: copper, aluminum, and bauxite. Copper has made possible the rapid growth in the resources available to Zambia for development, while aluminum made possible the Volta Project in Ghana and has provided an important proportion of Cameroon's export earnings. The Boké project for the large-scale exploitation and export of bauxite in Guinea could enable Guinea to make a new start in development in the next few years. The other metals, particularly iron ore, have given Liberia and Angola an opportunity to accelerate their development and perhaps will provide an even greater opportunity for Gabon in the next 10 years.

For the other exports, the growth rates have ranged down from three or four per cent. It is not surprising, consequently, that the general rate of growth for most African countries in the last seven or eight years has been in this vicinity.

The volume of external aid has remained fairly constant at around $1 billion a year for the countries south of the Sahara throughout the past decade. For Africa in general, aid has financed about one quarter of the total investment: but in the French-speaking countries, around one third of the total investment has been financed by external aid.

The international agencies, particularly the World Bank regional offices in Abidjan and Nairobi, and the Food and Agriculture Organization, UNESCO, and the United Nations Development Program, have devoted a great deal of attention to helping in the identification and preparation of projects. The stage is now beginning to be reached in many African countries where their experience and knowledge have grown so that their ability to put resources effectively to use has begun to exceed the capital available to them. In short, the absorptive capacity of the African countries for aid is growing while aid is not.

After 1960, the international private

capital markets no longer were willing to consider loans to African countries, with the result that they had to rely almost exclusively on bilateral official donors and the international financial agencies for loan capital. A few small loans in recent years have been floated in the Paris market by Gabon and Ivory Coast, but these bore the guarantee of the French Government. The first real breakthrough to the private capital market came in July, 1968 with a $10 million Eurodollar loan to the Ivory Coast Government from a syndicate of 10 international banks headed by the London office of the Bankers Trust Company.

Another transitional problem related to independence has been a reduction in the quantity and quality of economic research resulting from the departure of career expatriates, and the lack of suitable replacements. On balance, it is reasonable to say that the progress of knowledge about and of techniques to master the African environment is still below the pace reached shortly before 1960. But progress there has been. Among the most significant advances are the maize improvement scheme started in Kenya in 1958, and the new International Institute of Tropical Agriculture being created at Ibadan, Nigeria.

The Kenya Government, the Kenya Maize and Produce Marketing Board, the British Ministry of Overseas Development, the United States Agency for International Development, and the Rockefeller Foundation have joined forces in the maize program, which has developed an improved hybrid maize for Africa resulting in increases in yields of 25 per cent. The potential importance of the new agricultural research center at Ibadan being established by the Ford and Rockefeller Foundations is indicated by the success of similar programs which resulted in the improved Mexican wheat varieties and the IR-8 rice developed by the International Rice Institute in the Philippines. In 1943, when the Mexican wheat research program was inaugurated, Mexico imported half the wheat it consumed. At present Mexico is a wheat exporting nation, with output up from 300,000 tons to over 2 million tons. Similarly, IR-8 has contributed to drastically changing for the better the food outlook of India and the Philippines.

Quick miracles cannot be expected in Africa, but it is on progress in such fields as food research that economic development in Africa ultimately depends.

Finally, one further non-quantitative factor must also be included in any assessment of Africa's economic future—the thirst African's show for education and learning. The impact this will have on productivity, enterprise, and creative economic imagination can hardly be guessed at, but there is no doubt that it should influence forecasts to come out at least somewhat more optimistically than the cold figures would otherwise warrant.

Social–Cultural Patterns

B

ECONOMIC HISTORIANS often stress the role played by the traditional institutions of pre-industrial European countries in shaping their sequential patterns of development: that the costs, speed, and specific lines of development were influenced by what existed before industrialization.[1] However, we seem not to apply the lesson to exotic areas such as Africa. Economists rarely show interest in the voluminous anthropological literature concerned with the economic organization of primitive societies before Western impact. Yet it is these same primitive societies in Africa, Asia, and Latin America which are now so much the concern of the economics of development.

Although Western impact in the form of wage employment and dependence upon cash cropping have become widespread in Africa, it is probably still true (as it was in the early 1950's), that most Africans get the bulk of their livelihood from traditional modes of production within the framework of tribal societies.[2] It is with such relatively unchanged, primitive economies in Africa that this paper is concerned.

There are at least two kinds of development problems for the solution of which knowledge of primitive economic structure is useful:

1. What accounts for the marked difference in receptivity to economic and technological change among primitive societies? Why do some adopt Western institutions and techniques with ease and alacrity, while others resist the changes necessary to generate growth?

2. Why is economic development often accompanied by traumatic social change? Is it possible to reduce the social costs and dislocations by building compensators into the new economic forms?[3]

The point of this paper is to show how primitive economies in Africa differ structurally from developed economies in the West. Our concern is not so much with technological differences as with differences in the organization of production. And for either the West or primitive Africa, it is convenient to regard production of any kind as consisting of three component subprocesses: the allocation of labor and other factors; the work process of arranging and transforming

4

Traditional Production in Primitive African Economies

George Dalton

From The Quarterly Journal of Economics, *Vol. 76, No. 3 (August, 1962), pp. 360–378. Reprinted with permission.*

resources into products; the disposition of what is produced.

The Absence of Market Dependence

At the outset, we may summarize our main theme as follows. The absence of market exchange as the *dominant*[4] economic organization allows indigenous African production to take forms different from those in Western economy. These forms invariably entail social control of production by kinship, religion, and political organization. Therefore, change in primitive economic processes means inevitable change in social organization.

In primitive communities, the individual as an economic factor is personalized, not anonymous. He tends to hold his economic position in virtue of his social position. Hence to displace him economically means a social disturbance.[5]

It is necessary to emphasize the economic importance of indigenous social organization because production in tribal Africa is most frequently a community activity in MacIver's sense, and only rarely associational:

Association is a group specifically organized for the purpose of an interest or group of interests which its members have in common.

45

... Community is a circle of people who live together, who belong together, so that they share not this or that particular interest, but a whole set of interests wide enough and comprehensive enough to include their lives.[6]

We are used to thinking in terms of "production units" because the Western firm is an association, not importantly affected by kinship, religious, or political affiliation of participants. In Africa, however, production is often undertaken by intimate communities of persons sharing a multitude of social ties and functions, one of which happens to be the production of material goods. If we are not to prejudge the nature of production organization in African economy, it must be understood that none of those special characteristics of Western production due to the use of machines and reliance upon factor and output markets, need be found. The component processes exist: the allocation of factors; the arrangement of work; and the disposition of produce. How they are organized in the absence of market integration must be a matter for investigation. In a word, every society has production processes, but not necessarily production "units."

Indigenously, the most important production lines in Africa are agricultural, carried on without machine technology, and for subsistence purposes rather than primarily for market sale.[7] Unlike his counterpart in the American Midwest, the African farmer typically is not enmeshed in that kind of larger economy from which he extracts his livelihood as a specialist producer of cash crops, the money proceeds of which are used to recoup his costs of production, and the residual (his income proper), used to buy daily-used material items and services.

The absence of machines and of market dependence are related: as with hired labor or any other *purchased* factor, a machine represents a money cost which can be incurred only if the purchaser uses the machine to enlarge his money sales revenue from which he recovers its cost. The analytical point to be stressed is that without purchased ingredients of production, and without reliance upon market disposition of output, the input and output decisions of producers cannot be based on factor and output prices as guiding parameters. That neither factor nor product prices exist to constrain the indigenous African agriculturalist (as they do the Western) is crucial to understanding why it is that Africans can organize production in such seemingly bizarre "social" ways.

The absence of Western technological and market constraints means also the absence of the Western kind of material insecurity. It is not technological unemployment and depression which are the threats to the continuity of production and income, but rather physical environment—weather, plant disease. That there is no counterpart to depression-born unemployment is simply a reflection of the absence of dependence on market sale.

A related point of contrast is that, unlike the Western worker, the African is rarely a full-time specialist in one occupation or in one production group.[8] Not only is it typical for him to produce for himself a wide range of the items he uses—his own house and tools as well as his food—but during the course of a year he is frequently a part-time participant in several production activities: he may join sporadic work parties to do specific tasks such as clearing fields for friends, kin, and chief; he may be of an age set which is obliged to perform community services such as repairing roads;[9] he may go on seasonal expeditions to extract ore for metals.[10] In sum, it is frequently the case that during the year, an African will work in several production groups, no one of which is crucial to his own livelihood. It is also common for an African to receive substantial amounts of factors, goods, and services as gifts, or in forms other than remuneration for work performed.

Production and Social Organization

The negative point stressed above, that the absence of machines and market dependence means the absence of those kinds of constraints on production organization in the West, clears the way to examine two positive points stressed repeatedly in the literature of primitive Africa:

1. That neighboring societies sharing the

same physical environment often produce markedly different ranges of output,[11] with different technologies[12] used within differently organized production groups.[13]

2. That such economic and technological differences are largely attributable to differences in social organization: kinship, political, and religious institutions constrain and direct all phases of production, in the same sense that market structure and machine technology constrain and direct production in Western economy.

The connections between indigenous African production and social organization may be described in three ways:

1. In terms of the MacIver–Nadel distinction, production groups typically are not separate associations, but rather are integral parts of a community:

... obligations to participate tend to be obligations to associate with the group involved rather than specifically engage in production.[14]

The ties between producers tend to reach out beyond this common interest in the act of production and its rewards alone. A production relationship is often only one facet of a social relationship ... economic relations can be understood only as a part of a scheme of social relations.... Economic anthropology deals primarily with the economic aspects of the social relations of persons.[15]

... special organizations to carry out cultivation or manufacture need not be expected among the Bantu; the functions are always actively carried out, but often by organizations of which the family or household is the most important, which exist to carry out almost all necessary functions, including the religious, the legal, the political, and the educational, and which conduct manufacture and agriculture alongside of these other activities.[16]

2. The same point is generalized by Karl Polanyi in saying that primitive economy is "embedded" in society, in the sense that the economic system functions as a by-product of noneconomic institutions: that economy as a cohesive entity, a separate set of practices and relationships apart from social organization, does not exist in primitive life.[17]

3. If the organization of production in African economies is indeed an inextricable part of social community, it should be

possible to show how *each* component subprocess of production—the allocation of factor resources, the arrangement of work, and the disposition of produce—is related to social structure.

Allocation of Factors of Production

Production in all economies requires organizational devices and rules to direct labor, land, and other resources to specific uses. Resource allocation is never unstructured because continuity in the production of basic goods is never unimportant. One may gain insight into the special rules which mark off types of economy—say, the United States compared with the Soviet Union, compared with the Bantu of South Africa—by asking which transactional procedures channel resources to production lines: how are land, labor, and other resources allocated; how do they change hands or usage?

In our own economy, factors as well as products are marketable commodities. In tribal Africa, products are frequently marketed, but factors almost never. A distinguishing characteristic of such economies is that labor and natural resources have no separate "economic" organization: factor movements and appropriations are expressions of social obligation, social affiliation, and social right. A second characteristic is that typically, land utilization is organized differently from labor utilization. Unlike Western market economy, *each* of the factor ingredients may enter production lines through *different* institutional channels, the channels being structured social relationships. Both points are illustrated by the following examples.

In much of agricultural Africa, land for homesteads and farms is acquired through tribal affiliation or kinship right. One receives land as a matter of status prerogative; only rarely is land acquired or disposed of through purchase and sale.[18] The Bantu are typical in this regard:

Every household-head has an exclusive right to land for building his home and for cultivation. Generally he can take up such land for himself within the area controlled by his sub-chief or headman, provided that he does not encroach upon land already occupied or cultivated by others. Failing this, it is the duty of his headman to provide him gratuitously with as much land as he needs . . . He also has the right, subject to the approval of his headman, to give away part of it to a relative or friend, or to lend it to someone else. But he can never sell it or dispose of it in any other way in return for material considerations. Should he finally abandon the spot, his land reverts to the tribe as a whole and can subsequently be assigned to someone else. The only other way in which he can lose his right to the land is by confiscation, if he is found guilty of some serious crime.[19]

So, too, with the Tiv,[20] the Dahomeans,[21] the Nupe,[22] and the Kikuyu.[23]

What makes the African social integument so important for factor allocation (and therefore production) is that land may be acquired through one set of social relationships, while labor to work the land is acquired through others. In the same Bantu societies in which land is acquired from chiefs by all family heads as a matter of tribal affiliation, labor to work the land is acquired by marriage rights (wives do the sustained cultivation), and by kinship and friendship reciprocity (work parties to do specific tasks such as clearing fields and harvesting). Put another way, the "labor" to perform different tasks in growing the same crop—clearing the field, planting, harvesting—may be acquired through different social relationships.[24]

The extent to which various community relationships allocate factors to production lines is even greater than indicated above. Each separate production line—farming, cattle raising, house construction, road construction—may use somewhat differently institutionalized procedures for recruiting the labor and acquiring the land and material resources used in each; that is to say, labor for agriculture may be acquired in several ways, each different from labor used in producing other goods.

As will be pointed out below, such factor diversity born of multiple social obligations is also the case with the disposition of the goods produced. African economies are "multicentric"[25] in the allocation of both factors and produce. This multicentricity is expressed in two ways, both extremely common in primitive economy:

1. Resources and products are arranged in groups, the items in one group exchangeable with each other, but not with items in other groups;[26] indeed, there may be items which are not exchangeable at all. Typically, "subsistence" items form one or more exchangeable groups, and "prestige" items, others.

2. Each commensurable group of factors and products may be transacted by an essentially different socio-economic device or procedure (reciprocity or redistribution); each socio-economic procedure expressing the special social obligation which induces the material transaction and, where relevant, dictating the permissible ratios at which commensurable goods may change hands.[27]

Market exchange is also a common transactional procedure in tribal Africa, but differs sharply from reciprocity and redistribution in the permissible range of goods transacted in markets, the forces which determine exchange ratios, and in the absence of a social imperative connected with market transactions.

In summary, an African's role in each production process is usually defined by some aspect of his social status—tribal member, husband, cousin, friend, elder. The question, what forces, institutions, or rules direct labor, land, and other resources to specific lines of production, can be answered only with reference to community social organization.

Work Arrangement

The specific arrangement of work in any production line is the combined result of physical environment, technology, economic structure, and social organization. But the relative importance of each may differ between different production lines and between different types of economy. Here we will be concerned with one primary point of difference between Western and primitive economies. In our own system, the constraints imposed by economy-wide market integration and by machine technology are far more important in determining work organization than those imposed by physical environment and social structure. In tribal Africa just the opposite is the case: physical environment and social structure are all-important because of the absence of machine technology and of a larger market economy to enforce economizing decisions on local producers.

That physical environment imposes sharp constraints on African work organization is due to the great reliance by the Africans on production lines entailing little fabrication, such as agriculture and herding. Compared with their Western counterparts, the African agriculturalist and herder lack those devices of applied science (irrigation equipment, disease-resistant seeds, scientific stock breeding) which reduce ecological risks in the West.[28] Indeed, technology and science have allowed some Western farmers to organize farm work on something like a factory basis. However, the economic, as distinct from the technological differences between Western and primitive production, deserve emphasis. Dependence on market sale for income, together with reliance on purchased factors, force Western farmers into the same economizing choices of weighing costs against sales revenues that typify manufacturing processes. With us, farm production too is sensitive to market prices, which of necessity serve as guiding parameters for production decisions including efficient work organization as measured by least cost.

Where African producers do not use purchased factors and do not depend on market sale, economizing least-cost choices in work arrangement are not enforced by technological or economic necessity, as in the West. We are told frequently that in primitive economy, social relationships and values are important determinants of work organization:[29] that sexual division of labor is maintained, that magic and religion impinge on work schedules, that there is often a festive aspect to work parties, and that it is not uncommon for more labor to be lavished on a task than is strictly necessary. It is because of the absence of Western market and technological constraints that work *can be* arranged to express social relationships. The tribal producer does not have a payroll to meet. It is *not* that he is indifferent to material abundance or efficiency; rather, unlike the West, the larger economy neither compels producers to seek cost minimization, nor provides them with economic directives (factor and output prices) to make economizing decisions in work arrangement. It is important to understand this point in order to understand why economic development or Western "impact" induces such deep and wide social dislocation. When Western market economy comes to dominate some area of Africa—typically, through a land shortage forcing changeover to production of cash crops—there are socioeconomic repercussions because of the need to reorganize factor allocation, work arrangement, and the range of items to be produced, in accordance with market criteria.[30]

Disposition of Products

The apportionment of outputs is a concept familiar to Westerners. We are used to tracing through the yearly flow of goods to their final recipients as is done in national income accounting and input–output analysis. But as one economist who tried to measure product and income flows in primitive African economy points out, our Western categories of analysis are derived from our own very special market-integrated structure.

An attempt to examine the structure and problems of a primitive community in the light of the existing body of economic thought raises fundamental conceptual issues. Economic analysis and its framework of generalizations are characteristically described in terms appropriate to the modern exchange economy. It is by no means certain that the existing tools of analysis can usefully be applied to material other than that for which they have been developed. In particular it is not clear what light, if any, is thrown on subsistence economies by a science which seems to regard the use of money and specialization of labor as axiomatic. The jargon of the market place seems remote, on the face of it, from the problems of an African village where most individuals spend the greater part of their lives in satisfying their own or their families' needs and desires, where money and trade play a subordinate role in motivating productive activity.[31]

The absence of purchased factors (including machinery) and the lack of dependence on market sale for livelihood, together with the pervasive influence of the social integument, are reflected in the disposition of produce, as well as in the allocation of factors and the organization of work:

> The income-creating process is itself part and parcel of the income it yields, and the results of the process cannot be abstracted from the process itself.[32]

If the categories we use to describe output disposition are to be analytically revealing they must be derived from the special structural characteristics of indigenous African economies. We follow therefore, the African emphasis on the social obligations to pay and to give, and the rights to receive goods and services, built into social situations. In the succinct statement of Firth, "From each according to his status obligations in the social system, to each according to his rights in that system."[33]

In primitive economy, transactions of products are like those of factors in four ways:

1. Factors and products both may be transacted by different rules or mechanisms within the same economy.

2. Both may enter different transactional spheres, in the sense that the items in each sphere are commensurable and exchangeable only with other items in the same sphere, and not with items in different spheres.

3. The dispositions of factors and products cannot be understood outside the social situations which provide the impetus for their movement, i.e., transactions of both express underlying social relationships.

4. What might be called "socially guaranteed subsistence" is arranged both through factor resource and product disposition.

Illustration of each point is given below.

Factors and products are transacted by any of three socioeconomic rules or principles: reciprocity, redistribution, and market exchange.[34] Reciprocity is obligatory gift- and counter gift-giving between persons who stand in some socially defined relationship to one another. Indigenously, gifts of produced items and factors are regarded simply as one form—material, or economic—of expressing such social relationships. (In our own society, a birthday gift from father to son is just one among many ways of expressing their kinship relation.)

Reciprocity plays a much more important part in primitive African economies than in our own: the frequency and amount of such gifts are greater; the number of different people with whom one person may engage in gift exchange is larger; the social obligations (and sanctions) to do so are stronger; and, above all, such gift reciprocity may play an important part in production (especially in labor allocation), which is rarely the case in our own economy outside the family farm.

After describing the network of obligatory gift transfers of labor and material products among kin and friends at ordinary times as well as during festive occasions, Schapera and Goodwin explain the importance of reciprocal flows in Bantu societies:

> The main incentive to conformity with these obligations is reciprocity. In the relative absence of industrial specialization and consequent economic inter-dependence, kinship serves to establish greater social cohesion within the community, and to integrate its activities into a wider co-operation than obtains within the restricted limits of the household. The so-called "communal system" of the Bantu is largely a manifestation of this close bond of solidarity and reciprocity arising out of kinship and affecting well-nigh every aspect of daily life.[35]

The great variety of items and services transacted reciprocally helps to explain why "production" is invisible, so to speak, in primitive economies: from the viewpoint of the participants, the movement of resources and products is not regarded as an activity distinct from other social activities. A gift of labor to help a kinsman clear his land (part of production) may not be distinguished from a gift of cattle to help him acquire a bride; or, indeed, a gift of a song or a name. The pivotal matter is the social relationship between the persons which induces gifts of labor, cattle, songs, and names. When the source of the gift obligation is the same, there is no reason for the participants to mark off the labor gift as part of production. *It is only when production activities become divorced from activities expressing social obligation* that production becomes marked off as a peculiarly *economic* activity, apart from other activities (as, of course, occurs in market economy).

Redistribution

Redistribution entails obligatory payments of material items, money objects, or labor services to some socially recognized center, usually king, chief, or priest, who reallocates portions of what he receives to provide community services (such as defense or feasts), and to reward specific persons. Typically, but not invariably, the central figure is also endowed with the right to distribute unused land or hunting sites; these allocation rights are vested in him in the name of the community by virtue of his high political, juridical, military, or religious authority. As with reciprocity between friends or kin, the obligation to give over factors, such as labor for the chief's garden or new house, may not be distinguished from the obligation to pay over items such as food. Indeed, what appear to us as economic transactions of resources and products need not be distinguished indigenously from such as express the obligation to perform military service.

Among the Bantu the chief receives payments of specific goods and services from all his people, and payments of fines and blood-wealth. Such tribute payments are partly in recognition of his position as the steward of tribal landholdings, and of his juridical authority. The word "tribute" is important here in both its economic and social meanings: the goods and labor paid over are tribute, and the social recognition of authority is a tribute:

By virtue of his official status as head of the tribe he also played an important part in the economic organization. . . . He received tribute from his people, both in kind and in labor. He was given a portion of every animal slaughtered or killed in the chase; the *lobola* [bride-wealth] for his chief wife was paid by the members of his tribe; he had the right to call upon his subjects to perform certain tasks for him, such as building his huts or clearing the land for his wives' gardens; above all, he received fees for hearing cases and fines for misdemeanors, and, in cases of homicide the culprit paid compensation not to the relatives of the deceased but to him.[36]

His material receipts cannot be regarded apart from the chief's material obligations to his people. He uses the payments and fines for his own maintenance, but also to provide community services and to reward special service of his subjects:

. . . all this accumulation of wealth by the chief was really made on behalf of the tribe. One quality which was always required of the chief was that he should be generous. He had to provide for the members of his tribe in times of necessity. If a man's crops failed he would look to the chief for assistance; the chief gave out his cattle to the poorer members of his tribe to herd for him, and allowed them to use the milk; he rewarded the services of his warriors by gifts of cattle; his subjects frequently visited him in his kraal and during their stay he fed and entertained them.[37]

Just as an individual receives land from his chief and labor from his wives, kin, and friends as a matter of right, so too does he receive material aid in time of need as a matter of social right. Rarely in African societies are there special institutions to care for the disabled or the destitute.[38] Subsistence is guaranteed among the Bantu—as is the case widely in primitive Africa—in two ways: through socially structured rights to receive factors of production, and through emergency allotments of food from the chief and gifts from kin. It is these socially assured rights to labor and land, and to emergency subsistence, which has sometimes been mistaken for "primitive communism."[39]

Market Exchange

As with reciprocity and redistribution, market exchange is a common transactional procedure, especially in West Africa. However, indigenous market transactions differ sharply from those labeled reciprocity and redistribution, and differ also in important respects from market transactions in developed economies.[40]

Purchase and sale seem to us peculiarly *economic*—permeated by utility and material gain—precisely because market transactions are neither induced by, nor express social obligations or relationships. Unlike the partners to reciprocal and redistributive transactions, buyers and sellers in the market share no social tie which *obliges* them to engage in the market transactions. Therefore terms of trade may be haggled out without social disruption, both parties to the exchange being socially free to seek their own maximum material advantage.

Indigenous market exchange in Africa might better be called market-place exchange to point up the absence of labor and land markets. In primitive Africa, market exchange is usually confined to a limited range of produced items transacted by face-to-face buyers and sellers in market places. Moreover, the market exchanges are usually peripheral, in the sense that most sellers do not acquire the bulk of their livelihood, and buyers the bulk of their daily-used goods and services, via the market-place sales and purchases. Although the market prices are determined by familiar supply and demand forces, there is absent that crucial feedback effect which links change in market price to production decisions. Unlike the price mechanism in a market-integrated economy like the United States, prices formed in African market places do not serve to reallocate factors among production lines, because labor and land do not enter the market and basic livelihood is acquired in nonmarket spheres. Market-place exchange is found widely in Africa as a peripheral pattern in the same societies in which all important output and factor flows are carried on via reciprocity and redistribution.[41]

Colonial Impact and the New National Economies

It is necessary to consider the socio-economic impact of colonialism to understand the present situation in much of Africa. Two points especially must be made clear.

The destructive aspect of colonialism was not *economic* exploitation of Africans in the conventional Marxist sense; it could hardly be so, considering that material poverty was already the common lot before the Europeans arrived. It is, perhaps, our own cultural emphasis which makes us focus on the real-income component of welfare and regard it as the sole component. Typically, colonialism did not make Africans worse off *materially*; it destroyed culture and society of which the indigenous economy was an inextricable part.[42] It destroyed materially poor but unusually integrated ways of life, wherein economic and social processes were mutually dependent and reinforcing. This is something on a different plane from simple material betterment or worsening. The destructive colonial impact consisted in forcing socio-economic change which was not meaningful to Africans in terms of their traditional societies:

> For the sting of change lies not in change itself but in change which is devoid of social meaning.[43]

Despite any real income increases which may have resulted, European enterprise was devoid of social meaning for Africans because it required work which was not part of social obligation to kin, friends, or rulers. Work for Europeans was not done as a by-product of traditional social relationships, and work for Europeans meant not working at those traditional tasks which were expressive of social rights and obligations:

> Of [indigenous] labor itself, we can say ... that it is a socially integrative activity. ... Nor must we forget that wherever European and other more complex societies have encouraged primitive man, the carrot has been a bribe (and a pitiful indemnity) for those who must willingly neglect the performance of what are to them socially important functions so

Material income is important to Africans not only because it sustains life, but also—in Steiner's phrase—because the work processes which yield income and the transactional disposition of the labor, resources, and products are so organized as to express and strengthen social relationships and purpose: kinship, tribal affiliation, friendship and religious duty. It is noteworthy that in the few cases in which Africans have been able to work for Europeans without giving up most of their usual activities, traditional social life has remained intact.[45] Most frequently however, entering the newly created market economy as laborer, specialist producer of cash crops, or commercial trader buying for resale, has meant enlarged material income at the sacrifice of work activities which were necessary to traditional social organization, and so the latter deteriorated.

What has been called the "demonstration effect"—increased willingness to enter commercial activities in order to acquire Western material items—works in the same direction. In traditional society material wealth acquisition was largely a by-product of social status.[46] Typically, only those of higher social rank were permitted to acquire certain wealth items or an unusual amount of wealth. In the kingdom of Dahomey, for example, "The accumulation of wealth, except by those whose status entitled them to wealth, was deemed treason to the state."[47] A socially divisive impact of Western economy in Africa has been the democratization of wealth. Neither market organization, nor industrialism impose status criteria on wealth acquisition. Rather the opposite is the case (as Sir Henry Maine has long since told us).

It should be added that the force of socioeconomic change in Africa cannot be explained in the simple terms of changed ownership of property. To the extent that Africans sell their labor to European firms (and other Africans), they become proletarians. What strikes the Marxists is that the wage laborers engage in production processes the capital instruments of which they do not

own. This is true, of course, but the crucial point is not that the workers do not own the buildings and machines, but that they come to depend for their livelihood on the impersonal market sale of their labor. Material income thereby depends upon forces, people, and institutions outside of, and not controlled by, the indigenous social community. Work becomes a thing apart from the other aspects of life, organized as a separate association, and not merely one facet of community life.

What is important for our purpose is that the same is true where Africans do *not* become proletarians, but enter market economy by producing cash crops on their own land. Here they own the instruments of production, but like the wage laborers also come to depend for their livelihood on market sale for a money income. The latter mode of entering the exchange economy can be as disruptive to indigenous social and economic organization as wage labor, and for the same reasons. It is not alienation from the means of production which is socially divisive, but rather the dependence upon impersonal market forces unrelated to indigenous social control; the separating of economy from society by divorcing resource allocation, work arrangement, and product disposition from expressions of social obligation. And, to be sure, the consequent loss of socially guaranteed subsistence, as well.

In advocating policy measures for developing African economies one must avoid the vice of utopianism: to create a blueprint of what ought to be, which bears no relation to what is, and so is unachievable. However, to retain indigenous social organization in the new economies of markets and machines is obviously impossible. What is not impossible is to frame local economic organization and national policies which allow the expression of traditional values of reciprocity and redistribution within the new economic and technological context. As we are learning from our own welfare state experience, even within efficiency constraints, economic organization is capable of contrived flexibility to accommodate social values.[48] The extent of diversity among the already developed nations indicates the possibility of creating distinctive African forms that are viable economically and socially.

> The real task is not to force change, but to induce it in a manner which will be meaningful to the members of the societies it affects.[49]

The institutions being fashioned in the newly independent countries of Africa may appear somewhat suspect in the West. They include strong central controls, unions, producer's and consumer's co-operatives, and much else of the paraphernalia of welfare and socialist states, even at the very beginnings of development; indeed, even in countries without industrialization.

What deserves emphasis is that political and economic structures transplanted to Africa from the West are being adopted with major changes to suit African needs and traditions. Neither democracy nor the welfare state mean to Africans what they do to Westerners because Africans did not share those Western political and economic experiences, in reaction to which democracy and the welfare state came into being in the West.[50] To us, the welfare state is a reaction against the social and economic experiences of squalor, depression, and war resulting from industrialism within the economic context of the relatively uncontrolled market system. The Africans neither shared our experiences of the pre-1930 system, nor committed themselves to our laissez-faire ideology (which we so painfully had to unlearn).

We should not be overly eager to create in Africa an uncontrolled market idyll the blessings of which we so insistently deny ourselves. To Africans, the welfare state and policies of strong central control mean techniques for rapid economic development and political unification, which, at the same time, express social responsibility in accord with traditional usages. It would be unseemly to deny the Africans material aid or sympathy because—like us—they insist upon having institutions shaped by historical[51] experience and current needs.

This study was supported in part by the National Academy of Sciences—National Research Council, under Contract No. DA-19-129-AM 1309, with the Quartermaster Research and Engineering Command, U.S. Army. I am grateful to Karl Polanyi and Paul Bohannan for their comments on an earlier draft.

Notes

1. Alexander Gerschenkron, "Economic Backwardness in Historical Perspective," in B. F. Hoselitz, ed., *The Progress of Underdeveloped Areas* (Chicago: University of Chicago Press, 1952); W. W. Rostow, *The Stages of Economic Growth* (New York: Cambridge University Press, 1960).

2. ". . . between 65 per cent and 75 per cent of the total cultivated land area of tropical Africa is devoted to subsistence production." United Nations, *Enlargement of the Exchange Economy in Tropical Africa* (New York, 1954), p. 10.

3. On social aspects of economic development, see Paul Bohannan, "The Impact of Money on an African Subsistence Economy," *Journal of Economic History*, Vol. XIX (December, 1959), 491–503; N. Keyfitz, "The Interlocking of Social and Economic Factors in Asian Development," *The Canadian Journal of Economics and Political Science*, Vol. XXV (February, 1959), 34–46; Mary Douglas, "Lele Economy Compared with the Bushong: A Study of Economic Backwardness," in Paul Bohannan and George Dalton, eds., *Markets in Africa* (Evanston: Northwestern University Press, 1962); W. E. Moore, "Labor Attitudes toward Industrialization in Underdeveloped Countries," *American Economic Review*, Vol. XLV (May, 1955), 156–165.

4. By dominant is meant that source which provides the bulk of material livelihood. Market-place exchange occurs frequently in indigenous Africa, but typically provides sellers with only a minor portion of their income. The point is considered at length later in the paper. It should be emphasized that market-place exchange does *not* refer to long-distance trade, usually in prestige goods (gold, cattle, ivory), sometimes carried on by professional traders, sometimes under government commission. On such trade, see the writings of Karl Polanyi referred to throughout the paper.

5. Raymond W. Firth, *The Elements of Social Organization* (London: Watts, 1951), p. 137.

6. R. M. MacIver, *Society, Its Structure and Changes* (New York: R. Long and R. R. Smith, 1933), pp. 9, 10, 12, quoted in S. F. Nadel, *A Black Byzantium, the Kingdom of Nupe in Nigeria* (London: Oxford University Press, 1942), p. xi. The distinction goes back to Tonnies' *Gemeinschaft und Gesellschaft*, and to Max Weber, *The Theory of Social and Economic Organization* (Glencoe, Ill.: Free Press, 1947), pp. 136–137. Association and community are not

to be regarded as mutually exclusive, but as opposite ends of a range describing degrees of emphasis. What is here meant by community is characterized in a recent work, as diffuse, ascription-centered, and socially recruited. See Stanley H. Udy, *Organization of Work* (New Haven: Human Relations Area Files Press, 1959), pp. 39, 53.

7. United Nations, *op. cit.* The literature on indigenous nonagricultural production in Africa, is fragmentary. A good study of handicraft production is contained in Nadel, *op. cit.*

8. I. Schapera and A. J. H. Goodwin, "Work and Wealth," in Schapera, ed., *The Bantu-Speaking Tribes of South Africa* (London: G. Routledge, 1937), p. 153; also, M. J. Herskovits, "The Problem of Adapting Societies to New Tasks," in Hoselitz, *op. cit.*, pp. 94, 106.

9. Nadel, *op. cit.*, p. 248; M. J. Herskovits, *Economic Anthropology* (New York: Knopf, 1952), p. 113; Richard Kluckhohn, "The Konso Economy of Southern Ethiopia," in Bohannan and Dalton, *op. cit.*

10. Walter Cline, *Mining and Metallurgy in Negro Africa* (Menasha, Wisconsin: George Banta, 1937), p. 56.

11. E. H. Winter, "Livestock Markets among the Iraqw of Northern Tanganyika," in Bohannan and Dalton, *op. cit.*

12. Mary Douglas, *op. cit.*

13. Margaret Mead, "Interpretive Statement," in Mead, ed., *Cooperation and Competition among Primitive Peoples* (New York: McGraw-Hill, 1937); Udy, *op. cit.*

14. Udy, *op. cit.*, p. 104.

15. Firth, *op. cit.*, pp. 136–138.

16. D. M. Goodfellow, *Principles of Economic Sociology* (London: G. Routledge, 1939), pp. 7–8.

17. Karl Polanyi, *The Great Transformation* (New York: Farrar & Rinehart, 1944), Chap. 4, "Societies and Economic Systems"; "Our Obsolete Market Mentality," *Commentary* (February, 1947); "The Economy as Instituted Process," in K. Polanyi, C. M. Arensberg, H. W. Pearson, eds., *Trade and Market in the Early Empires* (Glencoe, Ill.: Free Press, 1957).

18. Paul Bohannan, "Africa's Land," *The Centennial Review*, Vol. IV (Fall, 1960); Herskovits, *op. cit.*, pp. 364–365.

19. Schapera and Goodwin, *op. cit.*, p. 157; see also, J. L. Sadie, "The Social Anthropology of Economic Development," *Economic Journal*, Vol. LXX (June, 1960), 297.

20. Paul Bohannan, *Tiv Farm and Settlement*, Colonial Office, Colonial Research Studies 15 (London: H.M.S.O., 1954).

21. M. J. Herskovits, *Dahomey, An Ancient West African Kingdom* (New York: J. J. Augustin, 1938).

22. Nadel, *op. cit.*

23. The Kikuyu came closest to Western concepts of land tenure, and land was sold on rare occasions. See, Jomo Kenyatta, *Facing Mount Kenya* (London: Seeker and Warburg, 1938); Bohannan, "Africa's Land," *op. cit.*

24. Schapera and Goodwin, *op. cit.*, pp. 149, 151–152.

25. "Introduction," in Bohannan and Dalton, *op. cit.*

26. Raymond W. Firth, *Human Types* (New York: T. Nelson and Sons, 1958), p. 69.

27. Polanyi, "The Economy as Instituted Process," *op. cit.*; George Dalton, "Economic Theory and Primitive Society," *American Anthropologist*, Vol. 63 (February, 1961).

28. Daryll Forde and Mary Douglas, "Primitive Economics," in Harry L. Shapiro, ed., *Man, Culture, and Society* (New York: Oxford University Press, 1956), p. 337.

29. Peter Lloyd, "Craft Organization in Yoruba Towns," *Africa*, Vol. XXIII (January, 1953), p. 31; also, Mead, *op. cit.*; and Udy, *op. cit.*

30. P. H. Gulliver, "The Evolution of Arusha Trade," in Bohannan and Dalton, *op. cit.*

31. Phyllis Deane, *Colonial Social Accounting* (New York: Cambridge University Press, 1953), pp. 115–116; the same point is made by Firth, *The Elements of Social Organization, op. cit.*, p. 121.

32. S. H. Frankel, *The Economic Impact on Under-Developed Societies* (Cambridge, Mass.: Harvard University Press, 1955), p. 41.

33. Firth, *The Elements of Social Organization, op. cit.*, p. 142.

34. Polanyi, "The Economy as Instituted Process," *op. cit.*

35. Schapera and Goodwin, *op. cit.*, p. 166.

36. I. Schapera, "Economic Changes in South African Native Life," *Africa*, Vol. I (1928), p. 175; see also, Herskovits, *Dahomey, op. cit.*, pp. 78–80.

37. Schapera, *op. cit.*, p. 175; see also, M. Fortes and E. E. Evans–Pritchard, *African Political Systems* (London: Oxford University Press, 1940), pp. 8–9.

38. Sadie, *op. cit.*, p. 297.

39. See, Polanyi, "Our Obsolete Market Mentality," *op. cit.*, p. 112; also Firth, *The Elements of Social Organization, op. cit.*, pp. 145–146. It should be added that the material insecurity which results from dependence on favorable weather and other aspects of physical environment, together with low productivity techniques and the lack of storage and processing facilities, also work in the direction of mutual aid and sharing. See Forde and Douglas, *op. cit.*, p. 337.

40. For an extended treatment of markets in primitive compared with developed economies, see "Introduction" in Bohannan and Dalton, *op. cit.*

41. Soviet economy provides an analogy: peasant market-place exchange of a few food and craft items which are bartered at freely fluctuating prices, is a peripheral pattern compared with the dominant central planning complex through which most goods are produced and almost all factors allocated.

42. There is a familiar parallel situation worth mentioning. Some literature of the British industrial revolution addresses itself to the question, "Did the English workers get better off or worse off during the period of rapid industrialization?" The writers then attempt to measure real income changes to find an answer. The ambiguity lies in implicitly defining better or worse off solely in terms of real income, despite the massive social dislocations involved in movement from a rural subsistence to an urban commercial way of life. See T. S. Ashton, "The Standard of Life of the Workers in England, 1790–1830," *Journal of Economic History*, Supplement IX, 1949.

43. Frankel, *op. cit.*, p. 27.

44. Franz Steiner, "Towards a Classification of Labor," *Sociologus*, Vol. 7 (1957), pp. 118–119.

45. William Watson, *Tribal Cohesion in a Money Economy* (Manchester University Press, 1958).

46. Douglas, *op. cit.*; Herskovits, *Dahomey*, *op. cit.*, p. 73.

47. Karl Polanyi, "Economy and Society in Historic Dahomey" (unpublished manuscript).

48. Gunnar Myrdal, *Beyond the Welfare State* (Yale University Press, 1960).

49. Frankel, *op. cit.*, pp. 78–79. Herskovits points out that the successful transition to market-oriented production in Ghana is characterized by, ". . . inner developments based on pre-existing patterns rather than development induced by the direct application of forces impinging from outside and cast in terms foreign to native practices. Here there is no lack of incentive to expand production." Hoselitz, *op. cit.*, p. 102. See also, Moore, *op. cit.*, p. 164; also, Kenyatta, *op. cit.*, pp. 317–318.

50. In much of Africa, creating conditions necessary for the success of democratic political institutions is likely to be even more difficult than creating the economic and technological bases for growth. Tribal, instead of national identification, widespread illiteracy, and the initial power assumed by the single parties and leaders who brought political independence, all militate against democracy as it is known in the West. Moreover, unlike economic development, political democracy must be fashioned almost wholly from within; there are really no equivalents in the political sphere to the massive economic aid and technical assistance to be had from abroad. However, the existence of single political parties should not be taken as *ipso facto* evidence of dictatorship. Diversity and dissenting views within unified political and juridical structures are not uncommon African traditions. One must hope for the substance of democracy, but not for the familiar forms.

51. Africa has two kinds of history: the conventional kind to be studied through European accounts of exploration, settlement, and colonial rule, and an unconventional kind to be studied through anthropological accounts of indigenous economic and social organization.

ECONOMISTS AND SOCIOLOGISTS, as well as practical business people, have often observed in underdeveloped countries an apparent lack of response of producers and wage earners to ordinary economic incentives. J. H. Boeke[1] states of prewar Indonesia:

> When the price of rice or coconuts is high, the chances are that less of these commodities will be offered for sale; when wages are raised, the manager of the estate risks that less work will be done; if three acres are enough to supply the needs of the household a cultivator will not till six; only when rubber prices fall does the owner of a grove begin to tap more intensively, whereas high prices mean that he will leave a larger or smaller portion of his tappable trees untapped. Examples might be multiplied indefinitely. *This inverse elasticity of supply* should be noted as one of the essential differences between Western and Eastern Economics.

But the "problem" does not seem to be peculiar to the East. In Africa, one often hears from employers of African labour, whether on plantations, on farms or in mines, in industry or in domestic service, that higher pay does not offer a dependable inducement to greater effort or more regular work. On the contrary, it is said that the incentive of a higher wage is likely to lead to greater absenteeism, extended periods of time being spent with the family in tribal surroundings. In the Caribbean areas, too, one sometimes hears complaints about the indolence of the West Indian agricultural worker or about his "traditional distaste" for agricultural work. One used to hear from mine operators in Mexico that higher wages merely accentuated absenteeism. But even in the case of self-employed peasant producers in many underdeveloped countries, the backward state of agriculture, to a large extent, is said to arise from lack of initiative and unwillingness of the peasant to improve his methods of production.

On the face of it, it might seem that an inversely elastic or backward-rising supply curve is characteristic not so much of "Eastern Economics" as of economics of underdeveloped countries in general. This, if true, presents a rather disturbing thought to all those vitally concerned with the economic development of such countries.

5

Economic Development and Economic Incentives

S. Daniel Neumark

From The South African Journal of Economics, *Vol. 26, No. 1, pp. 55–63. Reprinted with permission.*

For underlying our thinking on economic development is the assumption that people in underdeveloped countries will normally respond to what we regard as ordinary economic incentives in the ordinary way. But if the reverse is true, i.e., that the more economic incentives one offers, the less effort one obtains, would it not be more rational to try to promote economic progress in underdeveloped countries without economic incentives?

The fundamental issue of alternatives inevitably arises. The ideal, of course, would be a society in which each member could be relied upon to render freely his best service for the good of the whole. This has been possible in the case of either a family household, or a small idealistic community. In practice, however, any large society aware of, and aspiring to, the conveniences and comforts of industrial civilization could not long dispense with economic incentives as the chief driving force of what is called economic progress. Short of labour levies or of such economic pressure as taxation, it is difficult to see what could take the place of economic motivation. This somewhat gloomy prospect seems to be the logical conclusion of the assumption that a backward-rising supply curve is characteristic of underdeveloped economies. But is this assumption justified?

The object in the following pages is to

examine some of the evidence, and to bring out both what seems to be and what is really a lack of response to incentives, while also trying to delimit the sphere in which economic incentives are not effective. The problem of incentives in underdeveloped countries is examined along the following lines:

1. evidence of positive response to ordinary incentives;
2. particular circumstances responsible for lack of response;
3. character of exchange and demand for money in an economy which is largely self-supporting, i.e., an exchange economy still in the embryonic stage.

Response of African Peasants to Price

Evidence is not lacking to show that people in underdeveloped countries respond in the expected way to price incentives. In Indonesia, for instance, much evidence controverts Boeke's conclusion that inverse elasticity of supply is "one of the essential differences between Western and Eastern Economics." It is known that in prewar years, heavy export duties, if not the fall in international rubber prices, proved effective in reducing the smallholders' rubber production. More recently, "the reactions of the Indonesian rubber and copra producers to the Korean boom were completely normal according to Western standards,"[2] with production rising or falling in response to rising or declining prices.

In Africa, evidence of a "normal" response to prices is available for almost every African territory south of the Sahara. Such evidence is by no means confined to export staples like cocoa, coffee, cotton, peanuts and tobacco. It also extends to all food crops of which a surplus is produced for sale—local or export—as well as to livestock and livestock products. With the expansion of the exchange economy and the growth of local markets, this mode of behaviour is gradually spreading to activities which were formerly dominated almost entirely by subsistence

needs and social customs. With the growth of towns, the rural population in many African territories is able to avail itself of the increasing opportunities for finding an outlet not only for the surpluses of their traditional food crops, but also for vegetables, fruit and livestock. Mention should also be made of the increasing importance of such products as dried, smoked, and even fresh fish, for which there is a growing market, as well as firewood and charcoal. This shows a diversity of activities, both within and outside of agriculture proper, in which a peasant may profitably engage. A supply curve for a certain commodity on a certain market may appear to be perverse, but it may so appear only because the peasant has found more lucrative work.

An excellent illustration of a "normal" response to price change is the story of maize production in Uganda. Cotton and coffee have long been Uganda's main commercial crops; maize has only become a major commercial food crop since World War II. With a view to discouraging overproduction, all surplus maize offered for sale between 1943 and 1951 had to be marketed through government authorized channels, at fixed prices to growers, though some exceptions were made for certain large employers of labour who were authorized to buy their requirements direct from the growers at fixed prices. As has been the experience elsewhere with price control, considerable quantities of maize, in the form of grain and maize meal, were sold by growers at higher prices through "unofficial" channels. Hence, a correlation of official maize prices with quantities sold through official channels would not be a true indication of how Uganda peasants responded to price changes. A comparison of successively announced official prices with subsequent acreages would seem to be a much safer guide, though even here one must bear in mind that the Uganda peasant is not confined to a single crop. This comparison is shown in the following table.

In 1949 the price of maize to the grower was raised from 4 to 5 cents per pound,[3] while in the 1951–1952 season, the price to the grower was increased from 5 cents to 7 cents, or an increase of 40 per cent over the 1950 price. With a 25 per cent price increase,

Maize Prices, Acreage, and Marketed Surplus in Uganda—1948–1955[a]

Year	Prices to Growers (East African Cents)	Acreage	Estimated Marketed Surplus Tons
1948	4[b]	295,785	48,976
1949	5[b]	314,643	47,106
1950	5[b]	316,579	33,150
1951	7[b]	267,965	20,113
1952	14[b]	301,244	28,500
1953	15[b]	661,902	124,634
1954	10[c]	471,692	76,000
1955	15[cd]	379,564	35,000

[a] Figures of marketable surpluses are those given by the Department of Commerce. Acreage from Department of Agriculture.
[b] Guaranteed official price.
[c] Free market price.
[d] Average price to Buganda grower; in the Eastern Province the average price to growers was only 14 cents.

the acreage under maize rose from 295,785 acres in 1948, to 314,643 acres in 1949, while with a 40 per cent increase in 1951, the acreage under maize actually fell to 267,965 acres. Was this one of the perverse supply reactions to the 1951 price increase? Nothing of the kind. More likely it was a normal reaction to the increased prices of cotton and coffee. The price of cotton per 100 pounds was advanced from 31 sh. 75 cents in 1949–1950, to 43 sh. 16 cents in 1950–1951. Coffee prices advanced even more spectacularly. In May, 1950, an increase of 60 per cent in the price of coffee was announced and resulted in new plantings assuming considerable proportions in Buganda Province, the main producer of maize. In addition, coffee growers made a new effort to improve the condition of their existing coffee plots, many of which had been neglected.[4] The Annual Report of the Department of Agriculture for 1951, referring to Buganda, says:

> The high prices paid encouraged growers to pay more attention to better cultural practices, and many acres of neglected coffee were brought into a higher state of production, although much more would have been achieved in this respect if a more plentiful supply of labour had been available. Over a quarter of a million seedlings were sold and an increasing number of individual growers planted their own nurseries. Many growers were persuaded to construct drying tables for the preparation of their crop, and of those without tables, an increasing number dried their cherry on mats.[5]

There was also expansion of the area under food crops other than maize. The area under finger millet, for instance, increased by about 34,000 acres, while the area under peanuts increased from 344,895 acres in 1950, to 414,696 acres in 1951, the price of peanuts to growers having risen from 580 sh. per ton in 1950, to 674 sh. per ton in 1951. This well illustrates the fact that relative prices are the important factor, and that expansion of one type of output is often at the expense of other types in terms of land, labour, and capital. In this instance, however, and considering the slow change in farming methods and the availability of an ample reserve of land, as is common in Africa, the limiting factor was probably labour.

We now come to the second and most spectacular stage of the Uganda maize story. The disappointing response of the Uganda peasants to an increase of 40 per cent in the controlled price of maize in the 1951–1952 season brought home the fact that further increases in the price of maize were necessary to ensure an adequate supply. Early in 1952 it was officially announced that internal marketing of maize in the main producing areas would be freed from control during the 1952–1953 season, and, "in order to ensure that a reasonable price should be paid to the grower," the Commissioner for Commerce was prepared to purchase F.A.Q. maize at an f.o.r. price of 36 sh. per bag of 200 pounds. The guaranteed price to the grower for other than the main producing areas was 14 cents per pound. Although this represented a price increase of 100 per cent over that of the previous season, many growers were able to realize considerably higher prices. In fact, the largest proportion of the maize offered for sale was sold at 20 to 25 cents per pound.[6]

In 1953, in memory of the very high prices of 1952, and because a guaranteed price of approximately 15 cents per pound to the growers was announced before planting took place, the area planted to maize rose to 661,902 acres, as compared with 301,244 acres in 1952, an increase of about 220 per cent. The 1953 maize crop was estimated at nearly three times as large as the previous record crop produced within the Uganda Protectorate, while the marketable surplus offered for sale was more than four times that of 1952. The debacle caused by the flood of grain is also illustrated by the fact that 1,346,634 bags of maize were purchased from producers,[7] while the storage capacity of the grain-conditioning plant, the only available storage for grain of high moisture content, was only 155,000 bags.

We cannot go into the details of the rest of the story. What is important here is the Uganda peasant's response to price. By any standards, the verdict can only be an un-qualified "normal." But what is perhaps more remarkable is to find such a response in a country where commercial crop growing is barely fifty years old.

Specific Circumstances Responsible for Lack of Response

Circumstances responsible for lack of response to an economic incentive are not always apparent, especially to a casual ob-server. As noted earlier, the lack of response to an increase in the price of maize in Uganda in the 1951–1952 season was due to relative price changes of other crops, coffee and cotton, which offered even better profit opportunities than maize. In short, even from a purely economic point of view, the response —or the lack of it—to change in the price of a particular crop in any particular year is insufficient to establish a principle unless prices of alternative crops or alternative profit opportunities are taken into con-sideration.

Nor is there any reason why other circum-stances relevant to the production of a par-ticular crop should not also be taken into consideration. In the examples of Uganda maize, for instance, the change in maize acreages by Provinces and Districts during the period under discussion varied widely from area to area in response to the price increase in 1952–1953. Whereas some areas showed an acreage increase of 225 per cent, and others 50 per cent, in still others the acreage under maize remained unchanged.

To some extent, the differences in response as manifested in planted acreage can again be explained in familiar economic terms: the presence or absence of immigrant labour, the availability of tractors, transport facilities, and proximity to market.

In the West Indies, some labourers may not turn up for work on the sugar estates in spite of the fact that they depend greatly on seasonal employment. The reason is not necessarily something to be described as "traditional distaste" for agricultural labour. These seasonal workers usually have their own agricultural holdings, and when the employment on the estate conflicts with the work at home, they may give higher priority to the work on their own plots, very often as seasonal as the work on the estate.[8] Their behaviour is "ordinary" in economic terms.

Absenteeism has long been one of the serious problems with which industry in Africa has had to grapple. A bonus paid by a certain factory in Kampala, Uganda, for regular attendance did little to reduce the rate of absenteeism. But, as pointed out by Elkan, although this may, in part, be con-nected with intemperate living, some men would take days off because the loss in wages thereby entailed is more than compensated by gains of trade, harvest, or inheritance.

Kampala offers many opportunities to the occasional trader—to men who will peddle a load of fish sent them by relatives from across the lake or who have the occasional load of plantains for disposal. Men who have land nearby may gain more by taking days off during the planting and harvesting seasons than they lose in wages. Again, a man stands to gain more by being present at the division of a deceased relative's property than by being present at his place of work.[9]

On the other hand, there are situations which, though less easy to explain in obvious economic terms, are nevertheless real deter-rents to economic incentives and increased production. In the West Indies, for example, the low production of various foodstuffs for local consumption has long been attributed to "praedial larceny." A farmer is reluctant to grow foodstuffs because a large part might easily be stolen before being reaped by the rightful owner.[10] Here a social situation seems to dampen economic incentives. During a recent visit to the Kivu Province of the Belgian Congo, the present writer was shown how peasants were taught to look after their animals and to collect manure. From the demonstration plot nearby they could easily see that the application of manure resulted in a more than five-fold increase in the yields of manioc and beans. Nevertheless, they made no attempt to apply manure to their own field crops, though they did apply manure to their banana gardens. Further inquiries into this curious phenomenon brought to light the fact that it had to do with the prevailing system of land tenure. According to customary law, the ownership of the land is vested in the Chief; and while the peasant enjoys permanent tenure in respect of land on which a permanent crop like bananas is grown, he has no permanent tenure in respect of land on which he can only grow annual crops like manioc or beans. This being so, the peasant is very reluctant to increase the yield of an annual crop lest he may be deprived of his land by a covetous Chief. A social situation again dampens economic incentive.

Finally we have evidence to show that a good many people in underdeveloped countries, even when the circumstances relevant to the situation are favourable, either do not respond to economic incentives, or do not take advantage of obvious opportunities. Let us consider some aspects of migrant labour. Typically, a man will leave his village in Indonesia or his reserve in Africa to take employment for a period of time which will depend on the amount of money he needs for a specific purpose—in Africa, to pay taxes, to buy oxen to pay the bride price, to obtain a bicycle or a watch. Once the objective has been attained, he will—or may—leave to return to his old mode of life. As is well known, this has been at the root of the serious problem of labour turnover. Generally offered incentives to promote a dependable labour force will only aggravate the situation, since of many it will be true that the more they earn the sooner they can reach the target and quit the job. Unfortunately, too, on returning to their own holdings, the African migrants commonly do less work for themselves than they would do for their employers. As P. H. Gulliver says, in a recent study of labour migration in Tanganyika,

The Ngoni migrant learns little whilst he is away and he brings almost nothing in the way of new ideas and values, new techniques or standards, or a renewed spirit. He is content to be back home in the old life.[11]

Obviously, this phenomenon typically belongs to an economic category which is neither a purely household or tribal self-sufficient economy, in which economic exchange with the outside world is ruled out by definition, nor a full-fledged modern exchange economy. What is necessary to stress here, however, is that this lack of response to economic incentives does not arise from the innate characteristics of the people. As is shown later, it arises from the characteristics of an embryonic exchange economy which, in spite of its dealings with the outside world, operates only on the fringe of a modern exchange economy.

The problem may now be restated. In Western societies economic motivation is fairly general and constitutes the main driving force of what is called economic progress. How general is economic motivation in economically underdeveloped countries, and to what extent can it be relied upon to serve the purpose of economic development? Granted that lack of response to economic incentives could often be remedied by land reform, rural credit, better technical education, and better transportation facilities; granted also that better results in industry could be achieved by regular employment at a wage sufficient to provide for the essential needs of the worker and his family, plus better housing, and security for the worker's old age. Even so, before economic incentives can play as strong a rôle in the life of people in underdeveloped countries as in the life of Western people, money and things money can buy will have to acquire more nearly the same significance in the social life of the non-Western as in the Western world.

Nature of Exchange and Demand for Money in an Embryonic Exchange Economy

It has often been said that people in underdeveloped countries have fewer wants than

Westerners and that the problem, therefore, is how to make them less content with what they have. It is perhaps more true to say that non-Western people have different needs and obligations which may not be easily satisfied by the exchange media which are offered to provide economic incentives.

Perhaps the most important distinction is to be found in the different attitudes towards money. Basically the demand for money is a "derived demand," i.e., a demand for goods and services. But the demand for money in a developed exchange economy is in most cases nonspecific in the sense that money does not have to be embodied in real things, or even earmarked for any specific purpose, in order to exercise its influence as a spur to greater efforts. As the popular saying has it, money can buy everything, and the need for it seems to be continuous. As against this, the demand for money in an embryonic economy is largely derived from a demand for specific things for which there is a felt need. Such a demand for money may be called a *target demand*. Once a limited objective has been attained, any further exertion to earn money would be meaningless. By the same token, a reduction in the price of a commodity offered for sale or a rise in wages will mean that the desired objective can now be attained with less effort.

Now while it is true that individuals in developed Western societies may have a target demand for money, in addition to their regular demand, such a target demand is of relatively little social and economic significance in an economy in which a continuous flow of goods and services is ensured by a well-lubricated market mechanism. The essential feature of an embryonic exchange economy is that its target demand for exchange media is the only economic link with the outside world. It follows from this that the amount of labour or goods that members of an embryonic exchange economy are prepared to offer for sale is determined by a target demand for exchange media rather than by price, cost, and profit. This does not by any means make a person with a target demand indifferent to price changes. As we have seen, a fall in price will mean that the

objective can be attained with less effort, while a rise in price will mean additional effort. There is nothing perverse or irrational about such a behaviour. On the contrary, it is the inevitable logic of a situation dominated by a target demand.

The general problem of economic incentives in its bearing on underdeveloped countries would thus seem to crystallize around the following categories:

(1) Response to economic incentives demonstrably normal in the majority of cases.

(2) Apparent but unreal lack of response.

(3) Lack of response due to deterrents or circumstances over which an individual has no control.

(4) Lack of response arising from an economic system in which demand for money is a *target demand*.

The first two categories have evolved as a result of radical changes in the needs and obligations of people in underdeveloped areas brought about by changing economic conditions and by culture contact. The sphere of influence of these categories is steadily growing at the expense of the self-sufficient sector of the economy, as more and more people in underdeveloped areas are being drawn into the orbit of a continuous exchange with the outside world.

Categories (3) and (4) pose some serious problems. However, the nature of the problem in each category is quite distinct and each will require a separate approach. Thus in (3), where lack of initiative or response arises from circumstances over which an individual has no control, the problem is how to remove the impediments in question. In our example from the Kivu Province, the problem seemed to be one of land tenure, and a solution along lines of land reform is indicated. In our West Indian example the reason why a person would not plant more pigeon peas or more coconut or mango trees in a certain locality is that a part of the harvest might be stolen in the field. The remedy here is perhaps along the lines of social and economic improvement brought about by an all-round increase of production, as suggested by the present writer in 1950.[12]

In category (4), the question is not how to

clear away this or that particular obstacle in order to prepare the way for greater production. The nature of the problem is such that it does not lend itself to any single solution. For, an embryonic exchange economy is at any point in time also a "way of life," and what is involved here is really a general and pervading, probably slow, change in social and economic values.

Notes

1. J. H. Boeke, *The Structure of Netherlands Indian Economy* (New York: Institute of Pacific Relations, 1942), pp. 29–30. My italics.

2. G. van Zuiden, "A Brief Survey of the Economic and Financial Position of Indonesia" in *Indonesia in 1956, Political and Economic Aspects* (The Hague; Netherlands Institute of International Affairs, 1957), p. 62.

3. East African currency is expressed in pounds, shillings, and cents. £ = sh. 20. Sh. 1/- = 100 cents.

4. Uganda Protectorate, *Annual Report of the Department of Agriculture* for the year ending 31st December, 1950, p. 29.

5. Uganda Protectorate, *Annual Report of the Department of Agriculture* for the year ending 31st December, 1951, p. 28.

6. Uganda Protectorate, *Annual Report of the Department of Agriculture* for the year ending 31st December, 1952, p. 40.

7. Total production for sale was estimated by the Department of Agriculture at 1.5 million bags. Uganda Protectorate, *Annual Report of the Department of Agriculture* for the year ending 31st December, 1954, p. 4.

8. S. D. Neumark, "The Importance of Agriculture in Caribbean Economy," *Caribbean Economic Review*, October, 1951, pp. 6–7.

9. W. Elkan, *An African Labour Force* (Kampala, Uganda: East African Institute of Social Research, 1956), p. 20.

10. S. D. Neumark, "The Importance of Agriculture in Caribbean Economy," *Caribbean Economic Review*, October, 1951, pp. 11–12.

11. P. H. Gulliver, *Labour Migration in a Rural Economy*, East African Studies No. 6 (Kampala, Uganda: East African Institute of Social Research, 1955), p. 42.

12. S. D. Neumark, "The Importance of Agriculture in Caribbean Economy," *Caribbean Economic Review*, October, 1951, p. 12.

Economic Policy and Planning Techniques

SINCE ACHIEVING independence, almost all countries in the underdeveloped world have turned their attention from the struggle for political freedom to the problems of industrialization and economic growth. They are adopting economic planning as a tool; in some cases this is due to the socialist background of the leadership, but in most instances it is the result of the realization by the African leadership that only conscious and determined government policies will extricate their countries from the low-income trap in which they find themselves.

In Africa, each country has its plan for development. The article, "Economic Planning in Africa," by the U. N. Economic Commission for Africa, presents a survey of current development plans in various African countries, and includes information on the organization and operation of planning agencies, the patterns and techniques of planning, and the methods of financing the plans. Also discussed are the problems encountered in the organization and preparation of plans, as well as their execution at the national and regional levels. Particular stress is placed on the relationship of planners to regional committees, and on the enlistment of public co-operation, which is important to implementation as the raising of capital from domestic or foreign sources.

The plans of individual countries differ in time specified, organizational patterns, and techniques of implementation, including methods of financing. However, there are striking similarities on some important political–economic aspects, such as the role of government in the economic sphere, and the choice of words to describe the political–economic system underlying plans and economic policies. The governments have assumed dominant roles in economic matters. As Marcus explains in his paper, "The Economic Role of the Government in Independent Tropical Africa," some of the main functions undertaken by the governments are the direction of new enterprises and the active support of most new projects. The latter, in practice, means government ownership and operation, including utilizing hired foreign technicians to fill skill gaps. Marcus has given many reasons with which the increasing government intervention is justified by the African countries. Private enterprise is, however, encouraged. Foreign capital is welcomed and can be invested under private management and control.

The African countries are, however, realizing that a higher rate of development can come only if the government intervenes.

This increasing role of government is often considered synonymous with socialism. Some intellectuals may also express preference for this system on ideological grounds, and/or as a protest against certain social and ethical aspects of capitalism, such as colonialism; (colonialism and capitalism are considered two sides of the same coin). And, as Elliot Berg mentions in his article, "Socialism and Economic Development in Tropical Africa," capitalism is said to "rest on the exploitation of man by man. It leads to intolerable inequality ... It is inhuman, destructive of human dignity. It alienates each man from his brother and prevents a full flowering of human personality."

Socialism is also advocated for Africa on the ground that a socialist solution to Africa's development problems is fundamentally in harmony with the communal traditions of African societies. As Berg points out, there is little new about indictments of capitalism as a social and economic system; they are drawn from the mainstream of European socialism. The advocacy of socialism for Africa because of its consistency with African communal traditions is, on the other hand, more difficult to apprehend because of a lack of consensus in the definition of the term *communal*. While "socialists" in Africa share the use of the term socialism, it is not easy to define the specific meaning of "African socialism" in terms of concrete economic policies. Thus, as Berg notes, countries professedly socialistic have policies regarding nationalization of economic activities, the role of the private sector, and land tenure that are inconsistent with socialist doctrines. There is a considerable gap between theory and practice. Berg alleges that the gap occurs because the doctrinal bias cannot withstand the historical experience of economic deterioration after the adoption of a socialist policy. Berg further argues that at present a socialist model is inconsistent with maximum economic growth in Africa chiefly because of a serious shortage of trained and experienced personnel to manage governmental enterprises, and the physical, social and economic environment of African agriculture, which is generally uncongenial to mechanization and large-scale farming. Trade monopolies by the state are difficult to enforce because of the ease in smuggling of scarce goods in a continent having the highest ratio of frontiers to total area in the world. Thus, many of the socialist leaders of Africa—such as Sekou Touré of Guinea—have come to espouse *state capitalism* as a necessary prelude to socialism in Africa. Most other leaders have not advocated a transitional position; like Leopold Senghor of Senegal, they voice a philosophy, but follow a pragmatic course in their policies and plans for economic development.

I. Historical Introduction

THE HISTORY of economic planning in Africa is intimately tied with the practice by metropolitan countries of earmarking funds for their dependent territories. This practice in turn stems largely from the anticyclical policies followed by these countries during the Great Depression; in this respect, the experience of France and the United Kingdom, the two countries whose dependencies accounted for about two-thirds of the continent's area and population until the recent past, is very similar.[1]

The establishment in the United Kingdom of the Empire Marketing Board in 1926, following the Imperial Economic Conference three years earlier, seems to mark the first conscious effort at introducing some measure of central control to the economic sphere of the British Empire. But it was not until 1929 that the government took definite steps in earmarking funds to colonies with the declared purpose of encouraging economic activity. 1929, the first year of the Great Depression, Britain had been struck by widespread unemployment of both men and equipment. Britain's vast colonies presented themselves as a suitable field of investment for revitalising the metropolitan economy. This led to the enactment of a bill which made provisions for financial assistance to overseas territories. It was known as the Colonial Development Act of 1929, and in the words of the Act itself, this assistance was to serve the purpose "of aiding and developing agriculture and industry (a) colony or territory and thereby promoting commerce with, or industry in the United Kingdom." In 1945, the Colonial Development and Welfare Act replaced that of 1929. In both its financial provisions and the scope of the problems to which it applied, the 1945 Act was more generous.[2]

In France there were similar developments. The Imperial Economic Conference of 1934–1935 was primarily a result of the world-wide industrial crisis, and it was partly inspired by Britain's Colonial Development Act of 1929. The deliberations of this conference resulted in a number of detailed recommendations for the attainment of an integrated autarchic economy. Following the British experience,

6

Economic Planning in Africa

United Nations Economic Commission for Africa

From Economic Bulletin for Africa, Vol. 2, No. 2, 1962, pp. 29–44.

the Conference decided to set aside a Colonial Development Fund of 15 billion francs to be spent over a fifteen-year period.

It was under these circumstances that economic planning took roots in Africa. When in 1945 the Colonial Development and Welfare Act was passed for a second time, the United Kingdom committed itself to put up £120 million in the subsequent ten-year period. Immediately afterwards, the Colonial Office requested the territorial governments to draw up ten-year plans to facilitate the distribution of the fund. Hence, the coming into existence of ten-year plans for the various territories. In the case of France, a rather vague fifteen-year plan was drafted in Paris to allocate the 15 billion francs recommended by the Imperial Economic Conference to French overseas possessions. Expenditures envisaged were not linked with specific investment projects. A much more precise plan was introduced in later years for 1946–1956,[3] covering the whole of the French Empire including France itself.

This in short marks the prelude to economic planning in most of the African countries.[4] But two other factors also led to the widespread adoption of this practice.

The first is related to budget-making problems. In many countries there was the awareness that many items included in annual budgets were in reality of a multi-annual nature. Major construction works, projects for educational and agricultural development, for instance, extended over periods usually longer than a fiscal year. This brought home the idea that an annual budget is no self-contained list of revenue and expenditure items, but only a link in a long chain of budget periods. Therefore, economic planning was not merely desirable but quite necessary.[5]

The second factor is the successful introduction of economic planning in certain countries outside the continent as an efficient tool for policy formulation with regard to rapid economic development. This explains the strong commitment to economic planning in so many African countries as well as the constant increase in their number.

While it is true that economic planning for Africa in colonial times had a similar beginning in both France and the United Kingdom, it was not implemented in the same way in their respective dependencies. The French had a predilection for a single plan to cover the whole of the Empire. It was an emphasis put on a system rather than on its parts. This was understandable since the basic purpose was to create a self-sufficient economic system whereby a close working relation would be maintained between the different regions. Plans were drawn up in Paris, and the territories did little outside the implementation of these plans. The British approach presents a contrast. No central plan existed for the Empire. Allocations were made to the various territories, and plans were drawn up locally. There was, of course, some measure of control from the Colonial Office. The plans drawn up locally had to have the approval of London prior to their execution, but neither in scope nor in purpose was such control comparable with its French counterpart.

Further, what originally inspired the idea of economic planning for Africa by metropolitan countries was not so much a desire to develop the continent's economy, as it was the search for remedies for the industrial crisis of the early thirties. The idea of planning as a means of economic and social

development came at a much later stage. It would be going out too far afield to try to trace the circumstances which brought about this shift in objective; however, one of the major factors responsible for this seems to have been the emergence of new political forces (particularly the impending independence of territories from colonial rule) on the world scene in the postwar period.

Economic planning in Africa today is more widespread, more vigorous, and operates within a much larger scope of problems than in colonial times. As will be seen from this paper, however, it is still in its initial stage of growth. Both its administrative and technical aspects pose major problems to be solved. Some of these will be raised in later pages, but first a glance at the current situation.

II.   *Survey of Current Development Plans*

In the last few years a large number of new development plans have been launched, while others have been revised. Furthermore, it is known that a substantial number of plans are still being elaborated.

With regard to economic planning, it is useful to distinguish, on the one hand, planned perspectives indicating the direction of change in the economy within a relatively long period of time—e.g., 10 to 20 years— and, on the other, development plans covering usually 3 to 5 years.

A picture of the current development plans and those in preparation is presented in Table 1. It should be stressed that because of lack of adequate information, the following data may be incomplete.

Algeria, Cameroon, Senegal, Tunisia and UAR already have their planned perspectives as well as development plans, but some others, e.g., Dahomey, the Congo (Brazzaville), and Madagascar are in the process of preparing development plans on the basis of perspectives. The Congo (Leopoldville) has started to revise the perspectives for 1960–1969 prepared by the Belgian government, and to elaborate the new perspective and development plans relevant to the new political conditions. But in most of the African countries, planned perspectives have not been drafted.

The Algerian Plan de Constantine (1959–1963), published in 1960, took the Ten-Year Perspective 1957–1966 (*Perspectives Decennales*) several steps further by revising it in the light of changed conditions.

The Tunisian Three-Year Development Plan 1962–1964 is closely linked to and based on the Ten-Year Perspective 1962–1971, and its main target is to change economic and social structures in order to enable a smooth performance of the next Five-Year Development Plan 1965–1969.

The Four-Year Development Plan 1961–1964 of Senegal is based on research presented in the Report on the Perspectives of Development of Senegal in 1960–1980 by two French Research Companies (Compagnie d'Etudes Industrielles et d'Aménagement de Territoire et Société d'Etudes et de Réalisations Economiques et Sociales dans

l'Africulture). The Perspectives have laid a special emphasis on regional research and, in this way, have enabled the distribution of over-all targets by regions in the Four-Year Development Plan.

The Twenty-Year Perspective 1960–1980 of Cameroon elaborated by the French Research Company "Société Générale d'Etudes et de Planification" was the first step which enabled the drafting of the Five-Year Development Plan.

The three Madagascar development plans, namely, the Ten-Year Plan 1950–1960, the Four-Year Plan 1952–1956 and the Three-Year Plan 1959–1962 were never followed. But at present the government is drafting a new Ten-Year Perspective Plan and, on this basis, a Three-Year Development Plan, July 1963–June 1966.

In the majority of the countries of the

Table 1—Development Plans in Africa

	Planned Perspectives		Development Plans Current Plans		Plans in Elaboration	
Country	Period	Number of Years	Period	Number of Years	Period	Number of Years
Algeria	1957–1966	10	1959–1963	5		
Basutoland			1960–1964	5		
Cameroon	1960–1980	20	1961–1965	5		
Congo (Brazzaville)		20–30			1961–1963	3
Congo (Leopoldville)	1960–1969	10				
Dahomey		20			1962–1965	4
Ethiopia			1957–1961	5		
Ghana			July 1959 } June 1964	5		
Guinea			July 1960 } June 1963	3		
Ivory Coast					1962–1963	2
Kenya			1960–1963	3		
Libya					1961–1962	1
					1962–1963 } 1966–1967	5
Madagascar		10	1959–1962	3	July 1963 } June 1966	3
Mali			1961–1965	5		
Morocco			1960–1964	5		
Nigeria					1962–1967	5
Federation of Rhodesia and Nyasaland			July 1959 } June 1963	4		
Senegal	1960–1980	20	1961–1964	4		
Sudan					1961–1968	7
Tanganyika			1961–1962 } 1963–1964	3		
Tunisia	1962–1971	10			1962–1964	3
UAR (Egypt)	1960–1970	10	1960–1965	5		

continent, perspective plans have not been prepared, but in some (e.g., Ethiopia, Mali and Morocco) development plans have been influenced by certain long-run economic and social considerations.

A small group of countries have not had plans yet, but one of these, the Sudan, has had long-term specific projects, though it, too, will have a plan in 1962. In Libya, an interim Development Programme for 1961–1962 (and possibly 1962–1963) will be followed by the Five-Year Development Plan covering probably the period 1962–1963 to 1966–1967.

From Table 1, it may not be evident that the plans differ considerably in some major aspects. Some cover a wide range of problems and provide a fair amount of detail. This is the case with the plans of the UAR, Senegal, Morocco, Algeria and Tunisia. Others are deficient in both coverage and detail. But, on the whole, most of the plans share a common feature, namely that of being essentially public expenditure programmes.

III. *The Institutional Framework of Planning*

As might be expected, there is little uniformity either in the organization or in the operation or planning agencies of the various African countries. Differences reflect the peculiarities of each country as well as past associations with different approaches to planning. But there are certain similarities. These may not always embrace the majority of the countries in the continent, but they provide a basis for classifying countries into groups, and within such groups, they have a broad application.

Three related subjects will be discussed in the following few pages. First will be the organization and operation of planning agencies in the different countries; second, certain patterns in the drafting and implementation of development plans; and third, some weaknesses (chiefly organizational) of these agencies.

The planning institutions of the great majority of African countries can be conveniently classed into two major categories. The first would include those countries where the agencies set up for development planning constitute autonomous government bodies with no special link to any one ministry, and the second those countries where planning agencies are integrated into the traditional setup of ministerial administration. Each of these will be dealt with at some length.

The first category consists of countries like Ethiopia, the United Arab Republic, Ghana, Senegal and Madagascar. In Ethiopia, the Imperial Planning Board formulates the long-term development programme through its planning office. The office is divided into four sections—*viz.*, (1) General Economics (dealing with such topics as national income, balance of payments, the budgets, etc.); (2) Particular Economics (concerned with studies by sectors and branches, e.g., industry, energy, etc.); (3) Social Services, and (4) Statistics. The Board, presided over by the Emperor, includes ministers directly concerned with economic affairs (i.e., Public Works and Communications, Finance, Commerce and Industry, etc.) as well as the Ministers of Defence, Interior, and Foreign Affairs. It has a Planning Committee which meets under the chairmanship of the Prime Minister and which is composed of all the foregoing ministers—with the exception of those of Defence, Interior, and Foreign Affairs—the Governor of the State Bank of Ethiopia, and the Auditor-General. The committee reviews the draft development plan prepared by the Board's Secretariat (the planning office) and, as far as is known, the Board itself and its Planning Committee in an advisory capacity, supervise the implementation of the plan. In principle, therefore, it is the Board which formulates general objectives and follows up the execution of the development programme.[6]

In the United Arab Republic (Egypt), a similar organization exists. There is, first, the Higher Council for Planning which meets periodically under the chairmanship of the

President of the Republic and which decides the main objectives and targets of the plan. Then comes the Ministerial Committee for Planning, headed by the Vice-President and Minister of Planning. This is composed of the various ministers affected by economic planning and the Governor of the National Bank. This committee revises the framework of the plan in detail. And finally, there exists the National Planning Commission which is composed of four divisions—(1) documentation, training and accountancy; (2) programming, projects and follow-up; (3) national accounts; (4) economic structure, eighteen units and two research groups (i.e., Economic Research and Operation Research).[7] One of its most important functions is to draw up the plan and follow up its progress. The National Planning Commission seems to be well organized to follow the progress of the plan. Each of the major ministries has a planning unit (in which the National Planning Commission is represented) which sends periodic progress reports to the Commission. These form the basis for assessing the degree to which the development plan is implemented.

The institutions in Ghana have undergone drastic change. According to a recent reorganization, two major agencies have been set up. The first is the State Planning Commission,[8] which is to examine and evaluate all existing development projects, direct and supervise the formulation of a new comprehensive economic plan, and recommend urgent new projects for the national economy pending adoption of this plan. The second is the State Control Commission which will keep under constant review the financial and general economic position of the country and, in the light of this, recommend necessary adjustments in expenditure and taxation. Both commissions have the President of the Republic as their chairman.

This reform seems to represent an improvement on the old system. The responsibilities for preparing and implementing plans are now clearly defined, and it is also clear where these responsibilities lie. Further, a definite break has been made with the past practice of planning for the public sector alone. Behind these changes lies the desire to take economic planning much more seriously

than in the past, as well as the urge to ensure a rapidly expanding economy.

In Senegal, as in Ghana, some reforms have been recently introduced. Accordingly, a new Commissariat for Planning has replaced the old Ministry of Planning, Development and Technical Co-operation and is charged with the task of formulating and supervising plans. It gets general directives from the National Commission for Planning. The latter represents a wide range of interest of both of public and private nature. The Commissariat is subject directly to the office of the President of the Government. Projects drafted by it and approved by the government and the National Assembly become law. This reorganization was brought about mainly to facilitate the implementation of the Four-Year Development Plan launched in 1961.

In Madagascar, as in Senegal, the General Commissariat for planning which comes directly under the office of the President of the Government drafts and supervises the execution of the development plan. General directives for the plan will in the future come from the Supreme Council for Planning, which is to be set up shortly. The General Commissariat "is not an administrative unit in the usual sense of the word, but a planning and research organ at the national level".[9] It is composed of four divisions: Research Division, Development Division, Programme Division—which drafts annual plans—and Operations Division, which follows up the progress of the plan. The General Commissariat proposes and initiates policy measures for the achievement of targets laid down in the plan.

Turning now to the second category of countries, namely, those in which the administration of planning is incorporated within the traditional ministerial system, we find three groups, which are not always different with regard to operation, but which are quite distinct from the point of view of formal organization.

First, there is the case where development planning enjoys the status of an independent ministry. Not too many countries have adopted this practice, but Guinea is an example. Here, the Ministry of Planning assumes the responsibility of drafting plans and making sure that the most favourable conditions obtain for their implementation. Thus, the ministry has the duty of making proposals for institutional reform, of taking steps to ensure a balanced development in the economic and social field, making sure that priorities are adhered to, and, on the whole, regulating all government activity relating to the development programme. But all important policy decisions are taken by the Bureau Politique of the Parti Démocratique de Guinée and the government.

Secondly, there are those countries where one ministry is given the joint responsibility over development planning as well as some other major function. Tunisia has a Secretariat of State for Planning and Finance, Congo (Brazzaville), a Ministry of Planning and Supply, and Mali, a Ministry of Planning and Rural Economy. As far as the Tunisian Secretariat of State for Planning and Finance is concerned, there exist two sections for development planning. One is responsible for its drafting, the other for its supervision and co-ordination. The former function is discharged by the Planning Direction, and the latter by a section for the control of planning known as Sous Direction du Contrôle du Plan. The Planning Direction, which is composed of seven sections—namely, the sections for Agricultural Planning, Industrial Planning, Commercial and Financial Planning, Cadre Planning, Infrastructure Planning, Statistics and Regional Development—gets its general directives from the Supreme Commission for Planning. The membership of this Commission, which is chaired by the President of the Republic, is made up of the major ministries as well as representatives of workers and employers. The fact that planning and its finance are brought together under a single ministry seems to enhance the executive role of that ministry in relation to others.

In the Congo (Brazzaville), the Minister of Planning and Supply is responsible for the elaboration of the development plan, as well as for the supervision and co-ordination of its execution. The Commissariat for Planning, working in conjunction with the Ministry of Planning and Supply and subject directly to the authority of the minister, drafts the development plan. The directives for this originate in the Council of Ministers, but they are often based on the proposals presented by the Minister of Planning and Supply. It is the Council which also decides on priorities with regard to objectives and targets.

The third class embraces a larger group of countries than either of the preceding two cases. The distinguishing characteristic of this class is that a planning unit is established within a particular ministry (such as Finance or Economic Development), where the development plan is drafted. Such a unit usually does not independently discharge the function of supervising the execution of the plan. In most cases this is done by the parent ministry itself. The main difference between the preceding two classes and this one is that the former economic planning enjoys a higher administrative status than the latter.

There are several examples of this third group. In Tanganyika, a distinct division within the Treasury is chiefly responsible for development planning. The preparation and revision of plans, their continuity, progress reports on them, the allocation of funds between different projects, the preparation of annual development estimates, etc., all come under this division. Another major function of this division is to act as a secretariat to the Development Committee of the Cabinet. For some of its data it relies on the Economic and Statistics Division which is otherwise not directly involved in development planning. The services of the Economic and Statistics Division include economic analysis and project appraisal, long-term economic forecasting, special studies and special statistical series. The work of these two divisions is coordinated by the Deputy Secretary to the Treasury who also acts as Secretary to the Development Committee of the Cabinet. The latter is the policy-making body of the government on economic matters and, in this capacity, it decides on proposals to change existing plans. Eight ministers concerned with economic development constitute its membership and the Minister of Finance acts as chairman. Its decisions are presented to the whole cabinet for ratification.

With regard to co-ordination and control, the Treasury itself bears the responsibility.

Similarly, in Kenya the Development Section in the Treasury, in collaboration with the Economics and Statistics Division, drafts the development programme. This is done under the immediate direction of the Deputy Permanent Secretary to the Treasury and by Ministers concerned. The Development Committee of the Council of Ministers reviews the development programmes and makes recommendations on priorities to be followed and changes to be made in the development programme. The Council of Ministers goes over these recommendations and on their basis advises the Governor who finally issues directives. The membership of the Development Committee is made up of five ministers directly involved in development, the Leader of Government Business in the Legislative Council, and the Arab Advisor. The Parliamentary Secretary to the Treasury also attends meetings of the Committee.

Whereas each ministry concerned with economic affairs is chiefly responsible for the implementation of its own share of the development programme, the Treasury provides over-all co-ordination.

In Uganda, a Ministry of Economic Development has recently been established with a statistics and an economic planning branch. As the over-all government organization for development planning has not yet been settled in detail, however, it would be premature to present its description.

In Morocco, the Division of Economic Co-ordination and Planning in the Ministry of National Economy and Finance is at once responsible for drafting as well as for co-ordinating the execution of the plan. It is composed of three sections—planning, economic research and statistics. It also serves as a technical secretariat to the Supreme Council for Planning, which formulates general outlines for plans. The Council is made up of representatives of both public and private interests. Besides the Minister of National Economy and Finance and the other ministers concerned with economic affairs, the Supreme Council consists of representatives

of agriculture, industry, commerce, handicrafts and trade unions. With regard to the Ministry of National Economy and Finance, it is interesting to note that its control over the implementation of the plan is made more effective by the financial control it exercises over projects. This also seems to be the case in Tanganyika and Kenya.

In Nigeria and the Federation of Rhodesia and Nyasaland, planning is complicated by the federal system. In both cases, there are four development plans, one for the federal government and one each for the three territories or regions. While it is true that jurisdiction over economic affairs is constitutionally defined for the different governments, and thus obvious duplications avoided, the existence of separate planning agencies for each government raises serious problems of co-ordination.

In Rhodesia and Nyasaland, the Federal Ministry of Economic Affairs produces a co-ordinated federal development plan after making various assessments of potentiality and requirements with individual ministries. The executive agency for the plan is the Development Planning Committee of the federal cabinet. This has only three members and relies on the staff of the Ministry of Economic Affairs for economic studies related to development planning. In the three territorial governments, planning functions are discharged by the Ministries of Finance and/or the Development Secretariats. The activities of these and of the Federal Ministry of Economic Affairs are regulated by an Inter-Governmental Development Planning Group which furnishes the background information and studies for the preparation of the four plans and co-ordinates the activities of the planners so that the four plans are integrated and self-supporting.

The machinery for implementation and for providing general directives does not seem to be as strong as in other countries. With the exception of a biennial review of plans by planners, no formal machinery exists for direct and continuing supervision and co-ordination of the execution of development projects. Similarly, no particular body issues policy directives, except that the Development Planning Group and the Development Planning Committee, as a result of their interchange of views with ministries and territorial governments, make recommendations which may be accepted by Cabinets.

The Federation of Nigeria is now preparing the 1962–1967 plan. The planning unit within the Ministry of Economic Development is primarily in charge of this. It works in close co-operation with the Joint Planning Committee, which is a representative body of the federal and regional governments. It meets regularly under the chairmanship of the economic adviser to the Federal Prime Minister, and comes directly under the National Economic Council. The latter is composed of a number of ministers from each region and from the federal government who meet under the chairmanship of the Federal Prime Minister. In view of the fact that the new plan has not been launched and that the old ones were administered under different circumstances, little more can be said on the existing organization.

Although the first category of countries (i.e., Ethiopia, the UAR (Egypt), Senegal and Madagascar) is characterised by an autonomous government body responsible both for drawing up and supervising the execution of plans, and the second category (e.g., Morocco, Tunisia, Tanganyika, etc.) by other distinguishing features, it is to be noted that even in this second category there exists the tendency of establishing certain bodies at the head of planning units for the purpose of formulating a general outline for development planning. The Supreme Council for Planning in Morocco, the Supreme Commission for Planning in Tunisia, the Development Committee in both Tanganyika and Kenya are instances of this. It should also be noted, however, that the function of these bodies, in contrast to those in the first category, is restricted to providing a general guide, whereas in the other it consists of laying down general policies, as well as putting these in concrete form in a development plan and seeing to it that they are successfully implemented.

That in brief is what a quick glance would show about the organizational structure of planning institutions in the continent. As we have seen, there are broad organizational patterns into which most of the planning agencies seem to fit. This happens to be true also of the manner in which development plans are drafted and implemented.

PATTERN IN PLANNING

Broadly speaking, there exist two approaches concerning the distribution of functions in development planning within a government. In the first place, drafting as well as supervising the implementation of a plan are carried out by one agency. The National Planning Commission in the UAR, the Imperial Planning Board in Ethiopia, the Commissariat for Planning in Senegal, the Division of Economic Co-ordination and Planning in Morocco are instances of this. In other similar cases, these functions come under one Ministry, sometimes with distinct sections for each of these two functions. Tanganyika, Tunisia, Congo (Brazzaville) and Kenya are examples. Of all the cases in this group, that of the United Arab Republic represents perhaps the most effective system for following up the progress of the plan. As was mentioned earlier, planning units are set up within each major ministry. One of their more important functions is to send periodic reports to the National Planning Commission on the execution of the plan. This, coupled with the fact that a representative of the National Planning Commission takes part in the proceedings of the planning units, tends to keep the commission in close contact with current developments.

In the second place, distinct agencies are charged with the job of drafting and supervising the implementation of plans. There do not seem to be too many cases of this. But Ghana, and to some extent Mali, represent this class. As we have seen already, Ghana now has two distinct agencies for planning and implementation. The National Planning Commission will be engaged in the former task, and the State Control Commission in the latter. In Mali, the Ministry of Planning and Rural Economy produces the development plan, while the Ministry of Finance looks after its control and execution.

With regard to interests represented in the stage of plan formulation, we see a clear division between these countries which have had past associations with France on the one hand, and those whose association has been with the United Kingdom. In the former case, planning is a joint enterprise of both public and private interests. In Morocco, for example, various government departments, private businessmen, and trade unions are represented in the Supreme Council for Planning which formulates the general outline of the development plan. The same applies to the fourteen sectoral commissions which assist the Supreme Council. Similarly, in Tunisia this joint endeavour is evident on both the national and regional levels. The plan is first drawn up by the Planning Direction (a purely government agency) on the basis of directives originating from the Supreme Commission for Planning—consisting of representatives of government, private business interest, and trade unions— and passed on to the central and regional Consultative Commissions for comment. These Commissions are composed of representatives of trade unions and employers. The National Commission for Planning of Senegal also has a similar composition. In Guinea, the regional commissions for planning seem to reflect this same desire to bring economic planning to as wide a cross-section of the population as possible.

In sharp contrast to this stand those countries where planning is by and large a government affair—Tanganyika, Kenya, Nigeria, the Federation of Rhodesia and Nyasaland, Ethiopia, the Sudan, etc.[10] This is probably due to the fact that planning in these countries has on the whole been restricted to the public sector.

But there is one feature common to all the countries of the continent, that is the practice of seeking expert advice from outside government circles, and usually from outside a country itself. In some instances the experts are integrated into the planning institutions themselves, thus discharging the functions of ordinary civil servants. At other times, they maintain a more or less distinct identity. Whatever the form, the services they render

are basically the same.

In this connexion, it is worth noting the role that the International Bank for Reconstruction and Development is playing. The Bank has produced reports on a number of countries and, as is usual with such reports, their coverage has been comprehensive. They have often covered fresh ground and have gone a long way in providing as complete a picture as possible of the economies they describe. But one of their most interesting aspects has been the services they have rendered to planners. It may be an exaggeration to say that they have inspired planning, but they have quite often provided very crucial data that planners have found useful. Nigeria, for instance, followed for many years the Bank's recommendations in its development plans. Recently, in some countries the reports have gone even further than that. For instance, the latest plan for Tanganyika has this to say: "The report of the World Bank Mission entitled 'The Economic Development of Tanganyika' gave a comprehensive survey of the economy which served as an indispensable background to the work on the development plan."[11] That the Government of Kenya has now asked for a Bank Mission to write a report on the country's economy which will be followed by a development programme seems to be further evidence of this.

In some West African countries, private French research institutions have carried out social and economic studies and have, at times, gone as far as actually drafting development plans. Examples are Senegal and Cameroon (see Sec. II).

SOME WEAKNESSES IN ORGANIZATION

Despite the widespread commitment to the practice of planning, there are still weaknesses in organization. A few of these are the following.

In nearly all African countries, lack of adequate statistics has been one of the main obstacles to the preparation of plans and to the improvement in methods and techniques of planning. The situation has been made worse by the fact that planning institutions are often administratively separate from statistical agencies; it is this that sometimes accounts for the divergence between what the statistical agency produces, and what the planning agency needs for its purpose. There is a tendency in a few countries to bring these two functions within the planning agency as in the case of Morocco, Tunisia, the UAR, and Senegal, or within a given ministry as in Tanganyika, Kenya and Dahomey. Further, there is usually some degree of co-operation between planning and statistical agencies; but, on the whole, it cannot be said that the problem has been satisfactorily solved.

Two other major weaknesses are closely related to a very important phase of planning —implementation. The first is the general absence of planning units within ministries concerned with economic affairs. The UAR and Morocco seem to be the major exceptions. Kenya has a planning unit only within the ministry of agriculture, and Tanganyika is considering establishing such units in its major ministries, but has not done so yet. Without such units to draft projects, watch their execution, and prepare progress reports, economic planning would be deprived of an indispensable arm. The second weakness is much more important; it concerns regional planning.

Regional planning is not of course entirely absent from the continent. In Nigeria and the Federation of Rhodesia and Nyasaland, there are regional as well as federal plans. In Kenya, there is some degree of regional planning which is carried on by the provincial commissioners and their teams. In Morocco, Tunisia, Guinea, Senegal and Madagascar, preliminary steps have been taken for the establishment of regional planning institutions. In Morocco, regional working groups already exist in some provinces under the direction of provincial governors; they are to be re-organized under a new name (Regional Planning Commissions), and are to represent both public and private interests. In Tunisia, Regional Consultative Commissions have been set up; among their more

important functions is the examination of the plan before it is in final shape. In Guinea, regional planning commissions are actually engaged in drafting the early phases of the plan. In Madagascar, a good deal of attention is devoted to regional project and regional research. And finally, in Tanganyika, regional and district teams have been engaged in formulating projects for quite some time.

Yet, it cannot at all be said that regional planning has grown to full stature in any one of these countries. In the case of Nigeria and the Federation of Rhodesia and Nyasaland, it is not so much dictated by economic considerations, as it is by constitutional arrangements. In the remaining, it may be true that there is more awareness of the economic implications of the matter, but not much has been done beyond laying early foundations. And, of course, there are a large number of countries where regional planning does not exist at all.

It is important that regional planning be not overlooked in Africa. The particular geographic and demographic conditions of the continent are strong arguments in its favour. The wide area of many African countries, regional differences in climate, population density, and social and economic factors lend more weight to the argument. More significantly, it is on the strength or weakness of regional plans that the successful realisation of development plans depends so very much. The rather unimpressive history of plans in Africa in this respect lends more emphasis to this point. As is the case in so many other countries, the execution of plans has been much less noteworthy than their drafting. This is also due to forces other than just administrative weaknesses. But it seems that the first step to take would be to correct institutional inadequacies.

IV. Formulation of Development Plans

OBJECTIVES AND TARGETS

The shape of the development plans in Africa varies from country to country. Usually, in the more advanced development plans a description of aims, objectives and targets is preceded by a picture of existing social and economic structures and/or trends. But the scope of this picture and the way in which it is fitted into the development plans are different. In some development plans, a picture of the prevailing social and economic structure and trends is presented in a separate chapter preceding the description of planned targets and objectives. In other plans, the analysis of the current situation and existing trends is split between a general survey of current problems given in a separate introductory chapter, and detailed pictures of individual sectors presented at the beginning of chapters dealing with the sectoral planned targets. In development plans which represent only capital expenditure programmes, the social and economic structures are not described. In those programmes the introductory chapter is limited only to existing economic trends; some programmes, e.g. Federation of Rhodesia and Nyasaland, do not even include any information about social and economic structures, and current developments.

Some countries publish an annual or other periodic economic survey in addition to the development plan, where the current situation and existing trends are analyzed. In other countries, a speech or statement by the Prime Minister or chief of the central planning agency in introducing the development plan is an occasion for presenting a current economic survey.

In the more advanced development plans the description of the economy and its broad trends in a period immediately preceding is usually followed by a description of general aims and objectives of the development plan. For instance, in some plans, special emphasis is laid on the necessity of change in the social and economic structures as a pre-condition for accelerating economic growth. Traditional land tenure systems, customs and traditional attitudes, a high percentage of subsistence activities and a very limited scope of monetary transactions, extremely wide differences between standards of living in urban and rural areas constitute the common features of most African countries. These conditions for economic growth are aggravated by the dependence of many African countries on the export of one or two agricultural commodities whose prices undergo frequent fluctuations. The removal of these obstacles to economic development constitutes the most important aim in some development plans.

The place and weight given in development plans to the problem of changes in the social and economic structures varies from country to country and depends on the stage of economic and social underdevelopment, as well as on the planners' attitude. In all the development plans of those countries on the shores of the Mediterranean (Morocco, Tunisia, UAR) and in some others, e.g., Senegal, a necessity of change in the social and economic structures and modernization of the economy is stressed, although with different degrees of emphasis. In some development plans, the modernization of economic and social structure is considered necessary in order to consolidate the political independence recently gained.

Usually, a qualitative description of aims and objectives is followed by a quantitative one. In the development plans of Algeria, Morocco, Tunisia, Senegal, UAR, and Ethiopia, the general quantitative targets assume the form of aggregates like national income, value added in production, investment, consumption, employment, imports, exports, etc. In Tunisia, one of the main targets of the Development Plan is to assure the minimum of individual income of 50 dinars per head per year. In Ghana, the establishment of 600 industrial plants, producing a range of over 100 different products, constitutes the quantitative target of the industrialization programme.

In the North, and in some Western African countries, the targets are formulated by sectors (agriculture, industry, transport and communications, etc.), but the breakdown of the sectoral targets among sub-sectors and branches differs from country to country in its degree of detail. The sectoral targets for agriculture are usually distributed among: crop production, livestock production, forestry and fishery. The number of branches for output targets in industry depends on the planned structure of industry as well as on the planners' approach and the available statistical data.

In those countries where development plans are mainly public expenditure programmes the breakdown of capital expenditure is usually based on the institutional structure of governmental departments, and on the economic classification of investment (called also functional classification) which sometimes bears a close relationship with the sub-sectoral breakdown in the more advanced development plans. Only in few development plans do the over-all and sectoral targets cover both public and private activities, e.g., Algeria, Morocco, Senegal, UAR.

The over-all targets, covering some main aggregates, are expressed in value terms, but the sectoral targets are given in both measures: in terms of value—e.g., investment, value added, and in physical terms—e.g., cultivated area (in hectares or acres), planned crop production (in tons), planned industrial production by branches (in tons, metres), etc. Even in those plans which cover only public capital expenditure, usually expressed in monetary terms, some targets are set in physical units, e.g. beds in hospitals, classrooms, students, etc.

Regional planning has not yet found an adequate organizational solution (see Section III), but some regional targets are included in a number of development plans, even in those covering only public expenditure, e.g., Tanganyika, Kenya. These regional targets are formulated mainly for specific investment schemes linked closely with local resources and/or needs, e.g., hydro-electric projects, mining and transport programmes, etc. But even in the Four-Year Development Plan of Senegal, which seems to be one of the most comprehensive among African plans, the breakdown of investment by regions covers only public investment (about 57 per cent of total investment). As far as is known, the over-all and sectoral output targets have not been distributed in the development plans of Africa among regions in the form of regional quantitative targets.

Proper planning requires a considerable amount of information on an economy. Such information is lacking in most African countries, although governments are trying to set up the necessary institutional framework for collecting statistical data relevant to planning.

The tools used in the process of plan preparation are in most African countries very rough, and this is obviously due to an inadequate statistical documentation. But the deficiencies in statistics cannot justify completely the present state of techniques applied in planning in Africa. The often heard remark that highly sophisticated tools and techniques are not suitable to the underdeveloped economy of this continent need not obscure the fact that planning institutions have in general done very little in adapting these techniques to existing economic conditions.[12]

The methods and techniques of planning in use vary from country to country. In Algeria, Morocco, Tunisia, Senegal and the UAR, the available information and techniques applied in planning have enabled the elaboration of more comprehensive development plans as compared with other African countries. But most of the development plans in Africa are mainly public capital expenditure programmes, combined with a list of some development projects, which are not inter-related by means of economic calculations indicating the consistency of targets among themselves as well as with available resources.

Behind the more advanced economic plans lies the practice of preparing long-term perspectives indicating the directions of change in the economy within a comparatively long period of time (10 to 20 years), and these form the basis for shorter-term development plans. A small group of countries have already taken some steps in this direction. This group includes Algeria, Tunisia, Senegal, UAR (Egypt), where the methods and techniques of planning are more comprehensive than in other countries. But also in those countries applying rough techniques and tools of planning, a drift towards "perspective" planning exists and the preparation of development plans has been subject to some long-term considerations, particularly, demographic projections.

The development plans in the countries using more advanced techniques of planning (Algeria, Morocco, Tunisia, Senegal, UAR) contain projections of the main aggregates and data for the entire economy, as well as by sectors, and for some sectors even by branches. Estimated growth in population, as well as planned increases in employment, value added, investment and consumption, and changes in external trade, constitute the basic framework of the over-all targets. But on the basis of available information, it is difficult to say whether, and to what extent, sectoral targets (and sometimes branch targets) have been derived from the over-all targets. It seems that even those African countries which apply more advanced techniques, were not able to prepare their development plans only on the basis of the "programming approach".[13] The relationship between sectoral targets and over-all targets being mutual, development planning in those countries has involved a process of mutual adjustment back and forth of sectoral and over-all targets to each other. In this way, two techniques of planning have been combined: over-all comprehensive planning on the one hand, and project planning on the other; in other words, the "programming approach" and the "sectoral approach."

As can be seen from Table 2, input-output tables, as an analytic starting point for drafting development plans, have been computed in Algeria, Morocco, Mali, Tunisia and the UAR.

The fact that more advanced and comprehensive planning (including input-output tables) has been adopted by the countries on the shores of the Mediterranean seems to be due to:

1. the relatively more advanced stage of economic development in these countries as compared with many other African countries;
2. the emphasis laid on plans on the development of industry;
3. the influence of the French planning methods.

Most of the countries of the Mediterranean have in recent years faced the problem of unemployment complicated by the very rapid increase of population as well as by the heavy pressure on land. This has been the background for the drift towards industrialization, which is intended to create employment opportunities much faster than the development of agriculture. As the emphasis laid on industrialization in the development plans implies the wider and more complicated backward and forward links between industry and other sectors as well as within industry itself, an application of more progressive methods and techniques in planning (comprehensive planning, input-output tables) seems to become increasingly unavoidable.

It is worthwhile to notice that the input-output tables in Algeria and Tunisia have been used to determine the position of the

Table 2—Input–Output Tables in Development Plans

Country	Period Covered by Development Plan	Input–Output Table for the Year	Number of Columns (lines) in the Input–Output Table
Algeria			
Perspectives	1957–1966	1954 and 1967	27
Constantine Plan	1959–1963		
Tunisia			
Perspectives	1962–1971	1957 and 1970	29
Three-year plan	1962–1964		
Morocco			
Five-year plan	1960–1964	1958	30
Mali			
Five-year plan	1961–1965	1959	8
UAR			
Perspectives	1960–1970	1954	two tables :
Five-year plan	1960–1965		33 and 83

economy at the starting point of the development plan, as well as at the end of the planning period. This has been applied in order to check the consistency of the sectoral targets among themselves and with available resources.

The scope for using more advanced techniques is much wider at the stage of plan preparation within a central planning agency than within government departments. In most African countries the government departments involved in development planning merely draft their own projects and submit them to the central planning agency for inclusion in the development plan. But in some countries, as in the Congo (Brazzaville), Dahomey, Ethiopia, the Federation of Rhodesia and Nyasaland, Tanganyika and Kenya, this method of project planning is combined with an initiative originating in the central planning body (or government), which suggests to the Ministries and special agencies some development projects for detailed study and preparation. The extent of such central initiative in development planning is not the same in each country, and varies with changing circumstances. In Tunisia the Three-Year Development Plan has been based on the projects submitted for inclusion in the plan by ministries, but the part played by the central planning institution in the elaboration of the sectoral projects for the next development plan is supposed to be predominant. As far as the inclusion of a project in the development plan is concerned, the final decision rests usually with those bodies from which the general directives with regard to the formulation of the development plan originate, e.g., Cabinet of Ministers, Imperial Planning Board of Ethiopia, Supreme Council for Planning in Morocco.

V. Financing of Development Plans

One of the main obstacles in the execution of the development plans in Africa is lack of capital. The successful performance of plans depends not only on budgetary incomes, but to a great extent on the availability of capital from external and local sources. The purpose of this section is to examine in general terms the financial aspects of plans in Africa.

Development plans in most African countries generally cover capital formation in the public sector. Quantitative estimates of private capital formation or expenditure are to be found in the development plans of only a few countries, e.g., Morocco, Senegal, the UAR. A general picture of capital formation can, however, be formed from fixed capital formation series which exist for a number of African countries for the years covered by their earlier development plans. Fixed capital formation has been broken down into public and private in Table 3.

Private capital formation in the countries included in the foregoing table fluctuated from year to year, but never fell below 50 per cent of the total, except in Uganda and the Sudan. The trend of private capital formation cannot, however, be firmly forecast. Large proportions of private capital formation in African countries originate from foreign funds directly invested in industries for various industrial raw materials. The flow of this type of capital is influenced in present African conditions by noneconomic factors such as political stability and general state of confidence, which are not easily predicted. Direct foreign private investment has also been found to be generally sensitive to factors such as changes in demand for industrial raw materials in industrialized countries.[14] Recently, however, countries which have large internal markets and relatively developed industrial facilities have begun to attract foreign private investment into industries producing for local markets.

The tendency to create favourable conditions for private investment is characteristic of most development plans in Africa. The following statement in the Five-Year Development Plan of Morocco is indicative of this.

All activities in which interference of the State through B.E.P.I.[15] is not called for are open to the initiative of private industry. That is to say that the industry of Morocco constitutes a wide field of activities for private entrepreneurship, which is invited to construct, to produce, and to prosper. The State will inter-

Table 3—Fixed Capital Formation in Selected African Countries

Country and Year	Total	Private	%	Public*	%
Congo (Leopoldville) (million Belgian francs)					
1953	16,270	9,500	58	6,770	42
1954	15,250	7,970	52	7,280	48
1955	15,690	8,720	56	6,970	44
1956	16,320	9,510	58	6,810	42
1957	16,420	9,230	56	7,190	44
1958	14,270	7,340	52	6,930	48
1959	11,080	5,840	53	5,240	47
Ghana (£ million)					
1955	42.8	21.6	50	21.2	50
1956	45.7	26.3	58	19.4	42
1957	43.6	25.7	59	17.9	41
1958	41.0	24.8	60	16.2	40
1959	64.0	34.3	54	29.7	46
Kenya (£ million)					
1954	34.8	18.0	52	16.8	48
1955	43.1	24.1	56	19.0	44
1956	46.1	31.2	68	14.9	32
1957	47.0	30.6	65	16.4	35
1958	40.4	27.0	67	13.4	33
1959	42.8	28.7	67	14.1	33
Nigeria (£ million)					
1952	55.7	33.3	60	22.4	40
1953	54.7	32.1	59	22.6	41
1954	66.9	42.8	64	24.1	36
1955	78.3	44.0	56	34.3	44
1956	97.3	53.6	55	43.7	45
1957	101.1	68.9	64	38.2	36
Federation of Rhodesia and Nyasaland (£ million)					
1954	88.0	50.6	58	38.2	42
1955	112.1	70.1	63	42.0	37
1956	138.8	88.9	64	49.9	36
1957	152.2	88.2	58	64.0	42
1958	135.3	70.4	52	64.9	48
1959	130.8	77.5	59	53.3	41
Sudan (million Sudanese £)					
1955	21.2	9.8	46	11.4	54
1956	26.2	13.6	52	12.6	48
1957	42.8	21.5	50	21.3	50
1958	38.2	15.3	40	22.9	60
Tanganyika (£ million)					
1954	26.0	15.8	61	10.2	39
1955	28.9	18.0	62	10.9	38
1956	27.6	18.3	66	9.3	34
1957	29.5	19.7	67	9.8	33
1958	27.4	18.9	69	8.5	31
1959	29.1	20.0	69	9.1	31
Uganda (£ million)					
1954	18.5	4.1	22	14.4	78
1955	23.2	7.0	30	16.2	70
1956	21.7	8.4	39	13.3	61
1957	20.4	7.9	39	12.5	61
1958	19.6	7.5	38	12.1	62
1959	17.0	6.0	35	11.0	65

Source: *U.N. Yearbook of National Accounts Statistics*, 1959 and 1960.

* Public capital formation includes general government, public corporations, and government enterprises.

vene only in order to assist it and to protect it against competitors. For this country it would be a bitter disappointment if private capital and particularly the domestic one does not flow in sufficiently to play its part. Then the State would be obliged to extend its intervention and initiative.

In the Development Plan of Senegal it has been stressed that the State will employ all appropriate measures and create favourable conditions in order "to enable the necessary participation of the private sector in the execution of the Plan."

In Tunisia also, a wide field of activity is left to private capital. But it has been emphasized—as in the Development Plan of Morocco—that if the current performance of the plan shows that private capital is not inclined to take part in the process of economic development and to finance planned investment targets, public authorities will step in and carry out all these investment projects which are considered to be necessary for the achievement of the main planned objectives.

In introducing the Second Ghana Development Plan, the President expressed the hope that "overseas financial institutions and investors will study our plan with a view to considering in what way they can help us to realize our objectives."

In connexion with the elaboration of the Tanganyika Plan (1961–1962 to 1963–1964), it has been estimated that during the planning period of three years in which the Government has planned for yearly capital formation of £8 million, private capital formation would contribute £21 million in 1961, increasing at the rate of 5% per annum.

In the Federation of Rhodesia and Nyasaland, unlike in the foregoing countries, both the federal and territorial governments pursue a clear laissez-faire policy not only in the field of investment, but more generally in their outlook on economic problems. The 1959–1963 Development Plan, for instance, emphasizes that

...the Federation is not a "planned"

economy in the sense that development is controlled and directed in terms of a comprehensive programme of investment and allocation of resources, by a single planned authority. It is, in fact, a fundamental feature of the policies of the Federal and Territorial Governments that economic activity in the Federation should be privately owned and operated and that the activity of the Governments in the economic fields should in general be limited to providing the best possible climate for economic expansion, including the provision of services to facilitate that expansion.

Due to this approach the government is inclined to serve the needs of private enterprises rather than to incorporate the activities of private enterprises within the general framework of the development plan.

In common with other underdeveloped countries, African countries employ diverse measures calculated to attract foreign capital into industries. The more widely used devices are tax concessions, import duty rebates on essential imports of capital goods and raw materials, customs protection, government participation in the establishment of needed industries and the preparation of industrial sites with the provision of basic facilities.[16]

The main sources of finance for development programmes are (1) local resources in the form of budget surpluses and transfers from government agencies such as produce marketing boards in countries with marketing board organizations, (2) loans raised locally, and (3) external grants and loans. The percentage contributions from these sources to the development funds of selected African countries are shown in Table 4.

The figures on the financing of investment generally refer to a period different from that covered by the majority of the development plans discussed in this paper (see Section II).

The contributions by local sources on the one hand, and external grants and loans (including local loans) on the other, vary in different countries. The contributions from local sources is, for example, considerably higher in Ethiopia, Uganda, Morocco, the Federation of Rhodesia and Nyasaland, Nigeria, Ghana and Angola than in other countries—varying from 56 per cent in Ethiopia to 95 per cent in Angola. In Ghana, Nigeria and Uganda, the preponderance of funds from local resources is undoubtedly due to the development transfers from the produce marketing boards. Tanganyika, Basutoland, Kenya, Mozambique, the countries of former French Equatorial Africa and former French West Africa have depended largely on Foreign sources of finance.

The composition of external grants and loans also varies considerably in different development programmes.[17] Basutoland and Gambia depended almost entirely on grants from the British Colonial Development and Welfare Fund. In Tanganyika, the percentage share of grants in financing development plans is 31 per cent (1961–1964), Ethiopia 8 per cent (1957–1961), Congo (Leopoldville) 6.4 per cent (1950–1959), Nigeria 3.5 per cent (1955–1962), Uganda 2.3 per cent (1955–1960), Kenya 17.7 per cent (1960–1963). In the Portuguese territories, from 1953 to 1958 there were no grants in the development funds; in Mozambique, loans account for 58 per cent of the development fund.

There is not sufficient information on the percentage share of budget surpluses in

development funds, but it is to be borne in mind that more than any other component of capital development fund, the budget surplus is subject to fluctuation. The degree of the fluctuation depends on what happens to be the major source of the surplus.[18] If it derives chiefly from export and import taxes, as is the case in most African countries, the fluctuation is likely to be sharp. In fact, this has lately been the experience of some countries and, together with the necessity for larger development programmes, it has led to the running down of accumulated reserves and other overseas assets and to greater reliance on external loans and grants. In Ghana, for example, the recent fall in the world price of cocoa has meant some reduction in the availability of local investment funds and necessitated a recourse to overseas borrowing as well as to measures for compulsory saving. In order to stabilize the flow of development capital in the government sector and ensure its continuity, several countries, especially in

Table 4—Financing of Development Plans by Sources of Funds in Selected African Countries

Country and Period	Percentage Distribution Local Sources	External Sources
Angola 1953–1958	95	5
Basutoland 1960–1964	—	100
Congo (Leopoldville) 1950–1959	48	52
Ethiopia 1957–1961[a]	56	44
Former French Equatorial Africa and Cameroon 1950–1958[b]	20	80
Former French West Africa and Togo 1950–1958[b]	38	62
Gambia 1955–1960	6	94
Ghana 1959–1964	76[c]	24
Kenya 1960–1963	8	92[d]
Madagascar 1950–1958[b]	44	56
Mauritania 1960–1962	—	100
Morocco 1960–1964	56	44
Mozambique 1953–1958	42	58
Federation of Nigeria 1955–1962	60	40[d]
Federation of Rhodesia and Nyasaland 1959–1963	58	42
Tanganyika 1961–1964	20	80
Uganda 1955–1960	57	43[d]

Source: Congo (Leopoldville), Tanganyika, Ghana, Kenya, Federation of Rhodesia and Nyasaland, Ethiopia, and Basutoland—ECA Secretariat Questionnaire on Development Programming; Nigeria, Gambia, Uganda, Angola, and Mozambique—*UN Economic Survey of Africa Since 1950*, p. 246; Morocco—*Five-Year Plan, 1960–1964*; Mauritania—*The Three-Monthly Economic Review*, January, 1961 (The Economist Intelligence Unit). Former French Equatorial Africa and Cameroon, Madagascar and Former French West Africa, and Togo—*Economic Bulletin for Africa*, Vol. I, No. 2, p. 14.

[a] Financing of public and private investment.
[b] Figures refer to equipment expenditure.
[c] Including overseas assets.
[d] Including loans raised locally.

the British and former British territories, have established special capital development funds into which development grants, loans, budget surpluses in good time and other miscellaneous capital receipts are channelled. For the same reason, many African countries have adopted capital budgeting. The need for a capital budget, as already mentioned in the introduction, arose directly out of the requirements of development programming.[19] Since the development programmes consisted mostly of investment projects to be executed over a number of years, their financing presented a special problem for which the traditional annual budget was not adequate. Through the instrumentality of the capital budget, it became possible to lay down systematically planned capital expenditure for one or more years, and the corresponding capital resources or payments.

The capital budget usually forms a section of the Annual Budget Estimates in the British and former British territories. Its expenditure outlay corresponds to the portion of the development programme it is planned to fulfil within the fiscal year and its source of finance is the special capital development fund mentioned in the preceding paragraph. Also, in some French West African countries, e.g., the Republic of Togo, Ivory Coast and Senegal, the capital budget is annexed to the general government budget and is usually referred to as "capital and investment budget."[20]

In the early plans, little consideration was given to either the balance of payments effects of the plans, or their implications for recurrent government expenditure. In the first place, the economies of the dependencies were closely tied up with the economies of the metropolitan countries. The exports of the dependencies contributed substantially to the balance of payments position of the metropolitan countries; and productive investment in the development programmes were oriented to production for export either to the metropolitan countries, or to countries where earnings would benefit their balance of payments.[21]

With the attainment of independence by several former dependencies, the problem of financing development plans entered a new phase requiring new policies and new approaches to planning. The need for a structural balance between social and productive investment, and also between different productive sectors, arose in many countries. Hitherto, attention had been focused on exports leading in some cases, particularly in smaller countries, to one sector concentration, e.g., export crops or transport. Furthermore, independence brought with it larger expenditures on social infrastructure which are not only expensive, but have equally larger recurrent implications.[22] This problem was aggravated in many countries by the unfavourable trend of world prices of export commodities on which they depend for their development resources. The need to diversify the economy and to reduce dependence on the former metropolitan countries increased the import of capital goods, technical skills, and certain classes of raw materials.[23]

All these developments have put a strain on the limited resources of the countries and on their balance of payments. The consequence has been a general desire to plan more comprehensively by first assessing what the country needs, and examining the recurrent implications of the plan and its balance of payments effects. In some countries, e.g., Tanganyika, one of the main considerations in determining the size of the development plan was its recurrent effects on the budget: the cost of upkeep and maintenance of projects once they are completed and the servicing of loans where projects are financed with borrowed funds. Generally, considerations of balance of payments are made by preferring less capital intensive projects, where this is possible, and also industries that utilize larger proportions or local raw materials. Within this context, almost all the African countries try to maximize the inflow of private funds through tax concessions, subsidies, and sometimes granting monopoly rights. Additionally, several countries encourage nonfinancial investments in the form of community development works, promote rural investment in kind, and adopt measures to maximize domestic savings and channel them into productive investment.

V. Main Problems of Economic Planning by African Countries

As might be gathered from the preceding sections, economic planning has not gone far in evolving the organizational framework suited to African conditions. But a drift towards improving the existing planning organizations is taking place in a number of African countries. All attempts in this direction, however, face certain crucial questions. Among these are:

Should the functions of the central agencies which draft plans be extended to include supervisory as well as executive activities?

If the central planning agency is responsible only for drafting, which body is to supervise the implementation of plans, and how will the problem of co-ordination be tackled?

Should the statistical services come under the central planning agencies? If not, how is co-operation between them to be assured?

To what extent would planning units in those ministries directly involved in development planning bring closer together the central planning agencies and these ministries?

The successful execution of plans requires an appropriate regional implementation. This, in turn, implies a certain degree of decentralization of central executive power among regions and communities. But the scope of and the limits to decentralization depend on the level of education, skill, and professional training of the people employed in regional units. In this context some questions arise.

To what extent can the share of regions, provinces, and communities be allowed to play its part in the institutional framework of planning and its execution?

How should regional planning and its implementation be organized? Is it better to fit these activities into the existing regional administrative structure, or perhaps should the regional administration themselves be revised with the view of adapting them to the requirements of development planning?

In the development plans of some countries, a necessity for "mass mobilization" is stressed as a precondition for the successful execution of plans. But, if this political and social directive is not to be a mere slogan, a close link between the planning organization and regional communities seems to be necessary; hence the question arises:

How can the general public be associated with the formulation and implementation of the development plans?

In Africa, as well as in other areas, the preparation of plans is less difficult than their implementation.[24] Even in those countries where the techniques of planning are more advanced, the implementation of planning is far from being satisfactory. But an appropriate organizational pattern for the implementation of the development plans (adapted to specific requirements and national needs of individual countries) must be set up without much delay if the development plans are to be an efficient tool of economic policy, and not a sophisticated, analytical document for economists.

With regard to development finance, planners and those not directly involved in planning, face the crucial problem of tapping internal resources as well as taking recourse to foreign sources. In this connexion, the following questions may be posed.

What measures are to be taken in order to raise the level of capital formation originating from domestic sources?

Does the experience of countries suggest that development planning would, as a general rule, increase the prospects of obtaining foreign economic assistance on favourable terms, or does this depend on the nature and formulation of concrete projects incorporated in plans?

Notes

1. See *Colonial Planning*, B. Niculescu, George Allen and Unwin (London, 1958).
2. There was also the 1940 Act, but little was done to implement its provisions.

3. *Premier Rapport de la Commission de Modernisation des territoires d'outre-mer*, January, 1948. This is also known as the *Plan Pleven*.

4. It is also worth noting the impetus given to planning at this time by the Marshall Plan. One of the conditions laid down by the United States authorities for the Plan was that the European countries would have to submit a four-year recovery programme which included overseas territories.

5. See United Nations, Economic Commission on Africa, Document No. E/CN. 14/42, Add. 1, pp. 2–5.

6. The Planning Office of the Board has recently been brought under the Prime Minister's office, but this does not substantially affect the Board's autonomy.

7. Note the structural similarity between this and that of Ethiopia. The Imperial Planning Board, the Planning Committee, and the Planning Office of Ethiopia roughly correspond with the Higher Council for Planning, the Ministerial Committee for Planning, and the National Planning Commission of the United Arab Republic.

8. Now known as the National Planning Commission. This change in name symbolizes the extension of the Commission's activity to include all the country's social, economic and technological developments.

9. *Le Plan de Développement de Madagascar*, p. 9.

10. In accordance with a recent reorganization of planning administration in Ghana, non-governmental bodies are to participate in the work of the National Planning Commission. The Commission will consist of experts in the field of industry, agriculture, health, education, science and representatives from such key bodies as the ruling Convention People's Party, the trade union congress, the Bank of Ghana, and the Academy of Science.

11. *Development Plan for Tanganyika 1961/62–1963/64*, Government Printer, Dar-es-Salaam.

12. The following quotation is relevant in this respect. "When we come to composition [of plans], it appears that economic analysis could really come into greater play. For the technique of input–output analysis and possibly linear programming are well designed for the calculation of total repercussions, both on the supply and demand side, following expansion in each individual sector. It is not denied that serious problems need to be overcome in the use of these techniques in underdeveloped countries. But what is important is that if they are not faced, so that the total repercussions are not known, the planners are likely to find incomplete achievements of projects occurring through problems on the supply side and/or incomplete utilization through inadequate analysis on the demand side." —D. Dosser, "The Formulation of Development Plans in the British Colonies," *The Economic Journal*, June, 1959, pp. 255–256.

13. For a description of the technique of "programming approach," see *Economic Bulletin for Africa*, Vol. 1, No. 1, January, 1961, p. 74.

14. *U.N. Economic Survey of Africa since 1950*, Department of Economic and Social Affairs, New York, 1959, p. 228.

15. *Bureau des Etudes et Participations Industrielles*.

16. All the countries that replied to the ECA Questionnaire on Development Programming employ almost all of these devices; for a list of laws and codes to facilitate private investment, particularly foreign private investment in selected African countries, see Appendix to *Economic Development in Under-developed Areas—International Flow of Private Capital, 1958–1959: Report by the Secretary-General of the United Nations*.

17. For percentage shares of grants and loans in the development programme, see United Nations Economic Commission on Africa, *Economic Survey of Africa Since 1950*, p. 246.

18. *Economic Bulletin for Africa*, Vol. I, No. 2, Chap. I, Public Finance in African countries.

19. The link between budgeting and development programming in African countries is stressed in the ECA document: *Techniques of Development Programming in African Countries, 1959*, p. 3–5.

20. Pierre Sanner, *The Classification of Government Transactions in the French-speaking States of West Africa*, Chap. 11, Sec. 3, Operational Budget and Capital Budget—a paper submitted to Workshop on Problems of Budget Reclassification and Management in Africa, September 4–15, 1961.

21. *Economic Survey of Africa Since 1950*, op. cit., p. 239.

22. *Economic Bulletin for Africa*, op. cit.

23. In many instances the import of consumer goods, especially consumer durables, rose simultaneously.

24. The experience of the "planned economies" in Eastern Europe has proved that improvement in planning methods and techniques has gone much further than in the case of the supervision and co-ordination of the execution of plans.

7

By NOW IT IS a commonplace to preface any article on the underdeveloped areas with an introduction detailing the many problems and disabilities present. Overwhelming poverty, backward agricultural techniques, social and cultural inertia, rapid population growth, widespread ill-health—a mere check list is disheartening to any student earnestly interested in the well-being of his fellow men. Yet all observers agree that something must be done to induce these less fortunate countries to initiate a "take-off" into sustained growth, to begin the cumulatively upward movement into ever expanding production and well-being that the Western World has enjoyed for the past three centuries.

If the economist looks more closely at tropical Africa, however, he will find a serious prerequisite to such growth virtually absent—the lack of a local entrepreneurial spirit is a glaring obstacle to progress. The innovator, the man of daring, the risk-taker—call him what you will—is particularly inconspicuous, even in contrast with the Far East; the energetic native elements, such as in India and China, are present in Africa only in trade and transport. As a result, a greatly enhanced role for the government is called for, to supply the drive that the West relegates to the industrialist. Although superficially such intervention may resemble State socialism, actually it amounts to co-operation between public and private enterprise, each working in the sector that the other is either uninterested in exploiting or unfit to develop.

For our purposes tropical Africa will encompass the area south of the Sahara and north of the South Africa–Rhodesian white settler segments, akin to the French "L'Afrique Noire." It is peopled overwhelmingly by the Negro and Bantu groups—the Black Africans—comprising as high as 99 per cent and more of the total population of some of these lands. By Asiatic standards, the land is underpopulated, although there are a few exceptions, such as the former Belgian Trust Territory of Ruanda–Urundi. However, the poor farming techniques make for productivity as low as in the more overcrowded areas of the world, so that per capita living standards do not reflect the more advantageous man–land ratio.

The Economic Role of the Government in Independent Tropical Africa

Edward Marcus

From The American Journal of Economics and Sociology, *Vol. 24, No. 3 (July, 1965), pp. 307–315. Reprinted with permission.*

In certain respects tropical Africa is so diverse that it is impossible to talk of it as a unit. The tribal divisions are probably more fundamental than those separating the various European countries, while linguistic variations may result in as high as 1,000 different languages. Politically, the area has been influenced by several former European rulers—mainly the British, French, Belgian, Portuguese, and Spanish. West Africa has hardly any white settlers; the few are mostly temporary residents employed by the government or business. East and Central Africa have sizable white minorities, many of whom are permanent residents. Other alien groups are the Levantines in the West and the Indians in the East and Central regions.

Economically, too, there is diversity, in part the result of climatic differences. Some areas are blessed with mineral wealth, such as the coastal belts of West Africa and the rich Katanga–Northern Rhodesian copperbelt. A few are also rich in potential—or currently exploited—hydroelectric power, two in being (Kariba in the former Federation of Rhodesia and Nyasaland and Owen Falls in Uganda), with others still to be harnessed (Konkouré in Guinea, Kouilou in the former French Congo, Inga in the former

Belgian Congo, Volta in Ghana, Ivindo in the Gabon, and the Niger River in Nigeria). Hence, while a few have mining potentialities, many are certain to remain overwhelmingly agricultural, with some prospects of an industrialized sector as a subsidiary.

I

There are enough important similarities among the countries to warrant generalizations for the development-minded social scientist. All the indigenous elements are poor; the local foreign elements, in contrast, often being wealthy. While income differentials do exist, so that a cocoa-rich country like Ghana may have per capita income levels three or four times those of neighboring Upper Volta, both are still very low by Western standards. Concomitantly, there is the paucity of local savings and of investment capital. Morcover, what little funds do exist do not get mobilized for use in potential investment opportunities; few have the habit of entrusting their surplus funds beyond their own control. There is a beginning of a money market; Lagos, the capital of Nigeria, for example, does have a stock exchange, and the Nigerians are slowly becoming acquainted with share purchase. But this is at so restricted a level that for our purposes it can be ignored.

Probably equally serious, as already indicated, is the lack of entrepreneurs. The African is active in petty trade and transport —the colorful mammy traders and mammy wagons of West Africa have earned a place in any tourist's catalogue. But the willingness and ability to try new lines, in particular, manufacturing, is singularly lacking. Why this is so can best be answered by a psychologist, although it probably is related to the conservative tribal customs which discourage deviation from the accepted ways.

This preference for trade is re-enforced by the uncertainties that surround economic activity in an underdeveloped area like tropical Africa. The economy is dominated by the export of primary products, such as coffee, cocoa, copper, palm oil, and ground-nuts. These are subject to wide price swings, as small shifts in either supply or demand result in disproportionate impacts on income. Hence long-term projects become most hazardous, inasmuch as the shift in world markets abroad can nullify and even offset any efforts within the enterprise; the ability to forecast price trends is of far greater concern than the more long-run effects of efficient output. As a result, it is the trader, rather than the industrial organizer, who is better suited to cope with this hazard.

On the other hand, unlike the countries of Latin America or the Middle East, the land problem does not involve a conflict with a politically entrenched feudal aristocracy. Land ownership in the Western sense is a relatively new concept to the African; the traditional divisions were among the tribal groups, in which the individual had certain rights but not freedom to sell or alienate. While this concept is changing slowly, most notably in the newer urban centers, the rural attitudes are still not compatible with this development. Here land per individual is mainly a function of numbers rather than inheritance.

To the outside investor the two most serious obstacles are the lack of indigenous skills and the insufficiently developed infrastructure. Probably nothing impresses the newcomer so much, upon first arrival, as these deficiencies.

The first lack—a native group that has had sufficient technical training and experience— reflects both the inadequate education and the low level of industrialization. Since there is little employment for these skills, there is neither the incentive nor the finance to support a program that would produce a supply on which a newcomer could draw. Moreover, the colonial heritage has placed a status premium on white-collar—office—jobs, so that what technical capabilities do exist are primarily clerical, with a distinct prejudice existing against the manual opportunities.

This deficiency extends throughout the hierarchy. Executives, junior executives, foreman, the administrative cadre—all ranks, in brief, are in short supply. Hence, the newly established firm, even if on a small scale, must create its own staff training program, using whatever raw material is currently available or emerging from the local school system. This extra cost, of course, must be added to the more ordinary production expenses and, if too serious, could be sufficiently inhibiting to many would-be entrants. The only alternative is the employment of highly paid expatriate help, a costly substitute that may also create ill-will among the more nationalistically minded countries. Despite the inability of the locals to fill these posts, the feeling is still one of being robbed of the better-paying jobs by these foreigners.

The inadequate infrastructure is simply another manifestation of the lack of economic development. Railroads are few and river facilities poor. Most of the transport routes are designed for the evacuation of produce for export or the funneling of imports so that cross-country trade is insufficiently supported by the requisite transport network. Electricity, too, is inadequate to support any large-scale industrialization, for local coal supplies are scanty or nonexistent, and only a few areas have the potential inherent in hydro-electric power. As a result, most large-scale projects must include funds for their own transportation and power requirements, thus adding to the initial capital costs.

A factor that must dominate foreign capital's considerations to entry into Africa is the explosive possibility implicit in any large-scale alien ownership of business in newly independent countries. These are run by governments that have just emerged from political colonialism—where the former British, French, or Belgian rulers left less than a year or two before, often after a protracted struggle for self-rule. Hence, there is extreme sensitivity to allowing in a new form of colonialism disguised as foreign ownership of the economic sources of power, a strength that could be wielded subtly to exert the control lost at the political level. While few foreign companies envision their interests in such terms, the hypersensitivity of the local politician is such as to exaggerate this fear into an ever-present possibility. Any large-scale immigration of foreign firms would only fuel such latent hostility even more, so much so that it could break out into a drive for harassment and even confiscation, such as has occurred all too often

in Latin America and the Middle East. So far it can be said that no tropical African country has embarked on this path, despite rumblings in Ghana and Guinea, the two most leftward inclined of the newly emergent African States.

If we accept the disabilities of under-developed Africa—lack of an industrial entrepreneurial class, inadequate savings, latent hostility to expatriate capital—then the implication is quite clear. The state must assume the role normally allocated to private enterprise in Western economies such as the United States, the British Commonwealth, or the advanced countries of the Common Market. Two functions must be undertaken: the direction of new enterprise and the active support of most new projects. This latter, in practice, would mean government ownership and operation, perhaps utilizing hired foreign technicians to fill in the skilled gaps.

II

Government intervention, however, should not be undertaken in a doctrinaire fashion. For example, if local (native) capital does wish to enter new industrial fields, it should be encouraged. The case for state intervention is based on the supposition that little or no such energies will be available from the private sector.

More significantly, flexibility should be displayed in the forms of government participation. Joint ownership and licensing of new enterprises should be contemplated, as well as the more familiar form of complete government ownership. It should be noted that these various approaches are currently being tried, for example, in Nigeria.

Joint ownership is more than a partnership in the provision of capital, with the private member sharing the costs with the government. It also means joint risks, the loss being shared in proportion to the investment, and joint protection, since the state also has an interest in avoiding policies that threaten the enterprise with loss.

Where private capital from abroad is reluctant to enter on its own, joint ownership is a means of attracting it with a minimization of risk of loss. For example, its share of the investment could be in the form of equipment from the parent plant abroad, plus the necessary know-how needed to organize and initiate operations. If, in addition, the foreign partner is a source of the raw materials of partially fabricated components to be used by this new venture, its gain on these captive sales adds to the prospective profits picture.

An added attraction is present if—as is true in so many underdeveloped areas—the trade union movement is politically allied with the party in power. Partnership with the government thus includes an insurance against labor strife that could otherwise lead to production interruptions or excessively high wage demands. The Ghanaian labor situation may well be an illustrative example of this favorable possibility.

Licensing arrangements could serve as an alternative to joint ownership. Here the foreign corporation lends its know-how, patents, and processes and perhaps continues as a consultant to see that the production lines run smoothly. In return it acquires either a share in the firm or an income in the form of royalties based on output. Here, too, its commitment is a limited one, with the State putting up the capital, drawing on its foreign associate for the techniques that make the operation feasible. Obviously, this means that the State is running the entire risk of loss, but in return it has acquired know-how that might not otherwise be willing to come into the country.

Sole ownership, of course, simplifies the problem, but it entails the State undertaking the entire risk of loss and, at the same time, limits the usefulness of a given amount of capital. Joint ownership on a 50-50 basis, for example, would enable a given amount of government funds to go twice as far. But this requires the State to obtain a willing partner, and many foreign concerns prefer 100 per cent ownership rather than the sharing of control with a politically minded partner.

Furthermore, sole ownership throws the entire management responsibility on the State, although some of this can be lessened through management contracts with foreign organizations. In this case, the foreign staff is hired, but the risk of loss is still that of the State.

One of the major advantages of government ownership is its ability to plan the development along desired lines. For example, it is common for privately owned industry to locate in the capital and major port cities. The accompanying need is to attract labor from other centers, thus adding to the population problem, with attendant expansion of social costs—housing, water, streets, etc. Since some of these plants would be just as feasible economically if they were located in other, less populous centers, with a lessened need for migratory labor, the same degree of development could be achieved with a greater dispersal of its benefits. No longer would development along modern lines be a feature of a few "poles," with the remainder of the country a relatively untouched rural preserve. Such dispersal could be more certainly achieved by government-financed installations.

That government participation need not exclude the private investor can be illustrated from the dovetailing of interests in the currently projected Volta Dam in Ghana. This operation is to be on so vast a scale that it becomes feasible to use the various techniques suggested here. The power production is to be a government-owned operation and is to sell its output primarily to the aluminum smelter. This type of public utility has become increasingly government-owned, and the Ghanaian decision is in line with this trend. The more technical requirements of a smelter operation, in contrast, are those characteristic of private industry, and here a consortium of aluminum producers is participating as a group enterprise. Incidental by-products of this co-operation will be the development of a fisheries industry, which will help supplement the protein-deficient diet of the Ghanaians, and the utilization of surplus electric power to aid in the establishment of small industry complexes in the area served. It should be noted that small-scale enterprise will be aided through the by-product effects; here it is possible that indigenous enterprise will be induced to enter, thus perhaps stimulating the local entrepreneurial spirit.

This co-operation lends itself to the African environment. The leaders recognize the technical limitations inherent in so complex an enterprise as the production of aluminum and thus wisely leave both the production and the marketing problems to the more experienced private entrepreneur. Power production is a relatively simple operation, and its sensitive role in supplying the local consumer makes it a logical candidate for public ownership, whereas the almost negligible local market for aluminum makes this a less serious consideration.

Another institutional approach suited to the co-operation of government and private capital is the development corporation. This is generally a government-owned and -operated financing medium through which funds are channeled to specific new companies or the expansion of existing ones. The corporation can participate in any of the available feasible ways to initiate new installations. For example, it could serve as a silent partner, putting up a proportion of the funds jointly with a foreign firm. It could finance a local entrepreneur who may have obtained the license to produce some new item. Or it could establish a wholly owned facility and then either manage it or arrange for a management contract with outside advisers. Ideally, as its various projects become profitable it should try to sell off these assets, thus replenishing its funds for additional ventures. The success picture would presumably attract interest because of the proven record; the initial start-up risks have already been surmounted. Such disposal would also help enlarge the private sector of the economy and acquaint the local embryo industrialists with the experience of success in manufacturing. A beginning along these lines has already been attempted in Nigeria, where a large cement plant was sold through a public stock issue.

It should be noted that the licensing and managerial contracts are means of introducing foreign know-how where it might not come in on its own. The license means that the foreign company shares its knowledge with the local firm but does not risk any of its funds. In return, it would get a royalty. The managerial contract brings in executive talent on a basis not unlike that of any hiring corporation—a fixed salary plus perhaps profit sharing.

III

These various approaches reduce the stake that the foreign interest has in the outcome and thus should make it more amenable to a rapid Africanization of the staff, an objective emphasized by all African leaders. Since any loss resulting from too hasty a change-over would be shared with the African partner—entirely so where the foreigner's contribution is limited to a management or licensing arrangement—there would be less reluctance to entrust the local elements with greater responsibility. The resulting political advantage is obvious.

These approaches are also acceptable compromises with the nationalist pride and State-ownership leanings characteristic of much of the subcontinent. The African government is able to obtain the benefits of foreign know-how—and to some extent the additional capital where partnership is acceptable—without the onus of foreign dominance with its implications of colonial exploitation. The foreigner still has a profitable possibility while minimizing the capital he has invested, thus reducing the danger from confiscation and nationalization.

Moreover, it should be noted that there has not been a single significant case of expropriation in Africa, certainly nothing comparable with the Cuban situation. Even in strife-torn Congo (Leopoldville) the business interests have been virtually untouched, except to the extent that sales may have declined or employees fled as a result of the turmoil. But private property as such has been respected, and where operations have been feasible they have been maintained unhampered. Similarly in Guinea, accused of having virtually allied itself with the

Eastern Bloc, private enterprise has functioned with little hindrance. The most controversial illustration is the taking over of the Bauxites du Midi properties—an Aluminium Limited subsidiary. Here it is claimed that the company did not fulfill the terms of its concession—in effect, instituting a go-slow policy, while awaiting improvement in both the domestic political climate and general world aluminum marketing conditions. In Ghana, recently the target of critics because of new legislation, a requirement to reinvest earnings up to 40 per cent within Ghana is far less confiscatory than it appears. Most firms that plan to stay on in a country tend to reinvest a substantial portion, so that such legislation in practice would restrict only the "fly-by-night" operator.

Despite varying ideological professions by the different leaders, most of sub-Saharan Africa appears to be following the same basic approach—encouragement to private enterprise, where present, a welcome to foreign capital, but a realization that a greater rate of development can come only if the government intervenes, either directly in the establishment of new enterprises or indirectly through subsidies and tariffs. All will seek outside aid and therefore will be forced to draw up an over-all development plan, and all will probably have to borrow or guarantee loans from international institutions, thus adding to the degree of intervention in the economy. Hence, business will have to operate in a mixed environment, but not necessarily a hostile one. To the extent that it realizes this distinction and accepts the conditions, to that extent it will have adjusted successfully and thus made it possible for a profitable and workable operation.

Introduction

IT IS HARD these days to find an African statesman who does not advocate "a socialist path" to economic development. Among intellectuals, trade unionists and other politically aware groups, the enthusiasm for "socialism" is only slightly less widespread. On the ideological level, "socialism" has won the day in most of independent Africa.

That no two African socialists mean quite the same thing when they talk of socialism is by now clear. The gamut of conceptions runs from the very general Ujamaa ("Familyhood" or "Socialism" in Swahili) of Tanganyika's President Nyerere and the vague amalgam of Marxism, Christian socialism, humanitarianism, and "Negritude" of President Senghor of Senegal, to the more structured but heretical Marxism of Guinea's President Touré, which denies the presence of class struggle in Africa. There are also those, mainly university students and leaders of the "left opposition," who are more orthodox in their socialism. They see the emergence in Africa of unacceptable inequalities in income and power, and nascent class conflict. They question the meaningfulness of "African Socialism," and the ideological purity of "African Socialists." They are for socialism in Africa but not "African Socialism."[1]

Despite the diversity of socialist doctrine, most Africans who call themselves socialists do hold in common certain economic attitudes or preconceptions. All of them, first of all, view "capitalism" as an unsuitable system for Africa. It is the economy of the colonizers; capitalism and colonialism are really two sides of the same coin. It is old-fashioned, out of place in the modern world. It is inadequate to meet the pressing development needs of poor countries in general and Africa in particular. Individual enterprise cannot be counted on to mobilize resources on the scale required in Africa, and the market mechanism is a wasteful, highly imperfect regulator of economic activity. Development by the "capitalist," free enterprise route is too slow. There is too little private capital accumulation, too few entrepreneurs. Capitalism is—at least according to President Nkrumah—"too complicated." It would,

8

Socialism and Economic Development in Tropical Africa

Elliot J. Berg

From The Quarterly Journal of Economics, Vol. 78, No. 4 (1964), pp. 549–573. Reprinted with permission.

moreover, maintain and even intensify the hold of foreign capital, and the dominance of agricultural exports in the economy. In the absence of forced draft growth policies, which only the state can undertake, Africa will remain a permanent economic dependency of the outside world.

Even if all this were not true, even if the efficiency of capitalism as a model of growth could be satisfactorily demonstrated, it would still be unacceptable on social and ethical grounds. Capitalism rests on the exploitation of man by man. It leads to intolerable inequality, allowing the strong, the crafty, the well-placed to win a large share of society's goods without making corresponding contributions. It is inhuman, destructive of human dignity. It alienates each man from his brother, and prevents a full flowering of the human personality.

There is little that is specifically African about these ideas. They are general indictments of capitalism as a social and economic system, drawn from the mainstream of European socialism. The *African* quality of African socialist thinking in its economic aspects arises from two main sources. First, some of the universal critiques of capitalist economic organization receive special emphasis: the association of capitalism with colonialism, for example, and the un-productive, parasitic role of the merchant. But most universal and most basic is the general argument that a socialist solution to Africa's development problems is funda-mentally in harmony with the communal traditions of African society. African village life, the argument runs, is essentially socialis-tic. Land is held by the community, and much of the villager's work and play is organized on a group basis. Kinship ties remain strong, and among most African peoples firm class distinctions have not yet developed. Individualism has little place in traditional society. Even among those who have entered the money economy as cash crop growers or wage and salary earners, group loyalties remain deep. This social setting is a natural base for the construction of a socialist form of society, since Africans are by social instinct and economic cir-cumstances already socialists. All that is needed is to transform the old socialism, recast it into a new and modern mold.

Much remains vague in this formulation. Little is said about whether it is to be the village, the kinship group, the cooperative work societies which are to be harnessed and modernized. Less is said about how it is to be done. Some African socialists emphasize cooperatives, others communal cultivation. It is only the general tenor of the argument that is universal among "African socialists" if not among all socialists in Africa: some-how, the "communitarian" spirit of the villages must be retained and utilized to build a specifically African kind of socialist society. It is not an altogether unfamiliar argument. The Populists in Russia at the end of the nineteenth century were saying many of the same things: by building on the traditions of village socialism, society can skip a stage of history—the destructive, individualizing, capitalist stage.

Economic Policies: the Socialist Development Model

While most socialists in Africa share this general world view, it is not easy to define the meaning of African socialism in terms of concrete economic policies. Statements of socialist intent or doctrine rarely descend to the blueprint level, so they contain little in the way of specific policy proposals. Between theory and reality, furthermore, there may be a big gap; in Senegal and Tanganyika, among other places, the air is heavy with talk of socialism, but not much is done about it. In the area of actual economic policies, finally, different paths are being followed by African governments, all claiming to be headed in a socialist direction.

Thus socialists in Africa emphasize the need for planning. But so do non-socialists; planning of some sort is applauded every-where these days, even in strongholds of free enterprise. Socialists are sympathetic to nationalization of private industry, but few of them call for such nationalization on a wholesale basis, and they differ in their view of timing and the scope to be allowed to the private sector. All admit the need for private foreign investment, though with varying degrees of enthusiasm. Policies toward land ownership differ. In places like Senegal and Ghana, where individual tenure has made headway among peasant growers of export crops, there is no call for nationalization of the land. In Guinea, Mali, and to a lesser extent Tanganyika, individualization is dis-couraged. Under the banner of socialism, it seems, almost anyone can march.

But this is not quite true. It is possible to see in almost all socialist doctrine and practice a general policy orientation which gives some definable economic substance to socialist ideology. There is a "socialist road" to development, a "socialist model" of develop-ment, though it is a construct, an abstraction from which there are many departures in reality. The elements of this "socialist model" can be seen best in those countries which have most loudly and persistently announced their dedication to the building of a socialist society: Ghana, Guinea, Mali, to a lesser extent Senegal and Tanganyika. But the same elements are present as tendencies elsewhere, and are implicit in most socialist doctrine.

It is first of all clear that in all socialist approaches, the State is to be the driving force in development. Its area of action is to be enlarged. It is not only to undertake new initiatives, but to intensify existing controls over private economic activity.

In most of Africa, government has always been the major element in the economy, even though the public sector commands a smaller proportion of total output than in advanced Western countries. The presence of the state is exercised through its economic controls and regulations, and by its predominance in the money sector; between a quarter and a half of the recorded wage-labor force in most of the continent has long been employed by government. And the minimum tasks required in the continent's present stage of development (law and order, physical infrastructure, education, research) imply a very large government role even under the most "liberal." economic policies conceivable. But in the "socialist model" the state has a much greater place—in the creation and operation of industrial and agricultural enterprises, in control of marketing, in price regulation, and in general management of the economy.

Related to the predominance of the state is an emphasis on direct economic controls, underlying which is a belief in the efficacy of such controls, combined with a lack of faith in individual profit-seeking and the market mechanism as efficient instruments of resource allocation and mobilization. This is most strikingly evident in socialist policy tendencies in the distribution sector. Government monopoly of all or part of foreign and domestic trade is regarded as particularly desirable. In part this springs from a desire to reduce the influence of big foreign trading firms. But behind it is the conviction that private commerce is inefficient—that prices are too high, profits too great, and the number of traders too large, and that the merchant class is profoundly parasitic, a group of useless exploiters. For all these reasons it is necessary to "democratize the channels of commerce," as President Touré put it—i.e., nationalize trade.

This penchant for state take-over of the trading sector is stimulated by the belief that since trading is a simple matter its nationalization can provide an easy and rich source for development resources. Thus, in both Guinea and Mali, the planned profits of the

nationalized trading sector were to provide much of the local contribution to expenditures under the first postindependence development plans—in Mali about one-third of total domestic investment, in Guinea even more.

In agriculture, too, the policy tendencies of African socialists are definable. Agricultural development is not ignored; it comes in for reluctant recognition, reluctant because of the feeling that future price prospects for commodity exports are bleak, that true economic independence can come about in any event only when Africa no longer is dependent on the export of raw materials, and that industrial development is at bottom the only true engine of modernization. But in this socialists are not really different from most others in Africa and elsewhere in the developing countries. Where they part company is in method. The socialist road to agricultural development places little emphasis, or actually discourages, expansion of individual and family production, on the grounds (sometimes explicit, sometimes not) that to do so would involve the creation of a kulak class, a politically retrograde, exploitative rural bourgeoisie.

It is largely for this reason that African socialist thinking runs in terms of mechanization of agriculture, the big project, state farms, and development through conversion and activation of communal cultivation. This is clear, as we will see below, in Guinea, and it is becoming increasingly evident in Ghana, where the main source of planned agricultural expansion is to be in the state farming sector.

Origins of Socialist Attitudes

It is worth considering briefly the roots of these attitudes and ideas on economic policy. In part they rest on imported ideology. Much of the distaste and distrust with which African elites view "capitalism" reflects the Marxist world view—however modified or heretic in form—which colors the thinking of so many national leaders in Africa. Capitalism is to them simply the projection of colonialism and imperialism, much as Lenin said it was. Related to this are the personal and intellectual relations of African students and political leaders with European socialists, who most steadfastly fought their cause during the years of colonial rule. Development through expansion of the private sector also has political implications which many of the new elites find unpalatable: every foreign private enterprise harbors a latent neocolonial influence; and the emergence or expansion of a rich, energetic African capitalist class raises the specter of potential political opposition. Where there is money, Africans know, power is never very far away.

While all of these are important in explaining the "anticapitalist" spirit abroad in Africa, at least equally fundamental is the image of capitalism and the general economic attitudes inherited from the colonial period. Thus colonialism and capitalism are so closely identified in African thinking, not only, or even mainly, because of Marxist–Leninist doctrine, but because most Africans have seen it to be so. Behind them is a half-century of history cluttered with memories of price-fixing arrangements, government-bestowed monopoly privileges, restrictive wage and labor market policies, forced labor—all dependent on an alliance between colonial governments and private (almost exclusively foreign) enterprises, and most of them involving a sacrifice of African interests. It is hardly surprising that "decolonization" and a reduction of the role of private enterprise should seem related.

Moreover, the colonial experience in most of the continent was scarcely designed to encourage an appreciation of the economic potentials of individual initiatives in a relatively free market. Economic policy in colonial Africa was most often paternalist, *dirigiste*, anti-free enterprise to the core. More often than not, African peasants were told what to produce, who to sell it to, where, when, at what price. In a number of countries, even the African instinct of survival

was discounted; Africans were forced to grow some crops in excess of normal needs, as a guarantee against famine. Wage earners in much of the continent were not until recently thought by colonial officials or employers to be capable of spending their incomes "sensibly," nor were African farmers and traders presumed to be sufficiently alive to price and profit to assure urban food supplies at reasonable prices. Markets had to be "organized," commodity and labor supplies "regularized." Extensive price controls, monopolistic allocation of sales and purchases, regulation of entry into trade, commerce and industry—most of the armory of a benevolent *dirigism* found its way to Africa.

In the early years of the colonial presence this was no doubt inevitable and necessary. Preconditions for the effective functioning of markets had to be established. But it tended to persist, in much of the continent, when its utility was doubtful. That it did so reflected the economic tastes of colonial administrators in charge of economic policy, most of whom had little understanding of and sympathy for the struggles of the market place. They took a dim view of the competitive market, its "disorderliness" and seeming wastefulness; they rarely saw the point of having two sellers (or buyers) where one might do. And they had a particularly low estimate of the merchant, who—as they saw it—grew fat buying cheap and selling dear, exploiting the ignorance and improvidence of the ordinary African. The educational and disciplinary aspects of market decisions were never appreciated. And that the market might in some measure contain corrective tendencies, or reflect underlying forces of supply and demand, these and similar homely notions of the economist were badly received in Africa. When retail prices rose, the instinctive reaction was to damn the traders and look for conspiracy.

These are the habits of thought passed on to independent Africa by its colonial rulers: misunderstanding and mistrust of the market mechanism; an ingrained belief in the ability of government to manipulate economic variables, no matter how contrary the underlying market conditions; an inability to perceive the potential uses of the price system in allocating resources through decentralized decision-making. It is no surprise that so much African thinking on economic development policy runs in terms of state enterprise, direct state controls over production, marketing and prices, suppression of middlemen, and state-directed activity in general. Aside from the impulses in this direction arising from ideology and from internal political considerations, it represents continuity with the past.

The Guinea Experience

Consideration of socialist development policies in Africa invites a glance at the experience of the Republic of Guinea.[2] Alone of all the French territories in Africa, this small country of some three million proud and spirited people took its independence when offered it in 1958. Its dynamic political leadership was convinced of the efficacy of the socialist "model" as outlined above and was dedicated to economic transformation along socialist lines.

Its tasks were enormous. Despite their capture of political control, few Guineans had experience in dealing with economic problems, either on the level of the state or the firm; at independence, only a handful held high-level technical or administrative posts in government, and almost none knew managerial responsibility in the small private sector. The total stock of university-trained local manpower was probably less than 50 people, the number of high school graduates probably less than 500. In 1957 the high schools of the country produced only 30 graduates. Yet three months after independence, almost all French civil servants were gone. Gone too was French economic aid, which had provided most of the development finance during the postwar period, and the protected market in France for coffee and bananas—which accounted for 80 per cent of Guinea's export earnings in 1957.

The new government attacked its problems with vigor and confidence. One of its first acts, taken three months after independence, was to set up a state trading monopoly limited at first to trade in exports and key imports. This limited role of the state trading organization was soon found to be unsatisfactory; the domestic wholesale and retail trade remained in private hands, so the state had simply imposed itself on the existing "colonial" structure, adding, as it were, another middleman. The scope of state trading was thus extended; it was given a complete monopoly over foreign trade, and over domestic wholesaling.[3] The process was completed in 1960 by the extension of state shops to the retail level.

In mid-1960 a Three-Year Plan was initiated; it had been drawn up with the help of French Marxist advisors, and was implemented with the help of 1,000 to 1,500 communist technicians and over $100 million in credits from the communist countries. The planned investment was large ($140 million, later raised to $155 million), relative to either past investment rates or to GNP.[4] The sectoral allocation of planned expenditure was not much different from that found in most African development plans. But within the sectoral plans, the nature of Guinea's ideological options could be clearly perceived. Agriculture, for example, received 26 per cent of the total plan expenditure, but 90 per cent of this was allocated to the state sector—the main part of it for state-run farms.

The achievements of the plan period, and of the years since independence in general, have in some respects been considerable. The administrative machinery survived the shock of transition to independence. Guinea's government has made massive assaults on the education problem,[5] and if official figures are to be believed, the "human investment" program yielded substantial results—at least until 1962.[6]

The achievements of the new state, however, pale before its catastrophic failures in the area of economic policy and planning. In agriculture the state farms apparently never got off the ground, despite the import from the Soviet Union of hundreds of agricultural machines; by 1963 most of the equipment had been abandoned, so far as a visitor could tell, and the state farming enterprises quietly laid to rest. Far from meeting the ambitious agricultural goals of the Plan, agricultural output has fallen.[7] Nor has industrial progress been more notable; of the twenty-six plants listed in the Plan, less than a quarter were completed in mid-1963. By 1963 the country faced a severe balance-of-payments crisis. Imported consumer goods were scarce; it was difficult to see how Guinea could meet its debt service payments on loans from Soviet bloc countries, due to begin in that year. And all of this occurred despite an inflow of foreign aid of perhaps $50 million a year, which made Guinea one of the most "aided" countries per capita ($15–20) in the world during these years.

Part of this unhappy record is no doubt attributable to the precipitous withdrawal of the French. Part of it, too, is due to the methods and content of Soviet economic aid.[8] But the major burden of responsibility rests with the Guineans themselves. The state trading venture was an unmitigated disaster, afflicting the whole economy. An inexperienced Guinean management found itself in charge of what was in effect the largest trading firm in Africa. Despite some gallant efforts, the distribution system rapidly fell victim to a massive administrative muddle. Goods were ordered for which there was no demand, or in quantities far beyond normal needs. Desired staples were frequently in short supply because of inadequate inventory policies and irregular deliveries. The old "colonial" evil of the "tied" or "conditional" sale became common enough in state shops to call forth public denunciation by President Touré. Poor inventory control in warehouses resulted in the rotting of perishable items.

Thus Guinean urban consumers came to know shortages, poor quality goods, long queues, and black markets. Consumers of imports in the interior were even more badly served. And the export sector suffered from sparse and unreliable deliveries of pesticides, fertilizers, and other imported inputs.

The absence of consumer imports, or their low quality, combined with low prices fixed for meat and fish, affected the production and marketed supply of local foodstuffs and export crops. The flow of meat, fish and rice to urban centers shrank as producers either withheld their output from the market, or diverted their supply to the neighboring countries of Liberia, Sierra Leone and the Ivory Coast. Smuggling became the order of the day, absorbing not only the existing private traders who were hobbled and harassed by official regulations, but new entrants besides. Coffee found its way to the Ivory Coast; Guinea's 1962 export of coffee was half the level of previous years. Diamonds also left the country illegally. Some imports increased fantastically, for reasons that are not clear; imports of cotton prints, for example, rose from 158 million francs in 1959, to 2.3 billion in 1961 and 1.8 billion in 1962. Most of these textiles were almost surely smuggled out of the country to finance either smuggled imports from neighboring countries, or capital flight. The propensity to smuggle was aggravated by the drastic depreciation of the Guinean franc in (free and illegal) money markets in neighboring countries.

Troubles were compounded by price policies edicted with cheerful disregard for market forces and, in particular, without recognition of Guinea's geographical situation. Shortly after independence, for example, President Touré decided, as a symbol of the intentions of the new regime, to sell rice (a gift from the Chinese) at a price well below that prevailing in neighboring countries. In a matter of weeks the rice disappeared from the country, sold across the border at the higher prices prevailing there. Similarly, the government decided that certain basic goods, such as cement, would be sold in the interior either at the same price as in the port city of Conakry, or at a subsidized price. The aim was to favor consumers in the interior, on whom transport costs weighed heavily. But the subsidized items also found their way across the borders, since the delivered price in the Guinea interior was substantially lower than across the border.

Despite the obviously faltering performance of the economy, reform has proved difficult. In March, 1961 the system of internal distribution was on the verge of complete collapse. Imports were piling up in

Conakry, while the interior was without staples. The government was forced to commandeer all available trucks in Conakry to move goods to the interior. Shortly thereafter adaptations were made; the state trading organization was decentralized and a greater role for private traders was announced. But aside from some administrative reshuffling, little basic change occurred. Fundamental reappraisals were hindered by the need to maintain socialist purity, an unwillingness to look coolly at all alternatives. Official economic discussion, in fact, became increasingly divorced from reality.[9] It was not until the end of 1963, under the pressure of deepening economic crisis,[10] that a more basic reform was announced, involving changes in price policies and return of more of the distribution sector to private hands.

The costs of Guinea's false starts cannot be calculated only in terms of wasted resources and foregone growth. Much of the popular enthusiasm for the regime and the dynamism of its leadership has been dissipated. Cynicism and corruption have spread, and signs of disaffection appeared.[11] The moral and political cement binding the state together has been weakened as respect for the law, and for the regime, has diminished.

The Inapplicability of the Socialist Model

It is not the business of outsiders—at least economists—to quarrel about the suitability of the goals set out by socialists in Africa. This is their vision of the society they want (however vaguely delineated as yet), and is not open to question by others. What the observer from outside can legitimately consider, however, is the probable effectiveness of the "socialist model" in achieving the goals of economic growth and change which socialists, like most Africans, say they want. For a number of reasons, suggested in the Guinea story, the socialist path to modernization is not likely to bring success in this sense, for the major elements of socialist policy are ill-suited to present African circumstances.

The first and most obvious reason is Africa's scarcity of people equipped by training, experience or education to manage the economy. To an extent unmatched in most of the underdeveloped world, positions of skill and responsibility were until recently in the hands of non-Africans. This was true almost everywhere in the public sector until a decade ago, and remains true throughout the private, nonagricultural sector, with the possible exceptions of Ghana and Nigeria. One main reason for this was the limited availability, until recent years, of upper-level education. As late as 1958 there were only about 8,000 Africans graduated from all the academic secondary schools below the Sahara, and only about 10,000 others were studying in universities—more than half of these in Ghana and Nigeria. Educational intake and output have increased markedly since 1958, but in 1962 there were still few African countries where more than 200 Africans received full secondary diplomas. In only a handful of countries will the outflow from universities be more than 250 a year much before 1970.

In these figures lie the most severe indictment of colonial rule. African governments are trying to make up for it with an enormous educational effort. But trained people necessary to man the bureaucracies of the new states will not be available for at least a decade in most of the continent. It is not only the highly specialized technicians who will be in short supply; all professional and technical manpower will be sparse. And the vital middle levels, now exceedingly shallow, are likely to remain so for even longer, as universities continue to absorb most secondary school graduates. Under these circumstances, to put heavy and exacting new burdens on the state is to invite trouble—waste and inefficiency at the least, economic dislocation on the Guinean scale at the worst. This is the message not only of common sense; it is one of the inescapable lessons of the Guinea experience.

Contrary to President Nkrumah's view, socialism, with the larger state role that it assumes, is not less, but much more complicated than a "capitalist" or market system relying heavily on decentralized decision-making in the market. It is in particular much more demanding of trained human resources. Given the pressing scarcity of these resources, it is essential not to use them on tasks that can be performed by others. Where teachers are wanting, and general administration is shoddy, it is dubious wisdom to have trained and able people fixing and enforcing prices, authorizing import licenses, or even running industrial enterprises. This is especially pertinent to the extension of the state into the distribution sector. Where private individuals have the proven capacity and experience to perform efficiently, as do traders in most of the continent, the extension of state control represents a monstrous misallocation of trained manpower, even if government functionaries could do the job as well as the private traders —a most unlikely possibility.

Shortcomings in socialist approaches to agricultural development provide a second major reason for questioning the probable effectiveness of socialist policy. The lackluster record of agricultural development in socialist countries should by itself suggest caution to potential importers of development strategies; socialist achievement in agriculture has almost nowhere been impressive. But there are other reasons, closer to home, to question the efficacy of socialist solutions in agriculture.

The African physical and economic environment, first of all, has shown itself generally uncongenial to mechanization and large-scale farm projects. Most African soils are delicate, and little is known about them; the effects of continuous use of fertilizers, plowing and intensive cultivation, for example, have been adequately studied in only a few places. Within small geographic areas, African soils tend to vary widely in texture and chemistry, and many operations, such as tree stump removal, do not easily lend themselves to mechanization. Dust, heat and rain, combined with casual handling, sparsity of skilled maintenance men, and difficulties with spare parts all take a terrible toll on farm equipment. Machines do not in any case eliminate the need for labor, as Professor Frankel emphasized in his study of the East African groundnut scheme,[12] and unskilled labor tends to be scarce at planting and harvesting time, since most men have farms of their own that require attention.

These and other factors help explain why mechanization and big farm projects in Africa present an almost unbroken record of failure, and sometimes of disaster; Africa, indeed, is the scene of some of the world's most magnificent agricultural white elephants, such as the French-created Office du Niger in Mali, the Gambia poultry scheme of the early postwar years, and the East African groundnut scheme. The Guinea experience outlined above is perhaps even more relevant.

With growing knowledge and changing economic conditions, the prospects for mechanized, large-scale agriculture will no doubt improve; there are some places in Africa where conditions are already more favorable, and in all countries there is room for some effort in this direction. But as a major approach to agricultural development, it has little to recommend it. And when it is recalled that mechanized agricultural schemes eat up large amounts of Africa's scarcest resources—foreign exchange and human skill—they become even more questionable.

In addition to the dim prospects for expansion through state farming and mechanization, both of which are central to the economic thinking of most socialists in Africa, another set of considerations limits the applicability of socialist policies in African agriculture. More than any other region, Africa is a continent of subsistence farmers. The majority of Africans are only slightly committed to the money economy; they spend most of their lives in the village, where their main productive activity is the growing of food for their own consumption.

Under these circumstances, the key to agricultural modernization and growth is fuller peasant commitment to the money economy; villagers must be induced to use their land, their energies and their time differently from in the past, by growing more for the market. This transfer of resources within the village from subsistence production and traditional activities to cash crop production is, in Africa's present stage, the essence of development. It does not by itself guarantee self-sustaining growth, but it is a revolutionary step in the growth process; in the absence of major mineral resources it is an indispensable step.

There are plenty of examples of how an aroused peasantry shifting its energies to cash crops can work great economic transformations. In the space of two decades after the turn of the century, in a country almost without infrastructure and with very little assistance from government, Ghana's peasants made their country the world's greatest cocoa producer. In the Ivory Coast, the creation of a road network and a period of good prices led African farmers to a fivefold expansion of coffee production and a doubling of cocoa output in the fifteen years after World War II. The more recent surge in African export crop production in Kenya offers another example.

If one asks why more such transformations have not occurred, or why some, as in Uganda, seem to be arrested, half-finished, a number of obstacles become apparent: unsuitable soils and climate, including rainfall; expensive or inadequate transport and marketing facilities; lack of knowledge; absence of tools required for small technological changes (plows, for example), and others. Three factors, however, seem of particular significance and generality. The first is neglect of the peasant, the fact that in only a few countries have African villagers in the past received extension services, roads, marketing facilities and other assistance which government might give them. The second is land tenure; the "communal" nature of most land holding, and the difficulties of establishing individual title in some areas affect incentives and the ability of individual farmers to expand sales; in all areas it has limited African access to credit. Finally, rural Africans in most of the continent still have relatively few demands for new goods, and the money income needed to buy them; want levels remain low. It is not, of course, that they would not like more

money income; it is that they are not willing to make the changes in ways of life that are required to get more income.

This last point deserves special emphasis, for not only is it open to misinterpretation, but it is uncongenial to much thinking on development, among socialists as well as others. In order for marketed output to claim a larger share of village resources the peasant must be induced to switch from tried and proven activities to new and unknown ones. The peasant and his family must work harder, and give up "leisure" or customary pleasures and activities in the village. In addition to new outlays of effort, all of this involves uncomfortable departures from custom and may involve new risks, a greater dependence on the market, and even outlays of money. It is hard to see why he should make these changes unless he is first convinced that new goods and services are in fact important elements of a better life. His preference for more income as against his present way of life must be increased.

In these conditions, socialist attitudes and approaches lose most of their relevance. The socialist appeal for land redistribution, common in other parts of the underdeveloped world as a means of mobilizing the peasantry (politically, as well as in an economic sense), are devoid of meaning in sub-Saharan Africa where land is still relatively abundant, and landlordism is a rare problem. Approaches designed to squeeze the peasant into greater production for the market are unpromising. State levies on the agricultural sector, whether by price policies or direct deliveries, can be effective only where agriculture has become monetized and specialized. Peasants still mainly or largely in the subsistence sector cannot be bullied into the market; full retreat back to subsistence production is too easy. The ordinary African village is no Garden of Eden, and life there no idyll; disease is everywhere, famines strikes occasionally, comforts are few. But there is almost everywhere enough to eat, and the village provides the bulk of what most men feel they need. Since life in most African villages is not so oppressive as it is in many other parts of the underdeveloped world, and since many African villagers would find it possible to reduce their demands for goods from outside the village, the result of attempts to squeeze the peasant sector, and consequent peasant dissatisfaction, can easily be "sabotage" in the Veblenian sense—"a conscious withdrawal of efficiency."

The African peasant, then, cannot easily be pushed into the market. He must be pulled into it, encouraged, enticed by positive inducements, among which the most effective is no doubt that most banal of incentives— the possibility of higher real income. To the extent that this is true, it presents socialists in Africa with a fundamental contradiction of the utmost importance. It implies that agricultural transformation is not possible, or is possible only at a much slower rate, without some individualization of land tenure, the emergence of a rural bourgeoisie composed of the more energetic or more fortunate peasants, and the accentuation of rural income inequalities.

Socialists in Africa have not yet come seriously to grips with this set of problems. Their writing, and in a few places their policies, shows more concern with the dangers of individualism and the rise of rural moneyed classes than with the potential output effects of peasant awakening. They emphasize harnessing the communal spirit of the villages, and utilization of the co-operative work groups which perform much labor in traditional agriculture. They tend to rely heavily on appeals to larger social goals —Patriotism, National Construction, the General Good. It is, of course, possible that some considerable mobilization of peasant energies can be brought about in this way, more perhaps in Africa than elsewhere because of the strength of traditional culture there. But it is unlikely by itself to provide the kind of wrench from the past inherent in fuller commitment to the market.

Nor are abstract appeals likely to provide a continuous spur to increased effort. Experience with these methods of rural mobilization is not encouraging, either in Africa or

elsewhere. In addition to administrative and technical problems, there exist in all communal efforts powerful propensities to coercion, especially since lower level cadres tend to be overzealous. Unless these communal efforts are genuinely voluntary and devoted to local public works or other projects of immediate and obvious village utility, they may actually have negative effects on the release of peasant energies. Even where coercion is absent or mild, it often turns out that the list of useful projects which can be performed effectively by village communal labor is distressingly short in the absence of administrative aid, so that communal labor campaigns tend to fizzle out. The appearance of coercive elements and administrative and technical difficulties seem to explain the decline of Tanganyika's brief experiment in postindependence "self-help" programs,[13] and Guinea's attempts to utilize "human investment."

Large-scale transformation of the subsistence sector, then, is unlikely to be achieved unless villagers can see some close relation between their greater effort and a better life, and unless they come to believe that consumption of more goods is essential to this better life. To the extent that this is true, it raises serious doubts about the meaningfulness of most socialist prescriptions for agricultural development.

It is here, also, that socialist policies in the distribution sector are especially relevant. State trading companies are poorly designed to engage in the kind of want-creating activity that private merchants in Africa— indigenous and expatriate—have always undertaken. The agent of the state trading firm is unlikely to roam the remote villages with goods of tempting quality and style, and if necessary, with credit as well, in order to whet peasant appetites for money income and cajole them into new lines of production. He is not, in short, likely to be a creator of markets. So in the area where the distribution system has its most vital role to play— maintenance and expansion of the flow of marketed output from the villages through stimulating the demand for goods—a nationalized trading system is most deficient.

A third major pitfall for socialist solutions

in Africa has its basis in geography. Africa has the highest ratio of frontiers to total area of any continent. Goods and people have always flowed over these frontiers in the past, usually with few restrictions. Effective controls were scarcely possible, traders roamed at will between countries, and when prices in one country moved out of line with those in neighboring countries, smuggling on a large scale tended to develop.

The most striking examples are to be found in postwar West Africa, where bits and chunks of British colonies, with few import restrictions and relatively low price levels, jutted into the protected, high-price French African land mass. Trade between areas under British and French control existed before the colonial frontiers were established, and resourceful groups of African traders served these areas without regard to frontiers.

The mechanism and extent of smuggling is known only in broad outline, but there is enough evidence to indicate that it is a large-scale phenomenon, involving thousands of people, millions of dollars, and an institutional framework that includes specialized transport, established marketing channels, and free (illegal) foreign exchange markets in border towns and cities, almost all in African hands. Export commodities (cattle, smoked fish, cocoa, coffee, peanuts, diamonds, etc.) are involved, and consumer goods.

In West Africa, until the late 1950's at least, the foundation of the contraband trade was export of cattle and smoked fish from savannah regions in French West Africa (Niger, Mali, Upper Volta, northern Togo and Dahomey) to the British territories. These exports generated sterling, which was used to finance illegal import into the franc areas of textiles, bicycles, spirits, lamps, costume jewelry, cola nuts, matches and a wide range of other goods. A Franc-Sterling Study Mission estimated that total exports from British to French West Africa amounted to 12.2 billion metropolitan francs in 1956, of which 8.5 billion was contraband; British West African imports from French West Africa were estimated at 7.5 billion metropolitan francs, of which 4.5 billion was contraband.[14] French trading firms regarded

these estimates as undervalued, but in any event, something in the order of 20 per cent of total French African consumer goods imports were smuggled in the mid 1950's, and if only African-consumed goods are considered, the proportion would be substantially higher.

Not only consumer goods but export crops too passed over borders, whenever differentials in the prices offered to growers in the French and British areas made it profitable. Thus in some years in the 1950's, as much as 60,000 tons of peanuts crossed from Nigeria to French Niger to take account of the subsidized producer prices prevailing in Niger. In 1954 to 1955, it was estimated that 8,000 tons of Ivory Coast cocoa fled to Ghana, when the Ghana Marketing Board maintained its producer price at a high level compared with world (and Ivory Coast) prices. In 1960 the flow of cocoa from Ghana to the Ivory Coast may have been as high as 25,000 tons. And in 1962, an estimated 8,000 tons of export commodities were smuggled from Eastern Nigeria to benefit from higher prices in the Cameroons.[15]

Smuggling has up to now been less prevalent in other parts of the continent, mainly because price structures in southern and central Africa were less dissimilar, and exchange controls less widespread, and trade in East Africa has been relatively free. But recent Congo experience shows how quickly new channels of trade across neighboring frontiers can develop; with domestic inflation, an unrealistic rate of exchange and exchange controls (as well as new and chaotic political arrangements), a significant amount of Congolese production, both of manufactures and raw materials, left the country illegally, at least until the 1963 devaluation of the Congo franc. Its proceeds financed purchases of needed imports and hard currency balances abroad.

Suppression of smuggling is exceedingly difficult when conditions for its flowering are present. Frontiers are long. Often the ethnic groups are the same on both sides, which makes general restriction of movement of people hard to enforce. The smugglers are at least as inventive as the government officials trying to control them, and it is usually possible for the smuggler to find some customs officials who are willing to look the other way for a slight consideration. A government determined to crack down on smuggling can, of course, slow the contraband trade. But the expense of effective control is very considerable; even control of smuggling by sea, such as Nigeria is currently attempting, involves purchases of costly patrol boats and helicopters, as well as expansion of the customs staff. And control of smuggling from the sea is infinitely easier than control of the overland trade.

A control that was effective, moreover, might have serious political consequences. Almost everybody seems to benefit from smuggling. Producers of smuggled beef, fish and export crops get higher prices for their products. Consumers get cheaper, better, more varied goods. The level of employment and the wage bill is probably increased, since the ratio of workers and wage payments to sales volume is no doubt greater in the labor-intensive contraband trade than in legal commerce. Where African traders are the main agents of the contraband trade, there is also a redistribution of profit income from established (mainly expatriate) trading firms to African traders.

It is, of course, the government that is hurt: its customs revenues decline, its price policies are undermined, income is redistributed from public to private sectors, and respect for the law is diminished. But any government that successfully suppressed smuggling might find itself reaping a political whirlwind, for the list of injured private interests would be imposing.

The smuggler casts a long shadow in Africa. He imposes restraints, actual or potential, on independent economic policies. All of the instruments of direct economic control, as well as price policies generally, will—unless they are in harmony with those prevailing in surrounding countries—threaten to activate or enlarge the current of contraband trade. This will occur, for example, if

relatively low prices are paid for locally marketed goods, especially those which are easily transportable, or for export crops; or if austerity policies are introduced, restricting the import of luxury goods and raising their price; or if rate policies on railroads result in internal price distortions; or if exchange controls and restrictions on capital outflows become burdensome. The smuggler even threatens protected local industry with illicit competition.[16]

The Guinea experience is rich with examples. Guinea may be an extreme case, but it is not unique (the Congo provides many parallels), nor is it without relevance to other African areas. It is true that not every part of the continent has frontiers quite so permeable as Guinea's. Nor are there everywhere indigenous traders of such ingenuity and enterprise as Guinea's Dioulas. But comparable groups are found elsewhere, and where they are not, nothing is more calculated to nurture them than the opportunity for quick profit through smuggling.

The difficulty of framing independent economic policies under these circumstances is obvious. This is, of course, true not only for socialist policies, but for all public policies. As conceived in Africa, however, socialist policies involve a greater degree of direct economic control and manipulation of market variables, so the potential restraints implicit in the smuggling phenomenon have more bearing on them. Unless common policies are laid down by geographically related groups of African states, each of them is at the mercy of policies followed by their neighbors. In this sense, African states have a more limited command over their economies than is probably the case anywhere in the world. Socialism in one country is not possible in Africa.

Manpower scarcity, the inappropriateness of socialist approaches to agricultural development, and the constraints of external market forces on internal economic policies are the main but not the only bases for doubting the effectiveness of the socialist model in Africa. Several others deserve brief mention.

First, the efficient operation of state enterprises in Africa presents numerous difficulties in addition to those arising from trained manpower scarcity. Because of the primacy of politics in the recent history of these countries, public enterprises are subject to particularly intense political pressures of various sorts, all of which reduce their efficiency. The raiding of public corporations for support of political party activity, such as the Coker Commission recently revealed in Western Nigeria, is an extreme example. Political interference is also common in decisions on personnel, price and location policies. Employment policies are especially likely to be subject to external pressure; decisions on how many people are hired, or—more important—fired, and who they are, invite political intervention where unemployment is rife and highly particularistic loyalties persist.

The colonial heritage also raises special obstacles to efficiency, in the kinds of attitudes to work performance which it bequeathed. Under the colonial regime almost all employers and supervisors were white and alien, almost all workers African. Because the gap between the manager and the managed was so great, a sense of common enterprise rarely developed; poor work performance might, in fact, be justified in terms of the national struggle. It was an environment, in any case, uncongenial to the growth of an ethic of hard work and a dedication to ideals of craftsmanship. This has carried over into the independence period, and tends to be notably troublesome in the public sector.

In the public sector it is particularly hard to effect the "decolonization of work habits" necessary for improved work performance. The efficiency consciousness of management and supervisory staff tends to be less than in the private sector, partly because the public enterprise does not ordinarily have to meet the market test, partly because no personal resources are involved, but mostly because enforcement of discipline is harder in public enterprises subject to political restraints.

In addition to the efficiency question, and probably of a lower order of significance, is the fact that, at least for some decades, African economies will remain export-oriented. Between 25 and 60 per cent of marketed output in African countries is now

exported, and this is not likely to change soon. Trading in export markets is a highly specialized and delicate business, demanding quick decisions, high standards of quality control, close attention to timing of deliveries. It does not lend itself to the rougher arrangements possible if production is only for enclosed local markets.

The fact that Marketing Boards throughout the continent have for years adequately performed these functions suggests that foreign commodity trading can be done satisfactorily, so too much weight should not be placed on this argument. However, not all commodities lend themselves easily to state trading. The short, unhappy history of the Ghana Timber Marketing Board, whose policies were responsible in part for a drastic decline in timber exports, is suggestive. Among other difficulties encountered by the Board, foreign buyers complained about the consistency of quality grading.[17]

Finally, the degree to which socialist attitudes and policies are put into effect will influence the rate of inflow of private capital, which though not likely to be large in any case, has vital functions to perform. In addition to the conventional benefits (release of domestic resources for other uses, generation of new resources, increased foreign exchange through import substitution and greater export earnings), there are the general leavening effects that foreign private enterprises have in these societies, through their impact on skill development, and the transmission of ideas and techniques.

Conclusion

Ideology can provide a powerful impetus to economic development. By explaining today's struggles and sacrifices in terms of a vision of a better life tomorrow, it can give direction and hope, and inspire new effort. But ideology has its dangers too. It hardens thought. It restricts the search for alternatives, and makes changes of direction difficult. It might even be wrong—in its picture of the world and in its policy prescriptions.

This is the case with socialist ideology in Africa today. For contemporary Africa it is the wrong ideology, in the wrong place, at the wrong time. The state cannot and should not bear the burdens that most African socialists would put upon it. The trained people are lacking, and will not be available for some time. The capacity to control the economy is in any event restricted by African exposure to external market forces. Socialist approaches in agriculture are ill-suited to the special features of Africa's rural environment and are unlikely to effect that mobilization of the peasantry which is essential to continuing growth.

Thus far the predominance of socialist ideology has not had widespread effects on policy, except in a few countries. Guinea rushed along the socialist path after 1958. Ghana has proceeded more slowly, though the pace has picked up. The results are not yet evident, except in Guinea.[18]

The Guinea case is significant precisely because it represents the most extensive experiment in the kinds of policies socialists elsewhere in Africa recommend, and because the difficulties and shortcomings of these policies are illuminated with exceptional clarity there. Guinea's troubles also illustrate the blindfold effects of ideology, the extreme reluctance to abandon a patently unsuccessful set of policies when retreat from a hardened ideological position is involved. The economy of Guinea, and particularly its distribution system, has been in obvious disarray since 1960. Full consideration of alternatives was hampered by the continuing hold of economic ideology, and by the political need to repeat the ideological litanies. The 1963 reform, which is intended to return more of the distribution sector to private hands, will probably be more effective. But it is hardly a sign of flexibility or pragmatism—qualities often assigned to socialists in Africa—when it takes three years and movement to the edge of an economic abyss to adjust policies which have so obviously failed.

The fact that present African conditions make improbable the success of the kinds of policies generally called for by socialists in Africa does not leave only a complete laissez-faire alternative. The role of the state will inevitably be large in any development strategy. Planning is needed, in the sense of looking at the economy as a whole, understanding the ramifications of particular lines of policy, setting down rationally defined criteria for the allocation of public expenditures, stimulating the expansion of the private sector and guiding its direction. Nor does it mean that the socialist alternative will not have more promise of success in the future when trained people are more abundant, the agricultural sector monetized, and the state's capacity to control the economic environment more developed.

In reply to all of this African socialists might argue that the prime goals are social—the building of equalitarian and truly independent societies, where individualism is restrained, income inequalities and class lines are minimized, and the influence of the outside world reduced—and that all other goals, including economic growth, are subservient to these. With this there can be little quarrel. Nor could one object if African socialists recognized that these social goals are in some measure incompatible with maximum economic growth in Africa's present circumstances. But they believe that maximum growth can come only through socialist solutions, and this is almost certainly not true.

The prevalence of attitudes and policy inclinations which we have called the "socialist model" is a matter of no small significance for Africa's future. To the extent that these policies are applied they will lead to waste and misdirected effort, to mistakes few African countries can afford. They will increase political instability; by poor performance, a state that increases its activities in order to seek legitimacy will instead lose the legitimacy it has. Finally, those most firmly committed to socialist solutions are more often than not the most honest, dedicated and able people on the African scene, reformers, university students, and others inspired by a desire to reconstruct their society and make a better life for all their countrymen. This is the saddest part of it all—that these most admirable men are also those most firmly gripped by the illusion that socialism provides a quick and true path to economic development. Given power, they would lead their countries not forward but backward.

Notes

1. We are mainly concerned in this paper with the general economic content of socialist ideology in Africa, not with description and illustration of particular versions of socialism. We will therefore make few specific references. The main sources from which the description of socialist thought is drawn are *Africa Report: Special Issue on African Socialism*, Vol. 8 (May, 1963); A. Fenner Brockway, *African Socialism* (London: Bodley Head, 1963); Mamadou Dia, *Reflexions sur l'économie de l'Afrique noire* (Paris: Éditions Africaines, 1960); Kwame Nkrumah, *Building of a Socialist State* (Accra: Government Printer, April, 1961), and *I Speak of Freedom* (New York: Praeger, 1961); Colin Legum, *Pan-Africanism—A Short Political Guide* (New York: Praeger, 1962); Abdoulaye Ly, *Les Masses Africaines et l'actuelle condition humain* (Paris: Presence Africaine, 1956); J. Nyerere, "Ujamaa," speech at a TANU Conference on Socialism, April, 1962, excerpted in *Africa Report: Special Issue on African Socialism, op. cit.*, p. 24; Leopold Senghor, *African Socialism* (New York: American Society of African Culture, 1959), and "Negritude and African Socialism," in *African Affairs: St. Anthony's Papers*, No. 15, 1963, pp. 9–22; P. Sigmund, ed., *The Ideologies of the Developing Nations*, Introduction and Part III (New York: Praeger, 1963); Sekou Touré, *L'Experience Guinéene et l'unité africaine* (Paris: Presence Africaine, 1961); L. Hamon, "La voie africaine du socialism selon la pensée socialiste sénégalaise," in *Penant*, No. 695 (Janviers–Mars 1963), pp. 13–30; V. I. Potekhin, "Réflexions sur le socialism Africain," in *Recherches Internationales*, 1960.

W. H. Friedland and C. G. Rosberg (eds.), *African Socialism* (Stanford: Stanford University Press, 1964), should provide full case studies of socialist doctrine and policy.

It should be noted that the description and analysis in this paper refer to Africa south of the Sahara. While much of it has applicability to North Africa, conditions there are different in certain fundamental respects from those in countries below the Sahara.

2. This account relies heavily on personal observations and unpublished mimeographed documents gathered in Guinea. For further discussion see: J. Charriere, "La Guinée: Une experience de Planification," in *Cahiers Internationaux*, 1960; "Ou en est la Guinée?" in

Problemes d'Outre-Mer, 1 Juin, 1963, pp. 75–76; and J. Miandre, "L'experience guinéenne," in *Esprit*, October 1963, pp. 514–532.

3. It was reasoned that the state could "nationalize" importers' profit margins, earn 15 per cent on the sale of imports, and thereby raise 6 billion Guinean francs (about $24 million) in three years, or 60 per cent of the domestic investment component in the Plan.

4. Estimates of Guinea's GNP vary between $175 and $240 million. The plan was to be financed as follows: current budget surpluses and profits from state trading firms were to provide $40 million over the three-year period, free labor (*investissement humain*) $24 million, and foreign aid over $90 million.

5. The number of primary school pupils enrolled rose from 47,500 in 1958 to 160,000 in 1962, and secondary school attendance grew from 4,600 in 1958 to 10,400 in 1962.

6. The results claimed for *investissement humain* as of 1961 were: 2,000 buildings constructed, 14,000 acres of collective fields and 150,000 trees planted, and over 8,000 miles of road constructed. Much of this is surely fanciful, the road figure in particular. By 1962, in any event, official as well as popular enthusiasm for "human interest" had sharply declined, as coercive elements appeared, and as the usefulness of much of the work became questionable.

7. Rice production was to rise from 270,000 tons in 1960 to 315,000 in 1963; actual 1962 output is not known, but imports of rice had risen from $100,000 in 1957 to $6 million in 1962, a rise explainable only in part by the availability of P.L. 480 rice. Banana production of 60,000 tons in 1960 was to rise to 130,000 tons in 1963; actual 1962 output was 44,000 tons. The planned rise in coffee production was from 12,000 tons in 1960 to 16,000 tons (an output which had been achieved in the late 1950's); actual 1962 exports were 8,000 tons. Peanut production did rise from 2,000 tons in 1960 to 6,000 tons in 1962, but planned output in 1963 was 33,000 tons.

8. The first sugar sent from the Soviet Union was too soft; it melted and spoiled in the tropical heat. Later shipments were too hard; the sugar refused to melt in coffee. The first shipments of cement arrived unexpectedly; thousands of tons were dropped on unready Guinean docks, and were ruined by later rains. In Conakry, thousands of toilet units lay in the sun, unused and unusable in a country with little plumbing. Many Eastern bloc vehicles proved ill-adapted to African conditions, and scarcity of maintenance and spare parts led to a frightening mortality rate for them. Soviet projects were ill-planned, and proceeded very slowly.

9. The Economic Report of the 1962 Party

Congress, for example, recommended registration of each calf born in the country as a way of controlling smuggling; the formation of self-governed building co-operatives in the construction industry to raise productivity, and detailed work norms for agricultural production.

10. Late in 1963 there were reports of food riots in a number of urban centers.

11. In December 1961 discontent among some sections of the Teachers' Union and other intellectuals resulted in an outburst of violence, a charge that a communist plot was being hatched, and the closing of secondary schools for several months. Although not due directly to the state of the economy, this was at least in part a reflection of the sense of frustration engendered by economic deterioration.

12. S. H. Frankel, "The Kongwa Experiment: Lessons of the East African Groundnut Scheme," in *The Economic Impact on Under-developed Societies* (Oxford: Blackwell, 1953), pp. 141–153.

13. Cf. J. Nye, "Tanganyika's Self-Help," in *Transition*, Vol. III (November 1963), pp. 35–39.

14. Chambre de Commerce de la Côte d'Ivoire, "La Contrabande par Terre en Afrique Occidentale Française" (mimeo., n.d.).

15. *West Africa*, June 29, 1963, p. 733.

16. Gambian imports of matches, for example, amount to 55 boxes per year per capita; most of it is smuggled to Senegal, where the local product is higher priced and of poorer quality. The Federal Minister of Finance of Nigeria publicly estimated at 15 per cent the proportion of Nigerian cigarette consumption produced by smugglers in 1961, and emphasized the threat to the Nigerian tobacco industry.

17. See *West Africa*, March 17, p. 296.

18. It is interesting to note, however, that in the *Report of the Territorial Minimum Wages Board* of Tanganyika (Dar-es-Salaam, 1962), the harmful effects of a higher minimum wage on "emergent farmers," the most dynamic elements in African rural society, are discounted on the grounds that these highly individualistic, low-paying farmers have a doubtful place in a socialist society. Encouragement of cooperatives is recommended as more advisable.

Sectoral Development

THE ARTICLES IN THIS SECTION deal with the problems of the development of agricultural and industrial sectors of the African economies.

According to Svanidze, "African agriculture is the most backward in the world and its productivity is extremely low ... The yields of crops in Africa are appreciably below the world average." This low yield in agriculture is more or less uniform in most countries in the continent. Since, as is typical in underdeveloped countries, agriculture is the mainstay of the African economies, raising agricultural productivity is a *sine qua non* of initiating any progress during the initial stages of development. The article, "The Necessity for Agricultural Development in Africa and the Practical Difficulties," by the U. N. Food and Agriculture Organization, makes a strong plea for assigning priority to the development of agriculture in plans for over-all development of the continent. The article also presents a comprehensive survey of the major obstacles to agricultural development, including deficiencies in the natural environments, an insufficiency of protective humus, absence of effective anti-erosion measures, impediments to the use of fertilizers, severe climatic hazards and the inadequate irrigation facilities given arid lands. These lacks are compounded by nonphysical factors, such as the absence of appropriate infrastructures, human obstacles, such as peasant fatalism and the underemployment of labor. For each shortcoming cited, the Commission illustrates the nature of difficulty by reference to particular regions and offers suggested means for their removal as obstacles.

I. A. Svanidze, in his article, "The African Struggle for Agricultural Productivity," blames the backwardness of agriculture in Africa on the "system of shifting cultivation of land and nomadic livestock farming. The agrarian structure in a large majority of African countries is characterized by a diversified complex of widely ranging mostly precapitalist, types of land ownership and tenure ..." In view of the particular economic and political structures in African countries, Svanidze suggests dominant roles for government in raising the yield of agricultural products. He outlines efforts by governments to improve agriculture, with emphasis on mechanization of agriculture; the transformation of farming methods; improving livestock; and better land use through extension of irrigation facilities and reclamation schemes. Svanidze notes that an ". . . important prerequisite for increasing the efficiency of agriculture in Africa is progressive land reforms aimed at bringing land ownership in line with the vital needs of the working farm population. . . . African countries still face the problem of liquidating feudal-type land ownership and the abolition of the prerogatives and powers of the semi-feudal tribal nobility."

This brings us to the problems of land tenure, which are the subject matter of the article: "Problems of Land Tenure and Settlement," by the Food and Agriculture Organization of the United Nations (FAO). The F.A.O. makes the point that the present traditional land tenure systems in African countries, based on feudal, tribal and extended family arrangements, are increasingly at variance with the newly emerging socio-economic trends, namely, disintegration of the tribal order; change from abundance to a growing scarcity of land with the increase in population; the introduction of new technology, along with the development of a market economy; and the transition from subsistence to cash agriculture through the introduction of cash crops and urbanization. The exploitative elements implicit in the traditional tenure systems, such as "shifting cultivation" or "bush fallow," must end, giving place to forms of tenure which recognize the value of the land to the individual and also the individual's contribution to the value of the land. The paper by the F.A.O. also explains the changing patterns of African land tenure and emerging trends in different countries, although these trends are seen as peripheral and very slow in the direction of "individual holdings."

Whereas African countries have been advised to assign priority to agriculture in their development plans in the initial stages of development, it would not be advisable to ignore development of industries, especially major basic industries. This is necessary for the sake of balanced development, and the ability to "walk on both legs" towards economic advancement. The extract, "Industrial Development in Africa: Problems and Prospects," by the U. N. Economic Commission for Africa, presents a comprehensive survey of the present status and past growth rates of industrial development in Africa, plans for industrial development in different regions and countries, and recommendations for the future. The level of industrial development, as reflected in per capita industrial output, is very low in all African subregions (with the exception of southern Africa), when compared with the output per capita in the developed countries and even in many underdeveloped economies in Asia and Latin America. There are also wide differences in the degree of industrial development—as measured by the industrial output per capita—in different regions. By and large, industrial development in southern Africa has been much more pronounced than in North Africa, which is followed by East and Central Africa, with West African industry being less developed than that of the other subregions. Though there has been a rapid growth in industrial production in Africa—averaging around 7.4 per cent annually between 1938–1957 (compared with 4.5 per cent in the industrially advanced countries during the same period)—there has been no significant effect in bringing about a structural transformation of the African countries. The share of industry in the total output of Africa has not exceeded 15 per cent during the period in question. Even a large rate of increase on the small base of industrial production in African countries will not have substantial impact on total product and will not alter their structural position. The African countries have, however, planned for much higher rates of increase in manufacturing, mining and electricity. The following are the main features of the industrial plans of various African countries: (1) Governments have assumed greater roles in the development of their industrial sectors through direct investment of public funds; (2) considerable attention has been given, and sizable investment allocation have been devoted, to the improvement and expansion of transport facilities, power and water utilities, communication systems, and other infrastructure required for the removal of existing bottlenecks to economic development; (3) plans emphasize the development of heavy industries and industries producing import substitutes and export-oriented industries, based on the available mineral and forest resources; and (4) planning policies lean towards diversification in the development of heavy manufacturing industries. The United Nations Commission for Africa indicates that the path to industrialization has been substantially blocked by a lack of both capital and technology. Recommendations are made regarding choices in education and training, optimization of resource use, level of technology, and the most desirable industrial mix in order to accelerate industrialization.

Agriculture

As DEVELOPMENT PROCEEDS, agriculture's share of the economy, and of the active population, dwindles steadily. In the United States, the share was already less than 4 per cent of the gross national product in 1962, and it will decrease towards 3 per cent by 1970. This fact has prompted some states to grant instinctively the highest priority to industrialization. I do not wish to underestimate the value of industrialization, which, if achieved on an economically and technically sound basis, can bring about a much more rapid increase in labour productivity than agriculture. However, too many African industries do not at present fulfill these two essential conditions. The overall progress of the rural economy requires modern means of production; and the trend will have to be that most of these are provided by African industry, since Africa cannot make unlimited imports, as its balance of payments is already distinctly unfavourable and is becoming more and more so. Also, a substantial and rapid development of African industry is necessary, both to raise the average value of African exports, and to achieve the necessary reduction in imports of consumer goods (food, textiles, household goods). This principle appears to be indisputable; what is now needed is the knowledge of how to put it into effect.

We are now more familiar with the main reasons for the obstacles, difficulties and delays in African industrialization. First of all, this continent, like other backward areas, lacks the technical knowledge and the capital necessary for the rapid modernization of its economy (both industry and agriculture). Its fragmentation into very small countries (with the exception of Nigeria)[1] means that new industries have markets that are too restricted, especially when one considers the low purchasing power of the African population at present, above all in rural areas. It is a compelling and urgent need, and moreover a *sine qua non* of development, to harmonize the various industrialization projects of countries in the same part of Africa.

The Necessity for Agricultural Development in Africa and the Practical Difficulties

United Nations Food and Agriculture Organization

From René Dumont, African Agricultural Development— Reflections on Major Lines of Advance and the Barriers to Progress *(New York : United Nations Food & Agriculture Organization, 1966), pp. 12–41 (U.N. Doc. E/CN.14/342).*

Paul Bairoch has recently shown in a very interesting study,[2] that the Industrial Revolution in Western Europe was not fundamentally determined by technical progress, the role of the financial system or the impact of population growth—as has often been asserted. The increase in population in fact followed, not preceded, the Industrial Revolution. In the less developed countries, on the other hand, the population explosion is preceding the true industrial revolution, and so most of the available investments are being used to meet present needs. As the growth in population is so excessive, it is a hindrance rather than a stimulus to development.

I agree entirely with Bairoch that the increase in agricultural productivity at the end of the eighteenth century in Europe was the determining factor in the inception of development. It promoted and made possible the general and cumulative development of the economy. Bairoch shows that, on the other hand, the situation in the underdeveloped countries in 1965 makes this general development of the economy much more difficult than it was in England around 1780, or in France around 1820.

Moreover, the history of industrial development shows that it has always been a slow process. Thomas Balogh maintains that an industrial population has never yet been able to double in less than eight to ten years. If, as is the case in many African countries, the industrial population is still low or even almost nonexistent (less than 2 per cent of the total), it is an illusion to expect *great* industrial development to be achieved very rapidly, except in some unusually favourable cases. Such development could no doubt go ahead much more quickly in countries where it is already well established, and where the take-off stage is therefore being approached. As W. W. Rostow rightly points out, industrial development is much slower in getting under way when it has little or practically nothing to start on.

The recent history of industrial development in Africa provides us with practical confirmation of the great difficulties encountered. Efforts towards industrialization must be continued and intensified, however, since, without it, an economy remains too dependent and subordinate, but all this should be done only in so far as it is really worthwhile. On the other hand, it would certainly be a profound mistake to try to bring about a rapid development of the African economy solely by accelerating industrialization, that is to say, without any far-reaching modernization of agriculture. That might first slow down the over-all development of the African economy and, ultimately, even threaten the very possibility of such development.

Neither the present position of agriculture in Africa nor its recent development can be regarded as satisfactory. Even though exports have rapidly increased in volume, they represent only a modest share of total production, and the fall in prices has prevented revenue from keeping pace. Moreover, the meagre expansion thus achieved has been brought about almost entirely by extending the area under cultivation, while increases in yield per hectare have been confined to a few European or

evolués sectors, or to a few very small-scale experiments.

"Walking on Two Legs"—Industry and Agriculture

The inadequacy of recent agricultural progress in Africa is unhappily borne out by frequent rises in food prices and rapid and widespread increases in food imports. The latter factor dangerously limits the possibility of purchasing capital goods, and consequently of industrialization. Agricultural modernization and industrialization are closely linked. In 1965, there is no longer a question of continuing to set industry against agriculture; rather, each of them must be developed as well as possible and at the same time, which is by no means impracticable. This statement of principle is certainly not an adequate basis for advising a state what proportion of its total capital investment it should allocate to industry and what to agriculture.[3] Such guidance, *a fortiori*, cannot be given on a general or even on a regional basis; the proportions depend entirely on the particular situation in the country concerned.

In any case, there is now hardly any argument regarding the priority position of agriculture in the initial stage of development, even in countries where it was so long disputed, e.g., the socialist countries. It is true that the deliberate sacrifice of agriculture in the U.S.S.R., which was originally made to finance the industrialization of the country, seems to have helped it to build up its powerful heavy industry between 1929 and 1953. It remains to be proved whether such a sacrifice was indispensable for this development—which is impossible, as history cannot be lived over again. In any case, it was paid for dearly by the hardships of the Soviet people, who had to be subjected to an authoritarian regime, and cut off from the rest of the world, so that they would accept the burden. Such isolation is now practically impossible in Africa. Moreover, the starting-off level for agriculture is much lower than it was in Europe—even in Russia at the beginning of the five-year plans. Much more severe hardships would therefore have to be faced in Africa to attain anything like the same degree of industrial development; they would soon be rejected as unacceptable. Less would probably be achieved—and the fact that the continent is divided into states that are too small and, in many cases, have neither ores nor sources of energy would preclude any hope of comparable development—even if this heavier price were paid.

At the time of its most severe food shortages (1959–1962), China finally had to declare, and still maintains today, that agriculture was the basis of the economy,[4] while industry remained the driving force. In accordance with this principle, more and more factories (fertilizers, agricultural machinery, consumer goods, etc.) are being used to serve Chinese agriculture, even to the detriment of heavy industry, and especially the steel industry; the principle seems generally applicable in Africa. Not only agriculture, but also those industries that would permit its rapid modernization deserve high priority, to speed up the second stage of agrarian progress.

A first conclusion that may be drawn from this preliminary discussion is that countries should avoid any dogmatic application of principles and a priori theories, which were all evolved in nineteenth-century Europe under conditions very different from those prevailing in the Africa of 1965. It would seem inadvisable to grant absolute priority to any one sector; certain countries have done this without thorough economic study, some favouring agriculture and cottage industries, and some heavy industry. The first choice would normally lead to semi-stagnation, with the ultimate result of protracted underdevelopment and attendant poverty and ignorance, while the second would ignore the fact that steel-making is no longer the undisputed queen of industry it was a hundred years ago. Chemicals, especially petrochemicals and plastics, and aluminium can no longer be relegated to second place.[5] The Soviet Union is today paying very dearly for its backwardness in this field, and its overlong dogmatic devotion to steel.

All countries should strike a balance between agricultural and industrial development, which does not imply what branches of agriculture and what industries are best for any given country. It appears relatively easy to reconcile the two and "walk on both legs," as the Chinese say. In many countries, industry and the infrastructure will absorb a very large, if not dominant, share of the foreign exchange available. But, on the agricultural side, a first phase of expansion and rationalization can be achieved pending the arrival of modern equipment. This can be done by mobilizing latent productive forces, first of all by making optimum use of the land, water and cattle, and also of the labour force, which is often underemployed throughout the long dry season, rightly referred to by P. Viguier as "the long tropical winter."

This initial rationalization process, which is necessitated and made possible by the very low productivity of agricultural labour, can be launched fairly effectively with moderate quantities of imported goods; however, it will only be really effective if the main obstacles to agricultural development are overcome. These obstacles derive from the natural and economic environment, of course, but above all from the human environment. It is now time to try to describe and define the most important of them, at the same time, outlining the action necessary to eliminate them.

Obstacles Deriving from the Natural Environment: Soil Protection by the Provision of Humus, and Anti-erosion Measures[6]

Broadly speaking, the great majority of African soils are chemically poor, and even very poor. Their organic matter content and their exchange capacity are very low, as F. W. Hauck points out.[7] The nitrogen and phosphate content is normally not high, and, in the savannahs, the phosphate content is particularly low. The savannahs also lack sulphur, and the forests lack potassium and magnesium. This general statement by no means applies to all soils, however, so that particular attention should be given to the isolated areas of fertile land, in places where labour productivity could be much higher, technical facilities being equal. The brown tropical soils and, especially, the young soils derived from recent volcanic rocks, as in East Africa and at the foot of Mount Cameroon, for example, are highly prized, and with reason. The same holds true for the recent alluvial deposits in the valleys and deltas of the great rivers. However, the drainage and, occasionally, the irrigation projects essential for the use of these latter soils are very expensive, especially if work has to be done upstream to regulate the flow (flood and drought prevention) and attenuate erosion damage (silting up of dams).

Maritime alluvial deposits could also be used for the development of rice growing in Africa, in which Asian methods of rice cultivation might be copied with advantage. The greatest problems are the evolution of mangrove swamp soil, about which little is yet known, desalinization and sulphuration, and then the large-scale preparation and drainage work necessary to make the alluvium suitable for cultivation—especially as regards costs. A study of costs will enable each country to establish a more rational order of priorities for carrying out such work; based on cost and the various possibilities for effective and rapid utilization of the alluvium, taking into account the environment as a whole. In view of the population explosion, it is essential to avoid a repetition of previous errors, which are economically and psychologically costly and entail a serious loss of time.[8]

The black tropical clays or vertisols seem to be among the most interesting soils; they do not need any costly development work (occasional anti-erosive measures) and are very suitable for rice, cotton, etc.

The most widespread are the tropical ferruginous soils of the savannahs, which often have an underlying iron hard-pan. For this reason, they should always be kept covered with vegetation, but this is practically impossible with annual crops, which are almost all that is grown there. These soils are therefore very degraded already, and are in danger of becoming more so, if they continue to be misused. In forest areas, the ferralitic soils predominate; these can support rich industrial plantations in spite of the mineral impoverishment caused by leaching. Especially if fertilizers are used, they can support oil palms, rubber, coffee, cocoa, and bananas, pepper and kola nuts.

As the two soil types mentioned above are by far the most important in tropical Africa, more careful study must be devoted to them as a matter of urgency. This research should be more closely directed, than that of some pedologists, towards the possibilities of its practical application. The aim should be to draw up a list of suitable crops, in order of preference, and determine the best means of fertilizing and working the soil, with special emphasis on the heavy, more easily eroded soils. This would lead to the preparation of soil utilization charts, but not in random areas and not everywhere at once. As it would be a very long and costly operation to cover the whole of Africa, it is essential to start in areas where such work seems likely to be of most immediate value, e.g., over-populated areas, where everything must be put to use, even poor land,[9] or areas that, in the present state of knowledge, appear to be promising for early or more complete development. Above all, there should be no rigidity of mind with regard to the suitability of particular crops for particular areas; there will be unceasing development in this sphere.

Instability, as a result of the climate, is a feature of many African soils, which are exposed to the various dangers of erosion— by water wherever there is the least slope, even less than 1 in 100, and by wind wherever there is insufficient binding. This last point is linked with the ability of the soils to retain the often irregular rainfall and plant nutrients; and this in turn, like their stability, is linked with their content of fine elements, clays and humus. There is not much that man can economically do about these, with the exception of humus, which is very important.[10] Nor is there any reason why humus should always be produced by European methods, such as the use of farm-yard manure—which is so often badly made, too dry and also very costly, especially if it has to be carried on the head for long distances. Green manure and composts of all kinds have also been used, but the criteria for choice have so far been mainly technical. Increase of the humus content, which is inseparable from the use of draught animals, is not a panacea any more than is the use of fertilizers. Particularly in the tropics, this is a very slow process that has so far proved expensive.[11]

It is urgently necessary to make more careful economic studies of the various ways of providing humus, and also of the proposed methods of preparation and transport, for the different natural situations prevailing in Africa. Consideration must be given to the reaction of the peasant, whose preferences always affect the issue, especially in the early stages, even when his opinion might appear irrational to Flemings or Chinese. His aversion to handling human excreta, a valuable fertilizer, is justified by the risk of spreading amoebic and other intestinal affections. A study should be made of the techniques recently developed in North Vietnam, which remove the dangers, while permitting the collection of this fertilizer. Education can play a large part in the use of animal manure, but not immediately. Besides, the use of green manures grown on the spot is often more interesting.

With the provision of humus, the application of anti-erosion measures constitutes the most useful form of protection for African soils. The most advantageous methods of cultivation, such as the rational utilization of pastures and useful afforestation projects, are much more important for soil protection than protective measures proper, which play only an ancillary role. In a word, African agriculture must husband the soil, getting more from it, while giving it better protection; generally speaking, the two actions are not incompatible, if the peasants and the supervisory personnel have been given good technical training. Then anti-erosive works should be undertaken, a complementary task to good cultivation, and a logical order of priority would have to be established that would take both the urgency and the effectiveness of such action into account. Attention should first be given to protecting the most fertile soils, located in overpopulated areas, as well as those soils whose vulnerability presents the gravest threat to the country as a whole, its plains and its public works. In deciding which conservation techniques to adopt, the greatest attention must be given to the respective costs.

The Conditions for the Economic Use of Fertilizers

The use of chemical fertilizers will make it possible to turn to account soils hitherto considered rather infertile, especially when local extraction and manufacture are sufficiently developed in Africa. The physical properties of soils will then become of greater interest than the chemical nutrient content. The quickest return from the use of chemical fertilizers will be obtained in areas where a whole series of other conditions has been met, and where a certain amount of agricultural progress has already been made or at least is made concurrently. To be precise:

(1) The area must be reasonably accessible so that the cost of transport, fertilizers, and the resulting harvest is not excessive;[12]

(2) The area must be of fairly regular rainfall, or, more generally, climatic hazards must not be too serious;

(3) Plant varieties must be chosen that can respond favourably to the use of fertilizers;[13]

(4) The technical level of cultivation must already have begun to rise as a result of agricultural extension work. If fertilizers are to pay, plantations should be well established and well trimmed, and crops should be sown in good time, in well prepared soil, properly protected from disease, insects and weeds. In a limited number of cases, micro-nutrients, particularly zinc and magnesium, must be added. If fertilizers are to be economically interesting, there must be stabilization, not so much of agricultural prices expressed in absolute terms, but of their purchasing power for means of production (fertilizers, machines, pesticides, equipment for agricultural industries, etc.).

In short, the general use of fertilizers, especially phosphates and nitrogenous compounds, which are so essential for Africa, will only be fully economic under a certain number of conditions. The same applies to irrigation and the use of tractors. They must not be regarded as panaceas,[14] therefore, and the interaction of the various factors of production must never be overlooked. When the necessary conditions are fulfilled, the use of fertilizers does offer definite advantages, but it is still expensive. It thus requires very careful study, an example being the IRHO[15] study on groundnuts in Senegal. The hasty popularization of fertilizer mixtures that have not been thoroughly tested would expose the African peasant to disillusionment. What is even more serious, it might cause him to lose all confidence in technicians, even when their other recommendations would be most useful to him.

To sum up, the use of chemical fertilizers in Africa could, on the one hand, be considered as a very important step forward, but one that must be preceded and accompanied by a number of others. It becomes really valuable only when most of the other steps have been taken to ensure agricultural success. So, FAO's present study and demonstration programmes should preferably be carried out in areas where there is or has been a fairly intense and widespread agricultural extension campaign. Some of these tests would duplicate others, which are more thorough, as with groundnuts in Senegal.[16] It is reported that other FAO tests have been organized on ground that slopes too much for ploughing to be advisable. It would be better to spend a little more time on the study phase, than to give advice that would later prove misleading and discourage the peasants.

On the other hand, however, the effects of fertilizers, which are sometimes spectacular, can open the eyes of the African peasants, and make them keenly aware of the advantages of economic progress. Fertilizers also stimulate a great increase in the quantity of organic matter, thus becoming an economic source of humus. When fertilizers can to some extent supplant a belief in magic,

and thus stimulate the rapid general adoption of other good agricultural practices, they will become acceptable much more quickly. That would then justify subsidies, which, as in Northern Nigeria, could be recovered by levying export duty on products.[17] It will be shown later that the establishment of African fertilizer industries will require a much more rapid development than the local consumption of fertilizers, which justifies these subsidies. Furthermore, the rate of such subsidies (50 per cent in Senegal, 60 per cent in Nigeria) should be reduced progressively, but fairly quickly. Otherwise, the expenses involved will hamper the general modernization of these countries.

Conditions for the Successful Application of Irrigation

Just as there is no single type of African soil, so there is a whole range of African climates, which are remarkably diverse. In the extreme north of the continent, there is the Mediterranean climate, the greatest drawback of which is the disparity between temperature and rainfall. When the temperature is favourable for plant growth, there is not enough rain, and when the rain comes, it is often fairly cold. It is common knowledge that there is a very distinct gradation of climatic zones in the western areas south of the Sahara, passing from the most arid to the most well-watered zones, with the latter located along the coast or in Central Africa. East Africa is a still greater mixture of wet and dry zones, such as mountains, plateaus and plains, and the microclimatic areas form an even more complex mosaic.

In the whole of this tropical zone, where the problem of cold does not arise, the amount and distribution of rainfall are the determining factors for plant growth. In the evergreen forest zone, however, the limiting factor may be the lack of sunlight, which has quite a pronounced effect for instance on rice and oil palm in southern Cameroon. In other places, the presence of excess water causes difficulties, because of inadequate run-off and drainage. In all cases, excessive rainfall causes leaching and, therefore, impoverishment of soils; and often erosion also, if the soils are not protected when the slopes are cultivated.

The greatest disadvantage for most of tropical Africa is the low level, or at any rate, the frequent irregularity and very unfavourable distribution of the rainfall. I have already stressed the marginal, indeed much too marginal, character of agriculture in the sub-Saharan or north Sahelian zones. Even where rainfall is more abundant, as in the Sudanian region, it occurs over too short a period of time, and thus allows only one harvest per year. The consistently high temperature would make possible two or even three harvests, if an adequate supply of water could be provided all the year around.

Irrigation is thus an essential factor in African agricultural development, both for the Mediterranean zone and for the arid and semi-arid parts of the tropical zones. It is a factor that increases in cost, however, according to the scale of the operations, from wells with simple pumping installations, small-diversion streams, simple flood-control schemes (Niger valley type),[18] diversion dams with water distribution schemes (Gezira or *Office du Niger* type),[19] to whole irrigation networks based on storage dams (Maghreb, Egypt), which are the most expensive of all.

Certainly, in arid and overpopulated zones, where there is hardly any choice except between emigration and irrigation, as the possibility of local industries remains very restricted, one may be forced to carry out such projects even if they are very expensive. Foreign aid helps such work, as with the Aswan high dam. However, it would be desirable to study the economics of irrigation more carefully to improve the system of priorities and ensure a better return on such costly schemes, especially in the case of complementary irrigation, which is then only one of many intensification factors and therefore ought to pay. The conditions for economically successful irrigation appear to be even more stringent than for chemical fertilizers. Throughout the world, successes in irrigation have alternated with a greater number of setbacks. The main pitfalls that are to be avoided in Africa seem to be

(1) The antipathy of the people concerned, who often resist the efforts essential

for the transition to a more intensive cultivation system. New and unfamiliar techniques are involved, together with more intensive, and above all, more continuous work than was associated with the traditional, extensive systems. The cereal growers and graziers of the Beni-Amir in Morocco, like the peasants of the Upper Volta and the northern Ivory Coast, who are used to dry farming, have often under-utilized or sometimes even refused to utilize the irrigation facilities placed at their disposal at considerable expense by the public authorities. This antipathy sometimes stems from the fact that the system of irrigated cultivation has been dissociated from the traditional system, in an attempt to convert the farmer. It would have been better to try to associate the two systems and create complementarity, which would have facilitated an increase both in the production of human and animal food, and of income. In some cases, prominent local citizens benefit from the existing social situation, and therefore oppose hydraulic engineering projects in order to maintain their hold on the poor peasantry, as has already been mentioned in reference to north-eastern Madagascar (Lake Alaotra).

(2) Often there are no proper drainage facilities, which in some areas results from inadequate levelling (e.g., cultivation of cotton by the Office du Niger) and in others, from difficulties in the run-off of excess water (Beni-Amir). In some instances (Nile delta, lower Chélif in Algeria), this inadequacy can even cause noxious salts to rise to the surface; in Pakistan and India, millions of hectares in the Indus and Ganges valleys have become barren in this way (the *usar* soils in Uttar Pradesh, India).

(3) There is the inadequacy, or even absence, of anti-erosion measures in the catchment areas of large dams, which leads to rapid silting up of the reservoirs (certain Algerian dams), which become first partially and then completely unusable. This development has taken place within the space of ten years (the Ksob dam in Algeria), i.e., well before the additional harvests have been able

to pay off the very high construction cost.

(4) There must be highly intensive cultivation if the very costly irrigation process is to become economically interesting for Africa. This in turn means that all the conditions for agricultural success mentioned above in connexion with fertilizers must be met, and that fertilizers themselves must be applied on a large scale. The availability of water ensures a good yield from the use of fertilizers, while the latter are themselves indispensable for the economic viability of irrigation schemes. The multiplicity of crops and the intensity of cultivation really call for "gardeners," who are most likely to produce favourable results. Now a peasant, producing nonirrigated cereals, or still less a grazier, cannot suddenly become a gardener. In at least some of the regions where irrigation has recently been introduced, it is therefore advantageous to install settlers who come from well-watered areas and have good experience in the use of water.[20] The best Office du Niger settlers harvest ten times more cotton per hectare than the bad ones, and more than four times the average output on watered land.

In my opinion, factors (1) and (4) above seem to be the most important and, besides, are interconnected. With regard to (1), it is possible to test beforehand the willingness of the population to take advantage of the water supply when it becomes available by asking these people to participate without payment, or simply in return for food, in a substantial part of the work. Those who do not intend to make use of the facilities in the future will doubtless refuse to make such "advances of work," unless they are subjected to excessive pressure from government or political sources. If they accept, all of these volunteers should be guaranteed that they will benefit *directly and personally* from the fruits of their labours, in proportion to the contributions they have made. It has not been possible to sustain enthusiasm for human investment in Africa, often because in the first projects, which were badly designed and managed and were not accompanied by the necessary adjuncts (credit,

good marketing), promises could not be kept, nor the expected results achieved.

Of course, Africa has great rivers (Nile, Tana, Zambezi, Niger, Volta, Senegal, etc.) that carry a large volume of water through more or less arid zones, but their rate of flow is rather irregular. A carefully compiled priority classification is needed for all the innumerable large and small water schemes which could be carried out in Africa; this would be the only possible basis for more detailed studies. The total project cost per hectare and the productivity that may reasonably be expected are essential factors in such a classification. Other factors that must be taken into account are the condition of the local infrastructure, the population density, and in particular, the attitude of the people to the project; this last factor will often be difficult to assess, even with the test suggested above. The total cost as such is not of overriding importance; even when it is very high, it may still be acceptable if a large part of it is borne during the slack season, when there is no work, by the people who are to use the project.

In the great majority of cases,[21] calculation will show that small-scale water development schemes will deserve higher priority than large schemes. This category generally includes not only small irrigation networks but also moderate-depth pumping using animal power or motor pumps (electric or diesel). By these methods, full use can be made of the wide beds and banks of the large and small rivers, which are covered with fertile silt after the flood period. Priority for small-scale projects seems to be justified for at least three reasons. Their cost per hectare is usually much lower—five times lower on the average in India. A greater proportion of the work, such as simple digging,[22] can be allocated to the future beneficiaries than in the case of large projects. Finally, full utilization of the irrigation facilities is more rapidly and more easily achieved with small projects, which are particularly advantageous to their riparian populations, than with larger projects. This seems to apply even more to drainage projects (lower Guinea) or simple flood control (Niger, Senegal delta) than to irrigation proper. In some instances (upper

Niger), the economically most viable projects have already been carried out, and the more costly ones are still to be implemented.

However, there is still a wide range of small schemes deserving priority that can be determined by economic study. The large-scale schemes (Office du Niger, in Mali) often necessitate long and expensive movements of population over long distances and resettlement (of the Mossi of Upper Volta), a cost-increasing factor that must also be taken into consideration. However, if the beneficiaries build their own houses in the slack season, this cost is reduced. Large schemes will, however, be necessary in arid and populous zones, so that huge quantities of produce can be collected at one place for processing or export (Morovoay and Lake Alaotra in Madagascar). Moreover, many simple schemes that are set up to improve water supply from river flooding are not suitable for many crops other than rice and do not allow an increase in the number of crops. For cotton, drainage must be perfect, and for sugar cane, water must be available all the year round. Office du Niger expenditure of fr CFA 500,000 per hectare cannot be justified when the average annual harvest is less than fr CFA 30,000 of raw produce. In this country, nonirrigated cultivation can be improved at less expense per additional unit of yield. Supplementary irrigation is one of several factors of production, and its profitability should be assessed.

Comprehensive valley schemes often necessitate international agreements. They will be much more attractive economically when the production of hydro-electric energy is combined with irrigation. Exploiting the enormous energy potential[23] requires advanced industrialization, however. In both respects, irrigation and energy, it will thus be necessary to proceed by stages in pilot areas, providing training for farmers and technicians. In the case of the Niger, I proposed in 1961 a rough plan for a comprehensive scheme, to be carried out in successive steps, each step facilitating the financing of the following one. I should have liked to receive criticisms of my draft plan from my African friends in order to improve it, but unfortunately there was no response.[24] Admittedly, aid from outside Africa will more readily be

forthcoming for large schemes, but it is advantageous for such aid to be directed towards the sectors in which it will be most productive. The fact that money is a gift does not mean that it should be wasted.

I must again stress that, if a substantial contribution to the work on a project is to be obtained from its future beneficiaries, without excessive pressure being applied, it must be made clear to the people that they are in fact working for themselves. In my forthcoming study on the rural people's communes in China,[25] I shall show that, in 1957–1958, the peasants were moved, often far from their homes, for the sake of the "great leap forward"; this was done for giant collectives, the commune, or even the union of communes of the district.[26] Since 1962, most of the work required of the ·peasants has been at the level of the very small local collectives, the production teams (25–40 hectares of ploughed land, slightly more families and twice as many workers). When work is done outside these teams, it will from now on be paid for regularly by the benefiting organization. In 1958, it had been hoped that enthusiasm for communism would provide sufficient stimulus for the achievement of titanic, Herculean tasks with Lilliputian means. It was an overestimation of human nature to expect such idealism, and the Chinese authorities were soon forced to decentralize decisions and bring the motive of personal gain into full play so as to obtain sustained effort. This interesting lesson is worth bearing in mind for Africa.

To encourage the peasants using the water not to waste it, it is always preferable, wherever possible, to charge for the water by volume, i.e., by the number of cubic meters or cubic feet actually used, rather than by the surface area served. I have shown the wastage that resulted from the traditional method of charging by surface area in the Damodar Valley in West Bengal.[27] However, such a measure requires more intensive development, a greater stiffening with supervisory personnel and is scarcely practicable in the smaller village networks. In that case, however, the peasants, and not the community, must be made to carry out the simple maintenance work and to pay the other expenses, e.g., by a levy on harvests. The free distribution of water, which is quite common practice in tropical Africa, is an even greater incitement to wastage. Whenever a means of production is provided free, or at a price too far below its cost, it is very much underutilized. I have found hardly any exceptions to this rule anywhere in the world, even in the socialist countries.[28]

It seems that the improvement of the natural environment in Africa could be summed up in four terms—water, humus and fertilizer, on the one hand, and good anti-erosion and cultivation techniques on the other hand. It is still to be defined exactly where, when and how these can be provided at the lowest cost; the question requires a great deal of further study. I shall now examine some other sources of difficulty for African development, arising partly from the great distances involved, and the inadequate transport facilities, but chiefly from the *milieu humain*.

Costly Infrastructure

In East and South-east Asia, costs of production will rise at an increasing rate. The population density is often very high and is growing rapidly, which brings into full play the law of diminishing returns as far as labour is concerned. Thus productivity falls when the intensity of cultivation is raised too high, especially if there is a lack of technical knowledge and modern means of production, such as machinery and, especially, fertilizers. The African can often provide himself with food on his savannah clearings with less expenditure of calories than the Asian on his irrigated rice-fields.[29] Nevertheless, the low general density of population and the extreme unevenness of its distribution in Africa raise problems that are quite different, but still very serious. Admittedly, in underpopulated areas it is in the long run, advantageous for the population to increase. It is also necessary for this increase not to be too fast, so

that the present generation can support it, and so that its own level of living can be raised. Otherwise, the existing generation would be sacrificed to the coming generations, which implies very great enthusiasm for work, or a high degree of restraint. Demographic growth is already calling for a much more rapid modernization of agriculture, raising serious difficulties that cannot always be overcome. It should be recalled that the increase in food production since 1958 has in many cases been outstripped by population growth.

The ratio of road length to the number of inhabitants served is too high in areas of low population density, as are the costs of construction and maintenance. The cost per vehicle-user or per ton transported is even higher, because there is very little movement of trade in these regions. As too large a share of the budget must be allocated to roads or to financing the railway deficit, less money is devoted to projects that are more directly productive, such as land preparation, plantations and, above all, factories. Bearing this in mind, countries should not attempt to set up expensive lines of communication immediately in all their territories, including the most remote and most sparsely populated ones. There should be close co-ordination between the highway plan and the plan for the development of new areas, which should be chosen from amongst the most fertile. Intense development of the best land over a limited area generally seems more worthwhile than spreading the effort too widely and sprinkling the whole country with projects that are all inadequate. Increased participation by local labour in the construction and maintenance of roads, would make possible the more rapid establishment of a denser network.

The difficulty of overpopulated areas is also known in Africa, in several parts of Nigeria, in the mountains and in some places on the coast of West Africa, in some parts of East Africa (Rwanda, Kenya) and on the coast of North Africa. There is no doubt that a less uneven distribution of the population would often be more advantageous, for many areas with rich soil are used little and badly or not at all, while others, mediocre or fragile, are overworked, which finally makes necessary large-scale movements of population. However, to try to *impose* a better distribution immediately and arbitrarily, might involve considerable disadvantages. Such redistribution could, on the other hand, be *encouraged* with advantage, and thus achieved progressively. The types of resettlement adopted up to now by the Office du Niger in Mali, and in Ghana, Nigeria and the United Republic of Tanzania have been much too expensive for government resources. However, care must be taken not to create legislative obstacles that might hinder such movements of population, which will become absolutely essential, often in the near future.

Human Obstacles

With a great deal of capital and an abundant supply of technicians of all kinds, it is possible to implant a very modern factory in an "underdeveloped" area such as that of Fria in Guinea or Edéa in Cameroon. However, it is much more difficult to establish a technically very advanced agricultural system in family farms among people resistant to technical change; this requires both increased technical knowledge and a will to modernize, throughout the mass of the rural population. In Africa, moreover, the rural populations are at all stages of economic development, ranging from the Babinga, or Pygmies, who live in the dense forest by gathering fruits, hunting, and fishing, to the modern farmers of the North-African coast and the high plateaus of East Africa.

In tropical Africa, it is easy to find peasant populations that have themselves made substantial technical advances, one example being the empirical selection of the yam by the Baoule of the Ivory Coast. Elsewhere, as in the Congo Basin, which makes up the northern half of the Congo (Brazzaville), care of the few subsistence food crops, chiefly cassava, is traditionally left to the women; for this reason alone the activity is scorned. One must therefore be very wary of drawing general conclusions that are too superficial, and it would be the greatest mistake to consider all African peasants unsuited for progress. The establishment of cocoa plantations in Ghana and African cattle-rearing in Kenya, to quote only two examples, already provide proof to the contrary.

A natural environment that is generally hostile, or paradoxically, very fertile, together with the misdeeds of slavery and colonization,[30] have helped to maintain a mentality that is not very conducive to development. To quote from the report of the First FAO Regional Conference for Africa (Lagos, 1960, page 17), "The inertia bred of poverty and the frequently associated disbelief in the possibility of change were recognized as being difficult to overcome." At that time it was hoped that this mentality would change very rapidly in a direction favourable to development, when Africa finally belonged to the Africans, but these hopes have been disappointed.

Some Europeans believe that the granting of political independence might have engendered a more general enthusiasm, which could then have been directed chiefly towards the struggle against underdevelopment, the battle for production, which is so necessary for economic independence. In China, this kind of phenomenon did in fact produce notable results in spite of some extravagances of the "great leap forward," such as the small, country blast furnaces. Such results seem to have been distinctly better than those obtained in India, especially through the latter's community development programme. While it has been possible to arouse enthusiasm to a certain extent in Africa, notably in two or three more dynamic states of West Africa, the movement has unfortunately not become general enough, has not always been well managed technically; it has soon lost momentum. This, however, is not solely a result of ill-studied projects.

The mystique of independence seems to have been felt much more keenly in the towns, particularly by the various people who have benefited from it most directly in the civil service and political office. But it has not, in general, brought an increase of effort on their part. In the course of my various journeys between 1958 and 1965, I was struck by the very general apathy on the part of the rural population. They did not really win independence by a struggle—it is truer to say that it was granted to them. The social status of the country people has not been changed much by it, the main reason being that the *économie de traite*[31] has generally continued to weigh heavily upon them. The retention of their social position has even appeared to them as a relative regression, because at the same time they have seen some of their compatriots in the city rising in position so quickly.

In 1961 the same general impression was received from the statements of peasants as different as the Wolof of Senegal, the Betsiléo of the plateaus in Madagascar and the Bamiléké of Cameroon.[32] They all felt that they were "excluded" from a privileged urban caste, consisting mainly of merchants, officials, politicians and members of the liberal professions. Seeing the extravagant expenditure of these people, many of the peasants felt despised and downtrodden in comparison, especially if these privileged persons abused their dominant position and practised corruption.

They had all too often lost the hope of achieving a rapid and genuine enhancement of their social position by improving their production techniques, and in improving themselves in their craft as farmers. This is perhaps the most serious threat to the future of African agriculture. It is not enough, as has been suggested, for national leaders to stress the value and dignity of farming. Measures should also be taken to reduce the dangerous gap between town and country, by cutting down the privileges enjoyed by the urban population, for otherwise the status of the rural masses could not be quickly raised without compromising the volume of investments.

The major concern of African farmers is to send their children or nephews to school, so that at least one of them can enter what is regarded as a privileged caste, and afterwards be of assistance to the whole family. In some peasants this has created a fatalist attitude, which the vagaries of the climate have already helped to strengthen. What is the good of greater efforts when the harvest depends primarily on the rain? What is the good of working harder when the real privileges, the final results of work, will always be reserved for the town people?

This appears to be an even greater handicap to one like myself who had again in 1964 the opportunity to observe the hard work being done by Chinese and North Vietnamese peasants, and who has heard of the very rapid progress made in Japan. Ever since the nineteenth century, Japan has demonstrated a will to develop, which took root in a docile, still semifeudal society and then blossomed out in an economic framework that has become liberal. The great majority of the Chinese people, from the highest official to the humblest peasant, seem to be impelled by the same determination to achieve progress, but in this case the setting is one of somewhat authoritarian socialism, quite unlike the system in Japan. Africa will certainly not wish to be left further behind by Asia, and all Africans will therefore have to make greater efforts.

Underemployment in African Agriculture

Asking the peasants to do more work appears to be psychologically easier in China, where the level of living of almost *all* the population is very modest, as no one can display any luxury, and everyone toils hard with his own hands, at least for part of his time. As manual work is universally compulsory, it is not despised by the caste of the white-collar workers, or the new ruling caste. The drastic reduction of urban privileges (in Africa and elsewhere), thus seems to be an essential precondition for establishing or spreading as the case may be, a genuine will to work among the peasants. Some progress has already been made in this respect by certain African governments, such as Mali, the Central African Republic, and Rwanda, but it is not sufficiently widespread. If austerity is not imposed, I shall be obliged to adhere to the pessimistic reservations I made concerning the future of Africa.

In China, full employment in rural areas was difficult to reconcile with high productivity, in the year 1965, because considerably more than two workers are employed per hectare of ploughed land, and it is not easy to obtain much new land. In most parts of tropical Africa, however, there is no lack of land, and yet, the peasants are very much underemployed, as some recent BDPA[33] studies show. Although as a result of the long dry season, productive work is difficult during part of the idle periods in certain areas, that is by no means true for them all—far from it, indeed.

In Madagascar, for example, agricultural working times of less than 40 days per adult per year have been recorded, notably on the east coast where the permanent humidity would, in fact, allow cultivation all the year round. Sample surveys show that the average working time, for the country as a whole, is well *below 100 days per year*. Only some of the Betsiléo rice farmers are believed to have a working year of more than 200 days, and this figure is exceptional.

Persuading the African peasant to work harder, even with present techniques and tools, would permit an initial expansion of production that might assume considerable proportions. Such persuasion might be possible, if it were accompanied by increased austerity, exertion and economy in the towns. Such an atmosphere would at last make *animation rurale* more effective. The myth of independence could then truly begin to take shape and become a more definite reality for the African peasant. When that stage had been reached, it would doubtless be possible to mobilize him for the war on underdevelopment, poverty, sickness and ignorance. To do that, it would be useful first of all to make a few village leaders more conscious of these ideas, either by a mainly political approach [Ghana, Guinea, Mali, Congo (Brazzaville), Tanzania etc.], or by *animation rurale* that would take account of the difficulties encountered by IRAM[34] in Senegal, Niger and Madagascar.

The African peasants, thus guided[35] by their political or professional leaders—or preferably by their political *and* professional leaders—will then be better able to understand that ultimately they hold their fate in their own hands. This would be brought home to them if practical steps were taken to combat the main evils of the *économie de traite*. A kind of vicious circle is formed here, however, because the elimination of these evils often requires the establishment of sales co-operatives, which calls for a co-operative mentality, which is exactly what *animation rurale* is there to create.

Community Development or Human Investment?

An important form of approach, particularly in Ghana, Nigeria and English-speaking East Africa, is community development. I studied this technique in India where it has been most widely applied, and I showed that it was not nearly effective enough. The main reason for this seemed to lie in the continuance of the traditional forms of exploiting the Indian peasant, such as share-cropping and usury, and in the excessive concentration of effort on social amenities, i.e., roads and wells, schools and clinics. In some instance, the credit co-operatives fell (discreetly) into the hands of the money-lenders. The food situation in India towards the end of the third five-year plan seems to be even more critical than it was at the end of the first plan, although the rates of progress are comparable—and very slow. There is a tendency for a small, linear increase in production to be more than offset by a constantly rising population growth, the rate of which almost tripled in absolute terms between 1948 and 1964.

In this country, community development action has too much neglected the true "sinews of war" against underdevelopment, that is to say, direct and immediate action to increase agricultural production with greater speed. The best forms of this are small hydraulic engineering projects, anti-erosion measures, improved soil work and fertilization, parasite control, the elimination of the *économie de traite*, and the establishment of genuine credit and sales co-operatives. This could all come under the two headings of co-operative action and productive human investment. It should be repeated that human investment is more likely to be successful if everyone benefits from it in exact proportion to the effort made (e.g., in water development schemes), or if the work load is evenly shared by the whole population concerned (roads and schools). When the African political leaders, following the example of their Chinese or Malian colleagues, are not afraid to go and wield a pick, if only symbolically, by the side of the peasants, contempt for manual work (which is the main stumbling-block for African development) will begin to disappear.

In China, such human investment has made it possible to mobilize the most important latent productive force in the underdeveloped rural areas, namely, under-employment. Full employment has been achieved since 1958 in Chinese rural areas and is accompanied by a high rate of invest-ment.[36] The State takes 8 to 9 per cent of the gross harvest in the form of a land tax, which goes to finance national investments. Local investment is then provided partly by setting aside an amount equal to 3 to 6 per cent of the same production, and partly by assigning about 6 to 10 per cent of the total days worked in the year to investment tasks.[37] Even in its very different socio-economic setting, Africa could increase its investments considerably, especially if enthusiasm could be better aroused in country areas. Ad-mittedly, account must be taken of the universal imperfection of human nature. On the other hand, it would be very serious to forget that human nature can constantly, but slowly, be improved.

Notes

1. This country has coal, petroleum, ores, a railway network, a solid industrial infrastructure, and the largest market in tropical Africa. It can achieve large economies of scale and soon approach the take-off if it does not spoil its fine chances by corruption and internal discord.

2. *Révolution industrielle et sous-développe-ment* (Sedes, Paris, 1963).

3. Agriculture is said to receive 6 to 40 per cent of the total investment, according to the state concerned. The economic optimum lies somewhere between these two extremes, but varies considerably from country to country.

4. This approach was also adopted in Cuba from 1962 onwards.

5. This is especially true in a continent rich in bauxite and cheap water power to produce electricity.

6. For a more detailed treatment, see the FAO *Africa Survey*, 1962, and the studies on the African natural environment published by UNESCO.

7. *Soil Fertility and Fertilizers in West Africa* (E/CN.14/INR/70).

8. As was aptly pointed out by J. Guillard.

9. The areas of Kano in Northern Nigeria and Boukombe in North-Western Dahomey, to quote only two outstanding examples.

10. However, in the overpopulated areas of Southern China and North Vietnam, the authorities do not hestitate to bring in large quantities of more clayey alluvium to correct soils that are too sandy. In Africa, this technique is likely to be of interest only under certain particular conditions.

11. On a coffee plantation in Kenya, it takes 14 man-days to cut and carry the mulch produced on one acre, that is to say, one ton of dry grass for placing around the roots of the coffee shrubs.

12. Increasing the volume of harvests, and thus return freight, will reduce the cost of transporting fertilizers.

13. An FAO colleague writes: "These three conditions are generally met in most agricultural areas of North, West, Central and East Africa." The author in no way shares this opinion. While it is true that fertilizers are responsible for 50 per cent of European agricultural progress in the last hundred years, European agriculture was in a much better position to derive benefit from them than is African agriculture in 1965.

14. As N. S. Khrushchev regarded them in the Soviet Union from 1961 to 1964.

15. *Institut de Recherches pour les Huiles et les Oléagineux*, 11 Pétrarque Square, Paris 140.

16. It would have been better to popularize the fertilizer formulas determined by IRHO and IRAT, which were long established in the country, than to try out NPK in equal doses, as the economic utility of the latter is highly doubt-ful (FAO tests).

17. See also para. 23 of this report and resolu-tion No. 13 of the First FAO Regional Confer-ence for Africa, Lagos, November, 1960.

18. $160 per hectare.

19. More than $2000 per hectare.

20. See also the FAO Africa Survey, pp. 102–107, and especially the second column on p. 117.

21. With the exception of Egypt and its Aswan dam, and possibly Ghana and northern Nigeria, where reservations may in some cases be justified.

22. Which can be financed by means of the food supplied under the World Food Program.

23. 225,000 million kwh annual output for the Inga project on the lower Congo between the Stanley Pool, which is adjacent to the capitals of the two Congos and the sea.

24. Cahiers du Tiers Monde, 1961, *Reconversion de l'économie agricole du Mali*, pp. 171–180.

25. *Editions du Seuil* January, 1966.

26. There are stated to be about 1,800 districts in China.

27. In this connexion, see *Terres Vivantes* by René Dumont, Plon, 1961. See also, *Community Development Evaluation Mission in India*, report of a United Nations mission carried out at the request of the Indian Government, by M. G. Coldwell, R. Dumont and Margaret Read, published at New Delhi in November, 1969.

28. See *Sovkhoz Kolkhoz ou le problématique communisme* by R. Dumont.

29. In March, 1964, I noted 500 man-days per hectare of rice-fields for 25 quintals of paddy (in a co-operative in the province of Thai Binh, North Vietnam).

30. "Which should not be condemned *en bloc* the history of the developed and the underdeveloped world being the history of colonization," writes Dr. Autret. He adds: "Should economic development not be envisaged from the viewpoint of an ethic, of moral education? Professional ethics and the feeling of work well done are just as important factors as the bait of gain or the big stick."

31. This consists in the exportation of raw materials and the importation of manufactured goods.

32. This decided me to write the pamphlet, *L'Afrique noire est mal partie*, especially to take up the defence of the continually-exploited African peasant. I noticed this atmosphere again in the Central African Republic, in the summer of 1965.

33. *Bureau pour le développement de la production agricole. Sociéte d'Etat* (studies, training, technical assistance), 223, Blvd St. Germain, Paris. The Bambey Agronomy Centre has shown that every inhabitant of working age in the groundnut producing area works an average of 240 hours in the fields during the main growing season (May–November). In Kenya, an average of 90 days of work per peasant per year has been calculated, at the rate of 5 hours per day.

34. *Institut de recherche et application des methodes de développement*, 32 rue des Bourdonnais, Paris 1.

35. Is Africa not at a stage at which certain forms of enlightened despotism would be useful, if directed solely in the interests of national development?

36. This rate was, in fact, excessive—30 per cent of production around 1958–1959. It has no doubt fallen since, but in the absence of any published data, estimation has become even more difficult. It is certainly much higher than in all other underdeveloped countries, but doubtless lower than in Japan.

37. Irrigation works, reafforestation and anti-erosion measures, leveling, and planting of orchards, rural electrification, roads and tracks, buildings for community industries, etc.

10

The African Struggle for Agricultural Productivity

I. A. Svanidze[1]

From The Journal of Modern African Studies, *Vol. 6, No. 3 (1968), pp. 311–328. Reprinted with permission of the publisher, Cambridge University Press.*

AGRICULTURE IS the mainstay of the African economy. The well-being and even the lives of hundreds of millions of peasants, farmers, and farm-workers depend on the state of agricultural production. Exports of farm products are the principal source of foreign exchange for African countries.

African agriculture is the most backward in the world, and its productivity is extremely low. Thus, an individual engaged in farming in Africa feeds, on the average, 1–2 people by the products of his labour, compared with about 50 fed by a Canadian farmer.[2] The yields of crops in Africa are appreciably below the world average. The output of animal produce is also much lower than on any other continent.

The indigenous African population mostly uses the system of shifting cultivation of land and nomadic livestock farming. The agrarian structure in a large majority of African countries is characterised by a diversified complex of widely ranging, mostly precapitalist, types of land ownership and tenure; and this hinders economic progress.

The Role of The State

The state has to play a most important part in raising the yield of agricultural products in Africa, especially since the market does not affect the farming methods of the indigenous population to any great extent; the prospects of mechanising agriculture are limited, and there are a number of important social barriers hampering its successful development.

There are a variety of channels through which governments can exert their influence on agricultural production in Africa. The development of farming in African nations is directed and encouraged by state planning. Thus, in the U.A.R., out of £E4,152,000,000 to be spent by the state over the seven-year period 1965–1972, 16.5 per cent is allotted to agriculture. The plan provides for reclaiming 500,000 hectares of land at a cost of £E234,000,000, while £E51,400,000 is allocated for the projects carried on by the Ministry of Agriculture, £E1,000,000 to the Egyptian Cotton Development Fund, £E1,500,000 for livestock farming, £E3,500,000 to the Agricultural Credit Organisation, £E12,800,000 to the General Agrarian Reform Authority, and £E94,000,000 for irrigation and drainage projects. In terms of value, the annual output of agricultural produce is to go up to £E860,000,000 by 1969–1970.[3]

Governments also grant short-term and long-term loans to producers. Thus, by January, 1966, the Government of independent Kenya had granted £650,000 to African smallholders: £1,800,000 to African farmers resettled in the areas formerly occupied by Europeans, £60,000 to cotton-growers, £1,000,000 to African tea-growers, and £870,000 to Africans purchasing former European-owned farms.[4]

African governments organise purchases and sales of agricultural commodities, render technical assistance to peasants and co-operatives, and set up state-owned agricultural enterprises. The Sierra Leone Produce Marketing Board, for instance, is engaged in buying up and exporting palm products, coffee, and ginger; it participates in the production of groundnuts and other field crops, the groundnuts being delivered to the animal feed factory built by the Board in Moyami. Due to the Board's efforts since the country gained its independence, the total area under oil palm had increased, by mid-1965, from 1,200 to 14,800 hectares. Emphasis is placed on the development of large plantations of farm crops.[5]

Senegal, Guinea, and a number of other countries operate centers for mechanising agricultural production that provide peasants and cooperatives with machinery and supplies, including seeds and fertilisers. In the Malagasy Republic, state-owned organisations have been set up to bring new land into production (in Sakay, lower reaches of the Mangoky river, and near the Alaotra lake).

The funds needed for implementing agricultural projects and rendering aid to agriculture are derived by African governments from budget appropriations, exports, and, in a very large measure, from foreign aid programmes and private foreign investment (national private investment plays a lesser role). Thus in Senegal the implementation of the 1965–1969 development plan will require £174,000,000, of which 61 per cent will be accounted for by the Government and 39 per cent by private, mainly foreign, investors.[6]

It is common knowledge that highly productive farming necessarily involves large-scale production for the market. A subsistence or semisubsistence rural economy is necessarily accompanied by poverty, technological backwardness, a very slow rate of accumulation, if any, and economic stagnation. In terms of volume, subsistence goods still dominate in the gross farming output in Africa, although marketed output is expanding at a higher rate, so that over-all farming output by volume is steadily increasing from year to year. In Uganda, for example, between 1960 and 1965 the proportion of cash sales to the value of total farming output rose from 59.5 to 61.5 per cent.[7] In order to accelerate the transformation of agriculture to an exchange basis, the Sierra Leone Government is establishing an Agricultural Development Board backed up by a special U.N. fund.

The growing percentage of cash output in African agriculture is achieved through expanding farm production for both the foreign and domestic markets. It is expected that during the next few years a decisive attempt will be made to increase the output of goods intended directly for export. Subsequently, as the social division of labour progresses and the domestic market expands with the development of the nonagricultural sector of the economy (such as industries processing farm products), there will be a greater proportion of the population engaged outside farming, more geographical specialisation of agriculture, and further development of the national transportation network; consequently, an ever-increasing significance will be assumed by farm produce sold for consumption by the local population and local industries; that is, for the national market.

In expanding agricultural exports, African countries strive for their diversification and improvement. Thus, while the total value of farm produce exported by the U.A.R. between 1960 and 1965–1966 increased, the proportion of cotton—the country's main export—to total exports fell from 68 to 55 per cent, due to the higher share of other items.[8] African exports show a general trend towards a higher proportion of semi-finished agricultural goods and manufactures of local industries. In the year 1965–1966 the gross output of groundnuts in Nigeria rose from 1,214,000 to 1,317,000 tons; over the same period, the export of raw nuts dropped from 544,000 to 512,000 tons, whereas the export of extracted groundnut oil increased from 80,000 to 91,000 tons. Similar trends may be observed in groundnut exports from Senegal and Gambia.[9] Of great importance is the easing or lifting of trade barriers against exports of semi-finished and finished products from Africa.

As yet, the bulk of African farm exports goes to western capitalist nations, with which the African countries have long-standing economic ties dating back to colonial times. In the years to come, however, an increasing proportion of African products of farm origin can be expected to be exported either to the developing or to the socialist countries. As international transport facilities are improved and agricultural output becomes more diversified and rational, more farm products will be exchanged between regions and countries within the African continent.

If they are to catch up with the advanced western countries in production per capita, the African countries will have to treble, or at least double, the volume of their agricultural output. According to expert estimates made by the U.N. Economic Commission for Africa, under present social and economic conditions it will take the African countries a minimum of 40–50 years to solve this problem.[10] It has been estimated that Zambia, for example, in order to achieve present European standards by 1976, would have to double its agricultural output per capita and increase its industrial production by 20–40 per cent.[11]

The real growth of agricultural output in Africa is merely keeping pace with the rapid increase in population. In some African countries, agricultural output is growing rapidly because priority is given to the expansion of the exchange economy. Thus in 1965–1966 the value of farm produce in the U.A.R. was £E707,300,000, or 22 per cent more than in 1959–1960, while agricultural exports increased by 33 per cent between 1951–1952 and 1964–1965.[12]

Concurrently, the share of agriculture in the economy of African countries generally is decreasing, due to the priority development of the nonagricultural sector. In Nigeria, for instance, agriculture accounted in 1963–1964 for 64 per cent of the gross domestic product as against 64.7 per cent in 1962–1963. In the nonagricultural sector, the growth rate (8.6 per cent in 1962–1963 and 6.6 per cent in 1963–1964) is double that in agriculture, and the share of the agricultural sector in the gross domestic product was expected to drop to less than 60 per cent by 1967–1968.[13] In the U.A.R., the Ten-Year Development Plan indicates that agriculture will account in 1969–1970 for 24.4 per cent of the national income, as against 38 per cent in 1962–1963.[14]

The Mechanisation of Agriculture

Much work is required to transform the technical base of African agriculture. Arable land has to be substantially expanded and the productivity of agricultural labour sharply increased. Especially radical changes must take place in tropical Africa, where, as has been pointed out by the Egyptian economist

Samir Amin, the key problem in agricultural transformation is the transition from shifting cultivation of land by hoe to intensified tillage by plough.[15] Despite a number of difficulties, the plough has scored certain gains in tropical Africa. Thus, in Tanzania, the introduction of a simple ox-drawn plough has made it possible to expand substantially the arable areas in the Lake, Northern, and Western Provinces. In the Arusha district, up to 90 per cent of all cultivated land is now tilled by plough. In the North Mara district (Lake Province) farmers now use 15,000 ploughs, and in the Nzega district (Western Province), 4,000 ploughs.

There are a number of difficulties to be overcome before the plough can dominate throughout tropical Africa. These include, apart from the poverty of peasant households, the lack of draught animals in many areas and some adverse features of African soils. These obstacles can be overcome through the introduction of tractors and of specialised soil-tilling implements adapted to local conditions, such as disc ploughs and harrows, rotary hoes, and chisel ploughs. Since most African farmers cannot afford such facilities of their own, it seems reasonable that such facilities can be best utilised on a co-operative basis, the co-operatives being served by state-operated machine and tractor stations, or by centers for promoting modern agricultural production. Some encouraging experience in this direction has already been accumulated in Guinea and Senegal.

In an effort to mechanise farming, African countries have begun to step up their imports of tractors and other agricultural machinery, and have made their first steps towards the national manufacture of farm machines. In Zanzibar, the development plan for 1967 provides for the import of more tractors and for operating the available tractors in round-the-clock shifts, so as to meet the country's needs for food.[16] In 1965, the Nigerian Government allowed duty-free imports of tractors and farm machinery, as well as of spare parts and other farm equipment, in order to promote the introduction of mechanical tillage.[17] In Morocco, the *Caisse nationale de crédit* allocated in 1966 $20,000,000 to help privately owned households and co-operatives use up-to-date farming machinery and thus increase agricultural output. The bulk of agricultural equipment is bought abroad by state-owned agencies for foreign trade, but tractors are now assembled on the spot to save foreign currency.[18]

Considerable aid in reconstructing the technical base of agriculture in the emerging independent African nations is being provided by the socialist countries, which give priority in the supply of machinery and equipment to state-owned and co-operative agricultural enterprises, and offer advantageous terms to African countries. In 1964–1965 the Soviet Union supplied Libya with goods to the value of £1,000,000. These mainly included tractors, combines, and other agricultural machinery, as well as diesel engines and pumps for irrigation projects, equipment for drilling, and motor vehicles. In exchange, Libya supplied its traditional export commodities, such as wool, goat-skin, and castor-oil seeds.[19] Late in 1966 the U.S.S.R. sent the Sierra Leone Rice Corporation a consignment of tractors and equipment, which was followed by Soviet experts who came to train national specialists in the use of the equipment.[20]

Modernising the technical base of African agriculture involves the mechanisation of the laborious work of cattle farming, such as preparing the fodder, supplying water to the farms, milking the cows, shearing the sheep, and clearing the pastures.

A number of important rural electrification projects are now under way in Africa, which will mean a considerable increase in the power available for farm work. In 1967, when a new electric power station came into operation in Monrovia, Liberia, it was able to supply some of the rural areas for the first time. The transmission of electric power to villages has also been started in 1967 in Uganda (although it is, as yet, very expensive) and further provision is planned. In the U.A.R., the current plan envisages the provision of electric power for 1,400 villages by 1970.[21]

Raising Crop Production

To increase the production of farm crops, especially food crops, is a matter of great

urgency for Africa. More foodstuffs will raise African nutritional standards, which as yet are far from being satisfactory, and will also permit the African countries to dispense with imports of food crops from developed regions of the world.

Between 1958 and 1965 the production of millet, the main staple product of the Republic of Niger, increased from 621,000 to more than 1,000,000 tons. Over the same period, the yield of cassava doubled, to reach 150,000 tons, and that of rice grew from 293 to 600 tons. This increase in agricultural production has been mainly achieved since the country's independence.[22]

In Kenya, higher official buying prices, the use of better-quality seeds, and improved farming methods have led to a substantial rise in grain production. The country now meets in full its own requirements for rice; the area under wheat has increased in a few years from 92,700 to 123,000 hectares and is to be further expanded to 164,000 hectares. Today, Kenya is capable of meeting not only her home demand for wheat, but also that of Uganda, in addition to selling large quantities to Tanzania.[23]

The expansion of rice and cane sugar output is very important, but here much depends on adequate irrigation, and many African countries still have to import large quantities of these crops from abroad. Mauritania, however, is developing rice cultivation on irrigated lands in the Senegal river valley.[24] In the U.A.R., the yields of rice in 1956–1966 doubled, mainly due to the selection of seeds and the use of disease-resistant varieties. Agronomists in Arab countries have succeeded in developing new varieties of long-grain rice suitable for export, and also some varieties which will effectively withstand drought and can be conveniently grown in the summer months. Buying prices for rice have been raised by the state by 20 per cent. The government grants loans to rice producers and supplies them with high-quality seeds and fertilisers, including ammonium sulphate and superphosphate. The U.A.R. now exports 350,000 tons of rice annually, and is the fifth largest rice exporter in the world, after Burma, Thailand, China, and the United States.[25]

Rice is rapidly becoming an everyday food product in Nigeria and in many other countries of Western Africa. In Nigeria, the Five-Year Development Plan for 1962–1968 provided for modernising rice cultivation with a view to meeting the expected 15 per cent increase in demand by 1968. The difficulties in the way of raising rice production include the shortage of trained personnel, limited financial resources, under-developed transport facilities, and the lack of a system for organised marketing of rice.[26]

The U.N. Economic Commission for Africa has published a report on the needs and prospects for developing sugar production in 14 countries of Western Africa. Their total annual consumption of sugar is 298,000 tons, the bulk of this being imported. In 1964–1965 Nigeria's sugar imports increased from 40,000 to 90,000 tons and Ghana's from 40,500 tons to 56,000 tons. Sugar-cane factories function on plantations in Bacita (Nigeria), Komenda and Asutuare (Ghana), and Dougabougou (Mali). Enough sugar cane *could* be grown to satisfy local needs throughout Western Africa, except perhaps in Liberia, Gambia, and Niger. Plans have been made for increasing the production of sugar cane to 9,360,000 tons by 1980; of this, 4,000,000 will be produced by Nigeria, 1,680,000 by Ghana, 980,000 by the Ivory Coast, 820,000 by Senegal and Mauritania, and 556,000 tons by Upper Volta. As a result, the local demand for sugar will be met.[27]

In Tanzania a sugar factory is planned at a plantation near Morogoro, and the total area under sugar cane, 1,000 hectares in 1966, is to be doubled. This factory is to be commissioned in 1970 and will also process cane grown by neighbouring peasants. In Malawi, considerable progress has been made in sugar-cane growing, with the aid of irrigation. By the end of 1966, the area under sugar cane had reached 1,720 hectares, which means 30,000 tons of sugar a year. Of this quantity, 20,000 tons are consumed within the country.[28]

In Morocco, large sugar-beet plantations have been established in Sidi Sliman, where the first sugar factory in the country was commissioned in 1963, with a rated capacity of 35,000 tons a year. Another factory with a capacity of 40,000 tons, built with the technical assistance of Poland, is now operating at sugar-beet plantations in Beth. A total of 340,000 tons of sugar are now consumed in the country annually.[29]

African countries are expanding those cash crops in demand on the world market, while reducing or restricting the production of those crops whose export prospects are not good.

Tea, which not so long ago was a monopoly of European settlers and companies, is now being successfully introduced on African farms. In Uganda, the encouragement of tea growing is the responsibility of the newly created Tea Growers Corporation. To expand tea production in the country, the government, the I.B.R.D., and the Commonwealth Development Corporation have allocated £4,300,000. By the end of 1966, the total area under tea in Uganda amounted to 560 hectares, and it was planned to increase this by 800 hectares during each of the following four years.[30] In Kenya between 1960 and 1965, the area under tea on African farms increased from 600 to 5,200 hectares and is planned to go up to 10,000 hectares by 1968. Seventeen tea factories are planned, to process African-grown produce by 1970.[31]

Zambia has plans to produce 11,300 tons of tobacco annually. In Uganda, 2,000 farmers in Acholi and 900 in Lango were requested to sow 0.4 hectares each with tobacco in 1966, to obtain 680 tons of tobacco in 1966–1967. Tobacco leaves are processed at a new factory in Kampala. The government has advised the tobacco-growers to form co-operatives.[32]

In Nigeria, rubber trees are being planted on an increasing scale. In eastern Nigeria a *Hevea* plantation totalling 1,800 hectares is being established, adjoining 500 rubber farms of 3.2 hectares each. In western Nigeria, a large natural rubber research center is being set up. At the experimental station in Iyanomo, which has an area of 2,000 hectares, methods are being studied for increasing yields of latex and improving the quality of rubber. One of the objectives is to raise the output per hectare of plantation to 2.3 tons of rubber in place of today's 220–330 kg.[33]

Under a United Nations Food and Agriculture Organization (F.A.O.) project, Nigerian palm-oil production is to increase from 515,000 tons in 1965, to 900,000 tons in 1980. These figures have been arrived at on the assumption that approximately 350,000 tons of palm oil will be sold on foreign markets, while local consumption will rise from 360,000 to 535,000 tons. The amount derived from the existing trees can be expanded, both by increasing yields and by more efficient extraction methods. In addition, there is an extensive programme for replanting trees on old plantations, for example in an area of 236,000 hectares in eastern Nigeria, and for establishing new ones, including 78,000 hectares in western Nigeria.[34]

As far as coffee is concerned, African countries have to take into account the present world-wide tendency towards overproduction, especially of the lower grades. According to estimates of the International Coffee Organisation, unless appropriate limitations are imposed, world coffee production in 1971–1972 will go up to 2,256,000 tons, whereas world consumption of coffee will not exceed 2,080,000 tons. In Uganda, one of the leading coffee-growing countries of Africa, the government has decided to do away with the low-grade *robusta* coffee entirely, and to plant *arabica*, the high-grade variety, in its place. In Acholi alone, *robusta* is now being replaced on an area of 4,000 hectares.[35]

The Transformation of Farming Methods

The central problem of reforming African crop husbandry is to replace the traditional extensive shifting cultivation practised by the indigenous population of tropical Africa by modern intensive farming based on the continuous use of land. In fact, the rate of transition from extensive to intensive farming varies from one region to another and depends on the increase in the number and

density of the population, the introduction of ploughing and of cash crops (especially permanent ones), crop rotation, and the use of fertilisers. The transformation process is being promoted by consolidating plots of land belonging to individual families and to whole communities, allotting permanent land plots to farmers in Kenya and Zambia, amalgamating scattered settlements into villages in Tanzania, and by the Native Land Husbandry Act of 1952 in Rhodesia.

A decisive factor in increasing crop yields is the large-scale use of fertilisers. It has been estimated that exporting 500,000 tons of groundnuts and groundnut oil from northern Nigeria means a loss of 23,000 tons of phosphorus in the form of superphosphate for the nutgrowing areas. At the same time, the total consumption of fertilisers in northern Nigeria in 1964 was only 12,000 tons. Any agricultural export means the loss of a certain amount of valuable soil constituents, which have to be replaced, in one form or another. Another reason for the use of fertilisers is the steady intensification of farming: to step up agricultural production, more land is tilled, and this results in shortening the fallow periods, during which the soils start to exhibit signs of depletion.

The soils that respond well to chemicals include up to 40 per cent of tropical Africa. But supplies are scarce: "The use of plant nutrients in the developing countries now amounts to about 4.5 million tons, three times what it was ten years ago. But it is still far too low. If we aimed to increase fertiliser consumption in these countries to half the amount per acre that is used elsewhere, they would need at least four times as much as they have now."[36] The developing African countries have ample raw materials for the production of fertilisers. However, either the available deposits are not exploited or they are exported to developed countries in crude form. Therefore, African countries must prospect for new sources and exploit them quickly, set up enterprises to produce ready-to-use fertilisers, and organise "reasonable collaboration between those developing countries with the raw materials and those with the larger market for fertilisers."[37]

In Senegal, in 1963, the *Compagnie séné-galaise des phosphates de Taiba* produced 460,000 tons of calcium phosphate, in 1964, 667,000 tons, and in 1965, 867,000 tons. The mineral reserves in Taiba are estimated at 100,000,000 tons. In 1965, exports of the raw material for fertilisers amounted to 820,000 tons. Of these, 300,000 tons went to Great Britain, 253,000 to the Federal Republic of Germany, and 174,000 tons to Japan. In 1965, rock phosphate exports from Togo amounted to 981,000 tons; and, in the same year, 10,100,000 tons of phosphate were exported from Morocco.[38]

A number of independent African countries rich in raw materials are now establishing fertiliser factories. The International Finance Corporation, the Senegalese National Development Bank, and several European companies are financing the construction of a chemical fertiliser plant near Dakar—the first in Western Africa—which will supply fertilisers to both Senegal and the neighbouring countries. In Mombasa, Kenya, a chemical fertiliser plant is now being built by a West German capitalist firm. In Safi, Morocco, the chemical complex commissioned in 1965 produced, during its first year of operation, 125,000 tons of superphosphate; but only 10,000 tons of this were consumed locally.[39]

Livestock Problems

A great deal has to be done for the reconstruction of African livestock farming, and this could result in a considerable increase in the output of animal produce, primarily for the market. Today, Africa is still a big importer of meat and meat products. In many regions the shortage of livestock products has been accompanied by rising prices. The reasons for the present shortage are the extremely uneven distribution of livestock over the continent, inadequate transport facilities, the lack of meat-processing plants, and, finally, certain customs of the African community, rather than an actual scarcity of livestock.

For decades, Zambia (formerly Northern Rhodesia) imported meat from Rhodesia (formerly Southern Rhodesia), where the well-developed animal husbandry is run by Europeans. In 1966, after the Smith government had come to power in Rhodesia, the African Government of Zambia placed an embargo on the import of a number of commodities, including products of animal origin, from Rhodesia. Immediately, an acute shortage of beef was felt in Zambian markets. There are as many as 1,250,000 head of cattle in Zambia and, if the Africans had agreed to sell one animal out of ten to the Cold Storage Board, the "meat problem" would have been solved. Purchase prices for cattle have been considerably increased in Zambia, and in 1966 a fat animal could be sold for £50. And yet, by December, 1966, the Board had managed to buy only 1,215 head of cattle.[40] One reason was that the cattle-purchase programme was concurrent with the time of selling farm products by the farmers. More important was the fact that, in African rural areas, cattle by custom are regarded as traditional communal property, generally not to be sold. Cattle are often used as bridewealth, and mostly slaughtered on festive occasions in religious ceremonies.

Because of the difficulties in procuring cattle and meat in the African village, many African countries place emphasis on the development of large stock-raising farms. Thus Ghana, assisted by the West German Government, is establishing a cattle-rearing farm in the North, which will supply the meat-packing factory in Bolgatanga.[41]

Dairy farms are also being set up. In 1965–1966 the Uganda Company cleared and fenced 80 hectares of pasture land in Lubowa, where a dairy cattle herd is being formed, and where a mechanised dairy farm has been equipped. Measures are being taken to improve cattle breeds and quality. In Kenya, it was announced in 1966 that an official board was to be set up to promote the artificial insemination of cattle. It is recognised that Kenya has all she needs to become a supplier of pedigree cattle to the whole of Africa and to some Asian countries, too. Thus early in 1967, Uganda ordered 4,000 Kenya pedigree cattle.[42]

Wool production in Africa has been

developed so far only in the Republic of South Africa, but efforts to develop this highly profitable branch of livestock farming are being made in a number of African countries. For example, the Government of Tanzania has allocated for this purpose, £412,700, supplemented by £344,100 from the F.A.O. On the Kitulo plateau, Njombe district, 8,000 hectares of pasture have been allocated for sheep breeding. Here, 2,400 to 2,850 metres above sea level, a flock of 10,000 sheep is to be raised for wool within the next five years.[43]

There are also great potentialities in Africa for poultry breeding. In Nigeria, the Six-Year Development Plan provides for raising a million chickens annually in three centres—Kaduna, Jos, and Ilorin. The first of these is already in operation.[44]

Great efforts are being made to combat diseases and parasites affecting domestic animals. Cattle plague, in particular, is endemic to the animal-breeding regions of Africa. In 1928, 200,000 out of 250,000 cattle died of an epidemic that broke out in the Cameroons. Owing to the progress in veterinary science and the application of effective vaccines, no further epidemics have occurred in Africa. However, outbreaks of disease do still spasmodically occur each year in a number of cattle-breeding areas. For example, a few years ago, 6,000 to 8,000 head of cattle still died annually in northern Nigeria.

Under the auspices of the Organisation of African Unity, a huge international programme to combat cattle plague was initiated in Africa in 1961. The project of plague eradication is to be accomplished in four stages. The first stage involved the inoculation of 12 million cattle within a radius of 640 km. around Lake Chad in Nigeria, Niger, Chad and Cameroon. During the second stage, which started in 1965, 10 million cattle were inoculated in Nigeria, and in the northern regions of Togo, Dahomey, Ghana, the Ivory Coast, and eastern Mali. During the third stage, commencing in 1967, inoculations are being given throughout the entire territories of Mali, Mauritania, Senegal, Guinea, Sierra Leone, Gambia, and the Ivory Coast. Finally, the fourth stage will involve cattle inoculation over the whole

territory stretching from Chad to Sudan and Ethiopia. Each animal is inoculated three times.[45]

In Sabi-Lundi, Rhodesia, and in some other agricultural regions, pastures have for a number of years been treated with insecticides against the tsetse fly. The Agricultural Research Council of Central Africa is now conducting experiments on chemicals and radioactive agents which could be used to sterilise all male tsetse flies.[46]

Land Use and Ownership

There are immense reserves of unused land in Africa, which are now being drawn, though slowly, into economic use. According to an estimate, in 1961 the area of cultivated land, expressed as a proportion of the whole territory of the country, was 6.5 per cent in Mali, 33.8 per cent in Upper Volta, 6.8 per cent in Niger, 16 per cent in the Ivory Coast, 34 per cent in Dahomey, and 43 per cent in Togo.[47] According to an F.A.O. estimate, in 1965 cultivated land amounted to only 8.6 per cent of the total African territory.[48] Both these estimates take into account fallow land at various stages of regeneration under the African system of shifting cultivation.

Under present conditions, when the potential land reserves are still very great, the African countries in reclaiming new land give priority to irrigating alluvial soil, which has high fertility and is more readily available. Irrigation assumes special importance also in dry and semidry zones, which occupy a large proportion of the African continent.

In Ghana, a dam has been erected on the tributaries of the river southeast of Tamale, centre of the Northern Region, which will make possible the irrigation of 1,200 hectares for agriculture. In 1965, the Volta dam was put into service in Akosombo; more than 1,500,000 hectares around the water reservoir are now flooded each year, which provides excellent opportunities for rice growing.[49]

In Kenya, provisions have been made for

irrigating a total of 400,000 hectares. Late in 1966, surveys were completed and work is to be started soon on an irrigation complex in the lower reaches of the Tana, where 85,000 hectares will be irrigated, thus enabling about 150,000 hectares to be brought under cultivation. The main crops here will be cotton, sugar cane, groundnuts, some other oil-producing plants, and also cereals. In 1967–1968 the Government plans to spend £500,000 for irrigation projects on the Kano plain near Kisumu, where 12,000 hectares of highly productive land are to be sown to sugar cane, cotton, and rice. The first 800 hectares are to be sown within two years; 450 farms are to be built on this land, whose total annual produce, in terms of cost, will amount to £140,000.[50]

The Portuguese colonial authorities have launched a plan aimed at irrigating 300,000 hectares in the Zambesi river valley in Mozambique; a dam will be erected in Kwebrabasa.[51]

In 1966, Libya started work on a project aimed at irrigating 33,000 hectares in remote parts of the Sahara, based on boreholes. The first has been built in the Traghen region and is operating successfully. £10 million (Libyan) has been allocated for this project, from oil export revenues. Later, it is planned to irrigate a coastal area, 150 km. wide, by distilling Mediterranean water, using local oil and gas deposits.[52]

Early in 1967, the U.A.R. and the U.S.S.R. signed a protocol providing for Soviet supplies of pumping stations to irrigate 80,000 hectares west of the Nubaria canal. As part of this project, the U.A.R. Ministry of Irrigation has already started construction of an irrigation network in this region. It is envisaged that the U.S.S.R. will deliver the first three pumping stations in 1968; these will be the largest irrigation stations in the Middle East. In addition, the U.S.S.R. will supply 24 subsidiary pumping stations for watering the areas east and west of the Cairo–Alexandria highway. An additional protocol on the supply of three more pumping stations is to be signed later on.[53] The Assouan Dam, which has been built to the designs of Soviet experts and with extensive financial and technical assistance from the Soviet Union, is due for completion in 1968. As a result, 800,000 hectares of new land will be irrigated, and agricultural output in the U.A.R. is expected to increase by 50 per cent.

An important prerequisite for increasing the efficiency of agriculture in Africa is progressive land reform, aimed at bringing land ownership in line with the vital needs of the working farm population. Some African countries and regions still face, to a greater or lesser extent, the necessity of allocating land to those who work on it with their own hands—and the land will have to come from complete or partial expropriation of the various groups of big landowners. The greater part of the area still has to be gradually transformed from the now pre-dominant small-farm system to large-scale, modern, socialised agriculture.

In the Republic of South Africa, the minority of Britons and Boers (about one-fifth of the population) now enjoy the exclusive right of using over 87 per cent of the land. African agriculture is restricted to reserves or "Bantustans," where there is an acute shortage of land and the natural resources are rapidly depleted and destroyed. An average European agricultural enterprise has over 860 hectares;[54] this undoubtedly includes considerable spare land. There are farms exceeding 10,000 and even 20,000 hectares in area. In Rhodesia, the European minority (4 per cent of the population) have appropriated some 50 per cent of the territory for European settlement alone.[55] The average area of a European farm there is more than 2,000 hectares, of which at best 50 hectares is cultivated.[56] In Liberia, the American Firestone Tire and Rubber Company owns 400,000 hectares of concessions, of which only 50,000 hectares are used for growing rubber-bearing plants. Extensive land surpluses are also owned by non-African agricultural enterprises in Kenya, Zambia, Angola, and Mozambique.

A number of African countries still face the problem of liquidating feudal-type land ownership. Thus, in Ethiopia, the Emperor's family and the feudal nobility still own 60 per cent of the country's land, while the church and monasteries have another 30 per cent.[57] In the early 1960's, about one-quarter of the cultivated land (2 million hectares) in Morocco belonged to big and medium landlords who leased their land to sharecroppers, *khammasat*; more than half of the gainfully employed population had either to rent landlord-owned lands, which cost them up to four-fifths of the crop yield, or else they had to work as farm labourers for the landlord. Sharecropping was also practised by landlords in Tunisia, where 5,000 big Arab farmers owned 600,000 hectares of land.

Another pressing problem is the abolition of the prerogatives and powers of the semi-feudal tribal nobility—chiefs of tribes and districts, village headmen, and elders.

On the way towards large-scale socialised farming, a most important task is the co-operation of the broad masses of peasants. In principle, a co-partnership system can be developed among the bulk of the rural African population, for the sale and purchase of consumer goods, as well as for agricultural credit; this can also be drawn into producers' co-operatives, the highest form of co-operation. Getting the farmers to work together in producers' co-operatives is quite practicable, provided the authorities have sufficient patience and, most important, are able to arouse enthusiasm by demonstrating the practical advantages offered by joint work.

Co-operation is a reliable means of amalgamating the labour and resources of the peasants, intensifying the social division of labour in the village, and modernising agricultural production; and it is not accidental that the authorities of all independent African states are directly encouraging the development of co-operation as one of the most effective ways towards the promotion of agriculture.

From Kenya's independence up to mid-1966, more than 500 co-operative societies were registered. The total now exceeds 1,000 and their trade turnover is in excess of £30 million; by 1970 it is planned to raise the turnover of Kenyan co-operatives to £50 million so that their share in the gross domestic product will amount to 16–20 per cent.[58] In Guinea in 1963 there were 473 producers' co-operatives with a membership of 58,000, and their development has been followed by a steady increase in the propor-

tion of the economy which has been socialised, and a decrease in the share of the goods privately produced by co-operators.[59] Considerable progress has been made by the co-operative movements in Tanzania, Mali, Uganda, Senegal, and the Ivory Coast. In Algeria, it is planned to extend co-operative land ownership and the co-operative system of production to 19 million hectares of state- and privately-owned land.[60]

A second trend in introducing large-scale production into African rural areas is in the establishment of state-owned farms and plantations, which may in the initial phase be mixed enterprises, owned jointly by private capital and the state. Such enterprises may be set up on partly or fully nationalised farms formerly run by the settlers, on experimental farms established in colonial times, on confiscated or nationalised large-scale capitalist-type farms (as in Zanzibar), and finally on virgin and fallow lands where there are pioneering enterprises.

In Mali, *L'Office du Niger*, a large cotton- and rice-growing enterprise, formerly in the possession of the French administration, has been nationalised and is now being enlarged. The Tanzanian Goverment has started buying out controlling shares in the foreign sisal plantations, and these shares will from now on belong to the National Development Corporation.[61] In 1966 the state-owned sector in Algeria included some 3 million hectares of cultivated land, employing 300,000 permanent agricultural workers who received guaranteed wages.[62] In the U.A.R., large state-owned commodity farms are being set up on new lands at At-Tahrir and Inshas.

All these will be necessary steps: to achieve the state controlled agricultural production, to raise farm output, to modernise technique, to reconstruct livestock and crop farming, to reclaim new lands and to transform the agrarian system; as a result it should be possible for the productivity of agriculture in African countries to equal that of developed regions of the world within the present century.

Notes

1. Research worker at the Africa Institute of the U.S.S.R. Academy of Sciences, Moscow.

2. Èkonomika sel'skogo khozyaistva (Moscow, 1963), Vol. XII, p. 96.

3. *Africa Diary* (New Delhi), November 20–26, 1965.

4. *East Africa and Rhodesia* (London), April 28, 1966.

5. *Africa Diary*, September 4–10, 1965.

6. Ibid. March 14–20, 1966.

7. Uganda Government, *Background to the Budget, 1964–65* (Entebbe, 1964), and *ibid., 1966–67* (Entebbe, 1966).

8. *Africa Diary*, January 20–27, 1967.

9. *West Africa* (London), November 12, 1966.

10. Nezavisimye strany Afriki (Moscow, 1965), p. 95.

11. *East Africa and Rhodesia*, June 9, 1966.

12. *Africa Diary*, March 12–18, 1967.

13. *West Africa*, June 18, 1966.

14. *Al Ahram* (Cairo), October 29, 1964.

15. Samir Amin, *Trois Expériences africaines de développement: le Mali, la Guinée, et le Ghana* (Paris, 1965), p. 231.

16. *Africa Diary*, March 5–11, 1967.

17. *West Africa*, June 25, 1966.

18. *Africa Diary*, January 10–16 and 17–23, 1966.

19. *Ibid.*, January 3–9, 1966.

20. *West Africa*, December 31, 1966.

21. *Africa Diary*, November 20–26, 1965, January 20–27, and March 12–18, 1967.

22. *Ibid.*, January 17–23, 1966.

23. *Ibid.*, January 20–27, and March 19–25, 1967; also *East Africa and Rhodesia*, January 13, 1966.

24. *West Africa*, October 22, 1966.

25. *Africa Diary*, June 27, July 3, 1966.

26. *West Africa*, October 8, 1966.

27. *Africa Diary*, December 29, 1966, January 4, 1967.

28. *East Africa and Rhodesia*, April 14, and May 26, 1966.

29. *Africa Diary*, January 17–23, 1966.

30. *East Africa and Rhodesia*, July 14, 1966.

31. *Africa Diary*, April 18–24, 1966.

32. *Rhodesia and Eastern Africa* (London), September 1, 1966.

33. *West Africa*, April 23, and September 3, 1966.

34. *Africa Diary*, April 23–29, 1967.

35. *East Africa and Rhodesia*, June 16, and August 11, 1966.

36. *West Africa*, October 8, 1966.

37. *Ibid.*

38. *Ibid.*, April 30, and September 3, 1966; also *Africa Diary*, September 19–25, 1966.

39. *East Africa and Rhodesia*, January 13, 1966; *West Africa*, September 3, 1966; also *Africa Diary*, September 19–25, 1966.

40. *Africa Diary*, April 9–15, 1967.

41. *West Africa*, July 30, 1966.

42. *East Africa and Rhodesia*, March 17, and June 16, 1966; also *Africa Diary*, March 19–26, 1967.

43. *East Africa and Rhodesia*, July 14, 1966.

44. *West Africa*, July 30, 1966.

45. *Ibid.*, December 17, 1966.

46. *East Africa and Rhodesia*, May 26, 1966; also *Rhodesia and Eastern Africa*, September 1, 1966.

47. *L'Agronomie tropicale* (Paris, 1961), 2, p. 181.

48. *F.A.O. Production Yearbook, 1965* (Rome, 1966), pp. 3–7.

49. *Africa Diary*, February 14–20, 1966 and January 28, February 3, 1967.

50. *Ibid.*, January 10–16, 1966 and December 27, 1965, January 2, 1966; also *Rhodesia and Eastern Africa*, September 1, 1966.

51. *Ibid.*

52. *Ibid.*, April 2–8, 1967.

53. *Africa Diary*, February 28, March 6, 1966.

54. *Statistical Year Book, 1964* (Pretoria, 1964), pp. 1–3.

55. Lord Hailey, *An African Survey Revised 1956* (London, 1957), p. 705.

56. *Report on Agriculture and Pastoral Production of Southern Rhodesia, Northern Rhodesia, and Nyasaland, 1958–59* (Salisbury, 1960).

57. E. Luther, *Ethiopia Today* (London, 1958), p. 30.

58. *Rhodesia and Eastern Africa*, September 1, 1966.

59. *Horoya* (Conakry), December 28, 1962.

60. *Africa Diary*, November 7–13, 1966.

61. *Ibid.*, April 2–8, 1967.

62. *Al Ahram al Iktisadi* (Cairo), December 1, 1966.

Land Tenure

B

THE TRADITIONAL social framework and values, especially the land tenure systems in a large part of Africa, evolved under conditions which are increasingly at variance with present-day requirements. The situation of course varies widely in different areas. The feudal land tenure system of Ethiopia bears little relation to the tribal or extended family arrangements in large tracts of West or Central Africa. The alienation to foreign entrepreneurs, a problem of major importance in Central and Southern Africa, hardly arises in other parts of the region. Legislation and adherence to customary law also vary greatly. Nor are the differences simply differences from one country to another; in most West African countries, for instance, individual tenure is developing in the coastal regions, while in the rest of the country, tribal tenure prevails.

Until the recent growth of population, long-established customs and the traditional framework of African farming in fact protected and safeguarded soil fertility, and with it the social and economic security of Africans. But the increasing pressure on the land, the introduction of new technology, together with the development of a market economy and the rise of mercantile and speculative attitudes, are having an increasingly disintegrating effect on the tribal order. The clash of economic changes with time-honored values has undermined the viability and reduced the inherited authority and discipline of the tribal system, but as yet has given little compensating strength to the culture and social life of the people. And finally, the change from abundance, to a growing scarcity of land with the increase in population has created pressures for alternative land arrangements; toward forms of tenure which recognize the value of land for the individual and also the individual's contribution to the value of the land. In the African framework, the adoption of European legal institutions, such as unrestricted ownership, might give rise to forces leading to unbalance, inequality and unrest. It is a matter for serious consideration whether an evolution from traditional forms of social institutions to newer forms might not present

11

Problems of Land Tenure and Settlement

United Nations Food and Agriculture Organization

From Report on the Possibilities of African Rural Development in Relation to Economic and Social Growth *(Rome: United Nations Food and Agriculture Organization, 1962), pp. 61–65.*

a more suitable basis for balanced social and economic progress.

Land Tenure, Social Organization and the Traditional System of Exploitation

Since time immemorial, land has been the focus of the life of the tribe as a whole. In the famous words of a Nigerian chief, "Land belongs to a vast family of which many are dead, a few are living, and countless numbers are still unborn."

The system of exploitation which arose from the experience of ages is usually known as shifting cultivation, or bush fallow. Land was cleared and cultivated for a number of years consecutively, after which it was permitted to return to a state of bush to recover its fertility. As land was plentiful, the concept of ownership did not arise, because rights to exclusive use of land by a specific tribe were *de facto* not challenged. The amount of land which anyone could work was limited by the manpower of the family and the nature of the tools.[1]

The group which is entitled to determine land rights, that is, the right to cultivate, fish, hunt, or gather food, may be the tribe, the clan or the extended family. A number of different kinds of rights relating to the land are shared between the group and the individual. Custom requires that important decisions regarding land and its utilization be taken by all the members, though in practice it is often the chief or a council of elders that control the land for the group.[2] Alienation to outsiders can be challenged by any member of the group, and thus renders any rights acquired under customary laws highly insecure. It is a misconception of the fundamental role of the land to assume that a chief can alienate tribal lands to other tribes or for ownership or lease to foreign interests, though *de facto* he has been able to do so in many areas.

Disturbing Factors in the System

As the population grows and the money economy develops in importance, the relative abundance of land tends to decrease. The transition from subsistence to cash agriculture, i.e., the introduction of cash crops and urbanization, has had a profound influence on the land by giving it economic value.[3] As specialization increases, as for instance in the Ghana cocoa belt, land values rise. In the first stages, the economy acquires a dual aspect. Subsistence farming continues to supply the primary needs of the farmer, while the proceeds from his cash crops, in some areas at one time mainly required for tax payments, are now widely used to purchase consumer goods.

In a number of cases, the traditional systems of land tenure are still in harmony with present situations and are flexible enough to meet new needs, even of cash cropping, so long as population pressure does not lead to overcultivation. Generally, however, although family and group ownership remains prevalent in many areas, changes toward individualization of land tenure are apparent, especially in urban areas. In South Dahomey, for example, and in the cocoa areas of West Africa, marked adaptations are taking place in the original form of land tenure.

The technical experts who met at Arusha (Tanganyika) in 1956 and reported on African land tenure in East and Central Africa, recognized the arguments in favor of communal tenure. But where land is becoming scarce, they felt this system may carry within it grave dangers to the whole community and to the land available to it. These dangers are enumerated as follows.

It may, by its failure to provide adequate incentive to the individual to put effort or money into the land, militate against its conservation and improvement. It may, owing to the limitations to the form of security which it provides, delay the introduction of permanent cash crops, and, generally, of better farming methods. It may make it impossible for the farmer to raise loans on the security of his land for purposes designed to increase its productivity. It may, as scarcity enhances the value of land and an exchange economy begins to develop, place too great a strain on the public spirit of the traditional authorities charged with its allocation.[4]

The conclusion of the conference was that the old customary communal tenures must continue to evolve toward forms of tenure more conducive to economic development, if the agrarian revolution is to proceed without unnecessary impediment and friction.

Government Policy in Territories with Non-African Settlement

The present position and outlook is much influenced by the position of governments in relation to land and land rights; important issues in this respect have arisen, particularly with reference to land rights granted to non-indigenous settlers. While at first both in East and West Africa state ownership was used to make possible alienation and to encourage private enterprise, it has gradually evolved toward greater protection of the original rights of the inhabitants.[5]

In the former French territories, the principle of state ownership of vacant land prevailed down to 1955 and was applied specifically in Madagascar and West and Equatorial Africa. In 1955, however, new legislation re-organized land tenure in the French territories, recognizing the long-standing customary rights.

In the territories formerly under British administration, there was little uniformity of policy. However,

in general, the first object of British land policy has been to fix and stabilize the whole land situation by vesting supreme control on all land in the territory in the Governor on behalf of His Majesty, and thus to establish effective control by the State over the whole land of the territory and over all changes in it whether of tenure, title, alienation or transfer.[6]

In Uganda, for example, the Crown Lands Declaration of 1922 provides: "All lands and rights therein in the Protectorate shall be presumed to be the property of the Crown unless they have been or are hereafter recognized by the Governor by document to be the property of a person or until the contrary thereof be proved." In 1950, the Uganda Government declared that crown land outside Buganda was to be "held in trust for the use and benefit of the African population." In keeping with these policies, Africans are allowed to occupy crown lands in rural areas outside Buganda without lease or license, in accordance with tribal custom. Land occupied by Africans in Buganda must be held on lease or license and the rents so received are passed on to the Buganda government.

The degree of protection and recognition of the indigenous rights depended by their definition on the interpretation of words such as "vacant" or "unoccupied." Misunderstanding of the nature of indigenous rights and the existence of large underpopulated and apparently empty areas have sometimes contributed to the conception that all unoccupied land was no man's land available for concessions. The result has been that large areas in Central and Southern Africa were often occupied either simply through straight authorization, or else through agreement with chiefs or others who were supposed to represent tribal authority. The East African Royal Commission pointed out that the concepts of "Crown land" and "Public land" by transforming customary right holders to the position of occupiers at the will of the state, had given "the African a sense of insecurity in his land holding, notwithstanding the statements of policy and the complicated administrative machinery designed to reassure him."

The interpretation of vacant land in this sense recognizes only the areas in actual use by the African communities as occupied land, whereas in fact the territorial claims of these communities express themselves not only in the hunting, fishing and gathering rights of individual members, but also in the right to open up new land to the exclusion of non-members. This is illustrated by the traditional rule that the cultivating members of one lineage should not cross the line of advance of the cultivating members of another lineage.

In recent years, however, the tendency has been to consider all manifestations of customary law as rights to be respected. In the former French West and Equatorial Africa, the 1955 legislation provided a foundation in law for customary rights in land, including hunting and gathering rights and any other right exercised by the community according to customary law. At the same time, the law abandoned the presumption that vacant land is state land.

Similarly, the East Africa Royal Commission recommended the abolition of such concepts as Crown land, Public land and Native land, and rigid adherence to the safeguard under the law that all powers of disposition of land interests should be exercised with full recognition of *de facto* private interest in land. The recognition of African rights by statute has meant that they are established as a matter of law, rather than of policy, and they can thus be maintained more easily against encroachment by third parties.

It was in keeping with the new trend that most metropolitan governments had taken steps to control the transfer of rights in land to non-Africans. In the former British territories, the method often used was the proclamation of reserves to be retained for occupation by Africans only. However, the result was sometimes that the demarcated areas limited the expansion of African land tenure, and these often became insufficient to support the rapidly growing population. The extension of the cultivated area and the reduced bush fallow led to the deterioration of the soil. In Northern Rhodesia and in Nyasaland, the reserve policy was therefore abandoned and a system of "Native Trust Land" introduced. In other British territories, transfers of land to non-Africans were made subject to the consent of the governor.

In the former French territories, the alienation of lands is not allowed where customary law and the tribal system are effective. Furthermore, most alienations were subject to the consent of governors. However, the 1955 legislation provided that where individual customary owner rights have been officially adjudicated, these can be alienated.

Forest Tenure

A note may be added here on the situation in regard to forests. The terms "ownership" and "rights of usage," and indeed what is meant by the word forest itself in relation to agriculture and grazing in Africa, are still somewhat indefinite. The common presumption that vacant land is state land has had its influence on the establishment of state forests (national forests) and forest reserves. Reservation of land with or without transfer of ownership title or deed has in Africa often been done by the forest service. Adjustments to enlarge or sometimes to decrease forest reserves are now generally subject to proper land use surveys and plans. Government ownership has special importance in implementing long-range forest policy, since fragmentation and "circulation"—obstacles to sound forest land use—are not as likely to happen as under private or tribal ownership.

Full private forest ownership is not widespread. There are, however, extensive private forest plantations in Nyasaland and Southern Rhodesia, where plantations mostly of eucalyptus and pines cover about 80,000 hectares, compared with government plantations in the order of 25,000 hectares. It is

likely that an increase in private ownership will take more time in the closed forest area than in intensively managed small holdings with cash crops like coffee, cocoa, etc., and timber crops. In closed forest areas, the need for high investment has precluded Africans from pressing for ownership and has left the field clear for government action.[7] African tribal authorities, however, control a great portion of forest land. To regard these areas as communal forest, based on rights of law or customs, is sound, so that it may be said there is a three-fold pattern of forest ownership—state, communal and private.

Concessions or long leases are most important to open up forest areas. The initiative mostly comes from concessionnaires. Property rights on the soil are never transferred, but partnership arrangements could be developed. By planning forest plantations in closed forest and woodland areas, the introduction of co-operative schemes seems to be very feasible.

In Western Nigeria local authorities are recognized as owners of the produce of forest land. User rights, generally tribal or communal, in the forest reserves of Nigeria—except for the state forests of northern Nigeria—were not extinguished when reserves were established. The revenues from produce of the forest reserves are divided into fees and royalties, ordinarily in the ratio of 4:1, with the royalties payable to the "owners," i.e., the local authority, and the fees to the government communal reserve. Local authority rights can be inconvenient as far as orderly management is concerned. In Eastern Nigeria, a proposal has been made to purchase inconvenient user rights in parts of forest reserves where concentrated regeneration and formation of forest plantations is planned.

The land use policy in Liberia gives an example of withdrawing a portion of the existing forest area from circulation and setting this aside as national forests for the fulfillment of their protective and productive functions. This is an important step, for when the great mineral resources are exhausted, these renewable forest resources will be a main part of the national economy. The objective is that these national forests be managed and utilized by the Liberian Forest

Service with contractors. The forest land outside the national forests will be worked by concessionnaires in units from 4,000 to 30,000 hectares, under the supervision of the Forest Service (infrastructure planning, yield control, silviculture improvement, planning for timber processing plant). These concessions are long-term leases given to the lessee as the only practicable means of dealing with large forest areas, where utilization operations may require much capital in opening up the forest, in erecting plants, and in properly serving the local and export market.

The Pressure Toward Individualization

In the new circumstances of Africa, the customary system is often an obstacle to development. In the past, the members of a customary group—tribe, village or extended family—regarded their customary right—quite correctly—as an essential basis of social security. Under present conditions, the position of the individual actually cultivating the land has become equivocal. So long as he adheres completely to traditional methods of cultivation, he does not suffer, for under tribal tradition any piece of land was as any other, soon to be abandoned, and there was plenty to go round. In that framework, improved farming methods to increase production were not thought of or sought for. The need for increased output and at the same time to counter soil erosion, requires individual effort, and in most cases such efforts are not likely to be forthcoming if the individual who has made them is liable to see the land which he has worked on and improved passed on to someone else. Furthermore, rational agriculture requires that land should be grouped in economic units, while tribal land was often highly fragmented; fragmentation is particularly important, for example, in wide areas of Cameroon and in Nyasaland.

In the areas where cash crop production has reached a certain intensity and land scarcity is developing, the demand for individualization of tenure has become pressing. The East Africa Royal Commission recog-

nized and welcomed the trend toward individualization of land tenure in East Africa. It recognized that the traditional tribal form of agriculture was adapted to conditions of restricted subsistence production based on shifting cultivation. It considered, however, that once this system was no longer possible, a complete social and agricultural re-orientation was required. The mere expansion of production for the market was not in itself sufficient. It could lead to soil exhaustion, unless a proper fallow was maintained, and suitable crop rotations or economic methods of restoring nutrients to the land applied.

Over large areas of Africa, it is likely that the traditional tribal tenure will evolve into a system of individual tenure, as in other lands where old-established tenure systems have withered away as a result of new economic and demographic trends. But the process of individualization has to be distinguished from the establishment of full property rights. Individual tenure does not mean of necessity that negotiable rights in land have to be established. Nor does it mean that a uniform system has to prevail throughout a territory or country.

In Sierra Leone, for instance, in the areas of shifting cultivation, where rice is planted as a subsistence crop, the uncultivated bush of the extended family seems to be still included in the basic unit. Frequent bush disputes have shown, however, that the boundaries between individual family units are ill-defined. The allocation of land is still in the hands of the family head who makes his decisions along traditional lines. In such circumstances, to vest all negotiable rights in land in the head of the family might well lead to undesirable results, since it would enable the family head to dispose of land to his own advantage.

Various official reports suggest that in large areas tribal populations do not appreciate the importance of establishing and recording individual rights in land. It could be ventured that this resistance is not based on suspicion of the central authority, but rather on the awareness of the tribal groups of their economic weakness and their lack of bargaining capacity. There is a fear of concentration of land ownership and, also, that alien groups might buy agricultural land and establish large estates at the expense of the members of the tribe.[8]

The denial of traditional cultural ties, and the introduction of alien institutions is already in danger of jeopardizing harmonious communal development. An urgent solution is therefore required.

Land Settlement Schemes

The complexity of the social and economic problems involved in rural development has made drastic solutions attractive. If land tenure could be made secure, to serve the increase in efficiency, and if the African farmer could be helped toward modern methods in a suitable environment, a great stride would be made in raising productivity toward the level of more highly developed agricultures. This would not only contribute directly to further economic progress, but would have an immense indirect educational impact. These considerations explain the initiation of land settlement schemes in a number of countries since the war.

On the whole, these schemes have not had the desired success. Some, like the *paysannats* in the Congo (Leopoldville), were perhaps technically successful in the sense of increasing production while conserving the soil. But their success was largely dependent on European supervisors.

In Nigeria, the desire for a rural transformation has led to ambitious settlement schemes, in which the farmers receive education, training and material help (in the shape of regular wages for work performed in the initial period) to enable them to raise their output (partly mechanized) toward a goal of £500 per annum, against a national average of less than £50 per farming unit. The cost of these schemes, £3,000 (nearly $9,000) per family unit, could no doubt be reduced. But even at a fraction of the cost, such schemes would be self-defeating in a country where the population is growing at the rate of some

800,000 to 1,000,000 per annum, and with a *per caput* national income of at most £30 per annum. The demonstration effect is also very limited, since no ordinary farmer would have the capital to emulate the example of the settlers. The experiment is therefore liable to create a new small privileged class, the reverse of what was intended, though it is too early to reach a final conclusion.

By contrast, the Tanganyika Agricultural Corporation used the large areas opened up, cleared and prepared by the Groundnut Scheme, and some other areas as well, to initiate a supervised development scheme in order to educate Africans to see in modern land-use management their own salvation and prosperity.

The size of the settlement scheme of the Office du Niger in Mali has been reduced in scale, and the past level of expenditure much reduced. The results of the considerable research of the past are now being applied, and if adequate transport facilities for its output are secured, it is now in a position to make a valuable contribution to the economy.

Notes

1. Each adult (married) man of the group is entitled to open up as much of the common area of land as is required for his own and his family's subsistence, with exclusive rights to the return from his work. The clearing of a part of the *forest* generally establishes a right of priority or exclusiveness to cultivate the soil in favor of the member who carried out the clearing, as this is very arduous work. The right can be maintained against other members of the group and remains dormant even if the land is temporarily abandoned. Customary laws of succession and inheritance determine whether the land of a member who has died will come back to the community or will go to his heirs. Where livelihood is not based on hunting, fishing or gathering wild fruit, but on the harvesting of fruits of trees and plants cultivated on a patch of ground, the concept of ownership of the land does not necessarily emerge. In general, the private ownership of trees or crops planted and of yields obtained by a group member is recognized and respected, but the relationship to the land is not basically different. For all practical purposes, land has no, or a limited, commercial value in these circumstances.

2. One of the elders is generally known as the "land man." He usually is as much respected as the chief himself.

3. Speculation in land along motor arteries is acquiring considerable importance as, for instance, in Cameroon.

4. Special supplement to *Journal of African Administration*, October, 1956.

5. Hailey, *An African Survey*, 1957, p. 41: "So far as the native is concerned the crucial fact is not the manner in which the law is framed, but the spirit in which effect is given to it. The effect of a law professing to restrict the right of the State to the disposal of vacant lands varies according to the interpretation which practice places on vacancy; on the other hand, an outright assertion of full State proprietorship over all lands may, in spite of its apparent disregard for native rights, prove, when rightly used, to be the best machinery for protecting natives in the enjoyment of their lands."

6. United Nations Document T/AC, 36/L, 10, p. 29.

7. "As a commercial venture, sustained yield management of the ordinary run of unimproved tropical forest is likely to be little better than marginal, so that government management and investment may well be a necessary step in the first rotation for improvement and enrichment; the case for denationalization may be strengthened, as it has been for instance in Kenya as a result of the success of the government plantation program." W. A. Gordon, "Obstacles to tropical forestry—land tenure." *Unasylva* 15 (1961), 1: pp. 6–9.

8. In Sierra Leone, for instance, there is a fear in the major part of the country that the inhabitants of Freetown and its neighborhood (traditionally known as the colony) would buy agricultural land and dispossess the existing tribes.

Industry

C

WITH THE EXCEPTION of South Africa and a few other countries, the structure of output in Africa and its subregions is predominantly underdeveloped.[2] The high share of agriculture in gross domestic product, which is more pronounced in West and East Africa than in North and Southern Africa, is a manifestation of the low level of industrial development in the western and eastern subregions, in comparison with that in the northern part of the continent and, more so, in comparison with that of South Africa. In recent years, manufacturing and mining have accounted for about 20 per cent of the gross domestic product of the continent as a whole, whereas their share has been 8 per cent of gross domestic in West Africa, 15 per cent in East Africa, 20 per cent in North Africa, 21 per cent in Central Africa and approximately 39 per cent in Southern Africa, as is shown in Table 1.

One of the striking features made evident in Table 1 is that there are only narrow differences between subregions in the level of agricultural output per capita, whereas the mining and manufacturing outputs per capita show a wider range of industrial development in the same subregions. By and large, industrial development in Southern Africa has been much more pronounced than in North Africa, which is followed by East and Central Africa, with West African industry being less developed than that of the other subregions.

The fact that there are relatively small variations in the agricultural output per capita suggests that the differences in the over-all output per capita in the subregions mainly reflect the degree of development of the non-agricultural sectors.

With a population totalling about 272.8 million persons in 1963, and an industrial output of approximately $7.700 million in or about the same year (see Table 2), the industrial product per capita for the whole of Africa has been in the neighbourhood of $28,

Industrial Development in Africa: Problems and Prospects

United Nations Economic Commission for Africa

From Industrial Development in Africa (*New York : United Nations Economic Commission for Africa, 1967*), *pp. 3–28.*

on the average. Wide variations exist, however, in the industrial product per capita among the African subregions, ranging from $9 in West Africa, to about $158 in Southern Africa, in comparison with $11 for East Africa, $21 for Central Africa and $35 for North Africa.

Manufacturing development has been concentrated, thus far, in Southern Africa, which accounts for about 37.5 per cent of the total manufacturing output of the continent, followed by North Africa, which produces nearly 33.4 per cent of the total, and by East Africa, which produces about 12.5 per cent. Mining output has also been concentrated, with approximately 45 per cent of its total being in Southern Africa and about 32 per cent in North Africa. The distribution of mining and manufacturing output, in comparison with the distribution of population among the subregions, as shown above in Table 2, explains the wide differences in the degree of industrial development as measured by the industrial output per capita. East, West and Central Africa, although producing similar percentages of the total mining and manufacturing output in or about 1963 (about 8 to 12 per cent of the total in each), portrayed wide differences in population size. In West Africa, with 27.7 per cent of the total population of the continent, the industrial output per capita was lower than that of East Africa, with 28.4 per cent of the population. It was lower still in comparison with Central Africa, where only 10.9 per cent of the total African population produced 32.4 per cent of the total output of industry, and with Southern Africa, the most indus-

trialized area in the continent, where only 7.1 per cent of the total population produced about 39.5 per cent of the total output of industry in Africa during 1963.

A comparison of the main components of gross domestic product in the subregions of Africa with those of the industrially advanced countries presents striking differences. Table 3 shows the level of output per inhabitant from agriculture, industry and other sectors in the industrial countries and in the subregions of Africa.

Table 1—Industrial Origin of Gross Domestic Product in Africa, by Subregion[a]

Sector	Total Africa	West Africa	North Africa	East Africa	Central Africa	Southern Africa[b]
			(Thousand Million Dollars)			
Agriculture	13.8	4.5	4.5	2.8	1.2	0.8
Mining	2.3	0.2	0.7	0.2	0.2	1.0
Manufacturing	5.4	0.5	1.8	0.7	0.4	2.0
Other sectors	15.9	2.9	5.7	2.3	1.1	3.9
Total	37.4	8.1	12.7	6.0	2.9	7.7
			(Percentage of Gross Domestic Product)			
Agriculture	37	56	35	47	41	10
Mining	6	2	6	3	7	13
Manufacturing	14	6	14	12	14	26
Other sectors	43	36	45	38	38	51
Total	100	100	100	100	100	100
			(Dollars per capita)			
Agriculture	51	60	64	36	40	42
Mining	8	2	10	2	7	52
Manufacturing	20	7	25	9	14	106
Other sectors	58	38	80	30	37	206
Total	137	107	179	77	98	406

Sources: Various United Nations publications and documents; national plans and publications.

[a] The figures in the table indicate orders of magnitude in broad terms and represent only approximations in 1963 or thereabouts.
[b] 1962 at factor cost.

Table 2—Distribution of Manufacturing Mining and Population in Africa, by Subregion, 1963[a]
(Percentages of Totals)

Subregions	Manufacturing A	Mining B	A + B	Population
North Africa	33.4	30.0	32.4	25.9
West Africa	8.7	7.5	8.4	27.7
East Africa	12.5	10.2	11.8	28.4
Central Africa	7.9	7.9	7.9	10.9
Southern Africa	37.5	44.4	39.5	7.1
Total	100.0	100.0	100.0	100.0
	(Thousand Million Dollars)			*(Millions)*
Absolute totals	5.4	2.3	7.7	272.8

Sources: Various United Nations publications and documents; national plans and publications.

[a] These figures refer to the year 1963 or thereabouts. They are estimates of orders of magnitude rather than accurate data.

The level of industrial development as reflected in per capita industrial output is very low in all African subregions (with the exception of Southern Africa), when compared with the output per capita in developed countries.

While the level of agricultural output per capita in the industrialized countries appears to be about 2.3 to four times higher than that in the subregions of Africa, the industrial output per capita in industrially advanced countries is nearly sixty times as much as in West Africa, forty times as much as in East Africa and twenty-two times that in North Africa, but it is only seventeen times the level attained in Central Africa and about three times that reached in Southern Africa. These

figures illustrate the wide gap and the very low level of industrial output per capita in the various African subregions in recent years, in comparison with the industrially advanced countries and the advances these subregions must make in the years to come in order to reach, at some future time, the current level of average output in the developed countries.

A comparison of the changes in industrial output in Africa and in other areas of the world since the period prior to the Second World War is given in Table 4.

Table 3—Income per capita in African Subregions and in Industrially Advanced Countries, 1960[a]
(US$)

Area	Agriculture	Industry[b]	Other Sectors	All Sectors
Developed countries	120	480	600	1,200
Africa—Total	41	25	51	117
North Africa	48	22	62	132
West Africa	41	8	25	74
East Africa	31	12	29	72
Central Africa	37	28	38	103
Southern Africa	52	166	271	489

Source: United Nations Economic Commission for Africa, Research Division

[a] Figures refer to the year 1960 or thereabouts.
[b] Including mining and manufacturing, construction, power and water utilities.

Table 4—Changes in Industrial Output in Africa Compared with Other Areas, 1938–1960 and 1948–1960

	Index (1953 = 100)				Annual Compound Percentage Change	
	1938	1948	1957	1960	1938–1960	1948–1960
World						
Mining	63	80	120	132	3.4	4.3
Manufacture	50	72	121	140	4.8	5.7
Total industry	52	73	121	138	4.6	6.5
Industrial Countries						
Mining	66	85	114	112	3.3	2.3
Manufacture	47	73	116	131	4.8	5.0
Total industry	49	74	116	129	4.5	4.8
Africa						
Mining	69	73	123	150	3.6	6.2
Manufacture	30	67	127	—	7.9	7.4
Total industry	42	69	126	—	6.0[a]	6.9[a]
Africa Excluding Southern Africa						
Mining	47	65	115	141	5.1	6.7
Manufacture	29	74	140	—	8.6	7.3
Total industry	34	71	133	—	7.4[a]	7.2[a]

Source: United Nations, *Statistical Yearbook, 1960* (Sales No. 61.XVII.1).

[a] Up to 1957 only.

PAST RATES OF GROWTH OF INDUSTRY IN
AFRICA

The rapid rate of industrial growth in Africa over the past two decades has, thus far, had scarcely any significant effect in bringing about a structural transformation of the African economies. Although the growth rate of industrial output in Africa averaged about 7.4 per cent annually between 1938 and 1957, compared with 4.5 per cent in the industrially advanced countries, the share of industry in the total output of Africa barely exceeded 14 per cent in the twenty-year period, 1938–1958.

Taking the manufacturing sector alone, the annual rate of growth averaged 7.9 per cent for the whole of Africa and 8.6 per cent for the continent excluding South Africa, indicating a much higher growth rate than the

Table 5—Industrial Origin of Gross Domestic Product at Factor Cost in Countries of Africa, by Commodity Sector, 1960[a]
(Percentage of total gross domestic product)

Subregion and Country	Manufacturing	Electricity	Construction	Mining	Agriculture
North Africa					
Algeria	11.0	2.0	5.0	3.0	23
Libya	10.0	2.0	4.0	8.0	23
Morocco	13.4	2.2	4.0	6.6	32
Tunisia	12.0	2.0	5.0	3.0	29
Sudan	5.0	0.5	6.5	0.1	57
United Arab Republic (Egypt)	17.0	2.0	8.0	1.7	31
West Africa					
Dahomey	—	8.0	—	—	53
Ghana	8.2	0.4	4.0	4.4	49
Guinea	—	—	—	—	—
Ivory Coast	5.4	2.3	3.8	0.6	49
Mali	—	15.0	—	—	48
Mauritania	1.6	1.0	28.2	2.4	52
Niger	4.3	0.9	4.0	11.9	77
Nigeria	2.7	0.6	4.4	1.3	63
Senegal	8.5	0.7	4.7	0.7	28
Sierra Leone	—	—	—	—	—
Togo	—	19.0	—	—	52
Upper Volta	—	12.0	—	—	67
East Africa					
Ethiopia	5.2	0.4	2.0	0.2	76
Kenya	9.5	1.2	3.5	0.5	40
Madagascar	2.2	0.3	1.4	—	53
Malawi	5.1	1.0	3.5	0.6	—
Mauritius	16.0	2.0	6.0	0.2	23
Southern Rhodesia	14.7	3.4	5.4	6.4	—
Uganda	6.3	1.2	2.5	1.5	61
United Republic of Tanzania	7.2	0.6	5.9	3.8	59
Zambia	5.1	2.6	4.1	48.0	15
Central Africa					
Cameroon	8.1	1.9	4.0	—	46
Central African Republic	6.7	0.4	3.5	4.5	53
Chad	3.5	0.4	3.3	1.0	62
Congo (Brazzaville)	—	13.0	—	3.5	33
Congo (Democratic Republic of)	14.0	0.7	5.5	16.4	31
Gabon	3.0	1.9	9.0	17.0	27

Sources: United Nations, *Yearbook of National Accounts Statistics, 1963* (Sales No. 64.XVII.4); United Nations, *The Growth of World Industry, 1938–1961* (Sales No. 63.XVII.5); and United Nations Economic Commission for Africa, Research Division, national publications, 1965.

[a] Data refer to 1960 or thereabouts; some data are provisional estimates.

4.8 per cent per annum in the industrialized countries and in the world at large during the period 1938 to 1960 (see Table 4). It should be observed that the annual growth rates of manufacture were higher than those for mining in Africa and in the industrial countries, as well as in the world at large, throughout the period covered in Table 4.

It must be acknowledged, however, that the high relative growth rates of industry in Africa, as in the majority of other developing areas, mainly reflect small absolute increments on an initial low level. The size of the industrial sector in the subregions of Africa is rather small in relation to the output of their whole economies, and the impressive high rates of growth of their industrial output have not had a substantial impact on total domestic product. The small size of the manufacturing sector is demonstrated by its contribution to the gross domestic product in the largest number of African countries. The contribution of manufacturing to gross domestic product varies a great deal from country to country (see Table 5). Value added by manufacturing industries amounted to 15 per cent or more of the total output in only a few countries of Africa,[3] and in the largest number of countries for which data could be assembled, the contribution of manufacturing to total output ranged from about less than 5 per cent, to approximately 10 per cent of gross domestic product.[4] In a number of countries, the size of manufactured output has been even smaller than 5 per cent of gross domestic product in recent years.[5] In industrially developed countries, however, the share contributed by the manufacturing sector has accounted for 30 to 40 per cent or even more of the total output,[6] a fact which indicates also the wise disparity between the developed countries and the African countries with regard to the size of their industrial sectors in relation to the other sectors of the economy.

Plans for Industrial Development

PROJECTED INDUSTRIAL GROWTH IN CURRENT DEVELOPMENT PLANS

Bearing in mind that there is some relationship between the magnitude of a sector in the economy and the pace at which it is expected to expand, and the fact that the share of manufacturing in total output is rather small in the majority of African countries, the relatively high growth rates planned by these least industrialized countries could be attributed to the fact that they need to make less of an investment effort to attain a given growth rate than would be required in a more industrialized economy.

Table 6 shows a comparison of data obtained from national development plans with those referring to periods prior to the introduction of planning. In most countries, manufacturing is anticipated to grow at a more rapid pace than before the plan periods, pointing out the importance attached to the development of manufactures. Rather large increases in the planned growth rates of manufacture can be detected in North African countries (Morocco, Sudan, Tunisia and the United Arab Republic), as well as in West African countries (Ghana, Mali, Mauritania, Nigeria, Senegal and others). Generally, the same observation applies to East African countries, including Ethiopia, Kenya, Uganda, the United Republic of Tanzania and Zambia.

Some countries stressed in their plans the development of mining, and in a number of countries which originally had a small mining base, the planned growth rates for mineral production appear to be much higher than for manufacturing. An extreme example of this will be found in Mauritania, where the bulk of projected growth would originate in the mining sector, which is expected to expand at an annual rate of more than 148 per cent. In Ethiopia, the Sudan and the United Arab Republic, the current plans in operation contemplate growth rates of mineral output much higher than that of manufacture. Mining output has been projected to expand at an annual rate of about 53 per cent in Ethiopia, 25 per cent in the Sudan and 27 per cent in the United Arab Republic. It is to be noted that the share of mining in the gross domestic product is rather small in these three, being less than 1 per cent in Ethiopia and the Sudan, and less than 2 per cent in the United Arab Republic. Table 7 shows the planned growth rates of output in manufacturing and mining, electricity, gas and water utilities in selected countries of African subregions, in comparison with planned growth rates of gross domestic product.

In a number of countries where the mining sector is relatively more developed, the planned growth of mineral output has been much smaller than that for manufactured output. For example, in Zambia, where the share of mining accounts for almost 48 per cent of the gross domestic product, the planned growth rate of the sector is in the neighbourhood of 3 per cent per annum. In the Democratic Republic of the Congo, where mining has contributed about 16 per cent of the gross domestic product the planned annual growth rate has been set at 3 to 4 per

cent per annum; and in Morocco, where mining has contributed 6 to 7 per cent of the gross domestic product, the planned growth rate of the sector has been set at about 4.5 per cent per annum.

With the exception of a few countries, the current economic and social development plans in African countries call for an annual growth rate of industry which is substantially higher than the target growth rates of total output, i.e., the growth rates of gross domestic product (see Table 7).

The projected growth of gross domestic product ranges from 4 per cent to 9 per cent per annum, while the planned growth rates for manufacturing range from 8 per cent to as high as 30 per cent per annum in the different countries.

PLANNED INVESTMENT AND GROWTH PATTERN OF INDUSTRY

A significant indicator of the objectives and strategy of development in the plans of

Table 6—Planned Increase in Growth and Pre-plan Growth Rates in Manufacturing, Electricity and Mining, Selected African Countries (Annual Percentage)

	Manufacturing		Electricity		Mining	
Subregion and Country	Preplan[a] Growth Rate	Planned Increase Rate	Preplan[a] Growth Rate	Planned Increase Rate	Preplan[a] Growth Rate	Planned Increase Rate
North Africa						
Algeria	7.2	—	10.7	—	8.4	—
Morocco	2.5	6.1	3.2	3.9	5.1	−1.4
Sudan	6.0	15.8	10.0	13.6	—	25.0
Tunisia	4.6	3.4	5.3	−0.9	2.4	−0.4
United Arab Republic (Egypt)	7.8	5.5	11.4	23.0	7.7	20.0
West Africa						
Ghana	—	10.9[b]	19.2	—	6.9	—
Mali	—	19.0[b]	—	—	—	—
Mauritania	—	19.1[b]	—	—	—	148.0
Nigeria	7.3	—	13.2	—	5.1	—
Senegal	5.7	9.8[c]	—	—[c]	—	—[c]
East Africa						
Ethiopia	5.5	21.8	11.3	8.1	—	52.0
Kenya	2.6	5.3	2.1	1.7	−15.2	3.0
Malawi						
Southern Rhodesia	10.5	—	6.9	—	−5.8	—
Uganda	−0.5	—	15.1	—	16.7	—
United Republic of Tanzania	5.8	9.0	18.0	−6.0	−1.4	4.0
Zambia	8.0	23.3	—	—	—	3.2

Sources: National development plans; also United Nations, *Yearbook of National Accounts Statistics, 1963* (Sales No. 64.VXII.4); United Nations, *The Growth of World Industry, 1938–1961: National Tables* (Sales No. 63.XVII.5).

[a] Data refer to 1954–1958.
[b] Annual growth rate totals for all industrial sectors.
[c] Planned growth rates for all industrial sectors, 12.7 per cent per annum.

various African countries is the investment for the projected growth pattern of industry in the current and perspective plans. Most of the economic and social development plans, which present some detailed allocation of investment by economic sector and give information on the distribution of investment between public and private undertakings, illustrate the differences in development strategies, if not also in objectives.

Whenever it was possible to secure information concerning the share of industry in total public investment in preplan periods and in total planned investment, public investment in the development of industry, as a percentage of total public investment, has been considerably lower in the preplan period than in the plans of those countries for which data are available. An increasing number of countries of Africa have assumed a greater role in the development of their industrial sectors through the direct invest-

ment of public funds since they attained independence than they did before. The share of industry in total planned investment has also increased in different countries during the postindependence era of planning (see Table 8).

The distribution of capital expenditures among various sectors of the economy in the countries where data are available reflects the differences in the pattern of investment and in the priorities attached to the development of various economic and social sectors. Of strategic importance for the growth of the economy in the majority of African countries is the development of such basic facilities as power, transport and communication, and water supplies for the expansion of industries. In the economic development plans of a

Table 7—Planned Growth Rates in Output of Manufacturing, Mining, Electricity, Water and Gas, Selected African Countries (Percentage)

Subregion and Country	Plan Period	Gross Domestic Product	Manufacturing	Mining	Electricity, Gas and Water
North Africa					
Algeria	—	—	—	—	—
Morocco	1960–1964	7.0	8.8	4.5	7.0
Sudan	1961–1970	5.1	21.8	25.1	13.6
Tunisia	1962–1970	6.0	8.0	2.0	4.4
United Arab Republic (Egypt)	1960–1970	7.3	13.5	27.3	11.5
West Africa					
Ghana	1963–1969	5.5	8.5 [a]	—	—
Mali	1961–1965	8.0	21.0 [a]	—	—
Mauritania	1963–1966	9.2	30.0	148.0	10.0
Nigeria	1962–1968	4.0	—	—	—
Senegal	1960–1965	8.0	15.5 [a]	—	7.2
East Africa					
Ethiopia	1963–1967	4.3	27.3	52.6	19.4
Kenya	1964–1970	5.2	5.3	3.0	8.7
Madagascar	1964–1968	5.5	—	—	—
Malawi	1964–1969	—	—	—	—
Uganda	1961–1965	4.5	—	—	—
United Republic of Tanzania	1964–1969	6.7	14.8	4.2	12.3
Zambia	1966–1970	6.5	19.4	3.0	5.6
Central Africa					
Cameroon	1961–1965	5.5	—	—	—
Congo (Democratic Republic of)	1965–1969	7.0	14–16 [b]	5–6	—

The table has an overarching column header "Planned Annual Growth Rates" spanning the Gross Domestic Product, Manufacturing, Mining, and Electricity, Gas and Water columns.

Sources: National development plans.

[a] Including mining and electricity.
[b] Including construction and electricity.

large number of countries, considerable attention has been given and sizable investment allocations have been devoted to the improvement and expansion of transport facilities, power and water utilities, communication systems and other infrastructure required for the removal of existing bottlenecks to the growth of manufacturing, mining and other commodity-producing sectors. Allocations of planned investment, particularly in the 'public sector, for the development of these basic facilities have been large, often larger than the share of manufacturing in total planned investment. Table 9 shows the share of basic facilities, compared with the share of manufacturing and other industrial sectors, in the total planned investments in a number of countries in the subregions of Africa.

Although it is not easy to reduce the complexity and multiplicity of industrial activities and products into a few broad categories, such categorization has been attempted and followed in the United Nations study, *Patterns of Industrial Growth, 1938–1958*,[7] as well as in other studies concerning industrial development. Industry has been classified broadly into "consumer goods" and "producer goods," the latter comprising both intermediate products and capital equipment. Industry has also been subdivided into two groups, namely, "heavy" manufacturing and "light" manufacturing, the former corresponding to the intermediate and capital goods industries and the latter to the consumer-goods industries. Although these classifications are not fully satisfactory

Table 8—Share of Industry in Total Public Investment in Preplan Period and in Total Planned Investment, Selected African Countries (Percentage of Totals)

Subregion and Country	Share in Public Investment		Share in Total Planned Investment	
	Preplan Period	Plan Period	Private	Total
North Africa				
Algeria	2.5[a]	—	—	—
Morocco	2.1[b]	28	—	22.8
Sudan	9.0[c]	—	—	16.2
Tunisia	0.3[a]	—	—	—
United Arab Republic (Egypt)	2.1[a]	23	—	28.8
West Africa				
Cameroon	0.4[d]	10	—	—
Ghana	5.0	32	—	23.2
Guinea	—	18	—	—
Mali	—	14	—	14.0
Mauritania	—	50	—	41.0
Nigeria	9.0	29	—	13.0
Senegal	—	44	—	36.0
East Africa				
Ethiopia	2.0	28	28	28.0
Kenya	—	20	—	—
Madagascar	0.3[d]	5	36	16.0
Malawi	—	24	—	—
Uganda	—	19	28	21.0
United Republic of Tanzania	—	16	38	26.0
Zambia	—	7	70	51.0

Sources: National economic and social development plans; and United Nations, *Economic Developments in Africa, 1954–1955* (United Nations publication, Sales No. 56.II.C.3); *Economic Developments in Africa, 1955–1956* (United Nations publication, Sales No. 57.II.C.3).

[a] 1951–1953.
[b] 1954.
[c] 1939–1956.
[d] 1940–1955.

for analytical purposes, the "light-goods industries" include food, beverages and tobacco products, textiles, clothing, apparel and footwear, leather products, rubber products, printing and publishing. The "heavy-goods industries" cover paper, chemicals, non-metallic mineral products, basic metals, metal products, and machinery and equipment, both electrical and non-electrical.

A very broad and rough distribution of major groups of manufactures, comprising both the light-goods and heavy-goods industries among the subregions of Africa in 1958, is shown in Table 10. The figures show the percentage distribution of value added in each major group of industries for Africa as a whole, among its subregions. Neither the light-goods nor the heavy-goods industries are distributed evenly among the subregions.

Both categories of manufacturing have been concentrated in Southern Africa, followed by North Africa, with the three other subregions contributing together about 17 per cent of the output of light industries and a similar percentage of the output of heavy-manufacturing industries of the whole region.

The distribution by country of the value added from manufacturing among major groups comprising both light and heavy industries for 1960 or thereabouts, presents differences in the structure and development of the manufacturing sector (see Table 11).

In recent years, the share of value added

Table 9—Share in Total Planned Investment for the Development of Basic Facilities and of Industry, Selected African Countries (Percentage of Totals)

Subregions and Country	Plan Periods	Percentage of Total Planned Investment	
		Basic Facilities[a]	Industry[b]
North Africa			
Libya	1963–1968	38.6	4.0
Morocco	1957–1965	9.7	22.8
Sudan	1961–1970	39.7	—
Tunisia	1962–1971	—	—
United Arab Republic (Egypt)	1960–1970	27.8	28.8
West Africa			
Ghana	1963–1970	23.0[c]	20.0[c]
Mali	1961–1965	48.0	14.0
Mauritania	1963–1966	50.0	30.0
Nigeria	1962–1968	45.0[c]	12.0[c]
Senegal	1961–1965	—	—
Sierra Leone	1962–1967	37.0[c]	9.0[c]
Upper Volta	1963–1967	28.0	22.0
East Africa			
Ethiopia	1963–1967	35.0[d]	28.0
Kenya	1964–1970	23.0[c,d]	20.0[c]
Madagascar	1964–1971	50.0[d]	16.0
Malawi	1965–1969	33.0[c,d]	24.0[c]
Uganda	1961–1966	17.0[d]	21.0
United Republic of Tanzania	1967–1969	37.0[c,d]	16.0[c]
Zambia	1966–1970	40.0[c,d]	17.0[c]
Central Africa			
Cameroon	1961–1965	10.0[c]	41.0[c]

Sources: National development plans for the periods given.

[a] Including electricity, gas, water, transport and communication.
[b] Manufacturing and processing, and mining.
[c] Public investment only.
[d] Including also construction and housing.

originating in the various light-manufacturing industries has accounted for 75 per cent or more of the total value added in manufacturing in the majority of African countries —Burundi, Ethiopia, Ghana, Ivory Coast, Libya, Malawi, Mauritius, Rwanda, the Sudan, etc. In some of these countries, for example, Burundi, Ethiopia and Rwanda, the share of heavy industries has been as low as 7 to 10 per cent of the total manufactured output. This is probably also the case in such countries as Niger and Somalia, where the size of the manufacturing sector as a whole is also reported to be rather small, and industry is in the initial stage of development.

In those countries where manufacturing had an early beginning and the light consumer-goods industries have been relatively more developed, the shift of emphasis in more recent years towards the development of heavy-manufacturing industries can be detected in the change of composition of investment in manufacture, as is illustrated in the economic and social development plans of several African countries, among which the United Arab Republic, Tunisia and Senegal may be mentioned.[8]

The sectoral structure of manufacturing is more or less closely related to the level of industrial development. This is as true in African countries as it has been elsewhere in the world. In the earlier stages of development, light industries, including food, beverages, tobacco products, textiles, clothing and footwear, are generally favoured over heavy industries, such as chemicals, basic metals, metal products and engineering industries, because of the combined impact of capital intensity, the degree of skills required, and the size of the market for the supply of which the industry may be established. With the exception of a few countries in which basic metal industries have been developed on a large scale for exports (e.g., Southern Rhodesia and Zambia within the copper belt) and of South Africa, where metallurgy, chemicals and rubber are relatively advanced, as well as some North African countries where chemicals and certain basic metal and metal products industries have been developed, light manufacturing is preponderant in Africa at the current time. Thus, the share of heavy manufacturing varies from less than 10 per cent in some countries, to more than 50 per cent in a few others. Countries belonging to the latter group include South Africa,

Table 10—The Distribution of Output of Major Groups of Industries Among the African Subregions, 1958
(Percentage of Totals of Major Groups)

Major Groups of Manufacturing	Southern Africa	North Africa	Central Africa	East and West Africa	Total Africa
Light industries					
Food, beverages and tobacco [a]	37	39	17	7	100
Textiles	25	65	9	1	100
Clothing, foot-wear, apparel	79	15	5	1	100
Wood products and furniture	60	16	8	16	100
Paper and paper products [b]	78	16	4	2	100
Total	47	36	6	11	100
Heavy industries					
Chemicals, rubber, petroleum [c]	60	27	6	7	100
Non-metallic mineral products	49	26	20	5	100
Basic metals	54	4	36	6	100
Metal products, machinery [d]	73	19	7	1	100
Total	64	19	13	4	100

Source: Data derived from United Nations; *Statistical Yearbook, 1962* (Sales No. 63.XVII.1); see also International Labour Organisation, Second African Regional Conference, Addis Ababa, 1964, *Report of the Director General*, p. 127, Appendix Table 10.

[a] Including processing of agricultural raw materials in the subregions.
[b] Including printing and publishing in the subregions.
[c] Including petroleum and coal products.
[d] Including electric machinery and transport equipment.

Southern Rhodesia and Zambia, but it is only in South Africa that the branches of heavy industry can be said to be appreciably diversified.

However, in many countries at a low level of industrialization, increasing weight has been given in recent years to the development of a number of specific branches of heavy industries, including cement, non-metallic mineral products, fertilizers and other chemical products, in addition to a number of metal products, including table and kitchen utensils, simple tools and implements, or to the assembled production of some transport equipment, refrigeration units and other electric appliances based largely on imported parts for domestic assembly.

A variety of developmental undertakings for heavy industry along the lines cited are planned or are under way in a number of African countries with various degrees of industrialization. Planned development of cement and other non-metallic mineral products exists in the plans of Ethiopia, Ghana, the Sudan, Tunisia, the United Arab Republic and various other countries. Further development of chemicals and fertilizers has been planned or is under way in Ethiopia, Nigeria, Senegal, the Sudan, Tunisia and the United Arab Republic. Plants for the assembling of agricultural and transport equipment are incorporated in the plans of Mali, the United Arab Republic and a number of East and West African countries. Iron and steel mills are planned for Liberia and Nigeria in West Africa, for the Maghreb countries of North Africa and for Uganda and Zambia in East Africa, while in Southern Rhodesia and the United Arab Republic, substantial expansions in iron and steel production are being visualized. The aluminium metal and products industry is included in the plans for Ghana, the United Arab Republic and a few other countries.

The foregoing examples show the tendency towards diversification and selectivity in the development of heavy-manufacturing industries in various African countries. In a number of these countries, the planned growth rate of heavy industry has been set at a greater pace than the planned development of light-manufacturing industries. In formulating their current plans, many countries recognized the increasing volume and values of the intermediate products and capital goods required to attain the projected high growth rates for their economies and, accordingly, placed considerable emphasis on expanding the production of certain commodities in the capital-goods and the intermediate-goods industries.

The Influence of Foreign Trade on the Structure and Growth Pattern of Manufacturing Development

In most African countries, the bulk of development in manufacturing which took place during the Second World War and in the postwar period was largely oriented to produce import substitutes, and in a number of them, the outstanding growth was mainly in the export-oriented industries. Most of the export-oriented industries have been based on available resources in the countries, including a relatively abundant output of minerals or farm and forest products which are processed or manufactured for exports. The industries thus established have included both resource-oriented and market-oriented ones. Vivid examples of these include the basic non-ferrous metal industries in the copper belt, as well as in East and North Africa; the wood products industry in Gabon, Ghana, Ivory Coast, Kenya, Nigeria and South Africa; the fish processing industry in Angola, Morocco and South West Africa; and the vegetable oil industry in Nigeria, Senegal and other West and North African countries. These are in addition to the simple processing of cocoa beans, coffee beans, tea leaves, sisal into fibres and other agricultural products for exportation, which is undertaken by a number of countries, including Ghana, Kenya, Nigeria, Uganda and the United Republic of Tanzania, among others.

The development of light manufacturing, such as food, beverages, tobacco, textiles, clothing, footwear, furniture, soap, perfumery and other consumer goods, had been

Table 11—Structure of Manufacturing: Percentage Distribution of Value Added Among Major Groups of Light and Heavy Industries in Countries Under African Subregions, 1960[a]

Subregion and Country	Light Industries				Heavy Industries			Other Industries
	Food, Beverages, and Tobacco	Textiles, Clothing and Leather	Wood and Furniture	Paper, Printing and Publishing	Chemicals, Petroleum, Coal and Rubber	Non-metallic Mineral Products	Basic Metals, Metal Products, Machinery, etc.	
North Africa								
Algeria	40	11	4	3	5	9	23	2
Libya	50	11	—	—	5	—	20	1
Morocco	38	23	4	3	5	6	4	1
Sudan	62	5	—	5	9	10	18	—
Tunisia	38	19	5	3	10	5	18	2
United Arab Republic (Egypt)	24	46	2	4	10	5	8	1
West Africa								
Ghana	38	1	42	3	4	2	9	1
Guinea	—	—	—	—	—	—	—	—
Ivory Coast	47	14	14	2	8	—	10	4
Mauritania	—	—	—	—	—	—	—	—
Nigeria	37	4	17	—	27	4	5	7
Senegal	53	6	2	2	1	3	7	7
Sierra Leone	—	—	—	—	—	—	26	—

	Col 1	Col 2	Col 3	Col 4	Col 5	Col 6	Col 7	Col 8
East Africa								
Ethiopia	45	38	3	2	1	5	—	6
Kenya	38	8	10	3	12	11	18	1
Malawi	53	4	3	2	—	—	9	29
Southern Rhodesia	24	15	4	2	9	6	30	10
Uganda	—	—	—	—	—	—	—	—
United Republic of Tanzania	—	—	—	—	—	—	—	—
Zambia	33	3	5	—	—	14	38	7
Central Africa								
Cameroon	19	—	—	—	—	—	—	—
Central African Republic	—	27	—	—	—	54	—	—
Chad	—	—	—	—	—	—	—	—
Congo (Brazzaville)	—	—	—	—	—	—	—	—
Congo (Democratic Republic of)	—	—	—	—	—	—	—	—
Gabon	—	—	—	—	—	—	—	—
Southern Africa								
Mozambique	48	—	—	—	—	52	—	—
Rwanda-Burundi	80	11	—	4	—	2	—	3
South Africa	19	14	5	12	9	7	31	3
Africa as a region	25	25	8.6	1.2	5.2	7	21.3	6.0
Africa excluding Southern Africa	29	30	9.1	0.6	4.4	6.5	14.3	6.0

Source: United Nations.

a Data refer to 1960 or thereabouts.

Table 12—Changes in the Composition of Imports by African Countries, 1950–1960
(Percentage of Total Value of Imports for the Years Stated)

Subregion and Country	Food, Beverages and Tobacco			Other Consumer Goods			Fuel, Raw Materials and Semi-Finished Goods			Machinery and Equipment		
	1950	1955	1960	1950	1955	1960	1950	1955	1960	1950	1955	1960
North Africa												
Algeria	22	21	24	35	36	32	25	27	22	18	16	19
Morocco	25	24	21	28	33	27	26	28	38	21	15	14
Tunisia	16	21	19	39	37	30	27	29	32	18	13	19
Sudan	36	26	17	23	26	23	29	31	36	12	17	24
United Arab Republic (Egypt)	30	18	22	18	17	7	37	47	46	15	21	25
West Africa												
Ghana	—	22[a]	19	—	46[a]	42	—	15[a]	13	—	17[a]	26
Liberia	—	22	18	—	46	37	—	7	12	—	25	33
Nigeria	—	14[b]	14	—	54[b]	51	—	10[b]	11	—	22[b]	24
Sierra Leone	—	25[b]	23	—	46[b]	50	—	10[b]	10	—	19[b]	17
Togo	—	19	14	—	52	—	—	21	—	—	8	31
East Africa												
Kenya	15	—	8	42	—	40	18	—	34	25	—	18
Mozambique	—	14	—	—	40	—	—	17	—	—	29	—
Rhodesia and Nyasaland	—	10	8	—	47	46	—	9	10	—	34	36
Central Africa												
Cameroon	—	17	19	—	39	36	—	19	12	—	25	23
Congo (Democratic Republic of)	—	12	11	—	21	22	—	32	31	—	35	36
Southern Africa												
South Africa[c]	7	5	5	27	34	20	33	23	28	33	38	37

Sources: *Economic Survey of Africa Since 1950* (Sales No. 59.II.K.1); National publications of trade statistics; United Nations, *Yearbook of International Trade Statistics, 1960* (Sales No. 61.XVII.9); United Nations, *Economic Bulletin for Africa*, Vol. II, No. 1 (Sales No. 62.II.K.1).

[a] Data refer to 1957.
[b] Data refer to 1956.
[c] Data include South West Africa.

taking place in a wide range of countries in order to provide the domestic markets with substitutes for imports. More recently, in a smaller number of countries, the development of import substitutes has moved gradually into branches of manufacturing industries producing intermediate goods and a variety of capital goods, as mentioned previously.

African countries in the early stages of their industrialization rely upon enlarging the share of domestic production of consumer products, especially of light consumer goods for the domestic market, to reduce their dependence upon imports and to free foreign-exchange earnings for the importation of capital and producer goods, the production of which requires more intensive capital and relatively more advanced technologies, as well as a higher level of skills. Other countries at more advanced stages of industrialization move forward in the direction of the development of import substitutes of heavy consumer goods, producer goods and a variety of capital equipment. However, with the probable exception of South Africa, none of the African countries has reached the stage of industrial development where the expansion of industries for heavy consumer goods and the development of intermediate goods industries have not resulted in the increased growth of imports of semi-finished goods and raw materials required for the expansion of the established heavy industries.

Available data on the volume and composition of imports in several countries where import-substitute industries expanded between 1950 and 1960 indicate that the share of light consumer goods in total value of imports decreased between the 1950's and

1960's. By contrast, imports of intermediate producer goods and of capital equipment increased appreciably, resulting in a growing balance-of-trade deficit.

Table 12 shows the change in the composition of imports for the period 1950 to 1960 in a number of African countries at different stages of manufacturing development. Although the share of food, beverages, tobacco and some other consumer goods in the total value of imports fell between 1950 and 1960, the share of fuel, raw materials and semi-finished goods rose during the same period. In addition, the share of machinery and equipment in total value of imports has risen greatly in the majority of countries shown in Table 12.

Excluding Southern Africa, the value of imports in the rest of the continent increased by approximately 147 per cent between 1950 and 1963, the increase being much larger in the imports of machinery and transport equipment (by about 181 per cent) and in the imports of intermediate goods, which increased by almost 159 per cent in comparison with an expansion of only 143 per cent (in value terms) in the imports of consumer goods. During the same period, the share of consumer goods declined from 42 per cent to 35 per cent of the total value of commodity imports, whereas the share of imports of intermediate goods rose slightly, from 29 per cent in 1950 to 34 per cent of the value of imports in 1963. However, the share of machinery and transport equipment rose from 29 per cent of the value of imports in 1950 to 31 per cent in 1963 (see Table 13).

Table 13—Changes in the Structure of Imports of Manufactured Goods by Africa, 1950–1963[a]

Groups of Imports	Value of Imports (Millions of Dollars)		Percentage Change Between 1950 and 1963 (1950 = 100)
	1950	1963	
Consumer goods	976	2,000	143
Intermediate goods	705	1,958	159
Machinery and transport equipment	691	1,748	181
Total imports	2,372	5,705	147

Source: See annex.

[a] Excluding Southern Africa.

IMPORT-SUBSTITUTION OBJECTIVES

The target outputs in the development plans of African countries, whenever such targets have been stated, emphasize the goal of raising the manufactured output of light consumer goods, in general, and of a number of durable consumer goods to a lesser extent, in an attempt to reduce the share of consumer goods in total commodity imports. The projected annual growth rates of total imports and exports in the development plans of a variety of countries, in comparison with the growth rates of fixed capital formation and of consumption (both private and public), are given in Table 14. The figures show that for seven countries—namely, the Congo (Brazzaville), Ghana, Mauritania, Nigeria, the Sudan, Tunisia and the United Arab Republic—total imports are expected to grow at a much slower pace than total

exports. In their plans, stress has been placed on the rapid expansion of substitutes for imported consumer goods and, in a few of these countries, for a variety of producer goods.

On the other hand, in the plans of five countries—Ivory Coast, Kenya, Mali, Morocco and the United Republic of Tanzania—available data indicate that the projected rates of growth of imports are appreciably higher than those for exports, but much lower than the planned annual growth rates of capital formation. The rapid increase in the planned rates of capital formation—unaccompanied by a corresponding emphasis on the rapid growth of domestic output of heavy manufacturing of the capital goods and intermediate products required for the realization of the projected rapid growth of domestic product—necessitates a higher incremental rate of imports of these goods. Unfortunately, data are scanty on the composition of projected imports in the current plans of most African countries.

Table 14—Projected Rates of Growth of Imports and Exports in the Development Plans of Selected African Countries (Annual Compound Growth Rates)

Subregion and Country	Imports	Exports	Capital Formation	Consumption Private	Consumption Public
North Africa					
Morocco	7.0	4.8	19.4	4.4	6.4
Sudan	2.0	4.7	4.9	4.3	5.6
Tunisia	2.5	7.2	10.3	−4.0	—
United Arab Republic	−1.2	11.5	11.5	4.9	4.4
West Africa					
Ghana	4.8	5.3	8.0	−5.9	—
Ivory Coast	6.9	6.3	10.3	6.2	4.9
Mali	12.2	9.0	—	—	—
Mauritania	−0.5	49.4	−8.0	5.1	3.2
Nigeria	4.0	5.5	5.6	−4.4	—
Senegal	—	—	14.0	—	—
East Africa					
Ethiopia	—	—	12.2	3.3	7.5
Kenya	11.2 [a]	5.5	—	—	—
Uganda	—	—	—	—	—
United Republic of Tanzania	6.6	5.1	14.6	4.7	5.0
Zambia	—	—	8.6 [b]	6.0	8.6
Central Africa					
Congo (Brazzaville)	3.3	9.5	19.2	—	—
Congo (Democratic Republic of)	12–21 [a]	—	14–16	—	—

Sources: Data derived from national economic and social development plans of countries stated; also, United Nations Economic and Social Council, Economic Commission for Africa, "Outlines and selected indicators of African development plans (E/CN.14/336), 14 January 1965.

[a] Capital goods imports only.
[b] Government investment only, growth rates of private investment projected at 15.5 per cent per annum.

Data on the distribution of planned imports between consumer goods, producer goods and capital equipment are available, however, for a few countries—Ghana, Kenya, Mali, Nigeria, Senegal and the United Arab Republic. These data, which are given in Table 15, indicate that while imports of capital goods have to expand at an annual rate of 3.8 per cent in the United Arab Republic and at about 11.2 per cent in Kenya, in the latter country, imports of producer and consumer goods would increase by 6.1 per cent and 2.1 per cent, respectively. In the United Arab Republic, where planned expansion of manufacturing and mining not only stresses the rapid development of substitutes for producer and consumer goods, but also gives high priority to the production of capital equipment, the plan anticipates a reduction of imports of consumer goods at a rate of 1.2 per cent per annum, and a reduction of imports of producer goods at an annual rate of 4.0 per cent,

while imports of capital equipment would continue to expand at a rate of 3.8 per cent per annum.

Planned imports into Ghana, Mali, Nigeria and Senegal, taken together, indicate that the projected rates of growth of both producer goods and capital equipment are much higher than the rates for imports of consumer goods, which would be significantly cut down by the planned expansion of import substitutes in these countries. Table 16 shows the relative emphasis placed on the development of light and heavy manufactures as areas of import substitution in a number of African countries where available data permit such comparisons.

Manufactured imports still account for a very high percentage of gross manufactured output (in terms of value added) in African

Table 15—Annual Growth Rate Planned for Imports of Consumer Goods, Producer Goods and Capital Equipment

Country	Total Imports	Consumer Goods	Producer Goods	Capital Goods
U.A.R.	−1.2	−2.2	−4.0	+3.8
Ghana Mali Nigeria Senegal	+4.0	+0.6	+6.2	+6.2
Kenya	+5.5	+2.1	+6.1	+11.2

Sources: National plans of economic and social development.

Table 16—The Share of Light Consumer[a] and Heavy Industries[b] in Total Planned Investment[c] in Manufacturing and in Total Increase in Manufactured output, Selected African Countries
(Percentage)

Country	Planned Growth Rates		Share of Light Consumer Goods in Total Manufacturing		Share of Heavy Manufacturing in Total	
	Total Manufacturing	Light Consumer Goods	Increase in Output	Investment	Increase in Output	Investment
Ethiopia	27.3	22.3	69.2	37.5	30.8	62.5
Ghana	8.0	11.9	72.7	—	27.3	—
Senegal	15.5	8.0	45.2	36.5	54.8	63.5
Sudan	21.2	—	—	95.7[d]	—	4.3[d]
Tunisia	8.0	7.1	44.6	23.7[c]	55.4	76.3[e]
U.A.R.	13.4	7.6	28.4	22.7	71.6	77.3

Source: Based on national development plans of countries stated.

[a] Food, beverages, tobacco, textiles, clothing and foot-wear industries.
[b] Durable consumer goods, producer goods and capital-equipment industries.
[c] Gross fixed investment unless otherwise specified.
[d] Net public investment only.
[e] Net investment.

countries for which data are available (see Table 17). In recent years, imports of manufactured goods corresponded to between one-fourth and one-third of gross value of production of the domestic manufacturing sector in only a few countries (including the United Arab Republic and South Africa, where the rate of import substitution was highest in comparison with most other African countries). In other countries, the rate of substitution of manufactured imports through the development in this direction of domestic output of manufacturing has not resulted in larger declines in manufactured imports as a percentage of domestic manufacturing output. Manufactured imports amounted to between 55 per cent and more than 75 per cent of domestically manufactured output in Algeria, Gabon, Morocco and Tunisia (to cite some examples) and were higher than 92 per cent in Chad, Ghana, Nigeria and the Sudan (to cite other examples). In many other countries, the value of manufactured imports outstrips that of domestic manufactured output and, in some

cases, is more than double, as in Cameroon and the Congo (Brazzaville). These figures would indicate that greater perspective and wider scope for the substantial development of import substitutes industries exist, except in those relatively more developed countries where the manufactured imports constitute but a small percentage of domestic manufacturing output. For further manufacturing development of the latter countries, more attention should be devoted to the growth and expansion of export-oriented industries in future years. South Africa has been successful in the development of import substitutes and in the expansion of manufactured exports through the establishment of export-oriented industries. By 1960, the value of manufactured imports into South Africa amounted to about 485.5 million South African pounds, and the country exported in the same year domestically manufactured products valued at approximately £SA179.3 million, nearly 36.9 per cent of the value of its manufactured imports. In the United Arab Republic, where substitution for imports of light and heavy consumer goods has gone a long way in reducing the share of such

Table 17—Total Demand for Industrial Products and Share Contribution of Domestic Industries, Selected African Countries, for the Years Noted (Millions of Dollars)

Subregion and Country	Value of Imports	Value Added by Domestic Industry	Total Demand	Domestic Output as Percentage of Total Demand
North Africa				
Algeria[a]	237.0	303.9	541.0	56.1
Morocco[a]	122.0	207.5	329.5	63.0
Sudan[a]	15.1	16.4	31.5	52.0
Tunisia[a]	56.3	81.4	127.7	63.7
U.A.R. (Egypt)[a]	517.4	1,628.8	2,146.2	75.9
West Africa				
Ghana[a]	355.7	29.4	385.1	7.6
Nigeria[a]	547.0	44.0	591.0	7.5
Central Africa				
Cameroon[b]	76.5	36.5	113.0	32.3
Central African Republic[b]	20.4	21.2	41.6	51.0
Chad[b]	19.9	30.0	49.9	60.1
Congo (Brazzaville)	48.6	21.2	69.8	30.4
Congo (Democratic Republic of)	243.8	226.0	469.8	48.1
Gabon[b]	39.6	8.6	48.2	17.8
Southern Africa				
South Africa[c]	1,369.3	1,384.0	2,753.3	50.2

Source: United Nations Economic Commission for Africa, Industry Division, 1965.

[a] Data refer to 1960/1961.
[b] Data refer to 1963/1964.
[c] Data refer to 1960.

goods in total imports, attempts are being made to push forward manufactured exports of long-established industries like cotton and rayon textiles, leather and shoes, cement and furniture, as well as products of more recent industries, such as rubber products, chemicals, metal works and engineering industries, in an effort to secure the larger amounts of foreign exchange required to sustain higher levels of capital formation and accelerated rates of economic growth. In recent years, however, the value of manufactured goods exported by the United Arab Republic has accounted for only 10 per cent to 12 per cent of the value of imports of manufactured products. Table 18 shows the value of manufactured goods exported by a number of African countries in recent years.

Probably the greater number of imports used in manufacturing in Africa consist of intermediate goods which have not as yet reached the stage of final production by industries on the continent. However, Africa is a producer of a variety of the raw materials which go into the making of a long list of intermediate goods, which, in turn, are used in manufacturing on the continent. Nevertheless, a great number of African countries import from outside the region an increasing volume of intermediate manufactures, the basic inputs of which may have originated in Africa. Africa, as a whole, is a net importer of leather for shoes, wood for furniture and fixtures, wood-pulp for paper, metal products from non-ferrous metals, tanning materials for leather, dyeing products for textiles, etc. In the meantime, it is a net exporter of hides and skins, sawn wood, basic non-ferrous metals (including copper, tin, zinc, lead and aluminium), pigments, indigo, coal-tar dyes and other tanning and dyeing materials, all of which go into the corresponding imported intermediate goods. It seems that these input goods could be produced locally from domestic materials for use partly by the growing industries and also for exports at higher values than are obtained from their exportation in primary form. It is also evident that intraregional trade in such goods is very limited in extent, which partially explains the lack of co-ordinated development of manufacturing among African countries, in addition to the fact that production of inter-

mediate goods needed for inputs in existing industries is quite underdeveloped in many African countries.

EXPORT-DEVELOPMENT OBJECTIVES

It has been one of the stated aims of African countries to diversify their production and exports. One of the several forms that this policy has generally taken is the development of local processing of primary commodities and the expansion of industrial capacity. Progress in diversification of manufactured output has generally been felt in import substitution more than in the export trade. Steps which had been taken for the processing of primary products as an auxiliary to the export trade before independence had met, in some cases, with unfavourable reactions from the metropolitan country, resulting, for example, in import quotas and other forms of protection for the metropolitan industry. Actions of this type had been noted in Senegal in the ground-nut processing industry after the Second World War, and the rapid expansion of the same industry was discouraged in Nigeria until more recent times. Similarly, the Ghanaian attempt at diversification of exports had been confined within the extractive sector, but its current plan of development emphasizes the expansion of production for exports of cocoa products, timber, sawmill products and aluminium, in an effort to provide the base for the development of processing industries, they are projected to contribute significantly to the over-all industrialization programme.

The rather restricted range of exports in the majority of African countries gave rise in a number of them to the processing of primary products, as in the case of copper exports from the Democratic Republic of the Congo. Southern Rhodesia and Zambia; crude sugar and molasses from Mauritius and Mozambique, and to some extent, from Angola; fish products from Angola and South West Africa; and sawn woods from Gabon, Ghana, Nigeria and other West and Central African countries. These woods

Table 18—Value of Manufactured Exports in 1963, Distributed Between Groups of Industries, by Country

Subregion and Country	Currency Units	Food, Beverages, Tobacco	Textiles, Clothing, Leather	Timber, Wood Products	Chemicals	Metals, Metal Products	Oils, Fats and By-Products	Cement, Glass, etc.
North Africa								
Algeria								
Libya								
Morocco	Million dirham	241.1	13.4	—	23.8	18.2	0.3	1.5
Sudan	Million pounds	—	—	—	—	—	—	—
Tunisia								
U.A.R. (Egypt)	Million Egyptian pounds	25.0	29.2	0.2	0.3	—	1.2	2.0
West Africa								
Dahomey	Thousand million francs	0.1	—	—	0.02	—	0.47	—
Ghana	Million pounds	3.6	—	13.1	1.3	—	0.1	—
Guinea								
Ivory Coast	Thousand million francs	1.2	0.2	12.4	0.1	—	0.07	—
Mali	Thousand million francs	0.51	0.02	—	—	—	0.04	—
Niger	Thousand million francs	0.08	—	—	—	—	0.25	—
Nigeria	Million pounds	2.9	—	6.8	0.2	—	16.1	—
Senegal	Thousand million francs	2.6	0.2	—	0.09	0.32	11.52	—
Sierra Leone	Million pounds	—	—	—	—	—	0.03	—
Central Africa								
Cameroon	Thousand million francs	1.84	—	1.83	0.02	—	0.11	—
Congo (Democratic Republic of)	Thousand million francs	—	0.04	0.48	—	12.43	2.78	0.07
Gabon	Thousand million francs	—	—	9.46	0.12	—	—	—
East Africa								
Ethiopia	Million Ethiopian dollars	7.02	—	—	0.03	—	1.33	—
Kenya	Million pounds	4.53	—	0.14	2.04	0.70	0.26	0.50
Malawi ⎱ Southern Rhodesia ⎰ Zambia	Million pounds	5.33	2.11	—	—	129.8	0.39	—
Uganda	Million pounds	0.31	—	0.08	—	3.61	1.66	—
Tanganyika	Million pounds	1.20	—	0.31	0.39	—	1.50	—
Southern Africa								
South Africa	Million South African pounds	75.0	—	—	31.32	—	8.93	—

Source: United Nations, *Yearbook of International Trade Statistics, 1963* (Sales No. 64.XVII.4).

largely pass through simple shaping and rounding before exportation.

Simple preparation of natural rubber into crude rubber for exportation has been taking place in the major producing countries of Africa, namely, Cameroon, the Democratic Republic of the Congo, Liberia and Nigeria. The hides and skins which are being salted and dried for exportation in many countries of West, East and North Africa could have been the subject of expansion of the leather and leather-goods industries, adding to the value of their exports.

The value of exports of the simply prepared products of extractive industries, as well as of a number of manufactured goods proper, increased significantly in a large number of African countries between the 1950's and 1960's, as shown in Table 19. With a more advanced stage of industrial development, these manufactured exports tend to become more diversified, particularly in those African countries where the output of resources, including industrial resources, has attained some measure of diversification, i.e., South Africa since the early 1950's, and Algeria, Kenya, Morocco, Southern Rhodesia, and the United Arab Republic in more recent years. It is to be noted, however, that the bulk of exports of manufactured products is largely concentrated in a few commodities or a few major groups of industries. Thus, textiles, petroleum products and milled rice are by far the leading exports of manufacture in the United Arab Republic, accounting for about 82 per cent of Egyptian manufactured exports in 1963; non-ferrous basic metals, iron and steel products, meat products, clothing and footwear accounted for more than 96 per cent of the combined exports of manufactured products by Malawi and Southern Rhodesia in the same year. In recent years, more than two-thirds of the processed exports of Algeria and Morocco have belonged to the food, alcoholic beverages, pulp, leather, textiles and chemical industries.

Food products, oils, fats and by-products are predominant in the manufactured exports of Dahomey, Madagascar, Mali, Niger, Nigeria, Senegal and the United Republic of Tanzania. Crude metals and basic non-ferrous metals constitute the bulk of exports

of industrial products from the Congo (Democratic Republic of), Southern Rhodesia, Uganda and Zambia. Wood, lumber and products make up the highest percentage of industrial exports from Gabon, Ghana and Ivory Coast, and come second to vegetable oil exports from Nigeria. The so-called "industrial exports" of a number of countries would, however, more appropriately belong to mining rather than manufacturing output, as in the case of Guinea, Sierra Leone and the United Republic of Tanzania, in which unpolished and uncut diamonds account for the bulk of major industrial exports. Textile products have been substantial in the total value of manufactured exports of a few countries of Africa, including the former Federation of Rhodesia and Nyasaland, South Africa and the United Arab Republic, and, to a lesser extent, Cameroon, the Congo (Democratic Republic of), Ivory Coast, Mali, Morocco and Senegal, countries for which details of manufactured exports are more or less available.

A larger number of countries gained in exports of chemicals, but in only a few of them, e.g., Morocco and South Africa, do chemicals account for more than 10 per cent of total manufactured exports. Exports of non-metallic mineral products, such as cement, lime, ceramics and glass, appear in the foreign trade of a number of countries— the Congo (Democratic Republic of), Kenya, Morocco, Southern Rhodesia and the United Arab Republic—but most other countries endeavour to expand these branches for import substitutes more than for exportation.

Exports of domestically produced machinery, electrical machinery and transport equipment have been relatively developed in South Africa and are almost negligible in most other countries. A few countries of Africa recently attempted to produce for exportation a relatively small surplus of a variety of mechanical and electro-engineering products which belong to some branches of the three major groups of industries comprising machinery, electrical machinery and transport equipment. Cited cases in recent

Table 19—Development of Manufactured Exports in African Countries

Subregion and Country	Currency Units	Value of Manufactured Exports (in Current Prices)			Manufactured Exports as Percentage of Total Commodity Exports		
		1950	1959	1963	1950	1959	1963
North Africa							
Algeria	Million francs	67.7	—	—	68.3	—	—
Libya	Million pounds	0.44	0.59	0.13	12.0	16.1	0.1
Morocco	Million dirham	—	407	389	—	28.2	30.3
Sudan	Million pounds	1.41	2.16	4.28	2.9	3.2	5.3
Tunisia	Thousand million dinar	—	28.8	—	—	48.4	—
U.A.R. (Egypt)	Million Egyptian pounds	18.9	34.2	65.3	13.2	22.1	28.7
West Africa							
Dahomey	Thousand million francs	—	1.02	0.71	—	22.4	22.3
Gambia	Million pounds	—	0.11	0.10	—	3.9	3.0
Ghana	Million pounds	7.31	22.05	22.40	7.1	21.7	—
Liberia	Million dollars	—	4.14	7.63	—	6.2	11.2
Mali	Thousand million francs	—	1.15	0.62	—	33.4	23.7
Nigeria	Million pounds	20.9	22.9	36.7	24.7	14.2	19.8
Senegal	Thousand million francs	—	1.40	1.62	—	48.9	59.0
Sierra Leone	Million pounds	—	6.03	16.51	—	36.7	64.9
Togo	Million francs	—	316	246	—	8.8	5.5
East Africa							
Ethiopia	Million Ethiopian dollars	3.84	6.26	12.52	—	3.8	5.8
Kenya	Million pounds	} 4.29	} 12.82	11.61	} 63	} 10.7	26.5
Uganda	Million pounds			5.77			11.2
Tanganyika	Million pounds			10.19	12.1		16.3
Madagascar	Million francs		5,039	5,843		27.8	28.8
Malawi	Million pounds	} 101.97	} 123.48	} 140.36	} 70.9	} 67.6	} 69.9
Southern Rhodesia	Million pounds						
Zambia	Million pounds						
Mauritius	Million rupees	—	170	414	—	98.8	98.1
Mozambique	Million escudos	—	71.5	543.5	—	3.7	18.8
Southern Africa							
South Africa	Million South African pounds	89.1	180.4	—	29.2	45.1	—

Source: United Nations, *Yearbook of International Trade Statistics*, 1950, 1960, 1964 (Sales Nos. 51.XVII.2; 61.XVII.9; 65.XVII.2).

years can be found in Algeria, Southern Rhodesia and the United Arab Republic, for example.

One aspect of the problem of the creation and expansion of export-oriented industries is related to improvement of the conditions under which developing countries can sell such manufactured products abroad. Another aspect of the same problem relates to the choice of industries and of commodities which can succeed in developing and sustaining adequate export outlets. Industrial production for exportation in developing countries is generally successful when the producing industries have captured the domestic market, and so advanced in bringing down their cost structure, and have raised the quality of output to the level of their international competitors. Co-ordination in planning of such export-oriented industries between developing countries on a regional or subregional basis, as well as the institution of some common market arrangements for the countries involved, would provide some measure of success for their promotion.

The Employment Objectives of Industrial Development

Industrial development in many countries of Africa is apt to stress the employment objective of industrialization. In addition to the expansion of total output, output per capita and the rising per capita income from the development of the manufacturing sector,

emphasis has been laid on the creation of employment opportunities at higher rates than the growth rates of the labour force. The large majority of the labour force in African countries, as in many other parts of the world, is mainly dependent upon the availability of employment outlets to participate in the increase of production and to earn their income from work. Data on the distribution of the economically active population in major divisions of economic activity are available for only a few countries in Africa and largely refer to a number of scattered and seldom comparable years (see Table 20). They indicate, however, that the highest percentage of economically active population in individual countries are employed in the primary producing sectors, namely, agriculture and mining, and small percentages of them are employed in secondary sectors, including manufacturing, construction and electricity, gas and water utilities. The available data for the year 1960 or thereabouts show that, with the exception of South Africa, the economically active population engaged in secondary production accoUned for less than 10 per cent of the total engaged in most countries. Employment in secondary production in a number of countries at different stages of manufacturing development, such as Algeria, the Congo (Democratic Republic of) and the Sudan, accounted for 5 per cent or less of the total

Table 20—Distribution of Economically Active Population, by Source of Employment (Percentage of Totals)

Country	Year	Agriculture	Mining	Manu-facture	Electricity	Construc-tion	Services
Algeria	1954	82.1	0.4	2.9	0.1	1.7	12.8
Morocco	1960	56.6	1.3	8.0	0.3	1.6	32.2
Tunisia	1956	68.1	1.1	6.2	0.2	2.1	31.3
Sudan	1956	86.0	—	2.2	0.1	2.7	13.0
U.A.R.	1960	56.7	0.3	9.0	0.5	2.0	42.5
Ghana	1960	57.9	1.8	8.6	0.5	3.3	39.9
Central African Republic	1961	94.8	0.4	1.0	—	0.6	4.2
Congo (Democratic Republic of)	1955	85.2	1.4	2.8	—	2.1	13.5
Gabon	1963	92.5	3.2	2.2	0.1	1.8	6.2
South Africa	1960						
White		10.3	5.4	20.1	0.9	6.3	57.0
Non-White		34.7	11.9	9.9	0.6	4.5	38.4
Bantu		55.7	11.5	4.7	—	2.0	26.1

Table 21—Persons Employed in Major Divisions of Economic Activity
(Thousands)

Country	Year	Total	Agriculture, Forestry, Fishing 0	Mining, Quarrying 1	Manufacturing 2–3	Construction 4	Electricity, Gas, Water 5	Commerce 6	Transport, Storage, Communication 7	Services 8	Others 9
Chad	1959	1,340	1,140	1.2	5.0	6.2	—	4.7	2.5	29.9	105.5
	1960	1,340	1,135	1.0	4.3	7.4	—	5.1	2.0	20.1	165.1
	1961	1,380	1,140	1.5	4.3	7.4	—	5.0	0.1	20.0	198.7
Gabon	1956	37.3	14.5	4.6	2.5	1.9	0.1	2.1	1.4	6.6	3.6
	1957	41.5	12.9	6.2	2.4	3.8	0.1	3.2	1.6	6.5	3.5
	1958	38.1	12.9	4.6	2.2	3.8	0.1	3.3	1.7	6.5	2.8
	1959	41.3	13.0	5.1	3.2	2.9	0.2	4.1	2.1	6.4	4.3
	1960	42.8	14.7	6.2	4.2	3.1	0.1	4.4	3.0	6.7	0.5
	1961	42.0	13.8	6.5	3.8	2.3	0.1	5.1	2.8	6.1	1.0
	1962	42.8	13.3	6.5	3.9	3.7	0.1	5.5	2.6	6.4	0.8
	1963	44.0	13.4	6.5	4.2	3.6	0.1	5.7	2.7	7.0	0.9
Ghana	1954	244	34	37	15	50	5	24	22	58	—
	1955	245	41	12	16	57	7	26	23	63	—
	1956	267	42	32	18	47	8	30	23	68	—
	1957	277	41	33	19	48	9	29	26	72	—
	1958	292	44	33	21	51	10	29	29	76	—
	1959	319	45	31	22	60	12	32	27	80	—
	1960	333	58	29	24	62	14	31	31	84	—
	1961	350	48	28	29	63	16	38	33	94	—
Kenya	1956	596.7	235.2	9.0	55.4	39.7	2.3	35.8	52.5	166.2	0.6
	1957	614.4	253.4	7.9	57.0	36.6	2.5	36.8	54.6	165.2	0.4
	1958	593.1	249.5	6.4	55.6	34.2	2.5	36.4	48.1	160.1	0.3
	1959	596.9	251.7	5.4	53.7	31.5	2.5	37.5	45.9	168.3	0.4
	1960	622.2	271.8	5.0	52.3	33.0	2.5	39.0	46.4	171.8	0.4
	1961	589.4	252.0	3.8	42.5	28.6	2.5	43.2	44.2	172.4	0.2
	1962	581.2	245.5	3.5	45.3	12.6	2.0	42.8	46.2	182.8	0.5
	1963	535.1	219.7	3.1	40.7	18.8	2.4	42.0	45.3	162.4	0.7
Malawi	1954	135	48.8	0.4	15.8	19.4	1.2	12.2	3.9	33.3	—
	1955	147	54.7	0.5	17.3	21.4	1.2	12.4	4.3	34.9	—
	1956	164	63.5	0.5	18.7	25.4	1.4	12.6	5.3	37.1	—
	1957	167	63.9	0.5	18.6	26.4	1.4	13.5	5.9	37.3	—
	1958	167	62.3	0.6	17.8	26.4	1.4	14.5	6.4	37.2	—
	1959	163	61.7	0.5	16.7	24.4	1.6	14.6	6.5	36.9	—

	1960	158	60.8	0.4	16.2	22.4	1.6	14.2	6.7	35.5	—
	1961	152	57.9	0.5	15.0	20.4	1.6	14.2	6.9	35.1	—
Nigeria	1956	447.4	36.9	58.9	21.4	101.9	7.8	45.1	56.8	118.5	0.1
	1957	475.6	42.7	53.6	31.6	111.2	8.8	56.6	45.0	123.9	2.2
	1958	478.3	45.4	49.5	29.7	123.8	10.1	45.7	48.7	122.8	2.6
	1959	472.6	45.5	41.2	32.4	102.9	16.4	42.2	47.6	144.4	—
Southern Rhodesia	1954	625	235.9	65.3	75.6	58.5	6.4	42.7	19.9	120.6	—
	1955	649	243.4	62.5	80.2	61.1	6.5	45.7	21.7	128.2	—
	1956	685	246.6	64.0	89.4	66.6	6.6	50.4	22.7	139.0	—
	1957	710	245.0	63.7	94.6	73.6	7.3	53.6	24.4	148.0	—
	1958	724	249.4	60.0	95.4	73.0	7.8	57.3	25.0	156.3	—
	1959	723	252.0	55.3	95.9	67.2	7.9	59.4	25.6	160.4	—
	1960	734	260.8	55.0	96.8	64.9	8.2	59.9	26.4	162.7	—
	1961	710	252.5	51.2	97.0	51.0	7.5	58.2	26.5	166.2	—
Tanganyika	1954	401	218	15	18	16	1	11	7	113	—
	1955	375	201	15	17	12	2	11	6	111	—
	1956	387	207	15	17	13	2	9	7	116	—
	1957	380	211	13	18	11	2	10	8	107	—
	1958	447	216	13	22	11	2	14	9	120	41
	1959	445	222	10	21	12	2	15	10	118	36
	1960	404	201	12	19	10	2	15	7	108	30
	1961	460	189	11	20	—	7	19	19	—	92
Uganda	1958	243.0	58.4	4.2	26.1	38.0	2.4	13.8	11.3	88.7	—
	1959	239.5	56.8	5.5	25.4	33.0	2.3	13.7	10.5	92.2	—
	1960	244.5	61.3	5.7	25.8	30.3	2.2	14.7	11.1	93.6	—
	1961	236.1	55.7	6.1	27.0	29.3	2.0	15.0	10.6	90.3	—
U.A.R. (Egypt)	1958	—	—	—	565	119	—	631	223	1248	49
	1959	—	—	—	545	109	—	594	261	1146	59
	1960	—	—	—	537	105	—	579	214	1130	50
	1961	—	—	—	560	112	—	578	214	1151	28
	1962	—	—	—	600	113	—	578	225	1216	16
Zambia	1954	263	42.0	45.0	23.4	59.2	3.0	15.7	9.0	66.2	—
	1955	276	39.9	47.8	24.6	62.5	3.0	17.4	9.6	71.6	—
	1956	289	38.1	43.5	27.3	68.9	3.3	18.7	10.8	78.6	—
	1957	302	38.8	46.0	27.8	70.2	3.3	21.3	12.2	82.9	—
	1958	294	39.2	40.3	27.7	66.2	3.3	20.6	12.8	84.1	—
	1959	281	40.7	41.8	26.6	48.2	3.3	22.3	13.0	85.1	—
	1960	278	40.7	44.7	26.2	38.7	3.6	22.9	13.3	87.6	—
	1961	269	41.0	44.6	25.0	32.4	3.4	21.1	13.2	88.2	—

Source: International Labour Office, *Yearbook of Labour Statistics*, 1961–1964.

economically active population, but it was much higher in Tunisia (8.5 per cent), Morocco (9.9 per cent), the United Arab Republic (11.5 per cent) and Ghana (12.4 per cent) in or about 1955 to 1960, or more recent years.

Of the total labour force, those who were engaged in manufacturing alone represented less than 3 per cent of the total in the Democratic Republic of the Congo and the Sudan, but accounted for 6 to 9 per cent of the total in Tunisia, Morocco, Ghana and the United Arab Republic, arranged in an ascending order. In South Africa, however, the share of employment in non-agricultural commodity producing sectors has been appreciably higher than in other countries of Africa. In 1960, about 27.3 per cent of the economically active Europeans, and approximately 15 per cent of the economically active non-Europeans (except the Bantu population) were engaged in industrial employment.

Data on the distribution of wage and salary earners are available for more countries and cover a series of years. Although such data suffer also from known deficiencies and discrepancies, they may be used for general indicators of employment development in the non-agricultural sectors, including manufacturing. The total number of wage and salaried employees increased in almost all African countries between the 1950's and the 1960's, and their employment in absolute and relative terms had also risen in the manufacturing sector (see Table 21) in the majority of countries with reported data (see Table 22). Employment in manufacturing in a number of countries has, however, recorded a decline in recent years. Wage employment in manufacturing declined between 1958 and 1962 or 1963 in Cameroon, Chad, Kenya, Malawi and Zambia in absolute and relative terms, in contrast with the increases which it recorded in Gabon, Ghana, Nigeria, Southern Rhodesia, Tanganyika and the United Arab Republic. It is to be noted, however, that the size of wage employment in manufacturing has been rather small in most African countries, accounting for only 3 to 4 per cent of the number of wage earners in Tanganyika and Chad, respectively, and rising to about 7 to 8 per cent of total employees in Ghana and Nigeria, but accounting for between 9 and 10 per cent of the total in Gabon, Malawi, the United Arab Republic and Zambia. Their percentages have been much higher in Uganda and Southern Rhodesia, being approximately 11.4 per cent and 13.6 per cent in these two countries, respectively, in 1961–1962.

The share of manufacturing in total employment is indicative of the magnitude and relative importance of the stage reached in the development of industries. It is also evident that an accelerated rate of industrial development in African countries is as much hampered by the lack of skilled labour and the scarcity of managerial personnel, as by

Table 22—Structure of Employment in Manufacturing in African Countries in Recent Years
(Percentage of Total)

Country	Year	Food, Beverages, Tobacco	Textiles, Clothing, Leather	Wood, Furniture, Fixtures	Paper, Printing, Publishing	Chemicals, Fertilizers, Rubber	Cement, Glass, etc.	Metals and Products	Others
Algeria	1957	26.0	26.4	5.6	4.2	3.6	9.3	20.4	4.5
Libya	1958	32.9	17.9	6.9	2.8	0.9	3.9	32.1	2.6
Morocco	—	—	—	—	—	—	—	—	—
Sudan	—	—	—	—	—	—	—	—	—
Tunisia	—	—	—	—	—	—	—	—	—
U.A.R.	1958	22.8	49.5	2.5	4.8	6.1	4.6	8.3	1.4
Ghana	1959	12.0	1.4	55.3	9.7	3.2	3.2	13.8	1.4
Ivory Coast	1960	21.2	20.8	35.7	—	7.2	—	10.1	5.0
Nigeria	—	—	—	—	—	—	—	—	—
Senegal	1959	30.0	18.2	3.4	2.9	18.5	4.8	21.5	0.7
Ethiopia	1958	47.0	26.5	12.0	1.5	5.0	4.5	—	5.5
Kenya	1957	24.4	8.0	19.6	4.6	7.1	6.9	28.8	0.4
Rhodesia Nyasaland	1958	29.6	14.1	9.8	4.2	3.2	10.9	26.6	1.4

the lack of capital investment. It is now being recognized that raising productivity in the primary producing sectors in many African countries would require more and better equipment, as well as intensive application of more advanced techniques of production involving better inputs of capital and higher skills. It is necessary to introduce new techniques and new forms of organization, not necessarily involving larger inputs of labour. Thus, the further development of primary sectors in a great number of countries in Africa can scarcely bring about substantial employment outlets in agriculture or mining to accommodate the increasing labour force. Demographic pressures on land resources, which are already felt in parts of North, West and East Africa, in addition to the rising demand for higher output per capita, would call for shifting a sizable part of the labour force from agriculture, where its productivity is low or even negative on account of unemployment, to industry, where per capita output is higher.

It is true that unskilled labour is abundant in the majority of African countries, as it is in many other developing countries. It is evident also that the skilled labour required for industrial development is as scarce as capital. In many newly independent countries of Africa, "crash" programmes of education and training schemes have been visualized or even begun. Nevertheless, attention should be given to the planning of education and training in conjunction with planned development of capacities and output in the various sectors of the economy, to maximize the benefit from the utilization of resources earmarked for education in the planning and development of needed manpower. It takes a long time to "produce" skilled workers and highly trained personnel for vast developmental undertakings. However, developing countries of Africa could economize on the use of available skills and managerial abilities by the choice of industries which call for lower requirements of skilled labour in relation to the output. Examples of these industries include basic chemicals, chemical products, metal products, rubber products, pulp and paper, for which market and raw-material possibilities exist in various countries. The expanding non-agricultural

activities associated with the development of such manufacturing industries as construction and building, transport and communication, as well as distribution services, can afford more intensive utilization of labour in both the investment phase and the operational phase, in comparison with a range of industries for which developed technologies put limits on the number of workers needed to produce a specified level of output without sacrificing the productivity of labour. Export industries which need to meet the cost and quality of their foreign competitors will have to be relatively more capital intensive, utilizing more advanced technologies in comparison with the traditional industries, which are confined to the production of import substitutes under some measures of protection.

Expansion of non-farm employment opportunities for the growing labour force and the existing surplus manpower in agriculture is a major policy goal of industrialization in several countries of Africa, including Algeria, Tunisia and the United Arab Republic, where demographic pressure and underemployment or partial unemployment have existed for some time. In West Africa, Ghana and Nigeria also emphasized the expansion of employment opportunities through the development of the industrial sectors. In East Africa, the plans of Kenya, Malawi, the United Republic of Tanzania and Zambia emphasized also the employment objective of industrialization.

The development of industries to produce substitutes for imported light consumer goods might offer more labour-intensive possibilities when established to cater for the domestic markets than would be the case when they produce for regional or subregional markets. Noteworthy in this respect is the fact that the reports of the industrial coordination missions of the United Nations Economic Commission for Africa[9] to East and Central Africa, to West Africa and to the Maghreb countries in North Africa (Algeria, Libya, Morocco and Tunisia) made no reference to specific labour-intensive industries or processes in their review of the concrete possibilities of industrial development of these subregions.

More attention should be given to the possibilities of obtaining increased employment and output from existing unused capacities and through full utilization of available facilities, as a more economic alternative to the creation of additional units. In that way, available capital resources could be saved for the development of new lines of production and thus open further employment outlets for the available labour supplies. Current plans of some countries in Africa give due consideration to the degree of utilization of existing capacity, while others emphasize the creation of additional plants and equipments.

Problems of Choice and Balanced Growth

As is pointed out in a document recently presented to the United Nations Committee for Industrial Development. "There is no longer any substantial controversy about the importance of industrialization as the main long-run path of economic growth for the developing countries."[10] Contemporary thinking on the industrialization of less developed economies, while recognizing the importance of international division of labour and the accrued benefits from specialization, highlights the necessity of an industrialization policy oriented towards the creation of a diversified domestic industry. As expressed in another United Nations document, the ultimate objective of developing countries should be "to construct industrial economies as diversified as those which now exist in the advanced countries."[11]

Although the present study is concerned primarily with the problems and prospects of the industrial development of Africa, such problems and the measures to resolve them could only be assessed in the larger context of economic and social development. The more rapid growth rate of industries is visualized as an instrument and an important means for accelerated development of the African economies. The difficulties of attaining advanced levels of industrialization are, however, commensurate with the importance attached to industrial development and its requirements. African economies have been largely developed along primary production lines. Wherever secondary production has been developed, it has been based largely on import substitutes with little emphasis on export-oriented industries. This problem of choice concerning how to industrialize, like most other problems of choice, should be looked upon, from the short-run as well as the long-run point of view, as a part of the general planning problem of industrial development. Some of these problems are dealt with below.

IMPORT SUBSTITUTES AND EXPORT-ORIENTED
INDUSTRIES

As previously pointed out, the bulk of manufacturing development in Africa is based on the production of import substitutes. Export-oriented industries have mainly been involved in the simple processing of primary products of agriculture or of mining. However, a wide range of commercialized production of farm and forest products, as well as the bulk of mineral output, has been almost entirely exported in raw form to the outside world. Such resource- and export-oriented output in raw-material form, if manufactured gradually in the countries of origin, would greatly generate further value added, expand employment opportunities and result in larger foreign-exchange earnings, which are very much needed for the importation of machinery, equipment and other prerequisites of further growth in the developing countries of Africa.

The African share in world trade of beverage crops and of industrial crops is substantial, and its share in world production of minerals is relatively high. The bulk of African output of cocoa, coffee, tea, oilseeds, cotton, sisal, skins and hides, etc. is still exported in raw form. African output of cocoa, coffee, tea, oil-seeds, cotton, rock-phosphate and two-thirds of the chromite and manganese output. It produces more than two-thirds of the world output of cobalt and gold, about one-fifth of the world output of asbestos, half of the world production of antimony and the bulk of the world output of diamonds. However, such minerals are largely exported without being manufactured.

Greater diversity of economic activity through industrialization is becoming a major aim of most African countries. Although stress has been laid on the expansion of import-substitution industries, nevertheless, it must be borne in mind that only a part of the value of imports represents value added in the manufacturing sector, and to this extent, the substitution of domestic goods for imported ones might result in an enlargement of the contribution of the domestic manufacturing sector. This extent could be substantially narrowed, however, wherever import-substitution industries are highly dependent upon imported materials, labour and other requirements from abroad.

It appears that a higher degree of diversification of output and significant additions to value added from industry could be obtained through processing and manufacturing primary products before exportation. Depending in large measure upon technical and economic factors which are often beyond the control of African countries, the extractive output of Africa could provide a resource base for industrial development, oriented for relatively higher valued exports. These resource-oriented industries for export markets would have a greater comparative advantage over a number of established or contemplated industries destined to produce a variety of substitutes for imports.

A balanced development of industries would require a close examination of its requirements, as well as of its content. If increased consumption required the establishment of import-substitution industries, investment in such industries would necessitate larger imports of machinery, equipment, raw materials and other inputs which must be paid for in exports. Thus, consumption and investment would need to be harmonized through the establishment of some balance between import-substitution and export-oriented industries, in order to effect a balance between consumption and investment at a lower level of unfavourable balance of trade. It is to be emphasized that the problem is not confined to the choices between import-substitution or export-oriented industries to be developed, but

rather, it relates to the proper combination of these two categories of industries for more balanced and sustained industrial development. Import-substitution industries are largely oriented to domestic markets, but manufacturing of raw materials into semi-finished products or higher stages of output would involve the establishment of these industries mainly for exports. Needless to say, the expansion of raw-material processing industries on a large scale for the production of exports would call for a co-operative arrangement between developed and developing countries, and implies a new pattern in international location of industries and specialization based on a new division of labour.

LABOUR-INTENSIVE AND CAPITAL-INTENSIVE INDUSTRIES

Another problem in industrializing is related to labour-intensive and capital-intensive industries. Here again, the problem is not concerned with the choice of one as against the other, but rather the combination of the two. This combination would have to be guided by the principle of maximization of output and other benefits from the utilization of scarce given resources of capital, as well as of skilled labour, through time.

Labour at lower skills could be used where higher skills are not required, or in industries for which needed skills could be more easily acquired in a short period of time at a minimum cost. Capital-intensive industries normally require higher levels of skilled workers. Noteworthy is the fact that the combination between labour-intensive and capital-intensive industries is not merely a matter of composition of investment, but it implies also a pattern of allocation of labour skills, whether available or acquired.

Although the size of the market and the stage of industrialization, as well the state of technology which is accessible to the country, are decisive factors in determining the technique of production to be used, the majority of current development plans in African countries favour labour-intensive processes in a number of planned industries. Other countries of the continent recognize that modern techniques over a wide range of heavy industries are capital intensive and that more mechanization is required to improve production and qualities of output. Thus, the emphasis on labour-intensive utilization is advocated less in factory operations, but more in the building trade and other construction activities, as well as in material handling, distribution and other ancillary services associated with the development of manufacturing in general and of heavy industries in particular. In addition, a number of countries have emphasized the full utilization of existing idle capacities as a possible outlet for further employment.

In contrast to traditional industries, the manufacturing industries oriented to produce for the export market would have to be relatively more capital intensive, utilizing more advanced technologies and higher levels of skill than the rest of the sector. Manufacturing lines which were originally established to produce for the domestic market, before succeeding in capturing a sizable export outlet, would have to modernize their equipment and intensify the use of capital in production processes. The spinning and weaving of cotton in the United Arab Republic, the oil extraction in a number of West African countries and some of the food and beverage preservation industries in East Africa may be mentioned as examples. It should be noted that while labour-intensive techniques will normally produce increased output and larger employment in the short run, capital-intensive techniques are apt to result in relatively higher aggregate output and a higher level of output per worker, as well as a larger surplus for reinvestment. Thus, capital-intensive techniques are to be favoured whenever the objective is to attain the greatest long-run growth of output and employment in industry. To strike a balance and provide for an optimum combination in order to attain the short-run as well as the long-run objective of industrialization is a planning problem to which attention is hereby directed.

RESOURCE-ORIENTED AND MARKET-ORIENTED INDUSTRIES

Although primary production of agricultural and mineral output is predominant in African countries, stress has been laid in most countries on the development of import substitutes, largely of light consumer-goods for domestic markets. Wherever these industries are based on the processing of domestically produced raw materials, they would be both resource-oriented and market-oriented. Durable consumer-goods industries have been developed to a lesser extent in fewer African countries for the domestic market, but, in many cases, they are based on imported raw materials and skills, and in such cases they are market-oriented, not resource-oriented. Resource-oriented industries for export purposes are much less developed in most countries, excepting a few important industries based on the processing of the primary output of some mineral ores and a few agricultural products. In the long run, resource-oriented industries appear to have more possibilities for the accelerated growth of the industrial sector than do import-substitution industries. The problem concerning choices for the development of industries is not between resource-oriented as against market-oriented ones; rather, it is related to what combination of both should be attained to sustain accelerated growth. Thus, African countries, in the formulation of their industrial development plans, should endeavour to work out these plans with a view to saving foreign exchange by developing import substitutes and increasing their earnings of foreign exchange when they establish resource-oriented industries for exports.

Past attempts to improve the foreign-exchange position through the establishment of industries which were not basically resource oriented are often found to have had adverse effects on the international balances of a variety of countries. In recent years, for example, different assembly plants have been put into operation in an increasing number of African countries and have been contemplated in the development plans of others. These industries have been intended to produce substitutes for imports of such final

products as motor vehicles, bicycles, re-
frigerators, air-conditioners, radio sets,
electric fans, sewing machines and other
appliances or equipment, to save the foreign
exchange previously required for the importation of these products. It is to be noted, however, that such assembly production, as it
exists in a number of countries of North,
West and East Africa, has not been based on
established lines of manufacture capable of
producing various parts and other input
goods required for sustaining its growth. In
the absence of such input industries, assembly plants have to increase imports as
output expands, and under these circumstances, they turn out to be import generators
rather than import-substitution industries.
Furthermore, assembly production in such
cases would have very little backward linkage
with the other home industries which do not
produce the needed inputs. Moreover, the
bulk of assembly production, based on imports of parts to be assembled into final
consumer goods, has practically little forward
linkage except with repair and maintenance
establishments, which also depend upon imports. For lack of adequate planning to take
care of the backward and forward linkage
effects of such enterprises on other branches
of industry, as well as on the whole economy,
inaccuracies often exist in cost-benefit evaluation of projects, including the foreign-
exchange part. Furthermore, the existence of
inadequacies in other aspects of project
selection in the case of assembly production
in a number of African countries has often
resulted in high-cost, low-capacity utilization
and a mounting drain on foreign exchange.

LIGHT AND HEAVY INDUSTRIES

Another problem which is often raised
concerning how to industrialize relates to the
choice between light and heavy industries in
both the short and the long run. The argument for light industries usually emphasizes
the gradual approach to industrial development of countries in early stages, but it can
scarcely provide the push required to break
through the vicious circle of underdevelopment and gather momentum for accelerated
growth rates of the developing economies of
the continent. Heavy industries, which

largely produce input goods for other industries and final products of capital goods,
provide the possibility for further development of various branches of the economy, as
well as establish complementarity and closer
linkage between primary and final production. Industries belonging to the group of
intermediate manufacture, such as iron and
steel, basic chemicals and fertilizers, rubber
products and others, are among the heavy
industries which have high backward and
high forward linkage in the economy.

Vigorous growth of the industrial sector
usually requires a combination of heavy and
light industries to be established without
forsaking the principles of comparative
advantage, specialization and interconnec-
tions in the development of various economic
sectors. With a large portion of primary
production linked with the export markets
outside the national and subregional economies of Africa, its forward and backward
linkages are both low with reference to the
African economies, but are closely connected
to the economies of developed countries
which import such a production. However,
turning raw-material production into intermediate and semi-finished goods would
provide for a stronger industrial base at
home and enlarge the possibilities for better
exchange earnings from exports. These industries, however, are mostly capital intensive
and require considerable "know-how" and
industrial experience, in addition to some
security of expectation with regard to international markets, since domestic outlets are
often too small to absorb the potential output. In contrast to light industries for
domestic consumption that could be developed behind tariff walls and other measures of
protection or assistance on the national
level, export-oriented industries would have
to be competitive and would require measures
of international co-operation and action.

NATIONAL, INTRAREGIONAL AND REGIONAL
INDUSTRIES

With the exception of a few countries of
Africa, domestic markets are small. The

narrowness of national markets is manifest by the small population size, by low income per capita, by the sizable magnitude of the traditional and subsistence sectors, and by the prevalence of large numbers of small-size establishments in the manufacturing sector. In planning for industrial development, the majority of countries in the region have based their decisions on national considerations, and few of them in more recent years have realized the importance of subregional co-operation in the establishment of large-scale, capital-intensive industries which require a larger market for more economic operations. Examples of these may be found in the case of iron and steel plants which are under way or are being contemplated in the Maghreb countries and in countries of West Africa, the assembly production of engineering industries in Southern Rhodesia and neighbouring countries of East Africa and a number of heavy and light industries in Southern Africa, as well as in Central and North Africa.

Closer co-operation between countries located in the African subregions has been fostered by the United Nations Economic Commission for Africa and is being promoted by the formation of customs unions between a number of countries in East Africa, as well as in West and Central Africa. Nevertheless, efforts in this respect have been directed towards the creation of import-substitution industries on a subregional basis, while in the field of resource-oriented industries for exports, intraregional attempts have so far been negligible. Regional and subregional action on both fronts cannot be overemphasized. However, in planning for over-all development of industries in Africa, this important aspect cannot be overlooked.

It cannot be overstated that the establishment of subregional industries would require an adequate environment for mobility of resources and of products in order to reap the benefits accruing from specialization and diversification, and to effect a degree of integration on the national and subregional levels. Specialization and diversification on the national level, coupled with integration of industrial development on a subregional

or regional basis, are apt to result in minimizing socio-economic costs, on the one hand, and would serve for better distribution of benefits and of burdens, on the other hand.

Attention needs to be given to aspects of standardization in the development of national, subregional or regional industries with reference to specifications of materials, designs of plants, machinery and equipment, as well as final products. Regional and subregional co-operation is required to effect unified standards in the development of industries oriented to satisfy demand on a continental or subcontinental basis.

Problems of Co-ordination and Integration

The complex and multidimensional process of economic development through industrialization in Africa, as well as in other developing areas, is by necessity a long-term one, requiring adequate measures of comprehensive planning and deliberate policy action in the national sphere and on the international level. It has been increasingly recognized that for these countries to achieve rapid and sustained growth rates of their economies, some determination should be made of a set of interrelated industrial targets, and priorities should be assigned to resource and product allocation by a central authority to bring about harmony between objectives and action. Adequate co-ordination of efforts and reconciliation of objectives are essential elements in mobilizing available resources for industrial development in the context of over-all economic and social development. The need for adequate programming on the national level, if coupled with concerted action of the world community over periods of time, would set the pace for accelerated development and realization of mutual benefits.

Important problems of industrial programming stem from the lack of co-ordination and integration of objectives and of action on the national levels. Some of these problems originate with partial programming, which does not give due consideration to over-all development requirements. Others are related to the range of choices between complementary or alternative actions and the combination of lines of development based on such choices. It is to be stressed that the long-term view of industrialization of a national economy requires long-term planning in which proper combinations of resources and of objectives may result in vigorous development and sustained growth. What would appear to be alternative choices in the short run, as between import-substitution and export-oriented industries, between capital-intensive and labour-intensive undertakings, or between light and heavy industries, would, in a longer term view of industrial development, call for the establishment of some optimum combinations of all these through time. Sets of value priorities and time priorities are required for the formulation, evaluation and selection of industrial development programmes and projects, commensurate with the short-run as well as the long-run goals to be achieved.[12]

Comprehensive planning for industrial development has been inaugurated rather recently in the majority of African countries. Although the degree of comprehensiveness and coverage varies a great deal from one country to another, most development plans have been national in scope with rudimentary or little reference to corresponding plans of neighbouring countries of the continent. Absence of co-ordination on the subregional or regional level has been a common feature. Another common feature, though it appears less pronounced, is reflected in the lack of integration between declared national policies of industrialization and national programmes and projects designed for their implementation. Proposed programmes and projects often have been based on quick surveys of industrial opportunities without detailed feasibility studies and project evaluations.

Many plans recognize the importance of welding the financial, the material and the administrative aspects of programming for industrial development, but details of these have been often missing. The financial plans have seldom been dovetailed with the budgeting of material resources or fitted into a comprehensive growth framework of both the capital and the labour resources required

for realization of development and its objectives.

Although the plans for economic and social development in many African countries have recognized the scarcity of skills and high-level manpower, and provisions for the expansion of educational and training facilities have been incorporated in these plans in a variety of ways, nevertheless, little co-ordination actually exists between the projected expansion of education, in qualitative and quantitative terms, in relation to the requirement of planned undertakings which call for certain categories of skills, specialization and "know-how."

In the formulation of projects and programmes of development, due consideration should be given to co-ordination and integration, not only within the industrial sectors, but also between these and other related sectors of the economy. The assessment of the long-term growth prospects for the economy, as well as the determination of priorities in relation to objectives, should serve as a guide not only for co-ordinated development on the national level, but also for concerted action and co-operative efforts on international levels.

In all African countries, mixed economies prevail, with varying importance of the public and private sectors. Different degrees of emphasis have been placed in the implementation of current development plans on the role of each sector, as mentioned in a previous chapter. Co-ordination between private and public spheres of action is rather important for the attainment of socio-economic goals. Conflicting policy measures could well be avoided and replaced by complementary decisions which would ensure integration and co-ordination between the objectives of policy and the various means devised to achieve them.

The economies of African countries are largely open economies which are dependent upon the world market for exports and for supplies of variety of goods and services required for development. Their current development plans depend, to a large or small extent, upon the flow of foreign resources of capital, skills and know-how for implementation. Under these conditions, more co-ordination is needed between national development efforts and related international activities and institutions. In this respect, co-ordination between technical assistance from international sources and technical problems confronting planning and implementation on the national level would be warranted.

All those aspects of co-ordination and integration, as well as a few others, require comprehensive research and elaborate studies in which both national and international agencies can assist and take an important role. It should be mentioned, however, that planners and policy-makers for industrial development on the African scene are confronted with the familiar difficulty of inadequate statistical data and the rudimentary character of available information concerning industry and other economic sectors.

The need for subregional co-operation to foster economic development is being progressively emphasized by member countries of the continent and, in response, by the Economic Commission for Africa and other agencies of the United Nations family. Without closer co-operation between countries in the region, the formidable obstacles which confront many countries in Africa make it difficult to build viable economies within the strict confines of national boundaries. This derives from a variety of factors, including the narrow manpower base and the small size of national markets associated with the small populations in a large number of countries.[13] In addition, there is the fact that the natural-resource endowment is quite modest and rather undiversified in many of these countries. Closer co-operation between groups of these countries is needed to build up a strong industrial base for sustained economic and social development. An optimum situation would be for a group of neighbouring countries with a diversified but complementary resource combination and common interests to form among themselves a socio-economic entity for comprehensive planning. Alternatively, these countries would

need to integrate, or at least to harmonize and co-ordinate, their national development plans and thus provide for the more efficient use of available resources and create an environment more conducive to sustained and accelerated industrial growth.

Scope for International and Interregional Action

Solution of the intricate problems of industrialization of the underindustrialized countries in Africa, as in other areas, would require a variety of interrelated efforts, part of which should be at the national level, while others would call for international action on an intraregional or an interregional basis. Each country, in its own particular environment, would have to tackle a number of internal problems and obstacles which are national in character and participate with the world community in working out solutions for problems requiring concerted efforts and international action.

It is widely recognized that industrial growth can be accelerated in these developing countries only if they undertake deliberate action to plan the best use of their resources in the light of available markets, whether these are national, regional or world-wide. It is also important for each country to evaluate its own needs, assess its own resources, determine its own development objectives and closely assign priorities over time. There is little doubt, however, that many of these countries would need external assistance in the determination of their best industrial opportunities and in mobilizing available resources to realize these opportunities and reap their benefits.

One of the major obstacles to the promotion of industry in many of the newly emerging countries of Africa pertains to the absence of surveys of industrial development opportunities and the lack of adequately prepared programmes and projects which would attract the necessary financing from national or international sources. Over a wide area of industrial research, including the transfer or adaptation of modern technologies to the needs and circumstances of

It is becoming more clearly recognized
that developing countries can scarcely become
self-supporting at a high level of growth
unless they create new capacities for export-
oriented manufactures. Action directed towards the realization of this objective would
involve, on the one hand, concerted efforts
by developed and developing countries to
bring about a "modified international
division of labour, which is more rational
and equitable and is accompanied by the
necessary adjustments in world production
and trade."[14] It involves on the other hand,
concerted efforts by countries in the subregions of Africa to promote regional
specialization and exchange with a view to
realizing the economies of scale not available
to small developing countries acting independently of one another. In both those
spheres of action, considerable assistance
would be warranted on a national and on a
regional and worldwide basis, in the formulation of appropriate policies needed, as well
as in programming for their implementation.

There are many barriers in the individual
countries of Africa formed by history,
tradition, language, currency and even industrial specifications, in addition to other
natural or man-made obstacles which stand
in the way of closer co-operation and integration of industrial development activities.
Here again, regional and subregional efforts

to bring about effective co-operation through
co-ordination are needed to remove the
existing difficulties and to spur the tempo of
vigorous industrial growth. Many efforts are
being undertaken by the countries concerned, with the assistance of subregional
organizations as well as with the help of the
United Nations and its specialized agencies
and organs, each within its own field of
competence. Although programmes of research and avenues of direct assistance in
various aspects of industrial development are
expanding in response to the demands and
needs of underindustrialized countries, collaboration and co-ordination at the current
stage leaves much to be desired, at both the
international and the country levels.

A great deal of effort based on concerted
action at the national, regional and international levels is required in the formulation
and adoption of standard specifications for
various industries in Africa. The integration
of markets and products requires the application of unified standards not only for industrial products and their major input content,
but also in specifications concerning layout
of plants, power installations, transport
connections and other services closely related
to the development of industries on a subregional or regional basis.

ANNEX: Statistical Data on the Evolution and Current Structure of Industries in Africa, 1950–1963: Tables 23–27.

This is an attempt to produce a complete
statistical picture of the evolution and
current situation in the whole of Africa, with
the exception of Southern Africa, comprising
the following countries: Basutoland, Bechuanaland, South Africa, South West Africa
and Swaziland.

There are very few countries for which
series of data covering the whole period
exist, and where they exist, they are far from
satisfactory. Thus, the picture presented here
is an attempted reconstruction of the likely

pattern of movements, with many gaps being
filled in by estimates of figures extracted from
national development plans, the achievement
of which is not known so far. Therefore,
it should be understood that references to
dates, e.g., 1950 or 1963, are not intended to
be precise. Interpolation, extrapolation, and
back and forward projections have been used
when estimating the missing data for 1950
and 1963.

Data used for the tabulations and estimates
were derived, for the most part, from United

Table 23—Africa: General Statistical Data, 1950–1963

	Population (millions)	Industrial Gross Domestic Product (millions of dollars)							Industrial Gross Domestic Product as Percentage Total	Per capita (dollars)	
		Total[a]	Mining and Quarrying	Manufacturing Industries			Total	Grand Total		Total Gross Domestic Product	Industrial Gross Domestic Product
				Agro-allied	Light	Heavy					
1950											
Northern subregion	51.1	7,660	135	213	187	151	551	686	9	150	13
Western subregion	50.3	4,610	79	97	43	17	157	236	5	91	5
Central subregion	22.8	1,270	108	83	33	77	193	301	23	56	13
Eastern subregion	59.3	3,270	173	153	62	124	339	512	9	55	9
Africa[b]	183.5	16,810	495	546	325	369	1,240	1,735	9	92	9
1963											
Northern subregion	70.8	12,680	680	597	601	600	1,798	2,478	18	179	35
Western subregion	75.6	8,130	171	287	132	52	471	642	7	107	8
Central subregion	29.9	2,920	180	171	85	171	427	607	20	98	20
Eastern subregion	77.5	5,960	231	281	151	240	672	953	16	77	12
Africa[b]	253.8	29,690	1,262	1,336	969	1,063	3,368	4,680	15	117	18

a At market prices (1956–58).
b Excluding South Africa.

Nations documents and publications, and from national plans and publications.

Throughout the exercise, the data refer to prices prevailing in 1957 or thereabouts, i.e., 1956–1958. The gross domestic product is given at market prices. "Medium" population estimates have been used.[1]

Although an attempt has been made, it was impossible to produce a statistical review of data concerning capital formation (within the industrial sector), as well as regarding industrial employment. In both cases, not only the scarcity of the data, but also its substantial inconsistency, made the tabulation impossible.

Table 24—Evolution of the Degree[a] of Industrialization in Africa,[b] 1950–1963

	Class I $200 and over per capita				Class II $100 to 199 per capita				Class III $50 to 99 per capita				Class IV Less than $50 per capita				Total			
	Number of countries	Class' share in gross domestic product (%)	Class' share in population (%)	Average gross domestic product, per capita (dollars)	Number of countries	Class' share in gross domestic product (%)	Class' share in population (%)	Average gross domestic product, per capita (dollars)	Number of countries	Class' share in gross domestic product (%)	Class' share in population (%)	Average gross domestic product per capita (dollars)	Number of countries	Class' share in gross domestic product (%)	Class' share in population (%)	Average gross domestic product, per capita (dollars)	Number of countries	Subregion share in gross domestic product (%)	Subregion share in population (%)	Average gross domestic product, per capita (dollars)
1950																				
Northern subregion	1	33	18	296	5	67	82	119	—	—	—	—	—	—	—	—	6	45	28	150
Western subregion	—	—	—	—	5	39	23	148	8	57	69	76	1	4	8	45	14	27	27	91
Central subregion	—	—	—	—	—	—	—	—	6	85	82	87	1	15	18	49	7	8	12	56
Eastern subregion[c]	—	—	—	—	3	25	10	148	3	37	30	68	7	38	60	34	13	20	33	55
Total	1	15	6	296	13	46	32	128	17	30	39	69	9	9	23	36	40	100	100	92
1963																				
Northern subregion	3	42	24	310	2	49	57	150	1	9	19	90	—	—	—	—	6	43	28	179
Western subregion	1	20	10	217	6	31	22	149	6	47	62	82	1	2	6	39	14	27	30	107
Central subregion	1	5	2	301	3	30	22	134	3	65	76	84	—	—	—	—	7	10	12	98
Eastern subregion	2	18	6	236	2	21	11	142	6	26	42	70	3	35	41	42	13	20	30	77
Total	7	27	12	277	13	36	29	148	16	31	45	80	4	6	14	42	40	100	100	117

[a] For definition, see United Nations, *Patterns of Industrial Growth, 1938–1958* (Sales No. 59.XVII.6).
[b] Excluding Basutoland, South Africa, South West Africa and Swaziland.
[c] Excluding Reunion.

Table 25—The Growth of Industry in Africa, 1950–1963

Rates of Growth
(compound percentage per annum)

	Total Gross Domestic Product	Mining and Quarrying	Agro-allied	Light	Heavy	Total	Grand Total
				Industrial Gross Domestic Product			
				Manufacturing Industries			
Northern subregion	4.0	13.2	8.2	9.4	11.2	9.5	10.4
Extremes[c]	2.1–14.6	2.4–65.4	3.5–12.1	0.9–31.0	2.9–19.0	3.4–15.8	3.1–29.:
Western subregion	4.4	6.1	8.6	8.8	8.7	8.8	8.0
Extremes[d]	1.8–10.9						
Central subregion	6.7	4.0	5.7	7.6	6.3	6.3	5.5
Extremes[d]	5.0–4.4						
Eastern subregion	4.7	2.2	4.7	7.1	5.2	5.4	4.4
Extremes[c]	1.4–7.7	0–7.3	1.3–13.0	0.9–13.6	1.7–14.6	1.4–11.3	2.0–10.
Total	4.5	7.4	7.1	8.7	8.4	8.0	7.8
Extremes	1.4–14.6	0–65.4	1.3–13.0	0.9–31.0	1.7–21.1	1.4–15.8	2.0–29.

Growth per capita
(dollars)

Total Gross Domestic Product		Industrial Gross Domestic Product		Supply of Manufactured Goods[a]			
				1950		1960	
1950	1963	1950	1963	Domestic	Imported[b]	Domestic	Importe
150	178	13	35	15.4	19.6	55.8	34.2
91	107	5	8	22.4	9.6	20.4	19.6
56	98	13	20	9.9	13.1	18.6	19.4
55	77	9	12	11.3	9.7	13.1	15.9
92	117	9	18	15.1	12.9	27.5	22.5

[a] Excluding Southern Africa.
[b] Business gross output of c.i.f. prices.
[c] Minimum and maximum rate of growth acheived by individual country.
[d] The former French Equatorial Africa being treated as one unit by 1950 does not allow calculation of all rates of growth.

Table 26—Africa: Changes in the Structure of Manufactured Goods Supply, 1950–1963 [a]
(Percentage)

Consumer Goods

	1950					1963				
	North. Sub-region	West. Sub-region	Centr. Sub-region	East. Sub-region	Total	North. Sub-region	West. Sub-region	Centr. Sub-region	East. Sub-region	Total
Domestic demand	100	100	100	100	100	100	100	100	100	100
Import	39	18	42	38	31	19	28	33	44	27
Domestic supply	61	82	58	62	69	81	72	67	56	73
Export	26	—	4	21	13	8	2	3	27	9
Domestic production	87	82	62	83	82	89	74	70	83	82
Demand index [b]						372	151	256	179	234
Domestic-production index						379	138	297	178	234
Domestic-supply index						495	132	295	161	246

Intermediate Goods

	1950					1963				
	North. Sub-region	West. Sub-region	Centr. Sub-region	East. Sub-region	Total	North. Sub-region	West. Sub-region	Centr. Sub-region	East. Sub-region	Total
Domestic demand	100	100	100	100	100	100	100	100	100	100
Import	67	64	54	37	55	52	76	62	56	59
Domestic supply	33	36	46	63	45	48	24	38	44	41
Export	5	44	86	38	32	8	24	90	65	31
Domestic production	38	80	132	101	77	56	48	128	111	72
Demand index [b]						337	377	193	149	259
Domestic-production index						498	224	188	165	242
Domestic-supply index						495	247	157	102	236

Capital Goods

	1950					1963				
	North. Sub-region	West. Sub-region	Centr. Sub-region	East. Sub-region	Total	North. Sub-region	West. Sub-region	Centr. Sub-region	East. Sub-region	Total
Domestic demand	100	100	100	100	100	100	100	100	100	100
Import	89	100	100	100	95	79	100	100	82	86
Domestic supply	11	—	—	—	5	21	—	—	18	14
Export	1	—	—	—	—	1	—	—	4	1
Domestic production	12	—	—	—	5	22	—	—	22	15
Demand index [b]						321	302	161	266	281
Domestic-production index						585	—	—	6990	822
Domestic-supply index						626	—	—	40790	868

Total Manufactured Goods

	1950					1963				
	North. Sub-region	West. Sub-region	Centr. Sub-region	East. Sub-region	Total	North. Sub-region	West. Sub-region	Centr. Sub-region	East. Sub-region	Total
Domestic demand	100	100	100	100	100	100	100	100	100	100
Import	56	30	57	46	46	38	49	51	55	45
Domestic supply	44	70	43	54	54	62	51	49	45	55
Export	16	4	29	25	16	8	7	27	35	14
Domestic production	60	74	72	79	70	70	58	76	80	69
Demand index [b]						354	188	218	180	247
Domestic-production index						407	147	231	182	243
Domestic-supply index						501	138	250	148	251

[a] Based on business gross output and cif. rates.
[b] All indexes for 1950 = 100.

Table 27—Africa: Changes in the Structure of Industry, 1950–1963 [a]
(Percentage)

	Structure										Output Indexes [b] 1963					Structure Comparative Data			
	1950					1963													
	North Sub-region	West Sub-region	Centr. Sub-region	East Sub-region	Total	North Sub-region	West Sub-region	Centr. Sub-region	East Sub-region	Total	North Sub-region	West Sub-region	Centr. Sub-region	East Sub-region	Total	United Kingdom 1954	U.S.A. 1958	Italy 1958	Israel 1958
Mining and quarrying	20	33	36	34	29	27	27	30	26	27	502	217	166	133	255	8.4	8.8	3.8	3.2
Agro-allied industries	31	41	28	30	31	24	45	28	31	29	280	295	205	183	244	9.4	12.0	16.6	16.0
Light industries	27	18	11	12	19	24	21	14	16	21	322	302	259	244	298	30.6	29.7	29.4	46.0
Heavy industries	22	8	25	24	21	25	8	28	27	23	398	298	220	193	287	51.6	49.5	50.2	34.8
Total	100	100	100	100	100	100	100	100	100	100	361	271	201	176	267	100.0	100.0	100.0	100.0

[a] In terms of value added.

[b] 1950 = 100 (in terms of value added).

1. See also Annex to this paper.
2. In this paper, reference to South Africa indicates the Republic of South Africa. Southern Africa is taken to mean the subregion, including Basutoland, Bechuanaland, South Africa, South West Africa and Swaziland.
3. These countries include South Africa, the United Arab Republic (Egypt) and Mauritius, with the share of manufacturing accounting for 33 per cent, 17 per cent and 16 per cent, respectively.
4. These countries include Cameroon, Central African Republic, Dahomey, Ethiopia, Ghana, Ivory Coast, Kenya, Libya, Malawi, Senegal, the Sudan, Uganda, United Republic of Tanzania and Zambia.
5. Among these countries are Chad, Congo (Brazzaville), Gabon, Mauritania, Niger, Nigeria, Sierra Leone and Togo.
6. In 1960, industrial output accounted for more than 30 per cent of total output in New Zealand and more than 37 per cent in Canada, Denmark, the Netherlands and the United Kingdom of Great Britain and Northern Ireland.
7. United Nations (Sales No. 59.XVII.6).
8. The share of heavy industries in the economic development plan in the United Arab Republic accounts for about 71.6 per cent in the planned increase of manufactured output and for 77.3 per cent of total planned investment in industry. In Tunisia, the planned expansion of heavy industry would account for 55.4 per cent of the planned increase in manufactured output, for which 72.3 per cent of total investment in manufacture has been allocated. In Senegal, approximately 54.8 per cent of the planned increase in manufactured output is to come from the development of heavy industry, the share of which in the planned investment in manufacturing was about 63.5 per cent.

9. Documents E/CN.14/INR/1, E/CN.14/247 and E/CN.14/246 for these areas of Africa, respectively.
10. United Nations Committee for Industrial Development, "Industrial Development Problems and Issues" (E/C.5/75), Item 3(a) of the Provisional Agenda, Fifth Session, April 19, 1965.
11. United Nations, *World Economic Survey, 1961* (Sales No. 62.II.C.1), p. 3.
12. For theoretical analysis concerning these issues and others, see United Nations Committee for Industrial Development, "Industrial Development, Problems and Issues" (E/C.5/75) April 19, 1965.
13. In 1960, among the countries of West and Southwest Africa, Basutoland, Bechuanaland, Gabon, Liberia, Mauritania and South West Africa each had a population of a fraction of 1 million persons; Guinea, Ivory Coast, Niger and Senegal each had a population of less than 3.2 million; in Angola, Cameroon, Mali and Upper Volta, the populations ranged from 4 million to less than 5 million. In East Africa, the populations of Burundi, Malawi, Rwanda, Southern Rhodesia, Somalia and Zambia ranged from 2 million to less than 4 million; a few countries of the subregion—Ethiopia, Kenya and Tanzania—had populations of 8 million persons or more. In Central Africa, the population of the Congo (Brazzaville) amounted to a fraction of 1 million; that of the Central African Republic, to 1.2 million; and that of Chad, about 2.7 million.
14. *Proceedings of the United Nations Conference on Trade and Development*, Vol. 1: *Final Act and Report* (Sales No. 64.II.B.11), Final Act, para. 5.

Development of Human Resources

MANY PROBLEMS of economic and social development are closely related to population, labor force, and labor productivity. Unfortunately, despite improvements in recent years, population statistics and data on labor force and productivity trends are still defective and incomplete for most countries in Africa. The articles in this section attempt to provide information on some of these vital issues.

The article, "Population and Labour Force in Africa," by the International Labour Office, presents estimates on the size and density of population and other vital statistics on birth and death rates, distribution of population by sex and age, urban and rural population, and the proportion, in 1960, of the economically active population to the total population for different countries. Most of the demographic features in Africa—high birth and death rates, high proportion of rural population, high proportion of children in total population, etc.—are similar to those in underdeveloped countries in Asia and Latin America, with the exception of the higher proportion of economically active population with a greater ratio of labor force participation in the total population. These ratios are higher in most countries in Africa, because of the more active participation of women in the labor force. Hollister's article, "Manpower Problems and Policies in Sub-Saharan Africa," is concerned with problems related to manpower in the African countries. These are (1) the shortage of skilled manpower, (2) the rural–urban drift, or the problem of migrant labor, and (3) the malfunctioning of the wage system. Some possible solutions of these problems are also discussed in the context of economic and social structures of the societies. An integrated manpower policy, linking various manpower problems to the fundamental economic development objectives of the African countries, is proposed. Such a policy will necessitate a projection of manpower requirements and supply along with the increased educational needs. A technique for preparing such projections is suggested by Hollister. P. de Briey, in his article, "The Productivity of African Labour," addresses himself to another major labor problem: the extremely low productivity of African workers, which he feels accounts for their lower wages and poverty. Various economic and sociological explanations are examined, and de Briey concludes that the important elements are "Human Factors," namely, the worker's fundamental aptitudes, the life style he brings from his previous environment, and his internalization of physical, climatic, social, and moral circumstances. These human factors should receive serious consideration in framing labor policies for economic development. The rural–urban drift of labor, one of the major manpower problems mentioned by Hollister, is discussed in the article "Labour Migration in Africa," by Tom Soper. Soper discusses various factors responsible for this migratory character of a large section of the African labor force. He also describes the characteristics of the migrant workers and identifies principal factors underlying their decisions to leave traditional environments and seek only temporary employment in mines, towns, on plantations, planning, sooner or later, to return home. Soper also discusses the extent to which a class of permanent wage earners is developing in African countries, and the major factors responsible for this trend. William Brickman in his article, "Tendencies in African Education," presents a survey of varied patterns in the use of the meager funds that the African governments have been able to devote to education. Obviously, in Africa, as elsewhere, much yet needs to be learned regarding the relative advantage of investment in education over other governmental expenditures for maximizing developmental gains, and also the relative advantage of one type of educational investment over another.

Population Growth and Labor Problems

ABOUT 8 PER CENT of the total world population lives in Africa. According to recent estimates, in 1960 the population of the continent amounted to some 235 million persons.[1]

Africa has a larger population than Latin America (which had some 205 million inhabitants in 1960); but in the latter region a higher rate of increase is expected during the next 15 years, so that in 1975 it should have a population of some 310 million, or slightly more than that of Africa. However, since the available statistics for Africa are not very reliable, it may soon be necessary to raise the present estimate of population.

The populations of the various African countries, as estimated by official sources, are indicated in Table 1.

It will be noted that the sum of the national figures comes to about 247 million inhabitants—about 12 million more than the over-all estimate of 235 million given earlier. The reason is that the figure of 235 million is based on official statistics after adjustment to allow for possible overestimating or underestimating. For instance, it is considered unlikely that the population of Ethiopia exceeds 15 million; no census has yet been taken in that country. On the other hand, some of the figures for other countries seem to fall short of the truth. For instance, recent censuses in Ghana and Morocco proved that the official figures established prior to 1959 were too low. It may be inferred that in recent years the rate of growth of the African population has probably exceeded 2 per cent per annum, which is well above that for the industrialised countries (see the analysis of African population trends below).

The country with the largest population is Nigeria, with over 34 million inhabitants.

Over half the inhabitants of Africa are concentrated in eight countries or territories that have a population of more than 10 million each. They are Nigeria, the United Arab Republic (Egypt), Ethiopia, the Republic of South Africa, Congo (Leopoldville), Sudan, Morocco and Algeria. Gabon is the independent State with the smallest

Population and Labour Force in Africa

International Labour Office

From International Labour Review, *Vol. 84 (December, 1961), pp. 499–514. Reprinted with permission of the publisher, the International Labour Office, Geneva, Switzerland.*

population (440,000), but Gambia (300,000) —still a non-metropolitan territory—may soon take its place.

The mean density of the population in the African Continent is about 8 per square kilometre. This figure, however, means little for it gives no hint of the great divergences of the density in the different regions, which vary enormously as regards climate, facility of access and transport, natural resources and ways of life. For instance, the vast virgin forests of Equatorial Africa and the high tablelands of the southern Sahara are practically uninhabited, while the coastal zones of northern and western Africa and the banks of the East African lakes have a very high population density.

In many cases the distribution of the population is very irregular even in a given country or territory.

In the West African countries, over half the population lives in the relatively accessible coastal strip, which is about 200 miles wide. In some of the southern regions of Nigeria, Ghana, Liberia, Togo and Sierra Leone there are over 500 inhabitants per square mile. The same countries, however, have also some very sparsely populated zones, which bring the average density down to low levels ranging from 25 inhabitants per square mile in the Ivory Coast, to 100 per square mile in the Federation of Nigeria. In Tanganyika 63 per cent of the population lives on 10 per

Table 1—Population, Area and Density of Population in the Countries of Africa

Country or Territory	Population (Census or Estimate— in Thousands[a]	Total Area (in sq. km.)	Inhabitants (per sq. km.)
Algeria	11,020*	2,381,741	5
Angola	4,605*	1,246,700	4
Basutoland	685*	30,344	23
Bechuanaland	337	712,249	0.5
Cameroon	3,240*	432,500	7
British Cameroons	1,652*	88,270	19
Cape Verde Islands	195	4,033	48
Chad	2,660*	1,284,000	2
Central African Republic	1,185	617,000	2
Comoro Islands	185	2,171	85
Congo (Brazzaville)	795	342,000	2
Congo (Leopoldville)	14,150*	2,344,932	6
Dahomey	1,934*	115,762	17
Ethiopia	21,800	1,184,320	18
Gabon	440*	267,000	2
Gambia	301	10,369	29
Ghana	6,691*	237,873	28
Guinea	3,000*	245,857	12
Portuguese Guinea	565	36,125	16
Ifni	53	1,500	35
Ivory Coast	3,230*	322,463	10
Kenya	6,551*	582,646	11
Liberia (1956)	1,250	111,370	11
Libya	1,195*	1,759,540	1
Malagasy Republic	5,298*	590,000	9
Mali	4,100*	1,204,021	3
Mauritania	730	1,085,805	1
Mauritius	639*	1,865	343
Morocco	11,626*	443,680	26
Mozambique	6,310	783,030	8
Niger	2,850*	1,188,794	2
Nigeria	34,296*	878,447	39
Republic of South Africa	15,841*	1,223,409	13
Réunion	335*	2,510	133
Rhodesia and Nyasaland	8,330*	1,253,116	7
Ruanda–Urundi	4,780	54,172	88
Senegal	3,100*	197,161	16
Seychelles Islands	43	404	106
Sierra Leone	2,400	72,326	33
Somalia	1,990	637,661	3
French Somaliland	70	22,000	3
South-West Africa	525*	823,876	1
Spanish Possession in North Africa	146*	213	685
Spanish Possession in Equatorial Africa	218*	28,051	8
Sudan	11,615*	2,505,823	5
Swaziland	259*	17,363	15
Tanganyika	9,238*	937,061	10
Togo	1,442	57,000	25
Tunisia	4,168*	125,180	33
Uganda	6,682*	243,410	27
United Arab Republic (Egypt)	26,080*	1,000,000	26
Upper Volta	3,534	274,122	13
Zanzibar and Pemba	307*	2,643	116

Sources: I.L.O.: data supplied by Governments for the 1961 edition of the *Year Book of Labour Statistics*; United Nations *Statistical Papers*, Series A, Vol. XIII, No. 1, 1961; *Monthly Bulletin of Statistics*, June, 1961; *Statistical Year Book, 1960*

[a] The figures marked with an asterisk refer to 1960, the others to 1959, except where otherwise stated.

cent of the land, while two-thirds of the country is practically uninhabited.

Non-Indigenous Population

It is estimated that about 97 per cent of the inhabitants of Africa are of African descent. The percentage varies considerably, however, from one region to another. The non-indigenous populations are relatively numerous in the north and south of the continent, as well as in East Africa, where they find more favourable economic and climatic conditions. By far the most important non-indigenous group is made up of people of European descent, who are estimated to number about 6 million. More than half of them (3,122,000) live in the Republic of South Africa, while some 28 per cent of them live in North Africa (about 1 million in Algeria, some 400,000 in Morocco, 140,000 in Tunisia and 120,000 in Egypt). Europeans are relatively numerous in the Federation of Rhodesia and Nyasaland (308,000), Angola (110,000 in 1955) and Congo (Leopoldville) (some 110,000). Smaller groups are found in some East African territories (70,000 in Kenya, 70,000 in Mozambique and 30,000 in Tanganyika).

The European element is strongest in the Republic of South Africa (21 per cent). It is 13 per cent in Southwest Africa and about 10 per cent in Algeria. Elsewhere it is not of great significance.

The Asian elements, which are estimated to comprise about 1 million persons, are encountered chiefly in the south and west. About half of them (483,000) are settled in the Republic of South Africa and in Southwest Africa, where they make up 3 per cent of the total population. In the East African territories, such as Kenya, Tanganyika and Uganda, Asians are far more numerous than Europeans.

However small the non-indigenous population may be compared with the African, one must not forget that in most African countries it has played, and is still playing, a predominant part in the economic life of the nation. It is also worth noting that the non-indigenous population has increased very fast during the last 20 or 25 years.[2]

On the contrary, in such North African countries as Morocco, Tunisia and the United Arab Republic (Egypt) the non-African population has been falling since 1956. Recent events have slowed down or reversed movements of population from Europe to many countries located north of the Sahara.

Population Trends

It has already been stated that official statistics, in so far as they exist in Africa, are too irregular and unreliable to form a basis for a scientific analysis of the natural population trends. The records of births and deaths, in the few territories where they are kept, give figures which often fall short of reality by as much as 50 per cent.

Under these conditions it seems best merely to estimate, on the basis of the data supplied by censuses, sample surveys and such vital statistics as seem least incomplete, the limits within which the factors of demographic development for most African countries may be circumscribed without undue error.

According to the United Nations *Demographic Yearbook* for 1960, the mean birth and death rates for the whole of Africa, during the period from 1955 to 1959, were approximately 46 and 27 per thousand inhabitants, respectively. By way of comparison, the corresponding rates for North America, Oceania and the U.S.S.R. were 25 and 8 (or 9) per thousand; in Europe during the same period the birth rate was 19 per thousand and the death rate 10 per thousand.

FERTILITY

It is assumed that in many African regions fertility is close to that observed in collectivities where birth control is not practised. This is also borne out by the very high proportion of children in the total population (about 40 per cent).

Factors that favour high fertility rates include early marriage, which results in a long period of fertility, and the predominantly rural character of the African populations. Various sample surveys indicate fertility rates[3] of the order of 200 per thousand—for instance, 223 per thousand in Guinea (1955), 181 per thousand in the Bongouanou district of the Ivory Coast (1956), 193 per thousand in the lower valley of the Senegal river (1957), 197 per thousand in the Niger Valley in Mali (1957), 215 per thousand in Ruanda–Urundi (1952), 180 per thousand in Southern Rhodesia (1948) and 173 per thousand in the villages in the Northern Rhodesia brush zone (1950).[4] Since women between 15 and 45 years of age constitute about 25 per cent of the total population recorded by the censuses, the inference is that the birth rate for those countries ranges between 40 and 50 per thousand. Rates of this magnitude have been obtained in certain countries whose birth statistics are least incomplete: typical instances are 43.8 per thousand for the Moslem population of Algeria (1955), 46.5 per thousand in Mauritius (1950–1954), 45.2 per thousand in Réunion (1958), 43.8 per thousand in Egypt (1950–1954) and 46.8 per thousand in Tunisia (1959).

MORTALITY

The high death rate in many parts of Africa is due to malnutrition and to infectious and parasitic diseases. High infantile mortality is also an important contributory factor.

The fragmentary data available indicate that in some parts of Africa the gross death rate lies between 20 and 30 per thousand. According to reasonably representative sample surveys, the estimated death rate was about 22 per thousand in Congo (Leopoldville) in 1953, 28 per thousand in the Ivory Coast in 1958, 26 per thousand in the lower valley of the Senegal river in 1957, and 32 per thousand for the indigenous rural population of Northern Rhodesia in 1950. Estimates based on the results of censuses gave rates of 18.5 per thousand in Sudan in 1955 and 25 per thousand in Tanganyika and Uganda in 1947. In Ghana, in the urban zone where registration is compulsory (36 towns and municipalities), the death rate varies between

21 and 22 per thousand. In Tunisia, according to one estimate, the death rate was 26 per thousand in 1959.

POPULATION GROWTH

The foregoing proves that Africa is now passing through a phase of rapid expansion; but the rate of growth varies greatly from one country to another.

The annual rate of population growth between 1953 and 1959 was 2.6 per cent in Algeria and the Federation of Rhodesia and Nyasaland, 2.4 per cent in the United Arab Republic (Egypt), Ruanda–Urundi and Madagascar, 2.2 per cent in Congo (Leopoldville), 1.9 per cent in Morocco, Senegal and Nigeria, and 1.8 per cent in the Republic of South Africa and in Tanganyika. In other territories, such as Angola, Mozambique and Bechuanaland, the rate of growth has been estimated at a mere 1.1 per cent per year.[5] These figures, regardless of the accuracy of the data on which they are based, show that in most African countries the population is expanding very rapidly and that each country must frame its own economic and social policy in the light of this fact.

It is no easy matter to form an idea of present population trends; it is even harder to estimate future developments. It seems reasonable, nonetheless, to assume that the gap between fertility and mortality rates will continue to widen for several decades at least. It is expected that fertility will remain close to the present rate, and that in the countries where it has begun to decline it will not fall so fast as the death rate.

Mortality, on the other hand, whatever its present level, must be expected to fall as a result of the progress in hygiene and in the battle against infectious and parasitic diseases. Consequently, the immediate future will see the African population increasing even more rapidly than at present.

Distribution by Sex and Age

In many African countries and territories, the composition of the population by sex, as shown in various censuses or estimates, contains certain anomalies that are hard to explain. Thus, the masculinity rate (the number of males per hundred females) is 103 in Algeria (Moslem population), 107 in Tunisia, 102 in the Ivory Coast and Sudan, and 104 in the Republic of South Africa (Bantu population), whereas in Basutoland there are only 74 males for every 100 females, and in Ruanda–Urundi 86.

For Basutoland and the Republic of South Africa these imbalances may be ascribed to migration, which is more or less selective as regards sex. For other countries and territories, however, and especially Algeria and Tunisia, they cannot be explained by migratory movements.

These anomalies appear more significant when we examine the distribution by sex of the population in the three major age groups. The first interesting point is that in the oldest groups of the population in such countries or territories as Algeria, Angola, the Ivory Coast, Guinea, Morocco, Sudan and Tunisia, men predominate; this suggests that when a census is taken, old women are omitted more often than old men. Explanations based on a presumption that mortality is higher among women owing to the particularly hard conditions under which they live in Africa fall to the ground when the situation in other countries, where the living conditions of women appear to be the same, is considered.

In the group of persons aged between 15 and 64, however, there is a shortage of men, which is particularly noticeable in Congo (Brazzaville), Guinea, Ruanda–Urundi and Senegal. It is hard to explain this anomaly by migration alone, for the impact of this factor is limited. Adult males seldom leave their country for good. However, seasonal migration plays an important part where only the population actually present in the census area was counted. We must not forget that in Africa, adult males often evade registration because they suspect a connection between censuses and other population surveys and the obligation to pay taxes or supply compulsory labour; this may have affected recent censuses.

Concerning the composition by sex of the non-indigenous population, we find that the number of men exceeds the number of women in all the countries and territories for which information is available, with the sole exception of Algeria.

Leaving aside probable sources of error due to the fact that in most cases the inhabitants of African countries do not know their exact ages, the age structure of the African population reveals a very high proportion of children under 15 (40–42 per cent) and a low proportion of persons aged 65 years or over (3–5 per cent).

The composition by age of the population in a number of different countries and territories, as revealed by censuses or estimates, is given in Table 2.

These figures show that the composition by age of the African population is unfavourable from the economic point of view. On the one hand, the high proportion of children lays a heavy burden on the active population, while on the other, the relatively brief productive lifespan of the adults results in the wastage of a great part of the effort put forth by the collectivity for their education and training.

URBAN AND RURAL POPULATION

It is estimated that over 90 per cent of the inhabitants of Africa live in rural areas. Urban development is a relatively recent phenomenon and merely an aspect of the monetary economy introduced by the Europeans. Wherever Europeans have settled —for instance in the Republic of South Africa—towns, and particularly large modern towns, have rapidly grown up.

According to one estimate, in 1950, the total population of localities with 20,000 inhabitants or more was about 18,500,000 (or 9 per cent of the total population). The population of the large towns (100,000 inhabitants or more) rose from 1.4 million in 1900, to over 10 million in 1950—an increase of over 600 per cent.[6] However, the degree of urban development varies greatly from one African country to another. The urban population makes up about 30 per cent of the total population in Tunisia and Morocco, 33 per cent in the United Arab Republic (Egypt) and over 45 per cent in the Republic of South Africa. By contrast, in the non-industrialized countries, the urban population amounts to only about 5 per cent of the total. This is a major factor as regards the potentiality for economic development in those countries.

It is interesting to note that, owing to the rural exodus, the urban population is growing more rapidly than the population as a whole.

It is estimated that south of the Sahara at least 75 per cent of the Europeans and 70 per cent of the Asians and Arabs live in urban centres. In North Africa the proportion of Europeans living in urban centres seems to be even higher.

Consequently, the ethnic composition of the population of the towns is entirely different from that of the population as a whole. Many towns were built by European settlers as seats of civil and military administration or as trading or mining centres, to

which large numbers of Africans come—often for brief periods—to take up paid employment.

The Total Economically Active Population

It is hard to estimate with any certainty the total economically active population of the whole of Africa. Not only are data on the total population and its distribution by age groups frequently lacking, but difficulties arise in censuses and other surveys when it comes to distinguishing between unpaid family workers—particularly women and young persons—and the "inactive" population amid the great variety of conditions that prevail in the countries of Africa. Though subject to a sizeable margin of error, estimates of the total active population of Africa give a figure of some 102 million, or

Table 2—Composition of the Population by Major Age Groups in Some African Countries and Territories

Country or Territory	Year	Percentage of Total Population		
		0–14 Years	15–64 Years	65 Years and Over and Age Unknown
Algeria (Moslem population)	1954	42.6	54.3	3.1
Angola	1950	39.1	57.9	3.0
Cameroon (Yaoundé)	1957	39.2 [a]	54.2 [b]	6.6 [c]
Congo (Leopoldville) (African pop.)	1954	42.2	57.8	
Chad	1958	42.6 [d]	52.3 [e]	5.1 [f]
Guinea	1955	42.1	54.5	3.4
Ivory Coast	1960	42.9	49.6 [g]	7.5 [h]
Malagasy Republic	1959	43.7	56.3	
Mauritius	1959	44.2	52.7	3.1
Morocco (southern zone, Moslem pop.)	1952	41.0	55.4	3.6
Republic of South Africa (Bantu pop.)	1951	39.1	57.3	3.6
Réunion	1956	42.3	54.3	3.4
Ruanda-Urundi (African pop.).	1954	48.1 [a]	43.5 [i]	8.5 [j]
Senegal	1958	40.1	55.3	4.6
Sudan	1956	38.2	57.0	4.8
Tanganyika (African pop.)	1957	44.3	55.7	
Tunisia	1956	41.8	52.6 [k]	5.6 [c]
United Arab Republic (Egypt)	1947	38.0	58.6	3.4

Sources: United Nations: *Demographic Yearbook, 1956* and *1959*; I.L.O.: data supplied by Governments for the *Year Book of Labour Statistics*.

[a] 0–19 years.
[b] 20–59 years.
[c] 60 years and over.
[d] 0–17 years.
[e] 18–60 years.
[f] 61 years and over.
[g] 15–49 years.
[h] 50 years and over.
[i] 20–54 years.
[j] 65 years and over.
[k] 15–69 years.

43 per cent of the total population and 78 per cent of the population in the 15 to 64-year age bracket.[7] These proportions are high in comparison with the figures for other continents. They are due, firstly, to the small proportion of people aged 65 years and over in the total population, and, secondly, to the participation of large numbers of women and young persons in economic activities, particularly agriculture.

LABOUR FORCE PARTICIPATION

The labour force participation rates for men and women in certain countries are given in Table 3. The value of these figures for the purpose of international comparison is limited owing to the different statistical methods used. In some underdeveloped countries, where the methods of computing the size of the labour force used in industrialized countries cannot be applied, empirical procedures are sometimes employed. In Mali, for instance, one approximate estimate of the active population covered all men between 15 and 59 years of age and all women in that age group living in rural areas on the assumption that all of them, even the housewives, help to

cultivate the soil. In Upper Volta the figures for the active population are exactly the same as those for the total population between 15 to 65 years of age.

If we accept these data, we find that the participation rates vary considerably from one country to another. For instance, in Mozambique and the United Arab Republic (Egypt), the economically active population is only about 30 per cent of the total population, whereas it reaches 59 per cent in Gabon and 58 per cent in Cameroon. These divergences are due rather to differences in the methods used to define and count the active population, rather than on any actual differences in the relative numbers involved.

An analysis of participation rates by sex shows that, as a rule, the proportion of the male population participating in economic activities is high and, with few exceptions, varies little from one country to another. In this respect, the situation in Africa resembles that in the other continents in that the proportion of the total male population found in

Table 3—Labour Force Participation Rates in Selected African Countries (Percentages)

Country	Year	Men	Women	Both Sexes
Algeria :				
Europeans	1954	58.6	15.6	36.8
Moslems		51.7	25.2	38.7
Cameroon (African population)	1957	55.3	60.3	57.9
Congo (Leopoldville) :				
Non-indigenous population	1958	65.2	16.6	42.4
Indigenous population		48.9	49.8	49.4
Gabon	1959	61.1	57.6	59.3
Ivory Coast	1959	58.8	44.4	50.8
Malagasy Republic	1960	52.0	43.8	47.9
Morocco (Moslem population)	1952	53.6	24.5	39.0
Mozambique	1950	55.4	5.8	29.5
Nigeria[a] (indigenous pop.)	1952–53	54.4	41.7	47.9
Republic of South Africa :				
Whites	1951	58.1	16.3	37.2
Others		57.1	14.1	36.0
Senegal	1960	52.6	42.7	47.6
Sudan	1956	66.7	7.5	37.4
Tunisia	1956	52.3	19.6	35.8
United Arab Republic (Egypt)	1957–58	53.5	6.1	29.7
Upper Volta	1959	54.5	55.5	55.0

Source: I.L.O.: *Year Book of Labour Statistics, 1960*; data supplied by Governments for the 1961 edition.

[a] Including British Cameroons.

the active population tallies very nearly with the proportion found in the 15-to-64-year age group. In Africa this proportion is about 56 per cent, or approximately the same as in Latin America.

If the proportion of males of working age is taken into account, it appears likely that the rate given in the foregoing table for the male population of Congo (Leopoldville)—about 49 per cent—is an underestimate, whereas the figure for Sudan (66.7 per cent) is an overestimate. What probably happened, in the case of Sudan, was that a large number of boys were included in the active population.

As regards the participation rates for women, two widely different situations may be observed. In the United Arab Republic (Egypt), Mozambique and Sudan the proportion of women classified as active is very low (6 to 7 per cent of all women); censuses taken in some other Moslem countries gave similar results. By contrast, in other countries such as Cameroon, Gabon, Congo (Leopoldville) and Upper Volta, the rates range from 50 to 60 per cent. The reason would seem to be that in some countries, such as the United Arab Republic (Egypt), Mozambique, Sudan and the Republic of South Africa, the notion of economic activity has been interpreted restrictively in respect of the womenfolk in farmers' families, while in the other countries, all women of working age have been included in the economically active population. This inference is rather artificial, however, in so far as the terms "labour force" and "economically active population" as employed in industrialized countries are not really suitable for computing the number of economically active persons in Africa. For instance, the international definition of employment[8] excludes members of a family who work less than one-third of normal working hours; if this rule were applied, a large number of female agricultural workers in Africa would have to be classified as economically inactive.

It must be borne in mind that under the peculiar economic and social conditions prevailing in Africa, the number of economically active persons does not give a true idea of the size of the labour force; this depends on the length of time each member of the economically active population spends actually working.

Distribution of the Economically Active Population by Branch of Economic Activity— The distribution of a country's economically active population is to a great extent a function of its economic structure. Unfortunately, information on the latter subject is only available for a few African countries. The gap will be filled to some extent in the near future when the detailed results of the 1960 and 1961 censuses are known. For the present, except for the censuses taken in various countries between 1950 and 1956, only partial data are available—for instance, data on the European population in certain countries, or the results of sample surveys of limited geographical coverage.

Distribution of the Indigenous Labour Force— The criteria adopted for the definition of the economically active population and its classification by branch of activity vary from one country to another; consequently, the figures in Table 4 are only approximate. Nonetheless, a number of general conclusions can be drawn from them.

First of all, there can be no doubt that agriculture constitutes the main source of employment for the indigenous population. The proportion of the economically active indigenous population engaged in agriculture was 82 per cent in Algeria (1954), 85 per cent in Congo (Leopoldville) (1955), 77 per cent in Mozambique (1950), 71 per cent in Morocco (1952) and 64 per cent in Egypt (1947). In the Republic of South Africa, where the nonagricultural sector is more advanced, the proportion of persons engaged in agriculture is only 38 per cent. But in actual fact this proportion is probably higher, considering that when the census was taken, many women in the "African reserves" who undoubtedly do a certain amount of agricultural work were classified as "inactive." According to one estimate, in Libya, about 87 per cent, and in the Sudan about 90 per cent, of the active population is occupied in agriculture.

The "tertiary" sector (trade, transport, telecommunications and services) occupies a larger number of active persons than the

Table 4—Distribution of the Indigenous Population by Sex and Branch of Activity in Selected African Countries

Country	Total Indigenous Economically Active Population (in thousands)	Agriculture	Mines	Manu-facturing	Construc-tion	Water, Gas, Electricity	Trade	Transport	Services	Sundry and Ill-Defined
Algeria, 1954										
Total	3,157.4	82.1	0.4	2.9	1.7	—	3.2	1.0	2.2	6.5
Men	2,142.4	75.4	0.5	4.0	2.4	0.1	4.6	1.5	2.1	9.4
Women	1,015.0	96.3	—	0.5	0.1	—	0.2	—	2.5	0.4
Congo (Leopoldville), 1955										
Total	6,198.9	85.1	1.4	2.8	2.1	—	1.5	1.5	0.6	5.0
Men	3,042.0	69.8	2.9	5.7	4.3	—	3.0	3.0	1.2	10.1
Women	3,156.9	100.0	—	—	—	—	—	—	—	—
Morocco, 1952 (Moslems)										
Total	2,899.5	71.2	0.6	6.9	3.0	—	4.2	8.3	4.9	0.9
Men	1,979.5	65.3	0.9	6.2	4.2	—	6.0	11.4	4.9	1.0
Women	920.0	83.8	0.1	8.2	0.4	—	0.3	1.7	4.8	0.7
Mozambique, 1950										
Total	1,633.6	77.0	0.1	4.5	1.0	—	0.7	0.6	16.1	—
Men	1,484.1	75.0	0.1	4.9	1.1	—	0.8	0.6	17.5	—
Women	149.5	96.9	—	0.7	—	—	—	—	2.4	—
Republic of South Africa, 1951 (non-White population)										
Total	3,608.6	37.8	12.6	8.8	4.8	0.5	4.1	2.5	24.1	4.8
Men	2,915.5	43.4	15.5	9.8	5.9	0.6	4.9	3.1	5.4	11.4
Women	693.1	14.2	0.2	4.9	0.1	—	0.7	0.1	77.5	2.3
Tunisia, 1956										
Total	1,327.5	68.1	1.1	6.2	2.1	0.2	4.7	2.0	6.4	9.2
Men	941.3	59.3	1.5	6.8	3.0	0.3	6.3	2.7	7.5	12.6
Women	386.2	89.5	0.1	4.7	0.1	0.1	0.9	0.2	3.8	0.6
U.A.R. (Egypt), 1947										
Total	6,476.9	63.7	0.2	10.0	1.8	0.3	9.4	3.1	11.3	0.2
Men	5,827.8	62.5	0.2	10.3	1.9	0.3	9.3	3.5	11.8	0.1
Women	649.1	74.1	—	7.7	0.1	0.4	10.9	0.3	6.1	0.3

Sources: I.L.O.: *Year Book of Labour Statistics, 1960*; for Mozambique, United Nations, *Demographic Yearbook, 1956*.

Table 5—Distribution of Non-Indigenous Economically Active Population by Sex and Branch of Activity in Selected African Countries

Country	Total Non-indigenous Economically Active Population (in thousands)	Percentage Distribution by Industry								
		Agriculture	Mining	Manufacturing	Construction	Water, Gas, Electricity	Trade	Transport	Services	Sundry and Illdefined
Algeria, 1954 (non-Moslems)										
Total	354.5	11.1	0.8	17.2	9.7	1.2	20.8	8.8	25.2	5.2
Men	274.7	13.0	0.9	18.0	11.9	1.4	19.4	9.7	20.0	5.7
Women	79.8	4.5	0.2	14.4	2.0	0.6	25.6	5.4	43.3	3.9
Malagasy Republic, 1951 (Europeans: professional groups)										
Total	27.4	7.5	0.6	10.6	2.2	1.1	24.0	3.6	47.3	3.0
Men	24.0	7.5	0.7	9.6	2.4	0.8	24.8	4.1	47.0	3.0
Women	3.4	7.5	0.2	17.3	0.4	3.8	18.5	0.4	49.4	2.5
Morocco, 1951 (non-Moroccan population)										
Total	137.7	7.0	3.5	14.0	8.2	1.3	16.7	8.6	26.2	14.6
Men	107.5	8.4	4.2	5.2	9.9	1.5	15.0	9.5	24.3	12.0
Women	30.2	1.9	1.3	9.7	1.9	0.5	22.9	5.4	32.6	23.9
Mozambique, 1950										
Total	37.1	11.1	0.6	12.0	6.5	0.3	28.1	17.5	23.4	0.5
Men	33.1	11.9	0.6	12.0	7.2	0.3	28.6	18.5	20.5	0.5
Women	4.0	5.0	—	11.9	0.8	0.2	24.5	9.7	47.0	0.8

Northern Rhodesia, 1951 (Europeans)										
Total	16.7	8.0	29.2	9.6	7.4	0.4	12.7	9.1	22.7	0.8
Men	13.1	9.5	35.1	10.8	9.0	0.5	8.1	10.0	16.4	0.6
Women	3.6	2.5	7.4	5.2	1.6	0.1	29.7	6.2	46.0	1.3
Southern Rhodesia, 1956 (Europeans)										
Total	78.6	9.7	3.9	14.7	11.5	1.5	25.0	9.9	22.9	0.8
Men	56.6	12.7	5.1	16.8	15.3	1.9	9.2	11.0	17.4	0.6
Women	22.0	2.0	0.9	9.3	1.8	0.5	40.0	7.2	36.9	1.3
Republic of South Africa, 1951 (Whites)										
Total	983.6	14.8	5.8	18.6	6.8	0.7	18.2	11.5	20.8	2.8
Men	769.1	18.4	7.1	18.6	8.6	0.9	14.2	13.3	16.1	2.8
Women	214.5	1.8	1.0	18.5	0.6	0.2	32.5	4.9	37.4	3.1
Tanganyika, 1957 (non-indigenous population)										
Total	39.1	7.5	2.1	6.7	2.9	0.5	39.3	6.9	24.8	9.3
Men	35.1	7.9	2.1	7.2	3.2	0.5	41.4	7.3	20.7	9.6
Women	4.0	3.9	1.7	2.2	0.7	0.6	20.8	3.2	60.1	6.8

Sources: I.L.O.: *Year Book of Labour Statistics, 1960*; United Nations: *Demographic Yearbook, 1956.*

directly productive "secondary" sector (mining and manufacturing industries, water, gas and electricity supply). In the United Arab Republic (Egypt), in 1947, the tertiary sector occupied about 24 per cent of the active population and the secondary sector only 12.3 per cent. In Morocco, the corresponding rates in 1952 were 17 and 11 per cent. In the Republic of South Africa, where the secondary sector is more highly developed, the proportion of active persons occupied in that sector was 27 per cent of the total active population, the corresponding percentage for the tertiary sector being about 35.

Women play a very small part in economic activities outside the agricultural sector. The non-agricultural branches which employ relatively large numbers of women include manufacturing industry and various services (particularly domestic service).

Distribution of the Non-African Labour Force —The distribution of the non-African active population is totally different from that of the active population of African descent, as will be seen from Table 5.

The figures quoted in this table show that people of non-African descent are employed mainly in the branches of the tertiary sector. The majority of them are members of the liberal professions, civil servants or executives in commercial undertakings. The proportion occupied in the tertiary sector is 80 per cent in Tanganyika, 78 per cent in Madagascar and 70 per cent in Mozambique. In countries like the Republic of South Africa, Northern and Southern Rhodesia and Morocco, where mining and manufacturing industries are more highly developed, a substantial proportion of the nonindigenous population is employed in these branches as well.

Distribution of Paid Workers—One of the main characteristics of the labour force as analysed from the economic and social standpoints is the proportion of wage-earning workers in the total economically active population.

In order to investigate this problem, the active population of Africa must be divided into two groups: paid workers and others. The latter are occupied chiefly in the so-called

"subsistence" sectors of the economy and in family farms devoted mainly to the output of produce for sale.

As might be expected, in Africa the proportion of paid workers in the economically active population varies considerably from one country to another, depending on how highly developed the monetary economy is in each.

The available data reveal that the proportion of paid workers in the active indigenous population is 44 per cent in Egypt (1957–1958), 38 per cent in Tunisia (1956), 33 per cent in Algeria (1954) and 32 per cent in Morocco (1952). South of the Sahara, according to one estimate, the proportion of paid workers in the active male African population was 17 per cent in 1955, but there were considerable differences from one country or territory to another. In the Federation of Rhodesia and Nyasaland and the Republic of South Africa, over 50 per cent of all active males are wage earners. In Congo (Leopoldville), Angola, Mozambique and Kenya, the proportion of paid workers ranges from 30 to 40 per cent of the active male population, whereas in Cameroon, Ghana, the Malagasy Republic, Senegal, Tanganyika and Uganda it ranges from 10 to 20 per cent. In countries like Nigeria, Mali, Niger and Sierra Leone, where industrial activities are less highly developed and agriculture is organized in the form of family farms, the proportion of paid workers does not exceed 10 per cent.

On an estimation, about 70 per cent of all African paid workers are concentrated in the regions north of the Sahara (40 per cent)—especially in Egypt, Algeria, Tunisia and Morocco—and in the southern countries—particularly Northern and Southern Rhodesia and the Republic of South Africa. It is also obvious that paid workers are more numerous in the countries more intensely colonized by non-indigenous elements. One reason is that the latter have built up modern agricultural, industrial and transport systems, besides developing trade; another is that the increasing demographic pressure on the cultivated lands has forced the Africans to look for work outside the subsistence economy.

In Africa, women make up a very small fraction of the paid workers. The proportion

Table 6—Distribution of Paid Workers by Branch of Economic Activity in Selected African Countries
(Percentages)

Country	Total (in thousands)	Agriculture	Mining	Manu-facturing	Construc-tion	Water, Gas, Electricity	Trade	Transport	Services and Other
Algeria, 1954:									
Europeans	262.2	5.5	1.0	16.5	10.6	1.6	16.3	11.1	37.4
Moslems	1035.3	56.9	1.1	6.7	4.7	0.1	2.5	2.5	25.5
Cameroon, 1955	143.5	25.9[a]	3.1	4.6	14.5	—	9.5	5.4	37.1
Central African Republic, 1960	47.7	32.5	12.2	15.1	8.8	—	8.0	3.6	13.8
Congo (Brazzaville), 1960 (civil servants excluded)	45.7	19.5	5.0	11.8	9.4	1.5	17.9	10.9	24.1
Congo (Leopoldville), 1955 (indigenous population)	1182.9	24.2	7.4	14.0	11.1	—	6.7	7.7	28.9
Gabon, 1959	40.8	32.1	12.5	7.4	7.6	0.5	8.6	4.9	26.5
Ghana, 1959	319.5	17.2	9.8	6.8	18.9	3.8	10.0	8.6	24.9
Kenya, 1959	596.9	42.2	0.9	9.0	5.3	0.4	6.3	7.7	28.2
Malagasy Republic, 1960	194.5	24.4	2.9	9.4	5.0	1.0	14.5	8.5	34.3
Mali, 1959	31.4	20.7	7.3		15.0		11.1	11.8	34.0
Morocco, 1952 (Moroccan population)	928.2	38.0	2.0	10.6	8.2	—	2.5	25.1	13.7
Nigeria (incl. Brit. Cameroons), 1959	472.6	9.6[b]	8.7	6.9	21.8	3.5	8.9	10.1	30.6
Rep. of South Africa, 1951 (Whites)	754.4	3.2	7.3	22.4	7.6	0.9	19.4	14.4	24.8
Rhodesia and Nyasaland, 1959:									
Europeans	124.0	4.4	8.5	14.9	11.4	1.5	23.2	10.2	25.9
Africans	1083.5	33.8	8.3	11.3	12.3	0.9	5.5	2.5	25.4
Tanganyika, 1959	409.0[c]	54.3	2.4	5.1	2.9	0.5	3.7	2.4	28.9[c]
Tunisia, 1956 (Tunisian population)	501.9	35.9	2.7	8.3	4.4	0.4	4.8	4.9	38.5
Uganda, 1960	244.5	25.1	2.3	10.6	12.4	0.9	6.0	4.5	38.3
United Arab Republic (Egypt), 1947	2752.3[d]	51.8	0.4	13.6	3.3	0.6	4.6	5.2	20.5

Sources: I.L.O.: Year Book of Labour Statistics, 1960; data supplied by Governments for the 1961 edition; Annuaire Statistique de la zone franc 1949–1955, Vol. II (Paris, 1958).

a Salt works included.
b Large-scale undertakings only.
c Excluding domestic servants.
d In 1957–58, paid workers totalled about 3,060,000. See: "The Current Labour Force Sample Survey in Egypt (U.A.R.)," in International Labour Review, Vol. LXXXII, No. 5 (November 1960), pp. 432–449.

of women among the paid workers is barely 5 per cent in Algeria, Ghana, Niger, Nigeria and Tunisia; in the United Arab Republic (Egypt), it is less than 10 per cent; in Morocco, it reaches as high as 12 per cent and in Madagascar 17 per cent. About half the female paid workers are employed in the service sector.

The distribution of paid workers by branch of activity (shown in Table 6) reveals that in general, the greatest numbers of paid workers are employed in agriculture; yet, the proportion so engaged seldom reaches 50 per cent because the figures refer chiefly to commercial, agricultural and other undertakings. As a rule, the agricultural sector, in which the majority of the active population is generally employed, is essentially made up of family farms whose requirements in paid workers are extremely limited.

In Algeria, the United Arab Republic (Egypt) and Tanganyika, about 50 per cent of all paid workers are employed in agriculture. The proportion is equally high in Kenya, Morocco and Tunisia. Another major source of paid employment found in nearly all African countries is the service sector, which employs, as a rule, between 20 and 30 per cent of all such persons.

Even in the most highly developed countries—with one exception—manufacturing industry only employs between 10 and 15 per cent of all paid workers. In the exception— the Republic of South Africa—the proportion seems to be close upon 25 per cent (for whites alone, 22 per cent in 1951). The mines represent a relatively large source of paid employment in the Republic of South Africa, the Federation of Rhodesia and Nyasaland, Congo (Katanga), Ghana and Nigeria.

It must be said that most African paid workers are unskilled or semi-skilled. Characteristic of the situation is a low level of wages, a high rate of illiteracy, and the instability of the workers, due to the fact that a great many of them are migrants who, like a great many others, are to some extent tied to their subsistence economies; in addition,

there are vast reserves of cheap labour. On the other hand, the high cost of vocational training and the existence of a class of highly qualified nonindigenous workers who hold a practical monopoly in their respective trades, are additional factors explaining the lack of vocational training among indigenous workers. The repercussions of this situation are particularly evident today in the countries that have recently achieved independence, where the demand for highly qualified labour and civil servants able to cope with their new tasks has suddenly risen.

Notes

1. See "Projections of Population and Labour Force," in *International Labour Review*, Vol. LXXXIII, No. 4, April, 1961, pp. 378–399. See also United Nations: *Demographic Yearbook, 1960*, Table 2, where an estimated figure of 237 million is given for 1959. The annual rate of increase from 1950 to 1959 has been estimated at 1.9 per cent, which is greater than that suggested in the former study (1.6 per cent from 1950 to 1960).

2. Between 1935 and 1955 the European population increased from 58,000 to 110,000 in Angola; from 18,000 to 93,000 in Congo (Leopoldville); from 18,000 to 52,000 in Kenya; from 23,000 to 66,000 in Mozambique; from 54,000 to 155,000 in Southern Rhodesia; from 11,000 to 58,000 in Northern Rhodesia; from 1,970,000 to 2,856,000 in the Republic of South Africa. The same applies to the population of Asian descent. In Kenya today there are five times as many Asians as in 1935; in Tanganyika four times as many; in Uganda three times as many; and in the Republic of South Africa twice as many.

3. Ratio of births to the number of females between 15 and 45 years of age.

4. Robert Blang, *Manuel de recherche démographique en pays sous-développé* (published in French only), Commission for Technical Co-operation in Africa South of the Sahara (London, 1960), p. 32.

5. United Nations, *Demographic Yearbook, 1960*.

6. For statistics on the growth of the urban population in some towns south of the Sahara, see United Nations, *Report on the World Social Situation* (New York, 1957).

7. *International Labour Review, loc. cit.*

8. See I.L.O.: *The International Standardisation of Labour Statistics*, Studies and Reports, New Series, No. 53 (Geneva, 1959), p. 45.

IN THE SUB-SAHARAN African countries[2] there is rapidly accumulating evidence that three major problems related to manpower will be of central importance over the next five to ten years. These are

(1) the shortage of skilled manpower;
(2) rural–urban drift and unemployment;
(3) malfunctioning of the wage system.

The first two problems are distinct in one sense, but they are tied together by the third. An effective manpower policy will have to solve them jointly.

The Central Problems

SHORTAGE OF SKILLED MANPOWER

It is often dangerously misleading to generalise across a large, multinational region in attempting to describe socio-economic problems and possible solutions to those problems. But in some cases, strong similarities between countries suggest a common structural difficulty and generalisation provides an insight that outweighs the dangers of ignoring diversity. In the African countries under consideration, most investigators have come to the conclusion that shortages of skilled manpower are likely to be an effective constraint on economic growth.[3]

The nature of the shortages does vary. In the countries that were formerly colonies, the usual problems of generating enough of the skills required for rapid development have been aggravated by the postindependence exodus of expatriate skilled manpower from both the public and the private sector. In the few cases where a large-scale exodus has been avoided or reversed, there remains the problem of developing adequate indigenous sources to fulfil the natural desire to Africanise the skilled labour force. In some of the countries, the shortages of modern skills are evident at all levels. In others, the system for supplying the highest skills, i.e., those requiring university training, has been sufficiently developed to meet needs within the near future but there are indications of continuing major shortages of middle-level technicians.[4]

14

Manpower Problems and Policies in Sub-Saharan Africa

Robinson G. Hollister[1]

From International Labour Review, *Vol. 99, No. 5 (May, 1969), pp. 515–532. Reprinted with permission of the publisher, the International Labour Office, Geneva, Switzerland.*

RURAL–URBAN DRIFT AND UNEMPLOYMENT

While the lack of skilled manpower may be a factor limiting the rate of economic growth in Africa, the abundance of unskilled manpower can be an equally significant obstacle to the transition from a traditional to a modern economy. In sub-Saharan countries, the development of a modern sector has generally been accompanied by an increasing drift of the population from rural areas to urban centres. The rising urban, and therefore visible, unemployment presents a major challenge to many developing economies. This problem has become all the more dramatic in that growing numbers of the urban unemployed are primary school leavers.

Even where the growth rate of the gross domestic product (GDP) has been reasonably high, employment elasticity, i.e., the percentage change in employment in relation to the percentage change in GDP, has been low so that the proportion of the labour force in wage employment has generally been steadily declining and in some cases, the absolute level of wage employment has not risen. In a few countries the development plan documents show that the expected future growth in employment in the modern sector is less than half of the expected numbers of primary school leavers.

There is no question but that continued rural–urban drift and growing unemployment among primary school leavers will raise major policy problems in the near future. Some investigators have attributed the "flight from the land" to the effect of primary education upon the expectations and values of the rural populace. The educationist is likely to agree with this conjecture and, not surprisingly, to suggest a change in education policy as the answer to the problem. If the current type of education has led people to value urban life more highly than rural, then, some suggest, it is simply a question of changing the type of education so as to reverse their order of values. There seems to be a great deal of sympathy for the idea that the problem of rural–urban drift can be solved merely by introducing agricultural subjects into the curriculum of the primary schools, or by developing an extensive system of postprimary agricultural vocational schools. There are, in fact, strong arguments against accepting this oversimplified view, but in order to understand them properly, it will first be necessary to discuss the third problem—which is closely tied to the two already described—namely the malfunctioning of the wage system.

MALFUNCTIONING OF THE WAGE SYSTEM

In most of the African countries under consideration, the wage system in the modern sector of the economy has been distorted by the effects of foreign rule. In general, the wages paid to high-level manpower have been determined by the rates that were necessary to induce Europeans to enter the civil service or large private undertakings in these countries in colonial times. During the period of Africanisation, both before and after independence, the wage levels for high positions in the civil service were maintained even when expatriates were replaced. Since the public sector is, in general, by far the greatest employer in the high-level manpower market, the rates paid by it have dominated the wage structure, which is therefore characterised by extremely wide differentials between high-level manpower and manual workers and, in many cases, between the high and middle levels.

Even at the lowest level, wages in the modern sector have been higher than those in the traditional sector. Moreover, in spite of wide-scale unemployment, wages have been rising by about 4 per cent a year. The causes of this anomaly are not clear. It may be that, in public undertakings, managers have little incentive to resist even modest wage pressures and that, in the private sector, the entrepreneur's other preoccupations are such as to make minor adjustments in wage costs insignificant. However, these must be regarded as only the most speculative sort of hypotheses.

EFFECTS OF THE WAGE STRUCTURE ON SKILLED MANPOWER AND UNEMPLOYMENT

These peculiarities of the wage structure have very important effects on both the skilled manpower problem and the unemployment problem.[5]

On theoretical grounds one would normally expect wage differentials in a developing country to be wider than those in a developed country, since high-level skills are relatively more scarce in the developing country and differentials are helpful in encouraging people to seek training in these skills. However, it is quite clear that the differentials in the African countries are much greater than relative scarcity alone would dictate and greater than would be required to provide incentives for training at the highest levels.

Far from serving to provide a set of proper incentives for the growth of a rational spectrum of skills, the system has had serious adverse effects. First, because of the great differentials between high- and middle-level jobs, it has proved very difficult to encourage educated workers to enter middle-level careers, since with a little more training and luck they can hope to move into the stratosphere of the highest-level salaries. Secondly, the salaries for high-level manpower soak up a large part of the budget in the public sector. This feature of the wage structure has created a form of negative feedback to the educational system: in order to create more high-

level manpower, the secondary and university
systems must be expanded, but teachers'
salaries are tied to those of the civil service
and are therefore high, which makes the
expansion of the educational system at the
secondary level very expensive. The result is
that educational costs have been rising much
faster than school enrolments. The high cost
of secondary education limits the number of
secondary places that can be made available
and, therefore, the extent to which primary
school leavers can continue their education.
This forces them onto the employment
market in large numbers.

Rising wages in the modern sector at even
the lowest level have been increasing the
differentials between rural and urban wages,
and many feel that this plays a large part in
encouraging rural school leavers to seek work
in the towns. It is also suggested by some,
that these rising wages, to some extent, and
certainly the cost of high-level manpower and
shortage of middle-level manpower, encourage the adoption of more capital-intensive
techniques and, hence, keep employment
elasticity low.

The extensive damage caused by the
perversities of the wage structure in some
African countries would seem to make its
reform the central issue in manpower policy
and, perhaps, even in development policy as
a whole during the next five to ten years.

Solutions to the Problems

After this outline of the problems, some
possible solutions will now be briefly
discussed.

REFORM OF THE WAGE STRUCTURE

The measures that might be adopted to
reduce the effects of distortions in the wage
structure on the supply of skilled manpower
are as follows:

(1) a downward revision of the upper
salary scales in the public sector;
(2) a major increase in the supply of high-
level manpower in order to break the
dominance of the public sector in the skilled
manpower market;

(3) control of the distribution of high-
level manpower;
(4) revision of the requirements for high-
level manpower, by means of extensive job
analysis;
(5) inflation.

*Downward Revision of Upper Salary Scales
in the Public Sector*—Direct action to establish more reasonable, narrower differentials
between skill levels would obviously be the
most rational move. There are two major
obstacles to this: first, it seems highly unlikely that political pressure against such a
move could be overcome, since the highest-
level civil servants, who would lose most, are
the very persons who would have to plan and
implement such a move; and secondly, many
African countries still require rather large
numbers of expatriates in high-level positions
and it would be very difficult to pay them the
high salaries necessary to attract them while,
at the same time, paying their African
counterparts greatly reduced salaries. (Even
if the differential is made up of various
expatriation allowances or fringe benefits,
this does not disguise the fact that the
African officials are being paid less.)

It is conceivable that in certain countries
the political power of the leader may be
sufficient to accomplish such a move in the
name of a sacrifice for national development.
If it were possible to develop a multinational
or regional resolution to apply such a policy,
the inevitable resistance to it at the national
level might be overcome. This solution is
worth exploring, though the outlook for its
success is not bright.

*Increase in the Supply of High-Level Man-
power*—Some people argue that the wage
structure problem will be solved by the
natural increase in the supply of skilled manpower; that this increase will soon be large
enough to fill the vacancies in the civil
service and provide an excess supply for the
use of the private sector, so that the dominance of the public sector in this part of the
employment market, and hence the dominance of its distorted wage scale, could be

broken. However, this development does not seem very likely. In the first place, the short-term costs of producing a large amount of highly skilled manpower have already been shown to be very high: education is absorbing as much as 40 per cent of public budgets in several African countries, and the scope for further rapid expansion, therefore, seems limited. Moreover, even in the cases where supply is expanding rapidly, the possibility of breaking the dominance of the public sector would seem remote, for unless it is carefully controlled, the public sector will tend to respond to the increasing supply by increasing its "requirements." Finally, even if a large increase in the supply of high-level skills is eventually successful in inundating the market and, thereby, cutting the tie to the distorted public-sector wage structure, this will be an extremely expensive procedure in the short run.

Control of the Distribution of High-Level Manpower—Where the wage (or price) system fails to perform its proper distributive function adequately, the usual alternative is to resort to direct controls. It seems likely that the method used to alleviate the effects of the wage structure on the high-level manpower problem in the next five to ten years will be the establishment of some degree of such control. Indeed, several African countries are already applying a policy of this kind.

Allocative controls can be set up in varying degrees at various points of the system. The most obvious point is at the source of supply, namely in the education and training system. This can take the form of manipulation of the scholarship system to encourage movement toward careers in which the greatest shortages are foreseen, lump-sum payments to influence career choice, or direct allocation of students to particular education or training institutions. Secondly, allocative controls can be established at the point of entry into the employment market. Requests from the various public-sector agencies for new skilled manpower can be funnelled through a single agency, which can keep close control on the number of new entrants taken up by the public sector and reduce competitive bidding among the various agencies in this sector. Moreover, the controls at the point of entry into the employment market can be such as to favour private employers. Finally, controls can be established over the distribution of all high-level manpower. They may be limited to the public sector or extend to the private sector as well. In the public sector they can be used to inhibit the expansion of requirements for high-level manpower and prevent the escalation of average salaries that results from competitive bidding within this sector. (Some experts suggest that there is so much job switching among high-level civil servants that the net productivity of this scarce-skill group is seriously reduced.) Controls in the private sector can be particularly important as regards the use of expatriates and for ensuring the adequate development of training schemes in the sector.

The temptation to establish direct controls is great, but past experience with the use of such instruments in areas other than manpower has not been happy. It proves very difficult to keep control mechanisms efficient and flexible enough to respond to the dynamics of the economy.[6] So, although this method is the one most likely to be used, it would be wise to regard it as a last resort, to be applied only when the other options have been clearly ruled out, and to be strictly limited to the points where the desired results can be produced with the minimum of control machinery.

Job Analysis—The revision of the requirements for high-level manpower by means of extensive job analysis is a course of action that recommends itself regardless of the wage structure problems or the other measures taken to attack those problems. Job analysis can be of direct benefit in the public sector by achieving a more efficient use of manpower, for instance the allocation of less qualified assistants to lowly tasks currently carried out by highly qualified employees, and the breaking up of high-skill tasks into components that can be performed by groups of less skilled individuals. This type of analysis is very time-consuming and sometimes politically difficult, but it has already led to considerable savings in high-level manpower in particular ministries.[7]

Another way in which job analysis can help is by breaking the tie between salary levels and educational qualifications, which typifies many of the present civil service scales. Determining salaries in accordance with the responsibilities of the job rather than the educational attainments of the employee will reduce the upward drift of salaries that, under the present system, accompanies the natural growth in average educational qualifications in the civil service as a whole. *Inflation*—Under certain conditions a measure of inflation can reduce the malfunctioning of the wage system. In the simplest terms, the conditions required are that the salaries at the highest level should be tightly controlled, while the middle- and low-level wages are being adjusted upwards (the measure of inflation) so that the excessive differentials between high-level manpower and the other groups are narrowed.

There are several implications to such an approach. Because of the inevitable resistance to a downward adjustment of money wages, any attempts to reform the wage structure are likely to result in some degree of inflationary pressure. This potential impact of wage reform on other aspects of the economy, for example the balance of payments, should be clearly spelled out when such a reform is contemplated.

However, to the extent that there are already inflationary pressures at work in the economy, it may be possible to take advantage of the fact for the purpose of narrowing wage differentials: if the line can be held on high-level wages, particularly in the public sector, then the existing inflation can be allowed to push up low- and middle-level wages and thus reform the wage structure automatically.

It would, nevertheless, be rather reckless to suggest out of hand that inflation should be consciously generated solely to accomplish a reform of the wage structure. One cannot be sure of the ability of even the strongest government to control the character of an inflationary process. The degree to which the government is able to co-ordinate its responses to the pressures of various groups, each stressing its special need for a wage adjustment to offset rising prices, is a difficult political question. Inflation initiated

to counteract wage structure distortions may end by creating more distortions (both within the wage structure and in other areas of the economy, such as the pattern of investments, exports and imports) than it removes. Nevertheless, in situations calling for anti-inflationary measures, the calculation of the degree, character and timing of such measures should take sufficient account of the benefits deriving from the salutary effects that inflation may have on the distorted wage structure.

COMBATING RURAL–URBAN DRIFT AND UNEMPLOYMENT

In considering these two problems, the discussion will be much less specific and comprehensive, for the causes and possible solutions are much less clear than in the case of the wage structure problem.

First, it is worth repeating the warning against the oversimplification mentioned earlier, namely the idea that the rural–urban drift can be stopped merely by introducing more agricultural content into the curriculum of rural schools. The discussion of the problems relating to the wage system has shown that an important factor in the primary school leavers' preference for the town is the evident and growing differential between the standards of living provided by urban and rural jobs respectively.

This differential is only one manifestation of the fact that opportunities for upward mobility in the traditional sector are severely limited, for a number of reasons. Regardless of how much "love of the land" an agricultural curriculum may instil in the pupil, unless the career opportunities are clearly demonstrated, his rational choice will be to seek the more obvious openings in the urban areas.

In sum, the educational solution alone is not sufficient. A co-ordinated agricultural development programme is required in order to create real opportunities for improving one's standard of living through an agricultural career. Such a programme may include land reforms, the development of an extension service, the creation of reliable networks for supplying the modern requisites of agriculture and for marketing its products, and deliberate changes in the terms of trade for agriculture. There is no evidence that agricultural education alone will keep the people on the land, or that agricultural vocational education is either a necessary or a sufficient condition for creating modern, productive agriculture. An attempt to solve the rural–urban drift by changes in education alone can result in a considerable waste of resources.

Awareness of the unemployment problem leads to a suggestion for more careful consideration of the employment objective as an element to be considered in the selection of investment projects. There is a long-standing controversy concerning the extent to which the objective of maximising the growth rate of national income should be conditioned by the objective of increasing employment, but all that needs to be said here is that in African countries the unemployment problem is likely to grow in the near future and the pressure on development planners to give more weight to employment factors is therefore going to increase. To the extent that the wage structure distortions contribute to this problem, corrections of these distortions will help to relieve the pressure for shifting investment allocations to employment-creating projects. In addition, if those directing the education system are determined to pour resources into special types of education catering for the traditional sector, it may be wise for development planners to attempt to reallocate investments so that these resources will not be entirely wasted.

Since the continued rise of low-level wages in the face of large-scale unemployment seems to be a general African phenomenon, a major effort to explain and correct it would be worthwhile. Improved organisation of the low-wage employment market may help to alleviate this problem. At the very least, a critical eye should be cast on the nature of minimum-wage legislation and wage-fixing institutions to ensure that they are not creating conditions favouring this phenomenon.

To conclude this part of the article, one more general observation may be made. It is important for these problems to be attacked within the context of an integrated manpower policy. In the absence of such a policy, the different sets of experts view the various problems—those of education, manpower, development, investment, and so on—in a piecemeal fashion from different viewpoints and, thereby, overlook the important links among them. One example has been given to show how an approach from a single viewpoint, that of education, can lead to oversimplified solutions, which are likely to be ineffective (in this case, increasing the agricultural content of rural education). Similarly, employment market experts often create institutions, for example, minimum-wage standards, that exacerbate the more general problems, and development planners formulate plans without considering the skilled-manpower implications or without giving due weight to the employment effects. When these manpower problems are viewed as a whole, the necessity for designing solutions that are fitted to the peculiarities of the African context becomes much clearer and, therefore, the danger that visiting experts will simply replicate, untailored to African needs, the policies and institutions with which they were familiar in their own countries is much smaller.

In the discussion so far, the complex inter-relationship of the manpower problems that African countries will be facing over the next decade has been demonstrated. An attempt will now be made to indicate what the elements of an integrated manpower policy should be.

The Components of an Integrated Manpower Policy

MANPOWER PROJECTIONS

A manpower projection, of one type or another, serves a basic integrative function in a total manpower policy. The projection links the various elements of manpower policy to the fundamental economic development objectives of the country. In the past, this link has tended to work in one direction only, that is the development plan has determined the policies on education and the employment market.[9] If manpower projections are to be an effective integrative element, the link must lead to reciprocal influence with a two-way flow of information between the groups of policy makers, each group taking into account the constraints to which the other may be subject.

Techniques of Projection[10]—Many different techniques of projecting manpower requirements and supply, and hence educational requirements, have been used or suggested, and there have been heated debates among the proponents of the various methods. These controversies have, however, been largely unnecessary. Though the analytical starting points of the various schools of thought are very different, the underlying concerns are quite similar, and in any case, the actual choice of technique is largely determined in each country by the character of the data available or readily obtainable. The main techniques will now be briefly reviewed.

The fixed manpower coefficient, economic demand method. This generally starts with projections of gross domestic product, usually by economic activity, and proceeds to estimate the manpower requirements in each occupational category by making labour productivity assumptions and by assuming (and defining) a fixed coefficient for each occupational input in each economic activity. The occupational estimates are then converted into educational equivalents, and the net flow required from education is calculated on the basis of the difference between the manpower demand and the current stock minus death and retirements. The main disadvantage of this method is its rigidity: no allowances are made for possibilities of substitution among occupations, and relative costs are not taken into account.

The rate of return method. This generally uses a cross-section of earnings according to age and education (or occupation) to estimate lifetime earnings, which are then compared with costs of education in order to calculate internal rates of return (or present value) of the investment in this sector. The allocation of investment funds is then adjusted according to the relative rates of return. Major criticisms of this method are that current wages may not reflect actual current social

marginal product (for example, where the wage structure is distorted as in Africa), and that they may not be a good guide to relative social marginal products in the future.

The social demand method.[11] This usually amounts to attempting to estimate changes in the demand by various groups of the population for different types of education, either by extrapolating past trends, or by constructing behavioural models. The chief criticism of this method is that, as an instrument of planning, it is rather circular, since the trends in social demand in the past have been largely determined by the very policy parameters that the planner seeks to determine for the future. Future trends in demand should, it is argued, depend on future policies and not vice-versa.

Synthesis of projection techniques. The objective of manpower policy is to ensure that the pattern of the economy and the pattern of the human resources available are in reasonable conformity. All of the projection techniques have this objective, but they differ as to which factors they assume to be constant and which they allow to vary. Obviously, the ideal is to determine simultaneously the various policy elements with a view to the greatest social and economic gains. Progress in this direction can be achieved if the advocates of the different techniques are willing to adopt a more flexible approach and to determine policy, using an improved flow of information and an iterative process of decision making.

It is possible to reduce the rigidity of the fixed manpower coefficient technique so as to allow for substitution and take into account relative costs of education.[12] In this manner the manpower coefficient method approaches the rate of return method. Similarly, as has been noted in the first section of this paper, an integrated manpower policy must include an examination of the wage structure, with a view to increasing its efficacy as an allocative mechanism. This is certainly a first step towards improving the usefulness of rate of return analysis. Finally, even if one views the problem from the social demand perspective, where emphasis is laid upon giving maximum consideration to individual choice, it is necessary to determine the direction young people will take on leaving the education system; the question of whether school leavers can find appropriate employment in the economy is certainly important even from the viewpoint of social demand. Similarly, even the best manpower projections will be upset if individuals do not choose to fit in with the development plans, and therefore even the manpower economic demand method must take into account the incentives affecting individual choice.

In sum, it is possible either to look upon the lack of economic growth as the factor limiting the ability of the employment market to absorb effectively the growing numbers of school leavers, or to regard the lack of properly trained manpower as the factor inhibiting economic growth. In either case, the need for an integrated manpower policy follows, and, with sufficient flexibility on all sides, the common underlying aims will bring together the various viewpoints and methods.
Need for Flexibility and Revision—It is important to recognise that, in technical terms, the art of making manpower projections, whatever the technique used, is still at a rather primitive stage. This fact alone would recommend a more flexible approach to the use of manpower projections than has been typical in the past. The function of these projections is to assess the total implications of the policy alternatives that are being considered within each component of the manpower sphere; for example, the effect of changes in education on development objectives, of particular employment market institutions on the absorption of school leavers, and of changes in development investment on the need for various types of education. For this reason, too, projections must be flexible in form and the organisational links and information feedbacks among the various components must be carefully maintained. If projections are going to perform their proper integrative function, they must be periodically revised in the light of new information. (Though still primitive, the art of projection

is sufficiently systematised to be amenable to computer programming so that rapid revisions or sensitivity tests are feasible.)

Finally, it should be noted that though projections are the backbone of an integrated manpower policy, they are not the sum total of such a policy. In fact, now that some of the pioneering work has been done in this area, projection should take up a far smaller proportion of the total effort involved in manpower planning, programming and implementation than hitherto.
Special Manpower Projection Problems—The methods of projecting high-level manpower requirements that have been developed so far are primarily suited to the industrial sector of the economy. To date, little has been done with regard to two other sectors.

First, in African economies the public sector is the major user of high-level manpower. A large portion of this employment is related to public administration. Further study to discover the mechanisms that influence manpower utilisation in this portion of the sector might yield information of importance for manpower planning.

Secondly, a large portion of the total labour force in developing countries is involved in traditional agriculture, but very little is known about the extent to which agriculture and its supportive services can effectively utilise various types of skilled manpower and, in particular, what types of incidental, nonagricultural employment—skilled and semi-skilled—are generated by a process of modernisation in agriculture.

EDUCATIONAL PLANNING

The objective of the education component of an integrated manpower policy should be to ensure that the configuration of formal educational institutions and their student outflows are such that the economy can absorb and fully utilise school leavers so that the maximum social and economic gains are obtained for the minimum resource costs.
The Educational Pyramid—There are a great number of policy problems involved in the proper structuring of the various levels of education. One or two of these problems will be singled out here at each level. They belong

to those which, while long recognised, have not yielded to persistent and varied attempts at solution.

At the lowest level of the pyramid, one of the problems is to ensure that primary school leavers are employed in positions in which such education as they have acquired is not wasted and which, it is hoped, will provide opportunities for the acquisition of further skills through experience or informal training. Another, concerns the high dropout rates in the early school years. In almost every African country, an attack on this problem would bring about considerably increased efficiency in the use of educational resources.

With regard to middle-level manpower, one of the most difficult questions is to determine the extent to which the vocational content of education is provided in schools or by direct experience in industry. One of the objectives of an integrated manpower policy should be to develop collaboration between employment market experts and educationists, with a view to adopting a sensible and unified approach to this question. The establishment of middle-level manpower training institutions is perhaps the most difficult task confronting developing countries in the field of manpower, and the one in which there has been least success so far.

At the highest level, a problem often arises from the desire to create institutions closely modeled on those in advanced countries. This leads to an unnecessarily expensive type of education, ill adapted to the immediate needs of the developing country.

A major problem affecting the whole pyramid of formal education is to provide a proper balance of students over the spectrum of disciplines so as to match the spectrum of manpower needs. In particular, science and mathematics candidates prove difficult to encourage. A careful examination of ways of influencing the student's choice of subjects is important, and care must be taken to achieve the proper disciplinary flows from lower to higher levels. (Additional science places in the university will go unfilled if the science training in secondary schools is not adequate.) Curriculum development, examination procedures and scholarship policy can all play a role in properly shaping student flows.

Finally, a flow of information to the education sector showing actual training needs may help in the design of more appropriate curricular structures. (Even in developed countries such information flows are seriously lacking.)

The Teacher Supply—A great proportion of the trained manpower of developing countries is absorbed in their expanding education systems. An enormous waste of manpower and financial resources can occur if the teacher supply is not carefully planned. In this connection, one of the most difficult problems is to keep a balance in the structure of the teaching profession. In Africa, in particular, the fact that teachers' salaries are closely tied to civil service scales creates major financial difficulties in upgrading and expanding the teacher force. On the other hand, an imaginative teacher-training policy can enormously increase the efficiency of the entire system, since, by simple virtue of the fact that one teacher affects a number of pupils, such a policy has a large multiplier effect. This fact alone makes teacher training an obvious candidate for external technical and financial assistance.

Another important element in the planning of the teacher supply in Africa is the use of expatriate teachers. The policy in this matter can have important repercussions on wage scales and on the speed at which a country moves in developing its own sources of teacher supply. Very few countries have carefully projected their needs for expatriate teachers, or set up reliable recruitment systems for meeting these needs.

Finance, Costs and Efficiency—A major financial problem for education in Africa derives from the fact that rapid expansion of the primary system has usually absorbed a large part of the public budgets and left few resources for the balanced development of the secondary and higher levels. Earlier in this article a second problem was mentioned, namely the impact that distorted salary scales have on the costs of secondary education.

School building costs have varied very widely from country to country, but there is good reason to believe that major savings at all levels could be achieved through more careful planning.[13]

That the cost efficiency of educational systems in Africa has received relatively little attention is attested to by the fact that reliable data on costs per pupil or per class-room are rarely available. A proper alloca-tion of financial resources among manpower and development investments cannot be satisfactorily made until such data have been worked out.

EMPLOYMENT MARKET PLANNING

While some development of employment market planning and institutions has been carried out, it has rarely been viewed as an element in an integrated manpower policy; attempts to co-ordinate employment market planning with both educational and develop-ment planning have been rare. This lack of co-ordination makes it likely that the experts in each field will develop policies in isolation, based on experience in their own speciality, without taking into account the implications of these policies in the development context as a whole.

The Allocation Problem—The way in which a distorted wage structure adversely affects normal manpower distribution has been dis-cussed earlier in this article. A manpower policy that fails to take account of this is likely to founder.

Studies of manpower utilisation in the public and private sectors, including job analysis, can uncover considerable irration-ality in the allocation of skilled manpower and, at the very least, will yield information on the mechanisms by which school leavers are absorbed in the employment market.

Training Problems—As already noted, the development of training and education for middle-level manpower is one of the areas of manpower policy in which there has been least success.[14]

One way of improving the training process in general is to develop better sources and dissemination of vocational information. As was suggested in the first part of this paper, in connection with agriculture, a means of

guiding the flow of manpower into the occupations that are relevant to development is to provide them with a clearly visible career structure. Occupations that seem to offer little opportunity for upward mobility will not attract labour force entrants.

The fostering of training activities in the private sector is a challenge to employment market policy makers. Collaboration be-tween them and the development planners can help to ensure that foreign firms under-take to carry out training as part of their projects. Both advanced and developing countries are experimenting with various forms of incentive payments or taxes to en-courage vocational training.

Special pre-service and in-service training for ministries in the public sector should also be integrated into manpower policy.

Employment Market Organisation—To a certain extent, employment market organisa-tion develops automatically as the economy expands, but careful analysis and the creation of institutions (for instance a public employ-ment service) can certainly improve its efficiency.

It would be particularly helpful for de-veloping countries if trade union activities could be encouraged to serve vocational pur-poses with a minimum of industrial conflict. The problem is to achieve union participation in the creation of training systems that are free of the rigidities of the apprenticeship system, which hinders rapid skill develop-ment. Furthermore, the participation of union leaders in manpower policy boards may help to make the objectives of an in-tegrated manpower policy clearly understood among the rank and file of the employment market.

Similarly, on the employers' side, small-business management training constitutes an important task in itself and can help to rationalise the employers' approach to the recruitment of skilled and unskilled man-power.

It seems worth emphasising once more that employment market planning should not be carried out in isolation from educational or development planning. The employment market is the point at which many other components of manpower policy converge, and irrationalities in the market can destroy the proper development of these other components.

DEVELOPMENT PLANNING

While it has often been pointed out in development literature that the shortage of skilled manpower may be a constraint on economic growth, this has not been specifically taken into account in development planning documents. As noted earlier, the procedure to date has generally been to take development plans as given and then to derive manpower requirements. An integrated manpower policy requires a two-way process of plan determination. If skilled manpower is really a scarce resource, then development planning should take into account the relative manpower costs of alternative economic development patterns.

It is likely that development planners will be increasingly pressed to include employment creation in their investment criteria. A further consideration that might be included in project-selection criteria is the extent to which a project, through its training requirements, generates an experienced, skilled labour force (this is the classic example of external economies).[15]

It is worthwhile calling attention to recent developments in the economic literature which suggest that relative supplies of skilled manpower may play an important role, along with capital and natural resource supplies, in determining comparative advantage, and thereby, patterns of international trade.[16] The evidence available is much too fragmentary to enable one to come to any clear conclusion as regards development and manpower policy, but this aspect deserves further investigation.

PROGRAMMING AND IMPLEMENTATION

The discussion of an integrated manpower policy in this article has been primarily in terms of planning, but it should be evident from the nature of many of the remarks that projections and plan targets are only the starting point of a full manpower policy. The eal test of the policy comes at the stage of programming and implementation.

A distinction should be made between programming and implementation: by pro-

gramming is meant the development of a series of measures to be adopted during the plan period, and by implementation is meant the actual transformation of these measures into action.

It is possible to treat programming problems by formal quantitative methods (for example, dynamic programming, PERT[17] or critical path analysis), or by quite informal methods. So far, exploration of the various methods has been, as regards manpower policy, limited. Very few attempts have been made to define the alternative paths to manpower objectives and to make a rational choice of path according to economic efficiency or other criteria. This is a field in which even rudimentary methods might yield considerable gains, particularly when applied in the context of an integrated manpower policy.

A systematic approach to implementation problems[18] in the manpower field requires a careful examination of existing or potential instruments of implementation, and an attempt to think through the institutional requirements of manpower plans. It is true that implementation depends very much on imaginative force, but this does not mean that it should not also be approached systematically.

Particularly in the training of individuals who are to create and administer an integrated manpower policy, conscientious examination of programming and implementation problems will do much to counteract a rigid planning mentality, encourage flexibility in approach, and achieve the proper allocation of effort as between manpower planning, programming and implementation.

Notes

1. Associate Professor of Economics, University of Wisconsin.
2. Throughout this article "Africa" or "the African countries" should be taken to mean the sub-Saharan countries excluding Angola, Mozambique and the southern African countries.
3. Sometimes the importance of the skilled

manpower constraint is subsumed in the more general term "limits to absorptive capacity," but in the African context, the problem is specifically that of a lack of the human resources with which to plan and implement productive development projects.

4. This inability to produce middle-level technicians seems to be typical of countries that are trying to achieve sustained economic growth, even when income per head is at a relatively high level. For examples in Europe, see Organisation for Economic Co-operation and Development, Mediterranean Regional Project, *An Experiment in Planning by Six Countries* (Paris, 1965).

5. An excellent discussion of these problems can be found in A. R. Jolly: "Employment, Wage Levels, and Incentives," in UNESCO and International Institute for Educational Planning, *Manpower Aspects of Educational Planning: Problems for the Future* (Paris, 1968), pp. 236–247, and H. A. Turner, *Wage Trends, Wage Policies, and Collective Bargaining: The Problems for Underdeveloped Countries* (University of Cambridge, Department of Applied Economics, Occasional Papers, No. 6 (Cambridge University Press, 1965).

6. The best examples of problems that arise when direct controls are substituted for the price system are provided in the literature on import licensing. See, for example, Syed Nawab Haider Naqvi, "The Allocative Biases of Pakistan's Commercial Policy: 1953 to 1963," in *Pakistan Development Review* (Karachi), Vol. VI, No. 4, winter 1966, pp. 465–499, and Philip S. Thomas, "Import Licensing and Import Liberalization in Pakistan," *ibid.*, pp. 500–544.

7. See Robert L. Thomas, "Implementing a Manpower Programme in a Developing Country," in *Manpower Aspects of Educational Planning, op. cit.*, pp. 211–235.

8. The problems of the role of education in agriculture are discussed in considerable detail in Philip J. Foster, "The Vocational School Fallacy in Development Planning," in C. Arnold Anderson and Mary Jean Bowman, eds., *Education and Economic Development* (Chicago: Aldine Publishing Co., 1965), pp. 142–166, and Clifton R. Wharton, "Education and Agricultural Growth: The Role of Education in Early-Stage Agriculture," *ibid.*, pp. 202–228.

9. For examples of irrational planning that resulted from the manpower planners' acceptance of a unidirectional link between development and

manpower, see Organisation for Economic Co-operation and Development, *A Technical Evaluation of the First Stage of the Mediterranean Regional Project*, by Robinson Hollister (Paris, 1967).

10. George Z. F. Bereday, Joseph A. Lauwerys and Mark Blaug, eds., *The World Year Book of Education, 1967. Educational Planning* (London: Evans Brothers, 1967) contains a number of essays on projection techniques and other aspects of educational planning. See also M. Blaug, "Approaches to Educational Planning," in *Economic Journal* (London), Vol. LXXVII, No. 306, June, 1967, pp. 262–287, for a comparison of various projection techniques.

11. Some discussion of the social demand method as compared to manpower projections may be found in Organisation for Economic Co-operation and Development, *Human Resources Development: Manpower Forecasting in Educational Planning*, report of the joint EIP/MRP meeting, Paris, December, 1965 (Paris, 1967).

12. Some suggestions on how this might be achieved are made in OECD, *A Technical Evaluation of the First Stage of the Mediterranean Regional Project, op. cit.*

13. See Organisation for Economic Co-operation and Development, *School Building Resources and Their Effective Use: Some Available Techniques and Their Policy Implications*, by Guy Oddie (Paris, 1966).

14. For a discussion of these problems, see Mary Jean Bowman, "From Guilds to Infant Training Industries," in Anderson and Bowman, *op. cit.*, pp. 98–129.

15. See Robert E. Baldwin, "Export Technology and Development from a Subsistence Level," in *Economic Journal* (London), Vol. LXXIII, No. 289, March 1963, pp. 80–92.

16. See Donald B. Keesing, "Labor Skills and Comparative Advantage," in *American Economic Review* (Menasha, Wisc.), Vol. LVI, No. 2, May 1966, pp. 249–258, and idem, "Labor Skills and International Trade: Evaluating Many Trade Flows With a Single Measuring Device," in *Review of Economics and Statistics* (Cambridge, Mass.), Vol. XLVII, No. 3, August 1965, pp. 287–294.

17. Programme evaluation and review technique.

18. For a discussion of some of these problems see Robert L. Thomas, *op. cit.*, and A. and R. Hollister, *Factors Affecting Teacher Requirements and Their Supply* (Paris: International Institute for Educational Planning, October, 1965) (mimeographed).

Introduction

THE MOVEMENT of peoples to centres of economic opportunity in search of work as wage earners is no exclusive African phenomenon. In the contemporary African scene, however, there are two characteristics which differentiate these movements from the sort of labour mobility or labour turnover to which we have become accustomed in Europe. The first is that the movement is largely from a rural subsistence economy into wage labour in a money economy, and as such is a channel of entry into a completely different economic and social structure from what has formerly been experienced. The second is that the bulk of the movement into wage labour has not, until recently, been a permanent transfer of human resources from one region or occupation into another. The people who have gone out in search of wage employment have, in the main, left their wives and families behind them in the rural areas. They have then spent a period of time as wage earners, but with every intention, and indeed encouragement, to return home. In short, the wage labour force in Africa has traditionally been impermanent in its place of employment and, although, the individual concerned may have heavy family responsibilities elsewhere, as a worker he has been regarded as a temporary "bachelor" migrant. In Africa, indeed, the term "migrant labourer" connotes a worker whose permanent home is in his tribal area and who will return there at frequent intervals throughout his working life.

Extent of Wage Employment

The extent to which Africans have become absorbed in the modern money economy through wage labour is considerable. If one takes the territories of East, Central and Southern Africa, comprising Kenya, Tanganyika, Uganda, Northern Rhodesia, Southern Rhodesia, Nyasaland, the High Commission Territories, the Union of South Africa, the Belgian Congo and Ruanda Urundi, Portuguese East Africa and Portuguese West Africa, one sees a vast region in which some

15

Labour Migration in Africa

Tom Soper

From The Journal of African Administration, *Vol. II (1959),* pp. 93–99. Reprinted with permission of the Controller of Her Britannic Majesty's Stationery Office.

60,000,000 Africans live and work. Of these 60,000,000, only a proportion can realistically be regarded as a source of wage labour; indeed, by making allowance for women, children, aged Africans and those who are unfit for anything but the lightest manual work, a figure of between 12,000,000 and 13,000,000 is left representing what may be termed effective able-bodied adult males —i.e., the healthy members in the age group of broadly 16 to 45 years—and as such the core from which wage labour is drawn.

Turning to the individual territories, it is clear that the proportion of effective able-bodied adult males already engaged as wage labourers is very high. Looking first at the situation from the point of view of the extent to which the territorial economies have absorbed employees, in the Union of South Africa, some 1,800,000 or 95 per cent of the effective able-bodied adult males in the country are at one point of time wage earners. This is by far the highest percentage in the region under consideration, but very high proportions are also present in Southern Rhodesia, with 78 per cent of the effective able-bodied adult males in the territory employed, and Northern Rhodesia, with 57 per cent. These proportions are considerably higher than those of Nyasaland, Kenya, Tanganyika and Uganda, all of which have under

$33\frac{1}{3}$ per cent of their effective able-bodied males in employment.

These proportions are based on *de facto* population estimates and thus include African immigrants temporarily resident in a particular territory for purposes of employment. But when the analysis is made from the point of view of the extent to which the indigenous Africans of any territory are employed—whether inside their own territory or not—a different picture emerges in certain instances. In Nyasaland, for example, there are about 90,000 indigenous Africans working as wage earners inside the Protectorate, but some 152,000 are working abroad in Southern Rhodesia, the Union and elsewhere. Thus, taking the number of Nyasaland Africans working as wage labourers both inside and outside the Protectorate as a proportion of the estimated *de jure* African population, we find that over 50 per cent are in wage employment. For Southern Rhodesia well over 60 per cent of the indigenous Africans are employed both inside the territory and beyond it; for Northern Rhodesia the proportion is over 50 per cent; in the British East African territories the proportions are probably all below $33\frac{1}{3}$ per cent.

These figures are of necessity very rough calculations and they are intended to give only an indication of the magnitudes involved. What is quite clear is that the movement of Africans into wage labour has reached massive proportions. Furthermore, relatively few of the workers can regard themselves as being permanently divorced from their rural homes. Or perhaps it is more accurate to say that although more and more are becoming separated from their rural economies, relatively few can regard themselves as being permanently settled in their places of employment, or, indeed, permanently settled as wage earners even if their places of employment change. It is the object of this article to try to explain this phenomenon as it has developed in British East, Central and Southern Africa. Why is it in fact that over so much of its history labour movements in Africa have exhibited a constant movement back and forth?

To begin with, one should examine why it is that Africans have moved at all out of their tribal areas into employment as wage labourers. The obvious and basic reason for this has been the setting up and growth in places, frequently very remote from the centres of African population, of nonindigenous economic enterprises. This engendered a demand for labour on a far larger scale than had hitherto been dreamt of by the African people themselves. But having created this demand, there remained the problem of enticing people out from their own tribal subsistence societies within which the needs and aspirations of individuals could adequately be met. This was dealt with in various ways: through the offer of wages to people becoming steadily more conscious of the uses of and need for money, reinforced by the imposition of taxation on tribal economies that initially did not produce the needed commodity—money; through the activities of recruiting agencies; through government action; through the co-operation of chiefs with government; and through the pressure of disturbances caused by these and other factors to the tribal economy itself.

But the actual causes of the initial movement into wage employment are relatively well understood. What is interesting is why, instead of settling permanently in the areas in which they have found employment, have so many African workers subsequently continued as migrants moving periodically to and from their rural homes?

Perhaps the fundamental cause is that until recently all the parties concerned underwrote the system, and for very good reasons. The African labourer wanted it because he was at heart a peasant whose home was the rural area. It is understandable that he returned to his home as soon as he could. But having returned there, he went back again into wage employment either because the deficiency in his tribal economy that moved him originally appeared again, or because the new experience of wage earning was enticing, particularly to people for whom movement of some sort was of the natural order of things. Further, by contact with economically more sophisticated peoples his wants had been enlarged, and this in turn made the products of his traditional rural economy seem that much more inadequate. And if there was no possibility in his rural area to augment his income so as to satisfy these new wants, he had no alternative but to return to a spell of employment in wage labour. For the employer it was satisfactory because he did not relish the responsibility or cost of establishing permanent African communities outside their tribal environment. Governments wanted it for precisely similar reasons, and also because, when they adhered to the policy of indirect rule, they were determined not to weaken the tribal structure by the permanent divorce from the rural areas of the most virile elements of society. When African labourers immigrated from another territory, the fear of having to be responsible for them prompted the governments of the receiving territory willingly to make arrangements for their return; and the fear of losing the flower of their manhood prompted the government of the sending territory to insist on this. Thus, with all the interested parties anxious not to bring about settled African communities outside their tribal environment, it is easy to understand how the migrant system became part of the accepted order of things. And once having become established, an economic and social framework was created which itself perpetuated the system. In the centres of employment to which the Africans migrated, conditions were established which made it essential for him to look on the rural area as his real home and to maintain a foothold there even if he might wish to sever his ties with them. If he worked on a mine, he lived in a compound. In many cases this was for bachelors only, and thus the possibility of having a normal life with his wife and family was denied him. Even those mines which encouraged the employment of men with families did not solve the problem of insecurity because the African labourer could live only in a company house and he could acquire no permanent rights over land or property. When he lost his job, he lost his home, and thus in sickness or old age he had to look to his rural home again as his main support. In urban areas too, a similar situation existed. Instead of building up an established urban African community,

what must be regarded as little better than urban compounds came into existence. And when wives and families came to urban areas as well as the African employee himself, although facilities in the form of married housing were made available, the opportunity to acquire one's own home, to improve it and to live in it irrespective of the job one had was largely denied him. In short, for both the mine employee and the employee living in urban areas, home and security were in the rural areas. Workers on plantations, too, found themselves living under conditions not dissimilar from a mining compound, in tied housing which was the property of the estate company and as such could be regarded only as company accommodation that could be held only so long as the occupant was fit enough and young enough to be employed by the company concerned.

Only, indeed, among the employees of European agriculturalists was any element of stability maintained. Here, the system of labour tenancy did enable African families to settle near their place of work. The responsibility for them did not appear to the employer as an obstacle against settlement because they were given land that they themselves cultivated for their own needs. Thus, they could fend for themselves, as anyone else would have to, if changed economic conditions affected employment. Even so, while there was a considerable element of stability among them, there was also an element of instability. They were in fact only tenants-at-will who could, if need be, be uprooted at the mere whim of the employer. The fact that normally he did not want to uproot his labour force did not make the feeling of personal insecurity any the less. Again, therefore, there was a tendency for labour tenants still to keep some hold of their rights in their tribal areas and to return to them occasionally and eventually.

Changing Attitudes in Contemporary Africa

With the passing of time, however, the situation has gradually begun to change. For one reason or other, some Africans have been induced, or found it possible, to settle in the towns and other employment centres and to bring up their families there. There thus has grown up, slowly but at an increasing rate, a new generation of Africans whose natural environment is not the rural area but the town. "Home," T. S. Eliot has written "is where one starts from," and although the milieu from which this new generation of urbanised Africans has started has been in many instances sordid and insecure, it is none the less home. For them, the problem of breaking tribal ties has not arisen, since in their case such ties have little or no meaning. Meanwhile, on its side, government has no longer been able to take refuge behind the principle that settled urban communities were not to be encouraged, for in fact the communities already existed. Among employers, too, a new attitude has begun to emerge. On the one hand rapid expansion of economic activity, particularly after the Second World War, has made it increasingly difficult for them to command an adequate labour supply. On the other, their growing reliance on skilled or semi-skilled labour has meant that from their point of view the migratory system, with its high labour turnover, has become steadily less satisfactory. They have begun to recognize, in fact, that experienced labour and settled labour go hand in hand and that it is to their interest to support rather than to resist measures making for settlement.

Changing attitudes, however, have not necessarily been accompanied by a willingness on the part of those concerned to recognize and act upon the implications of the new trend. Africans still cling emotionally to the apparent security of their rural background. Governments have remained in the main unwilling to grant full land rights to urban Africans or the right to own property in urban areas. Employers, while ready to offer the prospect of long-term employment to married Africans, have been less ready to pay wages adequate to the needs of a family man in an urban environment. Challenged on this, they advanced the old argument that the low level of African productivity necessarily means low wages, thereby failing to recognise that low wages foster the migratory system and are therefore a cause, as much as a consequence, of low productivity. More than this, some employers when faced with a labour shortage have tried to extend the range of their recruiting operations and to bring in fresh supplies of unskilled and inexperienced workers from hitherto untapped areas. But it is becoming apparent that this expedient is less likely to attract labour of the type and on the scale now needed.

In the rural areas, too, economic development has tended, with the passage of time, to evoke new attitudes. In the past, governments were apt to favour the migratory system, because they were anxious not to denude permanently the rural areas of the fitter and more progressive males. But after the Second World War concern for the well-being of the rural areas led to a rather different conclusion. It came to be recognised, indeed, that the development of cash crop production and commercial farming made the migratory system just as inimical to rural enterprise as to urban and industrial enterprise. As M. Tondeur has expressed it, "This process (the migratory labour system) is clearly an obstacle both to the training of the skilled working class which modern industry needs, and to the evolution of the peasant class in the desired direction."[2] This outlook was accompanied, moreover, by a distinct movement away from the notion of each African being entitled to a piece of land of his own, to a belief that the main desideratum is the division of land into viable economic units. The old acceptance of subsistence farming and land fragmentation as the norm is giving way to a growing enthusiasm for the merits of efficient farming and the passing on of land by undivided inheritance. Further, the spread over the years of orderly administration, better health facilities and opportunities for gainful employment has brought about a growth of population to the point, in some regions, of serious overcrowding, and for this reason alone the tribal subsistence system and the traditional agricultural techniques that went with it are being viewed with growing—albeit nostalgic —official disfavour. In these circumstances, the feeling has grown that, insofar as it reduced the pressure of population and allowed better use of land in economic units, movement away from the land was not necessarily a bad thing in itself. What now seemed unsatisfactory, rather, was that those who moved away should keep coming back to impede the development of a more stable, progressive and productive rural community.

Stability in both urban and rural areas is now being seen as economically and socially desirable. But stability does not imply that there should be no movement at all between the rural and nonrural sectors. On the contrary, in many cases a sojourn in the towns by an individual has frequently resulted in his acquiring experience of the modern productive process and also a certain amount of capital which he can use or intends to use to good effect in the rural areas on his return to them. But it does demand a certain element of permanence in the particular sector of the economy in which a person is at one time working, and in many instances this lengthening of tenure will in fact become real permanence. For a person, however, to have the incentive to stay for a long period either in urban or rural regions, there must be an economic and social framework that makes him act in a way that supposes the possibility of permanence. There is no reason at all why an individual should not spend his life working in the towns and then, if he makes a success of it, retire to the country. While he is in the town, if he can own land and property he will do so and conduct himself as a fully urbanised person. At the end of his working life, he will then be in a position to decide for himself whether to continue living in town or to buy a small property in the rural areas. This situation, however, is a very different one from that which exists for most Africans today. They know—or fear—that they are some day to be turned out of their urban homes and that they will have to reestablish themselves in the rural areas. Thus they seek to ensure that they have a place there by maintaining as much physical contact with them as possible.

Since the Second World War, however, the factors making for the development of the migratory system have been losing much of their force. But it must be emphasized that even now they are far from dead and that the system continues to play a prominent part in African economic life. It does so in part, perhaps, because exceptional mobility of labour is a natural and unavoidable counterpart of rapid development in a vast underdeveloped continent. But it also survives because the territorial governments do not yet feel able to hasten those measures necessary for the permanent resettlement of the migrant labour force, and because social insecurity remains a basic condition of urban life for most of the Africans concerned. For many of them the town may indeed have become home, but it is a home in which few of them have any permanent stake and in which old age or unemployment can bring disaster. That many of them should try to retain a foothold in the tribal community of their origin is therefore only to be expected. But the pressure of events is making the maintenance of a dual urban–rural existence more and more difficult, and for this reason alone it seems likely that the days of the migratory system are numbered. Its effects are seen as deleterious to all alike.

There is ample evidence to show that during the interwar years, in certain regions, the migratory system impeded agrarian development and, indeed, weakened rural society by depriving it over long periods of the fitter and more progressive elements in the male population. Under the conditions then obtaining, this was broadly true, but the question was highly complex and it would be unsafe to regard this hypothesis as having been universally valid. Whatever its defects, the migratory system did have one advantage: most of the men who left to work in remote centres of employment also came back, in many instances, as agents of progress. Had their departure been permanent, the rural economy might well have collapsed: as it was, the migratory movement almost certainly contributed at that stage to its survival. The remittances sent or brought home by the migrants helped both to keep the community going and to furnish it with capital. The new wants they transmitted to their friends and relations provided the community with new incentives to break out of the age-old strait-jacket of subsistence economies. The ideas they brought back with them from mine or plantation enlarged the community's fund of economic experience and helped to develop a more mature approach to the process of production and exchange. Nor should it be forgotten that while they were away in the town or on the railway they helped to create a market for cash crops and thereby to create a situation in which a change from subsistence cultivation to commercial farming became possible.

Yet at this very stage of rural development the weaknesses of the migratory system began to make themselves apparent. The emergence of cash crop production meant that more skill and experience were required of the cultivator. Work which in subsistence cultivation could be left to the women, the young and the old, now gave way here and there to more complex operations beyond their scope. The ideas and methods brought back by the migrants were all too often apt to wither and die when they went away again. A situation indeed developed where, instead of having a rural peasantry which in theory was invigorated by its members having occasional sojourns in wage labour, or one which flourished by the regular removal of those people less suited to agricultural pursuits and the absorption of fresh talent from outside, many areas became little better than labour dormitories with the people, while looking on the land as their home, spending an ever increasing amount of their time earning incomes as wage labourers. And on their return to the rural sector they did not necessarily devote their time to improving their land but simply rested before leaving again for a further spell of work outside. This long absence not only made it physically impossible for the returned migrant to tend his land, but he soon became at heart less and less of a countryman and rapidly lost interest in the land except as a region of rest and a means of providing for his old age. When conditions were such that he did not

follow his path but reinvested his savings in the land and developed cash crop production, it seems likely—although not certain—that he became less and less migratory, and settled as a cash crop farmer.

In the field of wage employment itself, the long-term effects of the two-way movement of labour have been scarcely more satisfactory. Here, as in the rural sector, it has been a formidable barrier to the acquisition of skill. Except in the case of a fortunate minority, the intermittent nature of their employment has restricted migratory workers to unskilled occupations and hence low wages. The fact that their labour is cheap has produced among employers in general a somewhat casual attitude towards its training, supervision and management, so that, through no fault of their own, the productivity of the workers has remained low. Also the ability to always take on just one more apparently cheap labourer has discouraged investment in capital equipment in industry. On the other side of the equation, low wages have meant poor living standards and malnutrition; nor has the workers' energy been helped by the rigours of travel to and from the job. Finally, the migratory system has created a social framework in which the African working class has remained rootless, with little incentive or opportunity to become efficient or to acquire the specialised skills on which, in a modern context, productive efficiency so largely depends. The system has in fact brought about conditions and attitudes of mind which help to perpetuate it. And since that framework has now become so large, its improvement cannot fail to be a formidable and costly operation.

But however formidable and costly the operation might be, it is becoming transparently clear that the system has outlived its usefulness and is becoming more and more detrimental to the economic interests of all concerned. Without it, the African economy could not have grown so rapidly or, indeed, effectively in the past. In the very nature of things, the African population will continue to shift on a massive scale. Migratory labour will still continue to play a dominant role in the developing of African economies, but economic, social and political considerations alike now require that appropriate attention should be paid to the problems and tasks of settling an ever growing proportion of the wage-labour force.

Notes

1. I am greatly indebted in writing this article to the advice and guidance of Professor S. Herbert Frankel, Fellow of Nuffield College, and of Mr. L. C. Wilcher, Warden of Queen Elizabeth House, Oxford.

2. G. Tondeur: "La Conservation des Sols au Congo Belge," *Bulletin Agricole du Congo Belge*, June, 1947.

16

The Productivity
of African Labour

P. de Briey

From International Labour Review, Vol. 72
(August–September, 1955), pp. 119–137. Reprinted
with permission of the publisher, International Labour
Office, Geneva, Switzerland.

OVER the last 60–70 years, tropical Africa has undergone an economic revolution. Its 140 million inhabitants, who for centuries had been producing nothing more than the necessities for subsistence, have now begun living and producing with an eye to the outside world. In other words, a market economy has taken the place of the subsistence economy. This change was essential for progress. In the absence of any currency, some medium of exchange had to be found for the purposes of education, the treatment and cure of endemic and epidemic sickness, the opening of communications and the acquisition of a minimum of industrial equipment, or simply for the purchase of goods from Western traders. Africa, however, had no other medium of exchange to offer than its own farm produce or the labour of its people. While the resulting exchange has taken place partly through the sale of produce and partly through the hire of labour, "there is a marked tendency in most territories for one or the other of these two forms of commercialisation to dominate. Thus, for example, production for market plays by far the more important part in money earning in the indigenous agricultural economies in the Gold Coast, French West Africa, Nigeria and Uganda, while in Kenya, Northern Rhodesia and Southern Rhodesia

wage employment completely overshadows cash cropping."[1]

Thus a market economy made its appearance in Africa. The process was and still is extremely slow. Even now, in tropical Africa as a whole, the major proportion (approximately 70 per cent) of the resources of cultivated land and of labour (approximately 60 per cent) of the indigenous agricultural economies is still engaged in subsistence production.[2] Yet the development of a market economy is essential for any improvement in the standard of living of the people. In view of the rising population and the progressive erosion of the soil, to quote only the most obvious factors, there is a need to expand resources and acquire equipment, and this would be difficult in a subsistence economy. At the present stage of development, the need for fresh changes is becoming evident. It is clear that transport facilities will have to be improved if there is to be any increase in the export trade. Productivity will also have to be raised to ensure a flow of goods to foreign markets, meet the needs of workers employed in nonindigenous undertakings, and maintain the standard of living of the producers themselves. New sources of production will also have to be discovered, and the reserves of labour must be used more effectively than in the past, possibly by finding work for them in industry instead of on the land.

It is not possible to go into the details of these developments here; one of them, however—the raising of labour productivity—is well worth studying by itself, since opinions on the subject are extremely varied.

If the output of unskilled labour in industry were to be taken as a yardstick, the picture of the African worker's standards of productivity would undoubtedly be gloomy. It is unanimously recognised that the output of unskilled African workers is extremely low in almost all the undertakings that employ them. An attempt to measure the productivity of labour in a factory in Durban (Union of South Africa) showed that the output of the average unskilled migrant worker was only 29 per cent of the figure taken as the optimum.[3] The report of the commission of inquiry set up to investigate the protection of secondary industries in

Southern Rhodesia produced statistical evidence to show that output per head of local workers was considerably lower than in any other Commonwealth country.[4] A report published in 1946 expressed a similar opinion of labour in British East Africa (Kenya, Uganda and Tanganyika). It stated: "The dominant problem throughout East Africa is the deplorably low standard of efficiency of the worker"[5]—a view confirmed as far as Kenya is concerned by the report of the Committee on African Wages published in 1954. The Governor-General of the Belgian Congo, speaking before the Government Council in July 1949, was also sharply critical of the low output of workers in this territory.[6] An inquiry held in Duala (Cameroons under French administration) found that

As compared with a White worker's output, that of a Negro varies between one-third and one-seventh or one-eighth, depending on the employer and the trade (or within a given trade). The usual proportion is about one-quarter. In other words, it takes a Negro four days to do what a White does in one. And this opinion was confirmed by all the employers that we talked to.[7]

The output of the African wage earner is only one determining factor in the productivity of the population as a whole. Since his output is low, his wage is low—enough, perhaps, for his own subsistence but quite inadequate to meet the requirements of a family. This low level of output among the wage-earning population ought to be offset by higher productivity among the independent farmers, the more so since the number of the latter has been much reduced by the movement into wage earning employment in nonindigenous undertakings. Those that remain must consequently produce enough to feed the absent workers, meet the needs of the traditional communities and maintain a flow of goods for exchange on foreign markets. In fact, however, the productivity of the independent farmer has fallen off in almost every part of Africa south of the Sahara. An official inquiry held in 1949 into the economic circumstances of the population in a Ciskei Native Reserve in the Union of South Africa showed that only a very

small fraction (6.8 per cent) of the farmers' average income was derived from agriculture. In no village was the fraction more than 10.4 per cent. Much of the population's income (35 per cent) was derived from extra-reserve earnings (probably the wages of villagers who had found employment in areas some distance away). No indication is given of the other sources of income. Farm produce consisted of a little maize and kaffir corn, plus eggs and poultry; the main source of income, however, was the sale of wool.[8]

In the Native Reserves, the soil is becoming less and less productive. The official farm census returns show that a total of about 620 million pounds of maize and 148 million pounds of kaffir corn were produced between 1923 and 1927. The corresponding figures for 1935 to 1939, however, were no more than 478 and 122 million pounds respectively. In 1949 the average yields of maize in the area covered by the above inquiry were found to be as low as 30 pounds an acre.[9]

In Southern Rhodesia, the soil in the Native Reserves is almost as unproductive as in the corresponding areas of the Union of South Africa. For the years 1936 to 1946, maize yields in the Reserves are reported to have ranged from 1.5 to 2.0 bags an acre, as compared with a yield of 4.5 to 7.0 bags on the European farms. This means that two full acres are needed to support one person (at the desirable rate of 2,850 calories a day).[10]

The problem is aggravated by population increase. Unfertile land and the poverty that goes with it have led many of the younger members of the population to migrate. A report from Southern Rhodesia for 1948 states that a little over half the total male population is absent from the Native areas.[11]

This position is in no way exceptional. The work of Colin Maher and Humphrey [12] on Kenya, Clément,[13] Drachoussoff[14] and Malengreau[15] on the Belgian Congo, and Guilloteau[16] and Dumont[17] on French West Africa have shown that the exhaustion of the soil and the resulting drop in the incomes of African farmers are tending to become general. What is worse, it is clear that the native farmer is simply unable to increase his productivity, the limit to what he can do being governed by factors beyond his control. African farmers have neither the capital nor the technical knowledge, nor in some cases the cultivable land, to expand their output.

The result of this is that over large areas of tropical Africa, output is inadequate, and low living standards and instability are prevalent among both the independent farmers and the African wage earners. The peoples of Africa are poor because they do not produce enough. In order to create wealth they must produce more, so that the surplus production can be used to buy more efficient tools, pay for the cost of education and vocational training, acquire fertilisers for their land, extend the expectation of life through medical care, etc. As it is, they have to eat most of their own output of food or use it to buy clothing and other basic consumer goods.

The position is by no means hopeless. In Africa as elsewhere, the productivity of men depends on a few major factors:

(1) the amount of labour in relation to the available land;

(2) the amount of labour in relation to the available capital;

(3) the methods of production;

(4) the state of the labour force from the standpoint of health, intelligence and character, and its skill and training.

The first three factors must be studied if the productivity of the independent farmers is to be raised. However, in the case of the wage earners, whose opportunities are governed in the main by the society in which they are brought up and the undertakings for which they work, the human factor is the only one that matters. Moreover, in such a thinly populated continent as Africa the importance of man himself is preponderant. The following pages are accordingly devoted to an analysis of the human factor in productivity.

The productivity of an undertaking does not depend entirely on the workers it employs, but it is evident that the human factor is decisive, since no job can be done without a practical and intelligent approach. It follows that in any analysis of the factors governing productivity, particular attention must be paid to the worker's physical and mental health.

In the first place, the worker's fundamental aptitudes must be examined and, also, the kind of life he leads in his original environment, taking into account the attendant physical, climatic, social and moral circumstances. The next step is to try to understand what the transplantation to factory or city life means to him, and especially, the importance he attaches to his conditions of employment (wages, accommodation and so on), industrial relations, basic education and vocational training. Lastly one must attempt to estimate the violence of the shock he suffers on embarking on a way of life entirely different in conception, pattern and tempo from anything he has previously experienced.

The aptitudes of African workers have been the subject of much study. Attempts have been made to test the average development of their intelligence,[18] but a comparison of the results obtained with those yielded by similar experiments on Europeans has produced no conclusive evidence, and the most recent writers on the subject do not hide their scepticism.

It has indeed become abundantly clear in recent years that there is no present possibility of assessing the comparative general intelligence of Europeans and Africans in Africa; environmental differences are too many and too great, and have profound effects on traits (such as speed) and motives that influence the test achievement.[19]

The same author has been even more explicit in a recent booklet:

It has become increasingly clear in recent years that no fundamental differences between different groups of Africans, or even between Africans and Europeans, have yet been demonstrated. It is possible that intrinsic differences do exist but, if so, they are probably

quite slight and at present undiscoverable. . . .
The manifest differences that do exists a
between Europeans and Africans, and which
have been described by many writers, can be
well explained on the basis of experience, of
environmental factors. The chief environmental factors that account for the observed
diversities are climatic, infective, nutritional
and cultural. Of these, the last is overwhelmingly important, and in general it can be said
that the minds of men (unlike their bodies) are
mainly products of their cultures.[20]

The African's vocational aptitudes, however, are also important. A number of
interesting studies have been made in connection with short-course vocational training methods by an aptitude-testing mission
working in Brazzaville in French Equatorial
Africa, and Dakar in French West Africa.
The head of the mission has recorded the
following description of its findings:

(1) In an initial experiment conducted in
French Equatorial Africa, we found that the
aptitudes (mechanical, verbal, mathematical,
visual, etc.) that distinguish one European
from another were by no means easy to discern
in the young Africans we examined on
recruitment.

We then decided to measure their general
level of intelligence, or rather their powers of
adaptation. Judging by the success of the
training courses, this proved to be an efficient
method of selection. But the most interesting
thing we found was that when we resumed our
aptitude tests on the same subjects after four
months' training, not only were the results
more satisfactory, but the gifts of each subject
had become normally apparent—which seems
to confirm our suspicion that aptitudes are
impossible of measurement (at least by European standards) in the absence of any training
similar to that given in the place of reference.

(2) In this experiment, and in the other
experiments conducted later in French West
Africa, the standard set for the tests was lower
than is usual in France. The results obtained
at the beginning of the training were also
somewhat lower than those obtained in
France with corresponding courses. Even so,
it was only a few months before the progress
charts caught up with those we had plotted
for French workers, thus proving that the
African's initial difficulties are neither inherent nor insuperable. . . .

So far everything goes to show that, given
comparative equality of knowledge, the
African worker's basic intellect is the same as
that of his European counterpart—at least at
the level we have studied.[21]

The African is closely bound up with his
physical environment, and any assessment
made of him must therefore take account of
the climate in which he lives, the diseases he
suffers from, the food he eats, and the social
group from which he comes.

As regards climate, the view has been expressed that with freedom from malnutrition
and infection, and when other circumstances
are propitious, African society can rise to
splendid heights, and that Africans themselves are basically well adapted to their
climate.[22] Even if this view is considered
overoptimistic, the African climate would
not appear to be a major obstacle to the
productivity of labour.

In a study of labour productivity in the
Belgian Congo, Mr. Arthur Doucy has
described the physical condition of workers
from the Mayumbe, Tshuapa and Middle
Kwilu districts on arrival from their tribal
areas. He states:

(1) they all suffer from parasitic worms of
the intestines;
(2) some suffer from parasitic worms of the
blood;
(3) all have malaria;
(4) all have incipient yaws, for which they
have received little or no treatment;
(5) most have or have had gonorrhoea;
(6) many have syphilis;
(7) some of these conditions reduce their
haemoglobin level, which in many cases is as
low as 65 per cent, i.e., a red blood count of 3
to $3\frac{1}{2}$ million.[23]

This gloomy picture is unfortunately
generally true, though the specific infections
vary. Dr. Carothers, after mentioning the
main diseases to which Africans are subject,
adds:

Few Africans are free from all of these, and it
would be easy to find examples of persons in-
fected concurrently with malaria, hookworm,
bilharziasis, ascariasis, and taeniasis, with a
haemoglobin level of about 30 per cent, and
yet not complaining of ill health. "Normality"
in the African, even from the standpoint of
infection alone, is a rather meaningless
abstraction.[24]

This description of the pathological conditions found among a high percentage of Africans has a parallel in the reports that have come in from various sources concerning the effects of the chronic malnutrition so common in many parts of Africa. The fact that many African communities are underfed has been placed on record on numerous occasions, notably in 1939 by the British Committee on Nutrition in the Colonial Empire,[25] and in 1949 by the Inter-African Conference on Food and Nutrition held at Dschang in the French Cameroons. Dr. Carothers also writes:

> In summary, African diets are lacking in a variety of constituents necessary for physical and mental health. These deficiencies are most widespread and prominent in regard to protein, vitamin A, and certain members of the vitamin B complex. The chief sufferers are the infants and young children, but no age is immune. The classical deficiency diseases are seldom seen, but the bulk of the population lives on the verge of their development, and in periods of stringency they promptly appear.[26]

The main deficiency diseases referred to are pellagra and malignant malnutrition, also known as "kwashiorkor."

The effects of chronic malnutrition have not been accurately assessed in Africa, but it appears certain that in vast areas where malnutrition is an everyday occurrence, the inhabitants lack vitality and drive.

However far the low standard of productivity in Africa may be attributable to malnutrition and disease, it would be wrong to explain the inefficiency of the African industrial worker wholly in terms of his physical condition. The infections to which Africans are subject take a much stronger hold on them in the rural areas, where medical supervision is virtually nonexistent and malnutrition is also more acute. On the other hand, it would not be true to say that the African is generally incapable of sustained effort in his native environment. Many observers have testified to the contrary, among them Dr. Ombredane, who writes: "It has often surprised me to see Negroes working from 8 o'clock in the morning until 2 in the afternoon without any break for rest or refreshment, in an effort to finish a hut or a piece of raffia work, a hatchet, a hoe, an ivory figure or a mask that they had started making."[27] Mr. Ryckmans quotes the case of men who think nothing of a 12-hour walk into the jungle to fetch well over a hundredweight of brushwood.[28] Other illustrations can be found in the back-breaking job of clearing farmland and in the many other communal tasks that form a part of African village life. In the case of the farming population, as was mentioned earlier, the explanation of the low level of productivity lies in the inefficient farming methods and the desertion of the villages by the men. In the case of the wage-earning population, on the other hand, it seems that some other explanation must be found.

It is natural to look first for a connection between the African wage earner's indifference towards his job and the new setting in which he finds himself, involving as it does the payment of a wage as well as special housing, training, industrial relations and so on.

To a European worker wages are the fundamental incentive to work. It has often been said of the African worker that wages offer no inducement, and that less effort rather than more is likely to be the result of higher pay. This bare statement will not stand investigation. In a paper submitted to the Belgian Royal Colonial Institute, Mr. R. van der Linden has shown how wage increases in a Léopoldville shipyard between 1939 and 1950 were accompanied by an appreciable rise in productivity. What is true is that many Africans with crops or cattle to look after in their villages look for wage-paid employment with the sole idea of earning a little extra money with which to pay their taxes or to buy some article. If, having found a job, the wage is increased and they succeed in saving the requisite amount more quickly, they see no further point in working and either slacken off or try to leave. What is taken to be a lack of logic, or as a sign of indifference or laziness, is in fact the outward expression of a perfectly valid piece of reasoning. Even so, before wages can play the same part in the life of African workers as in the life of Europeans, money and economic forces generally will have to acquire the same significance in the African's social group as in the Western world. At the present time, Africans living in a subsistence economy can still dispense with wages and not starve. This, however, raises the problem of the African's relations with his social group—a point to be considered later.

There is no need to emphasise how much a worker's output can be affected by his housing. If an unstable worker is to settle, he has to be given a chance of finding accommodation near his workplace, and if he is to settle for any length of time, some arrangement must also be made to house his family. Some employers have recognised the benefits of a stable labour force and have arranged for suitable accommodation to be built for their employees. This, however, has not happened in the cities. In most cities the way the African population is huddled together in makeshift dwellings has to be seen to be believed.

However, while poor housing may discourage a worker from settling down, it should not be assumed that satisfactory housing will always have the opposite effect.

The value of training is self-evident. C. H. Northcott, writing of Africans in Kenya, states that men "who knew nothing of mechanics and until they reached Nairobi had never seen a railway train, are met in the railway workshops with a display of mechanism so great that it bewilders even a well-educated European."[29] The results achieved with training are in fact spectacular, but no worthwhile training can be given to a worker who stays only six months. Training presupposes a certain amount of stability; before a worker can be trained, moreover, he must be imbued with a desire to work.

It may be asked whether the problem can be solved by satisfactory labour-management relations. While an atmosphere of confidence and understanding can undoubtedly do much to encourage more effective and sincere co-operation on the part of African workers, it cannot guarantee success or higher output. There are certain over-riding factors influencing the conduct of the African worker, and even the best employer is powerless against them.

The analysis of the factors determining a worker's output leads to a fundamental question: Does the African want to work in an undertaking of the Western type? As one author has observed:

Men of all races work only to achieve some end. If that end is unobtainable, or not valued very highly, they either work light-heartedly or not at all. The African in town is in just this position. His expenditure is limited almost entirely to consumable goods, the kind of bric-a-brac that a traveller picks up on his travels. With none of the tribal sanctions capable of operation, with few kinsmen in town to remind the worker of his obligations, and with no urban public opinion, there is nothing, either in his own social system or in that of the West, to inspire him to greater effort.[30]

The above quotation emphasises the solitude of the normal Negro worker. He has lost his attachment to the land, he no longer takes part in tribal consultations, he no longer shares in the labour, joys and sorrows of his village. The significance of this isolation is difficult to grasp without some knowledge of the African's normal way of life in his natural environment and as a member of his social group. Carothers writes:

Life in Africa was highly insecure, but the individual did achieve some inner sense of personal security by adherence, and only by adherence, to the traditional rules—rules which received their sanction and most of their force from the "will" of ancestors whose spirits were conceived as powerful and as maintaining their attachment to the land. There were fears, of course, and misfortunes were almost the order of the day, but even these were seldom without precedent, and for each of these there were prescribed behaviour patterns which satisfied the urge to action, so that the African achieved a measure of stability and, within his group and while at home, was courteous, socially self-confident and, in effect, a social being. But this stability was maintained solely by the continuing support afforded by his culture and by the prompt suppression of initiative.[31]

Limits are placed on the freedom of the individual, for otherwise he would be lost to the community.[32] No culture is absolutely static, for a static culture cannot survive. The

African tribal system, like every other, has an infinite capacity for adaptation. But the fact remains that for a man brought up under a system deeply rooted in tradition and so vitally dependent on a code of social behaviour, the change to an entirely different way of living is a great strain. As Carothers observes, change has become a familiar feature of modern Europe and America. For an African, however, the shock is incomparably more violent, and it is natural that when he suddenly finds himself confronted with a way of life in which he is left alone to face a multitude of unknown risks, against which his tribal culture can afford him no protection, his first sensation is one of insecurity. This is a point on which all observers are agreed. Mannoni states that when a Malgache finds his traditional chain of authority in danger, if not actually disrupted, he falls a prey to panic, insecurity and a sudden sense of insufficiency.[33] Balandier also notes that the formation of an urban proletariat has gone hand in hand with a rising sense of insecurity. In a report on Elisabethville prepared on April 3, 1950, Grévisse writes: "The thought uppermost in the minds of the Bantu population of the towns is not a desire for individuality or freedom, as is often mistakenly believed; it is neither more nor less than a desire for some security."[34] But the security an African requires is not of a mystical or instinctive kind; it is physical and economic. What he wants is a guarantee against starvation and an assurance that he can live and grow old in peace with his family.

In Western civilisation, men work for money because of the security that it brings or because of the possessions and the prestige that a wealthy man can command. In African society men also sought security and prestige. These were likewise achieved only by hard work, although the concept of money did not enter into the situation. . . . The urban situation, however, demands that the African should work as hard as, or even harder than, he has ever done before but, at the same time, neither his work nor the money that he earns can provide him with the security or the prestige that he would like. The average urban African is unhealthy, badly housed, uneducated, and he lacks any security in town even if he happens to have been born there. . . . The bars to progress are very real to him and he knows that, under present conditions, town life in European employment can offer him little in the way of lucrative employment or future stability. Consciously or unconsciously, therefore, he refuses to cut himself completely adrift from his tribal kinsmen and his tribal background. This tendency to live and work in town while maintaining unproductive land in the reserves is referred to as the "foot in both camps attitude" and is largely condemned on the grounds that a man who attempts to retain a foot-hold in both places cannot be efficient in either. There is considerable truth in this assertion . . . the actual situation is that the urban Africans are poised between two different ways of life or systems of belief. They see clearly enough that the kinship system of tribal days and the monetary system of the West are incompatible. They see the two systems in conflict and they want to come out on the winning side. At present, however, neither side can offer any long-term advantage. The monetary system of the West offers goods but no security. The kinship system offers few goods but some security. This security, however, is already somewhat suspect because of the break-up of the tribal order. On the other hand, the precarious state of those who are completely detribalised, who have no country home to retire to in their old age, or who have no knowledge of country life, is fully realised. And so the majority of men continue to sit on the fence and attempt to retain such rural security as is available together with as many of the material benefits of town life as they can obtain. . . . Little change can be expected in the low level of efficiency, however, because the motives that are fundamental in prompting a man to work—the desire for security and self-respect—cannot operate.[35]

At first sight it would appear that the way to raise productivity is to do away with the alternative—to assist the worker in severing his tribal ties and to settle him, together with his family, at or near a centre of employment. To quote Carothers:

As things are, the chief incentive in the towns is to acquire money quickly with a view to a return to rural living. The ambition to improve one's skills and rise in urban industry cannot develop until the rural boats are burned; but I have no doubt that once these boats are burned and incentives are reoriented these people will work as competently, and ultimately as creatively, as any other men.[36]

This policy of stabilising African workers

near a center of employment has been adopted in the Belgian Congo for some years, and also, though more recently, in Kenya. The policy has been very clearly stated in the Report of the Committee on African Wages:

Of a total of some 350,000 adult male African workers in employment outside the reserves, it is estimated that more than half are of the migrant or "target" type; that is to say, they are workers who have left the reserves for a specific purpose—for example, to earn sufficient money to pay tax, replenish a wardrobe or acquire a wife . . . and return to the reserves once that purpose has been achieved. Many of them spend no more than six months outside the reserves in any one year and, for all practical purposes, they may be regarded as temporary workers. . . . It is only by retaining his stake in the reserve, and by returning there at frequent intervals, that the African worker can ensure, for both himself and his family, the minimum requirements of sustenance, a house in which to live, and security for old age. It follows that, if we are to induce the African worker to sever his tribal ties, and convert him into an effective working unit, we must be prepared to offer him, in his new environment, advantages at least as favourable as those he already enjoys in the reserve. . . . They are—the payment of a wage sufficient to provide for the essential needs of the worker and his family; regular employment; a house in which the worker and his family can live; and security for the worker's old age. At a later stage—when we have reached our objective—consideration will also obviously have to be given to the problems arising from unemployment among a stabilised working population.[37]

These changes may be expected to yield positive results. In the Belgian Congo, undertakings that have been employing stabilised labour for some years have reported an appreciable improvement in efficiency. Even so, it would not appear that the problem has been solved. For more than ten years the Union Minière has made it a practice to employ stabilised African labour, but one of its advisers, Mr. Fischer, stated in a report to the General Assembly of the Belgian Colonial Congress on June 6, 1952, that a spirit of tribal solidarity still persists even among many of the more enlightened workers and that in the majority of cases money incentives are ineffective.

What, then, is lacking? One writer has observed that "before wages can be fully operative as a factor in behaviour, they will have to find their proper place in a new pattern of society built up as a prolongation of the older order." [38] As the same writer has observed elsewhere in connection with the new wage-earning population, it should be possible to resettle them, re-establish their bonds of solidarity, and rebuild an organic community entitled to protect their interests and providing them with the guarantees that their original community is no longer able to afford.[39]

It is interesting to see the progress being made in the British West African territories, which offer many useful pointers for the future, inasmuch as development, and especially the development of African urban society, has been more rapid there than elsewhere. In these territories, as in the rest of Africa, the rural population have left their homes and families and gone into the towns in search of work. Statistics show that between 1931 and 1950, the population of Lagos increased by 80 per cent as a result of an influx from every tribal group in the country.

What has happened in consequence of this mingling of people and their shift from rural to urban pursuits is that a new social organisation has arisen. This is based on association, principally by occupation and by tribe, and it is taking responsibility for many of the duties traditionally performed by extended family and other kinship groups . . . Coleman reports similarly from Nigeria. There, too, these tribal associations have been organised spontaneously in the new urban centres. . . . "They are the medium," says Coleman, "for re-integrating the individual employed in an impersonal urban city by permitting him to have the essential feeling of belonging." These Nigerian tribal associations also provide mutual aid and protection, including sustenance during unemployment, solicitude and financial assistance in case of illness, and the responsibility for funerals and the repatriation of the family of the deceased in the event of death. . . . The fact that many kinship groups are no longer economically self-sufficient impairs their solidarity for other social purposes, and the result is that occupational and other associations which cut across tribal and kinship lines have taken over many of the activities previously performed by the extended family, the lineage, and similar traditional organisations.[40]

It would seem at first sight that this immense and diversified effort on the part of Africans to build up an entirely new and integrated social structure for their own protection when the older traditional society is beginning to disintegrate corresponds to former developments in Europe. One immediately calls to mind the rapid growth of the trade unions, the co-operative movement and the mutual benefit societies that came with the Industrial Revolution. There are marked differences, however, between what happened in the West and what is now happening in Africa. In the West the changes sprang from a more or less conscious impulse and developed naturally out of the economic and social movements of the past. The political and social structure was disturbed and, on occasion, underwent far-reaching changes, but there was continuity. In many respects the peoples of the West emerged from the ordeal with an even greater sense of national solidarity than before, and the community at large was also strengthened by the access of new sections of the population to the responsibilities of government. Nothing of the kind has happened in Africa. There was no preparation for the brutal changes that the community has undergone since 1850, and the changes came through the intervention of a foreign people. The new arrivals were not in any way concerned with preserving the foundations of traditional African society, and the result was unquestionably a weakening of the social structure. In the closing years of the nineteenth century and the beginning of the twentieth, settlement ceased to be confined to small and isolated groups of Europeans (such as explorers, missionaries and merchants), and the formation of an organised and stable European colony using the commercial and industrial techniques of Western Europe had a revolutionary effect on the indigenous population, to whom the advent of the European settlers revealed an alternative to farming and to the other traditional forms of tribal life. To the members of a strictly closed society such as then existed on the continent of Africa, the prospect of escape that was offered in this way could only serve to precipitate a crisis. The occupation of African territory by a foreign administration was also accompanied by interference in every aspect of their lives: religion, the organisation of society, feeding habits, farming methods, family relationships, the wisdom of the elders, the education of children—nothing remained intact. The African felt the ground shifting beneath his feet and suddenly perceived that the most stable elements in his experience had been shaken and were untrustworthy. Some of the officials sent out by the colonial Powers to administer and develop the new territories realised the extent to which the African community had been disturbed and tried to preserve as much of the political and social system as they could. Lord Lugard's "dual mandate" had its counterpart in Galliéni's orders for Madagascar and Lyautey's instructions for Morocco. But however well inspired such efforts may be, there are limits to what they can achieve; it is not always possible to preserve a system that is no longer in touch with present-day requirements or with the most progressive sections of the population. In a large part of tropical Africa, the social structure is disintegrating, if it has not already done so, and a new and improvised system of society cannot easily acquire the solidity and strength of one that is rooted in tradition. It may be argued that before doing away with the tribal basis of society an honest attempt should be made to give it new vitality and strength. Such an attempt, however, is not always possible. However poor and inadequate the new framework of society may be, it is always better than no framework at all. Consequently, where the traditional system seems to be declining, the possibility of remodelling the whole of indigenous society has to be considered.

All these factors have a direct effect on productivity. Every human being lives, works and dies within the framework of society, and, should it ever be threatened with collapse, his life and work are influenced accordingly. For the African, the problem of security is twofold—collective and individual.

The reason why collective security is such an urgent problem is that the primitive society was based on a code of neighbourly assistance that constituted a permanent guarantee for every member of the group. The spontaneous associations that are being formed among the mass of the detribalised working population hold out a promise for the future. In the economic and cultural sphere, the community development schemes and other similar ventures, and in the social sphere the mutual benefit societies, seem to have made a great impression, without having any specific political affinities, and should bring out the best leaders among the African population. The community principle behind these projects should make for consultation and so provide a safeguard against arbitrary action. Similarly, the efforts made to eliminate racial opposition and discrimination and build up a homogeneous society could undoubtedly do much, with time, to reduce one element of tension that makes for insecurity among the African population.

The African has also a problem of individual security. The straitened circumstances of their families now force the younger generation to make a rapid choice. Their own existence and that of their dependants are in danger; for them this is a new situation, since the livelihood of their fathers and forefathers had always been assured by the communities in which they lived. If the African decides to go to work in a factory, he encounters a new form of insecurity; whereas he naturally hopes to find the same neighbourliness and community spirit in his new surroundings that he was accustomed to find in his native village, he is suddenly confronted with antagonism.

When a tribal Negro agrees to enter the employment of a foreign master, he does so, perhaps without realising it, on the very real assumption that the master will take the place hitherto occupied by his tribal chief, or rather by the tribe in its entirety as represented by the chief, i.e. that he will take him over as he is, and be responsible for every aspect of his life —in fact, be a kind of father and mother to him. If we may be permitted to use precise and rather abstract terms, the Negro looks upon his wages not as payment for work done but as a token of a social contract.[41]

Mannoni gives a somewhat similar description of how relationships of dependency are formed in Madagascar.[42]

This feeling of insecurity can be partly overcome by the worker's belonging to a union; this gives him a new and vital sense of comradeship but stresses still further the antagonism that he finds so painful.

A number of rural employers in one of the provinces in the Belgian Congo have decided, with the assent of the African labour they employ, to replace the contract of employment by a contract under which the worker no longer enters into a personal commitment but simply undertakes to do a job.[43] The agreement is concluded between the two parties more or less on an equal footing, and the African worker has no difficulty in finding many precedents for it in tribal law. This is also true of other contracts, such as the contract of supply and certain contracts between landlord and tenant. There are, of course, many types of industrial employment to which contracts of this kind are hardly suited. Even so, the contract of employment itself is flexible enough in many ways. The modern world has ceased to regard it as the token of a sale in the ordinary meaning of the term and has recognised that the employer is not freed of all obligations when he has paid for the work. He is obliged to take account of the worker as a person, and the majority of Western laws require him to pay a pension to aged workers, compensation to workers injured at their work and even special allowances to workers with large families. Recreation facilities are also organised. All this is evidence that labour is not a commodity, and we are therefore forced to recognise that the African's reaction is essentially the reaction of a human being against an abstract and rigid legal concept. Yet it should be possible to make the human factor play an even greater part in the contract of employment by increasing the number of joint councils of employers and workers and by making them competent to deal with certain private matters of immediate concern to the workers and their families.

There are many other ways of encouraging the African worker to settle down in a normal social system, e.g., by schemes for providing housing at low cost, by affording facilities whereby the worker can become the owner of a house or land, by stabilising workers and their families at or near their places of employment, by paying wages adequate to support a family, by encouraging co-operatives, indigenous handicrafts, basic education, vocational training, and so on. Many of these suggestions are now being followed up in Africa, but there are two aspects of the worker's social life that have not been given the attention they deserve. The first is the position of the aged worker. There can be no question of security for a worker who knows that he has nothing to expect in the way of provision for his old age in the urban or industrial centre where he works. His natural inclination will be to keep open some line of retreat to his traditional environment. He will not work well, will be content to draw a meagre wage and will choose his own time to leave his employment. A great deal consequently remains to be done to guarantee detribalised workers a pension and, if possible, a house, and perhaps the chance of increasing their resources from market gardening.

Equal importance attaches to the facilities for workers' upgrading. Mr. Cumper, in his analysis of productivity in Jamaica, considers that the low standard of efficiency of local labour is to some extent attributable to the rigid system of social stratification, which in practice prevents any worker from rising above the foreman level.[44]

Exactly the same is true of Africa. In the Union of South Africa and in Southern Rhodesia law, tradition and the pressure of European labour all combine to keep the African worker in the semi-skilled or un-skilled grades. In Northern Rhodesia the position is the same, except that it has been brought about by the action of the European workers' unions. In British East and West Africa, the Belgian Congo and the French territories, the inadequate vocational facilities, the Negro's lack of general education and, in certain cases, the presence of European labour still keep the African in a posi-

tion of inferiority from which he has little prospect of escaping. Yet no man can be expected to reach a high standard of efficiency when he is denied the chance of improving his situation by work. The efforts already made to generalise vocational training might be coupled with an endeavour to introduce the principles of Training Within Industry as recognised and applied in Europe and America.

A worker's productivity, after all, is no more than a particular manifestation of human behaviour and should be studied in the context of the whole man. The African has had a very violent shock and has suffered considerably as a result. In a closed society where all precautions had been taken to safeguard the individual against all the hazards of life, a revolution has suddenly exposed him to a variety of hazards for which he is wholly unprepared. He cannot be expected to behave as if nothing had happened. The African of today has no assured future ahead of him and finds it impossible to pin his faith either in the values of the Western world, to which in any event he has hardly any access, or in the values of his former world, whose foundations have been shaken.

We are now in a position to see what is involved in raising the productivity of the African worker. Essentially it means restoring his self-confidence, and this will not be easy—the task of building up a feeling of security from nothing is beyond the powers of any human agency. Psychological adjustment must come first. However, much can be done to make adjustment easier. A number of possibilities have been mentioned in this article, and there are others. To seek out these possibilities, try them out and make them known is one of the most important duties of those who are helping to shape the destiny of Africa.

Notes

1. United Nations, *Enlargement of the Exchange Economy in Tropical Africa*, Document E/2557, ST/ECA/23 (New York, 1954), p. 4.
2. *Ibid.*, p. 3.
3. University of Natal, Department of Economics, *The African Factory Worker* (Cape Town: Oxford University Press, 1950), p. 99.
4. Quoted by B. Gussman in "Industrial

Efficiency and the Urban African," *Africa*, Vol. XXIII, No. 2, April, 1953, p. 135.

5. Colonial Office, United Kingdom, *Labour Conditions in East Africa*, report by Major G. St. J. Orde Browne (London: H.M. Stationery Office, 1946), p. 15.

6. *Bulletin du Centre d'étude des problèmes sociaux indigènes (C.E.P.S.I.)* (Elisabethville), 1949, No. 10, p. 96.

7. J. Guilbot, *Petite étude sur la main-d'œuvre à Douala* (Yaoundé, 1947), pp. 50–51.

8. See D. Hobart Houghton and D. Philcox, "Family Income and Expenditure in a Ciskei Native Reserve," in *South African Journal of Economics*, Vol. XVIII, No. 4, December, 1950, p. 427.

9. *Ibid.*, p. 433.

10. Sir Frank Engledow, *Report to the Minister of Agriculture and Lands in the Agricultural Development of Southern Rhodesia* (Salisbury: Government Stationery Office, 1950), p. 20.

11. *Report of the Secretary for Native Affairs, Chief Native Commissioner, and Director of Native Development, for the Year 1948* (Salisbury: Government Stationery Office, 1949), p. 7.

12. N. Humphrey, *The Kikuyu Lands* (1945), quoted in *East Africa and Rhodesia* (London), September 25, 1947, p. 57.

13. J. Clément, "Etude relative au paysannat indigène," in *Contribution à l'étude du problème de l'économie rurale indigène au Congo belge*, special issue of *Bulletin agricole du Congo belge* (Brussels), Vol. XLIII, 1952.

14. V. Drachoussoff, "Essai sur l'agriculture indigène au Bas-Congo," *Bulletin agricole du Congo belge*, Vol. XXXVIII, No. 4, December, 1947, pp. 855–856.

15. G. Malengreau, "Les lotissements agricoles au Congo belge," in *Contribution à l'étude du problème de l'économie rurale indigène au Congo belge, op. cit.*

16. J. Guilloteau, "La dégradation des sols tropicaux," in *Record of the XXVth Meeting held in Brussels on the 28th, 29th and 30th November 1949* (Brussels: International Institute of Political and Social Sciences [Comparative Civilisations]. 1950).

17. R. Dumont, "Etude de quelques économies agraires au Sénégal et en Casamance," in *L'agronomie tropicale*, Vol. VI, Nos. 5 and 6, May–June, 1951, pp. 232–233.

18. S. Biesheuvel, *African Intelligence* (Johannesburg, 1943).

19. J. C. Carothers, *The African Mind in Health and Disease*, (Geneva: World Health Organisation, 1953), Monograph Series No. 17, pp. 90–91.

20. *Idem: The Psychology of Mau Mau*, (Nairobi: Government Printer, 1954), p. 2.

21. R. Durand, "La formation professionnelle et la psychologie des noirs," in *Problèmes d'Afrique centrale*, No. 24, 2nd quarter 1954, pp. 105–106. For an account of similar experiments in the Belgian Congo, which gave similar

results, see A. Ombredane, "Principes pour une étude psychologique des noirs du Congo belge," in *L'Année psychologique*, 1951, p. 539.

22. *The African Mind in Health and Disease, op. cit.*, pp. 170–171.

23. Institut royal colonial belge, *Bulletin des séances* (Brussels, 1954), Vol. XXV, p. 785.

24. *The African Mind in Health and Disease, op. cit.*, pp. 32–33.

25. Economic Advisory Council, Committee on Nutrition in the Colonial Empire, *First Report*, Parts I and II, Cmd. 6050 and 6051 (London: H.M. Stationery Office, 1939).

26. *The African Mind in Health and Disease, op. cit.*, pp. 40–41.

27. A. Ombredane, *op. cit.*, p. 532.

28. P. Ryckmans, *Dominer pour servir* (Brussels: L'Edition universelle, 1948).

29. *African Labour Efficiency Survey, op. cit.*, p. 120.

30. B. Gussman, "Industrial Efficiency and the Urban African," *loc. cit.*

31. *The Psychology of Mau Mau, op. cit.*, pp. 2–3.

32. Rev. P. Charles, "Travail et psychologie africaine," in *Les missions et le prolétariat* (Brussels: Desclée de Brouwer, 1954), p. 169.

33. O. Mannoni, *Psychologie de la colonisation* (Paris: Editions du seuil, 1950), pp. 32–33.

34. Quoted by E. Toussaint in "Rendement de la main-d'œuvre indigène" (*Bulletin trimestriel du Centre d'étude des problèmes sociaux indigènes [C.E.P.S.I.]*), 1953, No. 21, p. xvi.

35. B. Gussman, *op. cit.*, pp. 141–143.

36. *The Psychology of Mau Mau, op. cit.*, p. 24.

37. Colony and Protectorate of Kenya, *Report of the Committee on African Wages* (Nairobi: Government Printer, 1954), pp. 13, 15 and 16.

38. Rev. P. Charles, "Problèmes de travail et réalités africaines," in *Bulletin bimestriel de la société belge d'études et d'expansion*, No. 152, August, 1952, p. 585.

39. "Travail et psychologie africaine," *loc. cit.*, p. 170.

40. Kenneth Little, "The Study of 'Social Change' in British West Africa," in *Africa*, Vol. XXIII, No. 4, October, 1953, pp. 277–279.

41. "Travail et psychologie africaine," *loc. cit.*, p. 173.

42. O. Mannoni, *op. cit.*, pp. 31–33.

43. Even if the idea of the employers was merely to evade their responsibilities under the legislation governing contracts of employment, the fact is interesting, since it shows that African workers prefer a situation that safeguards their independence even if it is less well paid.

44. G. E. Cumper, "Two Studies in Jamaican Productivity," in *Social and Economic Studies* (Institute of Social and Economic Research, Jamaica), Vol. 1, No. 2, June, 1953, p. 34.

Education

ALTHOUGH Western concern, especially in the United States, about the problems of education in Africa has expanded considerably during the past half decade or so, as the number of new nations has increased, it would not be correct to attribute relatively recent origins to the development of education in Africa. African education dates back to ancient times in Egypt, to the establishment of Moslem mosques in the centuries following the death of Mohammed, to the University of Timbuktu in the sixteenth century, to the schools of the Dutch on the Gold Coast and in South Africa during the seventeenth century, and to the missionary schools in the nineteenth century. The full story of the growth and progress of education over the centuries in the various parts of Africa still remains to be told. That a wealth of material is available is evident from the fact that the West has shown an interest in African culture from the Greco–Roman period right through the dawn of modern history.[1]

The attention given to African education in recent years is worthy of notice. During May 15 to 25, 1961, there took place in Addis Ababa, Ethiopia, a Conference of African States on the Development of Education in Africa, as recommended by the Eleventh General Conference of Unesco. At this historic meeting, representatives of 31 African governments and territories and of four European countries agreed upon the Addis Ababa Plan, a twenty-year program which would raise educational expenses from $450,000,000 (1960) to $2,200,000,000 (1980). Later, in the fall of 1961, the U.S. National Commission for Unesco devoted its Eighth National Conference to the theme "Africa and the United States: Images and Realities," which included serious consideration of the educational problems common to most African countries. In April, 1962, 31 ministers of education and three deputy ministers of 34 African nations met at the Paris headquarters of Unesco to follow up the Addis Ababa Plan. Most recently, during September, 1962, an Inter-African Conference on Higher Education met at Tananarive,

Tendencies in African Education

William W. Brickman

From Educational Forum, *Vol. 27 (May 1963),* *pp. 399–416. Reprinted with permission of Kappa Delta Pi, an Honor Society in Education, holder of the copyright.*

Madagascar, to plan the development of higher education in North and tropical Africa, especially with reference to the manpower needs of the rapidly growing nations.

In the meantime, the literature on African education began to multiply. Apart from the reports of the many conferences, there have appeared special African issues of educational journals, studies such as "Educational and Occupational Selection in West Africa" (edited by A. Taylor), historical monographs such as Franklin Parker's "African Development and Education in Southern Rhodesia," and a comprehensive survey of "The Educated African" (edited by Helen Kitchen), and other new publications. The rising demand for reading matter on African education was no doubt responsible for the issuance, late in 1962, of an abridgment by L. J. Lewis, of the University of London Institute of Education, of the "Phelps–Stokes Reports on Education in Africa."

Europeans and Americans are becoming better informed about African education through the presence and activities of the teachers exported in increasing numbers to Africa, as well as through the numerous African students in foreign universities. During the summer of 1962, two sizable delegations of educators, nearly all of them Americans, visited schools and universities in several African countries, by reason of the

alertness and initiative of Professor Gerald
H. Read of Kent State University, who has
made a lasting contribution as secretary–
treasurer of the Comparative Education
Society.

Interest in the problems and developments
of education in Africa is at a high pitch.
Information is available as never before.
There seems to be little reason for any
student of education to ignore Africa,
especially because of the crucial importance
of the continent for the future of world
civilization. In the following pages, the
present writer will endeavor to point up as
specifically as possible the more pressing
problems and tendencies in African education at the present time. The analysis is
based to an extent on visits to educational
institutions of all levels in East, Central,
South, and West Africa during August and
September of 1962. In addition, the writer
has made use of what he heard in discussions,
debates, and conversations with all kinds of
African educators and other informed
individuals. Finally, he has read a good deal
of source materials in several languages on
the historical background and the problems
and issues of education in Africa. However,
because of the lack of space it will not be
possible to cite directly all of the pertinent
references. While some of the comments may
be applicable to all or most of Africa, they
will be mainly concerned with the countries
of Africa south of the Sahara.

II

Perhaps the best clue to the common
problems of education in Africa may be
found in the proceedings of the Addis Ababa
Conference in 1961. According to the final
report of the conference, the urgency of the
basic problem lies in the fact that "today for
the African States as a whole, only 16 per
cent of the children of primary and secondary
school age combined are enrolled in school."[2]
Specifically, Niger had only 3.3 per cent of its
population between the ages of five and fourteen in school (1957–1958); Ethiopia, 3.8 per
cent (1958–1959); Upper Volta, 6.8 per cent

(1959–1960); Mauritania, 7.0 per cent (1957–
1958); the Northern Region of Nigeria, 7.4
per cent (1958); Mali, 7.7 per cent (1957–
1958); Somalia, 10.2 per cent (1958–1959);
Gambia, 10.7 per cent (1958); Sudan, 12.8
per cent (1959–1960); and Chad, 13.8 per
cent (1959–1960). At the other end of the
scale, Mauritius and the Western Region of
Nigeria attained 100 per cent in 1958, while
Basutoland had 90.5 per cent, Lagos Region
in Nigeria had 85.4 per cent, and Southern
Rhodesia had 83.5 per cent of its primary-age
children in school. Only three areas showed
an enrollment of more than ten per cent of
their secondary-age youngsters (ages fifteen
to nineteen) in secondary schools: Ghana,
29.4 per cent (1959); Mauritius, 18.1 per cent
(1958); and Lagos, 15.2 per cent (1958). The
Western Region of Nigeria had a figure of
8.8 per cent, Sudan one of 6.5 per cent (1959–
1960), and Zanzibar one of 5.0 per cent
(1958). All the other areas in Africa were
below five per cent, with the lowest figures
shown by Mauritania, 0.3 per cent (1957–
1958); the Northern Region of Nigeria
(1958); and Niger, 0.1 per cent (1957–1958).[3]
The figures speak for themselves. The
African need is obvious.

So far as higher education is concerned, the
facilities are "woefully inadequate to produce
the required manpower."[4] The Addis Ababa
report revealed that only 0.2 per cent of all
Africans of university age were attending
higher institutions of learning. The range of
attendance was from four in Ruanda–
Urundi (1958) to 1984 in Nigeria (1958). For
a developing and a developed Africa, of
course, it would be necessary to expand
facilities at home and to send more students
abroad. Interestingly, 25 out of the 34 sub-
Saharan (Middle African) countries and
territories have more students in foreign
institutions than in their own.[5]

There can be no doubt of the Africans'
eagerness for education on all levels. In all
countries, there is an avidity for advancement, which can only be attained, it is felt,
by the expansion of facilities. Africans want
more primary and secondary schools, technical institutes, colleges, and universities. In
speaking with African nationals in various
parts of the continent, one tends to wonder
whether what is desired is education itself or

the material advantages arising out of it in commerce, industry, and the civil service. Put in another way, do the Africans look for the advancement of their culture and for the enhancement of their understanding and appreciation of world culture, or do they seek the symbols of education, such as certificates, diplomas, and degrees? Everywhere, one hears more talk of these rewards of learning than of learning itself. Pupils and students are often impatient with teachers who deviate, however slightly, from the syllabus, upon which the examinations, grades, and diplomas depend, in an effort to introduce some life, ideas, and continuity into what seems to be a conglomeration of disparate data. Surely, the question of *educatio gratia educationis* versus education for practical purposes is one which can legitimately be asked of any national school system, especially that of a fully developed country. Why, then, raise it in the case of the new, emerging states of Africa? Mainly because the educators and other leaders in African countries tell themselves and their visitors that they are moving ahead on the educational front. If what they are promoting is practical training, they should not convince themselves that they are concerned with education.

Since World War II, most countries all over the world have been plagued by a shortage of school buildings, instructional materials, and textbooks. This has been true of the United States, as of the less affluent nations. A fundamental reason has been the scarcity of financial resources. In the words of the Addis Ababa report, "Current and future requirements go far beyond the resources in finance, material, and technical knowledge, on problems of school building construction now available in the African States. . . . Whatever the level of education, the need for equipment of all types is urgent. The problem is crucial in technical, vocational and higher education, in laboratories and shops, where at present many requirements can only be met abroad." [6] The visitor sees some new, modern, and well-equipped school and college buildings, the University of Ghana for example, but he cannot help observing substandard and poorly equipped buildings. One question that comes to mind

is why such a discrepancy should exist. Granted that new buildings cannot be erected everywhere at once, it is still difficult to comprehend why large sums are put into a few structures, while the majority languish in poverty. Perhaps, the spread of the limited budget among large numbers of schools together with the resistance to the temptation of erecting eye-catching edifices will help many a nation to alleviate its building and equipment problem. But, then, human nature being what it is—all the more so on the national level—it is too much to expect the withering away of the ego.

In connection with the need for textbooks, it is important to bear in mind that the developing nations require new books to fulfill the new educational objectives and curriculum content. Educational officials all over Africa pointed out, time and again, the lack of sufficient books in the first place, and the ill-suitability of the texts introduced by the European powers. What they wanted was a scholastic literature that reflected the conditions and values of African life and culture. Thus, a history book should stress African and national history, rather than that of Europe and of any particular European nation. Moreover, the primary readers should contain references to and pictures of lions and elephants, rather than of reindeer and grizzly bears. The production of a new textbook literature also involves the provision of more printing presses, as well as the training of competent textbook writers.

Another obvious need all over Africa is an adequate supply of well-prepared teachers. To some extent, the shortage is alleviated by the services of teachers and educators from a variety of sources: International Voluntary Services, Peace Corps, Teachers for East Africa, the Agency for International Development, the Afro–Anglo–American Program in Teacher Education, missionary groups, and other organizations. Eventually, it will be necessary for the new African nations to depend more and more upon their own teachers and administrators. In the meantime, some of the trained teachers are being attracted away to the commercial positions, the civil service, and the foreign service, with resultant gaps in teaching staffs in the schools of various countries.

Since the teacher is the key to the future of education in Africa, it is clear that a great leap forward must be made in teacher recruitment, education, in service training, and retention. In Tanganyika, the Director of Education increased "the qualified teaching staff by transferring qualified secondary teachers from administrative to teaching work and replacing them with less highly qualified teaching staff who had been given intensive courses in administrative work." [7] This is a drastic measure for the bureaucrat, but it seems very important for the upgrading of the secondary schools of the nation. Some similar steps would have to be adopted if the African countries are to realize their ambitious plans in education. The Addis Ababa Report indicates that one country would need to train 20,000 teachers in the next twenty years in order to achieve its goal of universally primary education by 1980. The teacher shortage is especially acute in the technical and agricultural fields in secondary schools, and it is hard to imagine how the new nations can grow to economic maturity without an adequate force of qualified instructors in these key subjects. The suggestion of the Addis Ababa Conference is that "an expanding supply of expatriate teachers is crucial in coming years to meet expansion plans, in addition to massive efforts now being made by certain non-African governments and nongovernmental organizations, especially missionary groups." The African authorities hope that the expatriates (foreigners) would supplement the African teachers, who are being trained at home and abroad. However, in the final analysis, the African leaders would have to plan for independence in teacher preparation as they have so successfully planned for political independence.

III

By the very nature of things, the existing curricula, which were developed under European educational authority, would have to be changed. The Three 'R's, the universal basic content of the primary school, are often considered as tools toward the acquisition of more advanced skills in technical and agricultural areas. In other words, whatever children learn must be of some value in the upbuilding of the technology and economy of the nation. When they graduate, they will naturally expect a higher standard of living than that possessed by their parents. However, it is too much to anticipate that all Africans will move from school to a world of comfort and culture. Consequently, there is a strong possibility that many African young people will experience a sense of frustration and annoyance. The Addis Ababa Conference sought to resolve this difficulty by a broad suggestion: "The attainment of universal literacy cannot be given the highest priority in the earliest stages of economic development as compared with the expansion of other skills at secondary and higher levels, but it is an objective in its own right, and every country should aim at having every child in school within two decades." [9] The problem of priorities is an extremely important one, and it may confront African political and educational leaders for a long time to come. As suggested by the Addis Ababa Conference, primary education would cover six years of instruction and would be so designed as to make it possible for the graduate to adjust himself vocationally in society even if he does not proceed to secondary school. Although the primary course of study should aim at general, rather than vocational education, "it should include elements which seek to develop an appreciation of the value of work with the hands as well as with the mind and to bring about a readiness for practical activity on which future vocational and technical education can be built." [10] It would seem that the expectation is that a relatively small percentage of primary pupils would go on to secondary school and higher education, to judge from this phraseology.

Considerable stress was laid at Addis Ababa on the secondary and higher education, as already outlined, even at the expense of the expansion of the primary school. The idea was that careful selection of the primary pupils would ensure a student body of quality in the secondary school. If the immediate objective of the new nations is rapid economic development, then this would depend upon the skills acquired by young people in the secondary and higher institutions. Consequently, "It is of the highest priority to ensure that an adequate proportion of the population receives secondary, postsecondary and university education; this should be put before the goal of universal primary education if for financial reasons these two are not yet compatible."[11]

The secondary school of the future, as envisioned at Addis Ababa, would consist of two three-year cycles. The curriculum in the lower stage would cover the mother tongue or national language, a foreign language, the social studies (history, geography, citizenship), natural sciences, mathematics, practical activities with hands and tools, music and art, health habits and physical education, and moral and/or spiritual values. This is a general course of study fitting the individual for the advanced stage or for entry into higher vocational life. At the higher secondary stage, there would be some common areas of study as well as opportunities for specialization toward future professions. The common studies comprise language, art, music, social studies, and practical wood or metal work for the academic students. Moreover, "the intensive study of the sciences and mathematics, required by a later technical or professional training, should start in earnest at the commencement of the higher stage."[12] Realistically, the African educators recognized the necessity, in some countries, of adding several years of pre-university study after the completion of the higher secondary school. This would be especially true of small, scattered, and inadequately staffed schools.

IV

There are certain curriculum problems which are controversial in nature. One problem is this: Should there be an emphasis on Africanization or on the Europeanization of studies? Another problem is the language of instruction. Should pupils be taught in the native language or in French or English where there are a number of languages in a country? There are more than five hundred languages spoken by African Negroes. What of the use of Swahili or another African tongue as an international or at least regional *lingua franca*? In East African countries, some ten million people speak Swahili.

There are arguments for and against an Africanized curriculum. From the standpoint of modern ethnology and human relations, it would seem most logical, pedagogical, and diplomatic to stress the languages, the traditions, and the content which are closest to the African people. On the other hand, there are many Africans who fear that such a curriculum will, in effect, isolate or segregate them from the mainstream of European and world culture. They seem to think that an Africanized education will consign them to a culturally low level, however proud they might be of their traditions. According to Professor Adam Curle, formerly of the University College of Ghana and now of Harvard University, it is unfortunate that "developing countries are apt to acquire an ambivalent attitude towards their own culture, both despising it for being 'primitive' and according it a patriotic excess of veneration."[13] He would like to have the studies of all aspects of native culture made "more widespread and objective." Naturally, the indigenous subjects must be taught and taught well, but the Africans will not be content until they will also have a solid background in those subjects which will enable them to communicate in an intellectual way with the rest of the world.

In a similar manner, there are differences of opinion with regard to the relative merits of a theoretical versus a practical course of study, a humanistic versus a scientific program. It is not too unreasonable to expect that, as time goes on, the African educators and political leaders will realize that an either-or solution is neither feasible nor advisable. What is likely to emerge is a synthesis of the old and the new, the African and the European.

As already pointed out, higher educational

facilities are a critical need all over Africa. The manpower requirements for research workers, professionals, administrators, and other important personnel are great and the potential future supply is rather low. According to the Addis Ababa experts, "present and projected crucial needs require that considerable numbers of African individuals undertake advanced studies overseas and that an expanded supply of expatriate staff be provided for new higher institutions, universities, technical colleges, research institutes and laboratories. Further, the expansion of higher academic and technological institutions in Africa should be geared not only to fulfilling the training needs of the States in which they are situated, but also to the requirements of other African States, intra-African hospitality in African universities today being a notable attribute."[14]

V

Higher education in Africa is growing rapidly everywhere. Of 34 Middle African countries and territories in 1951, only eleven had higher institutions of learning, and the combined enrollment was 2270. In 1961, nine more countries had higher educational institutions, and the total enrollment rose 700 per cent to 16,580. Four out of five North African countries had higher education in 1950, with a total registration of 40,470. In 1961, all North African countries had such facilities, and the enrollment jumped over 300 per cent to 132,820. For all of Africa, the enrollment increase between 1950 and 1961 was 350 per cent, owing to the expansion of existing facilities as well as to the opening of new institutions.[15]

The genesis and development of higher education in Africa must constitute an exciting experience to those who have taken part in the process. Even the reports of the founding and growth of these institutions make highly interesting reading.[16] It is an encouraging sign that material aid is forthcoming from foreign sources, such as the

recent grant of $2,300,000 by the Ford Foundation to the University of Ibadan, Nigeria, "for special assistance in university development and particularly to aid the growth of Ibadan as a center of research and graduate instruction."[17] Other signs of a healthy future for higher education in Africa are the colleges in Kenya, Uganda, and Tanganyika which constitute the University of East Africa, the new higher institutions in Southern Rhodesia, Ethiopia, Lovanium University in the Republic of the Congo (Leopoldville), and the new universities of West Africa. One might ask whether beautiful campuses and buildings (e.g., Ghana, Ibadan) make good universities. One becomes aware of pressures on faculty, as at Ghana, which bring about the departures to other countries. A visitor might even examine critically the contents of the library of a university which declares in its prospectus that it offers advanced degrees (eventually the Ph.D.) and discovers that the holdings hardly justify a B.A. program. Nevertheless, in spite of possible and actual problems and shortcomings, it is clear that the African governments will make a most serious effort to achieve at least an acceptable level of higher education.[18]

The recently issued report of the Tananarive Conference of 1962 throws some light on the future possibilities of higher education in Africa. This deliberative body of educational experts set as a goal of enrollment expansion a figure of 274,000 by 1980 or earlier. The current registration of about 31,000 will thus be increased, it is hoped, by close to nine hundred per cent. To bring about such a rise in student body it would be necessary, according to the estimate by the participants, for the Middle African universities to acquire an additional teaching corps of 21,000 and a financial investment of more than $1,500,000,000. No doubt, the African educators are aware of the problems faced by established universities all over the world with respect to recruitment of qualified faculty and the raising of funds. But this fact does not appear to deter them from making plans which they deem essential to the survival and progress of the new nations. Perhaps a degree of optimism and of extra effort might be salutary in an age of cynicism, disenchantment and disillusionment. It may be that the higher educational authorities have something to learn in this respect from the example of the Africans.

At the Tananarive Conference, educational officials from 31 African nations adopted a series of seven educational goals as a guide to the future development of their universities and other institutions of higher learning: the advancement of knowledge through instruction and research; the adherence and loyalty to the academic standards recognized all over the world; the ensuring of the unification of Africa; the encouragement of the interpretation and appreciation of African culture and heritage, and, through instruction and research in African studies, the achievement of recognition of the true status of the African heritage and culture; the full development of human resources toward the satisfaction of the manpower needs; the training of the "whole man" for the process of nation building; the evolving, over a period of time, of genuine African universities and other higher institutions of learning which are devoted to the advancement of Africa and its people, and which at the same time are promoting a feeling of kinship to human society all over the globe. So far as priorities are concerned, the report of the Tananarive Conference suggests manpower surveys as a source of information, but it also recommends that sixty per cent of admissions to higher education should be reserved for scientific and technical courses, while the rest of the places would be made available to students of the arts. "The most urgent need is to increase the flow of graduates into the teaching profession, particularly in the secondary schools."[19]

On the question of the relation of higher education to the development of African culture and nationhood, the report is quite specific. "African institutions of higher education have the duty of acting as instruments for the consolidation of national unity. This they can do by resolutely opposing the effects of tribalism and encouraging exchanges, and by throwing open the university to all students who show the capacity to benefit from a university education of internationally acceptable academic standards, and by resolutely ignoring ethnic or tribal

origins, and political and religious discrimination."[20] From this statement it appears that the African authorities are not interested in any sort of elite based on origins other than the professional, scientific, technical, or academic.

Curle makes a significant statement with regard to the curriculum of higher education. Apart from "vigorous and practical" instruction in the sciences, which would enable African students to understand and partially to control "some of the more undesirable side effects of social change," he would emphasize such fields as philosophy, literature, and comparative religion, the so-called "useless" subjects. "If such subjects are considered desirable in the older countries, how much more vital are they in the newer in which, through the rapidity of change, the moral pattern is confused."[21] As already mentioned, Dr. Curle desires the objective study of indigenous culture in addition to the "alien learning." This means that the curriculum should be national and international at the same time. Further, to meet the challenge of the modern world, the Africans must plan for a rapid assimilation of the latest techniques in the social and the natural sciences. Finally, there must be a firm grounding "in the needs of daily reality," e.g., in such fields as hygiene, home economics, and horticulture, which have a practical value, "provide a comprehensible base from which to explore the more complex theoretical issues," and "establish a functional link between the educational system and the community."[22] Such a program of studies appears logical, and it is up to the African educators to ponder this plan or to consider suitable alternatives. In any case, they will have to fill in the more precise details of the curriculum.

VI

The necessity of providing an adequate system of adult education in Africa is too obvious to require much comment. It is probable that at least 100,000,000 Africans are illiterate, and, accordingly, a rapid and efficient program must be instituted and promoted. As the Addis Ababa Report states, "every effort for the education of adults will have immediate effect on the economic and social development of the community."[23]

One of the recommendations of the Addis Ababa Conference, that of the acceleration of the educational and cultural programs for women, so that they contribute their full share to community welfare, implies also that there should be more attention to the education of girls. Traditionally, the girls have been neglected in Africa, especially in the Moslem areas, as in other parts of the world. Some of the opposition on the part of Moslem parents to the education of adolescent girls is gradually weakening. At the present time, girls constitute less than thirty per cent of the enrollment in primary schools and about 22 per cent in the secondary schools.[24] In the universities, as might be expected, women make up an even smaller percentage of the student population. In 1960, for example, they constituted six per cent of the total registration at the University of Ghana; seven per cent, at the University College of Ibadan; eight per cent, at the University College of East Africa; eleven per cent, at the University College of Sierra Leone; and fourteen per cent, at the University College of Fort Hare in South Africa. These figures pertain to African women, rather than to white ("European") women, who are much better represented in the universities of South Africa and Southern Rhodesia.[25] The immensity of the problem of the higher education of women in some parts of Africa, at least, is illustrated by the fact that, as of the early months of 1961, there were still no women college graduates in Ruanda–Urundi.[26] Since the African womanpower will be essential to the rapid development of the continent, it is clear that a campaign will have to be inaugurated for the education of girls and women on all levels.

To some extent, there has developed patterns of international cooperation in education among the new African nations, in view of the fact that many of them are not able to solve their problems entirely through their own efforts. Some states cooperate in the matter of provision of scholarships for students from other African areas. The University of East Africa, comprising higher institutions in Kenya, Uganda, and Tanganyika, is one promising venture which might serve as a stimulus for the creation of similar institutional arrangements in other regions of Africa. What especially interested the present writer and many of his colleagues during the visit of the Comparative Education Society to Africa in the summer of 1962 was the West African Examinations Council. The center at Accra, Ghana, represented a splendid example of the principle of cooperation by several nations in an important branch of educational activity. The testing programs are planned on the basis of pooled personnel, resources, and knowledge of the Africans themselves in conjunction with the help given by such foreign countries as Britain and the United States. This council will, in all probability, develop school certificate and other tests which will reflect fully the African aims, aspirations, and abilities in education. This type of cooperation might well be extended to other aspects of education and in other African areas. In isolation, the African nations will no doubt accomplish less than in mutual helping situations.

VII

Possibly the most dramatic educational problem in Africa is the question of racial discrimination and segregation. With few exceptions, the trend has been toward equalization of opportunity and integration. Thus, in Uganda, there has been a smooth process of integration in the secondary schools, even if diverse religions, languages, and backgrounds have discouraged any corresponding integration in the primary schools.[27] In Tanganyika, after the elections in 1958, the government appointed a Committee on the Integration of Education. A White Paper, approved in December, 1960, laid down the lines of racial equality in education which were to take effect in 1962. According to the new plan, all pupils, without regard to race, will be eligible to enter any school, subject to his ability to use the language of instruction.[28] As in Uganda, linguistic problems will not permit more than a gradual type of integration in the primary schools. It is interesting to note that private schools will not receive public aid unless they admit pupils of all races.

The trend toward integration is not universal. It is true that in Northern Rhodesia an interracial high school will be opened in 1963 by the Jesuits; but racial equality is not yet around the corner. While Africans seemed to have somewhat more freedom of movement in Salisbury, Southern Rhodesia—in the Jameson Hotel for example—racial segregation in education and other respects was still a patent fact. According to a recent observer who has studied the history and current status of African education in this territory, "Southern Rhodesia's official attitude is obviously colored by its proximity to the Union of South Africa, where both direct administration and restrictive segregation have become more and more rigid."[29] If the political situation in Southern Rhodesia should follow the trend of the developments elsewhere in Africa, there can be no doubt that the days of racial segregation in education will be numbered.

Except for the United States, no country has had the world spotlight on race relations as long as the Republic of South Africa. The Afrikaans word *apartheid* (racial separation) is perhaps the most widely circulated word in that language. South African scholars, nearly three and four decades ago, testified that the education of the Africans, Coloreds, and Asiatics was inferior to that of the whites in terms of financial support, staffing, facilities, and application of the principle of compulsory attendance.[30] In other words, the separate school systems were far from equal. During World War II, a German specialist observed that South Africa was maintaining the color bar in education in order to make certain that it has a cheap supply of Negro and Colored labor.[31]

With the passage of the Bantu Education Act of 1953, the movement to strengthen segregation may be said to have begun in recent times. While government officials and Afrikaner (white) educators were insisting

that the African Negro was being benefited by this law, the critically minded Father Huddleston claimed that the Bantu Education Act is "one of the chief instruments of a policy of racialism whose avowed aim is the establishment of an enduring white supremacy. It is, indeed, an education for servitude."[32] Some basis for this judgment could be seen in the adoption of the Separate University Education Act of 1957. On the international level, the United Nations issued in 1957 a report which stated that "one of the main effects of *apartheid* has been to increase and aggravate discrimination in education, particularly in regard to the Bantu group."[33] Although South African leaders continue to maintain that the Bantu are getting a better education than Africans elsewhere, there seems to be adequate evidence of an official and unofficial sort to lend weight to the hypothesis that the system of segregated schools has contributed to the subjection of the African Negroes and has prevented him "from raising his cultural and educational level to anything comparable to that of the European."[34] It should not be forgotten that the policy of racial segregation also affects the other nonwhite races, the Colored and the Asiatic.

The Republic of South Africa is determined to continue its policy of racially segregated school systems, not only in its own territory but also in the area of South West Africa, which is not regarded by the outside world as South Africa property. The government authorities point to the new schools and colleges which were constructed for the nonwhite races. One, the University College of the North, Turfloop, which was visited by the writer and his colleagues, has fine facilities and an adequate library.[35] On the other hand, it is difficult not to recall the dictum of the United States Supreme Court that separate schools are inherently unequal.

Except for the South African supporters of *apartheid* and some Bantu who have approved the education provided their race,[36] there are few who will speak up for the status quo in segregated education in South Africa. One Bantu has characterized *apartheid* as "an insult to human dignity"[37] and education under this philosophy as a movement toward barbarism. The Nobel Prize winner, Chief Luthuli, vows that "the struggle [against *apartheid*] must go on" and "I shall die, if need be for this cause."[38] There are South African whites who would like to join him in the struggle.

On the world level, there have been studies, reports, and other writings in opposition to *apartheid*. A Dutch scholar recently concluded the *apartheid* is basically wrong because "it completely lacks scientific and moral foundation."[39] The Security Council of the United Nations deplored in 1960 the policies of South Africa and called upon the government "to initiate measures aimed at bringing about racial harmony based on equality in order to ensure that the present situation does not continue or recur and to abandon its policies of apartheid and racial discrimination."[40] Recent observations of conditions in South Africa, conversations with South African whites and Bantu, and an examination of the literature do not give the present writer much ground for supposing that a change in policy will take place in the foreseeable future. No doubt, South Africa has been well aware all along of the anxiety all over the world with regard to *apartheid*.[41] Some of their leaders may indeed be aware of the conclusion of the recent report by the International Commission of Jurists to the effect that *apartheid* represents the "systematic violation of the most fundamental rights of mankind," not merely in South Africa itself but also in South West Africa.[42] Nonetheless, it does not appear likely that they will be swayed from their determination to perpetuate *apartheid* in education as in all other areas of life and society. Whether they will be able to go their way without serious opposition by the new nations of Africa and by the international bodies remains to be seen.

VIII

It is sometimes forgotten that modern education in Africa was promoted for a long time, especially since the nineteenth century, by Christian missionary groups. "Everywhere they were the pioneer teachers."[43] In addition, they were among the few who had taken the trouble to learn the native languages and to appreciate the heritage of African culture. Some missionaries, in fact, supplied written languages to tribes which did not possess one. Despite the lack of adequate facilities and personnel, and in the face of many difficulties, the mission schools managed to keep alive the tradition of education. This is not to say that all missionaries were effective educators; it is merely to call attention to an all-too-often overlooked fact that the roots of contemporary African education can be found in the efforts of the mission groups. Visitors to Africa can see today many missionary schools on all levels of instruction. These have helped to prepare Africans for their role today.

In a number of African areas, the church schools are running into obstacles for a variety of reasons. In South Africa, many were forced to be discontinued under the racial policies of the Bantu Education Act. Protestant schools faced difficulties in Catholic territories.[44] The tendency to secularism will no doubt lead to competition with new types of schools which will be more adequately supported by the state. Extreme African nationalism may become a source of opposition to schools which represent a foreign culture. Be that as it may, "the contribution of Christian schools to Africa up to this point is profound, ineffaceable and historically important as an element in the transformation now taking place. Few investments have yielded richer returns for a comparable expenditure of resources and effort."[45]

A very interesting development which deserves extended study is the education of Africans in foreign countries. President Kwame Nkrumah, who is himself an example of this tendency as a graduate of American universities, has recently called attention to the fact that Ghanaians studied in European universities during the eighteenth century.[46] Two Africans from the Gold Coast were reported as attending the College of New Jersey in 1774.[47] It was not until the end of World War II, however, that Africans began to come to foreign universities in significant numbers. With the increase of such students, there developed certain problems, such as racial discrimination in the United States and in other countries. The recent report by the Institute of International Education revealed a variety of economic and emotional problems facing the African students in the United States, but indicated that 79 per cent of the more than 1000 students surveyed were fully or mostly satisfied with their training programs. It is interesting to note the existence of friction between African and American Negroes, as well as the above-average performance by the African students in their academic work. Also of interest is the fact that close to half of the students came from Nigeria and Kenya, and that more than one-third (35 per cent) were pursuing studies in the social sciences." [48]

In February, 1963, reports from Sofia, Bulgaria, disclosed the ill-treatment of African students. A group of fifteen Ghanaian students charged that they had been called "black monkeys and jungle people," and "were treated like dirt"; and for these and other reasons they decided that "studying in Communist countries is a waste of time." [49] On the following day, six Ethiopian students left Bulgaria, and "hundreds more African students were reported waiting for funds or transportation to get out." [50] To those who have been following the fortunes of African students in the Soviet Union, this explosion does not come as a total surprise. At the University of Moscow and at the University of the Friendship of Peoples in the Name of Patrice Lumumba there have been incidents and actions of an unpleasant and discriminatory nature which led to the departure of African students. [51] It is clear that study abroad will not solve easily the problem of providing a satisfactory higher education for the many African students who look to greener pastures on other continents.

IX

The preceding pages have presented in brief outline some of the major tendencies, developments, and problems in African education at the present time. It is good that the various governments show a deep concern for the progress of education, which they conceive to be the key to national progress. This connection between education and material well-being has been underscored at Addis Ababa, where the delegates pointed up the significance of educational planning for the African nations. In the words of the Final Report, "education, far from being a mere consumer goods, is one of the most fruitful of investments," and, accordingly, "the development of education, both qualitatively and quantitatively, should constitute one of the essential elements in any plan for economic and social development." [52] The Conference gave some specific suggestions with regard to educational planning: definitions of terms and concepts, the problem of shortages of skilled manpower and surpluses of unskilled labor, the determination of priorities for the investment of resources in education, the particular steps in the planning process, and types of administrative machinery necessary for planning. Good advice and aid will be available to the African nations from their neighbors, from other continents, and from international groups. What remains is for each country to use its best judgment in adapting all the signs of goodwill to their objectives and needs. How education is to develop must, in the final analysis, be determined by each nation for itself. It is to be hoped that the political and educational leaders will exercise good judgment in the administration and organization of their school systems so that, while being true to their cultural heritage and national aspirations, they will reflect a deep interest in international understanding and harmony.

It is absorbing to observe at first hand the changes that are going on in African government, economy, society, culture, and education. Educators can learn a great deal by a visit to what was once called the "Dark Continent." But, in order to comprehend with any degree of depth the problems and trends of education in Africa, it is necessary for the educator to steep himself in a variety of source materials which throw light on the past and the present efforts of Africans to raise themselves to a cultural and educational level of which their ancestors could dream vaguely.

We need more scholarly studies of African education than we possess at present. We also need documentary collections, historical analyses, statistical compilations, and other types of literature for a better comprehension of education in Africa. With such a literature, it will be possible to enlighten students, educators, and the public in a specific way about the needs of Africans. Since we are convinced that we live in an interdependent world and that we have a moral obligation to help our neighbors, it is only right that we ourselves become as well informed as possible and that we do all we can to disseminate good information so as to enable others also to contribute toward the elevation of the education and the welfare of the world, of which Africa is becoming an increasingly important part.

Notes

1. Katherine George, "The Civilized West Looks at Primitive Africa: 1400–1800. A Study in Ethnocentrism," *Isis*, Vol. 49, March, 1958, pp. 62–72.
2. "Conference of African States on the Development of Education in Africa, Addis Ababa, 12–25 May, 1961: Final Report" (Paris: Unesco, 1961), p. 3.
3. *Ibid.*, p. 7. The Republic of South Africa is not represented in the statistics.
4. *Ibid.*, p. 8.
5. United Nations Press Release, UNESCO/ 1536, August 31, 1962. This later source indicates a total sub-Saharan African attendance of 27,541 in higher educational institutions during 1961–62. Of this figure, 14,678 study at home and 12,863 abroad. The ratio of students to the 20–24 population category ranges from 0.03 per cent in Niger to 1.6 per cent in Mauritius and in Zanzibar and Pemba.
6. "Conference of African States . . . Final Report," *op. cit.*, p. 4.
7. Betty George, "Education for Africans in Tanganyika: A Preliminary Survey," U.S. Office of Education, Bulletin 1960, No. 19 (Washington: U.S. Government Printing Office, 1960), p. 94.

8. "Conference of African States . . . Final Report," *op. cit.*, p. 5.
9. *Ibid.*, p. 11.
10. *Ibid.*, p. 45.
11. *Ibid.*, p. 10.
12. *Ibid.*, p. 49.
13. Adam Curle, *The Role of Education in Developing Societies* (Legon: Ghana University Press, 1961), pp. 25–26.
14. "Conference of African States . . . Final Report," *op. cit.*, p. 6.
15. United Nations Press Release, UNESCO/ 1536, August 31, 1962.
16. Kenneth Mellanby, *The Birth of Nigeria's University* (London: Methuen, 1958), and Kenneth Mellanby, "Establishing a New University in Africa," *Minerva*, Vol. I, Winter, 1963, pp. 149–158.
17. *News from the Ford Foundation*, February 19, 1963.
18. For examples of how West African universities are meeting the problems of secondary and higher education, see the relevant chapters in A. Taylor, ed., *Educational and Occupational Selection in West Africa* (London: Oxford University Press, 1962).
19. *The Development of Higher Education in Africa: Conclusions and Recommendations of the Conference on the Development of Higher Education in Africa* (*Tananarive, September 3–12, 1962*) (Paris: UNESCO, 1963), p. 22.
20. *Ibid.*, p. 12.
21. Curle, *op. cit.*, p. 25.
22. *Ibid.*, p. 27.
23. "Conference of African States . . . Final Report," *op. cit.*, p. 51. For a detailed analysis of the problem and suggested solutions, see pp. 51–61.
24. *Ibid.*, p. 6.
25. Martin L. Kilson, Jr., "Trends in Higher Education," in U.S. National Commission for Unesco, *Africa and the United States: Images and Realities* [Background Book for the Eighth National Conference, Boston (Washington: U.S. National Commission for Unesco), 1961], pp. 70–72.
26. William A. Payne, "Ruanda–Urundi," in Helen Kitchen, ed., *The Educated African* (New York: Praeger, 1962), p. 213.
27. Ruth C. Sloan, "Uganda," in Kitchen, *op. cit.*, p. 169.
28. See "Report of the Committee on the Integration of Education: 1959" (Dar-es-Salaam: Government Printer, 1960), pp. 9–11; see also Anonymous, "Tanganyika," in Kitchen, *op. cit.*, p. 156.
29. Franklin Parker, "African Development and Education in Southern Rhodesia" (Columbus: Ohio State University Press, 1960), p. 58.
30. Charles T. Loram, "South Africa," in I. L. Kandel, ed., *Educational Yearbook of the International Institute of Teachers College, Columbia University: 1924* (New York: Macmillan, 1925), p. 421; E. G. Malherbe, "Union

of South Africa," in I. L. Kandel, ed., *Educational Yearbook of the International Institute of Teachers College, Columbia University: 1936* (New York: Bureau of Publications, Teachers College, Columbia University, 1936), pp. 571–572.

31. Herbert T. Becker, "Des Schulwesen in Afrika," Band XIII/2 in Erich Obst, ed., *Afrika: Handbuch der praktischen Kolonialwissenschaften* (Berlin: Walter De Gruyter, 1943), p. 204.

32. Trevor Huddleston, *Naught for Your Comfort* (Garden City, N.Y.: Doubleday, 1956), p. 174.

33. Charles D. Ammoun, *Study of Discrimination in Education* (New York: United Nations, 1957), p. 11.

34. William W. Brickman, "Racial Segregation in Education in South Africa," in William W. Brickman and Stanley Lehrer, eds., *The Countdown on Segregated Education* (New York: Society for the Advancement of Education, 1960), p. 132.

35. See *Brief Review of Activities and Development, 1959–1962* (Turfloop: University College of the North, 1962), in Afrikaans and English; *Calendar, 1962, University College of the North: Yunibestiti Kholeji ya Lebva* (Pretoria: Government Printer, 1962), in Afrikaans and English.

36. Pablo Eisenberg, "Republic of South Africa," in Kitchen, *op. cit.*, p. 277.

37. I. B. Tabata, *Education for Barbarism in South Africa* (London: Pall Mall, 1960), p. 95.

38. Albert Luthuli, *Let My People Go* (New York: McGraw-Hill, 1962), p. 232.

39. K. L. Roskam, *Apartheid and Discrimination* (Leiden: Sythoff, 1960), p. 154.

40. *New York Times*, April 2, 1960.

41. See, for example, G. D. Scholtz, *Het die Afrikaner volk 'n Toekoms?* (Johannesburg: Vorwaarts, 1954), p. 132.

42. *South Africa and the Rule of Law* (Geneva: International Commission of Jurists, 1960), p. 82.

43. George W. Carpenter, "African Education and the Christian Missions," *Phi Delta Kappan*, Vol. XLI, January, 1960, p. 191.

44. *Ibid.*, pp. 193–194.

45. *Ibid.*, p. 195.

46. Kwame Nkrumah, *Flower of Learning* (Accra: Ministry of Information and Broadcasting, 1961), p. 3.

47. Laura Bornholdt, "African Students in the United States," in *Africa and the United States: Images and Realities*, Background Report, *op. cit.*, p. 91.

48. *IIE African Student Survey* (New York: Institute of International Education, 1961).

49. *Philadelphia Evening Bulletin*, February 15, 1963.

50. *Philadelphia Evening Bulletin*, February 16, 1963.

51. See, for example, Michel Ayih, *Ein Afrikaner in Moskau* (Cologne: Verlag Wissenschaft und Politik, 1961).

52. "Conference of African States . . . Final Report," *op. cit.*, p. 41.

Public Finance and Taxation

WITH THE INCREASING ROLE of African governments in economic development activities, including large outlays on economic and social infrastructure and mounting expenditures to meet insistent demands for additional social services, there has been rapid growth in government expenditures on both the current and development accounts, especially since 1950. Government revenues have not increased as fast as expenditures; this has given rise to growing budget deficits in most African countries. For the first few years, these deficits were covered by drawing on the past accumulated government savings. However, now indications are that past savings in most African countries have been depleted, and the governments are facing serious financial crises. The article, "Public Finance in African Countries," by the United Nations Economic Commission for Africa, presents a comprehensive survey of the situation, including a description of growing imbalances in the revenues and expenditures of many African countries. Efforts at raising additional revenues have not been very successful; and, because of the pressing and persistent demands for government services, especially social services, governments have found it difficult to reduce their expenditures on current accounts. Hence, most African countries are compelled to reduce development expenditures in relation to total government expenditure. This is a retrogressive step with serious implications for economic development. These countries have to take effective fiscal measures, including increasing their tax efforts, to raise additional revenues to meet vital development expenditures. The article "The Taxation of Low Incomes in African Countries," by Edward Arowolo explains the structure of various taxes in African economies. Arowolo discusses the difficulty of raising direct taxes, including the levying and collecting of income tax, when the majority of the population consists of peasants with low incomes from subsistence agriculture. Some African countries have turned to such measures as levying uniform per capita tax, poll tax, cattle tax, graduated per capita tax, consistent with their levels of economic and social development. Arowolo explains the administration of these taxes and the extent of their effectiveness in raising revenues.

18

Public Finance in African Countries

United Nations Economic Commission for Africa

From Economic Bulletin for Africa, *Vol. 1, No. 2 (June 1961), pp. 1–28.*

THE PURPOSE of this article is to analyse trends and problems in public finance in African countries. The analysis suffers from a number of limitations imposed by the weakness of the available data and should therefore only be considered as a first attempt to be followed by further analysis in subsequent years. It is hoped, however, that the present article may succeed in bringing out certain problems of serious concern to African governments. In so doing, it might contribute to increased interest on the part of governments in improving public finance data and in making these data available as soon as possible after the end of the fiscal year.

The scope of this article is confined to central government transactions and excludes accounts of local bodies, municipalities, etc. In the case of Nigeria and the Federation of Rhodesia and Nyasaland, however, accounts of the Federal Government as well as of regional governments are included.

The analysis is based on traditional budgetary data,[1] supplemented for certain countries by national accounting figures. These figures relate to the government sector as a whole.

The period covered, i.e., 1950–1958, was marked by political and economic changes of considerable importance. These changes have not been without repercussions on budgetary procedures, making it difficult to compare the data over the years. Similarly, the scope of government transactions has changed over the period and, probably, unevenly in different countries. This also reduces comparability, both between various countries at the same point of time and within one country over time. On the other hand, an important objective of public finance analysis would be to determine the effect of economic and political changes, including the attainment of independence, on the size and nature of government transactions. In the case of many countries, however, important changes are so recent that the appropriate analysis shall have to be undertaken at a future date.

The financial relationship between France and her former overseas territories in Africa changed considerably in the postwar period. For example, in 1945 the French Treasury took over from the overseas budgets totally or partially, the responsibility for development and current expenditure in respect of certain public services like maritime services, telecommunications, civil aeronautics, salaries of magistrates, governors, police, etc. The *Loi Cadre* of 1956 established a distinction between *Services d'Etat* and *Services Territoriaux*. The first category of services, which was financed by the French Treasury, included armed forces and most of the important public services except some social services like education and health and some economic services like agriculture, forestry, and veterinary. In general, the French Government took over responsibility in respect of expenditure on defence, foreign relations, major part of equipment expenditure, and some current expenditure. Thus a considerable part of expenditure in the overseas budgets, particularly capital, was financed by the French Treasury.

With respect to the French-speaking countries, two sets of data have been used in this article. Data on expenditure, except those on the structure of expenditure, were provided by the Banque Centrale des Etats de l'Afrique de l'Ouest.[2] These figures represent only "civil" expenditure, including most of such expenditure financed by France. The data are net of interbudgetary transfers and exclude military expenditure and expenditure of communes. Estimates of the equipment expenditure financed by the French Treasury are believed to be underestimated by ten per cent. The rest of the data, viz., those on revenue and on the structure of expenditure are derived from the sources mentioned in the General Notes.

The use of traditional budgetary data poses serious problems, both practical and conceptual, for international comparisons. Traditional budget classifications are designed primarily to serve the purpose of accountability. They do not necessarily reflect true magnitude of expenditure and revenue. For example, the use of appropriation-in-aid system would underestimate both expenditure and revenue. Other practical difficulties arise from the existence of numerous special funds and transfers to and from these funds, earmarking of specific revenues, and the like. The fiscal years are also different for different countries.

On the conceptual side, the most serious difficulty is to distinguish between current and capital expenditures. Most of the countries follow a double budget system based on a distinction between current account expenditure and capital or development account expenditure. This distinction, as made by the countries, has been adopted for the purpose of the present article. It should be noted, however, that the use of a separate budget for development expenditure is often dictated by consideration of safeguarding such expenditure against periodic fluctuations in current revenues and by the practice to earmark certain receipts like loan funds for such purposes. Expenditure of a capital nature can therefore be found on current account, and some current expenditures are included on the development account. Examples of other conceptual difficulties are the existence of double counting particularly in the case of ancillary agencies,[3] inclusion of repayment of debt on current account and revenue contributions to capital budget shown on current account as expenditures.

An attempt has been made to make corrections for some of these difficulties but no claim can be made for the perfection of the data. In view of these difficulties, however, the data presented in this article should be treated with caution and the broad conclusions reached should be looked upon as necessarily tentative. Certain conclusions have been tested by reference to national accounting data available for a few countries. It is not, however, suggested that the use of national accounting data lends any finality to the conclusions reached.

Growth of Government Expenditure and Revenue

GROWTH OF EXPENDITURE

The growth of government expenditures in African countries over the period 1950–1958 may be analysed in absolute terms and could be, further, related to other important economic variables—like exports, gross national product and prices—in order to present a more varied picture of the changes in government expenditures.

It will be readily seen in Table 1 that the growth of government expenditure was fairly rapid in absolute terms. Of the nineteen countries included in that table, thirteen countries experienced more than two-fold increase in government expenditures. Of these thirteen countries, five countries showed an increase of three-fold or more than three-fold. Relatively, the largest increase occurred in Ghana, Nigeria, Uganda, Sierra Leone and Madagascar. The countries which recorded comparatively small increase in government expenditure were Tunisia, Union of South Africa and former Trust Territory of Somaliland.

Government expenditure has been related to exports, in view of the fact that the latter constitute an important percentage share of commercialized production in many of the African economies. The relationship may be particularly significant in those countries whose export structure is relatively less diversified and which depend heavily on exports of one or a few primary products. The levels of domestic incomes, investment

Table 1—Growth of Total Expenditure

	In Terms of National Currencies				In Per Cent of Export Value				
	1950 (1)	1958 (2)	Increase[j] 1958/1950 (3)=(2)/(1)	Growth Rate (4)[k]	1950 (5)	1952 (6)	1957 (7)	1958 (8)	Average 1955–58[i] (9)
Algeria (billion francs)	89.2[e]	220.8	2.5	13.8	50.3	72.1	118.5	107.7	128.1
Congo (Leopoldville) (billion francs)[h]	4.3	12.4[d]	2.9	14.1	33.1	36.5[f]	51.9	61.4	53.0
Ethiopia (million Eth. $)	70.2	174.1	2.5	12.0	105.1	66.7	79.4	102.5	106.0
Former French Equatorial Africa–Cameroon (B CFA)	18.2	44.3	2.4	11.7	120.5	166.2	131.4[g]	103.3	139.7
Former French West Africa–Togo (B CFA)	31.4	89.2	2.8	13.9	96.9	158.8	116.3[g]	116.4	121.4
Ghana (£ million)	14.4	59.0	4.1	19.3	21.0	33.7	72.8	62.8	69.1
Kenya (£ million)	16.2	44.5	2.7	13.4	94.2	145.6[f]	192.0	151.9	161.2
Madagascar (billion CFA francs)	9.6	29.1	3.0	14.8	77.4	115.2	162.5[g]	144.1	173.2
Morocco (billion francs)	60.3	165.0[d]	2.7	11.3	90.8	79.6	99.5	113.7	132.8
Nigeria (£ million)	29.4	95.4	3.2	15.9	32.6	36.4[f]	52.6[g]	70.3	71.9
Federation of Rhodesia and Nyasaland (£ million)	54.6	86.3	1.6	12.1	⋯	49.5	53.2	63.5	53.5
Sierra Leone (£ million)	2.9	8.9[c]	3.1	17.3	37.2	⋯	48.4	⋯	57.8
Somalia (former trusteeship territory) (million Somalos)	100.0[a]	112.9[b]	1.1	2.5	⋯	⋯	131.8	118.6	145.0
Sudan (£ million)	30.0[f]	55.9	1.9	12.7	47.7	59.0[f]	80.0	120.7	105.3
Tanganyika (£ million)	11.2	24.1	2.2	10.1	102.0	38.6	57.1	57.8	59.4
Tunisia (billion francs)	40.4	65.9[d]	1.6	6.3	93.4	139.2	95.7	102.3	135.3
UAR (Egypt) (£ million)	163.8	309.9[d]	1.9	8.3		160.5	206.1	189.2	198.8
Uganda (£ million)	7.8	24.7	3.2	15.2	27.2	29.9	50.3	54.4	56.9
Union of South Africa (£ million)	222.2	378.0[d]	1.7	6.8	99.3	88.6	78.1	96.6	93.0

Source: See General Notes.

Note: *Former French West Africa–Togo*: Exports include trade between former FWA and Togo. *Former French Equatorial Africa–Cameroon*: Except for 1950, exports exclude trade between former FEA and Cameroon.

a 1955.
b 1959.
c 1957.
d Estimated.
e 1951.
f 1953.

g 1956.
h Current expenditure only.
i 1958 expenditure in per cent of average export value over 1955–58.
j 1954.
k Compound annual rate of increase.

Federation of Rhodesia and Nyasaland[a]
(£ million)

	Exports	Investment Expenditure	Tax Revenue
1955	171.4	17.9	53.5
1956	181.7	19.6	61.5
1957	156.1	23.5	68.7
1958	135.8	21.5	63.2
1959	186.9	17.9	58.9

[a] Federal and territorial governments.

and consumption in such countries are largely determined by the demand for their exports on the world market. Government revenue is largely derived from taxes on foreign trade transactions and hence any fluctuations in revenue originating from fluctuations in export earnings affect levels of government expenditures. It is, thus, through revenue that a direct relationship may be established between export earnings and government expenditure. The relationship, however, is not as simple and direct as it might appear. A steep rise in government revenue, due to an export boom, will as a rule not be translated into an immediate increase in government expenditure, but give rise to savings which may be used to finance outlays in later years. Moreover, decisions with respect to scale of government expenditures depend also on the availability of loans and grants, both internal and external.

The data on government expenditure in per cent of export value shown in Table 1 reveal some fluctuations over the period. It may be seen from column 9, however, that government expenditures increased considerably over the period in relation to exports. In considering these data, account should be taken not only of the comparatively large fluctuations in export value, but also of the time lag between fluctuations in export values and their impact on government expenditure. Because of the differences in crop years and fiscal years and owing to the delay in collection of revenue, the effects of a drop in export values in a particular year are seen on government revenue and expenditure, particularly capital, in the following year or even later years. This was true in certain cases during the 1957 recession in commodity prices. An example of such a time lag is provided by the following figures for the Federation of Rhodesia and Nyasaland.

An examination of national accounting data on government expenditures vis-a-vis the use of traditional budgetary data should help to indicate more precise magnitudes of increases in government expenditure. Unfortunately, such data are not available on a comparable basis for all the countries included in Table 1. However, the data shown for seven countries in Table 8 do lend support to the general conclusion indicated by the traditional data shown in Table 1. The growth of government expenditure in these seven countries was quite large and these data, further, indicate that Congo (Leopoldville) could be considered as one of those countries where the growth was relatively largest. It may be observed, further, from Table 14 that the growth of government expenditures in these countries was faster than that of gross national products, thus reflecting an increase in the size of the government sector in these countries over the period under review.

The growth of government expenditures has so far been considered in absolute terms and in relation to exports and gross national product. These relationships have been examined in current prices and it may be useful now to consider data on prices in order to have an idea of the extent of *real* increase in government expenditures. The importance of exports in African economies may suggest some relationship between export prices and government expenditure. Export prices would, however, affect only government earnings and not government expenditures. A significantly large part of government expenditure comprises of wages and salaries and this cannot be expected to vary with export prices. It is, perhaps, true in certain countries that export earnings, which are determined largely by export prices,[4] would influence levels of domestic incomes and hence internal price levels which are more relevant to the consideration of the growth of government expenditures. Import prices may, however, affect government expenditure depending on the import content of the latter.

An idea of the growth of government expenditure in relation to the internal price levels can be had from the data presented in Table 2. Data on cost of living, though available for most of the countries, are not a very good expression of the impact of price rise on government expenditure. Limitations of data put restraint on their use and interpretation. It may be only suggested that though prices did record an appreciable increase in most of the countries over the period 1950–1958, yet the increase in government expenditures was significantly more than could be accounted merely by price increases.

The experience of French-speaking countries is illustrated in Table 3. It may be seen that the growth of total government expenditure at constant prices was considerable, although much smaller than at current prices. A comparison between expenditure at constant prices and in current prices suggests that the implied rise in prices applicable to current expenditures was of the order of 68 per cent and that applicable to capital expenditures was approximately 87 per cent in 1958 over 1950. It may be perhaps correct

Table 2—Indices of the Growth of Government Expenditure and Prices: 1958
1950 = 100

Country	Government Expenditure[a]	Wholesale Prices[b]	Cost of Living[b]
Algeria	328[c]	143	168[c]
Congo (Leopoldville)	290	. . .	121
Ethiopia	250	96[d]	. . .
Ghana	410	. . .	124
Kenya	270	. . .	146[e]
Morocco	270	143	157[e]
Nigeria[f]	211	. . .	120
Federation of Rhodesia and Nyasaland[g]	160	. . .	115
Sierra Leone	310[h]	. . .	171[h]
Sudan[f]	190	101	116
Tanganyika	220	. . .	144[c]
Tunisia	160	140	152
U.A.R. (Egypt)	190	122	103
Uganda[f]	148	. . .	121[i]
Union of South Africa	170	141	137[c]

[a] Based on Table 1.
[b] *UN Statistical Year Book, 1959*, New York, 1959, pp. 434–446. Base year has been shifted from 1953 as given in this publication to 1950.
[c] 1949 = 100.
[d] Export goods.
[e] Europeans only.
[f] 1953 = 100.
[g] 1954 = 100.
[h] 1957.
[i] Europeans and Asians only.

Table 3—Growth of Government Expenditure at Constant Prices in French-Speaking Countries (in billion francs CFA)

Territory	Government Expenditure at 1958 Prices		Increase 1958/1950
	1950	1958	
Former French West Africa—Togo			
Current expenditure	33.8	68.2	2.02
Capital expenditure	21.2	21.0	0.99
Total	55.0	89.2	1.62
Former French Equatorial Africa—Cameroon			
Current expenditure	18.9	26.2	1.39
Capital expenditure	13.1	18.0	1.37
Total	32.0	44.2	1.38
Madagascar			
Current expenditure	11.5	22.0	1.91
Capital expenditure	5.2	7.1	1.37
Total	16.7	29.1	1.74

Source: Banque Centrale des Etats de l'Afrique de l'ouest.

to say that these countries experienced larger price increases than other countries in Africa.

An important explanation for the rapid growth of government expenditures seems to lie in the fact that in most of the African countries the development plans were initiated around 1950. It is true that some development plans were conceived in mid or late forties, but in most of the cases their implementation was deferred until around 1950. For example, though the Colonial Development Welfare Act of 1945 introduced the concept of planning in British overseas territories, yet "plans of an acceptable type only began to come forward in greater numbers towards the end of the forties and the beginning of the fifties." [5]

The principal reasons for the postponement of such plans were "shortages of administrative personnel and the general postwar shortages and uncertainties." [6] The first comprehensive postwar (ten years) French development plan for overseas territories was drafted in 1948 and the Belgian ten-year development plan for former Belgian Congo was prepared in 1949. It was, therefore, by 1950 that both metropolitan powers and their overseas territories were agreed

upon the need for planning, and human and material resources were being mobilized to implement development plans.[7]

An idea of the course of development expenditures over the period may be obtained by an examination of the shares of current expenditures in total expenditures. Table 4 depicts the percentage share of current expenditures in total expenditures of seventeen countries for selected years.

It may be observed from Table 4 that the course of current expenditures, and hence of development expenditures, was not altogether smooth. It is difficult to discern any general trend since the data exhibit different tendencies for different countries or a group of countries. In Algeria, Morocco, Sierra Leone, and former French West Africa, the growth of current expenditures continuously outstripped the growth of development expenditures. On the other hand, in Sudan since 1953, and in former Italian Somaliland (Trust Territory) since 1955, development expenditures increased faster than current expenditures. Current expenditures in Kenya, Tanganyika and Union of South Africa on one hand, and in Ghana and UAR (Egypt) on the other, show quite opposite tendencies. In the former group of countries current expenditures increased faster than development expenditures until 1956, while in Ghana and UAR (Egypt) an opposite tendency is

Table 4—Current Expenditure as Percentage of Total

Country	1950	1953	1956	1958
Algeria	53[a]	58	63	71
Ethiopia	96	91	98	83
Former French Equatorial Africa–Cameroon	62	60	62	59
Former French West Africa–Togo	64	65	74	76
Ghana	84	61	60	66
Kenya	75	78	85	82
Madagascar	71	65	66	76
Morocco	55	57	74	81
Nigeria	80	69	88	70
Sierra Leone	69	72	72	89[d]
Somalia (former trusteeship territory)	...	90[c]	89[d]	87[e]
Sudan	...	85	79	74
Tanganyika	70	79	81	78
Tunisia	70	56	...	72[d]
UAR (Egypt)	96	88[b]	87	91
Uganda	66	58	72	77
Union of South Africa	63	73	75	68

Source: See General Notes.   Note: Based on budgetary data.

[a] 1949.   [d] 1957.
[b] 1954.   [e] 1959.
[c] 1955.

observed. In Madagascar, the peak level of development expenditures was reached around 1953, and thereafter current expenditure increased faster than development expenditure. In general, it may be observed that in 1958, compared with 1950, the percentage shares of current expenditures in the total were higher in ten countries or group of countries out of fifteen for which data for the selected four years are available. In 1956, the number of countries in a similar situation was twelve out of fifteen. During the period under review, the peak level of current expenditures, in relation to the total expenditures, was probably reached in or around 1956.[8] Current expenditures were, therefore, generally rising faster than development expenditures, though in some cases, the absolute magnitudes of the latter were increasing.

Of the absolute magnitudes of development expenditures it may be said by way of a rough generalization that they showed a tendency to increase from year to year during the first half of the period, and most of the drops in these expenditures occurred during the latter half of the period. Generally speaking, the reasons for such cuts during

the latter half of the period were either the depressed state of the export markets, or special circumstances like attainment of political independence or domestic or external emergencies which made additional claims on the available resources. An examination of data for 1959 in the case of a few countries, however, shows that development expenditures were beginning to pick up.

National accounts data for a few selected countries lend further support to the general observations made in the earlier paragraphs. Data on fixed capital formation and on its share in total expenditure is shown in Table 5 for seven countries. Except in the Union of South Africa and Congo (Leopoldville) save for 1958, share of fixed capital formation is seen to be continuously diminishing. In other words, current expenditures in these latter countries were increasing at a faster rate than development expenditures.

Increases in current expenditures were generally of two types. Firstly, they increased partly because of assumptions of new functions or responsibilities or expansion of the

Table 5—Fixed Capital Formation as Percentage of Total Government Expenditure*

	1950	1953	1956	1958
Federation of Rhodesia and Nyasaland (£ million)				
Fixed capital formation	...	26.0[a]	32.2	36.7
Per cent of total	...	48	45	43
Ghana (G £ million)				
Fixed capital formation	...	18.5[a]	18.6	14.3
Per cent of total	...	41	36	26
Tanganyika (£ million)				
Fixed capital formation	...	10.2[a]	9.3	9.6
Per cent of total	...	46	38	35
Union of South Africa (£ million)				
Fixed capital formation	98[b]	122	149	211
Per cent of total	36	39	39	40
Congo (Leopoldville) (billion francs)				
Fixed capital formation	1,250	3,380	4,940	5,180
Per cent of total	28	37	37	32
Morocco (billion francs)				
Fixed capital formation	28[b]	26.3	28.4[c]	34.0
Per cent of total	44	38	32	27
Nigeria (£ million)				
Fixed capital formation	9.8	13.6	25.3	26.1[d]
Per cent of total	35	36	36	35

* Based on national accounting data. Fixed capital formation includes investment by general government and government enterprises. For Morocco only general government is included. For source see Table 8.

[a] 1954.
[b] 1952.
[c] 1955.
[d] 1957.

existing services by the governments. Secondly, completion of certain development schemes gave rise to recurrent expenditures in subsequent years.

Assumption of new responsibilities in some cases was the direct outcome of the attainment of political independence by the countries concerned. Examples of such countries are Ghana, Morocco and Tunisia. In all these countries, current expenditure on *general services*[9] registered the largest increase over the period 1950–1958.

This increase in all the three cases was largely due to the assumption of defence expenditures which had to be on their own account after the attainment of independence. Prior to the independence, all or most of their defence expenditures were borne by their metropolitan powers. This is one of the instances of new demands which are made on current revenues when a country attains political independence. Other examples are expenditure on diplomatic representation abroad, increased expenditure on legislative bodies and compensatory payments to expatriates consequent upon the adoption of the policy of Africanization after independence. The Government of Sudan, for example, made large payments in 1955–1956 in the form of gratuities, commutation of pensions and compensation to expatriates "who left the Government service on Sudanization."[10] The actual amount of such payments is not known, but the budgetary provision on this account during the fiscal year 1955–1956 amounted to £E 1.1 million.[11]

Political independence sometimes introduces new elements in public expenditure planning. This is more true in the field of social services like education, health and low cost housing. It is likely that such services may be subsidized to a larger extent after independence than before and they may be expanded considerably. A typical case in Africa is that of Nigeria, where it may be said that "independence started in advance." The field in which developments in Nigeria were particularly striking is education. Expenditure on education in Nigeria increased in absolute terms from £8.85 million in 1950

to £21.57 million in 1958 and as percentage of total current expenditure it increased from 9 per cent in 1950 to 22 per cent in 1958. The principal reason for such a rapid growth of current expenditure on education has been the emphasis placed on free and universal primary education.

Preliminary observations on the impact of political independence on government budgets have been made with respect to Nigeria and the four countries which became independent during the period under review. Since 1958, however, a number of other African countries have gained political independence. Independence has probably made or is making new demands on their resources in more or less similar directions as noted in the preceding paragraphs.

The second reason for increase in current expenditures was the emergence of recurring expenditures arising out of development projects. Most of the development plans conceived and implemented early in the decade were heavily weighted in favour of expenditure on transport and communications and on social services. The implications of such development programmes in terms of subsequent additions to the current budget must be considerable and, though such magnitudes cannot be firmly established, yet the fact helps to explain a part of the increase in government expenditure. The preoccupation with such recurrent costs of development plans was noticeable by mid-fifties. By this time, some of the countries[12] had started giving particular attention to recurrent implications of development plans. This aspect of the appraisal of development plans was partly dictated by limitations on current revenue and by falling reserves.

GROWTH OF REVENUE

The growth of current revenues between 1950 and 1958, both in absolute terms and in relation to exports, is shown in Table 6. Compared with the absolute growth in expenditures (see Table 1), current revenues did not increase as fast as expenditures. A three-fold or more than three-fold increase in revenue in 1958 over 1950 was observed only in four countries. Eleven countries recorded an increase of more than two-fold, while in

Table 6—Growth of Revenue

Country and Currency	In Terms of National Currencies				In Per Cent of Export Value			
	1950 (1)	1958 (2)	Increase 1958/1950 (3)=(2)/(1)	(4)*	1950 (5)	1952 (6)	1957 (7)	1958 (8)
Algeria (million francs)	41.9	157.3 P	3.7	17.9	40	44	75	77
Cameroon (billion CFA francs)[g]	3.1 E	9.4 E	3.0	14.9	38	60[b]	60	39
Congo (Leopoldville) (billion francs)	5.4	12.5 E	2.3	11.0	42	43	49	62
Ethiopia (million Eth. $)	66.0	138.9	2.1	9.7	99	70	80	82
Former French Equatorial Africa[g] (billion CFA)	4.2	10.1	1.7	6.5	91	103	64	53
Former French West Africa[g] (billion CFA)	24.4	RE 62.6	2.5	12.5	79	94	88	86
Ghana (£ million)	16.8	55.2	3.2	16.0	25	43	53	59
Kenya (£ million)	13.4	34.5	2.6	12.2	68	95	103	104
Madagascar[g] (billion CFA francs)	8.0	19.7	2.5	11.9	65	71	108	98
Morocco[f] (billion francs)	35.1	98.4[a]	2.8	15.9	53	60	84	89
Nigeria (£ million)	28.5	81.0	2.8	13.9	32	40	..	60
Federation of Rhodesia and Nyasaland (£ million)	50.6[c]	82.2	1.6	12.8	..	..	56	61
Sierra Leone (£ million)	3.0	9.6[a]	3.2	18.1	30	51	52	..
Somalia (million Somalos) (former trusteeship territory)	41.6[e]	64.8[d]	1.6	11.7	..	..	64	63
Sudan (£ million)	30.3[b]	47.4	1.6	8.3	..	60	89	102
Tanganyika (£ million)	10.7	18.8	1.8	7.2	46	34	43	45
Togo[g] (billion francs CFA)	1.1	2.2	1.7	9.0	71	60	83	69
Tunisia (billion francs)	17.9	46.5 P	2.6	12.7	5	67	77	72
UAR (Egypt) (£ million)	155.7	282.8 E	1.8	7.7	89	131	151	173
Uganda (£ million)	9.3	19.5	2.1	9.7	32	33	44	..
Union of South Africa (£ million)	155.2	308.3 E	2.0	8.9	69	75	66	79

Sources: See General Notes.

* Compound annual rate of increase.
Note: E = Estimates; P = Provisional; RE = Revised Estimate.
a 1957.
b 1953.
c 1955.
d 1959.
e 1954.
f Former southern zone only, except in column (8).
g Revenue of the local budgets.

six countries revenues failed to double over the period under review. The countries which recorded largest increases in revenue were Algeria, Ghana, Sierra Leone, and Cameroon.

Compared to 1950, in 1958 revenues as percentage of exports were significantly higher. The only striking exceptions were former French Equatorial Africa, Tanganyika, Togo and Cameroon. In the former French Equatorial Africa, revenue in relation to exports was much lower in 1958. In the other three countries, the percentages were practically the same in 1958 as those in 1950. Rapid growth of exports in 1958 over 1957 explains the lower percentages of revenue in 1958 compared to 1957 in former French Equatorial Africa and Cameroon.

It would be pertinent to inquire into the relationship between current revenues and gross national products since it may be argued that current revenue should increase faster than gross national product in view of the crucial role of governments in the development process. Such an examination is not possible in view of the paucity of national accounting data for most of the countries included in Table 6. In Table 14, however, current revenues are shown in

percentage of gross national product for several countries for selected years. It appears that current revenues increased faster than gross national product in Congo (Leopoldville), the Federation of Rhodesia and Nyasaland, and possibly also in Nigeria. In the other countries, the ratio of current revenue in gross national product either decreased or remained approximately unchanged.

Rules of traditional fiscal policy suggest that current revenue be at least sufficient to meet current expenditure. Considering the need for public savings in the developing countries of Africa, as in other developing countries, it may not be sufficient merely to balance the current budget, but to give rise deliberately to significant public savings in order to finance development programmes. An idea of the extent to which current revenues were sufficient to cover current expenditures and, further, create public savings can be had from Table 7. It may be seen from this table that in most of the countries current revenues were adequate to cover current expenditures. For example, out of seventeen countries included in that table, only three countries had deficits on current account in 1950, and six in 1958. But looking at the behaviour of current revenues and current expenditures, it is obvious that the former were, in general, continuously

Table 7—Revenue as Percentage of Current Expenditure

	1950	1953	1956	1958
Algeria	117.4 [a]	103.3	99.8	100.0 E
Congo (Leopoldville)	125.6	144.4	114.4	100.0 E
Ethiopia	98.2	102.0	100.2	96.0
Former French Equatorial Africa–Cameroon [d]	83.9	90.6	91.0	75.6
Former French West Africa–Togo [d]	126.9	115.9	98.1	95.0
Ghana	150.0	169.7	119.2 [c]	117.2 E
Kenya	110.7	98.2	86.8	94.3
Madagascar [d]	117.6	121.3	98.8	89.5
Morocco	106.7	125.5	104.5	97.0 E
Nigeria	121.3	160.0	107.8	123.7
Sierra Leone	150.0	148.6	145.8	...
Sudan	...	119.3	133.4	115.6
Tanganyika	137.1	102.9	100.0	100.5
Tunisia	107.8	100.0	...	100.6 [b] E
UAR (Egypt)	99.3	93.5	96.0	104.4 E
Uganda	182.4	126.6	112.8	105.4
Union of South Africa	110.3	117.3	116.5	119.7 E

E = Estimates.
[a] 1949.
[b] 1959.
[c] 15-month.

[d] Revenue of local budgets is related to total current expenditure, i.e., including current expenditure financed by France.

Table 8—Growth of Government Income and Expenditure on Goods and Services
ratios of increase = values for end years in column 1
values for initial years in column 1

	Government Expenditure			Government Income		Current Revenue as Percentage of	
	Consumption	Fixed Capital Formation	Total Expenditure	Current Revenue	Disposable Income	Consumption	Expenditure
Congo (Leopoldville), 1950–1958	3.38	4.14	3.59	2.18	2.07	157	101
Federation of Rhodesia and Nyasaland, 1954–1959	1.85	1.34	1.61	1.52	1.54	189	156
Ghana, 1954–1958	1.49	0.77	1.20	0.89	0.90	248	147
Morocco:							
1951–1955	2.16	1.32	1.78	1.33	1.26	204	126
1951–1958	3.23	1.58	2.51	...	...	...	...
Tanganyika, 1954–1958	1.49	0.94	1.24	1.21	1.20	144	117
Union of South Africa, 1952–1958	1.51	2.15	1.74	1.50	1.53	152	151
Nigeria:							
1950–1957	2.72	2.66	2.70	2.80	2.48	177	183
1952–1957	2.03	1.92	1.99	1.75	1.53	212	183

Sources: Congo, Morocco and Union of South Africa: *UN National Accounts Yearbook, 1959.* Federation of Rhodesia and Nyasaland, 1954–1959. Ghana: *National Accounts of the Federation of Rhodesia and Nyasaland, 1954–1957; Statistical Abstract, 1959;* Public Finance in Tanganyika, Dar-es-Salaam, 1959. Tanganyika: *Gross Domestic Product of Tanganyika, 1958.* Ghana: *Economic Survey, 1958.* Nigeria: *UN National Accounts Yearbook, 1958 and 1959;* Prest and Stewart, *The National Income of Nigeria, 1950–51.*

General Notes : Fixed capital formation includes investment by government enterprises except for Morocco where only general government capital formation is shown. For Ghana, railways and harbour are included. Disposable income equals revenue less subsidies and other current transfers.

273

declining in relation to the latter. The only significant exceptions to this statement are Nigeria and Union of South Africa. As a result of the slower growth of revenues, current surpluses which were quite high in many countries in 1950 had more or less disappeared by 1958. By 1958, rising current expenditures had caught up with revenues and the situation was practically even in that year.

National accounts data presented in Table 8 confirm the observations made above. Table 8 shows the ratios of increase between the two years indicated in column 1 of that table. The last two columns show current revenue as percentage of consumption expenditure for the same two years for each country. Current revenues in all countries were sufficient to meet consumption expenditures, but it will be seen that current revenues, except in the Union of South Africa, increased much less than current expenditures. Compared to current expenditures, current revenues had declined in the end years of comparison.

The increasing lag between revenue and current expenditure was partly due to the nature of development effort undertaken in the past which had a two-fold effect on government budgets. The development effort of the earlier period comprised of large investment in infrastructure in many countries.[13] One consequence of this investment in infrastructure, as already pointed out, was the emergence of additional recurrent expenditure in subsequent years. Moreover, infrastructure investment had no direct effect on revenue, while the indirect effect, i.e., the promotion of private investment and production, often fell short of expectations. It should be noted, however, that the position of the various countries in this respect seems to have varied widely and that the indirect effects have also depended upon the export situation and various types of policies adopted or pursued by governments. Thus, in the Federation of Rhodesia and Nyasaland mining and related industrial developments proceeded at such a rapid pace in the first part of the 1950's that infrastructure often

constituted a bottleneck in the economic development of the country. As regards policies, it has been argued that one reason for the relatively slow pace of industrialization in former French territories was the existence of a protected market for French manufacturers as a result of the arrangements of the franc zone. In this respect, the situation was different in the ex-Belgian Congo where Belgian manufacturers had to compete on equal terms with other foreign producers and therefore often found it profitable to start industrial enterprises in the Congo itself.[14]

THE GAP BETWEEN REVENUE
AND EXPENDITURE

Table 9 presents data on financing of total expenditure in certain selected countries over the period 1950–1958. The cumulative gaps between revenue and expenditure shown in column 3 of Table 9 obscure annual fluctuations in revenue and expenditure and the factors which determined their levels over the period. Some countries had accumulated public savings prior to 1950, and some were again quick to take advantage of high commodity prices during the Korean War period. These accumulated surpluses did affect the levels of expenditure during the subsequent years. In some cases, small gaps between revenue and expenditure may be explained partly by the adherence to cautious expenditure policies. For example, in British East African countries public development programmes were strictly geared to the available financial resources. Existence of over-all surplus or deficit does not necessarily speak, therefore, for either increased tax effort or lack of it in these countries. Some general comments can, however, be made and are important. Deficits occurred mostly during the latter part of the period, and the surpluses accumulated in the earlier years did enable some countries to meet subsequent deficits on their budgets. The West African countries included in the table had accumulated specially large reserves through savings in earlier years. In countries which had sizable over-all deficits, the most important source of financing these deficits was borrowing. Grants were particularly significant in

Table 9—Financing of Total Expenditure in Selected Countries: 1950–1958

Country and Currency	Total Expenditure (Cumulative) (1)	Total Revenue (Cumulative) (2)	Surplus (+) or Deficit (−) (3) = (2) − (1)	Net Borrowing (4)	Grants (5)	Other[a] (6)	Total Nonrevenue Receipts (7) = (4) − (6)	Increase (+) or Decrease (−) in Reserves[b] (8) = (7) + (3)
Uganda (£ million)	146.63	134.07	−12.56	11.08	2.37	3.16	16.61	+4.05
Union of South Africa (£ million)	2,640.5	2,211.4	−429.1	400.3	...	...	...	...
Tanganyika (£ million)	158.00	132.37	−25.63	11.46	8.56	4.31	24.33	−1.30
Kenya (£ million)[c]	356.03	273.38	−82.65	38.94	35.94	4.67	79.55	−3.10
Sierra Leone (£ million)[d]	47.26	49.39	+2.13	4.24	3.46	1.28	8.98	+11.11
Ghana (£ million)	368.79	379.57	+10.78	12.16[e]	20.35	11.94	44.45	+55.23
Nigeria (£ million)[c]	566.17	568.49	+2.32	5.68	26.85	...	32.53	+34.85
UAR (Egypt) (£ million)	2,258.22	1,947.73	−310.49	178.30	23.57[f]	31.03	232.90	−77.59
Sudan (£ million)	239.47	239.20	−0.27	...	0.11[f]	...	...	...
Ethiopia (Eth. $ million)	986.88	938.80	−48.08	24.06	12.80	8.80	45.73	−2.35
Italian Somaliland (million Somalos)	533.48	259.52	−273.96	...	254.49	6.25	260.74	−13.22
Morocco (billion francs)	887.05	663.80	−223.25	168.54[d]	...	34.11	...	...
Congo (Leopoldville) (billion francs)	126.40	88.81	−37.59	40.12	...	...	...	...

Source: See General Notes.

a Sales of assets, currency profits, etc.
b Including errors and omissions.
c 1946–1958.
d 1950–1957.
e 1951–1958.
f U.S. grants.

Kenya and in former Italian Somaliland. Perhaps the largest claim on reserves was made in UAR (Egypt), where E £70.4 million were withdrawn between 1950 and 1956 to cover the deficits of those years. These reserves were accumulated prior to 1950. A broad summary of events between 1950 and 1958 conceals the actual course of their development and it may be useful to study a few specific cases in order to throw light on the details of financing.

In Ghana, beginning from 1950, current revenues were increasing continuously until they reached an all-time peak of £75.20 million in the fiscal year 1954–1955. This was due to the extremely high price fetched by cocoa in 1954. The favourable revenue position resulted in budgetary surpluses until 1955. As a result of these surpluses, sterling balances of public authorities which stood at £17.8 million at the end of 1949 reached a peak of £82.0 million at the end of 1955.[15] Since the fiscal year 1955–1956, the revenue position deteriorated and Ghana had series of deficits thereafter. It was during this period that sterling balances were drawn upon and they fell to £58.2 million by the end of 1958. The fall in reserves did not equal the total amount of deficit during the last three years. The total deficit amounted to £28.72 million during 1955–1956 to 1957–1958. This is explained by resort to borrowing in spite of the extremely high position of reserves. The unbalanced portfolio of sterling securities partly dictated the use of loans for financing expenditures. A large part of these securities were invested in long-dated and low-rate stock and could be mobilized only at a considerable capital loss in case of immediate need.[16] The government's holdings of short-term assets never exceeded £4 to £6 million, and at the end of 1958 short-term assets amounted to only £0.7 million. Recently, attempts are, however, being made to diversify the sterling portfolio. The use of borrowing for development purposes was accompanied by practical measures to stimulate the growth of internal money and capital markets. Treasury bills were floated in Ghana for the first time in 1954. In 1957, Ghana

established its own Central Bank. The other monetary institutions in the public sector are the Ghana Co-operative Bank and the Post Office Savings Bank. These institutional changes have provided an outlet for the investment of private short-term funds. For example, the Treasury bills floated by the government in 1959 and in 1960 were fully taken locally.

In Nigeria, current surpluses were not fully spent until 1954, partly due to the shortages of constructional capacity in executing work programmes. The surpluses of revenue were saved and invested overseas. The tempo of development was quickened after 1955, and the subsequent plans were to be financed by the use of past savings. In 1955–1962 Development Plan, the total outlay envisaged is £339.1 million.[17] Out of this amount, the government was responsible for finding £275.8 million and £137.3 are expected to be obtained by contributions from revenue, including the use of past savings.[18] Until the end of 1958, however, there was no decline in the government's holding of sterling balances. The marketing boards play a very significant part in the development in Nigeria by providing grants and loans to the government for the financing of development programmes. By way of grants alone, the marketing boards are expected to contribute £12.8 million towards the financing of 1955–1962 Development Plan.

In Kenya, financing of development expenditure has largely depended on the availability of loan funds. During the period 1946–1953, gross development receipts totalled £35.9 million, of which loans accounted for £18.9 million. Colonial Welfare and Development grants totalled £2.6 million, and £11.6 million represented contributions from revenue including the use of the past savings. The General Revenue Balance of the Government increased from £2.2 million as at December 31, 1946, to £7.61 million on December 31, 1953. During the same period, public debt registered an increase of £17.55 million. Beginning from 1952, however, Kenya had to bear the burden of emergency expenditures. As a result of this, by 1954 the accumulated balances were exhausted and prospects of savings on current account were very dim. Beginning from 1954, Kenya had series of deficits on current account until the end of 1957–1958. In the 1954–1957 Development Plan, therefore, of total outlay of £21.6 million, £12.44 million were to be financed by loans, £1.6 million from C.D. & W. grants and £7.0 million from previous unspent balances. When the 1957–1960 Plan was drafted, the reliance on loans had increased, and at the same time there was tightness in London money market. Shortage of development capital induced a shift in favour of directly productive schemes. In the 1957–1960 Plan, loan funds accounted for £18.0 million out of the total size of the Plan of £23.3 million. Contributions from revenue were set at only £1.02 million. In the 1960–1963 Plan, loans are expected to contribute £18.50 million to a total outlay of 26.5 million. Contributions from revenue are expected to be only £1.3 million.

Throughout the period, Uganda had surpluses on current account, but these being small, particularly since 1953, financing of capital expenditure has depended on using the past savings. The past savings in question were those of the marketing boards which had accumulated reserves prior to 1953. From 1950 to 1952 (inclusive), the marketing boards had added £34.4 million to the Price Assistance Funds.[19] Cotton Price Assistance Fund was closed at £20 million in 1951 and the excess of £18 million was transferred to the government. This transfer alone provided a little more than a third of the government's capital expenditure programme during the period 1950–1959. The decline in sterling assets was £20 million between 1954–1958, and the General Revenue Balance had declined by £6.0 million during the same period. At the end of 1958, the government had only £11.8 million in budgetary funds and liquid sterling assets stood at a dangerously low level of £0.6 million.

The general conclusion seems to be that the use of past savings played an important role in the financing of expenditure during the period 1950 to 1958. The contribution of internal finance was quite high during the period. However, the recent situation indicates that past savings in most of the countries are fast approaching very low levels and hence the question of finance will be quite serious in future. It would, therefore,

be necessary to raise additional resources either at home or abroad.

Detailed data on financing of total expenditure in French-speaking countries are not available but the amount of government expenditure financed by French public funds is shown in Table 10. These data also illustrate the changes in the distribution of functions between France and these countries over

Table 10—Contribution of French Public Funds to the Government Expenditure in Former French Territories

	Billion Francs CFA			
	1950	1953	1956	1958
AOF–Togo				
Current	20.1	37.1	53.9	68.2
Capital	11.3	20.0	18.7	21.0
Total	31.4	57.1	72.6	89.2
AEF–Cameroon				
Current	11.2	19.1	21.1	26.2
Capital	7.0	12.7	12.8	18.0
Total	18.2	31.8	33.9	44.2
Madagascar				
Current	6.8	12.2	17.2	22.0
Capital	2.8	6.7	8.8	7.1
Total	9.6	18.9	26.0	29.1
	Per Cent of Expenditure Financed by France			
AOF–Togo				
Current	3.5	3.3	4.6	12.2
Capital	55.5	65.5	66.8	59.6
Total	22.2	25.1	20.7	22.4
AEF–Cameroon				
Current	5.0	6.5	10.3	16.1
Capital	64.9	74.9	94.4	86.9
Total	28.0	33.9	36.1	44.9
Madagascar				
Current	6.5	3.3	5.4	9.8
Capital	54.1	59.6	53.4	55.7
Total	19.8	23.3	21.5	21.0

the period considered. The extent to which current revenues of local budgets were sufficient to finance the total current expenditures has been indicated earlier in Table 5. The financial contribution of France to current expenditures, though not insignificant until 1956, registered a very noticeable increase in the two following years. This increased contribution reflects the implementation of the *Loi Cadre* of 1956. The role of external funds in the financing of equipment expenditure was very substantial. In the former French Equatorial Africa—Cameroon—the French aid to the equipment budget increased considerably over the period and on an average accounted for 80 per cent of equipment expenditure shown for selected years in the table. The average contribution from France, for the selected years, to the total equipment expenditure in the former French West Africa—Togo—and in Madagascar amounted to 62 per cent and 56 per cent, respectively.

The Structure of Current Revenue and Current Expenditure

STRUCTURE OF REVENUE

Table 11 sets out the structure of government revenue in African countries. It may be seen that tax revenue accounts for at least four-fifths of the total revenue in almost all countries. A particularly noteworthy fact is the excessive dependence on revenue from indirect taxes of a majority of countries. Direct taxes are significant only in a few countries.

Revenue from direct taxes is particularly important in Congo (Leopoldville), Union of South Africa, Federation of Rhodesia and Nyasaland, Kenya and Tanganyika. The principal reason for the importance of this source of taxation is the revenue obtained from company income taxation. Organized business on company lines is more important in the first three countries where a large part of the revenue accrues from companies established in the export sector of the economy. This revenue, therefore, represents a slice of export earnings taken by governments through income taxes rather than through export duties. The choice of the method of taxation of export earnings in these countries as against countries which use export duties reflect, therefore, mainly institutional differences in the export sector. In Kenya and Tanganyika, besides income taxation, other taxes like non-native educa-

tion taxes and African poll taxes are quite significant.

Taxation of personal and company incomes in Africa is relatively underdeveloped for various reasons. One reason is the absence of any large scale company business. Another reason is extremely low levels of per capita incomes and the relatively equal distribution of this income except where European population is found comparatively in large numbers. Under such circumstances, an extremely low level of exemption limit for income tax purposes would make collection of taxes too costly and a higher limit may not make it worthwhile. Absence of any systematic methods of accounting and bookkeeping render assessment of income more difficult and evasion easier.

Among the countries which depend heavily on revenue from indirect taxes, the most prominent are Algeria, Ethiopia, former French West Africa, Ghana, Morocco, Nigeria, Sierra Leone, former Italian Somaliland, Sudan, Togo, Tunisia, Uganda and Cameroon. These countries can, further, be split into two groups. In group one can be included those countries which derive a relatively larger part of their revenue from indirect taxes from duties on foreign trade transactions. Countries which derive a relatively larger part of their indirect tax revenue from taxes on domestic production can be said to belong to the second group.

The first group according to the above classification would include countries like Ethiopia, Cameroon, former French West Africa, Ghana, Nigeria, Sierra Leone, former Italian Somaliland, Sudan, Uganda and presumably Togo. Here again two groups of countries can be distinguished, viz., countries deriving larger revenues from import duties and, secondly, countries depending mainly on export duties. The contribution of foreign trade to the government revenues in either case is explained by the fact that a large part of incomes and expenditures in these countries passes through the ports. Import duties are relatively important in Ethiopia, Cameroon, former French West Africa, Nigeria, Sierra Leone, and former Italian Somaliland.

Export duties are generally a popular source of revenue in countries where export of one or two commodities constitute a significantly large share of total exports. The countries which depend heavily on export duties are Ghana, Uganda and Sudan. During the period 1950–1958, on an average, cocoa constituted 81.5 per cent of Ghana's exports, cotton accounted for 62.7 per cent of Sudan's exports and in Uganda during 1950–1957 exports of cotton and coffee accounted for 86.8 per cent of her total exports. Lack of diversification of exports in these countries also partly explains the existence of marketing boards. The marketing boards insulate to a large extent the impact of fluctuations in export prices on producers' incomes. This may have favourable effects on government revenue to the extent that producers' incomes and expenditures are maintained under unfavourable world conditions. On the other hand, the stabilization effort involves large fluctuations in government revenue from export duties.

The data on Sudan as they appear in Table 11 are slightly misleading. In the table, the share of export duties in total indirect taxes is not very significant. This is so because a large part of revenue derived from the sale of cotton overseas appears under nontax revenue. This revenue is in the form of government's share of profits from agricultural undertakings engaged in production and sale of cotton. The Gezeira Board, for example, contributes 40 per cent of its net profits to the government. If Sudan's traditional revenue data are reclassified, it is found that during 1953–1958, on an average, government revenue from cotton accounted for 33 per cent of total revenue.

Countries which derive relatively more revenue from taxes on domestic production are Algeria, Morocco, Tunisia and Egypt (UAR). Apart from domestic excises and sales taxes, one of the most favoured methods of raising such revenues has been the use of the device of fiscal monopolies. Fiscal monopolies of sugar and tobacco in Morocco and of tobacco and other product in Tunisia fetch substantial amounts of profits to the governments. Such trading profits are nothing but concealed indirect taxes. Fiscal monopolies are also practised in Sudan and Ethiopia in sugar and tobacco respectively. The commodities generally chosen for such trading purposes are those characteristic of mass consumption.

STRUCTURE OF CURRENT EXPENDITURE

Data on structure of current expenditure are presented in Table 12. The weaknesses of these data are clearly indicated partly by certain gaps in the table and partly by lumping together expenditure on economic services, community services like water, sanitation, roads, etc., and on social services other than education and health under "other current expenditure." It must also be pointed out that expenditure on identified functions does not represent the total expenditure on those functions. Traditional budgetary classifications are often presented on departmental or ministerial lines and there are often cases where expenditure on a particular function is incurred in various proportions by more than one ministry or departments. In order to get total expenditure on a function, it would, therefore, be necessary to trace expenditures incurred by various departments on that function. In view of the weakness of data set out in Table 12, any comments on the structure of current expenditure must be tentative.

It is difficult to distinguish any particular trends over the period. It can be said with some reservations that the share of expenditures on general services in 1958 was lower in most of the countries than in 1950. Significant exceptions were Ghana, Kenya, Morocco and Tunisia. Except in Kenya, the increased share of general services was due to the increased expenditure on defence following their political independence. In Kenya, the emergency lasting from 1952 to 1956 necessitated additional expenditure on the maintenance of law and order. Relatively increased expenditure on general services in countries which gained their independence during the period was, as already explained, due to certain new demands made by the fact of independence on their resources, e.g., expenditure on diplomatic representation abroad, increased expenditure on legislative bodies, etc.

Table 11—Structure of Revenue
(percentage of the total)

Countries	Year	Direct Taxes			Indirect Taxes				Nontax Revenue
		Income Taxes (1)	Other (2)	Total (3)=(1)+(2)	Import Duties (4)	Export Duties (5)	Other (6)	Total (7)=(4)+(5)+(6)	(9)
Algeria	1951	17.7	1.1	18.8	4.6	—	61.0	65.6	15.6
	1953	17.0	1.2	18.2	3.6	—	61.9	65.5	16.3
	1956	14.5	1.7	16.2	3.2	—	59.2	62.4	21.4
	1958 P	16.0	1.3	17.3	2.9	—	57.5	60.5	22.3
Cameroon	1950 E	...	...	25.6	...	...	...	61.7	12.7
	1953	...	...	25.6	25.9	25.6	9.1	60.6	13.8
	1956	...	...	21.0	32.4	25.1	8.1	65.6	13.4
	1958 E	...	...	20.3	...	...	...	62.0	17.7
Congo (Leopoldville)	1950	25.6	4.6	30.2	17.3	28.3	12.7	58.3	11.4
	1953	36.6	3.2	39.8	16.6	22.8	11.5	50.9	8.4
	1956	28.7	2.9	31.6	17.2	24.9	5.5	47.6	20.8
	1958 E	28.0	3.0	31.0	15.2	17.6	14.6	47.4	21.7
Ethiopia	1950	9.4	26.1	35.5	33.3	4.3	12.3	49.9	14.7
	1953	11.4	20.1	31.9	33.8	8.3	12.8	54.9	13.2
	1956	5.6	16.2	21.8	27.3	10.5	18.1	68.4 [a]	9.8
	1958	5.4	13.8	19.2	25.9	8.6	20.9	71.3	9.5
Federation of Rhodesia and Nyasaland	1954	56.9	...	56.9	...	...	4.5	20.8	22.3
	1956	55.6	...	55.6	...	...	4.6	23.1	21.3
	1958	51.9	...	51.9	...	...	5.0	25.0	23.1
French Equatorial Africa	1950	...	...	16.8	...	...	...	48.9	34.3
French West Africa	1952	...	...	19.5	21.6	9.8	15.7	47.0	33.5
	1955	...	...	36.0	25.9	9.5	23.2	58.6	5.4
	1958	...	...	37.5	22.8	8.1	25.1	56.0	6.6
	1950	6.1	10.9	17.0	30.9	10.0	20.7	61.6	21.5
	1952	7.0	13.4	20.4	26.0	10.6	24.2	60.8	18.8
	1956	...	...	25.1	26.3	11.1	34.4	71.8	3.1
	1958 E	7.3	12.2	19.5	41.6	14.7	17.2	73.5	7.1

Country	Year								
Ghana	1950	20.5	1.4	21.9	44.7	20.5	3.3	68.5	9.6
	1953	17.5	4.5	22.0	24.7	43.5	2.3	70.5	7.6
	1957	11.2	2.3	13.5	30.7	43.6	2.8	77.1	9.4
	1958	9.9	4.5	14.4	27.1	41.5	5.8	74.4	11.1
Kenya	1950	24.5	5.5	30.0	—	—	18.2	48.2	21.6
	1953	28.6	4.9	33.5	27.3	0.7	11.5	39.5	26.9
	1956	26.7	5.6	32.3	26.9	4.9	14.6	46.4	21.3
	1958	33.4	6.4	39.8	23.4	—	15.8	39.3	20.9
Madagascar	1950	...	...	42.4	...	...	...	47.6	9.9
	1952	...	...	31.2	...	...	...	55.6	13.2
	1955	...	...	32.5	...	...	...	49.5	18.0
	1958	...	...	29.9	22.7	7.4	16.0	46.1	23.9
Morocco[b]	1950	15.8	9.9	25.7	30.4	3.2	33.6	67.2	7.1
	1953	17.1	9.6	26.7	25.1	3.1	35.6	64.0	9.3
	1956	13.5	6.7	20.2	17.0	2.1	51.1	70.8	8.9
	1958 E	...	...	15.8	11.0	...	40.5	66.8	17.4
Federation of Nigeria	1953	13.6	0.8	14.4	29.1	28.1	7.7	64.9	20.7
	1956	9.2	2.4	11.6	40.9	19.7	16.6	71.2	17.2
	1958	12.4	8.2	12.6	42.9	15.7	10.3	69.2	18.2
Sierra Leone	1950	32.0	3.2	35.2	41.3	7.5	1.8	50.6	14.1
	1953	34.9	1.8	36.7	34.8	16.5	1.4	52.7	10.6
	1956	27.3	0.1	27.4	52.2	6.9	1.1	60.2	11.5
	1957	24.2	0.1	24.3	54.6	6.4	1.1	62.1	13.6
Somalia (former trusteeship territory)	1955	...	...	11.3	32.8	10.4	28.7	71.9	16.9
	1957	...	...	12.7	36.2	8.7	28.9	73.8	13.6
	1959	...	...	14.2	35.5	9.3	28.8	28.8	12.3
Sudan	1953	5.3	1.8	7.1	23.9	18.2	7.7	50.6	42.2
	1956	4.3	0.9	5.2	20.6	18.4	15.7	54.7	40.1
	1958	2.5	0.5	3.0	29.4	12.7	13.9	56.0	41.0
	1960 E	2.3	0.8	3.1	25.4	10.1	20.3	56.5	40.3

Table 11 (continued)

Countries	Year	Direct Taxes			Indirect Taxes				Nontax Revenue
		Income Taxes (1)	Other (2)	Total (3)=(1)+(2)	Import Duties (4)	Export Duties (5)	Other (6)	Total (7)=(4)+(5)+(6)	(9)
Tanganyika	1950	18.0	10.9	28.9	28.0	6.8	12.9	47.6	23.4
	1953	30.2	14.1	44.3	23.0	1.0	13.1	37.1	18.6
	1956	25.4	9.7	35.1	30.7	0.2	14.3	45.2	19.4
	1958	23.0	9.2	32.2	28.2	0.2	17.4	45.8	22.1
Togo	1950	...	...	12.8	...	...	...	59.6	26.6
	1953	...	...	15.7	...	...	...	69.3	14.3
	1956	7.2	1.7	8.9	35.2	7.2	40.5	82.9	8.2
	1958	5.4	1.4	6.8	36.0	7.6	38.6	82.2	11.0
Tunisia	1950	12.6	3.5	16.1	6.7	1.7	64.0	72.4	11.5
	1953	14.5	6.2	20.7	7.5	1.6	54.9	64.0	15.3
	1957	14.5	3.6	18.1	7.6	1.5	65.6	74.7	7.2
	1959 E	17.0	5.7	22.7	7.2	1.7	61.5	70.4	6.9
Uganda	1950	7.6	5.7	13.3	22.4	45.0	9.3	76.7	10.0
	1953	14.5	5.1	19.6	24.2	32.7	10.8	67.7	12.9
	1956	18.1	3.1	21.2	22.7	29.7	12.5	64.9	13.8
	1958	15.6	3.2	18.8	21.4	27.7	16.7	65.8	15.4
Union of South Africa	1950	48.4	6.2	54.6	11.7	0.5	15.7	28.0	17.4
	1953	51.0	4.7	55.7	11.1	0.8	15.1	26.6	17.7
	1956	47.9	4.5	52.4	13.5	0.3	15.8	29.6	18.0
UAR (Egypt)	1950	10.4	6.0	16.4	18.8	4.3	24.2	49.8	33.8
	1953	13.5	9.0	22.5	...	...	26.9	48.0	29.5
	1956	9.6	7.4	17.0	...	...	24.6	41.7	41.4
	1958 E	12.9	6.5	19.4	...	...	...	37.4	43.2

E = Estimate.
a This total includes Federal transaction tax 15.2 million Eth. $ for 1956 corresponding to a percentage of the total revenue of 12.5. This total includes Federal transaction tax 21.6 million Eth. $ for 1958 corresponding to a percentage of the total revenue of 15.9.
b Figures relate to southern zone only, except in 1958.

Table 12—Structure of Government Expenditure—Current Expenditure
(percentage of total current expenditure)

Country	Year	General Services Total	Of Which Defence	Education	Health	Other Current Expenses
Algeria	1950	48.9	—	13.4	6.8	30.9
	1953	38.2	—	18.0	9.7	34.1
	1956	36.2	—	16.2	9.4	38.2
	1958	43.4	—	14.5	9.4	32.7
Congo (Leopoldville)	1950	28.4	—	—	18.1	53.5
	1953	28.5	—	—	22.5	49.0
	1956	24.5	—	—	25.7	49.8
	1958 E	21.8	—	—	28.5	49.7
Ethiopia	1950	71.2	29.6	13.1	4.0	11.7
	1953	65.0	27.4	11.6	3.9	19.5
	1956	61.4	24.7	11.5	3.8	23.3
	1958	61.4	26.6	11.8	3.4	23.4
Former French Equatorial Africa [b]	1950	23.9	—	7.3	10.9	57.9
	1952	26.0	—	8.7	11.8	53.5
	1955	30.2	—	12.1	14.3	43.4
Former French West Africa [b]	1950	23.9	—	6.3	9.9	59.9
	1952	24.6	—	7.2	9.2	59.0
	1955 E	25.0	—	—	20.8	54.2
	1958 E	21.6	—	15.8	12.6	50.0
Ghana	1950	22.6	4.5	11.1	8.3	58.0
	1953	21.6	2.4	16.9	7.7	53.8
	1956 [a]	22.8	4.1	17.1	7.4	52.7
	1958 R	31.5	8.9	14.5	6.5	47.5
Kenya	1950	26.5	4.5	9.3	7.6	56.6
	1953	38.5	3.5	11.5	7.2	42.8
	1956	55.5	3.2	9.7	4.7	30.1
	1958	39.1	4.0	14.2	5.8	40.9
Madagascar [b]	1950	30.4	—	10.2	11.5	47.9
	1952	32.4	—	10.6	13.4	43.6
	1955	29.2	—	11.3	13.0	46.5
Morocco	1950	31.4	—	27.2	7.7	33.7
	1953	31.9	—	19.7	8.7	39.7
	1956	46.5	10.2	18.9	9.6	25.0
	1958 E	39.7	14.4	16.0	6.9	37.4
Nigeria	1950	18.8	3.0	8.9	6.3	66.0
	1953	21.8	3.9	10.3	6.9	61.0
	1956	18.1	2.9	13.9	7.1	60.9
	1958	20.0	4.1	21.6	6.4	52.0
Sierra Leone	1950	16.4	4.0	9.4	11.4	62.8
	1953	13.5	2.2	10.8	10.8	64.9
	1956	15.4	2.1	16.6	9.4	58.6
	1957	14.4	1.6	15.7	9.2	60.7
Somalia	1955	59.0	27.3	9.8	9.3	21.9
(former trusteeship territory)	1957	55.5	5.8	10.4	9.6	24.5
	1959	49.5	3.7	10.3	10.9	29.3
Sudan	1953	28.2	6.8	7.1	9.1	55.6
	1956	23.9	8.5	9.4	9.2	57.5
	1958	26.4	12.0	11.3	9.0	53.3
Tanganyika	1950	24.5	—	9.2	8.8	57.5
	1953	20.3	—	13.9	8.2	57.6
	1956	20.7	—	14.9	9.3	55.1
	1958	22.7	—	16.7	9.2	51.4
Togo [b]	1950	—	—	13.0	18.7	68.3
	1953	—	—	17.2	15.9	66.9
	1956	—	—	13.6	15.4	71.0
	1958 E	25.8	—	17.3	15.1	41.8

Table 12 *(continued)*

Country	Year	General Services Total	Of Which Defence	Education	Health	Other Current Expenses
Tunisia	1950	28.9	—	19.8	8.2	43.1
	1953	27.9	—	20.4	8.4	43.3
	1957	28.4	2.9	20.0	9.9	41.7
	1959 E	32.5	10.7	18.2	10.9	38.4
UAR (Egypt)	1950	34.7	22.6	12.1	5.5	47.7
	1953	27.4	17.4	11.3	3.1	58.2
	1956	41.5	31.0	11.5	2.9	44.1
	1958 E	35.3	25.5	13.7	3.4	47.6
Uganda	1950	27.4	4.3	11.2	11.6	49.8
	1953	23.3	4.2	15.1	9.8	51.8
	1956	23.9	4.6	20.5	8.7	46.9
	1958	25.0	3.7	21.8	10.4	42.8
Union of South Africa	1950	28.6	8.0	7.0	4.4	60.0
	1953	30.4	11.4	6.4	3.9	59.3
	1956	33.2	9.0	6.4	3.9	56.5
	1958 E	31.1	10.1	7.0	4.7	57.2

E = Estimate.
[a] 15 months.

[b] Includes only the expenditure of local budgets. Excludes expenditure financed by the French Treasury.

Percentages of total expenditure on education were in general higher in 1958 compared with 1950. Expenditures on health, in per cent of total, seem to have remained mostly either static or declined in some cases. There were very few increases.

It is possible to see among countries more differences with respect to expenditure on education in respect of expenditure on health. Important among countries which spent more on education are Morocco, Nigeria, Togo, Tunisia and Uganda. Expenditure on health was particularly high in Togo, Madagascar and former French Equatorial Africa.

"Other current expenditures" comprise of several items and, though it is observed that, in general, the share of these expenditures in the total had declined by 1958, yet it would not be proper to comment on this group of expenditures without the knowledge of the behaviour of different items that make up the group.

Levels of Revenue and Expenditure

TRADITIONAL BUDGETARY DATA

It is possible to think of two measures of levels of total government revenue and expenditure. Firstly, aggregates of revenue and expenditure can be related to population and expressed per head of population. Secondly, these aggregates can be related to gross national product and expressed in per cent of gross national product. In this article both the measures of level are used and the resulting data are presented in Tables 13 and 14. Per capita figures in Table 13 are based on traditional budgetary data while percentages in Table 14 are based on national accounting data for selected countries. Figures in Table 13 are expressed in national currencies and not converted into U.S. dollars. For purposes of comparison, countries have been grouped into common currency areas except for UAR (Egypt), which is shown separately. This has obviously restricted the choice of countries, but it is believed that the broad conclusions reached here will not be affected by the inclusion of other countries.

Levels of revenue and expenditure are at best rough indicators of the importance of public transactions in different countries. Measures of levels do not reflect certain factors like unit cost of services rendered, income distribution and institutional factors. For example, it is possible that two countries may have the same level of expenditure expressed per capita and yet the actual amount of services rendered may vary because of different unit cost of services. The cost aspect is particularly important in those African countries where Africanization of services has proceeded slowly and where the number of highly paid expatriates is significant in public services. The measure of level, therefore, does not necessarily indicate the degree of welfare.

One of the reasons for high cost of services in these countries is the presence of a large number of expatriates in public services and high wages paid to them. For example, in Congo (Leopoldville) it is estimated for 1957 that the average salary of a European in the economy was 30 times the average salary of an African.[20] In the Federation of Rhodesia and Nyasaland in 1956, 39,000 Africans in government administration accounted for a total wage bill of £3.41 million, while 9,780 Europeans accounted for a wage bill of £9.24 million. The average salary for a European in the economy as a whole was £1,084 as against £68 for an African. To give examples of former French territories, in former French Soudan in 1958–1959, 15.9 per cent Europeans in civil services claimed 33.5 per cent of wage bill as against 66.5 per cent of wage bill shared by 84.1 per cent Africans.[21] In Togo, a senior expatriate civil servant receives 76 times the national per capita income.[22] High levels of expenditure in these countries, therefore, do not necessarily mean provision of more services.

Within the currency areas, the countries in Table 13 are arranged in descending order of per capita national incomes. In view of the unreliability of national income data for some countries, this order should be considered as very rough and tentative.

It may be seen from Table 13 that there are considerable variations in the levels of expenditure and revenue among countries in the sterling area. Union of South Africa, a country more economically developed than others, has highest levels of expenditure and revenue. At the other extreme are Nigeria and Tanganyika. The countries (excluding Union of South Africa) can be broadly divided into three groups. Ghana and Federation of Rhodesia and Nyasaland belong to the first group where levels of expenditure and revenue are quite high. The

figures for Ghana in Table 9 are, however, overstated because the results of the recent census in Ghana show that population figures for earlier years were too much on the lower side. Kenya occupies a middle position. Nigeria, Tanganyika and Uganda constitute countries with relatively lower levels of expenditure and revenue.

The levels of expenditure and revenue in UAR (Egypt) are quite high. The rise in the level of total expenditure in UAR (Egypt) is, however, accounted primarily by the increase in the level of current expenditure.

In the North African countries of the franc zone, levels of expenditure and revenue were marked with fluctuations over the period. The level of current expenditures was perhaps highest in Algeria. Increased levels of current expenditures in 1958 compared with those of previous years reflect partly the increased expenditure on certain functions like defence in Morocco and Tunisia after independence, and in Algeria it presumably reflects the unstable political situation and the presence of large numbers of Frenchmen in the civil services. The level of development expenditure which was initially higher in Tunisia declined in 1954 and further in 1958. As far as levels of development expenditures were concerned, Morocco does not seem to have made great strides in 1958 compared with 1950. Algeria had again highest level of revenue, while Morocco seems to have improved its revenue situation considerably by 1958.

In other countries of the franc zone, levels of total expenditure were highest in the former French Equatorial Africa—Cameroon—though the level of current expenditure in Madagascar outstripped the corresponding level in other countries by 1958. The level of development expenditure was very high in the former French Equatorial Africa—Cameroon—and was nearly twice the corresponding levels in other countries. The level of revenue was, however, highest in Madagascar. By 1958, both in Madagascar and in the former French West Africa—Togo, the revenue levels had doubled.

Some broad conclusions may be drawn

Table 13—Per Capita Revenue and Expenditure
(in national currencies)

Sterling Area Countries	Current Expenditure	Development Expenditure	Total Expenditure	Current Revenue
Union of South Africa (£)				
1950	11.3	6.6	17.9	12.5
1954	16.0	6.9	22.9	18.1
1958	18.1	8.5	26.6	21.8
Ghana (£)				
1950	2.2	1.1	3.3	3.9
1954	4.9	4.7	9.6	9.7
1958	8.0	4.2	12.2	11.4
Federation of Rhodesia and Nyasaland (£)				
1954	5.7	3.4	9.1	7.3
1958	8.3	5.7	14.0	10.6
Kenya (£)				
1950	2.2	0.7	2.9	2.4
1955	6.4	1.2	7.6	4.7
1958	5.8	1.2	7.0	5.4
Nigeria (£)				
1950	1.0	0.2	1.2	1.2
1953	1.0	0.5	1.5	1.7
1958	2.0	0.9	2.9	2.4
Uganda (£)				
1950	1.0	0.5	1.5	1.8
1955	2.3	0.9	3.2	2.9
1958	2.9	1.0	3.9	3.1
Tanganyika (£)				
1950	1.0	0.4	1.4	1.2
1955	1.9	0.4	2.3	2.1
1958	2.1	0.6	2.7	2.1
UAR (Egypt) (£)				
1950	6.6	0.3	6.9	6.6
1954	7.6	1.0	8.6	7.7
1958	9.7	1.0	10.7	9.7

Franc Zone Countries	Current Expenditure	Development Expenditure	Total Expenditure	Current Revenue
(a) North African franc zone countries				
Algeria (francs)				
1951	5,106	4,884	9,990	6,027
1954	8,418	4,892	13,310	8,937
1958	15,325	6,188	21,513	15,324
Morocco (francs)				
1950	3,669	3,066	6,735	3,915
1954	6,085	3,425	9,510	7,146
1958	12,847	3,117	15,964	12,468
Tunisia (francs)				
1950	4,792	6,841	11,633	5,153
1954	9,478	6,709	16,187	8,981
1958	11,423	5,685	17,108	12,072
(b) Other franc zone countries (in Metropolitan francs)				
Former French West Africa—Togo				
1950	548	308	856	695
1953	…	…	…	…
1958	1,580	486	2,066	1,501
Former French Equatorial Africa—Cameroon				
1950	1,026	641	1,667	861
1953	…	…	…	…
1958	2,000	1,374	3,875	1,511
Madagascar				
1950	790	325	1,115	929
1953	1,343	738	2,081	1,629
1958	2,122	685	2,807	1,900

Source: *Demographic Yearbook, 1958 and 1959.* The recent census in Ghana indicates that the figures used here are too low.

Note: The table is based on budgetary data. Population figures are taken from UN.

from the differences in per capita expenditure and revenue among countries shown in Table 13. It may be said that these differences in levels reflect those in levels of development and in economic and social structure of the countries. In ancient days, the role of a government was mostly confined to the maintenance of law and order and to protect the sovereignty of the state. During the process of economic development, governments are seen to undertake increasing responsibilities. Examples of such increased governmental activity are increasing expenditure on social services like education and health, provision of social security, creation of infrastructure facilities and direct and indirect investment in productive fields like agriculture, industry, etc. With the increasing role of government in economic life, which is perhaps a concomitant of economic development in low-income countries, per capita government expenditure is likely to increase

over time. It is, therefore, perhaps correct to say that as a country develops, its government is likely to spend more on a per capita basis.

NATIONAL ACCOUNTING DATA

It is possible to develop the points made above by using national accounting data for a few countries. These data are presented in Table 14 where the share of various aggregate is expressed in terms of gross national product.

The cost aspect of government services may be brought into focus by relating aggregates of expenditure and revenue to gross national product. For example, Congo, though less developed than the Union of

Table 14—Government Expenditure on Goods and Services in Per Cent of Gross National Product at Market Prices[a]

		Government Expenditure			Government Income	
		Consumption (%)	Fixed Capital Formation (%)	Total (%5)	Current Revenue (%)	Disposable Income (%)
Congo (Leopoldville)	1950	9.53	3.71	13.23	14.93	14.45
	1954	11.99	7.50	19.50	19.05	18.11
	1958	18.19	8.69	26.89	18.45	16.88
Federation of Rhodesia	1954	8.4	7.75	16.16	15.92	13.36
and Nyasaland	1958	10.63	8.33	18.96	18.96	15.86
Ghana	1954	7.88	5.38	13.27	19.52	18.68
	1958	11.23	3.97	15.20	16.56	15.95
Tanganyika	1954	8.11	6.89	15.00	11.65	9.28
	1958[b]	10.08	5.43	15.51	11.79	9.32
Union of South Africa	1950	10.90	6.17	17.07	17.84	13.95
	1954	11.10	6.63	17.73	18.45	14.70
	1958	11.62	9.15	20.77	17.56	14.35
Morocco	1951	6.20	4.78	10.98	14.02	11.95
	1954	7.75	4.68	12.43	14.46	12.02
	1958	11.75	4.44	16.19	...	...
Nigeria	1950	2.97	1.61	4.58	5.27	4.76
	1952	3.46	1.94	5.40	7.32	6.72
	1956	5.30	3.00	8.30	10.28	8.25
Sudan	1955/56	7.42	2.49[c]	9.91	12.11	11.29
French West Africa	1956	12.13	4.29[d]	16.40	23.06	15.72
French Equatorial Africa	1956	9.86	4.64[d]	14.50	18.44	14.50

Source: Sudan: *The National Income of Sudan, 1955/56*, Khartoum, March 1959. Former FWA: *Outre-Mer, 1958*, and *Compte Economiques de l'AOF, 1956*. Former FEA: *Outre-Mer, 1958*, and *Compte Economiques des Administratives de l'Afrique Equatoriale, 1956*, Brazzaville, 1959.

Note: For source and other notes see notes to Table 8.

[a] Gross domestic product for Tanganyika.
[b] Provisional.
[c] Including public corporations.
[d] Excluding government enterprises and public corporations.

South Africa, absorbs higher percentage of gross national product for government consumption than the Union of South Africa. This is associated with the fact that the salaries of civil servants in the Congo (Leopoldville) are higher in relation to per capita national income than in the Union of South Africa. In general, high levels of government consumption expenditures may be explained partly by the relatively high unit cost of services rendered.

Except for Congo (Leopoldville), Nigeria and Sudan, the differences in the levels of consumption expenditure among other countries were practically small in or around 1958. The differences in the levels of total expenditure are largely explained by the different levels of fixed capital formation. The levels of total expenditure had increased by 1958 and, except presumably in Sudan and Nigeria, were at least 15 per cent of gross national product in or around 1958.

Percentages of revenue to gross national product depend partly on levels of income in these countries and partly on distribution of income and on institutional factors. In the Congo (Leopoldville), for example, the distribution of personal income was such that even relatively modest rates of taxation would result in comparatively high level or government revenue from direct taxes in relation to total personal income. Moreover, the country benefited to a large extent from export duties and company taxes. In Ghana, high percentages of revenue to gross national product not only indicate high per capita income, but also reflect the existence of Cocoa Marketing Board. The comfortable budgetary position in Nigeria also reflects upon the existence of marketing boards in that country.

The levels of revenue were quite high in all countries except in Nigeria. In the case of Tanganyika, the Union of South Africa and presumably in Morocco, the revenue levels were practically static over the period. The level was presumably static in Ghana also. 1954 was not a normal year for Ghana because the high revenue was due to the extremely high price fetched by cocoa in that year. The corresponding level of revenue for 1955 was 16.94, which indicates that the level has practically remained unchanged.

General Conclusions and Comments

The data presented in the preceding sections do not provide a satisfactory basis for an adequate analysis of problems and trends in public finance in African countries. Such an analysis would also have required a much more thorough examination of government transactions within the framework of the total economy of each individual country. Nevertheless, it might be useful to restate and to comment on some of the broad conclusions reached with particular reference to the countries of tropical Africa.[23]

The most conspicuous development in public finance during the period considered was the rapid rise in government expenditure in practically all the countries covered. Indeed, making use of various data available, it may be stated that government expenditure probably rose faster both at current and at "constant" prices, than any other major economic aggregate. This is in itself not so surprising in the case of developing countries. However, the trends observed during the past years pose several problems of concern to African governments.

The demands upon governments are very large in most African countries. No one can ignore the acute need for increasing outlays on economic and social infrastructure. Moreover, many African countries have no choice but to perform the functions of an entrepreneur in directing domestic savings into productive investments and even in assuming responsibilities of management.[24] However, in planning the nature and the rate of expansion of government activities, it is necessary to take into account the financial aspect of government spending and, above all, the effects of government transactions on the development of the economy in the short as well as in the long run.

It is frequently argued that government revenue should exceed government expenditure so as to leave a surplus for the financing of capital government expenditure. In 1958, most of the tropical African countries included in this article had no surplus on current account. Accepting for the moment the fiscal doctrine just referred to, the situation can be said to have deteriorated significantly since 1950. It may be assumed that this deterioration has continued in recent years, particularly since independence is usually accompanied by a substantial increase in certain types of current expenditure. There is also reason to believe that, in several countries, there has been a continued tendency for development expenditure to decline in relation to total expenditure. The question of finance is therefore of great importance in most countries of tropical Africa.

The failure of revenue to keep pace with both current and total expenditure reflects such factors as an inadequate tax effort on the part of governments, unfavourable export developments and a comparatively modest rise in national income. These factors are interrelated to some extent. An assessment of their influence on the course of events is also rendered difficult by the inadequacy of the data. However, rough indications of certain developments are given in the following paragraphs.

As regards the tax effort, it may be noted that a large part of the income and expenditure of these countries passed through harbours and that import and export taxes have accounted for a comparatively large share in total government revenue. Available data seem to indicate that during the period considered, most countries experienced a relatively larger increase in government revenue than in foreign trade. Taxation of foreign trade transactions might therefore have increased, although not necessarily in accordance with the requirements of economic development. Moreover, governments may not have given sufficient consideration to the possibility of developing or strengthening other forms of taxation.

At current prices, exports rose significantly during the first part of the period 1950–1958, but declined or leveled off in many tropical African countries in the subsequent years. The latter development contributed to the widening gap between government expenditure and revenue, through its effects on proceeds from export taxes as well as on private income and expenditure.

Reliable data on national income are not

available for a great majority of countries, but it is likely that the rate of increase of this aggregate was, as a rule, significantly smaller than that of government expenditure. The gap between government expenditure and revenue may therefore have widened even in the face of an increase in the latter in relation to national income.

It has been argued that in certain cases the comparatively small rise in national income reflected errors in government policies on expenditure. According to this argument, governments invested too heavily in infrastructure, especially at the beginning of the period considered in the present article, and did not take sufficiently into account the recurrent implications of this expenditure. As a result, the growth of current expenditure outstripped that of revenue. Regardless of the merits of this argument, it may be noted that the effect of infrastructure investment depends to a considerable extent on other factors, including measures adopted by governments to stimulate private investors to take advantage of the improvements in infrastructure.

In reviewing the experience of the past years, it seems appropriate to note that the usual distinction between current and development expenditure is not always a reliable guide for appraising the effects of the scale and nature of government spending and the magnitude of government revenue. Certain items of "current" expenditure, e.g., in the field of education, may be considered as investments, while certain types of "development" expenditure, for example on administrative buildings, may not make any significant contribution to economic growth. What is required is comprehensive development planning covering the economy as a whole and taking into account the relationship between the various economic and social sectors. The elaboration of such a plan would permit governments to take decisions on expenditure and revenue by reference to the short- and long-term requirements of economic development. It is a priori not excluded that economic growth may be promoted by accepting for several years a higher rate of increase of government expenditure on "current" as well as on "development" account than of government revenue, thus resulting in a growing gap to be financed by loans, grants and/or drawing upon reserves. The economic feasibility of such a course of action would in general depend on the extent to which two types of risks could be avoided or minimized.

The first risk is related to the internal balance. In many countries the absence of a domestic money market has constituted a serious obstacle to economic development. Governments should therefore make a determined effort to mobilize resources through borrowing at home. Such borrowing should, however, not be pursued so far as to create serious inflationary pressures which may upset the development effort itself. The second risk is related to the external balance. Borrowing abroad is always tempting in that it provides foreign exchange. At the same time, however, it involves commitments concerning the use of foreign exchange in future years. Governments must therefore give serious consideration to the ability of their economies to service the debts to be contracted abroad.

This being said, the need for increasing government revenue should be emphasized. The demands upon African governments are enormous and, other things being equal, an increase in government revenue would allow at least some increase in government expenditure. Governments would therefore be well advised to reconsider their tax systems with a view to increasing their efficiency in terms of both development policies and proceeds to the treasury. In particular, African countries need to pay more attention to the commodity structure of their imports.[25] Revisions of existing customs tariffs may produce both a more appropriate import structure and an increase in government revenue. Moreover, the continuing increase in money income should encourage the search for new forms of taxation.

There is also a need for a serious consideration of the cost of government services in African countries. This cost is still influenced to a considerable extent by the employment of expatriate officials whose salaries reflect the fact of expatriation and, sometimes, also "monopolistic" practices. Government expenditure in real terms may be increased and economic development promoted by making a clear distinction between expatriate and other officials in determining the salaries of civil servants. This would also increase the benefits to be gained from expanding secondary and higher education. Indeed, investment in education may be said to be particularly rewarding when accompanied by appropriate salaries for civil servants. In this case, Africanization would result not only in a reduction of the foreign exchange component of the government wage bill, but also in a decrease of the total cost of various government services.

General Notes

Signs: E: Estimates.
     P: Provisional.
     R: Revised.
Unless mentioned otherwise, the figures are actuals.
     ...Not available.
     — Nil or negligible.
Current Expenditure: Wherever possible transfers to Reserve Funds and Development Plans are excluded. PTT, where possible, is shown on a net basis. Debt redemption is excluded where such data were available otherwise are shown under "other current expenditure." Figures relate to Central Governments only except in Nigeria and the Federation of Rhodesia and Nyasaland where regional governments are included.
Development Expenditure: Usually as shown under development plans or capital or non-recurrent account by countries.
Revenue: In general exclude loans and grants and withdrawal from reserves. Profits of fiscal monopolies are treated as indirect taxes.
Fiscal Years: Year references in tables signify data for calendar years or years in which fiscal years end.

Notes

1. These data are given for fiscal years. The years presented in the table indicate the year in which the fiscal year ends.
2. These data are taken from an article on "l'Evolution des Depenses Publiques de 1950 à

1958 dans quelques pays Africains sous Administration Française," *Note d'Information* of June, 1961, of the *Banque Centrale des Etats de l'Afrique de l'Ouest.*

3. Agencies established to provide goods and services to other government departments.

4. Export earnings are also a function of quantity; particularly during 1956–1958 when export prices were generally declining, some countries maintained their export earnings by exporting increasing quantities.

5. Barba Niculescu and George Allen, *Colonial Planning* (London: Unwin, Ltd., 1958), p. 63.

6. *Ibid.*, p. 63.

7. *Ibid.*, p. 75.

8. In the French-speaking countries as a whole, development expenditure, both in absolute terms and in per cent of total expenditure, was highest in 1952. Thereafter current expenditure increased continuously faster than development expenditure, whose share in the total decreased from 40 per cent in 1952 to 28 per cent in 1958.

9. As defined in the *UN Manual for Economic and Functional Classifications of Government Transactions* (New York, 1958).

10. *Budget Speech, 1956/57,* Ministry of Finance and Economics, Khartoum, June 7, 1956, p. 5.

11. *Ibid.*, p. 9.

12. For example, see Uganda: The Capital Development Plan (First Revision), 1955–1960, and subsequent Three-year Expenditure Forecasts; Kenya: 1954–1957 Development Plan and 1957–1960 Development Plan; Ghana: See *Economic Surveys*, particularly after 1955.

13. For a description of development plans, see *Economic Bulletin for Africa*, Vol. 1, No. 1, Chap. B/II.

14. See Fernand Bezy, *Problèmes structures de l'économie Congolaise, Institut de recherches économiques et sociales.*

15. Throughout this paragraph book values of sterling balances for only public authorities, i.e., central government and local authorities, are quoted from *Quarterly Digest of Statistics*, Ghana, Vol. IX, No. 4, December, 1960.

16. See *Economic Bulletin for Africa* (Addis Ababa), Vol. I, No. 1, Chap. B/I, January, 1961, p. 66.

17. Includes federal government, regional governments, local bodies and statutory bodies.

18. *Economic Survey of Nigeria, 1959*, p. 89.

19. The total figure is derived from *Geographical Income of Uganda, 1950–1956 and 1957* (Entebbe: The Government Printer).

20. Information derived from an internal ECA study.

21 and 22. Jo W. Saxe, *The British and French Legacy to their West African Territories*, Centre for International Affairs, Harvard University, Cambridge, Mass., April, 1960 (mimeographed).

23. Africa excluding the North African countries and the Union of South Africa.

24. *Economic Survey of Africa since 1950*, p. 3.

25. See the *Economic Bulletin for Africa*, Vol. 1, No. 1, p. 20.

19

The Taxation of Low Incomes in African Countries

Edward A. Arowolo

From *International Monetary Fund* Staff Papers, *Vol XV (July 1968), pp. 322–343. Reprinted with permission.*

THE TAXATION of low incomes is peculiar to less developed countries where a high proportion (70–90 per cent) of the population is dependent on agriculture and where per capita incomes are low compared with those of the advanced countries. Using the rough index of low per capita incomes, most countries in Africa, Asia, and South America with an annual per capita income of, say, less than US $300 would be classified as less developed. The need for taxing people with low incomes in these countries arises partly because of the existence of fairly large subsistence sectors where production is for household consumption rather than for the market, hence the lack of a broad base for taxation, and partly because of the pressure to raise revenues in order to provide basic services and to undertake development projects. Because of the low per capita incomes of a large part of the potential tax-paying public, and because of the economic structure and social factors, the use of the normal income tax is severely limited.

Broadly, there are two types of problems connected with the taxation of low incomes. The first is the determination of the rate structure suitable to the income level and economic structure, taking into account the effects of tax rates both on the supply curve of effort and on the goal of achieving equity in taxation. The second is the ability of the authorities to achieve effective tax administration, under the economic and social environment of less developed countries. Given the tax rate structure, the maximization of the yield from any tax depends on effective administration.

This analysis covers only the direct taxes on low incomes, which in the context of African countries are referred to as personal taxes in contrast to the familiar individual income tax. No exhaustive treatment of income tax is undertaken, but references are made to the relationship between it and the personal taxes in the countries examined. The discussion also excludes indirect taxes and export taxes, which may be imposed upon the low income groups but which are not assessed on the basis of either individual resources or individual income. In order to appreciate some of the conditions of these economies, the economic structures of selected African countries as they affect their ability to raise revenues are examined. The influence of economic structure on the pattern of revenues is clearly shown in the relatively smaller proportion of direct taxes (taxes on individual and corporate incomes and all varieties of taxes on low incomes) in revenues. In the remaining part of the paper, the experience of a few African countries in imposing direct taxes on low incomes is examined.

Low Incomes and Economic Structure

The economies of many African countries are characterized by a heavy dependence on agriculture and a sizable proportion of agricultural output in the subsistence sector. For example, in 1965 the ratios of subsistence output to gross domestic product (GDP) at current prices in Uganda, Tanzania, and Kenya were 33 per cent, 28 per cent, and 23 per cent, respectively. (See Table 1.) In Sierra Leone the ratio was 40 per cent, while in Malawi it was 37.3 per cent. The high proportion of subsistence output in GDP further limits the productiveness of the normal income tax or any form of direct taxes and of indirect taxes as well. A large

Table 1—Selected African Countries: Indicators of Economic and Revenue Structures, 1965

(Amounts in millions of US dollars)

Country	Population (millions)	Population Dependent on Agriculture (per cent)	GDP at Current Prices	Output of Subsistence Sector	Share of Subsistence Output in GDP (per cent)	Per Capita GDP	Current Revenues	Direct Taxes	Personal Taxes	Ratio of Current Revenues to GDP (per cent)	Ratio of Direct Taxes to Current Revenues (per cent)
Kenya	9.4	75	805.3	182.8	22.7	85.7	147.0	43.4	—[a]	18.2	29.5
Liberia[b]	1.1[c]	90	217.3	19.2	8.8	197.5	40.5	15.5	1.5	18.6	38.3
Malawi	3.9[d]	75	174.7	65.2	37.3	44.8	25.7	8.5	2.8	14.7	33.0
Sierra Leone	2.2	75	325.5	130.2	40.0	148.0	46.9	9.4	—[a]	14.4	20.0
Tanzania[e]	9.9	80	669.8	189.8	28.3	67.7	99.4	25.5	9.5[f]	14.8	25.6
Togo[g]	1.7[c]	80	132.9	47.8	35.9	78.2	14.2	1.2	—[a]	10.7	8.5
Uganda	7.5	90	627.5	205.2	32.7	83.7	106.7[h]	12.3	—[a]	17.0	11.5

Sources: The East African Common Services Organization, *Economic and Statistical Review*, various issues, 1966; Kenyan Ministry of Economic Planning and Development, *Economic Survey, 1966* and *Statistical Abstract, 1966*; Tanzania, *Background to the Budget: An Economic Survey, 1966–67*; Ugandan Ministry of Finance, *Background to the Budget, 1965–66*; Malawi, *Budget 1966: Background Information* (Treasury Document No. 5); U Tun Wai and others, "The Economy of Togo," *Staff Papers*, Vol. XII (1965), pp. 409–69; International Monetary Fund, *International Financial Statistics*.

[a] Accrues to local governments.
[b] Data are for 1964.
[c] Estimate.
[d] Population in 1966 was estimated at 4.03 million.
[e] Excluding Zanzibar.
[f] Includes a development levy of US $5.6 million.
[g] Data relate to 1962.
[h] Excludes overseas reimbursements but includes appropriations-in-aid receipts.

segment of the population is dependent on agriculture; the ratio varies from a low of 75 per cent in Kenya, Malawi, and Sierra Leone, to a high of 90 per cent in Liberia and Uganda. (See Table 1, column 2.)

Per capita incomes, as could be measured roughly by the per capita GDP, are also low. Thus, in Malawi the per capita income in 1965 was only US $45, while in the three East African countries, per capita incomes averaged US $80. The higher per capita incomes in Sierra Leone (US $148) and Liberia (US $198) are explained by the importance of foreign economic enclaves—mining—in these economies.

The ratio of current revenues to GDP varies among countries, indicating different abilities to raise revenues, given the various economic and social factors. Of significance in this context is the low share of direct taxes in current revenues. In Kenya, the ratio of direct taxes to total current revenues in 1965 was 29.5 per cent, while in Liberia, Malawi, and Togo the ratios were 38.3 per cent, 33 per cent, and 8.5 per cent, respectively. This pattern of revenues is identifiable in many African countries, indicating heavier reliance on indirect taxes because of the limitations imposed by low incomes and associated factors on the collection of direct taxes.[1]

From the standpoint of direct taxation of income, low incomes within a country are relative to the structure of income distribution, the level of income tax rates, and the exemption limit for income tax purposes. In many countries it is possible for people with low incomes to pay taxes indirectly through customs and excise duties, sales taxes, consumption taxes, export taxes, etc. How productive such indirect taxes are depends on the size of the segment of the economy involved in cash transactions. However, the imposition of a normal direct tax on low incomes poses a problem; the level of personal exemptions may be so high as to eliminate most of the population from tax liability, as occurs in many developing countries (see Table 2), and it may be difficult to ascertain individual incomes for a large part of the potential tax-paying public under existing social and economic organization.

In the advanced countries, the question of the direct taxation of low incomes may not arise for obvious reasons: for example, the ratio of per capita income to the amount of exemptions is higher and, because there is a large number of individuals in the middle-income and high-income levels who are potential and actual income-tax payers, there is a great scope for productively imposing and income tax. Also, because of the relatively higher level of development, there are more companies and corporations capable of paying direct taxes on profits. In fact, in most developed countries there is no urgency to tax low incomes; on the contrary, social security payments (negative

Table 2—Selected African Countries: Relation of Per Capita Income Tax Relief to Per Capita Income, 1965

(Amounts in US dollars)

Country	Per Capita Income[a] (1)	Personal Exemption for a Single Taxpayer (2)	Tax Relief as a Multiple of Per Capita Income (3)
Burundi	53.0	182.8[b]	3.4
Kenya	85.7	604.8	7.1
Liberia	197.5	1,500.0	7.6
Sierra Leone	148.0	560.0	3.8
Tanzania[c]	67.7	604.8	8.9
Uganda	83.7	604.8	7.2

Sources: Table 1 and data supplied by the authorites of various countries.

[a] Per capita GDP.
[b] 1966.
[c] Excluding Zanzibar.

tax on low incomes) in different forms are made in many developed countries.

The question of taxing low incomes in many less developed countries is, however, an acute one. The income tax exemption limits are fairly high, so that, prima facie, most people in the middle-income groups may not be liable to pay income tax.[2] The extent to which this situation exists is indicated by relating per capita incomes to an unmarried person's exemption allowance. (See Table 2.)

In Kenya, the individual tax relief was 7.1 times the per capita income in 1965, while in Tanzania it was 8.9 times. The multiple is even higher for a married person; in Kenya it was nearly 20 times the per capita income. On the other hand, in Burundi and Sierra Leone, individual tax relief was, respectively, only 3.4 and 3.8 times the per capita income. In many African countries the effective exemption limit is substantially higher than these ratios indicate because the incomes of wives in most cases are negligible. The effect of the combination of generally low incomes and high personal relief is to exclude a high proportion of the working population from the payment of income tax. The problem is that in existing circumstances, a much lower limit for exemptions would make costs of collection unduly high, while the existing high limit makes income tax contribution to revenues relatively small.

In view of these problems, many countries in Africa have found it necessary, at either the central or the local government level, to design various ways of directly taxing low incomes. These types of direct taxes will be referred to simply as African Personal Taxes; the latest developments of these taxes, their rates, yield, assessment, and collection procedures in Tanzania, Nigeria, and Chad will be examined.

African Personal Taxes

NATURE OF AFRICAN PERSONAL TAX

The African Personal Tax (APT) is a common feature of the taxation systems in many African countries. It takes various forms, such as personal tax, poll tax, mini-

mum fiscal, cattle tax, income-rate tax, and, in its latest development, the graduated personal tax.[3] These taxes had their origin in the attempt to impose direct taxes on the incomes of Africans in conformity with their level of economic and social development so as to ensure a contribution to the revenue of the territory in which they were levied. In addition, the personal taxes were originally imposed, particularly in South and East Africa, with a view to stimulating the supply of unskilled labor for plantations and industrial undertakings. In general, however, the impact of the levy has been to help the reallocation of resources from the subsistence sector to the money sector, either through production for the market or through wage employment for unskilled labor. It should be added, too, that until the early 1960's direct taxation in most countries had a unique feature of distinguishing between Africans, who paid personal taxes, and non-Africans, who invariably paid income tax, sometimes in addition to non-African taxes. While the income tax laws were expected to be applied on a non-racial basis—except in Malawi (Nyasaland), Nigeria (other than Lagos and Colony), and Zambia (Northern Rhodesia) where Africans were specifically excluded—in practice, income tax was paid almost exclusively by non-Africans, partly because it was administratively difficult to apply it to Africans, and partly because only a few Africans had incomes high enough to require them to pay income tax.[4]

By its nature, the APT is a quasi-income tax because it is imposed on the individual on the basis of ascertained income, estimated income, or imputed income based on apparent wealth. The APT has evolved considerably, and what started as a hut or poll tax at a flat rate, payable by adult males, has been gradually modified to become a limited, graduated tax based on earned or imputed income. This development has been in keeping with the expansion of the money sector, higher levels of income, and the spread of literacy.

ADMINISTRATION

The administration of the APT differs widely among African countries, but the tendency has been improvement and uniformity in introducing graduated rates based on income. In Table 3, the similarities and differences in nomenclature, assessment, and collection arrangements among 22 countries are shown.

In the initial stages of the imposition of APT, the assessments of tax payers were based on tax rolls without individual income or wealth returns, a procedure that was necessary because of the high degree of illiteracy and low incomes which precluded the granting of personal relief in the determination of tax liability. Also, the administration of the tax was completely decentralized, and assessments were made by laymen at the local level, such as local assessment committees, village councils, or headmen; tax policy issues were determined as part of the over-all administration. Collection arrangements were also decen-

Table 3—African Personal Taxes: Nomenclature and Levying and Collecting Authorities[a]

| Country | Nomenclature | Governmental Authority for ||
		Levying tax	Collecting revenue
Former British territories			
Gambia	Yard tax, "strange" farmers' tax	Central and local	Local
Ghana	Poll tax	Local	Local
Kenya	Hut and poll tax, graduated personal tax (GPT)	Central[b]	Central[c]
Malawi	Hut and poll tax, minimum tax, GPT	Central	Central[c]
Nigeria	General tax, poll rax, income rate, personal tax[d]	Regional	Regional[c]
Sierra Leone	House tax, chiefdom tax	Local	Local
Tanzania	House tax, poll tax, GPT	Central[b]	Central[c]
Uganda	Hut tax, poll tax, GPT	Central	Central
Zambia	Native tax	Central	Central[c]
Former French West Africa[e]			
Dahomey	Minimum fiscal	Central[f]	Central[e]
Guinea	Personal tax	Central[f]	Central[e]
Ivory Coast	Personal tax, *taxe vicinale*	Central[f]	Central[e]
Mali	Minimum fiscal, *taxe de cercle*	Central[f]	Central[e,g]
Mauritania	Personal tax, *zekkat*	Central[f]	Central[e]
Niger	Minimum fiscal, *taxe de cercle*	Central[f]	Central[e]
Senegal	Minimum fiscal, personal tax	Central[f]	Central[e]
Upper Volta	Personal tax	Central[f]	Central[e]
Other countries			
Chad	Personal tax, civic tax	Central	Central
Congo, Dem. Rep. of	Native tax, additional tax, personal tax	Central	Central/provincial
Gabon	Head tax, commercial tax	Central	Central/local
Liberia	Hut tax	Central	Central
Togo	Capitation tax	Central	Local

Sources: Lord Hailey, *An African Survey, Revised 1956* Pierre Doublet, *Traité de Législation Fiscale dans les Territoires d'Outre-Mer*, Vol II (Paris, 1952); John F. Due, *Taxation and Economic Development in Tropical Africa*.

[a] Collection in all countries is carried out by local authorities, but centralized organization for collection tends to emerge with the introduction of the graduated personal tax.
[b] There is also a tax imposed by local authorities.
[c] Part of the proceeds are allocated to the local authorities.
[d] Other varieties are discussed in the text.
[e] Information relates to territorial governments existing before the attainment of independence in 1959. *Impôt personnel* is translated as "personal tax," while *impôt du minimum fiscal* is written simply as "minimum fiscal." All the countries imposed some form of tax based on cattle or livestock, hence cattle tax is a feature of the personal tax but is omitted from the nomenclature list.
[f] Refers to the territorial government.
[g] The proceeds of *tax spéciale de cercle* accrued to local budgets.

tralized, with great reliance placed on agents —an arrangement which probably minimized the collection costs. However, evasion was difficult to check, and effective administration was somewhat limited.

In most countries, the personal tax is administered separately from the normal income tax, and individuals with sufficiently high incomes pay both taxes. Only in Northern Nigeria has the personal tax been completely integrated with the income tax. In Kenya, Uganda, and Tanzania, such a development is unlikely as long as the collection of income tax remains the function of a supranational body (the East African Community), while responsibility for collection of the personal taxes varies between the central and local governments.[5]

APT IN SELECTED COUNTRIES

Tanzania—In mainland Tanzania, the Personal Tax Ordinance of 1955 replaced the provisions of the former Native Tax Ordinance, which had imposed the poll tax.[6] The new ordinance introduced a graduated system of personal tax with a minimum payment provision and is, in general, patterned along the lines of the East African Income Tax Law. With individual income as the basis of assessment, it is (as in Northern Nigeria) a quasi income tax, except that there is a ceiling to the tax payable.

The annual personal tax is imposed on every adult male and every unmarried woman, who is not exempt either by law or by proclamation, on the basis of his annual income.

Originally, there was provision for five steps in the graduation of the tax and the maximum tax payable was set at US $21, but with the revisions in 1961 and 1962, the steps were increased and the ceiling on personal tax payable was raised to US $62. The 1962 amendment to the law removed from the liability to pay tax persons earning less than £100 per annum. This relieved the administration of burdensome and expensive work in the collection of the minimum tax from numerous payers. In January, 1966, a new schedule of personal tax rates was introduced. (See Table 4.) The rates of tax are basically progressive in their effects, but they have a regressive element within each bracket as well as in the top bracket. While the closer interval between steps reduces the regressiveness of the tax structure as a whole, there still exists some element of regressiveness within each income range (see column 4 of Table 4). No personal relief is granted when computing tax liability.

Personal tax rates in Tanzania are not related to income tax rates, and in principle the APT is paid in addition to the income tax. Beginning in July, 1965, income tax rates were established on a two-tier system consisting of a flat rate of 12.5 per cent on

Table 4—Tanzania: Personal Tax Rates, 1966

Chargeable Annual Income in Pounds		Amount of Tax (*Shillings*)	Tax as Percentage of Income[a]	
Exceeding	But not Exceeding		Limit at Lower end of Bracket	Limit at Higher end of Bracket[b]
100	150	30	1.5	1.0
150	200	60	2.0	1.5
200	250	90	2.3	1.8
250	300	140	2.8	2.3
300	400	275	4.6	3.4
400	500	375	4.7	3.8
500	600	500	5.0	4.2
600	700	650	5.4	4.6
700	800	750	5.4	4.7
800	—	900	5.6	5.6

Source: United Republic of Tanzania, *Act No. 41 of 1965,* July 1965.

[a] Represents ratio within prescribed income range, e.g., £100–149 in the first range.
[b] Calculated on the maximum annual income, minus £1.

chargeable incomes and a surtax at progressive rates which vary from a minimum of T Sh 3 of surtax per T Sh 20 on chargeable incomes of between T Sh 20,000 and T Sh 40,000 to T Sh 12 per T Sh 20 on chargeable incomes above T Sh 200,000 (T Sh 20 = £1).[7] With the personal allowance for an unmarried person established at T Sh 4,320, income tax in addition to the personal tax is paid by an unmarried taxpayer only in respect of annual incomes in excess of T Sh 4,320; the point of liability to double taxation for a married man is T Sh 12,000.[8] Apart from the fact that the abolition of the personal tax on incomes of less than T Sh 2,000 removed many taxpayers from liability, the combined effect of the income tax relief is to remove a large number of taxpayers from double payment of tax on incomes below T Sh 16,000 a year. In effect, income tax proper is still payable by the high-income group; this is also shown by the fact that in 1964 only 22,209 persons were assessed for income tax out of a population of nearly 10 million and about 351,000 in wage employment.[9]

Each appointed collector is responsible for making assessments. He may require the filing of returns of income by taxpayers, but he may assess without such returns. Even where returns are filed, the collector can still raise a "best of judgment" assessment.

The collector is required to communicate the tax liability to each taxpayer before March 31 of each year by means of a demand notice, which requires the addressee to pay his tax before May 31, unless another date is specified. The penalty provision, 50 per cent of the tax due, serves as a deterrent to noncompliance. Defaulters can also be sued in court, while the collector has power to appoint an agent for collection. Provisions for checking evasion are adequate; individual receipts are issued in respect of tax paid, and a tax inspector[10] can request any taxable person to produce his tax receipt or exemption certificate. Failure to do so is regarded as evidence of evasion. The power conferred under this policing provision is stringent, especially the discretion to "detain" potential tax evaders until early evening of the day on which a tax receipt is demanded.[11]

Deduction of tax from earnings of employees was authorized in 1961. The procedure amounts to a selective withholding system, since it is applicable only to specifically approved employers (those who have more than ten employees) who are held responsible for the payment of tax not collected. The law provides that deduction can be made either in three installments or in one sum, as the collector may direct. A tax receipt is issued only after the full amount of tax due has been deducted. The scheme not only is restricted in coverage but also appears to present many opportunities for evasion where labor turnover is considerable.

The introduction of graduation has had a considerable impact on the revenue contribution of the personal tax. In recent years, however, personal tax proceeds to the Central Government have stabilized at about £1 million a year; in the fiscal year 1965–1966, they amounted to £0.97 million, representing 2.6 per cent of current revenues. *Northern Nigeria*—Northern Nigeria's Personal Tax Law of 1962 consolidated existing methods of direct taxation of Africans.[12] It reduced the variety of assessment procedures, and simplified the law and brought it into line with the political development of the region as a part of the Federal Republic of Nigeria. Prior to 1962, seven methods of assessing and collecting personal taxes were used, but the new law reduced these to three.

The law defines the personal tax as income tax, community tax, or cattle tax. The graduated personal tax approximates an income tax where incomes exceed £400; for lower incomes, other factors in addition to income form the basis of assessment. The law retains the assessment of relatively wealthy individuals and persons in the salary and wage-earning class by reference to scheduled rates (Table 5). The community tax is imposed where it is difficult to ascertain individual incomes or where existing differentiation in the incomes of individuals is narrow. In such circumstances a community tax is practicable from an administrative standpoint, while the apportioned tax is broadly equitable. Cattle tax is imposed in addition to, or in lieu of, any community tax payable.

The basis of assessment of the personal tax is global income. Chargeable income is ascertained by granting a consolidated personal allowance of £240 for a male individual liable for the graduated tax[13] and of other deductions, including special allowances for children's education, maintenance of relatives, life insurance premiums. All the deductions follow the income tax procedure, but a limit of £500 is set as the allowable deduction in respect of children. Where the total income of a taxpayer exceeds £400, tax liability is determined by reference to chargeable income and the schedule of rates as shown in Table 5. If total income is less than £400, the tax liability is a flat rate of sixpence per pound (2.5 per cent) on total income without granting the consolidated personal allowance.

Many employees come within the pay-as-you-earn (PAYE) system, and only those with incomes larger than £400 per annum or with other sources of income are expected to file returns.[14] The collection procedure for taxpayers who are within the PAYE system is simple. The employer deducts as directed the tax payable from an employee's earnings every month, the year's liability being spread over 12 months. The tax to be deducted need not be limited to that arising from wages and salaries but may include tax due on other sources of income, or even outstanding tax in respect of an earlier year. No separate individual receipts are issued in respect of deductions, but at the end of the year the employer normally issues a "certificate of pay and tax deducted" for the relevant

year. There is provision for the Revenue Division to adjust the tax liability at the end of the year, and refunds are made in the event of overpayment.

Continuity is provided when an individual changes his employment. The former employer is expected to send a "transfer certificate" to the Revenue Division and to provide two carbon copies of the certificate for the new employer, who sends one to the Revenue Division; the other copy is given to the employee as evidence of tax payment up to the time of his change of employment. This procedure ensures that tax deduction continues smoothly to the convenience of both taxpayer and the Revenue Division; it also assists the Division in locating taxpayers.

Unlike the past, present day coverage of the graduated personal tax is nonracial, since non-Africans are also liable. Proceeds of the tax are shared between the Regional Government and the collecting native or local authority in the ratio of 80:20, except that tax collected under the PAYE scheme is credited in full to the Regional Government.

Community tax remains as operated in the past. It is an "apportioned tax" as far as the individual taxpayer is concerned. Section 49 of the Personal Tax Law states, inter alia, that community tax "shall be levied upon and shall be paid by every such community or individual in respect of each year of assessment."[15] Students in full-time attendance at any training institution, indigent persons, persons under 16 years of age, and *any person who receives a notice of personal tax*

Table 5—Northern Nigeria: Personal Tax Rates, 1962

Chargeable Income		Amount of Tax (Shillings)	Marginal Tax Rate Within Range (per cent)
For every £1 of the first	£500	1.25	6.25
For every £1 of the next	£500	1.75	8.75
For every £1 of the next	£500	3.00	15.00
For every £1 of the next	£500	4.00	20.00
For every £1 of the next	£1,000	5.00	25.00
For every £1 of the next	£1,000	6.50	32.50
For every £1 of the next	£1,000	8.00	40.00
For every £1 exceeding	£5,000	10.00	50.00

Source: Northern Nigeria, *Personal Tax Law, 1962.*

assessment or who otherwise is liable for personal tax, either through the PAYE system or by intimation that he is liable for personal tax, are exempt.[16] The italicized clause brings into focus the point of contact between personal tax and community tax— a significant aspect in the evolution of the personal tax.

The responsibility for the determination of community tax for each area is that of the Provincial Commissioner, who is expected to act in consultation with the local or native authority. The Commissioner is guided in the determination of the community tax by such factors as the amount paid in the preceding year of assessment, the change in population, and any change in the "general state of prosperity." This assessed community tax must then be approved by the Minister of Local Government. The amount of tax and the time of payment is communicated to the local or native authority whose responsibility it is, in consultation with or by directions to district heads or village councils, to apportion "such amount of the community tax as may be just and equitable for each individual in the community to pay having regard to his wealth."[17] Collection is also carried out by the local authority. Any person who pays the personal tax at a flat rate of sixpence per pound under the PAYE system (i.e., whose annual income is less than £400) is allowed to deduct the amount of withheld tax from his apportioned community tax; thus, community tax is paid to the extent that it exceeds income tax. Proceeds from the tax are deposited in local treasuries until account is rendered to the Provincial Commissioner. Ultimately, the proceeds of community and cattle tax are shared between the Regional Government (12.5 per cent) and the collecting native or local authority (87.5 per cent).

No payment of cattle tax is expected where such cattle form part of the basis for the determination of the community tax for the area in which the cattle owner is registered; in practice, this applies largely to the nomadic Fulani tribe. Cattle, for the purpose of the Act, is defined to include oxen, sheep, and lambs. Rates of cattle tax vary according to the type of cattle and by group of provinces, except that there is a uniform tax of 2 shillings per head for sheep and lambs throughout the region.

The contribution of the personal tax to the revenue of the Regional Government has increased substantially in recent years. It increased from £1.7 million in 1962–1963 to an estimated £2.5 million in 1964–1965 and, in the latter year, accounted for about 10 per cent of the Government's current revenues.

Chad—In the Republic of Chad, a graduated personal tax (GPT) has been added to the existing capitation tax, and the personal tax system now consists of the civic tax (*taxe civique*), the cattle tax, and the GPT.

The civic tax is identical with the minimum fiscal of other countries that apply the French system and is administered along the same pattern. It is levied only on males who are 18 years of age and over and who derive an annual income, except in agriculture, of not more than 60,000 francs. Invalids and those with nonagricultural incomes of more than 60,000 francs a year who are liable for the GPT are exempt.

Lists giving the number of village taxpayers are compiled from the latest official census and corrected by additional information supplied by village chiefs. At present, it is estimated that 800,000 persons are liable for the tax, but on the average only 630,000 persons actually pay. The rate of the civic tax varies for difficult areas based on the ability of people in the particular area to meet the tax apportioned for the area. The current average rate is 900 francs but rates vary as follows: communes, 900 to 1,400 francs, principal cities of Departments, 900 francs—except in Borkou, Ennedi, and Tibesti, where the rate is only 360 francs; and in the districts, 900 francs.

Collection is the responsibility of the village chiefs under the direction of the regional authorities. The proceeds of the tax were 522 million francs in 1963. Except in the communes, where 25 per cent of the proceeds (e.g., of the GPT) goes into the "communal" budget, the tax revenue is credited to the general revenue of the Republic.

The cattle tax is imposed on all owners of cows, sheep, horses, and camels; animals which are under three years old are exempt. The tax is assessed on the number of animals owned and is collected in the same manner as the civic tax, with the proceeds credited in full to the national budget. The present rates per animal are 225 francs for horses and 20 francs for sheep; the rates are generally lower in the Borkou, Ennedi, and Tibesti regions.

As in Tanzania and those countries which now levy the GPT, the new personal tax in Chad is related to individual income. It is, however, essentially a proportional tax. (See Table 6.) The wide income ranges made the tax markedly regressive within each bracket level.

All males, and from 1965 females, with non-agricultural incomes in excess of 60,000 francs a year are liable for the tax. At present, more than 60 per cent of those liable are wage earners who also pay the "schedular tax." Only invalids and the maimed are exempt. Taxpayers are put on nominal rolls, but the tax is collected from most taxpayers by anticipation, that is, at the same time that the schedular tax (for wage earners) and the business fees are due. Only 13,000 persons pay the tax out of an estimated potential of 25,000 taxpayers, and the contribution of the GPT to revenue is still modest.

Trends in Revenue Contribution

The varieties of the personal tax make quite a significant contribution to the revenues of the central governments of many African countries. (See Table 7.) In addition, personal taxes add considerably to the revenues of the local governments. For example, in 1960 they accounted for 30 per cent to 46 per cent of the budgets of the local governments in Uganda.[18] In Kenya between 10 per cent and 31 per cent, and in Ghana about 20 per cent, of local government revenues accrued from personal taxes in 1960–1961.[19] In 1951–1952, more than 60 per cent of the revenues of local governments in Nigeria accrued from personal taxes.[20] In 1960–1961, the proportion was 48 per cent in Western Nigeria [21] and about 25 per cent in Eastern Nigeria,[22] where the taxation of low incomes below an established limit is the responsibility of the local governments.

The share of personal taxes in central government revenues depends on the fiscal arrangements between local and central governments. The relative share of personal taxes in the central government revenues of the former British territories has been declining, partly as a result of increasing scope of income tax proper, and partly as a result of the transfer, from the central governments to local authorities, of the power to tax low incomes. In Kenya the share of personal taxes in central government revenues declined from 8.9 per cent in 1947 to 3.6 per cent in the fiscal year 1962, while in Malawi it maintained a stable ratio of about

Table 6—Chad: Graduated Personal Tax Schedule, 1964
(In CFA Francs)

Annual Income		Amount of Tax	Tax as Percentage of Income	
From	To		Limit at lower end of bracket[a]	Limit at higher end of bracket
60,000	100,000	2,300	3.8	2.3
100,000	150,000	3,000	2.7	2.0
150,000	250,000	4,500	2.8	1.8
250,000	500,000	7,000	2.7	1.4
500,000	750,000	10,500	2.1	1.4
750,000	1,000,000	16,000	2.1	1.6
In excess of	1,000,000	24,000	2.4	2.4

Source: République du Tchad, *Propositions de Réforme Fiscal* (Paris, 1964), pp. 5–6.

[a] Ratio is calculated on the basis of the stated minimum in each range (except the lowest range), plus 10,000 francs.

Table 7—Selected African Countries: Contribution of African Personal Taxes to Central Government Revenues, 1960–1961 and 1963–1964

	1960–1961[a]					1963–1964[a]				
	Current Revenues (1)	Direct Taxes (2)	Personal Taxes (3)	Col. 3 as Percentage of Col. 1 (4)	Col. 3 as Percentage of Col. 2 (5)	Current Revenues (1)	Direct Taxes (2)	Personal Taxes (3)	Col. 3 as Percentage of Col. 1 (4)	Col. 3 as Percentage of Col. 2 (5)
	(Amounts in millions of pounds)									
Former British territories										
Kenya[b]	28.57	11.80	1.82	6.4	15.4	36.77	13.38	0.15[c]	0.4	1.1
Malawi	6.33	3.51	0.94	14.8	26.8	8.76[d]	2.27	0.94	10.7	41.4
Northern Nigeria[e]	3.92	1.35	1.02	26.0	75.6	25.41	4.11	2.56	10.1	62.3
Tanzania[b,f]	21.30	6.13	1.31	6.2	21.4	28.30	7.90	1.00	3.5	12.7
Uganda[b]	18.77	4.16	0.56	3.0	13.5	—	—	—	—	—
	(Amounts in millions of CFA francs)									
Former French territories										
Central African Republic	3,009	797	401	13.3	50.3	5,559	1,162	413	7.4	35.5
Chad	4,287	857	577	13.5	67.3	6,427	1,915	950[g]	14.8	49.6
Gabon	4,583	977	75	1.6	7.7	7,360	1,968	125	1.6	6.3
Niger	3,543	1,309	941	26.6	71.9	5,178	2,337	1,552	30.0	66.4
Senegal	25,560	4,470	867	3.4	19.4	33,902	6,420	1,063	3.1	16.6
Upper Volta	4,709	1,254	828	17.6	66.0	8,258	2,593	1,757	21.3	67.8
	(Amounts in millions of Mali francs)									
Mali	5,090	1,890	1,539	30.2	81.4	10,030	2,670	—	—	—

Sources: Annual budgets of various countries; "L'Economie Voltaïque en 1964–1965," Conjoncture Ouest Africaine (Paris), April 1965; Service de la Statistique Générale de la Comptabilité Nationale et de la Mécanographie, Bulletin Mensuel de Statistique (Bamako), various issues; Chambre de Commerce, d'Agriculture et d'Industrie de Bamako, Annuaire Statistique de la République du Mali, 1964, April 1965.

[a] Data are for calendar years 1960 and 1964 for former French territories.
[b] Fiscal year ends on June 30.
[c] The power of levy and collection of personal tax transferred to local authorities.
[d] Data relates to calendar year 1964; previous fiscal year, July–June, changed in January 1964.
[e] Fiscal year ends on March 31.
[f] Excluding Zanzibar.
[g] Estimate.

14 per cent until 1962, when it fell to 10.2 per cent. The same declining trend is evident in Tanzania where the ratio of 16.7 per cent in 1947 fell to 3.2 per cent in 1962. In Uganda the ratio was only 3.1 per cent in 1961–1962, a year before the power to tax was transferred to local governments. This trend is likely to continue in the future as a result of the increasing relative importance of other sources of revenue, such as indirect taxes and income tax proceeds, and the gradual abandonment of the personal tax field to local governments.

The same declining trend in the relative importance of revenues from personal taxes has been experienced in the former French African countries since the attainment of independence, although they still constitute a more significant source of revenue than in the former British territories. In Upper Volta, the ratio was some 17.6 per cent in 1960, and in Chad and Niger it was 13.5 per cent and 26.6 per cent, respectively. These three countries are landlocked and do not have as many alternatives for raising taxes as other countries. In fact, in 1964 the ratios in Chad and Upper Volta were about 15 per cent and 21 per cent, respectively. In Niger the ratio was 30 per cent in 1964, compared with 26. 6 per cent in 1960 and 46.7 per cent in 1950. In relation to direct taxes, the contribution is more significant for all the countries, with Niger and Upper Volta deriving more than 60 per cent, and Chad nearly 50 per cent, from personal taxes. With the fiscal reform of 1960, Ivory Coast has been able to dispense with the minimum fiscal as a source of central government revenue; in Senegal a larger part of the tax goes to the local authorities, while in Togo proceeds of the capitation tax accrue to the local government.

Conclusion

African personal taxes have proved quite effective in tapping the limited revenue potential of the low-income groups. The tax rates have been set in most countries at levels compatible with the normal supply of effort; in no country is there any evidence that there has been a contraction in the supply of individual effort to procure cash

income mainly as a result of the level of personal tax rates. On the contrary, in a few countries, one of the reasons for introducing the flat rate tax was to induce people in the subsistence sector to move into the money sector, either by producing surplus agricultural products for sale in the market or by coming into the labor market as wage earners.

The development in many countries has been the modification of personal tax rates, including limited graduation to reflect increasing levels of income; hence, tax policy has been suitably designed to conform to economic development. Nonetheless, the question of equity may be raised in view of the limited progressiveness in rates and the canon of ability to pay taxation. There is no doubt that the original, pure poll taxes were regressive, unfair to the poorer classes, and unduly advantageous to the wealthy, who had better ability to meet heavier tax burdens. But in economies with large subsistence sectors, these are taxes that are easiest to collect with a minimum of administrative cost, even if they cause discomfort in some instances, especially where the level of the minimum tax is high in relation to the general level of economic well-being. Moreover, measures have been taken in many countries to make the tax more equitable and to minimize the regressiveness through the adoption of limited graduation of rates. Rates of the GPT in Tanzania, Uganda, and Northern Nigeria show considerable improvement. Irrespective of the level of government that has jurisdiction over the taxation of low incomes, the degree to which progressiveness in the rate structure can be achieved will continue to be limited as long as the GPT has to exist side by side with income tax and has to be limited either by fixing a maximum payable tax or a maximum assessable income.

While there are no absolute criteria for appraising the efficiency of tax administration, indications are that the administration of personal taxes was related to the conditions of developing countries with predominantly agricultural economies, large subsistence sectors, limited wage systems, and mass illiteracy. In such an environment, a tax has to be simple, low in rate, and easy to administer. Tax administrative practices differ among countries and sometimes within the same country, reflecting the special situations in each area. The reliance on non-professionals and local personnel tends to lead to tax evasion in many areas. The general opinion, however, is that evasion was widespread before the introduction of the GPT. Little is known about enforcement activities, but it was not uncommon to detain taxpayers for a limited period of time (usually a day in some countries) if it was found that they failed to discharge their tax obligations. Penalties for non-compliance with the tax laws were imposed in some countries. In Malawi, up to 50 per cent of the poll tax is imposed as a penalty upon failure to pay on a prescribed date; in Northern Nigeria, a penalty equal to the amount of tax due is payable, while in Tanzania, the law provides for a penalty of 50 per cent of the tax due.

Through the imposition and extension of the APT, the fiscal objective of ensuring the contribution by the low-income groups to the financing of central government operations has been met successfully. A large majority of Africans have been even more adequately prepared for payment of income tax by the existence of the personal tax than by the tribute payments that preceded its introduction.

The importance of the APT in the tax revenue structure of the central governments in African countries will in all likelihood continue to decline, and the tax may be replaced eventually by the income tax. However, on the local government level a greater use can be made of the personal tax, particularly the GPT, if it is synchronized with the existing income tax. With the experience gained in administering it, the personal tax will fulfill a better role in providing a stable and an independent means of financing local government services than property taxes, the assessment of which is handicapped by a

lack of trained staff and by complicated systems of property ownership. Hence, the trend of abandoning the personal tax to local governments, as in Uganda, Kenya, Dahomey, and, to an extent, Mali and Senegal, may be preferred to a complete abolition of the tax.

Notes

1. See, for example, United Nations, Economic Commission for Africa, *Economic Bulletin for Africa* (Addis Ababa), June, 1961, and A. Abdel-Rahman, "The Revenue Structure of the CFA Countries," *Staff Papers*, Vol. XII (1965), pp. 73–118.

2. For example, in East Africa (Kenya, Tanzania, Uganda) out of a population estimated at 26.2 million in 1963 only 90,365 individuals (0.3 per cent) paid income tax in the fiscal year ended June 30, 1964. See F. H. Vallibhoy, *Tax Enquiry Report, 1964/65* (Entebbe, Ugandan Ministry of Finance, 1965), and the East African Common Services Organization, *Economic and Statistical Review*, June, 1966, p. 5.

3. See John F. Due, *Taxation and Economic Development in Tropical Africa* (Cambridge, Mass., 1963), p. 61; Ursula K. Hicks, *Development from Below: Local Government and Finance in Developing Countries of the Commonwealth* (London, 1961), p. 298.

4. See Lord Hailey, *An African Survey, Revised 1956* (London, 1957), pp. 645–646.

5. In Tanzania a development levy, which was first imposed as a flat rate tax on income in July, 1965, has been merged with the existing personal tax with effect from January, 1968. (See the budget speech for 1967–1968 by Tanzania's Minister of Finance, in *The Standard*, Dar es Salaam, June 15, 1967.) Efforts are being made to relate the personal tax rates to the income tax rates so as to secure an over-all elastic and more progressive rate of personal tax, taking into account the combined effect of the income tax.

6. Tanganyika, *Personal Tax, Chapter 355 of the Laws, Annual Supplement 1955* (Dar es Salaam, 1956), pp. 3–6. For the development of the personal tax system, see Great Britain, Colonial Office, *Development of African Local Government in Tanganyika*, No. 277 (London, 1951).

7. A new marginal rate of surtax of 65 per cent (T Sh 13 per T Sh 20) on chargeable incomes in excess of T Sh 300,000 was announced in the 1967–1968 budget (see budget speech cited in footnote 5).

8. The following main personal allowances are deductible from taxable incomes to arrive

at the taxpayer's chargeable income: single allowance, T Sh 4,320; married allowance, T Sh 12,000; for each of four children aged up to 19 years, T Sh 1,920; for fifth and sixth child, T Sh 960 (see the budget speech for 1965–1966 by the Minister of Finance, Dar es Salaam, June 15, 1966). Thus, a married man with, say, four children is not liable to pay income tax until his income exceeds T Sh 19,680, while a single person with two dependent children is not liable to pay income tax until his income exceeds T Sh 8,160.

9. *Background to the Budget: An Economic Survey, 1967–68* (Dar es Salaam, 1967). This is also borne out by the fact that of the total adult male employees (estimated at 254,200 in 1965), about 91.5 per cent earned less than T Sh 4,800 per annum, while 1.3 per cent earned T Sh 12,000 and more per annum.

10. Tax inspectors are not only those who are charged with the administration of the law—tax agents and tax clerks—but also police officers who are not below the rank of subinspector and are assigned for checking such evasion.

11. Until 1951, tax defaulters could discharge their liabilities by working on government undertakings, a continuation of a practice adopted in the 1930's.

12. Northern Nigeria, *Personal Tax Law, 1962*, N.N. No. 6 of 1962 (Kaduna). The law came into operation on April 1, 1962. Prior to the enactment of this law, seven types of direct taxes were imposed, namely, a locally distributed tax, a poll tax, a tax on ascertainable incomes, a wealthy trader's tax, a mines' labor tax, a strangers' tax, and a land revenue tax. See Great Britain, Colonial Office, *Annual Report on Nigeria, 1946–1949* (London, 1947–1950).

13. This consolidated allowance is granted to a female individual who has income of her own on which tax is payable, but a woman's income is not aggregated with that of her husband.

14. At present the scheme does not cover all employees or pensioners but only employees of designated employers, who are provided with requisite instruction or material. For a description of the assessment procedure, see *Personal Taxation of Individuals in Northern Nigeria* (Kaduna; Nigeria Revenue Division, Ministry of Finance of Northern Nigeria, September, 1964).

15. Northern Nigeria, *Personal Tax Law*, Section 49, p. 27.

16. The law is not clear on the liability for community tax of those who, in principle, are liable for the graduated personal tax but who, because of relief to which they are entitled, would not actually be called upon to pay. It can, however, be presumed that people in this category would be liable for the payment of the community tax.

17. Northern Nigeria, *Personal Tax Law*, Section 53, p. 29. A native authority can vary the amount allocated to an individual by a district head or village council.

18. Great Britain, Colonial Office, *Uganda: Report of the Year 1961* (London, 1963).

19. Hicks, *op. cit.*, pp. 299–300.

20. International Bank for Reconstruction and Development, *The Economic Development of Nigeria* (Baltimore, 1955), pp. 121 and 656–657.

21. Western Nigeria, *Statistical Bulletin*, Vol. V (June and December 1963).

22. Ministry of Local Government of Eastern Nigeria, *Annual Report, 1960–61* (Enugu, 1962), pp. 7–8.

VI

International Economic Relations

MOST AFRICAN COUNTRIES face persistent and chronic balance of payments problems arising essentially from their increasing demand for capital goods for development of industries and necessary infrastructure. In the article, "Balance of Payments Problem of African Countries," the U. N. Economic Commission for Africa presents a comprehensive survey of the current situation. The nature and major causes of unfavorable balances of trade, as well as deficits in the balances of payments are discussed. The Commission then considers the effectiveness of various proposed policies to ease the problem: foreign loans and grants, devaluation, and direct quantitative restriction of imports.

The balance of payments problems facing African countries are in many ways similar to those in the underdeveloped countries of Asia and Latin America. One way to overcome the problem is for an underdeveloped country to manufacture import substitutes. In most cases, tariffs on imports will be required to break through long established trade and marketing links with former colonial powers, to overcome established consumers tastes and habits, and to offset higher costs of domestic production. The local infant industries producing import substitutes will have to be granted protection during the period necessary to enable them to "stand on their feet." However, the real costs of protection are reduced when several developing countries integrate their trade and factor markets. Franklin Walker examines the benefits and problems from promoting import substitute industrialization through regional integration in the form of a customs union. He also examines the major existing treaties of integration in Africa, particularly with regard to how they are designed to achieve equity in distribution of benefits among member states.

20

Balance of Payments Problem of African Countries

United Nations Economic Commission for Africa

From Economic Bulletin for Africa, *Vol. 6, No. 2 (July, 1966), pp. 1–26.*

IT IS SOMETIMES asserted that African countries need not have balance of payments problems, that they may have balance of payments deficits, and that these deficits are innocuous when they are covered ahead of time by foreign loans and grants.[1] If it is at all meaningful to make a distinction between balance of payments problems and balance of payments innocuous deficits, it should be at once made clear that most African countries have balance of payments problems, more technically known as structural disequilibra. The consequence of the disequilibrium is a deficit. However, the deficit in most cases in Africa is not an innocuous one, if by innocuous is meant the absence of any such repercussions as may be considered injurious to the maintenance of the value of currency, the proper functioning of the monetary mechanism, and above all to the continuity of the process of economic development.

A fundamental contention of this paper is that it is not meaningful to dwell on distinguishing between harmful and innocuous balance of payments problems when discussing situations of developing countries in the course of implementing comprehensive development programmes. It may, however, be useful to differentiate certain types of balance of payments deficits. Apart from the purely academic interest in an exercise at definition, such differentiation helps to bring to light the exact predicament of African countries in balance of payments deficit. Here, the question at hand is not that of whether the deficit is due to an excess in autonomous outpayments over autonomous inpayments—in which case, according to Meade, it would be a true deficit—or to an excess in accommodating payments over accommodating receipts—in which case the deficit is not only untrue, but by Meade's token is in fact a true surplus.[2] It need not be laboured that it is in their autonomous transactions that the source of balance of payments deficits of African countries is to be found. Three types of the "true" deficit can be distinguished:

(1) *Planned Deficit:* This occurs when a country deliberately allows its autonomous outpayments to exceed autonomous inpayments, and finances the gap out of accumulated reserves and/or ascertained foreign source;

(2) *Accommodated Unplanned Deficit:* This occurs when the excess of autonomous outpayments over autonomous inpayments arising out of no deliberate action by the country is readily financed by an inflow of foreign capital whether it be grants or loans, short- or long-term, hard or soft;

(3) *Exigent Unplanned Deficit:* This is a deficit, arising out of no deliberate action on the part of the country, which cannot be readily eliminated through accommodating finances, and hence calls for emergency measures. The latter include the repressive measures such as all types of controls over imports and exchange, and the equilibrating ones such as the manipulation of the exchange rate and the level of internal prices, costs and incomes.

It can be seen from the above that the unplanned deficits (2) and (3) can be either temporary or chronic, depending on whether they are the result of transitional imbalances such as may be due to crop failures, floods, droughts and similar other seasonal irregularities, or whether the cause is a real disequilibrium in the structure and growth of imports and exports, a situation where the actual import propensity is higher than the feasible export propensity. Both (2) and (3) can be either innocuous or harmful depending on whether the deficit is temporary or chronic.

Moreover, it should be mentioned that due caution should be exercised in examining the consequences of what may be labelled "planned deficit." It is obvious that there is a limit past which the deficit can be no longer considered as planned, for instance when the foreign exchange reserves fall below the conventionally considered minimum safe level. Regardless of whether or not it continues to be considered a planned deficit, once that limit is passed, it is inevitable the deficit loses its innocuous character. Several African countries, especially those which had accumulated sizable foreign exchange reserves prior to independence, have since deliberately run down their reserves in what appeared to be a planned deficit intended to finance development plans. The point has been reached, however, when the profound concern of these countries over the state of their external finances has left no doubt as to whether any further deterioration can be considered planned action.

Balance of payments deficits of the majority of African countries are the result of structural disequilibrium, and hence they are persistent or chronic deficits. The shortfall in the external sector's current receipts is a phenomenon which is neither temporary nor sporadic. As recent trends amply indicate, the deficiency in meeting current external payments in Africa is *ceteris paribus* of a more permanent nature. Furthermore, this gap is generally widening. It is pertinent to consider the potential deficit, since the actual deficits sustained by most of the African countries are repressed to some, usually considerable, extent.[3] Presence of repression is manifest in the application of foreign exchange and import controls which are not only widespread but are increasing in intensity.

What is more serious is that the means of covering this chronic and growing deficiency are not always forthcoming. Contrary to the view held by some,[4] obtaining foreign loans and grants is not one of the easiest endeavours, least of all for the African countries with balance of payments deficits. Nor what has become available to Africa in foreign resources has always been adequate for the purpose of covering payments deficits. Moreover, the cost of such foreign resources has imposed an additional burden on the already strained current earnings. The burden, consisting of debt service charges and direct investment transfers, has been growing, and at an accelerated rate. The effect of all these factors has contributed to, or was exclusively responsible for, the depletion of foreign exchange reserves, which in certain instances has assumed alarmingly great proportions.

In the face of dwindling external reserves, there are only few alternatives open for coping with the situation, with fairly predictable consequences. If nothing is done, not only will the fall in reserves soon reflect itself in a depreciation in the real external (and probably also the internal) value of the currency, but it will also become eventually impossible to pay for imports of goods and services to the desired level. Default in discharging contractual obligations, such as debt service payments, may also occur. There have been some instances of debt renegotiation, or rescheduling of debt service payments, in Africa.

If currency devaluation is resorted to, the quantity of exports may as a result be increased and that of imports be decreased. But given the nature of the foreign demand for typical African export commodities and their supply conditions, and the nature of the African demand for imports, given the price —and income—elasticities of these demands and supplies elasticities, it is highly likely that the effect of devaluation will be to reduce total export proceeds and to increase the total import bill. The rise in the unit cost of imports does not only represent a further strain on the balance of payments, but can also aggravate the problem indirectly if the inflationary pressures which it is likely to set in motion are not effectively checked through appropriate monetary and fiscal policies. If deflationary measures are taken, they might result in paralyzing economic activity, hence arresting the process of development.

One other alternative widely adopted is to reduce the total cost of imports of goods and services through direct quantitative restrictions—by means of quotas and licensing, often combined with increased customs duties and foreign exchange controls. This policy usually succeeds in achieving its primary purpose, i.e., cutting down of aggregate imports. However, it usually makes it impossible to maintain a high and rising level of imports of capital goods and other intermediate production goods required for the fulfillment of development programmes. For effective results, the policy of direct import restrictions has in practice had to go beyond the category of consumer goods.

Several observations are called for. In the first place, even though imports of consumer goods, despite a considerable fall in their relative share in total imports in recent years, still represent the major category of imports of many countries, they cannot, however, be cut indiscriminately, for there is a minimum level of imported consumer goods which has to be tolerated as major incentives to human efforts.

Secondly, even if substantial cuts in imports of finished and semifinished consumer goods are feasible, it is possible and likely that such a measure will affect the availability of capital and intermediate production goods, and might thus frustrate investment plans. This can happen either directly through shortage of supplies imported as consumer goods which are also of industrial use, or, indirectly, through the impact of a deficient total effective demand on investment decisions. In the relatively more industrialized developing countries, the direct impact may also occur through diversion of home production from capital to consumer goods, while the availability of capital and intermediate production goods may be reduced indirectly through increased money demand for more expansion in domestic consumer goods at the expense of effective demand for investment goods.

Finally, it should be remembered that although imports of capital and intermediate

production goods do not account in all cases for the greater portion of total imports, they have, nonetheless, accounted, with only few exceptions, for the major part of recent import expansions. It is, therefore, probable that restrictive import measures will apply to them as well, especially when restrictions are applied to imports according to source. In fact, this has been frequently true of recent African experiences.

The fundamental shortcoming of the foregoing set of measures, aimed at preventing or alleviating drastic depletion of external reserves, is that if they lead to a reduction in imports of capital and intermediate production goods and, consequently, to a contraction in investment activities and industrial production, they will only have begged the question, indeed, they will have defeated the purpose. The rate of economic growth will have been slowed down. In addition, several other concomitant complications—in the price system, monetary mechanism, fiscal programmes and in the allocation of resources including human—will have developed. The initial deficit will have thus resulted in a situation which is far from being innocuous.

It should be remembered that balance of payments deficits of most, if not all, African countries have been caused by the attempt to speed up the pace of economic progress through the implementation of comprehensive development plans, with the result that imports of capital and intermediate production goods have experienced a phenomenal expansion far exceeding the export capacity to pay for. However, it should be borne in mind too that had it been always easy to secure the other means of meeting the rising cost of imports, namely, foreign financial resources, it would have been possible to avoid those harmful consequences—certainly to minimize them considerably. As will soon be evident, African countries have not been able to obtain such foreign financial resources with the ease and on the scale they had hoped for.

There should be no doubt that recent and

current developments in the balance of payments of many African countries should be appropriately referred to as problems, and in several cases as genuinely serious problems. These are examined in the remaining part of this paper.

Recent Trends in the Current External Transactions of African Countries—The Current Account

The African economies are characterized by a high degree of dependence on the outside world. This is manifest in the relatively large share of both exports and imports in gross national product. In 1961, Africa's total exports and total imports amounted, respectively, to about 21 and 26 per cent of the continent's (South Africa excluded) gross domestic product. These proportions naturally vary considerably among the individual countries, with some under 10 per cent and others well over one third. Still, however, the continental proportions are representative of the majority of countries. The corresponding ratios for Asia are in the tune of 12 and 14 per cent, and for Europe they are about 22 and 23 per cent.

The implications of this dependence are manifold. Of utmost significance is the direct impact of developments in their external transactions (current and capital) on the growth rate of the African economies. It may be pointed out that the degree of Africa's over-all dependence on foreign trade as generally measured by the ratios of exports and imports to GDP is itself not substantially higher than that of Europe, and is even less than the United Kingdom's, whose respective trade ratios are 27 and 26 per cent. Africa's dependence is, nevertheless, more acute, as it is not as yet possible to obtain capital goods locally and, hence, investment depends on imported equipment, the financing of which depends in turn on the proceeds of exports. It is thus the basic structure both of production and of foreign trade that renders the growth of the African economies highly sensitive to developments in the external sector. This dependence on foreign trade is, therefore, to be expected to perpetuate itself until such time as when the production patterns in these economies have been radically altered through industrialization.[5]

VISIBLE TRADE

Africa's (excluding South Africa) imports have continued to outrun her exports. Over the last decade, total imports registered an increase of 64 per cent, while the increase in exports amounted to a little over 58 per cent. The deficit grew from $230 million in 1953, to $581 million in 1963. The phenomenon is common to the majority of individual countries. As is demonstrated by Table 1, exports have in general only partially covered imports. Notable exceptions in this regard include Angola, Cameroon, Congo (Kinshasa), Gabon, Ivory Coast, countries of the former Federation of Rhodesia and Nyasaland, Tanzania, Uganda, and as of 1963, Libya. In three countries, the export value covered only one third or less of the value of imports, while in over one half of the cases the percentage coverage oscillated between 50 and 75 per cent.

Table 2 confirms the evidence afforded by Table 1 and, furthermore, it shows that the phenomenon of trade deficits is a persistent one. The deficits in several cases have been growing and have accounted for an increasing proportion of export earnings. Several factors are at work giving rise to the structural disequilibrium of Africa's trade balance.

One reason is to be found in the movement of the terms of trade. As is observed from Table 3, while the quantity of exports may have expanded, the value of exports has seldom increased commensurately, due to a downward trend in the prices of several major export commodities of African countries. Copper prices have tended to move upward, while the prices of most oil seeds and vegetable oils have either held their own or increased. On the other hand, Table 3 also shows that in the case of imports, both the quantity and prices have increased, hence the value.

In addition to deterioration in their terms of trade, several African countries have

Table 1—Foreign Trade of African Countries, 1962–1964

Countries	Exports (f.o.b.) (in million US $)			Imports (c.i.f.) (in million US $)			Exports as Percentage of Imports		
	1962	1963	1964	1962	1963	1964	1962 (%)	1963 (%)	1964 (%)
Morocco	348.4	384.1	432.1	433.7	448.7	461.4	80.2	85.6	93.6
Algeria	809.3	700.0	780.0	708.1	800.0	710.0	114.3	87.5	109.9
Tunisia	116.0	125.2	127.0	216.4	221.4	244.0	53.7	56.5	52.0
Libya	141.3	377.6	708.7	205.6	238.8	292.2	68.4	158.1	242.5
UAR (Egypt)	454.6	521.6	539.4	859.1	918.8	953.1	54.3	56.8	56.6
Sudan	226.7	225.9	196.0	256.5	280.3	267.7	88.3	80.6	73.2
Mauritania	2.8	16.1	45.8	35.7	30.0	15.7	7.8	53.7	291.7
Senegal	124.2	110.5	122.5	154.8	156.1	171.7	80.0	71.8	71.3
Ivory Coast	193.2	230.3	302.1	156.1	169.8	245.1	132.2	135.6	123.3
Upper Volta	7.9	9.3	—	34.7	37.1	—	22.8	25.1	—
Dahomey	10.9	12.8	13.2	26.8	33.4	31.4	28.6	38.3	42.0
Niger	14.5	27.4	21.3	25.5	29.5	32.9	55.6	92.9	64.7
Guinea	43.3	55.1	—	57.9	46.1	—	74.1	—	—
Togo	17.2	18.3	30.3	30.2	27.2	41.7	63.0	63.1	72.4
Gambia	10.0	8.7	—	12.5	11.8	—	76.9	73.7	—
Sierra Leone	56.6	81.9	95.1	85.2	83.5	99.5	67.1	97.1	95.6
Ghana	290.6	273.3	292.1	333.4	364.7	340.4	87.4	74.9	85.8
Nigeria	466.8	517.4	602.3	568.1	568.4	710.1	83.1	91.0	84.8
Cameroon	103.4	118.0	121.7	101.8	108.3	115.8	100.1	109.0	105.1
UDEAC	125.8	159.6	194.1	160.8	165.4	185.0	77.6	96.5	104.9
Congo (Kinshasa)	284.0	324.4	346.6	170.8	253.9	285.1	71.0	27.7	121.6
Rwanda	19.3	—	—	32.3	—	—	59.7	—	—
Angola	148.3	164.5	204.1	135.6	146.5	164.0	108.8	112.3	124.5
Rhodesia and Nyasaland Zambia, Malawi, Rhodesia	586.7	621.3	722.0	400.4	425.0	559.2	146.8	164.6	129.1
Mozambique	91.0	100.7	106.0	135.9	141.8	156.2	66.9	71.0	67.9
Rep. of Malagasy	94.3	82.1	91.8	121.6	127.5	135.5	77.0	64.9	67.7
Réunion	33.0	38.1	37.4	63.3	69.7	90.0	52.0	54.7	41.6
Tanzania	158.7	193.2	208.2	126.4	128.3	133.6	125.6	150.6	155.8
Uganda	114.0	151.6	186.0	73.4	86.6	91.9	157.5	176.2	202.9
Kenya	124.4	142.7	149.9	194.6	206.3	214.5	64.6	69.2	69.7
Somalia	25.5	31.8	36.1	37.8	44.7	54.7	65.8	71.1	66.0
Ethiopia	80.3	89.9	105.0	103.5	111.0	127.8	77.7	81.0	85.0

Sources: United Nations: *Monthly Bulletin of Statistics*, August 1964. Office Statistique des Communautés Européennes; *Associés d'Outre Mer*, Janvier–Decembre 1963.

313

Table 2—Trade Balances of African Countries
(in millions of US $ and [in parenthesis] as percentage of exports)

	1958	1959	1960	1961	1962	1963
Sudan	−26.1 −(20.2)	+54.6 +(27.9)	+6.0 +(3.2)	47.4 −(26.9)	−20.1 −(8.9)	−35.6 −(14.5)
UAR	−151.2 −(32.3)	−210.4 −(44.6)	−187.4 −(33.0)	−250.8 −(51.7)	−427.6 −(102.6)	−399.7 −(76)
Libya	−84.4 −(625.2)	−110.2 (918.3)	−166.5 −(1,473.4)	−130.9 −(1,681.8)	−65.5 −(46.4)	+96.8 +(28.7)
Tunisia	−1.2 −(0.8)	−16.9 −(11.8)	−68.6 −(53.2)	−100.8 −(88.0)	−85.3 −(73.0)	−96.9 −(79.4)
Algeria	−549.8 —	−740.5 −(201.2)	−706.1 −(125.6)	−310.7 −(45.7)	+54.7 +(7.1)	−888 −(125.6)
Morocco	−11.5 −(4.0)	+27.7 +(9.6)	−6.3 −(1.6)	−89.7 −(24.7)	−50.6 −(14.3)	−67.8 −(17.7)
BCEAO countries[a]	−93.0	−103.8	−48.6	−83.1	−78.8	−85.7
Gambia	— —	−0.5 —	−1.2 −(15.4)	−3.4 −(35.8)	−2.6 −(26.0)	— —
Sierra Leone	— —	−11.4 —	−0.8 −(1.0)	−20.6 −(25.1)	−38.6 −(68.2)	−12.4 −(15.3)
Liberia	— —	+22.0 —	+10.3 +(12.5)	— —	— —	— —

Ghana	−81.2 +(30.7)	+16.5 +(5.2)	−19.6 −(6.0)	+43.7 +(13.1)	−30.0 −(9.8)
Nigeria	−94.9 −(25.2)	−50.7 −(11.2)	−141.4 −(30.2)	−149.8 −(31.3)	−94.1 −(20.3)
Congo (Kinshasa)	+171.5 +(34.1)	+271.4 +(47.7)	— —	+110.3 +(31.5)	+124.8 +(38.7)
BCEAEC countries [b]	−32.1	−24.6	−49.5	−41.4	−30.6
Cameroon	+12.4 +(11.5)	+30.7 —	+15.5 +(16.0)	+6.1 +(6.2)	+7.5 +(7.2)
Zambia, Rhodesia. Malawi	−34.7 −(8.4)	+128.3 +(23.0)	+171.1 +(27.7)	+175.8 +(28.5)	+207.4 +(33.8)
Tanzania Kenya Uganda	+1.5 +(0.4) —	+16.5 +(4.6) —	+5.9 +(1.5)	+2.7 +(0.7)	+13.2 +(3.4)
Somalia	—	—	—	−9.1 −(34.6)	−16.5 −(65.5)
Ethiopia	−4.6 −(7.5)	−5.1 −(7.6)	+1.0 +(1.3)	−3.7 −(4.7)	−5.5 −(6.7)
Madagascar	−18.2 −(22.0)	−43.0 −(56.5)	−37.1 −(49.5)	−23.4 −(30.2)	−45.4 −(55.3)

Sources: International Monetary Fund, *Balance of Payments Yearbook*, *International Financial Statistics*, supplemented by national publications. The source for franc zone countries except Morocco and Tunisia is Comité Monétaire de la Zone Franc, *La Zone Franc*.

[a] Dahomey, Ivory Coast, Mauritania, Niger, Senegal, Togo and Upper Volta.
[b] Central African Republic, Chad, Congo (Brazzaville) and Gabon.

experienced severe fluctuations in their export earnings. The source of both problems is the high dependence in practically all African countries on one primary commodity or one group of such products with shrinking or unstable demand.

World demand for most of these commodities has not been expanding, the market showing signs of saturation, as in the cases of cocoa and coffee. Production of the latter commodities has continued to increase rapidly both in Africa and elsewhere, but the rate of absorption by the consuming countries, despite their steadily rising affluence, has been less than the growth rate of their economies. The demand for these and other tropical commodities by centrally planned economies has lagged considerably behind their rates of growth and of total consumption, in spite of these countries' declaration of intention to step up their demand for these commodities. A popular explanation of the centrally planned economies' low intake of tropical commodities is that their consumers have not yet developed a taste for these unfamiliar goods.

World demand for other African export

Table 3—Trade Indices of Selected African Countries

		1958	1959	1960	1961	1962	1963
Sudan	Volume of Exports	100	—	133	137	172	183
	Price of exports	100	—	110	105	105	99
	Volume of imports	100	—	102	144	156	161
	Price of imports	100	—	104	96	97	104
UAR	Volume of exports (cotton menafi)	100	131	162	128	114	158
	Price of exports	100	89	92	92	85	97
	Volume of imports	—	—	—	—	—	—
	Price of imports	—	—	—	—	—	—
Tunisia	Volume of exports	100	108	94	85	87	—
	Price of exports (phosphates)	100	113	110	109	109	—
	Volume of imports	100	110	136	151	163	—
	Price of imports	100	106	111	110	111	119
Morocco	Volume of exports	100	106	112	103	106	—
	Price of exports	100	94	111	114	113	118
	Volume of imports	100	85	102	108	106	—
	Price of imports	100	102	114	119	117	119
Ghana	Volume of exports	100	120	141	176	185	175
	Price of exports	100	91	78	62	58	59
	Volume of imports	100	133	153	164	137	156
	Price of imports	100	100	100	102	102	99
Nigeria	Volume of exports	100	120	118	140	149	154
	Price of exports	100	105	106	99	94	96
	Volume of imports	100	109	123	129	121	121
	Price of imports	100	98	103	103	105	109
Zambia Rhodesia Malawi	Volume of exports	—	135.1	145.5	151.5	156.3	—
	Price of exports	—	93.7	95.2	91.4	89.6	—
	Volume of imports	—	113.3	115.8	110.5	102.1	—
	Price of imports (1954 = 100)	—	105.4	107.8	111.6	111.4	—
Tanzania Kenya Uganda	Volume of exports	148	157	173	165	170	—
	Price of exports	81	79	78	77	76	—
	Volume of imports	103	102	108	117	117	—
	Price of imports (1954 = 100)	101	101	105	99	97	—
Ethiopia	Volume of exports	96	98	122	123	118	—
	Price of Exports	116	113	110.5	99.5	100	—
	Volume of imports	118	119.5	127	128.5	140	—
	Price of imports (1952/53 = 100)	120	126	121	129	133	—

Source: International Monetary Fund, *International Financial Statistics* supplemented by national publications.

commodities, notably cotton, has not only failed to expand, but has actually fallen, due to changes in tastes and to the development of synthetic substitutes in industrialized countries. Add to this that most of the cotton-producing countries have expanded their output. The consequence of all these developments is the marked downward trend in the prices of this commodity, which, like cocoa and coffee, is the mainstay of several African economies. Thus, one of the principal reasons for recent trade imbalances has been the depressed prices of cocoa for Ghana and Nigeria, coffee for Ethiopia, and of cotton for Sudan and UAR.

Cocoa, coffee and cotton are also the major export commodities, and constitute the backbone of the economies of several Franc Zone African countries, some of which have suffered the same problem; for instance, Cameroon with cocoa, Ivory Coast and Madagascar with coffee, and Chad and Central African Republic with cotton. Generally, however, the decline in export prices has been less steep for these countries, owing to price stabilization and subsidization measures which these countries have enjoyed within the framework of Franc Zone managed trading arrangements. As provided in the Convention of Association with the European Economic Community (EEC), France has, however, undertaken to liquidate the system of preferential commodity contracts.

Inflation-induced increases in costs of production have hindered the marketing of some African export commodities, especially manufactured and semifinished goods. The labour force employed in the production of the latter commodities is generally far more well organized than the labour force engaged in primary production, and union pressures have kept the wage level in close pursuit of the rising cost of living. General inflation and an overvalued currency in Franc Zone countries have rendered incompetitive even their primary agricultural products in markets outside the Franc Zone.[6]

Apart from inflationary pressures, the prices of Africa's manufactured and semifinished goods have not been competitive, owing to the low level of productivity. Failure to realize economies of scale, poorly trained manpower, inability to apply modern techniques due to either or both of the last two problems or to lack of capital, and the general waste of productive resources, including repeated loss of man-hours as a result of political and social unrest, are some of the important factors responsible for the low level of physical productivity. In monetary terms this has amounted to higher costs of production compared with other, especially extracontinental producers. The cost–price disadvantage has contributed a significant factor hindering the development of intra-African trade in manufacture and has, in fact, been responsible to a considerable extent for the development of chronic imbalances in some intra-African trade relationships, further aggravating payments difficulties.[7]

Export earnings of many African countries have fluctuated both with world demand, as a result of fluctuations in business activities in industrialized countries, and with supply conditions dictated by nature. Sizable trade deficits have been incurred during the downswing of these fluctuations. Deficits resulting from fluctuations are generally considered as temporary phenomena, and hence of no serious consequences. Nevertheless, considerable complications may build up and have in fact done so, in the wake of this type of imbalance. In the case of demand, the real cause has been in certain instances an actual shift rather than what apparently seemed to be reversible fluctuations. Supply failures, in addition to reducing current export earnings, have resulted in heavy drawing on reserves, impairing future financing of imports and threatening general financial stability. When supply failures extended beyond export commodities to other food crops, the problem was further complicated, as in such event imports would rise rather than fall as a result of increased importation of goods hitherto produced locally.

Imports of the overwhelming majority of African countries have registered substantial increases over the last decade both in value and volume. In exception to this, Algeria's imports dropped from $1,265 million in 1960, to $809 in 1962 and again to $780 million in 1964; imports of Congo (Kinshasa) stood at $284 and $347 million in 1962 and 1964, respectively, against $363 and $436 million in 1953 and 1957, respectively; and Madagascar's imports in the early 1960's have been more or less of the same value as they were in 1953. Liberation war in Algeria and the political crisis attending and consequent to Congo's independence, as well as the postindependence exodus of some one million French settlers from the former and of several hundred thousands of European settlers from the latter are the main reasons for the import contraction in these two countries.

The rising level of consumption throughout the continent, in fulfilment of the desire for better living and consequent to the rising level of money incomes of a growing proportion of Africa's population, has been met in part through increased importation of goods. Imports of consumer goods have increased in most countries at a high rate: in fact, the rate of growth of consumer goods imports in several countries has been higher than the growth rate of their national income, signifying that demand for imported consumer goods is elastic with respect to income. Notable exceptions in this regard include UAR, the former Federation of Rhodesia and Nyasaland, and to some extent Senegal, where import-substituting industries have already had effective results. For other countries such as Morocco, Tunisia, Ghana and Nigeria, whose imports of consumer goods have declined over the last three or so years, import substitution played a less significant part compared to the effect of direct restrictions necessitated by balance of payments problems. In Algeria, Congo (Kinshasa) and Madagascar, imports of consumer goods have followed the same trend as that of total imports.

Increased government consumption is another factor behind the rising trend of consumer goods imports. The expanded programmes of social services and amenities, particularly in the postindependence period, have called for an ever-growing expenditure on hospital furnishings, school supplies, office equipment, etc., most of which have so far to be imported.

Institutional inducement to increased importation of consumer goods, especially the durable ones, has been provided by the widely spreading hire purchase and installment payments facilities, which have made it possible to acquire, against future income, goods yielding immediate satisfaction.

In most countries, however, the growth of consumer goods imports has been less proportionate to that of total imports. This is explained by the greater expansion in imports of capital and intermediate production goods. Total imports increased by 90 per cent, between 1950 and 1960, while over the same period imports of consumer goods increased by only 41 per cent. Capital goods imports, on the other hand, increased by 204 per cent, while the corresponding increase in imports of intermediate production goods was 200. As a result of these variant rates of growth, the latter two categories of imports have accounted for a rapidly growing share in Africa's total imports. Their share increased from 30 per cent in 1950 to about 49 per cent in 1960, with capital goods' share rising from 13 to 21 per cent, and that of intermediate goods growing from 17 to 28 per cent.[8] Although data is not available on changes since 1960 in the structure of imports of the totality of African countries, yet it is clear that the 1950–1960 trend has continued in the same direction as indicated by developments in many individual countries.

Within the capital goods category, imports of machinery increased much faster (about 600 per cent increase) than imports of transport equipment (76 per cent increase), signifying the greater emphasis laid on investment in production compared to investment in infrastructure. Imports of chemicals and of metals have increased much faster than imports of the other two categories of intermediate production goods, namely fuel and basic materials. The percentage increases over the period 1950 to 1960 was 339 for chemicals, 261 for metals, 147 for fuel and 79 for basic materials. An increasing amount of Africa's needs of fuel and basic materials is being met by local production, while chemicals and metals continue to be obtained mainly from foreign sources, partly because of Africa's low level of industrial development and its poor scientific and technical know-how, which have barred the processing of available ores.[9]

Country-wise, the same general trends of changes in the structure of imports have prevailed and are more pronounced in those countries where industrial development has made greater strides than others, such as UAR, Ghana and Tunisia.

The main reason for the phenomenal rise in imports of capital goods and other intermediate production goods is the deliberate, and in some cases ambitious, effort to speed up industrial growth in most African countries. Industrialization is generally accepted by these countries to be the key to the self-sustained growth of their economies, the only situation in which fulfilment of their great aspirations for an ever-rising standard of living can be attained. The various development plans in the course of implementation in Africa bear evidence to this. The execution of industrial projects involves the utilization of resources which are for the most part unavailable locally and have thus to be imported, such as machinery, machine tools, fuel, chemical ingredients, essential raw materials and transport and other equipment. Not only have the imports of these categories of goods increased over the last decade, but as the development plans and other projections indicate, they will continue to expand as rapidly and perhaps even more rapidly than they have done over recent years.

In contrast to export prices, the index of import prices (unit values) has maintained its level over the last decade. Import prices have actually tended to rise. For all developing countries as a whole, available information indicates that the index has fallen by 3 percentage points between 1958 and 1962, and by the fourth quarter of 1964 and the first quarter of 1965, the index has climbed back to the 1958 level, the latter being 10 points higher than the 1950 level. The index for the developing countries does not seem to reflect the trend in Africa, for as Table 3 indicates, the index of import prices for many countries has risen by 5 or more percentage points between 1958 and 1964. By 1964 the rise in the price of imports into Morocco and

Tunisia was 33 and 32 per cent, respectively, and in the latter the index stood at 155 per cent in June of 1965.

Although no systematic information on import prices into Francophone tropical Africa is available, it can be established, by comparing unit value of imports of more or less similar goods, that on the whole, imports costs have been higher in these countries compared to other African countries. In addition to comparatively higher import prices, the commitment of these countries to import sizable quotas exclusively from France is not conducive to minimizing the over-all cost of their imports.[10] It has neutralized the favourable export prices they have managed to obtain under Franc Zone preferential commodity contracts.

INVISIBLE TRADE

With very few exceptions (UAR, Libya, and Tunisia) African countries have sustained sizable and often growing deficits in their invisible transactions (Table 4). Deficits are incurred on practically all of the principal classes of services comprising the major components of the invisibles account, i.e., freight, merchandise insurance, investment income and foreign travel.

Africa's invisible trade has accounted in recent years for between one fourth to one third of the continent's total visible trade. Receipts from transactions in services were a little less than one fifth of merchandise exports, while payments for invisibles amounted to over one third of merchandise imports. These proportions vary considerably among the individual countries.

On a world basis, there has been a tendency for invisibles to grow relative to visible trade.[11] Although present evidence does not substantiate this as regards Africa, there are, however, some other equally important tendencies that can be clearly observed. First, as is true with the rest of the developing countries, the invisibles account of most African countries shows a sizable deficit, for example, the total deficit of eight countries amounted to over $50 million in 1963.

Secondly, there has been a marked tendency for this deficit to grow. The total deficit of the seven countries increased from $48 million in 1958 to $449 million in 1963. Furthermore, it has absorbed a growing proportion of export earnings; 24 per cent in 1963 compared with 3 per cent in 1958.

A continuing deficit in their invisible trade, regardless of its absolute magnitude, represents undoubtedly a constant drain on the export proceeds of the African countries, which means, in turn, a lower real income and a reduced capacity to import. Hence, a growing deficit is tantamount to a progressive reduction in the potentially attainable level of both real income and importing capacity.

The problem of the deficit on invisibles account should be viewed in the context of the balance of payments as a whole, for as far as the developing countries are concerned, it only reflects the weak structure and the limited growth of their economies, and stems from traditional dependence of these countries on the international finance and service institutions of the highly developed countries. This is particularly evident in the

structure of the investment income component; indeed, the latter is a good index of the structures of the whole invisible account. But to follow the roots of the problems as reflected in the investment income component, it is inevitable to go beyond the invisibles account. An examination of the magnitude and implications of income transfers, even in the balance of payments context, would be incomplete without a search into the wider field of capital formation—including both the flow of foreign financial resources and the development of domestic savings. It is in essence a study of both the capital requirements of development programmes and the cost of financing these requirements from the various sources.

Interest and dividend payments on foreign private investment represent the largest component of the deficit in the invisibles account of African countries, "Investment Income" being the largest component of the account. Like the rest of the developing areas where the rate of domestic savings is low, African countries have sought investment funds in foreign high-saving countries. The reverse flow of interest and dividend payments have accounted for almost one half of the total services deficit sustained by African countries in recent years.

Table 4—Balance of Invisible Transactions (Services) of Selected African Countries
(In millions of US $)

	1958	1959	1960	1961	1962	1963
Sudan	−10.6	−14.4	−13.2	−17.5	−40.2	−39.9
UAR	+90.7	+75.2	+88.1	+63.1	+90.1	+119.4
Libya	+75.0	+87.5	+139.0	+112.3	+58.3	+103.8
Tunisia	+69.5	+33.4	+7.2	+21.6	+14.7	−9.9
Algeria	−129.9	−145.8	−381.6	−953.3	−1,557.5	—
Morocco	+89.4	+79.2	+41.2	−1.8	−11.1	−16.2
BCEAO	−118.8	−153.0	−186.8	−149.9	−127.0	—
Ghana	—	−45.1	−51.2	−88.5	−72.5	−78.6
Nigeria	−21.8	−42.6	−50.7	−40.9	−42.0	−57.4
Congo (Kinshasa)	−254.8	−277.2	—	181.8	−163.2	—
BCEAEC	−30.1	−48.7	−36.9	−74.4	−63.4	—
Cameroon	−30.8	+22.9	−48.7	−36.0	−38.4	—
Zambia ⎫ Rhodesia ⎬ Malawi ⎭	−139.4	−170.5	−188.5	−206.9	−220.9	−227.9
Tanzania ⎫ Kenya ⎬ Uganda ⎭	−47.5	−38.0	−33.5	−28.0	−35.1	−38.0
Somalia	—	—	—	−4.6	−12.3	−7.3
Ethiopia	—	−18.6	−11.8	−16.2	−21.1	−20.5
Madagascar	−34.5	−15.9	−22.5	−22.1	−21.1	—

Source: Same as Table 2.

For several African countries, the net balance on account of "Other Investment Income"—which covers mainly the various earnings on and payments for portfolio investments including exchange reserves and international loans—has been positive over the last five years. This balance has, however, tended to diminish and, in some cases, it has turned passive. This deterioration reflects two developments; one, the steady fall in earnings on investment of their international reserves as the latter tended to decrease, and two, the growing size of interest payments in connexion with the servicing of external debt.

External debt has been rising rapidly, and will continue to rise as rapidly, or even more, if the growth target as set out in the various development plans already under way in the continent are to be reached. The rate of increase of service payments has been twice that of the growth of debt, implying deterioration in the terms of borrowing which can be traced to two factors; the increase in the average level of the interest rates charged on loans and the tendency towards more shorter maturities.

According to calculations by the International Bank for Reconstruction and Development (IBRD), the cause of deterioration would be the growing proportion of medium and short maturities, while interest rates moved in the opposite direction. The average maturity is found to have been slightly more than 8 years, while the average weighted rate of interest amounted to about 4 per cent.[12] On the other hand, studies by the Organization for Economic Co-operation and Development (OECD) indicate that the cause of deterioration is high interest rates rather than short maturities. Interest rates of 5 per cent and more have been charged on 71 per cent of official loans extended by OECD, while the proportion of loans with a repayment period of 10 years and more has been in the neighbourhood of 70 per cent of total loans.[13]

Both IBRD and OECD calculations refer to all developing countries, and the findings are consequently influenced by trends in other areas. The interest component of debt service in all developing areas except Africa represented initially 1956, a smaller propor-

tion of the total than that accounted for by amortization—the proportion ranged from 15 per cent (Southern Europe), to 25 per cent (South Asia and the Middle East). For Africa this was as high as 74 per cent. Although the share of interest grew gradually in all other developing areas, still it accounted in 1963 for no more than 30 per cent for South Asia and the Middle East, and barely 20 per cent for Southern Europe; in Africa, interest charges accounted for 54 per cent of the total in 1963 and 61 per cent in the preceding year.

With the share of amortization growing from 26 per cent in 1956 to 46 per cent in 1963, it can be concluded that deterioration in the terms of borrowing by African countries is due to the tendency towards shorter maturities. Interest charges, though considerably diminished in proportion to total service, have nevertheless grown at a higher rate than outstanding debt, and it may thus be concluded that interest rates charged on loans to Africa, which were probably on the high side initially, have not been effectively reduced.

Another piece of evidence on the increase in the relative share of short-term credit in total indebtedness is provided by the steady growth, over the last decade, of the immediate repayments requirements relative to total outstanding debt. The pattern of development of the annual service charges on medium- and long-term external debt, contracted by seven African countries, as percentage of outstanding debts is as follows:[14]

1956	1957	1958	1959	1960
4.23	4.75	4.95	5.10	5.14

1961	1962	1963	1964
5.79	7.24	7.95	5.99

It is the inability to obtain the needed long-term credit that has induced resort to short- and medium-term borrowing to finance development programmes. This was either because the funds were not available on terms and conditions acceptable to both contracting parties, or because the pre-investment studies and surveys, such as project formulation and feasibility studies, were not adequately carried out. However, foreign investors cannot very well continue to advance the latter factor as an excuse for withholding long-term financing, as current development plans of many African countries give sufficient elaboration of the programmes and projects envisaged. Whatever the reason may have been, foreign suppliers have continued to make the needed equipment available on short-term credits, which are partly guaranteed by their own governments.

It is easy to draw an approximate line of demarcation between what is short and medium maturity and what is genuinely long maturity—thus 15 years may be taken as an average for long-term borrowing. Where the line should be drawn between high and low interest rates is a difficult matter; in particular, is there any unique average minimum rate. According to IBRD studies, 6 per cent is a fairly representative rate of conventional lending. Is the conventional rate high or low? Or indeed, is there a unique low rate other than zero? It is obviously a relative matter. The point at which interest rates begin to represent a high charge on the resources of a country would naturally depend on several factors, most important of which is the level of productivity in general, and in particular, the marginal returns to capital in the industries in which loan funds are invested. However, an indication that the rate of conventional lending of 6 per cent is a high one has been given by the United Nations Conference on Trade and Development (UNCTAD), which has recommended that "The interest rate on State loans should not normally exceed 3 per cent annually, and steps should be taken to ensure that loans to developing countries by international organizations are granted on favourable terms," [Recommendation I, E/CONF.46/141, Vol. 1. (Annex A.IV.3)].

Credit entries under the item "Direct Investment Income" cover all earnings accruing to African residents from direct private investment abroad, while debit entries cover all earnings accruing to nonresidents from their investments in Africa. In most cases there has been no credit entry under this item, as direct investment by Africans in foreign countries is practically nonexistent. The net balance on this account has therefore been practically always passive for all countries.

Information on foreign direct investment in Africa and, especially, on its distribution by sector is inadequate. From whatever scanty information and statistical data that are available, private direct investment emerges as an important component of the total flow of foreign financial resources into the continent. In fact, the present rate of net private lending and investment has far exceeded that of official net lending.

Although part of the flow goes into manufacturing industries producing import substitutes, primary export industries such as mining as well as the trade and services sector continue to attract the bulk of the investments. While a substantial part of the growing profits from investments in manufacturing industries is reinvested in productive assets, thereby enhancing the economies' productive capacity: the part which is not reinvested flows out in a rather uninterrupted manner. The outflow of profits from direct investment in manufacturing industries is therefore similar to that of debt service payments. Though not contractually fixed, it involves the same element of rigidity and its impact on the balance of payments and the state of liquidity. On the other hand, returns on investments in industries producing primary products for exports are not as high and therefore do not contribute to expanding the productive base of the economies through reinvestments. They, however, represent a lesser burden on the balance of payments and liquidity, because of their more flexible manner of outflow, profits fluctuating *pari passu* with export sales.

The return flow of profits from mining activities should not, however, be underestimated. Generally speaking, income transfers are especially large in countries where extractive industries represent a significant sector of economic activites, e.g., Libya, Algeria, Liberia, Congo (Kinshasa) and

Zambia. Mining concerns in these countries rest mainly on foreign investments, including both physical capital as well as the highly skilled and highly paid portion of the manpower employed in these massive businesses. It is thus the degree of foreign domination in the economy that determines the over-all size of the outflow of income transfers. Foreign elements are not limited, however, to investment in extractive industries. Plantation agriculture as well as export–import trade are other important areas. Hence the heavy flow out of Franc Zone tropical Africa.

It would be more advantageous for the balance of payments situation as well as for the efficiency of resource allocation to divert resources into manufacturing, drawing away from the trade and services sector, but also from mining. Although evidence is lacking, it seems that a larger part of the return flow of profits from mining activities in Africa can be ploughed back than is presently done.

To sum up the foregoing account: first, a continuing and increasing inflow of financial resources, both official and private, is a necessity for the desired accelerated development of the African economies. Secondly, an outflow in foreign exchange, of regular payments to service the hard-loan portion of official capital and a fluctuating—though still sizable on the average—outflow of profits from private investment are inevitable. Furthermore, these outflows will not be offset by inflows of service payments or private investment profits, hence a persisting deficit. Thirdly, the reduction of the deficit, eventually its elimination, cannot therefore be effected through immediate and drastic reduction of the inflow of financial resources; it has to come through other avenues, and it has to be considered in essentially the long-term context. Measures aimed at reducing the deficit incurred on debt servicing and private investment transfers fall into two main categories, (1) improving the terms of borrowing and (2) improving the efficiency of productive resources in the economy, including imported capital. A third possibility is, of course, to induce foreign investors to plough back a larger portion of their earnings in productive investments in the receiving country. This has a two-fold benefit; one, it directly reduces outpayments and, hence, the

deficit, and two, it contributes to improving the efficiency of productive assets.

Second to the one on investment income is the deficit on account of freight and merchandise insurance. Payments by African countries for freight and merchandise insurance have tended to be well in excess of their receipts (three times as much), because of institutional as well as economic limitations. Shipping and insurance represent some of the traditional and well-established industries in the highly developed countries, whereas, in industrially and commercially less developed countries, such as the African, financial and institutional factors have limited the development of these industries, necessitating dependence on industrialized countries.

Payments for freight and insurance together represent about one-tenth of the value of imports, but they are increasing both in absolute value as well as in relation to the value of the cargo. Similar to developments in other areas of invisible trade, both the volume of services as well as the upward movement of prices are accountable for the increase. Expansion in the volume of shipments is responsible for the general upward trend of payments, while the constantly rising freight rates have in addition, accounted in part for the increase in their relative value. Furthermore, the developing countries, including African, have been charged discriminatory high rates, allegedly to offset costs of the idle time of ships imposed by poor port facilities in these countries.

Another factor behind this deterioration stems from the general problem of marketing primary products. Although freight and insurance charges are normally paid by the importer, it is basically a matter of bargaining power, and African countries are likely to have been obliged in certain bargains to incur freight and insurance on their exports, indirectly by reducing the f.o.b. price so as to maintain the volume of sales. Although the effects of such bargains may not appear in the invisibles account in terms of additional payments, they represent, however, a further deterioration in the over-all current transactions account, as a result of loss of potential export earnings.

Foreign travel is another major deficit component in the invisibles account of African countries, with total receipts running at less than 50 per cent of total payments and the deficit of eight countries amounting to about $83 million in 1963—equivalent to 19 per cent of the over-all invisibles deficit. The bulk of payments and receipts is made on account of tourism, although the share of travel and maintenance expenses of government officials and students is not an insignificant one. Due to the total number of visitors and to the cost level both being higher in the case of Africans abroad, not only is total expenditure by Africans abroad greater than total expenditure by foreign tourists in Africa, but the continent's earnings from the tourist industry are also reduced by the outflow of various remittances. The tourist industry in Africa still rests to a considerable extent on foreign investments and expatriate managerial skills, judging by the ownership of hotels, airlines, travel agencies, tourist organizations, etc.

Another associated deficit arises in the services grouped under Balance of Payments item "Other Transportation." Most of these services such as handling, harbour anchorage, pilotage, towage, aircraft landing, provision of ships stores and bunker, etc., tend to yield a positive balance for African countries. They, however, are more than offset by the deficit on account of passenger fares, which, like in the case of ocean shipping, stems from Africa's dependence on foreign-owned carriers.

Certain other invisible transactions, including transfers of earnings of foreign migrant labour and of premiums paid on non-merchandise insurance have contributed a growing share of the total deficit. These services are grouped under Balance of Payments item "Other Services" and sometimes referred to as "Miscellaneous Transactions." The item, however, covers also all unallocated receipts and disbursements, and there have been certain erratic entries such as the inclusion of earnings accruing to the country from financial investments abroad and even merchandise insurance. Consequently, the item probably conceals some illicit capital flight operations.

Government transactions have shown a balanced pattern of payments and receipts, and for several countries receipts have exceeded payments by substantial margins. So far, it is the only surplus component of the invisibles account. In a few countries, local expenditure by foreign troops and related military personnel have contributed large earnings of foreign exchange. However, this is obviously a source which is likely to be dispensed with as recent political developments have clearly indicated. On the other hand, the trend of government expenditure abroad in the postindependence period is clearly for more spending—the number and size of African diplomatic missions in foreign countries bear evidence to this. The surplus has already shrunk, and the main reason has been the steady rise in government spending abroad. Although for certain countries such as Tunisia, government spending abroad decreased, this has been more than offset by the sharp fall in local expenditure by foreign governments resulting from the withdrawal of foreign troops.

Relatively more space is devoted in this study to the investigation of invisible transactions than is usually done in a study on balance of payments problems. The reason is simple. Invisibles have contributed a larger share in the overall balance of payments deficit of Africa than visible trade. In 1961, the invisibles deficit of some African countries was 43 per cent more than their visible trade deficit, while in 1963 it was more than 13 times as much. (Compare Table 2 and Table 4.)

The effects of the invisible trade balances for all countries on which data is available are shown in Table 5, which gives the combined balance of goods and services. All countries, including those whose visible trade balances are active, emerge with persisting deficits which are large and, in several cases, are growing rapidly. While payments for freight and merchandise insurance vary directly with the volume of imports, payments on account of investment income and

Table 5—Balance of Goods and Services and (in parenthesis) of Current Account of Selected African Countries

	1958	1959	1960	1961	1962	1963
Sudan (current account)	(−36.8)	(+40.2)	(−7.2)	(−64.9)	(−60.3)	(−75.5)
UAR	−60.6 (−60.3)	−135.2 (−121.4)	−99.3 (86.7)	−187.7 (−164.4)	−337.5 (−346.7)	−282.7 (−282.7)
Libya	−9.4 (+15.3)	−22.7 (+14.9)	−27.5 (+8.1)	−18.5 (+5.8)	−7.2 (+13.2)	−7.0 (+8.3)
Tunisia	+68.3 (+88.5)	+16.5 (+48.9)	−61.4 (−16.3)	−79.1 (−31.8)	−99.9 (−67.3)	−106.7 (−76.8)
Algeria	−679.7 (−713.6)	−886.3 (−932.2)	−1,087.8 (−1,144.0)	−2,407.1 (−2,436.0)	−1,399.2 (−1,446.9)	—
Morocco	+77.9 (+90.7)	+106.9 (+113.6)	+34.9 (+42.9)	−91.5 (−73.7)	−61.7 (−78.7)	−84.0 (−72.1)
BCEAO	−211.9 (−224.7)	−256.5 (−209.8)	−235.4 (−229.7)	−233.1 (−179.9)	−205.8 (−130.4)	—
Ghana	—	−28.6 (−31.6)	−70.8 (−74.5)	−132.2 (−147.6)	−63.0 (−79.2)	−108.6 (−128.2)
Nigeria	−116.8 (−114.8)	−93.2 (−98.0)	−192.1 (−194.3)	−190.7 (−203.0)	−136.1 (−117.6)	−92.4 (−84.6)
Congo (Kinshasa)	−83.3 (−111.5)	−5.8 (−66.1)	—	−71.5 (−54.0)	−38.4 (+33.1)	—
BCEAEC	−62.0 (−75.5)	−73.4 (−69.5)	−86.2 (−79.0)	−115.7 (−93.4)	−94.0 (−64.6)	—
Cameroon	−18.4 (−12.5)	−7.8 (−15.4)	−33.2 (−15.7)	−29.9 (−19.7)	−20.0 (−18.4)	—
Zambia, Rhodesia, Malawi (current account)	(−174.1)	(−42.0)	(−17.1)	(−30.8)	(−13.4)	(+40.3)
Tanzania, Kenya, Uganda	−47.5 (−47.5)	−38.0 (−37.9)	−33.5 (−32.8)	−28.0 (+24.6)	−35.1 (+21.0)	+38.0 (+76.8)
Somalia	—	—	—	−13.7	−28.8 (−3.4)	−22.8 (−5.6)
Ethiopia	—	−23.7 (−12.1)	−10.8 (−5.0)	−19.9 (−12.6)	−26.6 (−16.2)	−27.9 (−23.0)
Madagascar	−52.7 (−52.5)	−58.9 (−63.4)	−59.6 (−59.9)	−45.5 (−39.3)	−44.1 (−35.8)	—

Source: Same as Table 2.

foreign travel vary directly with the rate of investment and money incomes, respectively. All three independent variables have been increasing.

Due to institutional and economic limitations alluded to earlier, necessitating Africa's dependence on the service institutions of foreign countries, and the fact that demand for most of these services is relatively more inelastic compared to demand for physical commodities, it is not possible to subject services to direct controls and restrictions the same way visible imports are. The results are not comparable. Thus, even when the deficit on visible trade has been reduced, the invisibles deficit continue to mount.

On the other hand, it is generally more manageable to achieve a structural improvement in the invisibles balance (except for investment income) than it is with the visible trade balance, through reorientation of economic policy and investment priorities, without impairing at the same time the process of economic growth. It should be noted, however, that most measures which might be taken by African countries to improve their balance of payments on invisibles, particularly in the fields of shipping, insurance and tourist facilities, will require additional capital outlays, and probably also the employment of foreign personnel including experts. This should be expected with certainty in the short-run to entail a further strain on the balance of payments. One way of reducing the costs as well as spreading the benefits of such industries and facilities is to have them set up on a multinational basis.

TRANSFER PAYMENTS

One more element of the balance of payments on current accounts consists of transfers, i.e., receipts and payments for which no *quid pro quo* is demanded. As Table 5 shows, the effect of these transfers has resulted in a favorable current account balance in a few instances—Libya, Kenya, Tanzania and Uganda and, in 1962, Congo (Kinshasa). Generally, however, their effect has been to reduce the size of the deficits on goods and

services—Sudan, UAR, Tunisia, Morocco, the BCEAO countries, the BCEAEC countries, Zambia, Rhodesia and Malawi, Somalia, Ethiopia and, in recent years, also Nigeria and Madagascar. In certain cases, transfer payments have further aggravated the severity of the problem—Algeria, Ghana and until recently, Nigeria, Congo (Kinshasa) and Madagascar.

Transfers are made on both private and government accounts. Grants are the main component of transfers on governments' account. By and large, the United States has been the main donor country, extending cash grants through technical assistance programmes and grants in kind through provision of surplus foods. In Franc Zone tropical Africa, France is by far the principal supplier of all types of financial resources. The United Kingdom is another major donor country, though the grants go mainly to African countries of the Sterling Area, notably to Libya and East Africa and, on a smaller scale, to Ghana and Nigeria. Indemnities are far less frequent; they have been of particular significance only in the case of compensation payments to Sudan by UAR in accordance with the Nile Waters Agreement, and the reparations from Italy to Ethiopia. Government transfers have been on the whole a positive element, and have contributed to improving the balance of payments on current account.

Private transfers, on the other hand, have been in general a deficit component contributing to a further deterioration in the balance of payments. The major elements are migrants' transfers and expatriate remittances, the latter component representing an important element of outgoing transfers. Expatriate remittances are always fully covered by the Balance of Payments item "Private Transfers." Due to certain circumstances, expatriates may transmit part of their income without necessarily going through the proper transfer channels. For instance, when exchange controls are strict, expatriates may be tempted to transfer money abroad through devious routes, avoiding exchange control authorities. In general, expatriates appear to have been remitting sizable portions of their incomes, amounting at times to over 40 per cent and generally not less than

10 per cent of total income. In Gabon, for example, the 5,220 expatriates who accounted in 1960 for about 29 per cent of the country's GDP, transferred abroad about 47 per cent of their income. Accounting for fully one-third of the country's GDP, some 10,700 expatriates in Congo (Brazzaville) remitted about 17 per cent of their income. Similarly, about 10 per cent of the GDP of Central African Republic and about 7 per cent of Libya's GDP have leaked out in expatriate remittances. These remittances are not only a drain on foreign exchange earnings, but also a substantial leakage out of domestic savings.

Reducing the Deficit—Commercial, Monetary, and Fiscal Policies

There are several ways of countering a balance of payments deficit. Measures directed to this end can be generally grouped into two main categories: there are those which are aimed at reducing or eliminating a potential deficit in autonomous transactions, and there are others the aim of which is to finance an actual deficit. It goes without saying that the two are not entirely unrelated. However, distinction between the two sets of measures is of particular importance in the context of foreign trade-dependent economies, i.e., in the case of the developing countries of Africa—and other continents—whose economic growth derives its vital stimuli from the external sector. Thus, some of the deficit reducing measures, especially those aimed at the cutting down of import outlays, have the disadvantage of obstructing the process of growth, through their impact on the availability of imported development goods, and by reducing consumption goods they exact a disincentive effect on the human effort that is unfavourable to the general level of economic activities.

QUANTITATIVE RESTRICTIONS

Aggregate imports can be cut down through various measures, which can be generally grouped according to the impact they exert into four main categories of action or policies. All four policies have been adopted in varying combinations by African countries. The most popular and most direct of these measures is that of quantitative restrictions. These are administered through the establishment of global quotas for the various commodities or groups of commodities, setting the limit to the total amount or value of each which can be imported within a specified period of time, usually one year. Individual or bilateral quotas are often established within these global quotas, specifying amounts—usually maximum—that can be imported from individual countries, this being generally the case when trade exchanges are effected through bilateral agreements.

Import licensing is another method of quantitative restrictions. Under it the importer would be unable to clear his goods from Customs without the appropriate import licence, which is to be obtained in advance. The import licence is also a necessary document for obtaining the means of external payments when exchange controls are applied. Import licensing has frequently been instituted as a complementary requirement to the establishment of import quotas or to the application of exchange control, essentially to ensure that quota limits are observed and foreign exchange is being used for the approved purposes. Nevertheless, licensing has been pursued to the exclusion of quotas by several countries.

With the exception of Liberia, all countries in Africa have taken recourse to quantitative restrictions, through quotas or licensing, or both. In many countries, the purpose has been to reduce imports, and generally to plan its structure, in an effort to achieve, maintain or plan balances of payments equilibrium. However, as far as the Franc Zone countries of tropical Africa are concerned, quantitative restrictions are an integral part of their trading system, as imports from all sources other than France are only a residual quota, determined in its totality by the size of France's annual quota (accounting on the average for 75 per cent of their total imports), and for imports from non-Franc Zone sources, by the approval of the French Treasury. As such, quantitative restrictions are predetermined measures, directed more towards consistency with the objectives of France's commercial and financial policies than they are towards alleviating their own problems of trade imbalance. Indeed, these measures have, if anything, operated to perpetuate imbalances, evidence to this is the chronic and growing deficit of most of them *vis-à-vis* France.

Quantitative restrictions have been applied in certain instances to imports from individual sources. The most drastic recent experience of this is Nigeria's decision not to issue licences for any and all categories of imports from Japan. By bringing total imports from any particular source to nil, this measure has far reaching effects, not only in countering a trade deficit, but also on the structure of imports, especially if the source happens to supply a sizable share of total imports. Such is the case of Japan, who in 1963 supplied 13 per cent of Nigeria's total imports. Although more than three-quarters of imports from Japan consisted of consumer goods, they have included, nonetheless, about 4 per cent of Nigeria's total imports of capital and transport equipment; the short-run consequences of their absence on total investment it is not wise to overlook. Nigeria's trade deficit with Japan in 1963 amounted to about $69 million, almost twice the country's over-all trade deficit in the same year. Assuming that Nigeria will also lose her exports to Japan, which amounted to less than $7 million (less than 9 per cent of imports), the long-term effects of shifting purchases to other supplies may prove more advantageous for balance of payments equilibrium, if they result, in addition to reducing the over-all trade deficit, in a large supply of development goods and/or in additional exports into the alternative partners.

EXCHANGE CONTROL

Restrictions on imports are applied also through the rationing of external purchasing power, that is to say, through the imposition of exchange controls. By requiring the surrender of all foreign exchange earnings accruing to residents, the government controls the distribution of the means of external payments, which distribution is effected in accordance with set priorities of import policy. The fundamental objective is to keep imports to the level which it is possible for available means to finance. Generally, the granting of exchange permits is done with the view to cutting down of the nonessentials, especially of consumer goods, in favour of the essentials—capital equipment, intermediate production materials and foodstuffs. Permits for most invisible transactions are granted more readily although, however, another important objective of exchange control is to bar capital flight, and hence, the strict control over personal remittances.

Like the administration of import quotas and licensing, the operation of exchange controls is embedded in a complex machinery of procedures and office routine, involving the Central Bank, which is the top operator and authority being the custodian of foreign currencies, the Ministry of Commerce for verification of the type of goods to be imported, and the commercial banks who are the actual undertakers of the exchange transaction including correspondence with exporters and the direct financing of importation. These are costly and time-consuming operations. Nevertheless, with the single exception of Liberia, exchange control is operative throughout the continent. Not only is it widespread, but it has also grown more intensive over recent years. For instance, several countries have recently applied exchange controls to some members of their currency and trading area, trade with whom had hitherto been free of any restriction, e.g., Morocco and Tunisia in the Franc Zone, and Ghana and Kenya in the Sterling Area. Another example is the growing limitation on the amount of money individuals are allowed to transfer abroad.

Intensification of exchange controls is tantamount to increasing the degree of inconvertibility of the currency in question, which in turn perpetuates payments difficulties. The proliferation of exchange controls as well as of quantitative restrictions in Africa has, furthermore, encouraged and led to the wide usage of bilateral trade and payments agreements. More than three hundred such agreements have been concluded over the last ten years. The major part of the trade of several countries has been conducted through bilateral agreements. Although, on the whole, the utilization of bilateral agreements by African countries has helped in expanding their trade by opening new channels, bilateralism has brought new problems, most aggravating of which to Africa's trade and payments difficulties is the accumulation of inconvertible claims on bilateral partners.

IMPORT DUTIES

Another method of reducing the quantity of imports operates indirectly through raising the price of foreign goods by means of import duties. There is not one country in Africa that does not tax imports. All countries derive the major part of their fiscal receipts from this source. But in recent years, more countries have resorted to the manipulation of the customs tariff for restricting the flow of imports in order to redress trade imbalances. In addition to being indirect in their impact, import duties are also selective. They have generally been geared to reducing consumer goods imports by increasing their cost to the final consumer, while in order not to impede the flow of capital and intermediate production goods, relatively low rates of duties have been levied on them, and certain raw materials have been allowed free-duty entry.

Not only has the policy of high import duties been pursued as a measure of protection for domestic infant industries, but its success is in fact dependent on the availability and quality of domestic substitutes. In the absence of the latter conditions, import duties are bound to generate inflationary pressures without accomplishing the desired attenuation of the problem of trade imbalance. Moreover, these inflationary pressures, once transmitted to other sectors, especially the ones producing export commodities, can also jeopardize the country's competitiveness in export markets.

Not only have there been some instances

of failure of substitutes to bridge the duty-created gap, as is true of most Anglophone countries, but import duties have also been occasionally imposed or raised without provision for increasing local substitutes production—as in most of the Franc Zone countries as well as Ethiopia, where budgetary and internal balance objectives have been given over-riding consideration over those of external equilibrium.

CURRENCY DEVALUATION

Devaluation of currency is another method of raising the cost of imports, but in two respects it is different from import duties. First of all it is not selective except in the infrequent case of multiple exchange rates. Secondly, devaluation has dual direct effect; while raising the cost of imports, it simultaneously renders domestic exports cheaper, whereas the effect of import duties on exports is indirect through inflationary pressures and furthermore the result is more expensive exports.

The success of devaluation depends primarily on the elasticity of demand—foreign and domestic—and on the supply elasticity of export commodities. When the elasticity of domestic demand for imports is small, i.e., when demand is insensitive to changes in prices—such as Africa's demand especially for capital and intermediate production goods and for essential foodstuffs—devaluation would not only fail to reduce the quantity of imports sufficiently, but would also increase the total foreign exchange cost of imports.

If in addition, foreign demand for domestic goods is inelastic, such as in the case of most of Africa's agricultural export commodities, the lowering of export prices may not be compensated by a larger volume of sales; total foreign exchange earnings may thus be decreased rather than increased. The balance of payments implications of this are obvious —a larger deficit than before devaluation. Apart from commodity exports and imports,

devaluation invariably increases total payments for invisibles, except perhaps if provision is made that foreigners pay in foreign
currency for the services rendered, as for
instance, in UAR's Suez Canal arrangement.

Even if foreign demand is responsive to
price changes, export sales and earnings may
still fail to expand if the supply of export
commodities happens to be inflexible. Full
employment is the main reason for supply
inflexibility in the highly developed countries.
In Africa, the prevalence of inflexibilities is
dictated by the limited area of cultivable land,
seasonal limitations and crop rotation considerations as far as agricultural products are
concerned, and for these and other commodities, limitations on supply responsiveness
and mobility of resources have been set by
financial and technological bottlenecks, such
as the chronic shortage of investible funds
and skilled manpower as well as the inadequacy of existing techniques of production
to cope with rapid expansion.

Whatever its effects on exports might be,
devaluation is most unlikely to bring about
a significant reduction in import outlays for
African countries, and may possibly lead to
an increase in the total cost of imports. In
fact, this has been true of recent devaluations
in the continent, e.g., Morocco and Congo
(Kinshasa).

Generally, devaluation is most warranted
if the currency in question has already
appeared to be overvalued, such as in the
case of inflation, or if a major currency has
been devalued, especially if it happened to
be the currency of a major trading partner
or partners and/or if the currency in question
is linked to the devalued one. So far, all
recent devaluations in Africa seem to have
been warranted according to this criterion—
thus inflation in Congo (Kinshasa) and
Burundi, and adjustment to the French
Franc's devaluation and its impact on other
major trading partners in the Franc Zone by
Morocco and recently by Tunisia. Still,
however, neither has the value of imports
been reduced nor has that of exports been
always significantly increased as a result of
these devaluations.

One more set of measures aims at reducing
imports through the reduction of total
domestic demand or, in other words, the
reduction of total purchasing power. Although generally very little resort has been
made by African countries to effective deflationary policies, there have been some
instances of partial application. For instance,
in the fiscal sphere most, if not all countries,
have increased taxation, both the rate and
the base. This, however, would not be
regarded as a deliberate deflationary measure,
since in the great majority of cases, increased
taxation has been accompanied by increased
government expenditure. What is withdrawn
from private spending streams feeds into the
channels of government expenditure. When
surpluses appeared on annual budgets, they
have been invariably transferred to the
development budget. A major category of
development budget expenditure comprises
imports of capital goods and transport
equipment.

Some monetary restraints have been
occasionally applied, mainly through restriction of bank credit, particularly in
connexion with the financing of imports.
This credit policy has frequently lacked in
effectiveness. For one thing, it has not been
always consistent with other monetary and
fiscal measures, mainly because restrictions
on short-term credit for the financing of
imports have often been imposed over short
periods of time to offset what is essentially
a seasonal trade imbalance. Another source
of weakness has been the failure to secure
full compliance by banks, especially where
expatriate institutions are dominant.

Total purchasing power can be reduced
more directly by withholding part of the
earnings at the source. This procedure can
and has been applied in the situations where
the earnings of large groups of the labor
force—particularly farmers engaged in the
production of major export commodities—
pass through some administrative agency
such as the Marketing Boards in West Africa,
and the Gezira Board in Sudan. Again, the
effect of withholding portions of farmers'
earnings has often been offset by increased

spending, made possible by Boards' loans to the government, either directly or by acquiring government securities and Treasury Bills against payment in foreign exchange to the Central Bank.

Basically, all deflationary measures seem to be incompatible with the commitment to promote economic growth, through the prosecution of a wide range of development programmes, all of which call for increased spending. Deflationary measures could be warranted when designed to curb inflationary pressures. But then, is it possible to have economic growth without some inflation?

EXPORT EXPANSION

Increasing the export earnings is not only a desirable way of reducing the trade and payments deficit, but is in fact the long-term objective of economic policy of all African countries. To this end, each country has adopted one combination or another of price, income, production and marketing policies. The most fundamental, however, is the production policy, which is the essence of the comprehensive development plans, and on which all countries count most. The principal objectives of this policy are two: expansion and diversification, with import substitution as a corollary of both.

As mentioned earlier, export earnings of practically all countries have increased over the last decade and continue to rise. Increase in output of export commodities has been the cause, while export prices moved downward. The problem posed by weak and unstable world demands for the great majority of their export commodities has been fully appreciated by African countries, and a considerable emphasis has been laid on increasing the production of manufactured goods with a hopeful view to exporting them. Only this type of diversification is capable of accelerating the growth of export earnings to an extent comparable to, and possibly more than, the rapid expansion of imports.

PRODUCTION POLICIES

So far, there have been only very few instances of expansion in export earnings that may be considered remarkably substantial. These instances are limited to the mineral-producing countries and especially those where oil or natural gas have been recently produced in big quantities, viz., Libya, Algeria and Nigeria. Many countries have continued to seek expansion of export earnings in the introduction of new but essentially primary products, some of which are in fact major agricultural export commodities of other African countries. This policy has often been erroneously construed as one of diversification capable of speeding the growth of export earnings. The principal advantage of this policy is to guard against sharp fluctuations of earnings, since it is unlikely for world prices of all agricultural export commodities to move in the same direction over the same period, though it is possible. As far as earnings are concerned, more can be obtained from investing the resources in other sectors, especially manufacturing.

Apart from inflationary pressures and low productivity referred to earlier, the expansion of exports of manufactures by African countries has been seriously limited by the many obstacles which especially the developed countries have placed against the entry of these products into their markets. If these obstacles are not removed, and even more, if the developed countries do not accord Africa's exports of manufactures some measure of preferential treatment, the continent's industrial efforts will be fruitful only if greater economic integration is achieved, whereby larger markets are created.

INCOME POLICIES

Increasing importance has been attached to marketing policies. The ineffectiveness of both price and income policies in promoting export growth has been already alluded to in connexion with import policies. Suffice it to say, as far as income policy is concerned, that deflationary measures and, specifically, wage reduction or even freezing will not only be strongly opposed by political pressure groups, especially trade unions, but the effect on cost and prices if any will most likely be negated by diminished productivity as a manifestation of the disincentive which this policy is bound to create.

PRICE POLICIES

Devaluation, as stated earlier, is warranted in special situations, and its success is dependent on certain conditions that are not generally obtaining in the African economies. Moreover, its effects on export earnings have to be weighed against possible unfavorable effects on imports.

Subsidies on exports, especially of manufactured goods, cannot bring about lasting results, and may even prove to be self-defeating in the long run if costs of production continue to be high. The level of costs depends primarily on the level of productivity and has, therefore, to do with the availability of capital and the training of manpower. However, the bearing of productivity on the level of costs can itself be greatly reduced if production fails to expand to a scale permitting the realization of some economies. Hence the dependence of the level of costs on the availability of large markets.

MARKETING POLICIES

Most of the marketing policies and arrangements followed by African countries have been generally geared to expanding export sales. The stability of export earnings has been another important objective. Thus, one of the main functions of the Marketing Boards is to obtain better prices for the country's principal exports through increased bargaining power.[15] In most of the Franc Zone countries in Africa, the fundamental objective of the Price Stabilization Funds (Caisse de Stabilization des Prix) is to stabilize the prices of major export commodities. Bilateral trade and payments agreements adopted in the region have sought, as a primary objective, to expand trade, particularly on the export side. New outlets for exports have been found in the centrally planned economies, and additional connexions established in Western Europe through these agreements. The arrangements have not, however, prevented imports from outrunning exports.

Other countries, notably the Franc Zone members and Somalia have established arrangements with their major trade partners —France, and Italy in the case of Somalia— for the disposal of principal exports on a bilateral commodity contract basis, with the intention of ensuring growth of export sales and stability of prices. Most of the Franc Zone countries as well as Somalia have entered into agreement of association with the European Economic Community for easier access to the growing Common Market. In addition, several Commonwealth African countries have sought some accommodation with the EEC for the same purpose. Nigeria has already reached an agreement. An example of the limitation of this sort of arrangement is the fact, though unofficially reported, that some of Nigeria's principal exports, notably cocoa and palm oil, will not receive preferential treatment in the EEC.

Although some success has been achieved through manipulation of marketing arrangements in maintaining and expanding export sales and earnings in the face of falling, stagnating or otherwise unstable world demands, this has been more or less confined to traditional primary products. As pointed out earlier, world demand for mineral products has continued to grow, and Africa's export proceeds on this score have continued to increase steadily. Only few countries, however, have mineral products to export in big quantity. It is inevitable that exports of manufactures have the greatest potential, and for most countries represent the only way of increasing their export earnings to cope with, and provide for rapid economic growth. It is in this area that marketing arrangements have so far accomplished negligible, if any, positive results. The developed countries have kept their markets outside the reach of manufactured goods from Africa through superiority of local substitutes, or by placing trade barriers, and generally through both. In the developing countries, including in Africa, a combination of low purchasing power and protective duties and other trade barriers has rendered their markets unpromising.

As all the attempts to cut down imports to balance with exports without impairing the process of growth have met with very little success, so have the efforts to increase export earnings. The trade deficit has persisted and has been growing. As development-plans forecasts indicate, African countries realize that the deficit will not disappear very soon. It is, therefore, pertinent to direct attention now to the more realistic approach to countering balance of payments deficits, namely to those measures aimed at financing deficits.

Financing the Deficit—The Capital Account

Drawing on reserves of foreign currencies is obviously the simplest way of financing an external deficit. It is a way, however, that cannot be resorted to indefinitely, for when the deficit persists, the reserves are steadily exhausted. Many African countries have experienced rapid depletion of reserves in recent years. Some, particularly Ghana and Nigeria, have deliberately run down their reserves which had been accumulated in pre-independence periods. The reserves of these two countries had in fact stood at, by every measure, high level, but they have now reached the critical point. In 1959, the reserves of Ghana and Nigeria represented about 200 and 125 per cent of their respective imports, i.e., six and a little less than four times as high as the conventional minimum safe level. The reserves to money supply ratio then stood at about 300 and 200 per cent for the two countries, respectively. Indications are that their reserves' position will deteriorate further past the conventional safe point. Many other countries have already passed that point. The question of reserves' levels will be further considered.

FOREIGN FINANCIAL RESOURCES

As mentioned in connexion with investment income transfers, foreign financial resources are a vital necessity in augmenting national resources and in providing the foreign exchange portion of development outlays. This is explicitly stated in the reports on the financing of development programmes.[16] National resources, including domestic savings and the disposable foreign exchange reserves, are not adequate to meet the financial requirements of these programmes. The question is, therefore, whether the present flow of financial resources is adequate; no doubt it is not, given the planned rates of growth which have to be reached and maintained, and the short-fall of local resources which has to be made good. As Table 6 shows, foreign financial resources have in many instances failed to cover the gap between current receipts and payments. Not only has the inflow of capital been inadequate, but it has been further diminished by the reverse flow of debt service charges and direct investment transfers.

It has become evident, as a result of theoretical studies on the question of external financial resources in relation to economic growth,[17] that the flow of financial resources to developing countries will have to be increased substantially and for a considerable number of years, if these countries are to reach the stage of self-sustained economic growth. Specifically, for a typical developing country, the flow has to increase at an accelerated rate for a period of fifteen years; it would continue to rise for a further ten years, though at a decelerating rate, and only then would the total net flow begin to diminish, returning to zero in the thirty-sixth year. The assumption in the theoretical model as developed by the International Bank for Reconstruction and Development (IBRD) being a zero flow of external resources in the first year.

According to the IBRD model, total debt service payments increase in a manner similar to the increase in the flow of debt. The ratio of total debt service payments to exports rises rapidly from zero, attaining a peak value of more than 50 per cent in the middle years of the debt cycle, and declines thereafter. Depending on a number of variables, the pattern of development of debt service ratio may differ from the model's typical case. For example, an initially higher ratio of exports to national product (a more open economy) and a higher rate of export growth will cause the general level of service ratio, including peak level, to be lower. Regardless of these two variables, a higher rate of domestic savings, particularly an accelerating one, a lower (average) rate of interest on capital inflow and a longer repayment period would result in a lower level of debt service ratio; due to the first, the need for external capital will be less, and to the second and third the size of annual service payments (interest charges and amortization) would be smaller and net resources received greater. What is most crucial is a high rate of marginal savings, i.e., the proportion of the increment in income which is ploughed back as savings. With a higher marginal rate of savings, not only would the borrower's ability to service external debt be enhanced, but it would also be quite likely to simultaneously narrow the savings–investment gap, hence reducing the need for foreign capital.

African countries are in fact different from IBRD's model. For one thing, present indebtedness is substantially above zero. As it has been pointed out earlier, the terms of borrowing have deteriorated, mainly because of the tendency toward shorter maturities while interest rates remained at conventional levels. Of more significance is the fact that the present rate of growth of the inflow of financial resources into Africa is not high enough, and by no means is it one with which the debt cycle can be completed in thirty-six years. Indeed, as revealed by Table 6, the flow of foreign resources has not as yet shown a persistent increase, much less an accelerating rate of growth.

On the other hand, African countries have been able to obtain foreign resources partly in the form of grants and soft loans. Grants carry no service obligation, while soft loans, such as those repayable in the recipient's currencies, do not commit the recipient's foreign exchange earnings. Obtaining resources in this form in a growing proportion relative to total required inflow is one certain way of reducing the magnitude of service payments. The proportion of grants and soft loans to total financial resources which were made available to Africa by OECD member countries and Japan on a bilateral basis rose from 50.8 per cent in 1960 to 55.3 per cent in 1961. As a percentage of total official bilateral flow only, grants and soft loans have not increased over the period 1960 to 1962, remaining at 81, and their value has actually dropped in both dollar and relative terms in 1963, when they represented about 78 per cent of the total.

Total private lending to Africa by OECD dropped by about 5 per cent between 1960 and 1961. Although guaranteed export credits have more than doubled between 1960 and 1961, it is not clear whether total private lending has increased. Net lending and investment, which accounted for 92–24 per cent of the total had in fact dropped by some 3 per cent between 1960 and 1961. Figures on net lending and investment by OECD in 1962 and after are not available, but it appears that the downward trend has continued through 1962 and 1963, at least in some countries. Private long-term capital has fallen off in Nigeria, the former Federation of Rhodesia and Nyasaland and in Sudan, while short-term private capital contracted in Ethiopia, Libya, the former Federation and Tunisia.

It is a characteristic feature of private capital movements to fluctuate frequently and sharply in response to changes in economic conditions and the political atmosphere. The latter changes have at times prompted large-scale outflow of private capital. Changes in the political atmosphere, actual or imminent, are the main cause of capital flight. The factors which have discouraged a larger inflow of long-term private capital into the continent include unfavourable or otherwise nonexistent or incoherent investment laws, lack or absence of industrial concessions, uncertainty about transfer of profits and repatriation of capital arising from the proliferation of exchange restrictions, fear of nationalization, low level of productivity in receiving countries, the inadequacy of supporting services and inefficiency of the infrastructure, and insufficiency of reported economic facts and reliable statistical data about the country.

Despite unfavourable circumstances attending its flow, private capital has far exceeded official bilateral lending, amounting to about three times as much as the latter. It has accounted for a sizable share in the total flow of financial resources, about one-third. The contributions of the various multilateral agencies have so far represented but a small proportion of the total inflow (about 5 per cent), and, therefore, in the immediate future, any significant increase in the flow of external resources has to be borne by the other sources.

DRAWING ON RESERVES OF EXTERNAL CURRENCIES

Total net inflow of financial resources from all sources has so far failed—except in Ethiopia, Madagascar and some other CFA countries—to finance fully the growing

current account deficits. Consequently, most countries have resorted to utilization of foreign exchange reserves. Repeated drawing has brought the reserves of some countries down to 50 per cent or less over the last few years. Although the absolute level of reserves is not of very much importance for balance of payments considerations, particularly for the financing of imports, it nevertheless has a significant bearing on general confidence in the currency and the economy as a whole. Flight from currency, capital flight, currency smuggling and black marketing are some of

Table 6—Net Movements of Capital and (in parenthesis) of External Reserves in Selected African Countries

(in millions of US $)

	1958	1959	1960	1961	1962	1963
Sudan	+23.0	+33.9	+41.9	+50.3	+50.3	+32.4
	(−12.6)	(+73.8)	(+33.0)	(−14.1)	(−8.3)	(−44.5)
UAR	−1.1	+40.2	+48.2	+122.8	+240.8	+215.5
	(−79.2)	(−65.1)	(−55.7)	(−62.0)	(−117.4)	(−67.2)
Libya	−0.6	+1.2	+1.3	−0.1	−6.2	+3.8
	(+10.5)	(+18.2)	(+12.1)	(+7.5)	(+2.8)	(+27.2)
Tunisia	−0.9	−0.7	+18.3	+21.7	+46.8	+53.3
	(+20.4)	(+49.5)	(1.9)	(−15.8)	(−25.7)	(−23.0)
Algeria Public funds	+730.6	+836.1	+987.1	+1,309.4	+1,348.4	—
	(+17.0)	(−96.8)	(−156.8)	(+16.5)	(−107.5)	—
Morocco	+18.8	+30.2	+40.7	+46.2	+41.5	+47.0
	(+23.3)	(+53.9)	(+81.8)	(−44.1)	(−32.8)	(−42.5)
BCEAO Public funds	+160.4	+194.6	+237.8	+231.9	+211.2	—
	(−64.3)	(−15.0)	(+8.1)	(+52.0)	(+80.8)	—
Ghana	−28.5	+9.5	+20.2	−50.7	+78.1	+68.2
	(−2.6)	(−17.9)	(−45.9)	(−209.7)	(−4.5)	(−68.6)
Nigeria	+114.2	+118.4	+164.1	+177.8	+85.1	+81.5
	(+5.0)	(+29.4)	(−33.6)	(+14.8)	(−37.0)	(−30.5)
Congo (Kinshasa)	+94.7	+25.9	—	−3.9	−6.0	—
	(−16.8)	(−40.6)	—	(−54.6)	(+27.0)	—
BCEAEC Public funds	+65.3	+17.9	+90.9	+103.7	+104.9	—
	(−10.3)	(+2.5)	(+11.9)	(+10.3)	(+40.4)	—
Cameroon Public funds	+16.1	+21.0	+36.8	+29.4	+33.8	—
	(+3.6)	(+36.4)	(+21.1)	(+9.7)	(+15.4)	—
Zambia Rhodesia Malawi	+161.6	+36.4	+5.3	+93.2	+13.4	−13.7
	(+5.9)	(−6.4)	(−45.4)	(+45.6)	(+8.7)	(−16.3)
Tanzania Kenya Uganda	+70.1	+59.4	+195.3	+52.7	+65.7	+44.2
	(−2.2)	(+11.8)	(+44.5)	(−17.8)	(−16.2)	(+5.2)
Somalia	—	—	—	+7.6	−1.3	+11.6
	—	—	—	(+7.4)	(−4.8)	(+2.7)
Ethiopia	+14.7	+1.8	+9.2	+14.2	+29.9	+26.2
	(+6.8)	(−9.8)	(+3.8)	(+1.6)	(+9.2)	(+1.0)
Madagascar	+52.3	+61.4	+53.5	+48.9	+96.8	—
	(−0.5)	(−2.0)	(6.4)	(+9.5)	(+61.1)	—

Source : Same as Table 2.

the harmful consequences of drastic depletion of reserves.

In relation to the financing of imports, the foreign exchange position of many countries is now equally unsafe. It has been generally accepted that countries ought to maintain a minimum of foreign currency reserves equivalent to four-months' imports. Reserves of several African countries have already fallen to or below one-third their annual imports. As Table 7 shows, the reserves of certain countries stood at even less than one-sixth of their imports in 1964.

It is prudent for these countries to halt this dwindling of reserves. As a first step to replenishing reserves; they should refrain from further drawing. Ideally, all countries should have been continuously augmenting their reserves in order to maintain the minimum safe level, the latter has continued to rise with the steady growth of imports.

OTHER MEASURES

The gravity of the situation has led to the adoption of other measures, most important

of which are those based on the facilities or sponsorship of the International Monetary Fund (IMF). But the problem has also encouraged further intensification of restrictive practices.

In addition to normal outright drawings in the gold and credit tranches,[18] some African member countries have also taken recourse to drawing under Stand-by arrangements initiated in 1952. Indeed, most of the recent and current Fund drawings have been made under Stand-by arrangements. The following African countries have entered into such arrangements over the period May, 1964 to September, 1965: Burundi, Liberia, Mali, Morocco, Somalia, Tunisia and the UAR.

Under these arrangements, countries are assured that drawing may be made up to prescribed amounts and within an agreed period, if they undertake to observe the conditions, pursue the policies and implement the measures required by the Fund. The latter requirements, set out in what is called a letter of intent, oblige the benefiting country to follow certain policies in the fields of exchange, monetary and fiscal matters, and provides the Fund with a sanction against misuse of its resources.[19] Liberalization and

Table 7—Foreign Exchange Reserves of Selected African Countries (in millions of US $ and [in parenthesis] as percentage of Imports)

	1959	1960	1961	1962	1963	1964
Sudan	131.9	166.6	152.7	145.7	101.2	71.1
	(99.9)	(91.0)	(64.2)	(55.8)	(35.5)	(26.5)
UAR	357	291	221	217	227	139
	(55.0)	(43.6)	(31.6)	(28.8)	(24.8)	(14.6)
Libya	69.7	82.4	87.4	96.0	121.9	171.9
	(61.1)	(48.8)	(58.7)	(46.6)	(51.0)	(58.9)
Tunisia	84.8	85.4	74.3	61.9	63.4	33.4
	(55.4)	(44.7)	(35.2)	(28.6)	(28.4)	(13.5)
Morocco	143	206	185	174	110	53
	(42.7)	(49.9)	(40.9)	(40.1)	(24.6)	(11.5)
Mali	—	—	—	10.6	3.5	2.7
				(23.2)	(10.2)	(7.4)
BCEAO countries	—	—	—	159	147	134
				(34.5)	(30.8)	(22.1)
Ghana	432.7	387.89	191.4	208.8	127.7	128.2
	(136.9)	(106.8)	(48.6)	(62.7)	(35.0)	(37.7)
Nigeria	—	448	369	320	248	256
		(74.1)	(59.1)	(56.2)	(42.7)	(36.0)
Kenya, Uganda	136.2	133.6	138.9	144.6	170.5	183.9
Tanzania	(39.9)	(35.6)	(36.7)	(38.1)	(42.1)	(42.9)
Somalia	—	11.4	16.5	16.2	19.1	17.0
		(37.7)	(51.2)	(42.7)	(42.7)	(31.1)
Ethiopia	51.1	52.7	54.9	36.6	64.3	75.9
	(64.7)	(62.7)	(61.0)	(63.6)	(58.4)	(61.7)

Source: International Monetary Fund, *International Financial Statistics.*

convertibility are the Fund's basic objectives in the field of exchange; some Stand-by arrangements called for devaluation of currency, e.g., Tunisia, others reestablished the par value, e.g., Burundi. In most cases, countries have indicated the intention to pursue certain deflationary policies in the monetary and fiscal fields. As pointed out earlier, some inflationary pressures are unavoidable under conditions of rapid economic growth, and it is, therefore, of utmost importance to distinguish between what are genuinely counter-inflationary measures and outright deflationary measures. The line is indeed very thin and it is a difficult task, but the failure to do so, and in particular the imposition of exaggerated deflationary measures, can only stifle economic growth, and, as a matter of course, prolong payments disequilibrium.

The IMF has also assisted in the renegotiation of outstanding debt, with the objective of rescheduling of debt service payments. Many countries in Africa are presently faced with immediate debt repayment requirements which are very heavy in comparison with their potential foreign exchange earnings. The source of the problem is the structure of debt which, as mentioned earlier, has been increasingly influenced by short-term credit. It is neither the Fund's duty nor is it within its means to refinance debts, and the Fund has only provided technical assistance in connexion with debt negotiation, consisting of presentation of the payment problem and showing in particular the short-term and medium-term balance of payments prospects. In many instances, however, debt renegotiation has represented one aspect of a general stabilization programme, featuring also some financial assistance from the Fund, e.g., Liberia's Stand-by arrangement which, together with debt renegotiation, represented complementary support for a comprehensive programme of financial reform.

Like the Stand-by arrangements, rescheduling of debt service payments is conditional upon some general requirements, most apparent of which is the avoidance of further short-term credit. The view is sometimes held that although it may, and generally does, serve to obviate default and

improve a country's financial and credit position, a formal renegotiation of debt, by its very occurrence, may also serve to cast doubt on the country's credit-worthiness, for "it may not suffice to restore the debtor's credit-worthiness to the level at which it would have been if renegotiation had not been necessary."[20] But surely no stigma could be attached to a country's credit-worthiness because of renegotiation, so long as it honored its obligations. Debt renegotiations, especially during recent years, have arisen because of excessive debt servicing burdens resulting from deterioration in terms of borrowing. It is, therefore, necessary to devote more attention and effort to forestalling heavy and rapid accumulation of short-term credit, the actual source of excessive external debt burdens, while similar attention and effort be devoted to promoting the growth of genuinely long-term credit.

This fact has been widely acknowledged by UNCTAD, not without some dissension on the part of the capital-lending industrialized countries. UNCTAD has also recommended that, "Repayment (of loans) should be spread over a considerably long period which should normally be not less than twenty-seven years, and with a certain grace period, taking into account the specific nature of goods. Existing loans should, where necessary, be mutually re-studied and revised with a view to consolidation and renegotiation, where the economic condition of a recipient country so justifies it."[21]

None of the foregoing, essential *ad hoc*, measures has provided the solution to Africa's balance of payments problem which is basically a structural disequilibrium. Reserves continue to be diminished, import restrictions tightened, exchange controls intensified and the bilateral channelling of trade and payments steadily increased.

It may be observed that the figures in Table 5—current account balances—and those in Table 6—capital and reserve movements combined—do not always offset each other. The discrepancies are referred to as "errors and omissions," and normally they are supposed to be within narrow limits. They, however, can be no longer considered as errors and omissions if they reach such high levels as shown in Table 8. One plausible explanation of such discrepancies, though only when negative, is the presence of illicit flight of capital. The latter is not only a symptom of balance of payments problems, but is certainly capable of aggravating and complicating these problems. The genesis of these errors and omissions could of course also be bad statistical reporting of exports and imports.

Conclusion

To recapitulate, Africa's balance of payments problems are in the majority of cases a symptom of economic growth. Only in a limited sense do they represent an instance of planned deficit, as it is deliberately intended for economic growth to outstrip the expansion of domestic resources, creating thereby a savings–investment gap that is widening. Commodity imports have run well in excess of export capacity. Payments for invisibles have averaged about twice as much as receipts from invisibles. Only if an adequate inflow of foreign capital—grants and loans—is forthcoming, will it be possible to tackle these problems without slowing down the tempo of economic development.

The domestic resources gap is often inappropriately thought of to represent only the difference between gross domestic savings and gross capital formation. First of all, domestic savings that are relevant are gross retained savings, since private transfers abroad, servicing charges on external loans as well as direct investment transfers, are all a charge on gross savings. In addition, the domestic resources gap should ideally be taken to include an estimated annual increment to the foreign exchange reserves, or alternatively, gross domestic savings should be charged with this increment, which would maintain a conventionally acceptable minimum safe level of reserves *mutatis mutandis* with development in imports.

In the absence of adequate inflow of capital to fill this gap, imports have to be cut down to the limits permitted by current domestic capacity, with the consequent tapering off of the growth rate of total output. This paper, it is hoped, has fully revealed the crucial importance of foreign capital for the development of the African economies. But it has also demonstrated beyond doubt that so far the inflow of foreign financial resources into Africa has not been adequate· In addition, the cost of servicing the hard-loan portion of the inflow has been rising rapidly, due to deterioration in the terms of borrowing which has resulted mainly from the tendency towards shorter maturities, but also because interest rates have remained at conventional levels which are still relatively high. This has represented a further diminution of the already insufficient financial

Table 8—Balance of Payments—Errors and Omissions
(in millions of US $)

	1958	1959	1960	1961	1962	1963
UAR	−17.8	+16.1	−17.2	−20.4	−11.5	−2.1
Tunisia	−67.3	+1.2	−0.02	−5.8	−5.3	+0.4
Morocco	−86.2	−89.9	−1.8	−16.6	+4.3	−17.4
Ghana	—	3.9	−10.9	−11.5	−3.4	−8.7
Nigeria	+5.6	+9.0	−3.4	+40.0	−4.5	−27.4
Zambia Rhodesia Malawi	+18.5	−0.8	−33.3	−16.5	+35.6	+42.8
Tanzania Kenya Uganda	−24.8	−9.7	−117.9	−59.6	−70.5	−126.2

Source: Same as Table 2.

resources and an additional burden on the strained balance of payments.

In order to redress their balance of payments problems while maintaining the growth rate of their economies at the desired level, African countries, individually, collectively and inevitably, in collaboration with the capital-lending countries and the international and regional financial institutions, have to aim at (1) increasing the flow of foreign financial resources and (2) improving the terms of borrowing, or, in other words, reducing the cost of these resources. The two objectives are obviously interrelated.

Notes

1. Erin E. Jucker–Fleetwood, *Money and Finance in Africa*. (London: George Allen and Unwin Ltd., 1964) Ch. XXV.

2. J. E. Meade, *The Balance of Payments*, Oxford University Press, 1955.

3. This is a case where the potential or possible deficit is larger than the actual deficit. See Meade, *op. cit.*

4. Jucker–Fleetwood, *op. cit.* p. 292.

5. For more detailed discussion of the importance of foreign trade to Africa see, "Balance of Payments Problems in Developing Africa," in the United Africa Company, *Statistical and Economic Review*, No. 29, April 1964, ch. I.

6. ECA, *Bilateral Trade and Payments Agreements in Africa*, Document No. E/CN.14/STC/24/Rev.1, Paras. 27–42.

7. *Ibid.*, Ch. II.

8. There is no information on import prices by categories, i.e., according to end-use. The index of total import prices has risen over the period. It is probable, therefore, that there has been a price-effect in the growth of capital and intermediate goods' imports, but this is also true of consumer goods' imports. Consequently, most of the growth in capital and intermediate goods' imports is to be explained by a real increase in volume. That the percentage increase in import prices (10 points) was much smaller than the percentage increase in the value of imports—total as well as each and every category—strongly reinforce this view.

9. ECA, *Industrial Growth in Africa*. Document No. E/CN.14/INR/1/, Rev. 1, Table 8.

10. ECA, Document No. E/CN.14/STC/24/Rev. 1, *Loc. cit.*

11. Ely Devons, "World Trade in Invisibles," *Lloyd Bank Review*, April, 1961.

12. International Bank for Reconstruction and Development, *Economic Growth and External Debt—A Statistical Presentation*, Document No. E/CONF.46/40, p. 15.

13. Organization for Economic Co-operation and Development (OECD), *The Flow of Financial Resources to Developing Countries in 1961*.

14. International Monetary Fund, *Annual Report—1965*, p. 25.

15. "Due not so much to the ability to withhold supply but basically to the fact that these Boards have access to more technical, commercial and financial resources than single individuals or single firms." See: ECA, Document No. E/CN.14/STC/13, *State Trading in Africa* and ECA, Document No. E/CN.14/STC/CS/1, *National Stabilization Measures—National Marketing Boards and Price Stabilization Funds in Africa*.

16. ECA, *The Development Plans of African Countries:* see also ECA, *Outlines and Selected Indicators of African Development Plans*, Document No. E/CN.14/336.

17. International Bank for Reconstruction and Development, *Economic Growth and External Debt—An Analytical Framework*, Document No. E/CONF.46/84.

18. "A drawing which does not increase the Fund's holdings of a member's currency above the amount of its quota is said to be in the gold tranche; a drawing which increases the Fund's holdings above the amount of the quota is said to be in the credit tranches." IMF, *Introduction to the Fund*. Washington D.C., 1964.

19. This sanction is established mainly through the practice of phasing the right to draw over specified periods of time. Stand-by facilities cannot be used at once. J. Marcus Fleming, *The International Monetary Fund, Its Form and Functions*, IMF, Washington D.C., 1964.

20. IMF, *Annual Report—1965*, p. 27.

21. Recommendation 1.2, E/COMF.46/141, Vol. 1,—Annex AIV.4.

Regional Economic Integration in Africa

Franklin V. Walker

ALL MODERN industrial nations owe their development in part to policies and activities of economic integration. Haberler[1] finds three overlapping waves of market unification have occurred in the last two hundred years. First, modern nations were formed by combining smaller states and removing internal feudal restraints on commerce, power was centralized in national governments, and labor was cut free from traditional ties to the land. Development of national transportation and communication networks further served to extend local trade into national markets.

Competition between localities brought specialization by comparative cost advantage and this division of labor increased the wealth of nations. In the words of Adam Smith, "division of labor is limited by the extent of the market." Further gains would come with extension of national markets to form world markets, bringing nations to specialize by comparative advantage. Haberler's second wave began in the mid-nineteenth century when Great Britain, confident of her lead in manufactures, led the movement toward free trade among nations.

Germany and other continental powers returned to protective policies after the 1870's and Haberler's second wave was in ebb, but Dell[2] points out that the integration movement continued in a discriminatory form as a central feature of colonialism. By treaty or administrative practice, preferential markets were secured for home country

manufactures, security and profit were obtained for investment of European capital, and raw materials were made available with little effective competition from the industrialists of rival powers.

Currency difficulties and the Great Depression brought substantial disintegration of world markets between the two world wars. Haberler's third wave began after World War II and is still continuing. It has taken two forms. First, there is revival of the drive toward universal free trade through liberalization of tariff policies and removal of quantitative restrictions in imports of manufactures, promoted by the General Agreement on Tariffs and Trade (GATT) and embodied in a series of multinational reciprocal trade agreements.

The second contemporary integration movement is regional. Contiguous countries with similar degrees of economic development and compositions of output have elected to merge their markets in various degrees of integration. It began in Europe, with simultaneous formation of the European Economic Community (EEC) and the European Free Trade Association (EFTA), but the movement soon proved catching among the developing countries. South America and Mexico have the Latin American Free Trade Association (LAFTA) and there is a Central American Common Market. Several integration treaties exist in continental Africa, which will be reviewed later. The United Nations Economic Commissions for Latin America and Africa are both actively promoting regional integration in their respective parts of the world.

The purpose of economic integration in developing countries is to facilitate and promote industrialization. Rightly or wrongly, their governments believe creation and expansion of manufacturing activities will accelerate the rate of economic growth and enhance national power. Many modern manufacturing processes are subject to substantial economies of scale, so that large markets are needed in order to obtain acceptably low capital and production costs. By extending markets, regional integration makes possible establishment of such industries, while it also increases the scope for local specialization by comparative advantage and may bring the gains of increased competition as more producers in small-scale enterprise vie with each other.

Both universal trade liberalization and regional integration provide these gains, but the latter policy is also one of protection against imports from outside the region. From this standpoint, regional integration runs counter to the gains from trade and it is possible that the real costs of protection will exceed the benefits of integration. Moreover, when two or more countries integrate their markets, one may enjoy most of the benefits while the other feels unfairly burdened by the costs. Such mal-distribution and inability or unwillingness to overcome it by administrative measures is the principal reason for failure of regional integration schemes of developing countries.

Some Characteristics of African Economies

Before considering further the benefits and costs of regional integration in Africa, some relevant characteristics of the economies of independent African states should be understood. Thirty-six independent countries of continental Africa are here considered, excluding South Africa, Rhodesia and three small nominally independent territories that are economically tied to these two countries. These states are identified in Table 1, which gives their area, population, density of settlement and gross national product (GNP) for 1963, the most recent year for which comparable GNP data are available for these countries. More recent data would not substantially change the picture.

The first thing to note is that these countries are very small, with a few exceptions, both in population and gross national product. This is particularly true of those in the three regions of sub-Sahara tropical Africa. North Africa has somewhat larger countries, particularly the three Maghreb states of Morocco, Algeria and Tunisia, and the United Arab Republic (Egypt). Most of the North African people live within a hundred miles of the Mediterranean Sea or in a narrow belt along the Nile River. Scarcity of arable land and high net reproduction rates

burden the North with excess population, a problem not generally met with below the Sahara.

In the three regions of tropical Africa, there are 30 countries with a combined population of about 200 million people. Three have nearly half this population: Nigeria, Ethiopia, and the Democratic Republic of the Congo (capital at Kinshasa).* The three countries of former British East Africa (Kenya, Uganda and Tanzania) have a combined population of 26 million persons served by the oldest common market on the continent.

The remaining two dozen countries have an average population of only three million persons and an average GNP of $330 million. A. J. Brown[3] has estimated that the income of a median African state is equivalent to that of an English town of 100,000 inhabitants. To bring the comparison closer to home, in 1963 the people of Vermont received personal incomes totalling $847 million, the lowest of all continental United States, but greater than the GNP of any of the 24 African states except Ghana. The combined GNP of all two dozen states was no higher, in total, than the personal income of the people of Georgia in 1963.

Density of settlement varies widely in the tropical countries, a dimension important in identifying the sizes of markets because of transportation costs and economies of urbanization. Very low densities occur in the coastal countries of Mauritania and Somalia, and the landlocked countries of Mali, Niger and Chad. These all reach into the Sahara desert and their populations are concentrated at a few points along the coast, in the first two countries, and near the southern boundaries of the last three. The tropical forest areas of Gabon, Congo (capital at Brazzaville) and the Central African Republic also show low density. On the other hand, Nigeria has a fairly heavy population density, particularly in its coastal areas, while the small interior states of Rwanda and Burundi have densities comparable to those

*The name of the Republic was changed to Zäire in 1971.

Table 1—Area, Population and Income of African Countries in 1963

	Area (th. sq. mi.)	Population (millions)	Density (pop./area)	G.N.P. ($ millions)
North Africa				
Morocco	171.8	12.7	74	2,362
Algeria	919.6	11.6	13	2,743
Tunisia	48.3	4.5	93	942
Libya	679.4	1.5	2	731
UAR	386.1	28.0	72	4,331
Sudan	967.5	12.8	13	1,333
West Africa				
French Group				
Mauritania	419.2	0.8	2	108
Senegal	75.8	3.4	44	708
Mali	463.9	4.4	9	329
Guinea	94.9	3.4	35	333
Niger	489.2	3.1	6	260
Upper Volta	105.9	4.7	44	220
Ivory Coast	124.5	3.7	29	764
Dahomey	43.5	2.2	52	167
Togo	21.9	1.6	72	135
English Speaking				
Gambia	4.0	0.3	75	26
Sierra Leone	27.7	2.2	79	295
Ghana	92.1	7.3	80	1,667
Nigeria	356.7	55.6	156	4,163
Liberia	43.0	1.0	24	192
Central Africa				
French Group				
Chad	495.8	2.8	6	213
Cameroon	183.6	4.6	25	603
Central African Republic	238.2	1.3	5	148
Congo	132.0	0.8	6	153
Gabon	103.1	0.5	4	138
Other				
Zäire	905.6	15.0	17	1,768
Equatorial Guinea	9.8	0.3	27	n.a.
East Africa				
British Group				
Kenya	225.0	8.8	39	898
Uganda	91.1	7.2	79	534
Tanzania	361.8	9.8	27	708
Zambia	288.1	3.5	12	532
Malawi	46.1	3.8	81	155
Other				
Ethiopia	457.3	21.8	48	1,078
Somalia	246.2	2.3	9	160
Rwanda	10.2	2.8	280	117
Burundi	10.7	2.6	247	123

Source: United Nations, *Statistical Yearbook*, except Equatorial Guinea.

Table 2—Principal Exports and Largest Market of African Countries
(percentage of export value in 1966)

	Principal Export Commodities	Largest Market
North Africa		
Morocco	Phosphates (25), citrus (15), vegetables (15)	France (42)
Algeria	Petroleum (57), wine (12)	France (75)
Tunisia	Phosphates (25), olive oil (18)	France (35)
Libya	Petroleum (99)	Germany (33)
UAR	Cotton (55)	U.S.S.R. (24)
Sudan	Cotton (49), oilseeds (21)	Italy (13)
West Africa		
French Group		
Mauritania	Iron ore (93)	France (21)
Senegal	Peanuts and products (78)	France (74)
Mali	Cotton (24), cattle (21)	Ivory Coast (36)
Guinea	Alumina	U.S.
Niger	Peanuts and products (72), livestock (11)	France (55)
Upper Volta	Livestock (52)	Ivory Coast (52)
Ivory Coast	Coffee (39), wood and lumber (24), cocoa (20)	France (39)
Dahomey	Palm products (49), cotton (11)	France (53)
Togo	Phosphates (43), coffee (22), cocoa (19)	France (40)
English Speaking		
Gambia	Peanuts (36), vegetable oils (37)	U.K. (61)
Sierra Leone	Diamonds (53), iron ore (16)	U.K. (62)
Ghana	Cocoa and products (66)	U.K. (16)
Nigeria	Petroleum (33), peanuts and products (18), palm products (13)	U.K. (37)
Liberia	Iron ore (64), rubber (19)	U.S. (33)
Central Africa		
French Group		
Chad	Cotton (77), cattle (10)	France (49)
Cameroon	Cocoa (25), coffee (21)	France (44)
C.A.R.	Diamonds (54), coffee (24)	France (37)
Congo	Wood (49), diamonds (39)	Germany (26)
Gabon	Wood (31), manganese (31)	France (45)
Other		
Zäire	Copper (38), other metals (14)	Belgium (40)
Eq. Guinea	Cocoa, coffee, wood	Spain
East Africa		
British Group		
Kenya	Coffee (30), tea (14)	U.K. (20)
Uganda	Coffee (52), cotton (23)	U.S. (25)
Tanzania	Cotton (21), coffee (18), sisal (14), diamonds (11)	U.K. (27)
Zambia	Copper (93)	U.K. (32)
Malawi	Tea (26), tobacco (26)	U.K. (38)
Other		
Ethiopia	Coffee (56), hides and skins (13)	U.S. (44)
Somalia	Bananas (42), livestock (24)	Italy (46)
Rwanda	Coffee (56), tin ore (32)	Belgium (33)
Burundi	Coffee	U.S.

Source: United Nations, *Yearbook of International Trade Statistics*, except Guinea. Equatorial Guinea and Burundi from the *Statesman's Yearbook*.

of Austria, Czechoslovakia and Denmark. Overpopulation is a problem in these three countries.

Table 2 shows the principal export commodities and export markets of these economies, with percentages of export value in 1966 shown in parentheses. It is apparent that a few primary raw or semiprocessed materials dominate the export earnings of nearly every country. Principal agricultural exports are cocoa, coffee, cotton, peanuts (groundnuts), palm products and wood or lumber. Some countries rely heavily on earnings from mineral exports: Guinea and Ghana (alumina), Cameroon (aluminum), Zäire, Zambia and Uganda (copper and other non-ferrous ores and metals), Mauritania and Liberia (iron ore), Libya, Algeria and Nigeria (petroleum).

It is also apparent from Table 2 that most of these countries find their principal export markets in the European nations of which they were once colonies. In general, they also obtain most of their imports from these nations. Trade connections established by colonial integration continue to prevail. These are reinforced by preferential tariff policies. The United Kingdom accepts imports from her former colonies free of duty or at substantially lower tariff rates than apply to the same commodities from other sources, and her former colonies reciprocally give more liberal tariff treatment to British goods. Similar arrangements exist between the European Economic Community and the former colonies of France, Belgium, and Italy.

Less than a tenth of recorded trade of African countries is with each other, and this small trade is of substantial importance only to a few landlocked grazing countries. Mali, Niger, Upper Volta and Chad obtain a large part of their export earnings by selling livestock and some other foodstuffs to adjacent coastal states. Trade between the latter is frustrated by the lack of adequate transport, a lack which must be overcome if regional integration is to extend markets effectively. Existing transportation routes were built, in the colonial period, to drain raw materials directly to the sea for shipment to Europe.

The United Arab Republic is the most industralized of the 36 countries in northern and tropical Africa, with a fifth of its GNP originating in manufactures, while the three Maghreb countries of Morocco, Algeria and Tunisia come next, with a seventh of their GNP from manufacturing. Besides a broad range of light consumer goods and foodstuffs, these countries produce textiles, heavy industrial chemicals, cement, and petroleum products. They assemble motor vehicles and a few other consumer durables, and Egypt has a small integrated iron and steel complex.

Of all the countries of tropical Africa, only Kenya has as much as ten per cent of its GNP originating in manufacturing. The modal figure for the other economies is six per cent, with activities confined to food processing, beer brewing, and production of cigarettes, footwear and a few other light consumer goods not subject to important economies of scale. Kenya has a dairy industry. Textiles, cement and petroleum products are produced in a few of the larger states. Except for isolated facilities reducing ores to metal for export, there are virtually no large-scale enterprises in tropical Africa.

In summary, the typical independent African state is very small in population and income, depends heavily on a few primary exports which it sells largely to the nation with which it was linked in colonial integration, and buys the largest part of its imports from that source. It does little trade with its neighbors and its small manufacturing sector is confined to light commodities that can be produced economically on a small scale.

Benefits and Costs of Regional Integration

Several degrees of regional integration are distinguished in economic literature. A free trade area is formed when countries agree to remove restraints on trade between themselves, but retain autonomy in establishing tariffs and other limitations on trade with nonmembers countries. If they not only trade freely among themselves, but also adopt a single set of tariffs and other restric-

union may, itself, be part of a common
market, in which labor, capital and enterprise are allowed freely to move from one
member state to another. Finally, in order to
remove disparities in resource allocation and
reduce payments imbalances, the member
governments may agree to co-ordinate or
harmonize fiscal, monetary and other
economic policies. In this case, they form
an economic union or economic community.

While economists may agree on the meaning of these classifications, treaties that bear
their names often contain provisions that
depart from these descriptions. Thus, a
"common market" agreement may fail to
provide for unrestricted factor mobility and
may permit member states to impose
limited tariffs on internal trade. Such an
arrangement is better termed a "preferential
tariff area." Much of existing economic
theory of regional integration concerns
customs unions, strictly defined, and the en-
suing discussion will begin with this case.

TRADE CREATION AND TRADE DIVERSION

Following Viner's[4] analysis, the static
welfare theory of customs unions weighs
the gain from trade creation among the
member states against the real cost of trade
diversion from third-country sources of
supply. When two countries remove tariffs
on mutual trade, they gain from realization
of scale economies, reallocation of resources
by comparative advantage, and possibly increased competition among producers. The
gross national product obtainable from a
given supply of resources is increased by
their more efficient employment.

On the other hand, producers within the
union are able to underbid competitors outside the union because consumers do not
pay duties on internal output. Purchases by
consumers in one member country will be
diverted to supplies from another member
country, even though the latter are produced
at higher opportunity costs than must be
paid for these goods from sources outside
the union. By thus producing goods in
which it has a comparative disadvantage, the
union employs its resources less efficiently

and reduces the GNP it can obtain from
them.

To illustrate, suppose Ivory Coast and
Upper Volta form a union. A certain type
of cotton cloth is available from Europe at a
landed price of $10.00 a bolt (franc price
converted to dollars for convenience) in
both countries. Prior to union, suppose each
country imposed a 100 per cent tariff on this
cloth, but Ivory Coast buyers found it
cheaper to buy from her infant textile industry since the latter was able to produce
and market cloth at $15.00 a bolt. It is
assumed this price fully measures the opportunity costs of cloth production. That is,
if the same resources were reallocated from
cloth to cocoa production they would earn
$15.00 in foreign exchange.

When the union is formed, Upper Volta
consumers stop buying European cloth,
which costs them $20.00 inclusive of tariff,
and start buying the $15.00 cloth from Ivory
Coast. To buy European cloth, Upper Volta
would need to export goods worth only
$10.00 for each bolt, but she now must earn
$15.00 in foreign exchange for each bolt
from Ivory Coast. The purchasing power of
exports is reduced and, by the same token,
the real income Upper Volta realizes from
employing her resources is reduced.

In passing, it should be noted that this
illustration of trade diversion also indicates
another problem for the government of
Upper Volta. The custom revenues that were
obtained from imports of European cloth
were not a real cost to Upper Volta citizens,
since they were used to finance internal output or redistributed in some other way to
the benefit of Upper Voltans. However, with
trade diversion, the government loses these
tariff revenues and must either impose other
taxes to replace them or cut back on government activities. Since tariffs are an important
source of revenue in developing countries,
the government of Upper Volta may be
seriously disadvantaged by this result.

ACCEPTANCE OF APPARENT COST

There is some reason to believe that in
the early stages of an African customs

union, trade diversion costs will exceed trade creation gains. The members will have similar degrees of development and cost structures, and they will lack industries subject to economies of scale. Removal of internal duties will do little initially to create more trade within the union.

On the other hand, trade diversion is apt to be greater if only because the volume of trade with Europe is much larger. Moreover, the union will probably establish a common external tariff which is higher, on a number of commodities, than for any one country prior to the union. These countries will now want to promote establishment of industries subject to economies of scale that would previously not have been acceptably efficient within the confines of national markets.

However, in some cases the apparent cost of trade diversion may exceed the opportunity cost. In the illustration previously cited it was assumed that resources used in cloth production were valued at opportunity cost. This will not be true if the labor would otherwise have been unemployed and if the capital had been attracted from abroad only in response to the profits available from protected cloth production. Or, if the labor had been employed in agriculture, the value of its exportable output may have been much less than what it adds in value to cloth production. Overpopulation of arable land means a low marginal product for labor and some workers can be drawn from agriculture with little reduction in food and fiber output. One of the motives for regional integration is to increase employment and attract foreign capital, and to the extent this is successful, the real costs of protection are negligible.

Even in the case that a union initially costs more than it gains, it is the long-run outlook that matters. Comparative advantage is subject to change, and infant industries, if properly selected, will achieve economies in time that will give them a cost advantage over foreign producers. Labor must be brought to higher levels of general education and specific skills, rehoused in urban areas and conditioned to accept the disciplines and incentives of an industrial labor force. It

takes time to train management. Capital becomes available at lower cost as continued success of enterprise reduces the perceived risks of investment.

As a number of infant industries are formed in a locality, external economies are realized through common use of transportation, power and communication facilities, establishment and growth of financial and marketing institutions, and pooling of labor. Increased employment and concentration of population in urban areas expands markets and reduces transportation costs.

Finally, the purpose of regional integration by developing countries is not to achieve efficiency in resource use, but to promote industrialization. Establishment of import-competing manufactures may be the means to maximize the rate of economic growth, particularly if resources would remain otherwise unemployed or underemployed. But industrialization may be valued as an end in itself, supported by considerations of national prestige and power or by the belief that industrial societies bestow a higher quality of life.

Distribution of Gains

Manufacturing enterprises tend to congregate in urban localities, where they enjoy external economies, access to transportation hubs, and the heaviest density of demand for their products. When an initially more urbanized and industrial country integrates with less developed neighbors, it is likely to receive the lion's share of further industrial development. The poorer members of the union find themselves disadvantaged in a number of ways. First, they receive little of the new industry and the direct benefits it offers. Second, they may pay a higher real price for diverted trade, and their governments are deprived of customs revenues. In addition, they lose to the industrial center profits and income taxes they would have obtained from domestic establishment of the industry. Finally, if the union involves a common market, they lose their younger and more able workers to the urban center, which also attracts the savings of their population.

Why, then, should poorer countries of Africa be willing to enter into union with their more affluent neighbors? In the longer view, there are likely to be gains for them. First, they can expect to obtain what Myrdal[5] terms "spread effects." As incomes and material input requirements of the industrial center expand, the peripheral countries gain larger markets for primary outputs. Second, once infant industries achieve a comparative advantage, diversion costs will be replaced by gain for all members of the union. Finally, there are diseconomies of agglomeration at existing manufacturing centers which may eventually lead to establishment of other centers in the initially disadvantaged countries.

If such market forces alone are not enough to attract or hold poorer countries, the more developed states may induce them to accept integration by sharing the benefits through redistribution funds or fiscal policies. Dispersal of manufactures may be promoted by planning new industrial locations, allowing poorer countries to offer tax advantages or subsidies, or using licensing systems to limit manufacturing enterprises in one country and guarantee union-wide markets to firms willing to locate away from the center.

A union development fund or bank can develop transportation systems and local infrastructure facilities that serve to establish new growing points within the poorer countries. Finally, the union may depart from strictly free internal trade by permitting disadvantaged states to impose limited tariffs on goods from other members that compete with its own existing or prospective infant industries.

Harmonization of Policies

In order to realize greater net gains and reduce causes of dissension, African states may agree on other measures of integration besides a customs union. A common market for labor and capital improves intra-union allocation of resources, by attracting factors to the points and employments where rewards are greatest, if the rewards reflect social valuation of output. Harmonization of fiscal, monetary and other policies provides

two results. First, it helps ensure that trade and factor movements are in comformity with social gain. Second, it reduces balance of payments disequilibria that would tempt a deficit country to limit imports from other members and restrict capital outflows. Co-operation in development planning prevents competitive bidding by governments for new enterprises (that can result in waste of resources), and such co-operation can be used as a means of diversifying new industry among the member economies. These are important reasons for going beyond a simple customs union to form an economic community.

Fiscal harmonization means use of similar or equal tax structures within each of the member countries. Income and profits tax rates are equalized so that differential tax treatment will not lure industries away from localities in which they have a comparative cost advantage. Production excise taxes are made equal for the same reason. Taxes levied at the point of consumption do not conflict with optimum resource allocation, but they may be equalized to avoid discrimination against consumers in some countries and to prevent smuggling.

The principal difficulty with fiscal harmonization is that each state surrenders tax autonomy and thus accepts restraints on its budget that may be out of line with conceived needs for financing internal development. Even with equal tax rates, polarization of manufactures in one country yields it the highest revenues, while the poorer countries are apt to feel the greatest need for revenues to finance development of infrastructure facilities in order to gain manufacturing centers of their own.

In the absence of monetary union, harmonization of monetary policies is needed for balance of payments reasons. If member states go their own way in determining the quantity of money and terms of credit, some may pursue more expansionary policies than others. Balance of payments deficits are likely to occur for the countries with expansionary policies, as imports increase more than exports and capital flows out to efficiently link supply and market localities in separate countries.

take advantage of higher interest rates in the countries restricting credit. To stem its loss of reserves, the expansionary country will be tempted to resort to escape clauses that permit it to restrain imports or even abrogate the union treaty if it does not provide such escapes. It may impose exchange controls and prevent capital exports. Or it may resort to devaluation. To avoid such disruptions to trade and payments, the member countries agree to co-ordinate monetary policies.

Although harmonization may prevent sustained payments imbalances, short-term deficits will occur from such events as crop failures, strikes, or establishment of a competing producer in a partner country. To enable a member to weather such a period without resort to restrictions, the union may include a payments agreement in which the members agree to extend short-term credits to each other when deficits occur.

Co-operation in development planning can prevent wasteful competition for industrial enterprises. For example, suppose a union of two countries provides a market adequate for one large cement producer. In the absense of co-operation, both states may succeed in attracting a cement enterprise, resulting in overcapacity. Or if only one initially gets a plant, the facility may be deliberately constructed at less than optimum scale to minimize the cost of excess capacity in the event that the second country establishes a plant. By co-operating, the member states can agree to allocate large-scale industries and to provide market guarantees that will induce producers to install larger and more economical units.

Co-operation in planning can also serve two other ends. It can be used deliberately to disperse industries and provide infrastructure investments in the countries not initially favored by existing manufacturing centers. Second, it can take advantage of complementaries and external economies. Development of hydro-electric power in one country, for example, may be keyed to establishment of power-using industries in another. Railroads may be planned so that they most

Treaties of Integration in Africa

Africa has had no shortage of plans and attempts at integration, ranging from co-operative development of water resources or marketing of livestock, to proposals for continental trade integration. The more important regional integration treaties will be reviewed here.

THE EAST AFRICAN ECONOMIC COMMUNITY

The three former British East Africa countries of Kenya, Uganda and Tanzania (federation of Tanganyika and Zanzibar) have a common market and common services dating from the 1920's, which were reorganized to form the East African Economic Community in 1967. At that time, the *de facto* common market was given legal status as the East African Common Market within the Community.

The Community has a stronger administrative structure than other integration arrangements in Africa, including three cabinet-rank ministers named by the member governments to administer Community affairs through several Councils. It has a Legislative Assembly, to establish policy subject to assent by the Heads of the three member countries, a Tribunal to adjudicate disputes, and a permanent headquarters at Arusha, Tanzania.

Some of the common services inherited from the colonial period—railroads, harbors, airline, post and telegraph—are established as self-supporting corporations. Other common services, supported by tax revenues, are administered by the community administration.

The Common Market provides for a common external tariff and, except for a so-called transfer tax, unrestricted internal trade in manufactures. The transfer tax is in fact a limited tariff, which one member can impose on imports from another under certain conditions. First, the tax can only be applied by a member whose trade in manufactures is in deficit with respect to the other two members. The value of imports subject to tax can be no greater than the deficit. Second, once the deficit is reduced to less than 20 per cent of the member's manufacturing trade with other members, no further taxes may be imposed. Third, the tax on any one import can be no higher than 50 per cent of the rate applicable to similar goods imported from outside the union. Fourth, the tax can only be levied on imports which compete with existing or soon-to-be-established manufacturing capacity in the deficit country. Finally, no single duty can be retained longer than eight years, and the right to levy such taxes will lapse after 1982.

While departing from the strict definition of a customs union, the transfer tax represents a practical solution to the problem of distributing the gains from integration. Kenya is considerably more industrialized than Uganda and Tanzania, with manufactures polarized around Nairobi. In the past, the rate of economic growth has been substantially greater in Kenya, and the other two countries have felt unfairly burdened with the trade diversion and revenue costs of the customs union.

Immediately prior to granting independence to the three countries, Great Britain appointed the Raisman Commission to investigate this distribution problem. The Commission, reporting in 1961, agreed that Kenya had received the greatest benefit from the customs union, but argued that the other two countries gained because the spread effect more than offset the costs of trade diversion. Moreover, they could expect to gain much more by remaining in the union than by attempting to industrialize independently. Following the Commission's recommendation, a Distributional Pool was established which redistributed some tax revenues in favor of Uganda and Tanzania.

This compensation was not enough and, upon gaining independence, Tanzania threatened to leave the market. To prevent this, the three countries entered into extensive negotiations leading to the Kampala Agreement of 1964. This Agreement provided for some reallocation of production among existing plants in the three countries,

dispersal of several new industries, temporary use of quotas on local imports by deficit members, and appointment of a commission to investigate the long-run problem of equitable industrial allocation.

Only the first provision of the Kampala Agreement was implemented. When Kenya seemed to ignore the rest and the three countries were unable to agree on monetary union, Tanzania independently imposed quotas and other restraints on trade that appeared to spell the end of the common market. Then, in late 1965, the three governments established a commission under the chairmanship of Professor Kjeld Philip of Denmark to find ways of preserving the common market and common services. The recommendations of this commission resulted in the Treaty for East African Co-operation of 1967, which established the present East African Economic Community and provided the transfer tax as its principal feature to deal with the distribution problem.

The requirement that a deficit country can impose the transfer tax only on intraregional imports which compete with its own existing or imminent production will largely limit use of this tariff to protection of smaller-scale industries. The Treaty provides no machinery to prevent future polarization of large-scale manufacturing at Nairobi. However, it does establish an East African Development Bank, which is to give priority, wherever feasible, to industrial development in the less developed states, to finance projects that make the partner economies increasingly complementary in industry, and allocate more than threefourths of its loans, loan guarantees and investments to Tanzania and Uganda. While the Bank cannot dictate the locational pattern of private capital, its financial power and the investigations of its research department can be employed to induce dispersal of enterprise.

Finally, the Treaty continues a high degree of fiscal integration, inherited from the colonial period, and seeks to ensure harmonization of monetary policies by the three central banks. For the most part, excise, income and profits tax rates are uniform in the region. Changes in these rates, and in the common external tariff schedule, are made by joint agreement of the partner governments. Customs receipts, on imports from outside the union, and excise tax revenues are allocated to the country of final destination of the goods taxed, while income taxes go to the country in which the income is earned. Monetary policy harmonization is promoted by provisions that the governors of the central banks confer together quarterly and that the central banks extend limited credits to each other in times of temporary deficit.

THE CENTRAL AFRICAN CUSTOMS AND
ECONOMIC UNION

Congo, Gabon, Central African Republic and Chad were formerly joined in the Federation of French Equatorial Africa. For administrative convenience, the Federation had a common currency, common services, a common market, and a system of redistribution of revenues to the benefit of poorer inland territories. This Federation was dissolved when the countries became independent, but the latter were able to agree on conventions which preserved a monetary union, common services and the customs union.

The fifth French-speaking state of Central Africa, the Federal Republic of Cameroon, was formed by uniting the French Cameroon mandate with part of British Cameroon in 1961, shortly after the larger French country became independent. French Cameroon had had close economic ties with the French Equatorial African countries and shared their common currency. The new state of Cameroon entered into a convention with the other four states to continue in monetary union, and progressively, to integrate its market with theirs. These five countries later formalized the arrangement with a treaty establishing the Central African Customs and Economic Union (UDEAC), which came into effect at the beginning of 1966.

The Union has a policy-making and administrative structure, of which the Steering Committee, consisting of Ministers of Finance of members countries, decides on the operation of the customs union, the level of import duties, enterprises which are to be classified as serving the whole union, harmonization of taxes, and the level and distribution of the Solidarity Fund, a device for redistributing revenues to the poorer states. In principle, there is to be a common external tariff and free trade within the union of regionally produced manufactures. However, there remain some exceptions to the uniform external duty, and internal trade is hampered by various restrictions, particularly between Cameroon and the other four countries. In time, these departures from a strict customs union may be overcome, particularly as the Cameroon economy is integrated with the others, and a higher degree of harmonization of excise and income tax rates may be obtained.

National industries that are classified as serving the whole Union are accorded special tax and allocation treatment. First, they are exempt from import duties on their materials and all national excise taxes; instead, they pay a single tax established by the Steering Committee. Second, when one of these enterprises is to be established, the Steering Committee undertakes a detailed study of production economies available at various locations, existing capacity within the union, and possible compensation to states that may suffer economically from establishment of the enterprise elsewhere. Such co-ordination and allocation of major industrial enterprises, to avoid excessive polarization, is a uniquely important part of the treaty.

Believing that they received insufficient benefit from the Union, Chad and Central African Republic resigned in April, 1968, and announced they were joining the Congo Republic (now Zäire) in a Union of Central African States. However, in December, the Central African Republic returned to the UDEAC. The outlook for UDEAC continues to be favorable, even if these two states should leave, because the largest gains are likely to occur for Congo, Gabon and Cameroon.

The third apparently succeeding integration arrangement in Africa involves the four Maghreb countries of Morocco, Algeria, Tunisia and Libya. In 1964, with help from the Economic Commission of Africa, they established a Standing Consultative Committee at Tunis. The Committee, which makes its recommendations to a council of the Ministers of Economic Afairs of the four governments, was charged with promoting co-ordination of development plans of the four states, with emphasis on harmonization of industrial development, co-operation in energy production and mining, preparation of a plan for trade integration, and working out of a common approach to development financing. Few of these goals were close to accomplishment after five years, though the Committee did complete several detailed feasibility studies of heavy industries, obtained co-operation in transportation, communication and tourist policies, and developed a joint policy for negotiating a trade agreement with the European Economic Community.

Late in 1967 the Committee was instructed to draw up a draft agreement containing a list of products to be freely traded among the Maghreb countries and standardization of protective measures on trade with outsiders. This degree of integration remains unrealized and trade between the countries continues to be very small compared with their trade with France and the rest of continental Europe.

THE ARAB COMMON MARKET

In 1950, to gain military and economic strength against Israel, Egypt entered into a Treaty of Joint Defense and Economic Co-operation with six other members of the Arab League located in the Middle East. The Treaty established an Economic Council and provided for co-operation in exploiting mineral resources, expansion of mutual trade, and co-operation of economic activities. Seven years later, a Council for Arab Economic Unity was established to draw up proposals of economic integration, which then led to creation of the Arab Common

Market in January, 1965. Despite its name, it is actually a free trade area containing the United Arab Republic, Iraq, Jordan, Syria, Kuwait and (later) Sudan. Trade among these countries is very small, and attempts at co-ordination of industrial development and other aspects of economic co-operation remain unfulfilled.

ATTEMPTS AT INTEGRATION IN WEST AFRICA

Eight countries of West Africa—Mauritania, Senegal, Mali, Guinea, Niger, Upper Volta and Dahomey—were united in the Federation of French West Africa prior to independence. As in the Federation of Equatorial Africa, administrative convenience had created a common currency, a range of common services, a customs union and redistribution of revenues from wealthier coastal territories to the inland areas.

This Federation was dissolved in 1959, when the countries gained independence, but the monetary union was preserved with establishment of a common central bank and currency. Guinea opted out of the monetary union, but Togo, a former French mandate, later joined it. Except for Guinea, the former Federation states also agreed to keep the customs union. However, they were unable to agree on allocation of customs revenues and the union soon dissolved.

A second attempt was made in 1966, when the same countries agreed to establish a West African Customs Union. More a preferential tariff area than a customs union, this agreement permitted members to tax noncompeting imports of regional products up to fifty per cent of combined tariff and excise rates on comparable imports from outside the union, or up to seventy per cent if the regional products competed with their own industry. The members soon fell into discord over measurement of the base for these internal tariffs and the Union was stillborn.

Yet another attempt came in 1967, this time including the English-speaking states of Ghana, Liberia, Sierra Leone and Nigeria, as well as the former Federation states (except Guinea) and Togo. They signed articles of agreement establishing an Economic Community of West Africa with the ultimate objective of creating a customs union. In the meantime, the Community was charged with developing proposals for policy harmonization and co-ordination in the areas of agricultural production, industrialization, development planning, trade liberalization, identification and financing of joint projects, and education.

The Economic Community will presumably be subject to the same sources of disharmony, arising essentially from the distribution problem, as beset the two previous ventures. In addition, stresses may develop from inclusion of English-speaking countries, with their different institutions and cultures, competing preferential arrangements with the United Kingdom, and separate currencies. On the other hand, there are more potential gains from integration across these boundaries. For example, Niger has more existing and potential trade links with English-speaking Nigeria than with other French-speaking countries.

Summary and Conclusions

The reason African countries look to industrialization as the means of economic growth is not hard to understand. Demands for their primary food and fiber exports are inelastic with respect to both income and price. Dependence on one or two primary exports brings "feast or famine" conditions, as quantities and the terms of trade fluctuate in response to wars and business fluctuations abroad. Individual exports, such as sisal and rubber, are subject to displacement by development of synthetic substitutes.

Industrialization might take the form of processing raw materials into semifinished or finished manufactures principally for export. This is already done to some extent, but the prospects are again limited by inelastic demand conditions. Moreover, "escalation" of tariff structures in industrial countries means that processed exports must sur-

mount much higher effect rates of protection than raw materials. The industrial countries are also prone to place high tariffs and quotas on labor-intensive manufactures, such as footwear and textiles, to protect domestic producers from "unfair competition from cheap foreign labor." These are precisely the manufactures in which labor-abundant and capital-scarce developing countries are likely to have a comparative advantage.

Thus, African countries look to manufacturing that substitutes for imports as the available form of industrialization. Tariffs are needed to break through long-established trade and marketing links with former colonial powers, to overcome established consumer habits reinforced by advertizing, and to protect infant industries while they achieve internal economies through experience and external economies through complementary development. The real costs of protection are reduced when developing countries integrate their trade and factor markets, bringing the gains of scale economies, intraregional specialization, greater competition, and employment of resources at the points where they add most to the value of output.

There is little doubt the small countries of Africa will find regional integration the most efficient road to industrialization by import substitution. Achieving equity in distribution of the benefits and costs of a union is the largest problem confronting such unions. More developed states, such as Kenya in East Africa, Congo (Brazzaville) in the UDEAC, and the larger coastal countries in West Africa will tend to gain the lion's share of industry and tax revenues. Need to harmonize fiscal, monetary and other policies requires a surrender of sovereignty that the poorer states, in particular, may be reluctant to make without compensation.

Compensating reallocations of tax revenues occur in the East and Central African Common Markets, but they are not sufficient, alone, to solve the distribution problem. The poorer countries want industry, too, and to be viable, an integration treaty may be required to depart from the strict definition of a customs union. Member states may be permitted to impose limited protective tariffs, as in East Africa and the proposed West African Common Market, or industries may be deliberately dispersed by an allocating authority, as in the UDEAC. Efficiency costs can be minimized or possibly eliminated, and private capital may be induced away from the traditional manufacturing center, by creation of transport networks and other forms of social overhead capital that serve as the base for new industrial locations. Such development of infrastructure may be financed by a development bank or through co-ordinated planning and allocation of government investment.

In conclusion, regional integration is needed, but will only succeed if all partners believe they will grow more rapidly with union than without it. The more advanced countries must be willing to share industrialization, even if the gain in equity comes at some loss in efficiency.

Notes

1. Gottfried Haberler, "Integration and Growth of the World Economy," *American Economic Review*, March, 1964.

2. Sidney Dell, *Trade Blocs and Common Markets* (New York: Knopf, 1963).

3. A. J. Brown, "Should African Countries Form Economic Unions?" in E. F. Jackson ed., *Economic Development in Africa* (Oxford: Basil Blackwell, 1965).

4. Jacob Viner, *The Customs Union Issue* (New York: Carnegie Endowment for International Peace, 1950).

5. Gunnar Myrdal, *Economic Theory and Under-Developed Regions* (London, 1957).

ABOUT THE EDITORS

J. S. UPPAL is a Professor of Economics at the State University of New York at Albany. He is the co-author (with Kuan-I Chen) of *India and China: Studies in Comparative Development*, also published by The Free Press.

LOUIS R. SALKEVER is a Professor of Economics at the State University of New York at Albany, where he serves as Vice President for Research and Dean of Graduate Studies.